LEE THE SOLDIER

LEE
THE SOLDIER

★ ★ ★

Edited by

Gary W. Gallagher

UNIVERSITY OF NEBRASKA PRESS

LINCOLN AND LONDON

Acknowledgments for the use of previously published material appear on page xv–xvi.

Library of Congress Cataloging-in-Publication Data
Lee the soldier / edited by Gary W. Gallagher.
p. cm.
Includes bibliographical references and index.
ISBN 0-8032-2153-3 (cl: alk. paper)
1. Lee, Robert E. (Robert Edward), 1807–1870. 2. Generals—United States—Biography. 3. Generals—Confederate States of America—Biography. 4. Confederate States of America. Army—Biography.
I. Gallagher, Gary W.
E467.1.L4L48 1996
973.7'3'092—dc20
[B]
95-31874
CIP

Dedication

With love for Eileen Anne Gallagher,
who, as she often observes, has visited
Gettysburg far more often than did R. E. Lee

Contents

Illustrations

Maps

Acknowledgments

I am pleased to acknowledge the help of several individuals who took an interest in this project. T. Michael Parrish and Robert K. Krick shared their thoughts about which selections would make the strongest collection—though my final choices deviated from both of their lists. Alan T. Nolan and Charles P. Roland, both friends and mentors, encouraged me to put the book together and cheerfully agreed to let me include selections from their writings about Lee. Mary Tyler McClenahan stepped in at a crucial point and made it possible for me to add two chapters to the book from her father's *R. E. Lee: A Biography*. Jack Davis, Scott Hartwig, Carol Reardon, and Andy Trudeau joined Bob Krick and Mike Parrish in taking time from very busy professional lives to write original contributions for the collection. Finally, Eileen Anne Gallagher helped with proofreading and other tedious aspects of preparing the manuscript. My debt to her, already large beyond repayment, continues to grow.

Permission to publish the following memoranda is gratefully acknowledged:

Allan, William, "Memoranda of Conversations with Lee," courtesy of the Robert E. Lee Papers, Special Collections, James G. Leyburn Library, Washington and Lee University, Lexington, Virginia.

Gordon, Edward Clifford, "Memorandum of a Conversation with Lee," courtesy of the Southern Historical Collection, Wilson Library, the University of North Carolina at Chapel Hill.

Johnson, William Preston, "Memoranda of Conversations with Lee," courtesy of the Robert E. Lee Papers, Special Collections, James G. Leyburn Library, Washington and Lee University, Lexington, Virginia.

Sources for the following reprinted works are gratefully acknowledged:

Alexander, Edward Porter, "Letter on Causes of Lee's Defeat at Gettysburg," from *Southern Historical Society Papers* 4, no. 3 (September 1877).

Bruce, George A., "Lee and the Strategy of the Civil War," from Papers of the Military Historical Society of Massachusetts, 14 vols. (1895–1918;

reprint with new index volume, Wilmington NC: Broadfoot Publishing, 1989–90).

Castel, Albert, "The Historian and the General: Thomas L. Connelly versus Robert E. Lee," from *Civil War History* (March 1970), with permission of The Kent State University Press.

Connelly, Thomas L., "Robert E. Lee and the Western Confederacy: A Criticism of Lee's Strategic Ability," from *Civil War History* (June 1969), with permission of The Kent State University Press.

Early, Jubal A., "Reply to General Longstreet," from *Southern Historical Society Papers* 4, no. 6 (December 1877).

Freeman, Douglas Southall, "The Sword of Robert E. Lee" and "Why Was Gettysburg Lost?" from *R. E. Lee*, volumes 3 and 4. Copyright 1935 by Charles Scribner's Sons; copyright renewed © 1963 Inez Goddin Freeman.

Gallagher, Gary W., "Another Look at the Generalship of R. E. Lee," revised from *Why the Confederacy Lost*, edited by Gabor S. Boritt. Copyright © 1992 by Gabor S. Boritt. Used by permission of Oxford University Press, Inc.

Gallagher, Gary W., "If the Enemy Is There We Must Attack Him: R. E. Lee and the Second Day at Gettysburg," from *The Second Day at Gettysburg: Essays on Confederate and Union Leadership*, edited by Gary W. Gallagher (1993). With permission of The Kent State University Press.

Lawley, Francis, "General Lee," from *Blackwood's Edinburgh Magazine* 111, no. 677 (March 1872).

Longstreet, James, "Lee in Pennsylvania," from [A. K. McClure, ed.], *The Annals of the War Written by Leading Participants North and South* (Philadelphia: The Times Publishing Company, 1879).

Nolan, Alan T., "General Lee," reprinted by permission from *Lee Considered: General Robert E. Lee and Civil War History*. Copyright © 1991 by Alan T. Nolan. Chapel Hill: The University of North Carolina Press, 1991.

Nolan, Alan T., "R. E. Lee and July 1 at Gettysburg," from *The First Day at Gettysburg: Essays on Confederate and Union Leadership*, edited by Gary W. Gallagher (1992). With permission of The Kent State University Press.

Roland, Charles P., "The Generalship of Robert E. Lee," from *Grant, Lee, Lincoln and the Radicals*, edited by Grady McWhiney. Evanston: Northwestern University Press, 1964. Used by permission.

Wolseley, Field Marshall Viscount, "General Lee," from *Macmillan's Magazine* 55, no. 329 (March 1867).

Introduction

GARY W. GALLAGHER

R. E. Lee's Confederate military career has attracted intense scrutiny for more than a century and a quarter. Beginning with soldiers who fought both with and against him, writers have analyzed his strategic and tactical abilities, probed his character for traits that affected his performance as a field commander, and measured his impact on the fortunes of the Confederacy. The resulting literature, both vast and uneven, looms like Janus before readers who hope to understand Lee. The dominant strain of this historiography presents a soldier of almost preternatural gifts who compares favorably with the world's great captains. A smaller part of the literature, the influence of which may be found most often in the academic arena, casts Lee as a general whose weaknesses seriously compromised, and sometimes more than offset, his undeniable talents. Was Lee the mainstay of the South's military resistance, forging a record on the battlefield that enspirited Confederate citizens while stretching Northern resolve nearly to the breaking point? Or did each of his renowned victories lead to no deeper result, obscuring more important events elsewhere while inflating their architect's reputation?

Lee the Soldier originated from the belief that anyone hoping to answer such questions lacked a good place to begin their quest. Although entering a manifestly crowded—many would say saturated—field, the book seeks to serve both professional historians and lay readers by providing convenient access to assessments of Lee's generalship that reflect the interpretive sweep of the literature. A single volume admittedly cannot address every historiographical twist and turn, but it can set forth the major debates, identify the crucial figures who shaped those debates, and point readers toward other pertinent titles. To achieve these goals, *Lee the Soldier* combines the general's unvarnished postwar testimony about his campaigns, sixteen previously published selections by historians and American and British contemporaries of Lee, five new essays by specialists in Civil War military history, and an annotated bibliography of two hundred key titles relating to Lee.[1]

A few words about the development of rival interpretive traditions concerning Lee's Civil War service are in order before introducing the material in *Lee the Soldier*. For the heroic tradition, we should begin with Confederate testimony. Twelve days before the battle of Antietam, Col. Robert H. Jones of the Twenty-second Georgia Infantry suggested to his wife that "everything is staked on this army. We have the best leader in the Civilized world—Genl Lee stands now above all Genls in Modern History. Our men will follow him to the end." Nine months later, as the Army of Northern Virginia marched toward southern Pennsylvania in its second raid across the Potomac River, another Confederate soldier affirmed that "language is inadequate to convey an idea of the supreme confidence this army reposes in its great and good leader." Defeats might lurk ahead, thought this man, but because "Lee is there, directing with his steady hand, which no crisis can make tremble, all will be well." In the wake of just such a crisis at Gettysburg, Jefferson Davis implored R. E. Lee to ignore critics who questioned his conduct during the campaign. Refusing to consider replacing Lee, who had suggested that another commander might better serve the Confederate cause, Davis alluded to his general's brilliant "achievements which will make you and your army the subject of history and object of the world's admiration for generations to come."[2]

Davis's prediction proved remarkably accurate—though he scarcely could have foreseen the degree to which Americans North and South, together with like-minded people in Britain, would embrace Lee as a military figure of fabulous proportion. After the war, former Confederate soldiers understandably looked upon their old chief with a combination of affection and reverence anticipated by the army's medical director shortly after Appomattox. "Under your guidance, the true and good men of the Army of Northern Virginia were ever ready to follow whether our march led to victory or defeat," wrote Surgeon Lafayette Guild amid the wreck of the Confederacy in early May 1865. "To belong to General Lee's defeated Army is now the proudest boast of a Confederate soldier." Lost Cause warriors, such as Jubal A. Early, John Brown Gordon, and others, worked tirelessly through the late-nineteenth century to burnish Lee's image in the South as a soldier of unparalleled skill—an easy task because most white Southerners had considered Lee an unrivalled captain since before the mid-point of the Civil War.[3]

Works of art reinforced the efforts of Lost Cause speakers and writers in the years following Lee's death. Monuments to the general appeared across the former Confederacy, most notably Edward Valentine's recumbent study at Washington and Lee University, unveiled in 1883, and imposing statues at New Orleans and Richmond dedicated in 1884 and 1890 respectively.[4] In countless Southern homes, engravings of Lee, or of the general at the center of groupings of Confederate luminaries, hung on walls as reminders of glory won on storied battlefields against imposing odds.[5]

Southern efforts to honor Lee continued in the twentieth century. His birthday became widely celebrated as a holiday. The state of Georgia flanked him with Jefferson Davis and Stonewall Jackson in plans for the colossal Confederate sculpture at Stone Mountain outside Atlanta. The Robert E. Lee Memorial Foundation, established in 1928, purchased and began to restore his birthplace at Stratford Hall; statues went up in Dallas and Austin, Texas, in Charlottesville, Virginia, and elsewhere; and Virginia selected him to join George Washington as the Commonwealth's heroes in Statuary Hall at the national Capitol. A firm belief in Lee's preeminence as a soldier and admiration for his qualities as a man animated those who sought in these and other ways to keep his memory alive in the former Confederacy, as evidenced on the 125th anniversary of Lee's birth when J. A. Garber of Virginia spoke in the House of Representatives about the "beautiful and perfect symmetry of character" of "the matchless soldier . . . [whose] genius for war at once placed him in the front ranks of the soldiers of all ages."[6]

Douglas Southall Freeman's massively detailed *R. E. Lee: A Biography*, which won a Pulitzer Prize in 1935 and sold surprisingly well for a work of its bulk, quickly became the most influential study of Lee. Portraying his subject as an uncomplicated Christian gentleman who possessed stunning military gifts, Freeman solidified a cluster of positive images that had been nurtured by the general's admirers over many decades. Dumas Malone, who as editor of the *Dictionary of American Biography* had seen Freeman's shorter sketch of Lee and eagerly awaited the larger work, later recalled the experience of reading *R. E. Lee* for the first time: "Great as my personal expectations were, the realization far surpassed them, and never did I devour a major historical work with such insatiable appetite and more unalloyed satisfaction. The book reached the full stature of the man." Malone also noted that while Lee was a national figure, "to everybody it seemed fitting that he had been most fully described and most adequately portrayed by a son of the Confederacy who lived in Richmond." The impact of Freeman's biography cannot be overestimated; it has remained in print for sixty years, inspiring generations of readers to share its high estimate of Lee as a soldier.[7]

Clifford Dowdey succeeded Freeman in the 1950s and 1960s as the leading chronicler of Lee and his campaigns, bringing to his work a comparably positive estimate of the general. A Virginian with deep family roots in the Commonwealth, Dowdey had worked for Freeman at the Richmond *News Leader* and frankly admitted he was "awed at the prospect of trying to offer any supplement" to *R. E. Lee: A Biography*. He nonetheless wrote a one-volume life of Lee as well as studies of the Army of Northern Virginia during the Seven Days, Gettysburg, and Overland campaigns—all of which reached substantial audiences. Like Freeman, Dowdey saw Lee "as a simple man, whose character grew in proportion to his commitment to the life-task he felt God had assigned him. . . . He assumes heroic stature because he was a product of an age in which men and women held heroic concepts of life and its meaning." Bold, decisive, and able to inspire boundless confidence among the men he commanded, wrote Dowdey, Lee exhibited "the quality of a powerful force, complete and harmonious."[8]

White Southerners were not alone in accepting Lee as a military genius. Many of his opponents in the Army of the Potomac undoubtedly considered him the conflict's best soldier. Conditioned to lose under a succession of commanders in 1862 and 1863, these men achieved victory under Ulysses S. Grant without necessarily seeing him as Lee's equal. As late as 24 March 1865, with the Army of Northern Virginia obviously staggering toward defeat, a soldier in Grant's army warned: "[W]e must bear in mind that we have not yet rendered it impossible for Gen. Lee to win another victory." Writing on the day of Appomattox, Col. Charles S. Wainwright employed language that presaged Lost Cause writers in implying Lee really had not been beaten: "The Army of Northern Virginia under Lee . . . today . . . has surrendered. During three long and hard-fought campaigns it has withstood every effort of the Army of the Potomac; now at the commencement of the fourth, it is obliged to succumb without even one great pitched battle. Could the war have been closed with such a battle as Gettysburg, it would have been more glorious for us; . . . As it is, the rebellion has been worn out rather than suppressed." Similarly, New Englander Stephen Minot Weld took pains to explain to his sister why he had reacted in muted tones to Lee's surrender. "To tell the truth, we none of us realize even yet that he has actually surrendered," admitted Colonel Weld. "I had a sort of impression that we should fight him all our lives. He was like a ghost to children, something that haunted us so long that we could not realize that he and his army were really out of existence to us. It will take me some months to be conscious of this fact."[9]

By the end of the nineteenth century, as growing numbers of Northerners urged reconciliation with the South, the context of Lee's fame shifted from regional to national.[10] Frederick Douglass had complained as early as Lee's death in 1870 about "bombastic laudation of the rebel chief. . . . We can scarcely take up a newspaper . . . that is not filled with *nauseating* flatteries of the late Robert E. Lee." The extent to which many in the North accepted Lee as an admirable foe radiated from Charles Francis Adams's address at Washington and Lee University on 19 January 1907. Speaking on the one-hundredth anniversary of Lee's birth, this descendant of two American presidents and veteran of the Army of the Potomac praised his subject as a soldier and a man. Adams even forgave Lee's devoting his military talents to the cause of disrupting the Union, assuring his Virginia audience "that under similar conditions I would myself have done exactly what Lee did. In fact," added Adams, "I do not see how I, placed as he was placed, could have done otherwise." Across the Atlantic and half a century, Winston Churchill echoed Adams's assessment when he called Lee "one of the noblest Americans who ever lived, and one of the greatest captains known to the annals of war."[11]

A sketch published during the Civil War centennial pronounced Lee "the most universally revered of American soldiers in all parts of the country," a statement difficult to prove though probably accurate. With that superlative as his point of departure, Glenn Tucker sought to understand what made Lee "both a great military man and a magnificent person." Tucker's approach underscored that during the 1960s, in the popular imagination at least, Lee's military reputation overshadowed reputations of Grant and all other Union and Confederate generals. "Few men in history are freer from an element of hate," observed Tucker in a passage remarkably like many penned by Lost Cause writers nearly a century before, "though no man administered to American armies more numerous or mortifying defeats on the field of battle or brought the United States nearer to humiliating disaster than did Lee—humiliating because virtually all the while he commanded only a single army of a nation . . . which did not possess more than one-tenth the resources or wealth nor one-fourth the military manpower of the United States." The thirty years since Tucker's article appeared have wrought no major change in Lee's status. "With only occasional and essentially unheeded dissent," argued Alan T. Nolan in 1991, "a belief in Lee's paramount greatness as a general is the most intense and enduring aspect of the Lee tradition."[12]

Often obscured by the chorus of praise for Lee's generalship is the parallel body of more critical writings about his military career. Union veterans who believed him the primary agent of rebellion seldom extolled his virtues as a soldier. They looked to Ulysses S. Grant or William Tecumseh Sherman—or perhaps to Virginian George H. Thomas, whose loyalty to the Union at high personal cost contrasted starkly with Lee's decision to join his native state—as their preeminent military heroes. Grant himself denied that his most famous opponent excelled even among Confederate officers. "I never ranked Lee as high as some others of the army, that is to say, I never had as much anxiety when he was in my front as when Joe Johnston was in front," commented Grant in 1878. Stung by Jubal Early's strident attribution of Union victory to an overwhelming edge in men and material, Grant insisted that Lee "had everything in his favor. . . . He was supported by the unanimous voice of the South; he was supported by a large party in the North; he had the support and sympathy of the outside world. All this is of an immense advantage to a general." Sensitive as well about invidious comparisons between himself and Lee, Grant alluded to a "cry . . . in the air . . . that the generalship and valor were with the South." He thought Lee manifested a "slow, conservative, cautious nature, without imagination or humor, always the same, with grave dignity." "I never could see in his achievements what justifies his reputation," concluded Grant. "The illusion that nothing but heavy odds beat him will not stand the ultimate light of history. I know it is not true."[13]

A few ex-Confederates also criticized Lee's generalship. P. G. T. Beauregard, who entertained a lofty opinion of his own merits as a strategist, praised Lee's "great nerve, coolness, & determination" but, echoing Grant, thought him "perhaps a little too cautious in civil as well as Mil[i]t[ar]y matters" and depreciated his "powers of deduction." Conspicuous in his postwar willingness to criticize Lee, James Longstreet boldly challenged his former chief's aggressive strategy and tactics and proclaimed Joseph E. Johnston more skillful (Johnston likely would have agreed with Longstreet's assessment). Longstreet's often intemperate statements about Lee at Gettysburg and on other battlefields helped transform "Old Pete" into the arch villain of Lost Cause writers and their successors, who habitually used him as a scapegoat for southern defeat. In 1907 Senator Charles A. Culberson of Texas asked the forty-three Confederate generals then living whom they considered "the greatest commander developed on the Southern side in the war." Thirty-four of forty responses named Lee, a strong confirmation of his primacy but indication as well of appreciable sentiment at odds with the dominant Southern white celebration of Lee's flawless generalship.[14]

Several twentieth-century historians raised serious questions about Lee's Confederate operations—though nearly all of them conceded his unusual ability to fashion striking battlefield triumphs. Three examples will serve to illustrate major themes. In 1933 Maj. Gen. J. F. C. Fuller's *Grant and Lee: A Study in Personality and Generalship* foreshadowed later critiques by challenging Lee's strategic vision and emphasizing his quixotic search for decisive victories. Fuller cast Lee as a man crippled by his Virginia mentality, unaware of the importance of events beyond the Appalachians, and willing to spend freely of his army's blood for transitory tactical gain in his native state. Thomas L. Connelly's *The Marble Man: Robert E. Lee and His Image in American Society*, published in 1977, built on Fuller's arguments about Lee's obsession with Virginia and waste of precious manpower. A Tennessean and historian of the Army of Tennessee, Connelly especially resented that Lee and his army dominated the military literature on the Confederacy. Assailing nearly every facet of Douglas Southall Freeman's interpretation of Lee as a soldier and a man, Connelly claimed that the general's historical standing owed nearly as much to postwar machinations by Lost Cause warriors as to his deeds on the battlefield. One reviewer predicted that Connelly's book would "make some people angry, delight intellectual Lilliputians, and stimulate future biographers of Lee."[15]

Fourteen years elapsed between the publication of Connelly's book and the appearance of Alan T. Nolan's *Lee Considered: General Robert E. Lee and Civil War History*, a frank reevaluation of several elements of the Lee orthodoxy. Although written in restrained language, Nolan's study alienated Lee's partisans with its suggestion that much of what had been written about the general obscured more than it illuminated. Nolan developed Fuller's theme of wasteful offensive battles at great length, declaring that Lee's oft-praised qualities—"devotion to the offensive, daring, combativeness, audacity, eagerness to attack, taking the initiative"—in fact harmed the larger Confederate war effort by trading irreplaceable manpower for short-term success when only a protracted war that undermined Northern morale could have brought Southern independence. Nolan's book elicited warm praise as well as harsh rebuttals, including, in the latter category, one outraged reader's recommendation "that anyone with a copy of Mr. Nolan's book burn it."[16]

The polarity of reaction to *Lee Considered* reflected the persistent tension between admirers and critics of Lee's military record[17]—which brings us back to the rationale for *Lee the Soldier*. Readers will find in the material that follows a broad range of arguments for and against Lee's greatness as a general. The emphasis is on analysis, though several selections employ a narrative framework within which the authors make their analytical points. As a collection of interpretive writings, *Lee the Soldier* complements the *Official Records*, *The Wartime Papers of R. E. Lee*, and other works that contain Lee's wartime letters and reports. Once familiar with dominant historiographical themes, readers can canvass contemporary documents with an eye toward deciding which authors have best portrayed Lee's stature as a soldier and his influence on the course of the war.[18]

The book is organized in four parts. The three selections in part 1 are notes from a series of postwar conversations in which Lee spoke candidly about his campaigns. Especially valuable because of Lee's well-known reticence about wartime events, these comments reveal strong opinions about his lieutenants, policies adopted by the Confederate government, and the published writings of former Confederate officers. The sections on the 1862 Maryland campaign and Gettysburg are especially enlightening. For example, although in July 1863 he had taken full responsibility for the result at Gettysburg, Lee's statements to William Allan demonstrated the extent to which he held "Jeb" Stuart and, to a lesser degree, his three corps commanders accountable. Lee undoubtedly believed that a concerted effort on the part of his key subordinates would have carried the field at Gettysburg. In addressing his strategic thinking prior to both raids into the North, the general described a broad defensive posture within which the forays across the Potomac would act to disrupt Union plans and relieve Confederate logistical problems. Apart from strictly military subjects, Lee twice mentioned his support for early emancipation and the enrollment of black men in the Confederate army as steps certain to strengthen the struggle for Southern independence. He also discussed at length events surrounding his decision to resign from the United States Army in April 1861. Overall, these conversations shed light not only on Lee's military operations but also on his postwar frame of mind.

I chose the eleven essays in part 2 as important summary analyses of the quality and effect of Lee's generalship. Jubal A. Early's "The Campaigns of Gen. Robert E. Lee," first delivered at Washington and Lee University in 1872 and subsequently distributed widely as a pamphlet,[19] stands as the quintessential Lost Cause statement of Lee's greatness. In this address, Early emphasized the importance of Northern human and material resources—advantages that rendered Lee's successes all the more compelling. What of the relative abilities of Lee and Grant? Early claimed that one might as well "compare the great pyramid which rears its majestic proportions in the valley of the Nile, to a pigmy perched on Mount Atlas." A former lieutenant general who had commanded the Second Corps of the Army of Northern Virginia through much of 1864, Early played a vital part in the postwar process by which white Southerners came to terms with defeat. As president of the Southern Historical Society, frequent speaker at commemorative gatherings, and widely acknowledged (across the South) expert on the operations of Lee's army, he wielded considerable influence over the development of early Confederate military historiography. Early waged a tenacious war in print against James Longstreet and all others who questioned Lee's brilliance as a commander, prompting one former comrade to comment that "no man ever took up his pen to write a line about the great conflict without the fear of Jubal Early before his eyes."[20]

Francis C. Lawley and Garnot Wolseley contributed two of the earliest British evaluations of Lee. Lawley wrote first, drawing on his experience as a London *Times* correspondent covering the American war to write "General Lee" for *Blackwood's Edinburgh Magazine* in 1872.[21] Frequently in the company of Lee and other generals in the Army of Northern Virginia, Lawley witnessed major battles in the Eastern Theater and developed a deep admiration for the Confederate cause. His essay reflected that admiration, though he judged Lee's conduct at Fredericksburg and Gettysburg flawed and pronounced him less able than Napoleon and Frederick the Great. Jubal Early immediately challenged Lawley's conclusions, enclosing a copy of his Washington and Lee address for the British author's edification. Lawley's friendly response to Early reaffirmed his high regard for Lee but gently suggested that the general's own character, "the very purity, unselfishness & modesty of Gen. Lee as a man diminished rather than enhanced his greatness" as a soldier.[22]

Fifteen years after publication of Lawley's piece, Field Marshall Wolseley's "General Lee" appeared in *Macmillan's Magazine* as a review of Armistead Lindsay Long's *Memoirs of Robert E. Lee: His Military and Personal History*.[23] Coming from the pen of a renowned British military officer, this short sketch carried the weight of a professional's competence to judge Lee's merits. A meeting with Lee in the fall of 1862 had left an indelible mark on Wolseley, who dwelled on the Virginian's personal characteristics as much as his generalship. Even Jubal Early could have asked for no more favorable conclusions—Wolseley's Lee faced formidable odds, won historic victories, and demonstrated the qualities of a model Christian gentleman indicative "of a man who was cast in a grander mould, and made of different and of finer metal than all other men."[24]

The tone of George A. Bruce's "Lee and the Strategy of the Civil War" contrasts sharply with the first three readings in part 2.[25] A Union staff officer during the Civil War and a politician in postwar Massachusetts, Bruce wrote a detailed history of the Twentieth Massachusetts Infantry and delivered several papers to the Military Historical Society of Massachusetts. Unimpressed by arguments about Lee's superior generalship, Bruce anticipated J. F. C. Fuller, Alan T. Nolan, and other later critics by stressing the heavy losses that attended Lee's offensive movements. Impulsive, audacious, and even reckless, Lee's "temperament . . . was in conspicuous display from the day he took command of the Army of Northern Virginia until the Wilderness, in 1864, enforced caution and restraint." Beyond the activities of his own army, insisted Bruce, Lee exerted little influence on the course of the war: "He can never be placed in the ranks of those great captains who have affected the fortunes of nations, for good or ill, as commander of the national forces. In this respect he falls far below Washington and Grant."[26]

Douglas Southall Freeman consciously avoided comparisons to other famous soldiers in "The Sword of Robert E. Lee," the summary chapter on Lee's Confederate service from *R. E. Lee: A Biography*. Yet Freeman's catalog of Lee's military virtues suggests a ranking very near the top of any roster of captains. High intellect, a sure grasp of strategic details, boldness, willingness to commit his entire force to any contest, and skill as an administrator highlighted but did not exhaust Freeman's list. Like Jubal Early, Freeman alluded to Northern numbers and industrial power; unlike Lee's fervent Lost Cause admirers, he also discussed the general's failures and miscalculations, including what he termed an "excessive amiability" that prevented his dealing harshly with troublesome subordinates.[27]

Freeman's analysis remains the essential starting point for most evaluations of Lee's military career—a fact borne out by the essays of Charles P. Roland, Thomas L. Connelly, and Albert Castel. In "The Generalship of Robert E. Lee," first given as a paper at Northwestern University during the Civil War Centennial, Roland presents a thoughtful expansion of Freeman's points.[28] Suggesting that Lee's critics often directly contradict one another, he sketches a soldier fully aware of the large strategic picture and supremely talented as a theater commander. In "Robert E. Lee and the Western Confederacy: A Criticism of Lee's Strategic Ability," published in 1969, Connelly asked rhetorically how much Lee's "personality and reputation" had been "enhanced by the literary ability of Douglas Freeman." Because of its vigorous attack on Lee's strategic grasp, this article earned Connelly a reputation as one of the general's leading critics—a reputation solidified eight years later by his book *The Marble Man*. Freeman and Lee both considered Virginia the prime arena of military action, insisted Connelly, a serious misreading of the actual strategic situation. Lee's costly battles in Virginia and refusal to allocate more resources to the Western Theater raised the question whether "the South may not have fared better had it possessed no Robert E. Lee."[29] Albert Castel answered Connelly in "The Historian and the General: Thomas L. Connelly versus Robert E. Lee," which appeared in the March 1970 issue of *Civil War History*. Mounting an all-out assault, Castel disputed not only Connelly's conclusions but also his use of evidence. Without Lee's "military genius," stated Castel in summary, the Confederacy "would have crumbled much sooner than it did."[30]

Alan T. Nolan's "General Lee" and my "Another Look at the Generalship of R. E. Lee" differ as strikingly as the essays by Connelly and Castel. In the longest chapter from *Lee Considered*, Nolan carries forward the interpretive tradition of George A. Bruce, J. F. C. Fuller, and Connelly. Cutting through more than a century's rhetoric about how Lee's audacious gambles resulted in breathtaking victories over larger Federal armies, Nolan states that too much offensive action and too many casualties more than offset individual battlefield successes. Lee drained the Confederacy's limited manpower and thus undermined its struggle for independence. My essay, a revised version of a broader piece on Civil War generalship,[31] acknowledges that Lee's battles were bloody and that he sometimes acted too aggressively but denies that he pursued a deeply flawed strategic vision. I believe that he saw clearly the importance of his victories in the Eastern Theater and adopted a strategy calculated to inspirit the Confederate populace while demoralizing the North. Historians too often overlook the fact that Lee's generalship fit the temperament of the Confederate people—an important factor when examining the performance of any military figure in a democratic society. I join Charles P. Roland and Albert Castel in asserting that Lee's contributions lengthened the life of the Confederacy.

William C. Davis closes the second section of this volume with a new essay on the relationship between Lee and Jefferson Davis. More than any other officer who headed a Confederate army, Lee understood the need to subordinate himself to the chief executive. He kept the president informed, solicited his advice, and otherwise demonstrated a deft reading of his superior's personality. Davis responded with consistent support for his most trusted general, deferring to Lee in ways unthinkable with Joseph E. Johnston or P. G. T. Beauregard. Davis's essay effectively conveys the degree to which political acumen supplemented military ability in making Lee a successful commander.

The ten essays in part 3 narrow the focus from Lee's broad military career to specific campaigns. Three questions guided my selection of military operations. Was a campaign important in Lee's military development? Did it figure prominently in the larger framework of the war? Did it inspire a significant literature? Five campaigns met one or more of these criteria. The Seven Days marked Lee's debut as an army commander; Antietam capped a summer's continuous campaigning and hugely affected the political landscape of the war; Chancellorsville displayed the Lee-Jackson partnership at apogee; Gettysburg ended a string of victories that had brought the Army of Northern Virginia to a peak of confidence and power; and the confrontation between Lee and Grant from the Wilderness through Appomattox went a long way toward settling the fate of the Confederacy. Six of the ten essays relate to Gettysburg because of the imposing size and extreme contentiousness of the literature on that famous operation.

A trio of new pieces cover the period down to Gettysburg. In "From 'King of Spades' to 'First Captain of the Confederacy': R. E. Lee's First Six Weeks with the Army of Northern Virginia," Carol Reardon finds that most accounts of the Seven Days have taken Lee on his own terms. Failures among Confederate subordinates and the conduct of George B. McClellan have dominated analysis, diverting attention from Lee's own actions. Lee turned the enemy back from Richmond, states Reardon, but whether he bungled a larger opportunity in the process deserves much closer attention. D. Scott Hartwig's "Robert E. Lee and the Maryland Campaign" takes a fresh look at the sequence of decisions that brought the Army of Northern Virginia to the ground at Sharpsburg on 17 September. Answering historians who maintain that Lee attempted to accomplish too much with a weakened army in September 1862, Hartwig states that the campaign was not "doomed from the start" and might have yielded larger results.[32] "Lee at Chancellorsville," by Robert K. Krick, openly admires the general's determination to risk everything in a series of breathtaking gambles along the Rappahannock River in May 1863. After a fumbling opening during which Joseph Hooker stole a march on the Army of Northern Virginia, Lee quickly seized the initiative and kept Hooker off-balance with unexpected moves. "Lee did things that Hooker could not imagine him doing," writes Krick. "In the process he won his greatest victory."[33]

Chancellorsville capped a remarkable ten-month run during which Lee and his soldiers won all of their famous victories. Gettysburg injected a dose of reality into the Army of Northern Virginia, which learned that even Lee's presence could not guarantee triumph. Lt. Gen. James Longstreet, Lee's senior corps commander throughout the war, held his chief accountable for the defeat at Gettysburg. In "Lee in Pennsylvania," published in the Philadelphia *Weekly Times* in November 1877, Longstreet expressed "the greatest affection for General Lee, and the greatest reverence for his memory" but charged him with numerous mistakes—"not so much matters of deliberate judgment as the impulses of a great mind disturbed by unparalleled conditions." Lee's decision to continue the tactical offensive after 1 July was what most upset Longstreet, who believed the Confederates should have tried to force the enemy to attack them.[34] Longstreet's article provoked a quick and overwhelming reaction in the South, helping to ignite the "Gettysburg Controversy" that raged for years among former Confederates. Jubal Early orchestrated a campaign to discredit Longstreet, using the pages of the *Southern Historical Society Papers* as his prime forum. Printed in the December 1877 issues of the *Papers*, Early's "Reply to General Longstreet" typified Lost Cause portrayals of Longstreet as slow and willful on the battlefield and dishonest in his postwar descriptions of events on 1–3 July 1863.[35]

Although most former Confederates joined the anti-Longstreet forces, a few sought to steer a more dispassionate course between the antagonists. Edward Porter Alexander's "Letter on Causes of Lee's Defeat at Gettysburg" fell into this category. Alexander had been the premier artillerist in the Army of Northern Virginia; he admired both Lee and Longstreet, and shunned extravagant statements in his voluminous postwar writings. In this letter, he pointed out that the Northern public would have forced Meade to take the offensive, affording Lee the luxury of selecting a strong defensive position and exploiting a repulse of the enemy with a counterattack. Lee's costly attacks on 2–3 July were thus unnecessary, though only delays and poor execution denied him victory on 2 July. Events on that second day had "been the subject of much crimination and recrimination among survivors as to the greater or less responsibility for them," noted Alexander with some distaste, "but, to history, of course the general commanding is the responsible party."[36] In later correspondence with the historian Frederic Bancroft, Alexander reiterated his belief that Lee erred in attacking on 2–3 July, adding perceptively that "Longstreet's *great* mistake was not in the *war*" but after the war in "his awkward & apparently bitter criticisms of Gen Lee." He accurately noted that "[m]any an old soldier will never forgive Longstreet such a sentiment."[37]

Douglas Southall Freeman often relied on Alexander's writings but disagreed with the Georgian in the case of Gettysburg. "Why Was Gettysburg Lost" summarized the campaign in Freeman's biography of Lee, giving readers a list of factors that compromised the Confederate effort. Freeman mentioned Longstreet's sulking on 2 July most prominently but also apportioned blame to Richard S. Ewell, Jeb Stuart, A. P. Hill, and a group of artillerists. Lee's failure to prod the balky Longstreet into action on 2 July revealed the commander's "greatest weakness as a soldier." "No candid critic of the battle can follow the events of that fateful morning and not have a feeling that Lee virtually surrendered to Longstreet," wrote Freeman, "who obeyed only when he could no longer find an excuse for delay." In a concluding statement that has colored untold accounts of the battle, Freeman suggested that the greatest blow to Confederate fortunes at Gettysburg came two months earlier "at Chancellorsville when Jackson fell."[38]

The final pair of essays on Gettysburg focuses on the first and second days respectively. Alan T. Nolan's "R. E. Lee and July 1 at Gettysburg" disapproves of the strategic movement across the Potomac, holds the commanding general rather than Jeb Stuart largely responsible for failures of reconnaissance during the campaign, and argues that Lee's tactical lapses on the first day set the stage for later defeat. The cataclysmic battle in Pennsylvania was unnecessary, believes Nolan, because Lee enjoyed the option—as he had in December 1862 and would again in May 1864—of choosing a good defensive position along the Rappahannock and waiting for the inevitable Federal advance.[39] In " 'If the Enemy Is There We Must Attack Him': R. E. Lee and the Second Day at Gettysburg," I second Porter Alexander's view that Lee should have taken a defensive position after the first day's smashing tactical victory. Political pressure would have forced Meade to attack, which might have yielded a decisive opening for a counterstroke. I do not argue that Lee's decision to resume the offensive on 2 July was entirely foolish, however, because Confederate momentum and morale stood so high. Lee understood that those two factors had brought victory on other fields and expected that they might do so again.[40]

Gettysburg marked Lee's last major strategic offensive. Ahead lay a protracted defensive campaign that is the subject of Noah Andre Trudeau's new essay, " 'A Mere Question of Time': Robert E. Lee from the Wilderness to Appomattox Court House." The literature on Lee's military career generally lauds his ability to adapt to defensive fighting beginning in May 1864. Forced to resist his naturally aggressive impulses, goes a common argument, Lee masterfully employed position and entrenchments to ward off Grant's relentless pressure. Trudeau fully credits Lee's leadership amid increasingly trying circumstances, yet he reveals a number of lapses that he considers indicative of eroding self-confidence. Some episodes, believes Trudeau, such as the futile assaults at Fort Stedman in March 1865, seem inexplicable except as strange mutations of Lee's innate combativeness.

Anyone who digests the text and notes of these essays should have a reasonably good sense of how the literature has evolved. Those who emerge from the experience eager to read more will enjoy T. Michael Parrish's "The R. E. Lee 200: An Annotated Bibliography of Essential Books on Lee's Military Career," which constitutes part 4 of this volume. As with all such lists, Parrish's is idiosyncratic and certainly will not suit everyone. Only a relative handful of books could be included. Some readers will use the list as a guide to build a basic collection of books on Lee, while others will prefer to quibble about titles included or left out. Both exercises are enjoyable and worthy diversions.

A brief comment about the texts of the reprinted items is pertinent. Some of the pieces contain a few errors of fact or unusual spellings of personal and place names. I have not burdened them with a new layer of scholarly apparatus to correct such shortcomings. I selected the texts because of their points of view—which remain vigorous despite the presence of niggling errors. With that cautionary note, I invite readers to explore this sampling of interpretive writings about R. E. Lee the soldier.

NOTES

1. *Lee the Soldier* differs radically in intent and content from Stanley F. Horn's *The Robert E. Lee Reader* (Indianapolis: Bobbs-Merrill, 1949), which to the unwary might appear to be a comparable work. Horn presented, in the words of others, an uncritically favorable biography of Lee, fitting together excerpts from various published sources to give "a readable and accurate picture of the true Robert E. Lee"—whom Horn saw as "not merely a great general; he was a great citizen" (p. 7).

2. Robert H. Jones to My Dear Wife, 5 September 1862, typescript of original in private hands, provided by Keith H. Bohannon, Smyrna, Georgia; letter signed "G" in the Augusta (Georgia) *Daily Constitutionalist*, 18 June 1864; Jefferson Davis to R. E. Lee, 11 August 1863, in Jefferson Davis, *Jefferson Davis Constitutionalist: His Letters, Papers, and Speeches*, ed. Dunbar Rowland, 10 vols. (Jackson: Mississippi Department of Archives and History, 1923), 5:589.

3. Lafayette Guild to R. E. Lee, 5 May 1865, Medical Department, Letters Sent, Medical Director, Army of Northern Virginia, 1863–5, Chapter VI, vol. 642, RG109, National Archives, Washington DC. Although different strains of Lost Cause myth-making developed after the war, they agreed on Lee's perfection as a soldier and his centrality to any attempt to place the antebellum South and the Confederacy in the best possible light. For a full treatment of this topic, see Gaines M. Foster, *Ghosts of the Confederacy: Defeat, the Lost Cause, and the Emergence of the New South* (New York: Oxford University Press, 1987), especially chapters 4–7.

4. Foster, *Ghosts of the Confederacy*, 88–92, 100–102, discusses the circumstances surrounding the creation of these monuments.

5. Chapter 11 of Mark E. Neely Jr., Harold Holzer, and Gabor S. Boritt, *The Confederate Image: Prints of the Lost Cause* (Chapel Hill: University of North Carolina Press, 1987), offers an excellent discussion of the postwar Lee iconography. "Lee's image dominated all" Confederate subjects, observe the authors (p. 159); in the mid-1890s, one New York catalog of engravings listed no fewer than nine prints of the general. (Although purchased in the South, most engravings depicting Confederate heroes were published by northern firms.)

6. Michael Kammen, *Mystic Chords of Memory: The Transformation of Tradition in American Culture* (New York: Alfred A. Knopf, 1991), 491, 405; Thomas L. Connelly, *The Marble Man: Robert E. Lee and His Image in American Society* (New York: Alfred A. Knopf, 1977), 126; Ralph W. Widener Jr., *Confederate Monuments: Enduring Symbols of the South and the War Between the States* (n.p.: Privately printed, 1982), 211 (the statue in Austin, erected in 1933), 216 (Dallas, 1936), 240 (Charlottesville, 1924); Roy Meredith, *The Face of Robert E. Lee in Life and Legend* (New York: Charles Scribner's Sons, 1947), 135–36; J. A. Garber, *Robert E. Lee:*

Speech of Hon. J. A. Garber of Virginia in the House of Representatives, January 20, 1930 (Washington DC: GPO, 1930), 3.

7. Douglas Southall Freeman, *R. E. Lee: A Biography*, 4 vols. (New York: Charles Scribner's Sons, 1934–35); Dumas Malone, "The Pen of Douglas Southall Freeman," in Douglas Southall Freeman, *George Washington: A Biography*, 7 vols. (New York: Charles Scribner's Sons, 1948–57 [vol. 7 written by John Alexander Carroll and Mary Wells Ashworth]), 6:xviii–xix. Among the many printings of *R. E. Lee: A Biography* were two "Pulitzer Prize Editions"; Scribner's also published a one-volume abridgment by Richard B. Harwell titled *Lee* (1961) and a version for younger readers titled *Lee of Virginia* (1958).

8. Clifford Dowdey, *Lee* (Boston: Little, Brown, 1965), x–xi; Dowdey, *Lee's Last Campaign: The Story of Lee and His Men Against Grant—1864* (Boston: Little, Brown, 1960), 6. Dowdey's other books on Lee and his army were *Death of a Nation: The Story of Lee and His Men at Gettysburg* (New York: Alfred A. Knopf, 1958) and *The Seven Days: The Emergence of Lee* (Boston: Little, Brown, 1964).

9. Wilbur Fisk, *Hard Marching Every Day: The Civil War Letters of Private Wilbur Fisk*, ed. Emil and Ruth Rosenblatt (Lawrence: University Press of Kansas, 1992), 318–19; Charles S. Wainwright, *A Diary of Battle: The Personal Journals of Colonel Charles S. Wainwright, 1861–1865*, ed. Allan Nevins (New York: Harcourt, Brace & World, 1962), 520–21; Stephen Minot Weld to Dear Hannah, 24 April 1865, in Stephen Minot Weld, *War Diary and Letters of Stephen Minot Weld, 1861–1865* (1912; reprint, Boston: Massachusetts Historical Society, 1979), 396. See also Michael C. C. Adams, *Our Masters the Rebels: A Speculation on Union Military Failure in the East, 1861–1865* (Cambridge: Harvard University Press, 1978), which considers why so many Union soldiers remained enthralled by Lee.

10. Among many factors that promoted the spirit of reconciliation in the North were a desire to get beyond the bitterness of the war, racial assumptions shared with southern whites, and unhappiness with political and social elements of the emerging industrial nation. On the North and reconciliation, see Nina Silber, *The Romance of Reunion: Northerners and the South, 1865–1900* (Chapel Hill: University of North Carolina Press, 1993), and chapter 4 of Connelly, *The Marble Man*.

11. David W. Blight, "'For Something Beyond the Battlefield': Frederick Douglass and the Struggle for the Memory of the Civil War," in *Memory and American History*, ed. David Thelen (Bloomington: Indiana University Press, 1990), 40; Charles Francis Adams, *Lee's Centennial: An Address* (Chicago: Americana House, 1948), 14; Winston S. Churchill, *The Great Democracies*, vol. 4 of *A History of the English Speaking Peoples* (New York: Dodd, Meade & Company, 1958), 169. Lee's counseling former Confederates to accept defeat and work toward reconciliation enabled Northerners to emphasize his symbolic role in reuniting the nation. Congressman Louis Cramton of Michigan, who proposed the legislation that established the Lee Mansion National Memorial at Arlington in 1925, spoke to this point: "I believe it is unprecedented in history for a nation to have gone through as great a struggle as that was, and in the lifetime of men then living to see the country

so absolutely reunited as is our country. . . . [T]here was no man in the South who did more by his precept and example to help bring about that condition than did Robert E. Lee." National Park Service Division of Publications, *Arlington House: A Guide to Arlington House, the Robert E. Lee Memorial, Virginia* (Washington DC: U.S. Department of the Interior, 1985), 7.

12. Glenn Tucker, "Now He Belongs to the Entire Nation," *Civil War Times Illustrated* 4 (April 1965): 4, 6; Alan T. Nolan, *Lee Considered: General Robert E. Lee and Civil War History* (Chapel Hill: University of North Carolina Press, 1991), 60. By far the most widely read popular magazine in the field, *Civil War Times Illustrated* devoted a special expanded issue to Lee in November 1985. Mark Grimsley's title, "Robert E. Lee: The Life and Career of the Master General," suggests the tenor of his piece.

13. "Heroes of the War. General Grant's Opinions About the Men Who Led the Armies For and Against the Union," *Philadelphia Weekly Times*, 3 August 1878. For an example of Early's argument about northern numbers, see Jubal A. Early, "The Relative Strength of the Armies of Lee and Grant," in J. William Jones and others, eds., *Southern Historical Society Papers*, 52 vols. and 3-vol. index (1876–1959; reprint, Wilmington NC: Broadfoot Publishing Company, 1990–92), 2:6–21 which reprints Early's letter dated 19 November, 1870 to the London *Standard* disputing Adam Badeau's figures.

14. P. G. T. Beauregard to Thomas Jordan, n.d. 1868, quoted in T. Harry Williams, *P. G. T. Beauregard: Napoleon in Gray* (Baton Rouge: Louisiana State University Press, 1955), 305; William Garrett Piston, *Lee's Tarnished Lieutenant: James Longstreet and His Place in Southern History* (Athens: University of Georgia Press, 1987), 26–27, chaps. 7–8; Lowell H. Harrison, "How the Southern Generals Rated Their Leaders," *Civil War Times Illustrated* 5 (October 1966): 27–35. Thomas L. Connelly's *The Marble Man* suggests that during the war and in the early postwar years a number of other Confederate generals rivalled Lee as heroes in the South—an interpretation that overlooks voluminous evidence to the contrary.

15. J. F. C. Fuller, *Grant and Lee: A Study in Personality and Generalship* (1933; reprint, Bloomington: Indiana University Press, 1957); Albert Castel, review of *The Marble Man* in *Civil War Times Illustrated* 17 (June 1978): 50. Connelly's book consists of two quite separate parts—the first an examination of the process by which Lee became first a Southern and then a national hero, the second a psychological interpretation of the general. Both include valuable insights as well as conclusions that reach far beyond the author's evidence.

16. Nolan, *Lee Considered*, 106; Confederate Historical Institute *Dispatch*, May–June 1992, p. 6. For a representative positive reaction to *Lee Considered*, see the review by Drew Gilpin Faust on the front page of the *New York Times Book Review*, 7 July 1991.

17. A major biography of Lee by Emory M. Thomas will appear sometime in 1995. Thomas's preliminary findings suggest that he will find an interpretive middle ground between rapt admirers of Lee's generalship and critics who believe his actions harmed the Confederate cause. In one essay, Thomas noted that "[s]omewhere

between Freeman's simple saint and Connelly's collection of complexes was the 'real' Lee. The challenge is much more than simply adding Connelly's 'Lee' to Freeman's 'Lee' and dividing by two, to arrive at an average 'Lee.'" Emory M. Thomas, "Marse Robert at Mid-Life," in *The Confederate High Command & Related Topics,* ed. Lawrence L. Hewitt and Roman J. Heleniak (Shippensburg PA: White Mane Publishing, 1990), 112. See also Emory M. Thomas, "Young Man Lee," in *Leadership During the Civil War*, ed. Lawrence L. Hewitt and Roman J. Heleniak (Shippensburg PA: White Mane Publishing, 1992), 38–54.

18. The principal sources for published letters and other wartime documents by Lee are numbers 103, 104, 112, 113, 114, and 188 in the bibliography at the end of this volume.

19. Jubal A. Early, *The Campaigns of Gen. Robert E. Lee. An Address By Lieut. General Jubal A. Early, Before Washington and Lee University, January 19th, 1872* (Baltimore: John Murphy & Co., 1872).

20. Robert Stiles, *Four Years Under Marse Robert* (1903; reprint, Dayton OH: Press of Morningside Bookshop, 1977), 191–92; Early's quotation is in "The Campaigns of Gen. R. E. Lee," this volume.

21. Francis C. Lawley, "General Lee," *Blackwood's Edinburgh Magazine* 101 (March 1872): 348–63. Lawley wrote in response to an invitation from the magazine to review John Esten Cooke's *Life of General Robert E. Lee* (New York: Appleton & Company, 1870).

22. Francis Lawley to Jubal A. Early, 14 May 1872, Jubal Early Papers, Library of Congress, Washington DC. William Stanley Hoole, *Lawley Covers the Confederacy* (Tuscaloosa AL: Confederate Publishing Company, 1964), examines Lawley's experiences in the Confederacy.

23. Field Marshall Viscount [Garnot] Wolseley, "General Lee," *Macmillan's Magazine* 55 (March 1887): 321–31.

24. Wolseley's quotation is in "General Lee," this volume. For a compilation of his writings about the Civil War, see Field Marshall Viscount Wolseley, *The American Civil War: An English View*, ed. James A. Rawley (Charlottesville: University Press of Virginia, 1964).

25. Excerpted from George A. Bruce, "The Strategy of the Civil War," a much longer piece that appeared in the Military Historical Society of Massachusetts's *Papers of the Military Historical Society of Massachusetts*, 14 vols. (1895–1918; reprint with new index volume, Wilmington NC: Broadfoot Publishing Company, 1989–90), 13:391–483. Bruce's examination of Lee has been given a title appropriate for this collection.

26. Bruce's *The Twentieth Regiment of Massachusetts Volunteer Infantry, 1861–1865* was published in Boston in 1906.

27. Freeman, *Lee* 4:165–87. Freeman's quotation is in "The Sword of Robert E. Lee," this volume.

28. Charles P. Roland, "The Generalship of Robert E. Lee," in *Grant, Lee, Lincoln and the Radicals*, ed. Grady McWhiney (Evanston IL: Northwestern University Press, 1964), 31–71.

29. Thomas L. Connelly, "Robert E. Lee and the Western Confederacy: A Criticism of Lee's Strategic Ability," *Civil War History* 15 (June 1969): 116–32. Connelly's article appears in this volume.

30. Albert Castel, "The Historian and the General: Thomas L. Connelly versus Robert E. Lee," *Civil War History* 16 (March 1970): 50–63. Castel's article appears in this volume.

31. The foundation for this essay is Gary W. Gallagher, " 'Upon Their Success Hang Momentous Issues': Generals," in *Why the Confederacy Lost*, ed. Gabor S. Boritt (New York: Oxford University Press, 1992), 79–108.

32. Hartwig's quotation is in "Robert E. Lee and the Maryland Campaign," this volume. See the essays by Robert K. Krick and Gary W. Gallagher in Gallagher, ed., *Antietam: Essays on the 1862 Maryland Campaign* (Kent OH: Kent State University Press, 1989) for examples of scholars who doubt that Lee's army was sufficiently strong to make the expedition into Maryland a success.

33. Krick's quotation is in "Lee at Chancellorsville," this volume.

34. Longstreet's quotations are in "Lee in Pennsylvania," this volume. His article was reprinted in *The Annals of the Civil War Written by Leading Participants North and South*, ed. Alexander Kelly McClurel (Philadelphia: The Times Publishing Company, 1879): 414–46, and in *Southern Historical Society Papers* 5:54–86.

35. Early's article appeared in *Southern Historical Society Papers* 4 (December 1877): 282–302.

36. Edward Porter Alexander, "Letter on Causes of Lee's Defeat at Gettysburg, in *Southern Historical Society Papers* 4 (September 1877): 97–111; quotation from p. 100.

37. Edward Porter Alexander to Frederic Bancroft, 20 October 1907, typescript at Kennesaw Mountain National Battlefield Park, Marietta, Georgia.

38. Freeman, *Lee*, 3:135–61. Freeman's quotations are in "Why Was Gettysburg Lost," this volume. In *Lee's Lieutenants: A Study in Command*, 3 vols. (New York: Charles Scribner's Sons, 1942–44), 3:187–89, Freeman softened his treatment of Longstreet at Gettysburg.

39. Alan T. Nolan, "R. E. Lee and July 1 at Gettysburg" in *The First Day at Gettysburg: Essays on Confederate and Union Leadership*, ed. Gary W. Gallagher (Kent OH: Kent State University Press, 1992), 1–29.

40. Gary W. Gallagher, " 'If the Enemy Is There We Must Attack Him': R. E. Lee and the Second Day at Gettysburg" in *The Second Day at Gettysburg: Essays on Confederate and Union Leadership*, ed Gary W. Gallagher (Kent OH: Kent State University Press, 1993), 1–27.

1. Lee circa 1850–52, while a captain of engineers in the United States Army, a pose widely reproduced as an engraving in the popular press during the Civil War. Francis Trevelyn Miller, ed. *The Photographic History of the Civil War*, 10 vols. (New York: Review of Reviews, 1911), 10:55.

2. Lee in 1862, a portrait that underscores the marked change in his appearance from the time he sat for the photograph in plate 1. Miller, *Photographic History*, 10:61.

3. A full-length view of Lee in martial dress by Minnis and Cowell, probably early 1863. As was his custom, Lee wears the insignia of a full colonel on his collar rather than the wreath and stars of a Confederate general. Miller, *Photographic History*, 2:235.

4. A full-length view taken by Julian Vannerson, probably in 1863, that presents a less-impressive figure than the booted and spurred portrait in plate 3. Courtesy of the Library of Congress.

5. Perhaps the best-known portrait of Lee, from the same sitting as the image in plate 4. Courtesy of the Library of Congress.

6. Lee in Richmond in April 1865, shortly after his surrender at Appomattox, in one of a series of poses for Mathew B. Brady. Miller, *Photographic History*, 10:69.

7. A profile of Lee taken at the same sitting as in plate 6. Miller, *Photographic History*, 3:23.

8. Lee on Traveller, taken in Lexington, Virginia, by Michael Miley in September 1866. Lee wears a Confederate uniform from which all insignia had been removed. Miller, *Photographic History*, 9:121.

LEE THE SOLDIER

★ I ★

TESTIMONY

OF R. E. LEE

Biographical and Editorial Notes

GARY W. GALLAGHER

Biographical Note

William Allan (1837–89), a native of Winchester, Virginia, earned an M.A. from the University of Virginia in 1860 and served as chief ordnance officer of the Second Corps of the Army of Northern Virginia under "Stonewall" Jackson, Richard S. Ewell, Jubal A. Early, and John Brown Gordon. Named professor of applied mathematics at Washington College in 1866, he taught in Lexington until 1873, when he became the first principal of the new McDonogh Institute in Baltimore, a position he held until his death. Among the most important Confederate writers, Allan collaborated with Jedediah Hotchkiss on *The Battlefields of Virginia: Chancellorsville* (New York, 1867) and on *History of the Campaign of Gen. T. J. (Stonewall) Jackson in the Shenandoah Valley of Virginia* (Philadelphia, 1880). His most ambitious work, titled *The Army of Northern Virginia in 1862*, appeared posthumously (Boston and New York, 1892).

Edward Clifford Gordon (1842–1922), a native of Richmond, Virginia, attended the University of Virginia before enlisting in the Richmond Howitzers in April 1861. An artillerist until March 1863, he transferred to staff, serving with John Echols's brigade and later with Jubal A. Early. Ordained a Presbyterian minister in 1872, he headed congregations in Virginia and Georgia before moving to Missouri, where, among other posts, he held the presidency of Westminster College and acted as secretary and treasurer for Home Missions, Synod of Missouri. His "The Battle of Bethel," an address delivered to the Richmond Howitzer Association in December 1882, was published as pages 14–84 of *Contributions to A History of The Richmond Howitzer Battalion. Pamphlet No. 1* (Richmond, 1883).

William Preston Johnston (1831–99), the eldest son of Confederate general Albert Sidney Johnston, was born in Louisville, Kentucky, and educated at Yale and at the law school of the University of Louisville. He spent most of the Civil War as a colonel and aide-de-camp to President Jefferson Davis, a great admirer of Johnston's father. Captured with Davis and imprisoned for several months after the war, he accepted the chair of history and English literature at Washington College in 1867, remaining in that position for a decade. He subsequently served as president of Louisiana State University and later of Tulane University. His publications included a biography of his father titled *The Life of Gen. Albert Sidney Johnston* (New York, 1878).

Editorial Note

The following transcriptions adhere strictly to the originals in almost all respects. William Allan was quite irregular regarding punctuation, sometimes using apostrophes and sometimes leaving them out, placing commas and capitalizing words according to no strict conventions, and pursuing a haphazard course with periods after abbreviations. He also misspelled a number of names—both of individuals and places—and took little notice of when he should begin new paragraphs. The fact that Allan wrote quickly to get down as much of Lee's conversation as possible explains the somewhat chaotic nature of the document. Punctuation, spelling, and similar elements of Allan's text have not been corrected silently, nor will the reader find a procession of "sics" or bracketed editorial intrusions.

The typescript of William Preston Johnston's memoranda is littered with misspelled words and other errors, many of which have been corrected in ink on the original. These corrections were incorporated in the current transcription; however, misspelled words that eluded the earlier proofreaders were not corrected, nor was Johnston's paragraphing changed. Similarly, the typescript of E. C. Gordon's memorandum, which is much cleaner than Johnston's, was not altered.

In sum, these texts may read a bit awkwardly in places. That seemed preferable to making wholesale alterations. Anyone who cites the memoranda, of course, enjoys the option of adopting a different editorial approach.

In terms of scholarly apparatus, the endnotes contain information pertinent to a full understanding of the texts. Persons, events, books, and articles are identified within the context of the memoranda. The notes offer no summaries of the lives and careers of prominent officers or other figures who are included in standard biographical reference tools. Lesser known figures are identified more fully. Occasionally, notes guide the reader to other

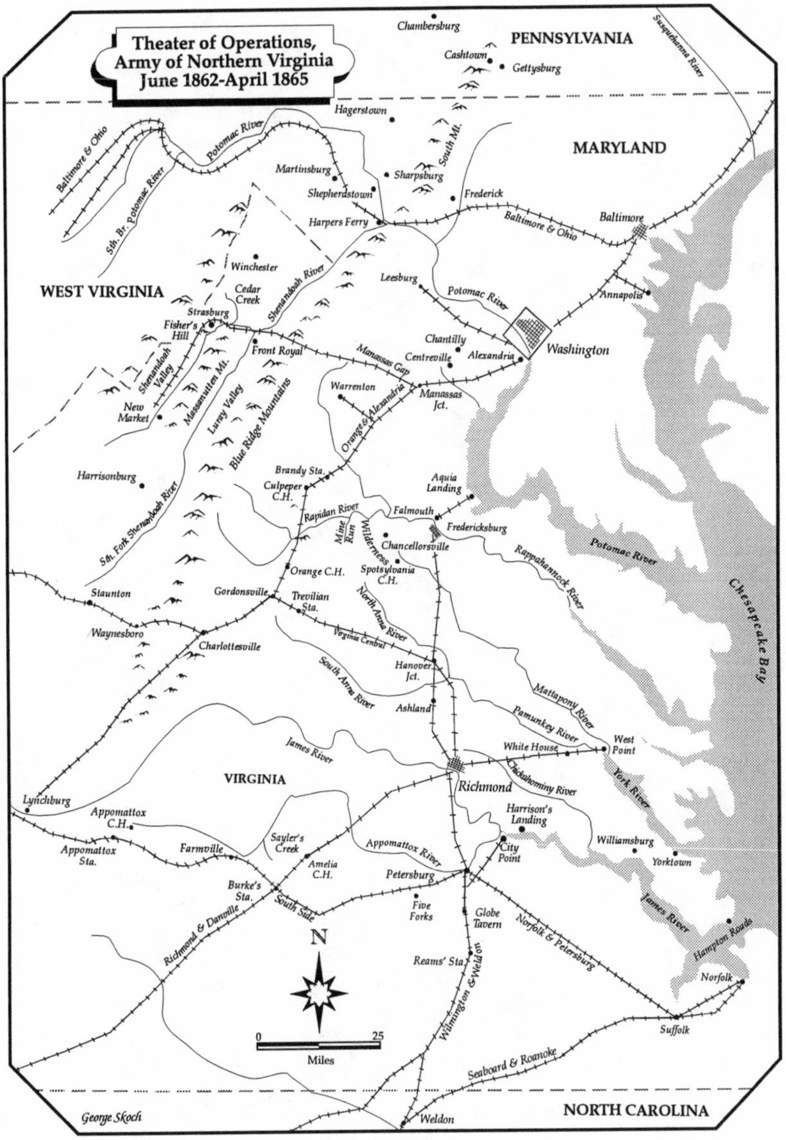

material that illuminates a point raised by Lee, but there are no extensive historiographical discussions of the sort that overwhelm too many edited documents.

Memoranda of Conversations with General Robert E. Lee

WILLIAM ALLAN

Memda of a conversation with Gen. R. E. Lee, held Feb. 15 1868

On going in to see the Genl,[1] after talking on other matters, he asked me if I had seen a piece in D. H. Hill's magazine, entitled Lost Dispatch in reference to the first Md. Campaign (1862), and said that there were many mistakes in it.[2] "Hill (the author) says the loss of the dispatch was advantageous to the C.S. cause, but he takes an entirely different view from me." The Genl then gave an outline of this campaign. He said that after Chantilly (about Sept. 1) he found he could do nothing more against the Yankees unless he attacked them in their fortifications around Washington, which he did not want to do, and he therefore determined to cross the river into Maryland, and thus effect two things—1st To relieve Va. from both armies, as he thought such a movement would force Genl McClellan[3] over the river—and 2nd to live for a time on the abundant supplies in Maryland. That in reference to this he talked to Gen. Jackson,[4] who advised him to go up into the Valley and cross the Potomac at or above Harper's Ferry, clearing out the forces at Winchester &c. He (Lee) opposed this, because it took him too far from McClellan, and might not induce the latter to cross over, which was his main object, and he therefore ordered Jackson to take command in advance & cross in Loudon and move towards Frederick, destroying the canal &c. He sent Stuart[5] with him, and had just ordered D. H. Hill, (who had just come up from Richmond) to White's Ferry in anticipation of this. He told Jackson to take Hill with him. He came on with remainder of the army as soon as he could. At Frederick he made

Stuart divide his cavalry and threaten both Baltimore & Washington on both flanks of McClellan, giving out on each flank that he (Lee) was behind with his whole force. Stuart reported McClellan near Rockville, advancing very slowly, meanwhile covering Balt. & Washington, uneasy & uncertain. The Yankees still holding Harpers Ferry &c in the rear. He formed a plan to overwhelm them by sending three columns, Walker, McLaws and Jackson to center at Harpers Ferry and if possible catch them.[6] Jackson was to take his own three divisions only—Lee kept D. H. Hill & Longstreet[7] & Stuart with himself, Stuart still to demonstrate and deceive the enemy. He had the orders sent from his own Head Quarters to Hill, as the latter was now under his immediate command, & it was perfectly proper for Gen. Jackson to do so too, to inform Hill that he was no longer under his (Jackson's) orders. The orders named the points to be reached by the divisions concentrating at Harpers Ferry, and indicated the purpose, but this had all been fully *explained* to Jackson, verbally, and no one could imagine that the order did not contemplate just what Jackson did. He then retired from Frederick as McClellan advanced, and held the Gap in the mountain with Hill,[8] keeping Stuart to watch and deceive the enemy. He then took Longstreet & went to Hagerstown, to capture flour and stores there which were being run off to Pa. Longst did not like marching, and said "Gen. I wish we could stand still and let the d——d Yankees come to us!" The night he was at Hagerstown he recd a dispatch from Stuart, saying that McClellan had taken the advance, & was pushing with his whole force, & that he, (Stuart) was falling back. Later, an alarming dispatch was also received from Hill to same effect. Lee then wakened Longstreet and began to march back at day light. Hot day & troops tired when they reached Boonesboro but gap was held. Stuart informed him of report of a Md. gentleman, who said he was at McClellan's H. Qr.s when Lost Dispatch was found, and that he (McC.) openly expressed his delight.[9] This night Lee found out that Cobb[10] had been pressed back from Crampton's Gap, and this made it necessary to retire from Boonesboro Gap, which was done next morning and position at Sharpsburg taken. Message was sent to hurry up Jackson, (who was a day later than expected,) & battle was given at Sharpsburg with a tired and weakened force, (about 35000 men) & not all on the ground till late in the day. Had the Lost Dispatch not been lost, and had McClellan continued his cautious policy for two or three days longer, I (Lee) would have had all my troops reconcentrated on Md. side, stragglers up, men rested & I *intended then to attack McClellan*, hoping the best results from state of my troops & those of enemy. Tho' it is impossible to to[11] say that victory would have certainly resulted, it is probable that the loss of the dispatch changed the character of the campaign. He spoke very highly of Jackson, said D.H. Hill had such a queer temperament he could never tell what to expect from him, & that he croaked. This was the case around Petersburg in 1864 when Beauregard complained of it to Gen. Lee.[12]

Speaking of Chancellorsville

He said that Jackson at first preferred to attack Sedgewick & Co[13] in the plain at Fredericksburg, that he told Jackson he feared it was impracticable, as he had thought at the first battle of Fredericksburg Dec 13. Hard to get at the enemy and harder to get away if we drove him into the river. But told Jackson if he (J.) said it could be done he would give orders for it. Jackson asked to be allowed again to examine the ground & enemy, did so during the evening, and at night came to Lee and said he thought He (Lee) was right, it would be inexpedient to attack there. "Then," said Lee, "move in the morning up to Anderson."[14] Next day he found Jackson on skirmish line, driving in Yankee Skirmishers around Chancellorsville. He, (Lee) wanted to attack on his right, to cut Hooker off from the river, and rode down & examined Yankee lines all way to the river, but found no place fit for attack, returned at night & found Jackson, and asked him if he had found any place to attack. Jackson said no. Lee said then we must get round on his (Yankee) right. Jackson[15] said he had been enquiring about roads by the furnace. After a while Stuart[16] came and said he would go down to furnace and see what he could learn about roads. He soon returned with Dr. Lacy who said a circuit could be made round to Wilderness Tavern and a young man living in the county and then in the cavalry was sent for to act as guide.[17]

On Feb 25th (Tuesday) Gen. Lee sent for me, showed me a Globe with Cameron's statement about his conduct at beginning of the war, and read me a letter he had just written to Reverdy Johnson, denying Cameron's charge.[18] He stated to me all the circumstances connected with his resignation from the old army and his acceptance of command from Virginia. Gen. Scott[19] sent for him in the winter, (he was in Texas,) and he reached Washington a day or two after Lincoln's inauguration. Scott told him he wanted him to revise (in connection with others) the army regulations. Lee had asked him upon his arrival in Washington what he (Scott) wanted, and stated that he (Lee) could not go on duty against the South. Scott told him as above about revising the regulations, and showed him a mass of correspondence between himself and Lincoln and others, which made Scott think there would be no war. Among other letters shown was that one of Scott about "wayward Sisters" &c., and one from Seward, very *pacific* in tone.[20] Gen. Lee went to Arlington much relieved, as he had intended resigning if there were any intentions of putting him on War duty, and wanted to do this before any orders should be determined on, as he did not desire to resign under orders.[21] Scott's talk made him think there wd not be war. He could not realize that the people would fight. Matters went on unchanged, (he waiting for Gen. Smith and other members of the revising board)[22] until in April, on a Thursday which must have been the 18th he went at old Mr. Blair's request to see him at young B's house, opposite War Depart.[23] Had long interview with old Blair, who told him Mr. L. and Cabinet wanted Gen. Lee to be Commander in Chief in field, (as Scott was too old) and tried in every way to persuade him to take it. Talked all over the Secession question & the slavery question—appealed to his ambition—spoke of the looking of the country to him as the representative of the Washington family &c.[24] Lee replied courteously all the time, agreed about the folly of Secession, and deprecated War. Said as far as the negro was concerned he would willingly give up his own (400) for peace[25]—spoke kindly of the Govt and how he had never had reason to complain of it &c., but at the same time said distinctly that he would not take arms against the South. After a long interview in which B was very wily and keen, Lee went direct to Scott's office, who was busy, but at once admitted him and received him kindly. Lee told S. what B. had just said, and that he had declined the place and also stated the reason. Scott expressed his deep regret, but said he had rather expected it from what Lee said on his return from Texas. Lee went home, and thinking over the matter concluded he ought to resign, as he was not willing to obey orders in a certain contingency, wrote his resignation next day, but kept it by him another night to reflect fully, did so, and on Saturday morning enclosed the resignation in a note to Gen. Scott and sent it to him. Thro' an aid of Scott's who lived with Lee, (Williams by name)[26] he heard at dinner Saturday that the resignation had been received by Scott, approved & forwarded to the War Depart. and that all the Depart. were in a stir over it. He remained at Arlington until Monday. On Sunday night Judge Robinson[27] came to see him, and told him about Secession of Virginia, officially, said Convention had sent him to see Scott, and ask him to Richmond to command her forces. Scott had refused, and he (Robn) had been instructed in such a contingency to see Lee and invite him to Richmond. Had little talk as it was Sunday night, (this was first communication ever received about or from the Va. side,) promised to meet Robinson at Alexandria next morning. Did so, taking valise, and after a talk got on the cars and went to Richd. Met Letcher[28] and accepted command. Never drew any pay from time of return from Texas till resignation. Hoped and believed even after resignation that there would be peace, and intended to live in retirement. One reason of going so promptly to Richd was a visit to White House[29] which had been some time contemplated. Never had any conversation about command of U.S. Army with any one except as above, & refused to advise young Williams & brother what to do in the emergency.

Tuesday March 3. Gen. Lee, upon my showing him a letter from Gen. Lilly[30] in which it was stated that Gen. Ewell had given $500 to be applied to the increase of his (Lee's) Salary, said he was obliged to Gen. E but could not accept it, would be glad for the College to have it, but that he already received more than enough for his services.[31] He then talked of Gen. Ewell, of whom he spoke very kindly, said he had known him long in the west, & that he had long known his faults as a military leader—his quick alternations from elation to despondency his want of decision &c. He said that in the campaign of 1863, after he had sent Ewell ahead, and had given him full instructions, and told him that he had sent him ahead confiding in his judgment, and that he must be guided by his own judgment in any unforseen emergency, that at Winchester Ewell, after sending him very encouraging messages about entrapping Milroy, and detailing Rode's & Early's movements, suddenly sent a dispatch stating that upon closer inspection he found the works too strong to be attacked, and asking his (Lee's) instructions![32] (Gen. Lee had feared the old habit of E. when he assigned him to the Corps, but had hoped he had gotten over it, & talked long and earnestly with him when he assumed command.) Again at the wilderness of May (5?) 1864, he urged Ewell to make the flank attack, made later in the day by Gordon, several times before it was done. He (Lee) intended it to be a full attack in flank, & intended to support it with all Ewell's corps and others if necessary, and to rout the enemy. Early, Lee thinks kept Ewell from pushing this matter, until very late; when Gordon did go, it was too late in the day, and he was not supported with sufficient force to accomplish anything decisive.[33]

On May 12 Lee found Ewell perfectly prostrated by the misfortune of the morning, and too much overwhelmed to be efficient, and on May 17 or 18 when E. went out on Grant's flank, to attack, and did get into a corps or two of troops, he lost all presence of mind, and Lee found him prostrate on the ground, and declaring he cd not get Rodes div. out. (Rodes being heavily engaged with the enemy.) He (Lee) told him to order Rodes back and that if he could not get him out, he (Lee) could. When the Corps was about to come to the Valley E. applied to be reinstated in Command. Lee tried to put him off by sickness, but when E. insisted, he told him plainly he could not send him in command. *Rodes had come to Lee and protested against E's being again placed in command.* After this Gen. Lee recd an anonymous letter, appealing to him by his long friendship &c. to reinstate Ewell. Gen.

Lee had heard that Ewell thought hardly of his treatment, and he (Lee) was very reluctant to displace him, but felt compelled to do so.[34] He expressed the kindest personal feeling for E. and wrote a kind letter thanking him for his kind offer to increase his salary, but declining it.

March 10. Went into the Gen.'s room on business—After a bit he showed me an extract from some N.Y. paper that had been sent him, abusing him severely for his conduct in taking the C.S. side. The said piece evidently from some violent radical sheet wh. was taking as a text the movement on foot by Beecher & Co. for the benefit of the College.[35] The Gen. said he never noticed newspaper reports, nor the speeches of such men as Butler,[36] (who had made he said statements similar to those in the piece he was reading) but that these people repeated the same old falsehoods against him & he supposed wd do so. First, they said he was educated by the Gov. at W.P. True, he says, but he was sent there by Va. who was entitled to this, and he could not see that it at all lessened his obligation to obey her. 2^d^ He was never on Gen. Scott's staff except a little while in the city of Mexico, when Maj. Smith[37] the Chief Engineer wad disabled or removed. 3^d^ He only recollects seeing Scott twice after his return from Texas, (Mar. 1861) before he went to Rich^d^ once directly after his return when he reported to Scott, & then the only confidential talk was that he asked Scott what was going to be done, and told him that if he (Lee) was to be placed on duty against the South he wanted to know so that he might at once resign. Scott then showed him Lincoln's & Seward's letters, and made him (Lee) believe, and as he (Lee) thinks believed fully himself, that a peaceful solution would be attained. One of Seward's letters was very emphatic, & stated that he (Seward) would not remain in the cabinet if he thought any thing but peace contemplated. Lee saw no more of Scott, (and was in no manner in his confidence) until the day B. offered him command of the army. Then he went to Scott & told him that he had declined, when S. said "he was afraid so," & then he (Scott) told him that he intended to remain and gave his reasons for it—that he did not think there would ever be so good a gov^t^. in the country if the present were broken up &c. Lee did not blame Scott, for there were powerful reasons on both sides, and it was a hard thing for him even, thinking as he did that Secession was foolish and the war wrong, to break loose and come South. He knew the country was unprepared—Told Mr. Davis often and early in the war that the slaves should be emancipated, that it was the only way to remove a weakness at home and to get sympathy abroad, and to divide our enemies, but Davis would not hear of it.[38] Thinks highly of Davis, but blames him for not conciliating his opponents & trying to unite all in the Cause. Mr. Davis' enemies became so many as to destroy his power and to paralyse the country &c.

April 15, 1868

Mema. of conversation just had with Gen R. E. Lee about Gettysburg &c. occasioned by a letter of inquiry addressed to him by W. M. McDonald, and the answer to which he submitted to me.[39] McD. asked—1st Why in 1862 Lee at Frederick City turned round to Harpers Ferry and did not march at once on Baltimore. 2d Why Burnside[40] was not attacked in the plain at Fredericksburg after his repulse—3d Why Gettysburg was fought and lost.

In regard to the first Gen. Lee said—he had never invaded the North with an eye to holding permanently the hostile portions of it.[41] That especially in 1862 his object was not primarily to take Baltimore or to undertake any very decided offensive movement. It was in the first place to get the enemy away from the works in front of Washington, which he tho't it folly to attack from the Manassas side, next to subsist our own army. He says he could not stay where he was at Manassas, from want of supplies and adequate transportation. He could not go forward for he thought it injudicious to attack the fortifications—To have retired up into Loudoun was giving the enemy possession of Fairfax &c. and inviting him to flank him towards Richmond. By crossing the river, and thus threatening Baltimore and Washington, he drew the enemy from their works, thus relieved Va. from their presence, and got ample supplies from Md. for his own troops. Once there, in order to remain for any time or to be in proper position for a battle when he chose or should be forced to deliver it, his communications were to be kept clear through the Valley, and to clear them, and capture the detached force at Harpers Ferry, was the object of his movement then. He would have fought McC after H's F. if he had had his troops all in hand, and McC. out so that he could get at him. Sharpsburg was forced on him by McC. finding out his plans and moving quickly in consequence.

2. In regard to Burnside, he stated as he had said before to me, that it was folly to attack the enemy under the guns on the Stafford side. That the larger part of our losses at Fredericksburg resulted from pursuing the enemy too far into the plain, that he had carefully examined the whole river, and was convinced nothing of that sort could have been judiciously attempted, unless by night when the enemy was retiring. This effort he wd. have made but did not know of their retreat till morning. He did not expect them to retreat. Hoped they would have tried his lines again.

3rd As for Gettysburg—First he did not intend to give general battle in Pa. if he could avoid it—The South was too weak to carry on a *war of invasion*, and his offensive movements against the North were never intended except as parts of a defensive system. He did not know the Federal army was at Gettysburg, *could not believe it*, as Stuart had been specially ordered to cover his (Lee's) movement & keep him informed of the position of the enemy, & he (Stuart) had sent no word. He found himself engaged with the Federal army therefore, unexpectedly, and had to fight. This being determined on, victory wd. have been won if he could have gotten one decided simultaneous attack on the whole line. This he tried his utmost to effect for three days, and failed. Ewell he could not get to act with decision, Rodes, Early, Johnson[42] attacked and were hurt in detail. Then Longstreet & Hill[43] &c. could not be gotten to act in concert. Thus the Federal troops were enabled to be opposed to each of our corps, or even divisions in succession. As it was, however, he inflicted more damage than he received, and broke up the Federal summer campaign.[44] When he retired he would have crossed the Potomac at once if he could have done so. It was so swollen as to delay him, and hence his works &c. at Hagerstown. He would not have been sorry if Meade[45] had attacked him there, but he did not stop specially to invite it, but because the river was high. Meade's failure to attack showed how he had suffered. In regard to going into Pa. at all, he thought it was far better than remaining at Fredericksburg. He had twice been attacked there, and succeeded, but he did not wish again to remain there to risk another attempt. The position was to be easily flanked, and the plan Grant afterwards pursued might have been tried at any time.[46] He thought it best to improve the advantage gained by going North, thus drawing away the enemy from the Rappahan^{k} exciting their fears for Washington, and, by watching his opportunities, baffle and break up their plans. To have lain at Fredericks^{g}. would have allowed them time to collect force and initiate a new campaign on the old plan. In going into Pa. he diverted their attention, kept them thinking of Washington instead of Richmond, & got ample supplies for his army. He did not want to fight, unless he could get a good opportunity to hit them in detail. He expected however probably to find it necessary to give battle before his return in the Fall, as it would have been difficult to retreat without it. He had no idea of permanent occupation of Pa. He was troubled as it was to forage, so weak was the force he cd spare for this purpose. He expected therefore to move about, to manoeuver & alarm the enemy, threaten their cities, hit any blows he might be able to do without risking a general battle, & then towards Fall return nearer his base.[47]

Stuart's failure to carry out his instructions *forced the battle of Gettysburg, & the imperfect, halting way in which his corps commanders* (especially Ewell) *fought the battle, gave victory,* (which as he says trembled for 3 days in the balance) *finally to the foe*. He says that one day, (I think the second) he consulted Ewell and told him that if he could not carry his part of the line, he would move the 2^{d} Corps to the right of Longstreet and threaten their communications with Baltimore, but that Ed. Johnson and Ewell said the line then held could be carried. Johnson, Rodes, Early however attacked in succession, and were not able to hold any advantage. Gen. Lee talked feelingly of the criticism to which he had been subjected, said 'critics' talked much of that they knew little about, said he had fought honestly and earnestly to the best of his knowledge and ability for the 'Cause' and had *never allowed* his own advantage or reputation to come into consideration. He cared nothing for these, success was the great matter. Instanced Gen. Joe. Johnston's sensitiveness on this score, and how wrong and unwise it was.[48] He referred to a reported conversation of Longstreet, in which the latter stated that Gen. Lee was under a promise to the Leut. Generals not to fight a general battle in Pa. The Gen. said he did not believe this was ever said by Longstreet. That the idea was absurd. He had never made any such promise, and had never thought of doing any such thing.[49]

Dec. 17. 1868—I went into the Generals office this morning to talk about the proposal of the Ins. Co.[50] and while there urged him to prepare his History.[51] He talked of the difficulties and referred to the many errors which had become rife, and which it would be necessary for him to correct, as one of the disagreeable things which stood in his way. He spoke of the mistakes in Dabney's Life of Jackson,[52] & told me about the campaign of 1862. He said that when he took command, (on Johnston's wounding,) he found it wd. be necessary to strike a blow, that most of the Genl^{s} in the army were opposed to this, that Whiting[53] for instance was for holding the lines and retiring gradually before the enemy. But he (Lee) thought that would never do, and he proposed to Mr. Davis to bring down Jackson, & gather all and make an attack on McClellan. Mr. Davis hesitated and held back, came out to see him and talked the whole matter over, and after considering another day, granted finally his permission. Jackson had written proposing to go into Md. and push for Washington, but Lee told him the movement wd be premature, and that it was necessary first to get rid of McClellan, and that he wanted him to hit the Yankees in the Valley, so as to keep them quiet, and then bring everything down to join him. To deceive the enemy he sent troops to Jackson, sending them round by Lynchburg & knowing that the news wd reach the enemy, and induce the belief that Jackson was to be pushed North. All of Jackson's movements were in accordance with letters from him, (of which Dabney says nothing.) He sent for Jackson to come to Richmond to see him, met him there, and arranged the plan for the attack on M^{c}C's right. Jackson appointed a certain day to be up, and then Lee was to meet him with the mass of the army before Richmond. Lee told Jackson that he had not given himself time enough, and *insisted* that he should be allowed 24 hours more. With this under standing he prepared everything, &

moved a part of his troops over at Mechanicksville to attack in conjunction with Jackson. He was disappointed in not finding J.[54] Stuart who had been sent over to join him & to assist him, reported him not up. Lee was then uneasy for fear the enemy seeing his movement and the stripping of his Richmond lines, would push forward and reach the city, and so he attacked at Ellyson and Mechanicsville with what troops he had, and in spite of the formidable works, in order to occupy the enemy and prevent any counter movement. His Eng^r reported against attacking there, but he was obliged to do *something*. So again the next day Jackson was still not up, and now the two Hills &c. all being over the river he was forced to push forward and attack at Gaine's Mill with all his energy.[55] Otherwise with a large part of his army really farther from Rich^d than McClellan[56] was, disaster was to be apprehended. He had communicated too with Jackson, and hoped to have his attack soon supported. Jackson did not get in till late in the afternoon, hence the severe fight that A. P. Hill had in the morning to himself.

He referred to the pieces lately in the papers about a proposed night attack at Fredericksburg on Jackson's part. He said this was not so, and that when he and Jackson were talking over the matter the day after the fight, *he* asked J. if it would be possible to pick[57] a body of troops and attack in the night, and that Jackson advised against it, and said that his (J's) troops even in the twilight of the evening before, (that of the day of the fight) had gotten into such confusion in the plain as to fire into each other.

He also referred to the fall of Petersburg, and said the immediate occasion was Longstreet's delay in coming over, that he had written to L. several times telling him that the enemy had mostly left his front and were on the South side, but that L. would not be convinced, and insisted they were still before him. This however only hastened what would soon have come any how.

February 19, 1870

Went by appointment to see Gen Lee, who told me he wished to give me Cutt's report on the Va. Boundary, which Pierce had just sent him.[58] After this he read me another letter from Fitz John Porter, and his own reply in regard to the second battle of Manasses.[59] He then talked nearly an hour about that and other battles—said he breakfasted before day on the morning of Aug. 29, on the west side of Thoroughfare Gap & while at break fast received word from Longstreet that the Gap was open and that he was putting his troops in on the march. The General said that on his arrival there the evening before, he found some Federal troops and artillery ready to dispute his passage, but knowing the country well, he sent a division by a path over the Mountain that night, though the circuit was 5 miles. The division got over and camped on the Washington side, and their presence doubtless induced the enemy to withdraw. He started forward by daylight and passed the gap, and got in the neighborhood of Gainesville he thinks by nine oclock, meeting Stuart & riding on with him. He sent back word to Longstreet to put his troops in order as they came up. Then sent Stuart to the extreme right, who after a while returned and reported a heavy force demonstrating there. He went then himself, and saw troops (Porter's as it turns out,) did not think them disposed to attack. They were peaceable looking as he expressed it. Told Stuart so, but ordered Longstreet to send some troops to support Stuart, and told the latter to make all the show he could, & prevent the enemy attacking, and if he did attack to hold him in check. Thinks Longstreet was in position by noon. Received after this word from Jackson that he was hard pressed, & asking reinforcements. He then ordered Long. to attack, & Hood & Evans[60] were put in on Jackson's right. Hood did not like the place and said so, but Lee said he must attack any how and relieve Jackson. Hood and E. did so, and drove the Yankee's handsomely, and after night returned to Lee[61] delighted & excited, and said the enemy were lying thick "like a bed of roses," (they were the Zouaves.)[62] Next day ordered every thing to attack late in the evening, after the assaults of the enemy had been repulsed, & carried every thing before him. Said he did not care about Pope's[63] or Porter's quarrel. That Porter was not a strong man, wd. do well enough with somebody to tell him, but rather timid under responsibility. Anderson's troops got up during the battle, but were hardly engaged. D. H. Hill did not arrive until after Ox Hill. Knew Porter quite well. He was his Adj. while Sup^{t} at West Point, after Gen. Seth Williams[64] left.

Spoke feelingly of Gettysburg, said much was said about risky movements—Everything was risky in our war. He knew oftentimes that he was playing a very bold game, but it was the only *possible* one. Said he had urged the Gov^{t}. before going to Penn. in 1863, to bring Beauregard to Manasses with all the troops that could be got, & threaten Washington in that quarter. Mr. Davis promised to do so, but it was never done, probably the difficulties were too great. Did not expect much more than a demonstration, but Beauregard with a few troops there, wd. have produced a great diversion, and a great moral effect. Mr. Davis did not like the movement northward said he was afraid Lee could not get away, that the enemy would attack. Lee said he had no fears about getting off, the only trouble was about Richmond, but that he thought by concealing his movements and managing well, he could get so far North as to threaten Washington before they could check him, & this once done he knew there was no need of further fears about their moving on Rich. Succeeded in this, but failed at Gettysburg from a variety of causes. 1. Stuart failed to give him information, and this deceived him into a general battle. Then he never cd. get a simultaneous attack on the enemy's position. Often thinks that if Jackson had been there he would have succeeded.

Said that at Chancellorsville, which was another "risky" movement, he told Jackson they must either make a *night* attack on Sedgewick in front, or move off and attack Hooker at C. Jackson went & reconnoitered & returned & reported against an attack in front, especially against a night attack, & then it was decided to move at once to Chancellorsville.

NOTES

1. Allan's memoranda are in Robert E. Lee Collection, Special Collections, James G. Leyburn Library, Washington and Lee University, Lexington, Virginia [repository cited hereafter as LL-W&L]. Anna Brooke Allan prepared five typed copies of the manuscript volume of Allan's memoranda in 1946, presenting one to the Southern Historical Collection at the University of North Carolina at Chapel Hill, and distributing the others to members of the family. The meetings recorded by Allan took place in Lee's office, usually in the morning, and Allan prepared his memoranda the same day.

2. The article to which Lee reacted was [Daniel Harvey Hill], "The Lost Dispatch," *The Land We Love* 4 (February 1868): 270–84. (Hill edited the magazine, in which all the articles, including this one, were unattributed.) A major general and division commander in Lee's army during the 1862 Maryland campaign, Hill wrote this piece as a vigorous denial that he had mislaid a copy of Lee's Special Orders No. 191 during the operation. He was prompted to do so by Edward A. Pollard's statement that "A copy of the order directing the movement of the army from Frederick had been sent to D. H. Hill; and this vain and petulant officer, in a moment of passion, had thrown the paper on the ground. It was picked up by a Federal soldier, and McClellan thus strangely became possessed of the exact detail of his adversary's plan of operations." Edward A. Pollard, *The Lost Cause* (New York: E. B. Treat & Company, 1866), 314.

3. Maj. Gen. George Brinton McClellan, a native of Pennsylvania, commanded the Army of the Potomac during the Maryland campaign.

4. Maj. Gen. (later Lt. Gen.) Thomas Jonathan "Stonewall" Jackson of Virginia, who led the left wing (subsequently the Second Corps) of the Army of Northern Virginia during the Maryland campaign.

5. Maj. Gen. James Ewell Brown "Jeb" Stuart, a Virginian and Lee's chief of cavalry during the period from June 1862 to mid-May 1864.

6. Brig. Gen. (later Maj. Gen.) John G. Walker and Maj. Gen. Lafayette McLaws, natives of Missouri and Georgia respectively, commanded divisions in James

Longstreet's wing of the Army of Northern Virginia. Lee placed them temporarily under Jackson's command in the movement against Harpers Ferry.

7. Maj. Gen. (later Lt. Gen.) James Longstreet, born in South Carolina and often associated with Georgia or Alabama, led the right wing (subsequently the First Corps) of Lee's army.

8. Hill's troops defended Turner's and Fox's gaps, located just southeast of Boonsboro, Maryland, in the South Mountain range.

9. In *Landscape Turned Red: The Battle of Antietam* (New York: Ticknor & Fields, 1983), 349–52, Stephen Sears argues that Lee did not learn of the loss of Special Orders No. 191 until several months after the Maryland campaign ended. Lee's comments to Allan concerning this subject, concludes Sears, suggest that "the general unintentionally let the knowledge of events gained through hindsight cloud his memory of the exact contents of Stuart's dispatch reaching him that eventful night almost five and a half years before."

10. Brig. Gen. (later Maj. Gen.) Howell Cobb of Georgia led a brigade from his native state in Lafayette McLaws's division. Cobb performed very poorly at Crampton's Gap on 14 September.

11. The manuscript includes this double "to"; Allan may have meant to write "impossible too to say victory would certainly have resulted."

12. Gen. Pierre Gustave Toutant Beauregard, a native of Louisiana and the fifth ranking officer in the Confederate army, directed the defense of Petersburg during the 1864 Overland Campaign. L. Hal Bridges, *Lee's Maverick General: Daniel Harvey Hill* (New York: McGraw-Hill, 1961), offers a generally positive assessment of its subject. For a more critical reading of Hill's military personality, see the introduction by Gary W. Gallagher in the University of Nebraska Press reprint of Bridges's book (Lincoln, 1991), p. xv–xviii.

13. Maj. Gen. John Sedgwick, a native of Connecticut, commanded the Federal troops who remained at Fredericksburg while Maj. Gen. Joseph Hooker shifted the bulk of the Army of the Potomac around Lee's left flank during the opening phase of the Chancellorsville campaign in late-April 1863.

14. Maj. Gen. (later Lt. Gen.) Richard Heron Anderson, a South Carolinian, commanded a division in James Longstreet's First Corps. Remaining with the Army of Northern Virginia while Longstreet and part of his corps conducted the Suffolk campaign in the spring of 1863, Anderson and his troops fought at Chancellorsville and Salem Church on 1–4 May 1863.

15. This sentence first began with "Jackson," which was crossed out and replaced with "Stuart," which in turn was changed back to "Jackson."

16. This sentence first began, "After a while Jackson came"; "Jackson" was crossed out and replaced with "Stuart."

17. The Rev. Beverley Tucker Lacy, Jackson's favorite chaplain, was familiar with local roads because his brother, J. Horace Lacy, owned extensive property in the area. The "young man" almost certainly was Charles Beverly Wellford, a former artillerist rather than a cavalryman, whose family had extensive holdings

in the county. Catharine Furnace, to which Lee refers, was named after Wellford's mother.

18. Lee had read a copy of the *Congressional Globe* containing remarks made on 19 February by Senator Simon Cameron of Pennsylvania, former secretary of war under Abraham Lincoln and the leading Republican politician in his state. Lee wrote to Democratic Senator Reverdy Johnson of Maryland on 25 February to thank him for questioning Cameron's statements about Lee. For the text of Lee's letter to Johnson, see Alan T. Nolan, *Lee Considered: General Robert E. Lee and Civil War History* (Chapel Hill: University of North Carolina Press, 1991), 178–79.

19. Brevet Lt. Gen. Winfield Scott of Virginia, the ranking officer in the United States Army at the beginning of the Civil War. On Scott's high opinion of Lee, see Douglas Southall Freeman, *R. E. Lee: A Biography*, 4 vols. (New York: Charles Scribner's Sons, 1934–35), 1:294, and Charles Winslow Elliott, *Winfield Scott: The Soldier and the Man* (New York: Macmillan, 1937), 712–14.

20. In a letter to Secretary of State William Henry Seward dated 3 March 1861, and widely reprinted in the northern press, Scott suggested that one of Lincoln's options was to "Say to the seceded States, Wayward Sisters, depart in Peace!" See Winfield Scott, *Memoirs of Lieut.-General Winfield Scott, LL.D., Written by Himself*, 2 vols. (New York: Sheldon & Company), 2:625–28, and Elliott, *Winfield Scott*, 697–98. Chapter 49 of Elliott's *Winfield Scott* and chapter 17 of Glyndon G. Van Deusen's *William Henry Seward* (New York: Oxford University Press, 1967) examine Scott, Seward, and the crisis of March–April 1861.

21. The text first read "did not want to resign."

22. The Civil War intervened, and the revising board did not do its work.

23. At Abraham Lincoln's request, Francis Preston Blair Sr., a long-time Democrat who had been a close adviser to Andrew Jackson, invited Lee to discuss his possible appointment as commander of a large United States army soon to be raised. The two men met at 1651 Pennsylvania Avenue, home of Montgomery Blair, the elder Blair's son and Lincoln's postmaster general. On this meeting, see Freeman, *R. E. Lee* 1:436–37, and William E. Smith, *The Francis Preston Blair Family in Politics*, 2 vols. (New York: Macmillan, 1933), 2:17–18.

24. Lee's marriage in 1831 to Mary Ann Randolph Custis, the only daughter of Mary Washington's son George Washington Parke Custis, gave Lee a strong connection to George Washington.

25. Allan or some other person placed a question mark above the figure 400, indicating uncertainty about the number of slaves Lee stated he would liberate in the pursuit of peace. Although part of the slaveholding aristocracy of Virginia, Lee himself never owned more than a few slaves. His father-in-law, George Washington Parke Custis, died in October 1857 leaving an estate that included 196 slaves and instructions that these people be freed within five years. As executor of the will, Lee carried out Custis's wishes, completing the process of emancipation during the winter of 1862–63.

26. Lt. William Orton Williams, a kinsman of the Lee family, resigned his commission to join the Confederacy, proposed marriage to Agnes Lee during the

war (she refused him), and was executed as a spy by the Federals on 9 June 1863. After the war, Lee wrote Williams's sister Martha about his continuing bitterness concerning the execution: "[M]y blood boils at the thought of the atrocious outrage, against every manly & christian sentiment which the Great God alone is able to forgive. I cannot trust my pen or tongue to utter my feelings. He alone can give us resignation." R. E. Lee to Martha C. Williams, 1 December 1866, in R. E. Lee, *"To Markie": The Letters of Robert E. Lee to Martha Custis Williams, from the Originals in the Huntington Library*, ed. Avery C. Craven (Cambridge, Mass.: Harvard University Press, 1933), 71–72. See also Freeman, *R. E. Lee*, 3:211–13.

27. John Robertson (not Robinson), a three-term Whig representative from Virginia in the U. S. House of Representatives during the 1830s, served as judge of the circuit court of chancery for Henrico County. See Freeman, *R. E. Lee*, 1:637–38 on Robertson's visit with Lee.

28. A native of Lexington, Virginia, and former U. S. congressman, John Letcher served as governor of his state from January 1860 through 1864.

29. William Henry Fitzhugh "Rooney" Lee, the general's second son, inherited the 4,000-acre White House plantation in New Kent County, Virginia, from his grandfather G. W. P. Custis.

30. Robert Doak Lilley of Virginia rose to the rank of brigadier general in the Confederate army and later served as chief financial agent of Washington College (his alma mater) during Lee's tenure as president.

31. A native of Georgetown DC, Richard Stoddert Ewell served in the Army of Northern Virginia through much of the war, rising to the rank of lieutenant general and succeeding Jackson in command of the Second Corps. Ewell's gift of $500 went into the college's endowment.

32. Maj. Gen. Robert Emmett Rodes and Maj. Gen. (later Lt. Gen.) Jubal Anderson Early, both of Virginia, commanded divisions in Ewell's Second Corps during the Gettysburg campaign. Lee's allusion is to the battle of Second Winchester, fought on 14–15 June 1863, at which Ewell's Second Corps defeated Federals commanded by Maj. Gen. Robert H. Milroy, a native Indianan.

33. Brig. Gen. (later Maj. Gen.) John Brown Gordon of Georgia led a brigade from his home state in Early's division of Ewell's Second Corps during the battle of the Wilderness on 5–6 May 1864. For a careful discussion of the controversy surrounding the timing and scale of Gordon's assault against Grant's right on 6 May, see chapter 7 of Gordon C. Rhea, *The Battle of the Wilderness, May 5–6, 1864* (Baton Rouge: Louisiana State University Press, 1994).

34. On Lee's problems with Ewell during the Overland Campaign, see Gary W. Gallagher, "The Army of Northern Virginia in May 1864: A Crisis of High Command," *Civil War History* 36 (June 1990): 101–18.

35. Henry Ward Beecher, abolitionist and minister of the Plymouth (Congregationalist) Church of Brooklyn, ranked among the premier orators in the mid-19th century United States. At a meeting at New York's Cooper Institute on 3 March 1868, Beecher called for northern donations to Washington College, which under Lee's leadership, he said, would provide an excellent education to young southern men.

36. Benjamin Franklin Butler, a native of New Hampshire and, after William Tecumseh Sherman, the Federal general most hated by Confederates, represented Massachusetts in the U. S. House of Representatives in 1868.

37. Lee became the ranking engineer with Scott's army in Mexico when Maj. John Lind Smith, a native of South Carolina, fell ill just prior to the final battles for Mexico City in September 1847.

38. On Jefferson Davis's and Lee's roles in the debate over black emancipation in the Confederacy, see Robert F. Durden, *The Gray and the Black: The Confederate Debate on Emancipation* (Baton Rouge: Louisiana State University Press, 1972). Lee's support for enrolling black men in the Confederate army with a promise of freedom did not become public knowledge in the wartime South until a letter from Lee to William Barksdale dated 18 February 1865 was published in several newspapers.

39. Lee's response to William M. McDonald was published in J. William Jones and others, eds., *Southern Historical Society Papers*, 52 vols. (1876–1959; reprint with 3-vol. index, Wilmington NC: Broadfoot Publishing Company, 1990–92), 7:445–46.

40. Maj. Gen. Ambrose Everett Burnside, a native of Indiana, commanded the Army of the Potomac during the Fredericksburg campaign.

41. For Lee's contemporary discussions of his reasons for crossing the Potomac in 1862 and again in 1863, see R. E. Lee to Jefferson Davis, 3, 4, 5 September 1862, Lee to Jefferson Davis, 10, 30 May, 25 June 1863, and Lee to Secretary of War James A. Seddon, 10, 30 May, 8 June 1863, in R. E. Lee, *The Wartime Papers of R. E. Lee*, ed. Clifford Dowdey and Louis H. Manarin (Boston: Little, Brown, 1961), 292–96, 482–83, 496, 498, 505.

42. Maj. Gen. Edward "Allegheny" Johnson of Virginia led one of Ewell's three Second Corps divisions at Gettysburg.

43. Lt. Gen. Ambrose Powell Hill, a Virginian who commanded the Third Corps in the Army of Northern Virginia at Gettysburg.

44. Lee commented on the damage inflicted on the Army of the Potomac at Gettysburg in a conversation with John Seddon, brother of the Confederate secretary of war, shortly after Gettysburg. Acknowledging his own army's heavy loss, Lee made an "emphatic gesture" and said, "[S]ir, we did whip them at Gettysburg, and it will be seen for the next six months that *that army* will be as quiet as a sucking dove." Henry Heth, "Letter from Major-General Henry Heth, of A. P. Hill's Corps, A.N.V.," in *Southern Historical Society Papers* 4:154–55. Lee was mistaken about the relative casualties—the Federals lost slightly fewer than twenty-three thousand men and the Confederates at least that many.

45. Maj. Gen. George Gordon Meade, born in Spain and subsequently associated with Pennsylvania, commanded the Army of the Potomac at Gettysburg.

46. Lee refers to Lt. Gen. Ulysses S. Grant's repeated shifts around the Confederate right flank during the 1864 Overland Campaign.

47. The end of this sentence first read "return & recover his base."

48. Gen. Joseph Eggleston Johnston of Virginia, a life-long friend of Lee who

nonetheless resented his comrade's greater renown, was notoriously prickly about rank, reputation, and perceived slights. Johnston's *Narrative of Military Operations, Directed during the Late War between the States* (New York: D. Appleton and Company, 1874), reveals in stark fashion this side of his personality.

49. Lee erred in thinking Longstreet had made no such claims about the Gettysburg campaign. In a conversation with the Northern writer William Swinton shortly after the war, Longstreet asserted that "in entering upon the campaign, General Lee expressly promised his corps-commanders that *he would not assume a tactical offensive*, but force his antagonist to attack him." William Swinton, *Campaigns of the Army of the Potomac: A Critical History of Operations in Virginia, Maryland and Pennsylvania, from the Commencement to the Close of the War, 1861–5* (1866; reprint ed., Secaucus NJ: The Blue & Grey Press, 1988), 340.

50. In late 1868, the Knickerbocker Life Insurance Company offered Lee the position of supervisor of their agencies at a salary of ten thousand dollars a year (his compensation from Washington College had been less than five thousand dollars in 1866–67).

51. In late July 1865, Lee sent a circular to some of his former officers asking for materials pertinent to the campaigns of the Army of Northern Virginia. He envisioned writing a history of his army—"the only tribute that can now be paid to the worth of the noble officers and soldiers." By December 1868 he had made little progress on the project, though Allan and many others still hoped he would complete it. See Allen W. Moger, "General Lee's Unwritten History of the Army of Northern Virginia," *Virginia Magazine of History and Biography* 71 (July 1963): 341–63 [quotation on p. 343], and Freeman, *R. E. Lee*, 4:418–19.

52. Robert Lewis Dabney wrote his *Life and Campaigns of Lieut.-Gen. Thomas J. Jackson (Stonewall Jackson)* (New York: Blelock & Company, 1866) at the request of Jackson's widow, Mary Anna Jackson. For a discussion of Lee's reaction to the book, see Douglas Southall Freeman, *The South to Posterity: An Introduction to the Writing of Confederate History* (1939; reprint ed., Wendell, N.C.: Broadfoot's Bookmark, 1983), 37–40. A copy of Lee's careful letter to Mrs. Jackson, dated 25 January 1866, in which he mentions problems with Dabney's book is in the Jedediah Hotchkiss Papers, microfilm reel 5, Library of Congress, Washington DC.

53. Brig. Gen. (later Maj. Gen.) William Henry Chase Whiting, a Mississippian, commanded a division during the Seven Days campaign.

54. Someone in a different hand spelled out "Jackson" here and substituted a semicolon for the period between "J" and "Stuart."

55. D. H. Hill and A. P. Hill commanded divisions during the fighting at Mechanicsville on 26 June and at Gaines's Mill on 27 June.

56. The text first read "McClelland"; the "d" has been crossed out.

57 The text first read "to push."

58. Richard Dominicus Cutts of the U. S. Coast and Geodetic Survey, a nephew of President James Madison, wrote treatises published by the government in the 1870s on surveying fieldwork, triangulation, instruments, and related topics.

59. Fitz John Porter, a native of New Hampshire, led the Army of the Potomac's

Fifth Corps during the summer and early fall of 1862. Relieved by Maj. Gen. John Pope for "disobedience, disloyalty, and misconduct in the face of the enemy" at Second Manassas, Porter served under McClellan at Antietam before being dismissed from the army in January 1863 following a politically charged military trial. He labored for years to clear his name, asking Lee and many other former Confederates to supply details about Second Manassas that would bolster his case. Much of the text of Lee's 18 February 1870 response to the letter from Porter that Allan mentions is reproduced in the entry for item 96, Sotheby's Auction Catalog, 31 October 1989. Another letter from Lee to Porter on this subject, dated 31 October 1867, is printed in Otto Eisenschiml, *The Celebrated Case of Fitz John Porter: An American Dreyfus Affair* (Indianapolis and New York: The Bobbs-Merrill Company, 1950), 195–96.

60. Brig. Gen. (later Gen.) John Bell Hood and Brig. Gen. Nathan George "Shanks" Evans, natives of Kentucky and South Carolina, commanded a division and a brigade respectively in Longstreet's wing of the army at Second Manassas.

61. The text first read "handsomely, out and after night returned to see Lee."

62. Lee probably was confused in his allusion to dead Zouaves. Among the units Hood's troops faced on 29 August was the Fourteenth Brooklyn, which wore Zouave uniforms. Because the action occurred after dark, however, it is unlikely Hood would have commented about the casualties from the Fourteenth "lying thick like a bed of roses." Hood's statement probably referred to action on 30 August, when the Fifth New York (Duryee's Zouaves) lost 120 men killed and mortally wounded in fighting against his division—the highest loss of life suffered by any infantry regiment on one battlefield during the war.

63. A native of Kentucky related by marriage to Mary Todd Lincoln, Maj. Gen. John Pope commanded the Army of Virginia as well as Porter's corps and other units from the Army of the Potomac at Second Manassas.

64. Seth Williams, a native of Maine, served as adjutant at West Point from 1850 to 1853 and adjutant general of the Army of the Potomac under a succession of commanders before becoming U. S. Grant's inspector general in early 1864.

9. Lee in *Harper's Weekly*, 24 August 1861, an engraving based on the antebellum photograph in plate 1.

ROBERT EDMUND LEE,
COMMANDER-IN-CHIEF OF THE CONFEDERATE FORCES.

10. Lee in the *Southern Illustrated News*, 17 January 1863. This portrait, the first seen by many people in the Confederacy, showed Lee as he had looked ten years earlier and gave readers an incorrect middle name.

11. *The Illustrated London News* ran this sketch of Lee in the field, by its artist Frank Vizetelly, on 14 February 1863. *Harper's Weekly* printed the same engraving on 14 March 1863, over the caption "The Rebel General Lee," alerting its readers that it differed "very materially from the portraits which are current in the North, which are taken from old photographs made before the war."

SOUTHERN ILLUSTRATED NEWS

Vol. II. RICHMOND, SATURDAY, OCTOBER 17, 1863. No. 15.

GEN. ROBERT EDMUND LEE.

GENERAL ROBERT EDMUND LEE.

12. Confederate readers of the *Southern Illustrated News* found this current portrait of their general in the magazine's 17 October 1863 number. The engraving is based on the photograph in plate 2 (or a variant pose from the same sitting).

13. Detail of plate 12, showing that the engraver replaced the colonel's insignia on Lee's collar with the appropriate insignia for a general officer. *Southern Illustrated News*, 17 October 1863.

14. Engraving by Frank Vizetelly based on the Minnis and Cowell portrait in plate 3, which appeared in *The Illustrated London News* on 4 June 1864, and in *Harper's Weekly* on 2 July 1864. The caption in both publications gave Lee's middle name as Edmund.

15. Grant whipping Lee in a cartoon from *Harper's Weekly*, 11 June 1864. Recent events at Cold Harbor did not support this view of the relative success of the great antagonists.

16. Detail of a sketch of Lee in the field observing an artillery exchange at Petersburg, drawn by Frank Vizetelly and printed in *The Illustrated London News* on 3 September 1864.

Memorandum of a Conversation with General R. E. Lee

EDWARD CLIFFORD GORDON

Memorandum of a conversation held with Genl. R. E. *Lee at Washington College, Lexington* V^{a}, *15* Feb *1868—In regard to operations of the* So. Army *in* Maryland *preceding the battle of* Sharpsburg *and the* "Lost Dispatch"[1]

Copy of a Mem: *sent to me by* Rev. E. C. Gordon Nov *22, 1886*[2]

Interesting Memorandum of a conversation held with Genl. R. E. Lee in Lexington Va on the 15$^{th.}$ of February 1868.

Going into the Genl's' Room on business as usual, when about to leave I asked him if he had read Genl. D. H. Hill's article in February (1868) No. of the "Land we Love," entitled "The lost Dispatch." He replied that he had not read it all, but had noticed the principal points in it; That he had not read Mr. E. A. Pollard's book, and was not able to judge of the merits of the question at issue between him and Genl. Hill, but that he was sure that Genl. Hill's account of the matter was not correct in several particulars.[3] At some length Genl. Lee then described his movement across the Potomac, the capture of Harpers Ferry, and the operations preceeding the battle of Sharpsburg. He stated that McClellan was up to the time of his finding the dispatch in complete ignorance of the whereabouts and intentions of the Southern army. That his, McClellan's army widely extended, with its left on the Potomac, was moving only a few miles every day, feeling its way with great caution. Stuart with his cavalry was close up to the enemy and doing everything possible to keep him in ignorance and to deceive him by false reports, which he industriously circulated. That he (Genl. Lee) proposed as soon as possible after the reduction of Harpers Ferry to collect his troops, and deliver battle, and although Harpers Ferry had not fallen so soon as he had hoped, still if McClellan could have been kept in ignorance but two or three days longer, he did not doubt then (nor has he changed his opinion since) that he could have crushed the army of McClellan, which was to a great extent disorganized and demoralized. That McClellan was informed of his movements, and the position of his troops by the Dispatch to Genl. Hill there could be no doubt. That he himself had gone to Hagerstown at which place there was a quantity of flour, and while there, he received dispatches almost simultaneously from Genl. Stuart and Genl. Hill stating that McClellan had changed his tactics, and was endeavouring to drive back Genl. Hill who was near Boonsboro. That Genl. Hill *ought to have* had all his troops up at the mountain, while in fact part were back at Boonsboro. Soon after this intelligence reached him in regard to McClellan, another dispatch arrived from Stuart, stating that he (Stuart) had learned from a gentleman of Maryland, who was in McClellan's head quarters when the dispatch from Genl. Lee to Genl. Hill was brought to McClellan, who after reading it, threw his hands up and exclaimed—Now I know what to do— That he (Genl. Lee) had been much surprised at the sudden change in McClellan's tactics, until he learned that he (McC) had thus found out his (Lee's) position, and in consequence he cannot agree with Genl. Hill that the losing of the dispatch was advantageous, but on the contrary a great misfortune. That according to Genl. Hill's account, if another dispatch had been lost, the South would have been victorious!! That Genl. Hill is mistaken in his remark in regard to his not receiving orders from him (Genl. Lee) directly. That Genl. Hill had moved up from Richmond, and not being then regularly incorporated in a corps, had been ordered by him to cross the Potomac and had done so in advance of the army—that when Genl. Jackson afterwards crossed he had taken command of all the troops then north of the Potomac and thus for a time Genl. Hill was immediately under his command, but that by the very order in question, Genl. Jackson moved with his three divisions together and Genl. Hill was left to bring up the rear and thus removed from Genl. Jackson. That he is confident the order was sent directly to Genl. Hill and that he supposes Genl. Jackson also sent a copy of the order to Genl. Hill—that he, Hill, might know through him that he was no longer under his command. That he cannot suppose the order was lost by a courier as couriers were always required to bring receipts to show that written orders were safely and surely delivered. That Genl. Hill is also mistaken in regard to Genl. Jackson's move to Harpers Ferry being contrary to or without orders. That even if he did not receive written orders to that effect, he remembers distinctly that in a private conversation with Genl. Jackson, the movements were agreed upon and that Genl. Jackson with his usual promptness executed them. Finally in regard to the point made by Hill that it is strange Genl. Lee did not have him cashiered for such great carelessness Genl. Lee said that he did not know that Genl. Hill had himself lost the dispatch and in consequence he had no grounds upon which to act, but that Genl. Stuart, and other officers in the army were very indignant about the matter.[4]

E. C. GORDON

NOTES

1. William Allan wrote this description of Gordon's memorandum on the back of the document. It has been moved to the beginning of this transcript because it provides a good title for Gordon's account of his conversation with Lee. A typescript of Gordon's memorandum is in the William Allan Papers, #2764, vol. 3, pp. 22–24, Southern Historical Collection, Wilson Library, University of North Carolina, Chapel Hill. Allan placed Gordon's memorandum with those recording his own conversations with Lee.

2. A parenthetical note on the typescript, which appears just after this line, states that "[t]he following memorandum was copied in some handwriting other than Colonel Allan's."

3. See note 1 in William Allan's memoranda for full citations to Hill's article and Pollard's book.

4. In a letter to Allan dated 18 November 1886 [typescript copy in Allan Papers, #2764, vol. 3, pp. 26–27, Southern Historical Collection], Gordon explained how he had prepared his memorandum and mentioned further details about Lee's comments: "I went directly from Gen. Lee's office to my own, & at once as rapidly as I could put down all that Gen. Lee had said respecting the 'Lost Dispatch—' The conversation made a great impression on me. Then only did Gen. Lee ever talk to me particularly about the war. He was excited, & somewhat indignant with Gen. Hill, particularly with his strictures on General Jackson." Gordon had omitted from his memorandum Lee's estimate of McClellan—"the substance of which was that he was an able but timid commander; nor could I have entered upon the *Mem.* the flashing of his eyes when he said: 'I went into Maryland to give battle, and could I have kept Gen. McClelland in ignorance of my position & plans a day or two longer, I would have fought and crushed him—' " Gordon's strong impression was that Lee blamed the failure of the campaign on the lost dispatch. Tempted more than once to publish his memorandum, Gordon had been "restrained by the fact that it would arouse D. H. Hill's anger, & do Gen. Lee no good." Gordon said he lacked the time to engage in controversy but gave Allan free rein to use the memorandum "in defending Gen. Lee from any unjust and unworthy assaults."

Memoranda of Conversations with General R. E. Lee

WILLIAM PRESTON JOHNSTON

General R. E. *Lee, Memoranda of Conversation May 7, 1868*

General Lee talked with me today about the operations of his army.[1] He said that at the Wilderness, Ewell showed vacillation that prevented him from getting all out of his troops he might. If Jackson had been alive and there, he would have crushed the enemy. He said Longstreet was slow in coming up "next day" (I think he said); that if he had been in time he would have struck the enemy on the flank while they were engaged in front. He said Longstreet was often slow. He said that when his line was attacked there while Longstreet was relieving Hill (or vice-versa) that the men received a blow that injured their morale. He always felt afraid when going to attack after that.[2] He spoke of Grant's gradual whirl and change of base from Fredericksburg to Port Royal, thence to York River and thence to James River, as a thing which, though foreseen, it was impossible to prevent. He said that this campaign had been compared by General Johnston to his retreat from Dalton. "I do not propose to criticize him," said he, "but I fought the enemy at every step. I faced him and I protected Richmond.[3] Stay-at-home critics may censure my army," said he, "but I believe I got out of them all that they could do or all that any men could do. After Gettysburg, the Herald announced that the army could not be out maneuvered and must be crushed; and that policy was soon after adopted."

He spoke pretty freely of the policy of the war. He claimed that he knew the strength of the United States Government; and saw the necessity at first of two things—a proclamation of gradual emancipation and the use of the negroes as soldiers, and second the necessity of the early and prompt exportation of the cotton. I mentioned the difficulty of a "Confederate Government" resisting a centralized one, to which he assented. He regretted that Breckinridge[4] had not been earlier made secretary of war. "He is a great man", said General Lee. "I was acquainted with him as Congressman and Vice-President and as one of our generals, but I did not *know* him till he was secretary of War, and he is a lofty, pure, strong man."

General Lee says he is an "American citizen," that he is not factious, but that he cannot and will not say that the Radicals are right. He does not think that the movement of Baldwin, A. H. H. Stuart and others (now) to ask for negro-suffrage and general amnesty will do any good.[5] I expressed this view to which he agreed, and added that immediately after the war he had advised them to adopt "impartial suffrage," (which, he said, would have excluded[6] ten negroes and one white man), say on some restricted franchise basis, and these gentlemen scouted the idea. Old Mr. Wickham[7] said they ought to demand a reopening of the African Slave Trade," which just shows," said he, "how mad men were." He spoke, however, of the good intentions of Stuart and the others.

I spoke to the general of writing his history of the war which elicited the above[8] remarks. He spoke of the difficulty of getting the documents to verify his statements, and his wish to be able to prove all he said; but he told me it was his purpose to write a history of his army. He explained to me his business arrangements, seizure of Arlington, etc.

The General had been talking with me about the various offers to induce him to enter the insurance business; but the sacredness of such a trust, as he expressed it, and the difficulties of conducting it, made him averse to trying it.

I wish I had taken down more of the converstions of General Lee. No man can talk to him when he opens his mind in full confidence without feeling that he is a proud, pure, strong man. He is confident of his own ability on the battle-field. His capacity is far far above his usual conversation.

W. P. J.

Lexington, Virginia, Friday, March 18, 1870.

Tuesday last, General Lee said to me at his office where I had called on some little matter of routine, that if he did not get better, he would be obliged to resign his position as President of Washington College. I expressed my hope and confidence that he would speedily recover if he would relieve himself of some part of the burthensome labor he takes on himself, but I was called off at once by my hour of lecture. I called next day to hand him a letter I had prepared at his request for his signature. I then took occasion to say to him, after an apology for that liberty, that his words had impressed my very deeply, (as in fact, they had, for I knew that with his reticence and poise he would not have uttered them without much purpose) and that I was greatly pained. I added that his first duty was to himself and his family, but that I was confident his illness was due to overconfinement and want of relaxation and change of air and scene and begged that he would either visit his many friends at Savannah, as I knew Miss Agnes wished, or that he would visit General Rooney Lee at the White House.[9]

He said his trouble was partly rheumatic (in his back) but that an adhesion of the membrane of the heart to the pleura impeded his breathing, so that while he could walk down hill, any ascent made it necessary for him to stop and rest, even between the chapel and his house. When he came here, he could and did easily walk to Thornhill,[10] or to my house; and now, though he rode easily, he scarcely walked at all. He alluded to his age, his wish to rest, and, on some little farm, to enjoy the outdoor life of the country. He said he could not go to Savannah without meeting more people than he wanted to.

He was evidently labouring under great depression of spirits, as is always the case with him, when sick.

I tried to point out to him as delicately as I could, that what we wanted here was his control, and not work; that he had everything in such excellent running order, that in his absence the machine would run for a while by its own momentum, with the inspiration of his headship to which we all all[11] looked.

He paid the Faculty some compliments. He mentioned that he wished to visit Alexandria to settle up Mr. Custis' estate.[12] My conversation on these and other topics lasted an hour and a quarter. I saw from this conversation that if he was not turned from his purpose that he would resign.

Yesterday, after a conference with White and Allan,[13] who had both been spoken to on the same subject by him, we agreed to call an informal Faculty meeting today and present him our regrets at his state of health and ask him to take at once a journey and a couple of months' relaxation. Colonel Allan consented to draw a paper to that effect, and did so presenting it in the Faculty meeting today at 3 P. M. where all were present except Professor Campbell, absent by some mistake. Professor Kirkpatrick was in the chair, and we adopted the resolutions suggested, and also requesting him to have a professor to attend to his duties during his absence.[14] I (as chairman) White, and Allan were appointed a committee to wait on him, which we did about five o'clock. The General was not looking well. After a few words of ordinary conversation, I told him that the Faculty, in view of his health, had had a meeting and deputed us to present him the letter I then handed him. He playfully replied that we were an irregular body as the President was absent; and, in the same spirit, I told him we had guarded his rights, and only acted as individuals as he would find. He read the paper, and in brief repeated what he had said to me more fully in private, rather evading a direct answer to our request and speaking of horseback exercise, etc. I also substantially, but very briefly and pointedly, repeated my former conversation and told him that it had been frequent matter of comment with us all that he was doing work no wise suited to him; that he ought to be relieved of all clerical labour; and that we felt his true work to be in his supervision and control and the zeal which his mere presence created among us all, and that what we wanted was his wisdom and example to guide us. I also, suggested that the best monument to his fame would be a history vindicating our cause; that it was due to himself and the country, and while his residence here might well afford him the best opportunity for the work, it would incidentally benefit the College.

The General replied that he was old. Spoke of our aid in attending to his correspondence and again spoke of the manner in which the Faculty had done their duty. He said he was hardly calculated for a historian. He was too much interested and might be biassed. I said that every body would at least give him credit for trying to tell the truth, at which he laughed. He spoke of his efforts to get correct copies of the Confederate records now in Washington and the difficulties, and alluded with some feeling and despondency to the demoralization of the country and his fear that worse was ahead. By the bye, the other day, he spoke to me of the "vindictiveness and malignity of the Yankees, of which he had no conception before the war." He said today also, that General Scott was induced to believe that pacification was intended by Mr. Lincoln and Mr. Seward, and tried to persuade him that Mr. Lincoln would recede. He was told that Mr. F. P. Blair asked in the caucus, "In that event what is to become of the Republican Party?" The same question now animates the North to cruelty. He finally alluded again to his age, ill-health, wish for rest and desire to make some permanent home for Mrs. Lee, "who is very helpless", he said.[15] He also said that he felt he might at any moment die.

I answered that whatever was his final resolution, he had done a good work here, and we would be satisfied of the wisdom and good feeling on which it was based.

During the latter part of the interview, his eyes were often moist, and we all laboured under a good deal of feeling. He promised to consider the communication. And now it is my belief that his purpose is fixed and that we shall soon lose General Lee at Washington College. I begged him last Fall to take a trip, but could not persuade him.

WILLIAM PRESTON JOHNSTON

NOTES

1. A typescript of Johnston's memoranda is in Robert E. Lee Collection, Special Collections, LL-W&L. W. G. Bean edited the memoranda for *Virginia Magazine of History and Biography* 73 (October 1965): 474–84. Although note 9 on p. 477 of Bean's article indicates that he worked from the typescript at Washington and Lee, his text departs from it in both punctuation and substance. Long after he prepared his memoranda, William Preston Johnston published "Reminiscences of General Robert E. Lee" in *Belford Monthly* 5 (June 1890): 84–91. That piece should not be confused with the memoranda.

2. Edward Porter Alexander, Longstreet's perceptive chief of artillery, commented after the war that Lee's placement of the First Corps at Mechanicsville, "far behind our *left flank*, fully 33 miles in an air line & 43 by the roads we had to use" from the Wilderness battlefield, resulted in the "first day's battle necessarily [being] fought without our presence." Edward Porter Alexander, *Fighting for the Confederacy: The Personal Recollections of General Edward Porter Alexander*, ed. Gary W. Gallagher (Chapel Hill: University of North Carolina Press, 1989), 348–49.

3. Joseph E. Johnston opened his 1864 campaign against William Tecumseh Sherman at Dalton, Georgia, retreating during the period from early May to mid-July from there into the defenses of Atlanta. For an excellent comparative estimate of Johnston's and Lee's performances during the spring and summer of 1864, see Albert Castel, *Decision in the West: The Atlanta Campaign of 1864* (Lawrence: University Press of Kansas, 1992), 561–62.

4. John Cabell Breckinridge of Kentucky, who held a major generalship in the Confederate army before becoming Davis's secretary of war on 4 February 1865.

5. John Brown Baldwin and Alexander Hugh Holmes Stuart, brothers-in-law and former Whigs who had served as delegates to Virginia's secession convention in 1861, were part of the "Committee of Nine" that pressed for the state's full restoration to the Union on the basis of "universal suffrage and universal amnesty." See Jack P. Maddex Jr., *The Virginia Conservatives, 1867–1879: A Study in Reconstruction Politics* (Chapel Hill: University of North Carolina Press, 1970), 67–70.

6. The transcript reads "exceeded ten negroes"; the word "excluded" was added in ink above "exceeded." The original transcriber undoubtedly made an error in this instance.

7. William F. Wickham, father of Charlotte Wickham, the first wife of Lee's son William Henry Fitzhugh, and of Williams Carter Wickham, who served as a brigadier general of Confederate cavalry and after the war became a Republican.

8. The typescript includes a question mark in pencil above the word "above."

9. Eleanor Agnes Lee, the general's third daughter and fifth child, accompanied him on a trip to the Carolinas, Georgia, and Florida in the spring of 1870. Departing on 24 March, Lee was back in Lexington on 28 May.

10. Located several miles south of Lexington, Thornhill was the home of Judge John W. Brockenbrough. Brockenbrough conducted a private law school in Lexington that in 1866 became affiliated with Washington College.

11. The typescript repeats the word "all"; in the absence of Johnston's handwritten manuscript, it is impossible to determine whether this repeated word is a mistake in the original or in the subsequent transcription.

12. Freeman, *R. E. Lee*, 4:385–90, details Lee's attempts to settle Custis's estate.

13. James J. White and William Allan were professors of classics and mathematics, respectively.

14. Professor John Lyle Campbell, the most eminent of the college's faculty, taught chemistry and geology; John L. Kilpatrick was professor of moral philosophy.

15. During Lee's years in Lexington, Virginia, Mary Custis Lee often was confined to a wheelchair.

★ II ★

ASSESSMENTS OF LEE'S OVERALL GENERALSHIP

The Campaigns of Gen. Robert E. Lee. An Address by Lieut. General Jubal A. Early, before Washington and Lee University, January 19th, 1872

JUBAL A. EARLY

LADIES AND GENTLEMEN:

MY FRIENDS, COMRADES AND COUNTRYMEN:

Though conscious of my inability to discharge, in a suitable manner, the duty assigned me on this occasion, yet, when asked to unite in rendering homage to the memory of the great Confederate Captain, I did not feel at liberty to decline the call. I have realized, however, most fully and sensibly, the difficulties of the position I occupy. All the powers and charms of eloquence and poetry, combined, have been called into requisition, to commemorate the deeds and virtues of him whose birth-day we celebrate. They are not at my command, and the highest eulogy which I am capable of pronouncing upon the character of our illustrious Chief, must consist of a simple delineation of his achievements, couched in the plain, unadorned language of a soldier, who bore an humble part in the many events which marked the career to which your attention will be called. I must, therefore, throw myself upon your kind indulgence, and bespeak your patience, while I attempt to give a sketch of those grand achievements which have placed the name of Robert E. Lee among the foremost of the renowned historic names of the world.

I do not propose, my friends, to speak of his youth, his early manhood, or his career prior to our late struggle for liberty and independence. These have been, and will continue to be, far better portrayed by others, and I will content myself with the remark that, together, they constituted a worthy prelude to the exhibition, on a larger theatre, of those wonderful talents and sublime virtues, which have gained for him the admiration and esteem of the good and true of all the civilized world.

Most men seem to have a just appreciation of the domestic virtues, the moral worth, the unselfish patriotism and Christian purity of General Lee's character; but it has occurred to me that very few, comparatively, have formed a really correct estimate of his marvellous ability and boldness as a military commander, however exalted is the merit generally awarded him in that respect. I will, therefore, direct my remarks chiefly to his military career in our late war, though I am unable to do full justice to the subject. I can, however, contribute my mite; and it may, perhaps, not detract from the interest of what I have to say, when you know that I was a witness of much of which I will speak.

I must, necessarily, go over much of the same ground that has been already explored by others, and repeat something of what I have already said in an address before the "Survivors' Association of South Carolina," and in some published articles. I will, also, have to give you some details and statistics, to show what was really accomplished by our army under the lead and through the inspiration of its great Commander. Flowers and figures of rhetoric may captivate the imagination, but material facts and figures only can convince the judgment, and the latter I will endeavor to render as little tiresome as possible.

The commencement of hostilities in Charleston harbor, the proclamation of Lincoln, calling for troops to make an unconstitutional war on the seceded States, and the consequent secession of Virginia found General Lee a Colonel in the United States army, with a character and reputation which would have ensured him the highest military honors within the gift of the United States Government. In fact, it has been said that the command of the army intended for the invasion of the South was tendered him. However, rejecting all overtures made to him, as soon as he learned the action of his native State, in a dignified manner, and without parade or show, he tendered his resignation, with the determination to share the fate of his State, his friends and kindred. The then Governor, at once, with the unanimous consent of the Convention of Virginia, tendered him the command of all the forces of the State. This he accepted, and promptly repaired to Richmond, to enter upon the discharge of his duties, knowing that this act must be attended with a very heavy pecuniary loss to himself on account of the locality of his estates. Those who witnessed his appearance before the Convention, saw his manly bearing, and heard the few grave, dignified and impressive words with which he consecrated himself and his sword to the cause of his native State, can never forget that scene. All felt at once that we had a leader worthy of the State and the cause.

As a member of the military committee of the Convention, and afterwards as a subordinate under him, I was in a condition to witness and know the active energy and utter abnegation of all personal considerations with which he devoted himself to the work of organizing and equipping the Virginia troops for the field. While he bore no active part in the first military operations of the war, yet, I can safely say that, but for the capacity and energy displayed by General Lee in organizing and equipping troops to be sent to the front, our army would not have been in a condition to gain the first victory at Manassas. I do not, however, intend, by this statement, to detract from the merit of others. The Confederate Government, then recently removed to Richmond, did well its part in bringing troops from the South; and I take pleasure in bearing testimony to the fidelity and ability with which the then Governor of Virginia coöperated with General Lee in his efforts to furnish men as well as the munitions of war.

His first appearance in the field, as a commander, was in Western Virginia, after the reverses in that quarter. The expectations formed in regard to his operations there were not realized, and, though he met with no disaster or defeat to his troops, the campaign was regarded as a failure. The public never thought of inquiring into the causes of that failure, and it is not to be denied that an impression prevailed among those who did not know him well, that General Lee was not suited to be a commander in an active campaign. There were some editors who while safely entrenched behind the impregnable columns of their newspapers, proved themselves to be as fierce in war as they had been wise in peace, and no bad representatives of the snarling Thersites, and these hurled their criticisms and taunts, with no sparing hand, at the head of the unsuccessful commander. It would be profitless, now, to inquire into the causes of the failures in Western Virginia. It is sufficient to say that they were not attributable to the want of capacity or energy in the commanding General.

He was, subsequently, sent to the Southern sea-board, for the purpose of supervising the measures for its defence, and he proved himself a most accomplished engineer, and rendered most valuable services in connection with the sea-board defenses in that quarter.

In March, 1862, he was called to Richmond, and charged with the conduct of military operations in the armies of the Confederacy, under the direction of the President. Just before that time, the evacuation of Manassas took place, and, subsequently, the transfer of the bulk of the opposing armies in Virginia to the Peninsula, the evacuation of Yorktown and the line of Warwick River, the battle of Williamsburg, and the transfer of the seat of war to the Chickahominy, in the vicinity of Richmond, occurred.

On the 31st of May and 1st of June, the battle of Seven Pines was fought, and General Johnston was so severely wounded as to be disabled for duty in the field for some time. Fortunately, the eminent and patriotic statesman, who was at the head of the Government, well knew the merits of General Lee, and at once assigned him to the vacant command; and then in fact began that career to which I invite your attention.

When General Lee assumed command of the army, which before that time had borne the name of the "Army of the Potomac," but was soon re-christened by the name of the "Army of Northern Virginia," he found the Confederate Capital beleaguered by an army of over one hundred thousand men, with a very large train of field and siege guns, while his own force was very little more than half that of the enemy. Nevertheless, he conceived the idea of relieving the Capital of the threatening presence of the besieging army, by one of those bold strategic movements of which only great minds are capable. General Jackson, by his rapid movements and brilliant operations in the Valley, had prevented the march of a column of about forty thousand men, under McDowell, from Fredericksburg on Richmond, to unite with the besieging army; and a part of McDowell's force, and Fremont's army from Northwestern Virginia, had been sent to the Valley, for the purpose of crushing Jackson. It was very apparent that J .ckson's force, then consisting of his own command proper, Johnson's command from Alleghany Mountain, and Ewell's division, could not long withstand the heavy forces concentrating against it, and that, when it was overwelmed, the enemy's troops operating in the Valley and covering Washington, would be at liberty to move on Richmond; while the detachment, from the army defending that city, of a force large enough to enable Jackson to contend successfully, in a protracted campaign, with the forces accumulating against him, would, probably, ensure the fall of the Confederate Capital. Preparations were, therefore, made to attack the besieging army, with the forces covering Richmond and in the Valley, by a combined movement. Some reinforcements were brought from the South, and three brigades were sent to the Valley, for the purpose of deceiving the enemy, and facilitating the withdrawal of General Jackson. Fortunately, that able and energetic commander had been enabled to prevent the junction of Fremont's army with the troops sent from McDowell's command, and, taking advantage of their separation and the swollen condition of the water courses, had defeated both forces in succession, and so bewildered their commanders by the rapidity of his movements, that they retreated down the Valley, under the apprehension that Washington was in danger. Leaving all of his cavalry but one regiment to watch the enemy and mask his own movement, General Jackson, on the 17th of June, commenced his march towards the enemy's lines near Richmond, in compliance with the plan and orders of General Lee; and on the 26th of June, less than four weeks after General Lee had been assigned to the command of the army, his attacking columns swung around McClellan's right flank, and fell like an avalanche on the besieging army. Next day, Jackson was up, and then ensued that succession of brilliant engagements which so much accelerated McClellan's famous "change of base," and sent his shattered army to Harrison's Landing under cover of the gun-boats on the James.

To give you some idea of the boldness and daring of this movement, and the impression it made on the enemy, I will call your attention to some facts and figures.

In his report, dated in August, 1863, and printed in 1864, McClellan gives the strength of the troops under his command at Washington, on the Potomac and within reach, on the 1st of March, 1862, as:

"Present for duty, one hundred and ninety-three thousand one hundred and forty-two."

A portion of this force had been left to operate in the Valley, another to cover Washington; and he puts the strength of "The Army of the Potomac," which designation his army bore, on the 20th day of June, 1862, just six days before the battles began, at:

"Present for duty, one hundred and five thousand eight hundred and twenty-five."

He further says that he had sixty batteries with his army, aggregating three hundred and forty field pieces. Besides these he had a large train of siege guns.

General Lee's whole force, of all arms, including the troops of Magruder, Huger, Holmes and Jackson, when the latter arrived, did not reach eighty thousand effective men, and of these, Holmes' command, over six thousand strong, did not actively engage in any of the battles. There were thirty-nine brigades of infantry in all engaged on our side in the battles around Richmond, inclusive of Holmes' command. The strength of twenty-three of them is given in the official reports, and was forty-seven thousand and thirty-four, including the batteries attached to a number of them. In these were embraced the very largest brigades in the army, as for instance, Lawton's. The sixteen brigades, whose strength is not given, were four of A. P. Hill's, two of Longstreet's, two of Huger's and eight of Jackson's. Taking the average of those whose strength is given, for the eight brigades of A. P. Hill, Longstreet and Huger, and an average of fifteen hundred for Jackson's eight brigades—which would be a very liberal estimate for the latter, considering the heavy fighting and long and rapid marches they had gone through—and it will give about seventy-five thousand men, including a number of batteries attached to the brigades. The cavalry with the army was less than two brigades, and that, with the artillery not included in the reports of brigades, could not have reached five thousand men. The field guns with our army, which were all that were used, were not near half as many as those of the enemy, and many of them were of inferior metal and pattern. We had not, then, had an opportunity of supplying ourselves with the improved guns of the enemy. Much the largest portion of our small arms consisted of the smooth bore musket, while the enemy was well supplied with improved rifle muskets.

From the data I have given, you will perceive that I have not underestimated the strength of the forces at General Lee's command; and this was the largest army he ever commanded. The idea of relieving Richmond, by an attack on McClellan's flank and rear, was a masterly conception, and the boldness, not to say audacity, of it, will appear when we take into consideration the relative strength of the two armies, and the fact that, in swinging around the enemy's flank, General Lee left very little over twenty-five thousand men between the Capital and the besieging army. Timid minds might regard this as rashness, but it was the very perfection of a profound and daring strategy. Had McClellan advanced to the assault of the city, through the open plains around it, his destruction would have been ensured. As it was, his only chance for escape was in a retreat through the swamps and forests, which concealed and sheltered his columns on their flight to the banks of the James. Notwithstanding the favorable nature of the country for his escape, McClellan's army would have been annihilated, had General Lee's orders been promptly and rigidly carried out by his subordinates. The bloody battle of Malvern Hill would not have been fought; and when it was fought, a crushing defeat would have been inflicted on the enemy, had the plans of the commanding General been carried into execution, as I could demonstrate to you, if it were profitable to enter into such a disquisition. McClellan was glad enough to escape from that field with his shattered forces, though he pretended to claim a victory; and the pious Lincoln gave "ten thousand thanks for it."

McClellan always insisted that we had overwhelming numbers against him, and this hallucination seems to have haunted him until the close of his career, if he is yet rid of it. On the night of the 25th of June, he telegraphed to Stanton, as follows:

"I incline to think that Jackson will attack my right and rear. The rebel force is stated at two hundred thousand, including Jackson and Beauregard.

I shall have to contend against vastly superior odds if these reports be true. But this army will do all in the power of men to hold their position, and repulse any attack."

In his report, he says:

"The report of the chief of the 'secret service corps' herewith forwarded, and dated the 26th of June, [1862,] shows the estimated strength of the enemy, at the time of the evacuation of Yorktown, to have been from one hundred thousand to one hundred and twenty thousand. The same report puts his numbers, on the 26th of June, at about one hundred and eighty thousand, and the specific information obtained regarding their organization warrants the belief that this estimate did not exceed his actual strength."

He missed it by only one hundred thousand, and his statement shows the impression made on him, by the fighting of our army under General Lee, and which he never got over. All the time he was at his "new base," he was afflicted with this dread phantom of overwhelming numbers against him, which, according to his account, were being constantly increased, and he begged most earnestly for reinforcements. Halleck, then lately appointed commander-in-chief at Washington, visited Harrison's Landing about the last of July, and after he got back, he reported, in writing, to the Secretary of War, that McClellan and his officers represented our forces, then, at not less than two hundred thousand, and his own force at about ninety thousand.

A new commander had now appeared in Virginia, on the north of the Rapidan, in the person of Major-General John Pope, whose head-quarters were in the saddle; who had never seen anything of the "rebels" but their backs; and who felt no concern whatever about strength of positions, bases of supplies, or lines of retreat. All he wanted to know, was, where the "rebels" were, so that he might "go at them;" and he left the lines of retreat to take care of themselves, while the "enemy's country" was to be the base of his supplies. His army, according to his own statement, amounted to over forty-three thousand men. General Jackson had been quietly sent up to Gordonsville, with his own and Ewell's divisions, which were soon followed by that of A. P. Hill. While McClellan was trembling at the idea of vastly superior numbers accumulating against him, Pope telegraphed to Halleck:

"The enemy is reported to be evacuating Richmond, and falling back on Danville and Lynchburg."

General Jackson soon began to show Pope some things that were entirely new to him. The battle of Cedar Run or Slaughter's Mountain, was fought on the 9th of August, and "a change came over the spirit" of Pope's dream. In fact, he began to see some remarkable sights, with which he was destined to soon become familiar. About this time, McClellan sent a despatch to Halleck, in which is this striking passage:

"I don't like Jackson's movements; he will suddenly appear when least expected."

There were not many, on that side, who did like General Jackson's ways. The authorities at Washington were completely bewildered by his new eccentricities, and the evacuation of the "new base," which had been assumed with so much ability and celerity, was peremptorily ordered.

Burnside soon arrived at Fredericksburg with thirteen thousand men, brought from North and South Carolina, eight thousand of whom, under Reno, were sent to Pope. In the meantime, General Lee had been watching McClellan's force, and, having become convinced that there was no immediate danger to Richmond, he determined to move against Pope, for the purpose of crushing him before he could be reinforced, and entirely relieving Richmond, by forcing McClellan to go to the defence of Washington. Leaving D. H. Hill's and McLaws' divisions, two brigades under J. G. Walker, a brigade of cavalry under Hampton, and some other troops at Drury's and Chaffin's Bluffs, to watch McClellan, General Lee moved with the remainder of his army to the Rapidan. Getting wind of the intended movement against him, by the accidental capture of a despatch to Stuart, Pope fell back behind the Rappahannock, and the two armies soon confronted each other on its banks. A raid by Stuart to Pope's rear, resulted in the capture of the latter's head-quarters and his correspondence, which latter showed that McClellan's army was hastening to Pope's assistance. D. H. Hill, McLaws, Walker and Hampton, were ordered forward at once, and while Pope was looking steadily to the front for the "rebels," without thought for his base of supplies, and in utter oblivion of any possible line of retreat, General Jackson was sent on that remarkably bold and dashing expedition to the enemy's rear, for the purpose of destroying Pope's communications and preventing the advance of McClellan's army to his assistance. Pope now found it necessary to look out for his supplies and his line of retreat, and then ensued that series of engagement called "the second battle of Manassas." Pope had already been joined by two corps of McClellan's army, Porter's and Heintzelman's, the one by the way of Fredericksburg and the other over the railroad; and Jackson's three divisions, numbering less than twenty thousand men, after cutting the railroad, and destroying several trains of cars and immense stores at Manassas, which could not be removed for want of transportation, withstood for two days, beginning on the 28th of August, Pope's entire army, reinforced by Reno's eight thousand men and McClellan's two corps, while General Lee was moving up with Longstreet's and Anderson's commands. Never did General Jackson display his leading characteristics more conspicuously than on this occasion, and he fully justified the confidence of the commanding General, in entrusting him with the execution of one of the most brilliant and daring strategic movements on record. Every attack by Pope's immense army was repulsed with heavy slaughter, and during the 29th all the fighting on our side was done by Jackson's corps, except an affair about dusk between a part of McDowell's corps and the advance of Longstreet's command, which began to arrive between eleven and twelve in the day, but did not become engaged until at the close, when an advance was made, along the Warrenton Pike, by one of McDowell's divisions, under the very great delusion that Jackson was retreating. On the morning of the 30th the attacks on Jackson's position, on the line of an unfinished railroad track, were renewed, and continued until the afternoon, with the same result as the day before. Longstreet did not become engaged until late in the afternoon, when, by a combined attack, Pope's army was driven across Bull Run in great disorder and with immense loss.

Pope's report and telegraphic correspondence afford a rich fund of amusement for those acquainted with the facts of his brief campaign in Virginia, but this I must pass over.

He claimed to have entirely defeated and routed Jackson on the 29th, and he actually had one corps commander cashiered, for not cutting off the retreat and capturing the whole force, which he claims to have routed. In a despatch to Halleck, dated 5.30 A. M., on the 30th, he says:

"We have lost not less than eight thousand men, killed and wounded; but from the appearance of the field, the enemy lost at least two to one. He stood strictly on the defensive, and every assault was made by ourselves. The battle was fought on the identical field of Bull Run, which greatly increased the enthusiasm of the men. The news just reaches me from the front that the enemy is retiring toward the mountains. I go forward at once to see. We have made great captures, but I am not able, yet, to form an idea of their extent."

He went forward, and saw more than was agreeable to him, and found that he had captured a "Tartar."

In a despatch dated 9.45 P. M., on the 30th, after the great battle of that day was over, he said:

"The battle was most furious for hours without cessation, and the losses on both sides were very heavy. The enemy is badly whipped, and we shall do well enough. Do not be uneasy. We will hold our own here."

To this Halleck replied on the morning of the 31st:

"You have done nobly. Don't yield another inch if you can avoid it. All reserves are being sent forward."

Yet, after all of McClellan's troops, except one division left at Yorktown, had arrived, and before another gun had been fired, Pope telegraphed to Halleck, at 10.45 A. M., on the 31st:

"I should like to know whether you feel secure about Washington, should this army be destroyed. I shall fight it as long as a man will stand up to the work."

The army that had been so badly whipped on the 30th, was soon advancing against Pope again. Jackson, by another flank movement, struck the retreating army at Chantilly or Ox Hill, and the shattered remains of it, now reinforced by two fresh corps and a division of McClellan's army, were hurled into the fortifications around Washington.

Major General John Pope had now seen as much of the "rebels" as he cared to look upon, and he disappeared from the scene of action, in many respects, "a wiser if not a better man." To get him as far as possible from the dangerous proximity, he was sent to the extreme Northwest, to look after the red men of the plains. When we recollect the bombastic proclamations and orders of Pope, at the beginning of his brief campaign, and the rapidity with which he was brought to grief, there appears so much of the ludicrous in the whole, that we are almost tempted to overlook the fiendish malignity which characterized some of his orders and acts.

In his report, after saying:

"Every indication, during the night of the 29th, and up to 10 o'clock on the morning of 30th, pointed to the retreat of the enemy from our front."

He further says:

"During the whole night of the 29th and the morning of the 30th, the advance of the main army, under Lee, was arriving on the field to reinforce Jackson, so that, by 12 or 1 o'clock in the day, we were confronted by forces greatly superior to our own; and these forces were being, every moment, largely increased by fresh arrival of the enemy in the direction of Thoroughfare Gap." So that this was another case of overwhelming numbers on our side.

Pope's army was originally, according to his statement, forty-three thousand, and, according to Halleck, forty thousand. He had been reinforced by eight thousand men under Reno; a body of troops from the Kanawha Valley, under Cox; another from Washington, under Sturgis, and all of McClellan's army, except one division, say eighty-five thousand men. General Lee had then between one hundred and thirty-five thousand and one hundred and forty thousand men to deal with on this occasion. The whole of McClellan's force was not up at the battle of the 30th, but all of it, except the one division of Keyes' corps, left at Yorktown, was up by the time of the affair at Ox Hill, on the 1st of September. General Lee's whole force, at second Manassas, did not exceed fifty thousand men. Neither D. H. Hill's, nor McLaws', nor Walker's division of infantry, nor Hampton's brigade of cavalry had arrived, and neither of them got up until after the affair at Ox Hill. We had only twenty-nine brigades of infantry and two of cavalry present at second Manassas, one of the latter being very weak. One of the infantry brigades, Starke's Louisiana brigade, had been formed of regiments attached to other brigades at the battles around Richmond, and another had arrived from the South during July. This latter brigade constituted all the reinforcements, except men returned from convalescence, received after these battles, and was twenty-two hundred strong, the last of July. The whole force in the department of Northern Virginia, on the 31st of July, 1862, was sixty-nine thousand five hundred and fifty-nine for duty. Deduct, rateably, for the twelve infantry brigades, with their proportion of artillery, and the one cavalry brigade absent, besides troops on detached duty at various points, and you will see how General Lee's army must have been under fifty thousand at second Manassas. Yet it had sent the combined armies of Pope and McClellan into the defences of Washington, in a very crippled condition, and thrown the Government there into a great panic in regard to the safety of that city. Fredericksburg had been evacuated, and the remainder of Burnside's corps brought to Washington, while a call had been made for three hundred thousand new troops.

Notwithstanding the exhaustion of his troops from the heavy tax on all their energies, the heavy losses in battle, and the want of commissary stores, General Lee now undertook the bold scheme of crossing the Potomac into Maryland, with his army reinforced by the eleven brigades of infantry, under D. H. Hill, McLaws and Walker, and Hampton's cavalry, which were coming up. On the 3d of September, our army was put in motion, and, passing through Leesburg, it crossed over and concentrated at and near Frederick city, by the 7th of the month. This movement threw the authorities at Washington into great consternation and dismay. McClellan had been assigned to the command of all the troops in and around Washington, and the correspondence between himself and Halleck, conducted mostly by telegraph, shows how utterly bewildered they were. Both of them were firmly impressed with the conviction that our numbers were overwhelming, and they did not know where to look for the impending blow. McClellan moved out of the city with great caution, feeling his way gradually towards Frederick, while a considerable force, which was constantly augmented by the arrival of new troops, was retained at Washington, for fear that city should be captured by a sudden *coup* from the South-side. A considerable force had been isolated at Harper's Ferry, and General Lee sent Jackson's corps, McLaws', Anderson's and Walker's divisions, in all twenty-six brigades of infantry, with the accompanying artillery, to invest and capture that place, retaining with himself only fourteen brigades of infantry, with the accompanying and reserve artillery, and the main body of the cavalry, with which he crossed to the West side of the South Mountain. The order directing these movements, by some accident, fell into McClellan's hands on the 13th, and he hurried his troops forward to attack the small force with General Lee, and relieve Harper's Ferry if possible. A sanguinary engagement occurred at Boonsboro Gap, on the 14th, between D. H. Hill's division, constituting the rear guard of the column with General Lee, and the bulk of McClellan's army, and Hill, after maintaining his position for many hours, was compelled to retire at night with heavy loss, the troops sent to his assistance not having arrived in time to repulse the enemy. That night, Longstreet's and Hill's commands crossed the Antietam to Sharpsburg, where they took position on the morning of the 15th. In the meantime, Harper's Ferry had been invested, and surrendered on the morning of the 15th—our victory being almost a bloodless one, so far as the resistance of the garrison was concerned; but McLaws and Anderson had had very heavy fighting, on the Maryland side, with a part of McClellan's army. As soon as General Lee heard of the success at Harper's Ferry, he ordered all the troops operating against that place to move to Sharpsburg as soon as practicable. Leaving A. P. Hill, with his division, to dispose of the prisoners and property captured at Harper's Ferry, General Jackson, late in the afternoon of the 15th, ordered his own division and Ewell's, the latter now under Lawton, to Sharpsburg, where they arrived early on the morning of the 16th. Walker's two brigades came up later in the day. The ten brigades brought by Jackson and Walker made twenty-four brigades of infantry, with the fourteen already on the ground, which General Lee had with him when the battle of Sharpsburg opened on the morning of the 17th of September. Jackson's division was placed on the left flank, and Hood's two brigades, which were next to it on the right, were relieved by two brigades of Ewell's division during the night of the 16th, and these were reinforced by another very early the next morning. General Jackson's whole force on the field consisted of five thousand infantry and a very few batteries of his own division. One brigade, my own, numbering about one thousand men and officers, was detached, at light, towards the Potomac on our left, to support some artillery with which Stuart was operating; so that General Jackson had only four thousand infantry in line, and D. H. Hill was immediately on his right, holding the centre and left centre with his division, then three thousand strong. General Lee's whole infantry force on the field, at the beginning of the battle, did not exceed fifteen thousand men, including Jackson's and Walker's commands. On the left and left centre, McClellan hurled, in succession, the four corps of Hooker, Mansfield, Sumner and Franklin, numbering, in the aggregate, fifty-six thousand and ninety-five men, according to his report; and a sanguinary battle raged for several hours, during which, Hood's two brigades, my brigade, Walker's two brigades, Anderson's brigade of D. R. Jones' division, and McLaws' and Anderson's divisions, successively went to the support of the part of the line assailed, at different points, the last two divisions having arrived late in the morning, during the progress of the battle. And all the troops engaged, from first to last, with the enemy's fifty-six thousand and ninety-five men, on that wing, did not exceed eighteen thousand men. At the close of the fighting there, our left was advanced beyond where it rested in the morning, while the centre had been forced back some two hundred yards.

In the afternoon, Burnside's corps, over thirteen thousand strong, attacked our right, and, after gaining some advantage, was driven back with the aid of three of A. P. Hill's brigades, which had just arrived from Harper's Ferry. At the close of the battle, we held our position firmly, with the centre slightly forced back, as I have stated. We continued to hold the position during the 18th, and McClellan did not venture to renew the attack. In the meantime, heavy reinforcements were moving to his assistance, two divisions of which, Couch's and Humphrey's, fourteen thousand strong, arrived on the 18th, while General Lee had no possibility of being reinforced except by the stragglers who might come up, and they constituted a poor dependence. The Potomac was immediately in his rear, and as it would have been folly for him to have waited until an overpowering force was accumulated against him, he very properly and judiciously retired on the night of the 18th, and recrossed the river early on the morning of the 19th. A very feeble effort at pursuit by one corps, was most severely punished by A. P. Hill's division on the 20th.

This was one of the most remarkable battles of the war, and has been but little understood. You will, therefore, pardon me for going somewhat into detail in regard to it. When General Lee took his position on the morning of the 15th, he had with him but fourteen brigades of infantry, besides the artillery and cavalry. The official reports show that D. H. Hill's five brigades numbered then only three thousand men for duty, and six brigades under D. R. Jones only two thousand four hundred and thirty men. The strength of three brigades is not given, but they were not more than of an average size—and estimating their strength in that way, it would give less than seven thousand five hundred infantry with which, and the artillery and cavalry with him, General Lee confronted McClellan's army during the whole of the 15th and part of the 16th. The arrival of Jackson's and Walker's commands, did not increase the infantry to more than fifteen thousand men, and they brought very little artillery with them. During the day, McLaws, Anderson and A. P. Hill came up with thirteen brigades, making thirty-seven brigades which participated in the battle. The official reports give the strength of twenty-seven of these, amounting in the aggregate to sixteen thousand nine hundred and twenty-three men. Taking the average for the other ten—and they were not more than average brigades, if that—and it would give about twenty-three thousand infantry engaged on our side from first to last. The cavalry, consisting of three brigades, which were not strong, was not engaged and merely watched the flanks. A very large portion of our artillery, which had been used against Harper's Ferry, had not arrived, and did not get up until after night-fall, when the battle was over. We had in fact comparatively few guns engaged, and the enemy's guns were not only very numerous, but of heavier metal and longer range. Taking the whole force, including the cavalry and the artillery, when all of the latter had arrived, and we had less than thirty thousand men of all arms at this battle, from first to last. General Lee, in his report, says that he had less than forty thousand men; but, for reasons that can be well understood, he never did disclose his own weakness at any time, even to his own officers.

When our army started for Maryland, after the affair at Ox Hill, it was out of rations, badly clothed, and worse shod. At the time of the battle of Sharpsburg, it had been marching and fighting for near six weeks, and the straggling from exhaustion, sore feet, and in search of food, had been terrible, before we crossed the Potomac. When it is recollected that the entire force at the end of July, in all the Department of Northern Virginia, was only a very little over sixty-nine thousand men, of which sixty thousand, including D. H. Hill's, McLaws' and Walker's divisions, would be a liberal estimate for all that were carried into the field, you will see that a loss of thirty thousand in battle, from Cedar Run to South Mountain, inclusive, and from the other causes named, is not an unreasonable estimate. In fact, at the end of September, when the stragglers had been gathered up, and many of the sick and wounded had returned to duty, with the additions from the conscripts, the official returns show only fifty-two thousand six hundred and nine for duty in the whole Department of Northern Virginia.

McClellan, in his report, gives his own force at eighty-seven thousand one hundred and sixty-four in action, and he gives an estimate of General Lee's army, in detail, in which he places our strength at ninety-seven thousand four hundred and forty-five men and four hundred guns at this battle. Truly, our boys in gray had a wonderful faculty of magnifying and multiplying themselves in battle; and McClellan could not have paid a higher compliment to their valor, and the ability of our commander, than he has done by this estimate of our strength, as it appeared to him.

In giving his reasons for not renewing the battle on the 18th, he says:

"One division of Sumner's corps, and all of Hooker's corps, on the right, had, after fighting most valiantly for several hours, been overpowered by numbers, driven in great disorder and much scattered, so that they were for the time somewhat demoralized."

I have shown how they were outnumbered.

Burnside, in his testimony before the committee on the conduct of the war, said:

"I was told at General McClellan's headquarters, that our right had been so badly broken that they could not be got together for an attack, and they would have to wait for reinforcements; and that General Sumner advised General McClellan not to renew the attack, because of the condition of his corps; and it was also stated that very little of General Hooker's corps was left."

This was on the night of the 17th, after the battle was over. On the 27th, McClellan wrote to Halleck as follows:

"In the last battles the enemy was undoubtedly greatly superior to us in numbers, and it was only by hard fighting that we gained the advantage we did. As it was, the result was at one time very doubtful, and we had all we could do to win the day."

Win the day, indeed! He had not dared to renew the attack on the 18th, and he did not venture to claim a victory until the 19th, when he found General Lee had re-crossed the Potomac, and then he began to breathe freely and to crow, at first feebly, and then more loudly. Who ever heard of a victory by an attacking army in an open field, and yet the victor was unable to advance against his antagonist who stood his ground?

To give you some idea of the immense difficulties General Lee had to encounter in this campaign, and the wonderful facility the enemy had for raising men, and reinforcing his armies after defeat, through the agencies of the telegraph, railroads and steam-power, let me tell you that a certified statement compiled from McClellan's morning report of the 20th of September, 1862, contained in the report of the committee on the conduct of the war, shows a grand total present for duty, in the Army of the Potomac, on that day, of one hundred and sixty-four thousand three hundred and fifty-nine, of which seventy-one thousand two hundred and ten were in the defences of Washington, under Banks, leaving ninety-three thousand one hundred and forty-nine with McClellan in the field on that day. A very large portion of this force had been accumulated, by means of the railroads, after the defeat of Pope. You may understand, now, how it was that our victories could never be pressed to more decisive results. It was genius, and nerve, and valor, on the one side, against numbers and mechanical power on the other; even the lightning of the heavens being made subservient to the latter.

You may also form some conception of the boldness of General Lee's movement across the Potomac, the daring of the expedition against Harper's Ferry in the face of so large a force, and the audacity with which he confronted and defied McClellan's army on the 15th and 16th, and then fought it on the 17th, with the small force he had.

Sharpsburg was no defeat to our arms, though our army was retired to the South bank of the Potomac from prudential considerations.

Some persons have been disposed to regard this campaign into Maryland as a failure, but such was not the case. It is true that we had failed to raise Maryland, but it was from no disaster to our arms.

In a military point of view, however, the whole campaign, of which the movement into Maryland was an integral part, had been a grand success, though all was not accomplished which our fond hopes caused us to expect. When General Lee assumed command of the army at Richmond, a besieging army of immense size and resources, was in sight of the spires of the Confederate Capital—all Northern Virginia was in possession of the enemy—the Valley overrun, except when Jackson's vigorous and rapid blows sent the marauders staggering to the banks of the Potomac for a brief interval; and Northwestern Virginia, including the Kanawha Valley, was subjugated and in the firm grasp of the enemy. By General Lee's bold strategy and rapid and heavy blows, the Capital had been relieved; the besieging army driven out of the State; the enemy's Capital threatened; his country invaded; Northern Virginia and the Valley cleared of the enemy; the enemy's troops from Northwestern Virginia and the Kanawha Valley had been drawn from thence for the defence of his own Capital; a Confederate force had penetrated to Charleston, Kanawha; our whole army was supplied with the improved firearm in the place of the old smooth bore musket; much of our inferior field artillery replaced by the enemy's improved guns; and, in addition to our very large captures of prisoners and the munitions of war elsewhere, the direct result of the march across the Potomac was the capture of eleven thousand prisoners, seventy-three pieces of artillery, and thirteen thousand stand of excellent small arms, and immense stores at Harper's Ferry. And at the close of the campaign, the Confederate commander stood proudly defiant on the extreme northern border of the Confederacy, while his opponent had had "his base" removed to the Northern bank of the Potomac, at a point more than one hundred and seventy-five miles from the Confederate Capital, in a straight line. In addition, the immense army of McClellan had been so crippled, that it was not able to resume the offensive for six weeks. Such had been the moral effect upon the enemy, that the Confederate Capital was never again seriously endangered, until the power of the Confederacy had been so broken in other quarters, and its available territory so reduced in dimensions, that the enemy could concentrate his immense resources against the Capital.

All this had been the result of that plan of operations, of which the invasion of Maryland formed an important part. Look at the means placed at the command of General Lee, and the immense numbers and resources brought against him, and then say if the results accomplished by him were not marvellous? If his Government had been able to furnish him with men and means, at all commensurate with his achievements and his conceptions, he would, in September, 1862, have dictated the terms of peace in the Capital of the enemy. But all the wonderful powers of the mechanic arts and physical science, backed by unlimited resources of men and money, still continued to operate against him.

A certified statement from McClellan's morning report of the 30th of September, contained in the document from which I have already quoted, showed, in the Army of the Potomac, a grand total of one hundred and seventy-three thousand seven hundred and forty-five present for duty on that day, of which seventy-three thousand six hundred and one were in the defences of Washington, and one hundred thousand one hundred and forty-four, with him in the field; and a similar statement showed, on the 20th of October, a grand total of two hundred and seven thousand and thirty-six present for duty on that day, of which seventy-three thousand five hundred and ninety-three were in the defences of Washington, and one hundred and thirty-three thousand four hundred and forty-three with McClellan in the field.

At the close of October, according to the official returns, now on file at the "Archive Office" in Washington, the whole Confederate force for duty, in the department of Northern Virginia, amounted to sixty-seven thousand eight hundred and five. A considerable portion of this force was not with General Lee in the field.

At the close of October, McClellan commenced a new movement with his immense army, across the Potomac, East of the Blue Ridge, while General Lee was yet in the Valley. As this movement was developed, Longstreet's corps, and the cavalry under Stuart, were promptly moved to intercept it, Jackson's corps being left in the Valley. McClellan was soon superseded in the command by Burnside, and when the latter turned his steps towards the heights opposite Fredericksburg, Jackson was ordered to rejoin the rest of the army. In the meantime, Burnside's attempt to approach Richmond on the new line had been checkmated, and he soon found himself confronted on the Rappahannock by the whole of General Lee's army. That army had to be stretched out, for some thirty miles, up and down the river, to watch the different crossings. The enemy began his movement to cross at and near Fredericksburg, on the morning of the 11th of December, and the crossing was resisted and delayed for many hours, but owing to the peculiar character of the country immediately on the South bank, and the advantage the enemy had in his commanding position on the

North bank, from whence the wide plains on the South bank, and the town of Fredericksburg, were completely commanded and swept by an immense armament of heavy artillery, that crossing could not be prevented. Our army was rapidly concentrated, and took its position on the heights and range of hills in rear of the town and the plains below; and when the heavy columns of the enemy advanced to the assault on the 13th, first on our right, near Hamilton's crossing, and then on our left, in rear of Fredericksburg, they were hurled back, with immense slaughter, to the cover of the artillery on the opposite heights, and every renewal of the assault met the same fate. In this battle, we stood entirely on the defensive, except once, when the enemy penetrated an interval in our line near the right flank, and three of my brigades advanced, driving and pursuing the enemy into the plains below, until he reached the protection of his artillery and the main line. Burnside's loss was so heavy, and his troops were so worsted in the assaults which had been made, that his principal officers protested against a renewal of the attack, and on the night of the 15th, he re-crossed to the North bank.

In this battle, he had all of McClellan's army, except the twelfth corps, which was eight or ten thousand strong and had been left at Harper's Ferry, and in lieu of that he had a much larger corps, the third, from the defences of Washington. In his testimony before the committee on the conduct of the war, he says he had one hundred thousand men across the river, and he was doubtful which had the superiority of numbers. In reply to a question as to the causes of the failure of the attack, he frankly said:

"It was found to be impossible to get the men up to the works. The enemy's fire was too hot for them."

Our whole force present was not much more than half that of the enemy, which crossed over to the South side of the river. This signal victory, in which the enemy's loss was very heavy and ours comparatively light, closed the operations for the year 1862.

Some newspaper critics and fireside Generals were not satisfied with the results of this victory, and thought Burnside's army ought to have been destroyed before it went back; and there were some absurd stories about propositions alleged to have been made by General Jackson, for driving the enemy into the river. That great soldier did begin a forward movement, about sunset, which I was to have led, but just as my men were moving off, he countermanded the movement, because the enemy opened such a terrific artillery fire from the Stafford Heights and from behind the heavy embankments on the road leading through the bottoms on the South side of the river, that it was apparent that nothing could have lived in the passage across the plain of about a mile in width, over which we would have had to advance, to reach the enemy massed in that road. According to the

statements of himself and officers, before the committee on th
of the war, Franklin, who commanded the enemy's left, had,
our right, from fifty-five to sixty thousand men, of whom only a
thousand had been under fire. The bulk of that force was along th
Green road, running parallel to the river through the middle of the
and behind the very compact and thick embankments on each si
road. He had taken over with him one hundred and sixteen pieces of
and there were sixty-one pieces on the North bank, some of which
very large calibre, so posted as to cover the bridges on that flank and
the plain in his front. Some of these were also crossed over to hi
General Hunt, Burnside's chief of artillery, says, fifty or sixty more p
could have been spared from their right, if necessary. The attempt to
this force into the river, would have, therefore, ensured our destruction

Franklin had eight divisions with him, while at Fredericksburg, c
fronting our left, were ten divisions, fully as strong, certainly, as Frankli
eight, and there were quite as many guns on that flank. It is true the enemy
loss there had been double that in front of our right, but he still had a larg
number of troops on that flank which had not been engaged. The characte
of the ground in front of our position, on that flank, was such that our troops could not be moved down the rugged slopes of the hills in any order of battle, and any attempt to advance them must have been attended with disastrous consequences. Burnside's troops were not so demoralized, as to prevent him from being anxious to renew the attack on the 14th, and the objection of his officers was not on account of the condition of their troops, but on account of the strength of our position. Nothing could have gratified him and his officers more, than for us to have surrendered our advantage and taken the offensive. General Lee, ever ready to strike when an opportunity offered, knew better than all others when it was best to attack and when not to attack.

It is a notable fact about all those people who favored such blood-thirsty and desperate measures, that they were never in the army, to share the dangers into which they were so anxious to rush others.

About the close of the winter or beginning of the spring of 1863, two of Longstreet's divisions, one-fourth of our army, were sent to the South side of James River; and, during their absence, Hooker, who had succeeded Burnside in the command, commenced the movement which resulted in the battle of Chancellorsville, in the first days of May. Throwing a portion of his troops across the river just below Fredericksburg, on the 29th of April, and making an ostentatious demonstration with three corps on the North bank, he proceeded to cross four others above our left flank to Chancellorsville. Having accomplished this, Hooker issued a gasconading order to his troops, in which he claimed to have General Lee's army in his power, and declared his purpose of crushing it. Leaving my division, one brigade of another, and a portion of the reserve artillery, in all less than nine thousand men, to confront the three corps opposite and near Fredericksburg, General Lee moved with five divisions of infantry and a portion of the artillery to meet Hooker, the cavalry being employed to watch the flanks. As soon as General Lee reached Hooker's front, he determined to take the offensive, and, by one of his bold strategic movements, he sent Jackson around Hooker's right flank, and that boastful commander, who was successively reinforced by two of the corps left opposite Fredericksburg, was so vigorously assailed, that he was put on the defensive, and soon compelled to provide for the safety of his own defeated army.

In the meantime, Sedgwick, whose corps numbered about twenty-four thousand men, and who had a division of another corps with him, making his whole force about thirty thousand, had crossed the river, at and below Fredericksburg, with the portion of his troops not already over, and, by concentrating three of his divisions on one point of the long line, of five or six miles, held by my forces, had, on the 3d of May, after repeated repulses, broken through, immediately in the rear of Frederickburg, where the stonewall was held by one regiment and four companies of another, the whole not exceeding five hundred men. General Lee was preparing to renew the attack on Hooker, whose force at Chancellorsville had been driven back to an interior line, when he was informed that Sedgwick was moving up in his rear. He was then compelled to provide against this new danger, and he moved troops down to arrest Sedgwick's progress. This was successfully done, and on the next day, (the 4th,) three of the brigades of my division, all of which had been concentrated and had severed Sedgwick's connection with Fredericksburg and the North bank, fell upon his left flank, and drove it towards the river in confusion, while other troops of ours, which had come from above, closed in on him and forced his whole command into the bend of the river. His whole command would now have been destroyed or captured, but night came on and arrested our progress. During the night, he made his escape over a bridge which was laid down for him. General Lee then turned his attention again to Hooker, but he also made his escape, the next night, under cover of a storm. Thus another brilliant victory was achieved, by the genius and boldness of our commander, against immense odds.

It is a little remarkable that Hooker did not claim, on this occasion, that we had the odds against him; but when he went back, under compulsion, he issued an order, in which he stated, that his army had retired for reasons best known to itself, that it was the custodian of its own honor and advanced when it pleased, fought when it pleased, and retired when it pleased.

In his testimony before the committee on the conduct of the war, he made this curious statement:

"Our artillery had always been superior to that of the rebels, as was also our infantry, except in discipline; and that, for reasons not necessary to mention, never did equal Lee's army. With a rank and file vastly inferior to our own, intellectually and physically, that army has, by discipline alone, acquired a character for steadiness and efficiency unsurpassed, in my judgment, in ancient or modern times. We have not been able to rival it, nor has there been any near approximation to it in the other rebel armies."

This was the impression made by that army under the inspiration of its great leader on "fighting Joe," as he was called. The impression made on Lincoln, at that time, may be gathered from a telegram sent to Butterfield, Hooker's chief-of-staff, who was on the North of the river. The telegram was sent, when Hooker had taken refuge in his new works in rear of Chancellorsville, and Sedgwick was cut off in the bend of the river, and is as follows, in full:

> "Where is General Hooker? Where is Sedgwick? Where is Stoneman?
>
> A. LINCOLN."

Hooker had with him what was left of the army of Burnside, except the ninth corps, which had been sent off; but two other corps, the eleventh and twelfth had been added, besides recruits; and his whole force was largely over one hundred thousand men. General Lee's army, weakened by the absence of Longstreet's two divisions, was very little if any over fifty thousand men, inclusive of my force at Fredericksburg.

As glorious as was this victory, it, nevertheless, shed a gloom over the whole army and country, for in it had fallen the great Lieutenant to whom General Lee had always entrusted the execution of his most daring plans, and who had proved himself so worthy of the confidence reposed in him. It is not necessary for me to stop here, to delineate the character and talents of General Jackson. As long as unselfish patriotism, Christian devotion and purity of character, and deeds of heroism shall command the admiration of men, Stonewall Jackson's name and fame will be reverenced. Of all who mourned his death, none felt more acutely the loss the country and the army had sustained than General Lee. General Jackson had always appreciated, and sympathized with the bold conceptions of the commanding General, and entered upon their execution with the most cheerful alacrity and zeal. General Lee never found it necessary to accompany him, to see that his plans were carried out, but could always trust him alone; and well might he say, when Jackson fell, that *he* himself had lost his "right arm."

After General Jackson's death, the army was divided into three corps of three divisions each, instead of two corps of four divisions each, the ninth division being formed by taking two brigades from the division of A. P. Hill and uniting them with two others which were brought from the South. These two brigades constituted all the reinforcements to our army, after the battle of Chancellorsville, and previous to the campaign into Pennsylvania. Longstreet's two absent divisions were now brought back and moved up towards Culpeper C. H., and General Lee entered on a campaign of even greater boldness than that of the previous year.

While Hooker's army yet occupied the Stafford heights, our army was put in motion for Pennsylvania, on the 4th of June, Hill's corps being left for a while to watch Hooker. This movement was undertaken because the interposition of the Rappahannock, between the two armies, presented an insurmountable obstacle to offensive operations on our part, against the enemy in the position he then occupied, and General Lee was determined not to stand on the defensive, and give the enemy time to mature his plans and accumulate a larger army for another attack on him.

The enemy was utterly bewildered by this new movement, and while he was endeavoring to find out what it meant, the advance of our army, Ewell's corps, composed of three of Jackson's old divisions, entered the Valley and captured, at Winchester and Martinsburg, about four thousand prisoners, twenty-nine pieces of artillery, about four thousand stand of small arms, a large wagon train, and many stores. It then crossed the Potomac, and two divisions went to Carlisle, while another went to the banks of the Susquehanna, through York. The two other corps soon followed, and this movement brought the whole of Hooker's army across the Potomac in pursuit. The two armies concentrated, and encountered each other at Gettysburg, east of the South Mountain, in a battle extending through three days, from the 1st to the 3d of July, inclusive. On the first day, a portion of our army, composed of two divisions of Hill's corps, and two divisions of Ewell's corps, gained a very decided victory over two of the enemy's corps, which latter were driven back, in great confusion, through Gettysburg, to the Heights, immediately South and East of the town, known as Cemetery Hill. On the second and third days, we assaulted the enemy's position at different points, but failed to dislodge his army, now under Meade, from its very strong position on Cemetery and the adjacent hills. Both sides suffered very heavy losses, that of the enemy exceeding ours.

Our ammunition had drawn short, and we were beyond the reach of any supplies of that kind. General Lee therefore desisted from his efforts to carry the position, and, after straightening his line, he confronted Meade for a whole day, without the latter's daring to move from his position, and then retired towards the Potomac, for the purpose of being within reach of supplies. We halted near Hagerstown, Maryland, and when Meade, who had followed us very cautiously, arrived, battle was offered him, but he went to fortifying in our front. We confronted him for several days, but as he did not venture to attack us, and heavy rains had set in, we retired across the Potomac to avoid having an impassable river in our rear.

The campaign into Pennsylvania, and the battle of Gettysburg, have been much criticized, and but little understood. The magnanimity of General Lee caused him to withhold from the public the true causes of the failure to gain a decisive victory at Gettysburg. Many writers have racked their brains to account for that failure. Some have attributed it to the fact that the advantage gained on the first day was not pressed immediately; and among them is a Northern historian of the war, (Swinton,) who says: "Ewell was even advancing a line against Culp's Hill when Lee reached the field and stayed the movement." There is no foundation for this statement. When General Lee, after the engagement, reached the part of the field where Ewell's command had fought, it was near dark, and no forward movement was in progress or contemplated. Two fresh corps of the enemy, Slocum's and Sickels', had arrived at 5 o'clock, at least two hours before General Lee came to us after the engagement. There was a time, as we know now, immediately after the enemy was driven back, when, if we had advanced vigorously, the heights of Gettysburg would probably have been taken, but that was not then apparent. I was in favor of the advance, but I think it doubtful whether it would have resulted in any greater advantage than to throw back the two routed corps on the main body of their army, and cause the great battle to be fought on other ground. Meade had already selected another position, on Pipe Clay creek, where he would have concentrated his army, and we would have been compelled to give him battle or retire. Moreover, it is not impossible that the arrival of the two fresh corps may have turned the fate of the day against the troops we then had on the field, had we pressed our advantage. General Lee had ordered the concentration of his army at Cashtown, and the battle of this day, brought on by the advance of the enemy's cavalry, was unexpected to him. When he ascertained the advantage that had been gained, he determined to press it as soon as the remainder of his army arrived. In a conference with General Ewell, General Rhodes and myself, when he did reach us, after the enemy had been routed, he expressed his determination to assault the enemy's position at daylight on the next morning, and wished to know whether we could make the attack from our flank—the left—at the designated time. We informed him of the fact that the ground immediately in our front, leading to the enemy's position, furnished much greater obstacles to a successful assault than existed at any other point, and we concurred in suggesting to him that, as our corps (Ewell's) constituted the only troops then immediately confronting the enemy, he would manifestly concentrate and fortify against us, during the night, as proved to be the case, according to subsequent information. He then determined to make the attack from our right on the enemy's left, and left us for the purpose of ordering up Longstreet's corps in time to begin the attack at dawn next morning. That corps was not in readiness to make the attack until four o'clock in the afternoon of the next day. By that time, Meade's whole army had arrived on the field and taken its position. Had the attack been made at daylight, as contemplated, it must have resulted in a brilliant and decisive victory, as all of Meade's army had not then arrived, and a very small portion of it was in position. A considerable portion of his army did not get up until after sun-rise, one corps not arriving until 2 o'clock in the afternoon, and a prompt advance to the attack must have resulted in his defeat in detail. The position which Longstreet attacked at four, was not occupied by the enemy until late in the afternoon, and Round Top Hill, which commanded the enemy's position, could have been taken in the morning without a struggle. The attack was made by two divisions, and though the usual gallantry was displayed by the troops engaged in it, no very material advantage was gained. When General Lee saw his plans thwarted by the delay on our right, he ordered an attack to be made also from our left, to be begun by Johnson's division on Culp's Hill, and followed up by the rest of Ewell's corps, and also by Hill's. This attack was begun with great vigor by Johnson, and two of my brigades, immediately on his right, which were the only portion of the division then available, as the other two brigades had been sent off to the left to watch the York road, moved forward promptly, climbed the heights on the left of Gettysburg, over stone and plank fences, reached the summit of Cemetery Hill, and got possession of the enemy's works and his batteries there posted. One of my other brigades had been sent for, and got back in time to be ready to act as a support to those in front: but though Johnson was making good progress in his attack, there was no movement on my right, and the enemy, not being pressed in that direction, concentrated on my two brigades in such overwhelming force as to render it necessary for them to retire. Thus, after having victory in their grasp, they were compelled to relinquish it, because General Lee's orders had again failed to be carried out; but one of those brigades brought off four captured battle flags from the top of Cemetery Hill. This affair occurred just a little before dark.

On the next day, when the assault was made by Picket's division in such gallant style, there was again a miscarriage, in not properly supporting it according to the plan and orders of the commanding General. You must recollect that a commanding General cannot do the actual marching and fighting of his army. These must, necessarily be entrusted to his subordinates, and any hesitation, delay or miscarriage in the execution of his orders, may defeat the best devised schemes. Contending against such odds as we did, it was necessary, always, that there should be the utmost dispatch, energy and undoubting confidence in carrying out the plans of the commanding General. A subordinate who undertakes to doubt the wisdom of his superior's plans, and enters upon their execution with reluctance and distrust, will not be likely to ensure success. It was General Jackson's unhesitating confidence and faith in the chances of success, that caused it so often to perch on his banners, and made him such an invaluable executor of General Lee's plans. If Mr. Swinton has told the truth, in repeating in his book what is alleged to have been said to him by General Longstreet, there was at least one of General Lee's corps commanders at Gettysburg who did not enter upon the execution of his plans with that confidence and faith necessary to success, and hence, perhaps, it was that it was not achieved. Some have thought that General Lee did wrong in fighting at Gettysburg, and it has been said that he ought to have moved around Meade's left, so as to get between him and Washington. It is a very easy matter to criticize and prophecy after events happen; but it would have been manifestly a most dangerous movement for him to have undertaken to pass Meade by the flank with all his trains. In passing through the narrow space between Gettysburg and the South Mountain, we would have been exposed to an attack under very disadvantageous circumstances. I then thought, and still think, that it was right to fight the battle of Gettysburg, and I am firmly convinced that if General Lee's plans had been carried out in the spirit in which they were conceived, a decisive victory would have been obtained, which perhaps would have been secured our independence. Our army was never in better heart, and when it did retire, it was with no sense of defeat. My division brought up the rear of the army, and it did not leave the sight of the enemy's position until the afternoon of the 5th. One of Meade's corps followed us most cautiously, at a respectable distance, and when, at Fairfield, near the foot of the Mountain, I formed line of battle to await it, no advance was made. There was none of the indications of defeat in the rear of the army on the march, and when we took position near Hagerstown to await Meade's attack, it was with entire confidence in our ability to meet it with success.

Meade's army at Gettysburg numbered at least one hundred thousand men in position. The whole force in the department of Northern Virginia, at the close of May, four days before our movement North began, was sixty-eight thousand three hundred and fifty-two. No reinforcements were received after that time, and, of course, the whole force was not carried out of Virginia. General Lee's army at Gettysburg numbered considerably less than sixty thousand men of all arms.

This campaign did not accomplish all that we desired, but, nevertheless, it was not unattended with great and advantageous results. It certainly had the effect of deferring, for one year at least, the advance on the Confederate Capital, and had it not been for the fall of Vicksburg at the same time, and the consequent severance of all the States beyond the Mississippi from the Confederacy, for all practical purposes, the public would not have taken as gloomy a view of the results of the campaign as it did.

So far from our army being defeated or broken in spirit, when the invading army of the enemy again advanced into Virginia, General Lee intercepted it, and taking position on the South bank of the Rapidan, effectually prevented any further advance until May, 1864, when, as I will show you, the power of the Confederacy had been so crippled in other quarters, as to allow an unusual accumulation of men and resources against the Army of Northern Virginia.

You must understand that the line of the Rappahannock and the Rapidan was the only practicable line of defence in Northern Virginia, because the possession and control of the Potomac and Chesapeake Bay, which the enemy's monitors and iron-clads gave him, without let or hindrance, would enable him to flank and turn any line of defence which might be assumed North of those rivers. Beyond that line General Lee, in 1862, had driven the invading army, and there he had retained it up to the time of which I am speaking. This was all that a defensive policy could accomplish, and it was only when he assumed the offensive, as in the campaigns of Maryland and Pennsylvania, that the enemy could be hurled back on his own border, in order to defend his territory and Capital. The results of the campaign into Pennsylvania left General Lee in possession of his legitimate line of defence, with the enemy's plans all thwarted for that year. In fact so satisfied was the latter of his inability to accomplish anything, by an attempt to advance on Richmond, that two of Meade's corps were detached for the purpose of reinforcing Rosecrans at Chattanooga, and General Lee held his own line by such a certain tenure, that he was able to detach Longstreet's corps, and send two divisions to Bragg, and one, first to the South side of James river, and then to North Carolina. After Longstreet had gone, occurred the movement which caused Meade to retire to Centreville, and about the last of November he crossed the Rapidan and moved to Mine run, but retired just in time to avoid an attack which General Lee had prepared to make on his flank.

At the close of the year 1863, the enemy was no farther advanced in his oft-repeated effort to capture the Confederate Capital, than when Manassas was evacuated, early in the spring of 1862; but in the Southwest, the fall of

Vicksburg, the disaster at Missionary Ridge, and the failure of the campaign in Eastern Tennessee, had not only severed the trans-Mississippi region from the remainder of the Confederacy, but had left all Kentucky and Tennessee firmly in the power of the enemy, and rendered all the lower basin of the Mississippi practically useless to us. The main army of the West had been compelled to retire to Dalton in the Northwestern corner of Georgia, and, for all useful purposes, the Confederacy was confined to Georgia, North and South Carolina, and the portion of Virginia held by us. It is true that we held posts and had troops in Alabama, Florida and Mississippi, but they could contribute nothing to the general defence, and the resources of those States were substantially lost to us, at least so far as operations in Virginia were concerned. This state of things left the enemy at liberty to concentrate his resources against the two principal armies of the Confederacy. Grant was made Commander-in-Chief of all the armies of the enemy in the spring of 1864, and took his position with the Army of the Potomac in the field, while Sherman was assigned to the command of the army at Chattanooga, which was to operate against ours at Dalton.

By the 1st of May, Grant had accumulated an army of more than one hundred and forty-one thousand men on the North of the Rapidan; and General Lee's army on the South bank, including two of Longstreet's divisions, which had returned from Tennessee, was under fifty thousand men, of all arms.

Grant's theory was to accumulate the largest numbers practicable against us, so as, by constant "hammering," to destroy our army "by mere attrition if in no other way." Besides the army under Grant, in Culpeper, there were near fifty thousand men in Washington and Baltimore, and the military control of the railroads and the telegraph, as well as an immense number of steam transports, rendered it an easy matter to reinforce him indefinitely.

On the 4th of May, he crossed the Rapidan on our right to the Wilderness, to get between us and Richmond. General Lee advanced promptly to attack him and thwart his purpose; and then ensued that most wonderful campaign from the Rapidan to the James, in which the ever glorious Army of Northern Virginia grappled its gigantic antagonist in a death struggle, which continued until the latter was thrown off, crippled and bleeding, to the cover of the James and Appomattox rivers, where it was enabled to recruit and renew its strength for another effort.

Two days of fierce battle were had in the Wilderness, and our little army never struck more rapid and vigorous blows. Grant was compelled to move off from our front, and attempt to accomplish his purpose by another flank movement, but General Lee promptly intercepted him at Spotsylvania Court House; where again occurred a series of desperate engagements, in which, though a portion of our line was temporarily broken, and we sustained a loss which we could ill afford, yet Grant's army was so crippled, that it was unable to resume the offensive, until it had been reinforced from Washington and Baltimore, to the full extent of forty thousand men. But General Lee received no reinforcements, and yet Grant, after waiting six days for his, when they did arrive, was again compelled to move off from us, and attempt another flank movement, under cover of the net work of difficult water courses around and east of Spotsylvania Court House. Never had the wonderful powers of our great Chief, and the unflinching courage of his small army, been more conspicuously displayed than during the thirteen trying days at this place. One of his three corps commanders had been disabled by wounds at the Wilderness, and another was too sick to command his corps, while he himself was suffering from a most annoying and weakening disease. In fact, nothing but his own determined will enabled him to keep the field at all; and it was there rendered more manifest than ever, that he was the head and front, the very life and soul of his army. Grant's new movement was again intercepted at Hanover Junction, and from that point he was compelled to retire behind the North Anna and Pamunkey, to escape his tenacious adversary by another manœuvre. He was again intercepted at Pole Green Church; and at Bethesda Church, and on the historic field of Cold Harbor, occurred another series of most bloody battles, in which such carnage was inflicted on Grant's army, that when orders were given for a new assault, his troops in sullen silence declined to move; and he was compelled to ask for a truce to bury his dead. Though largely reinforced from Butler's army, Grant was now compelled to take refuge on the South side of James River, at a point to which he could have gone, by water, from his camps in Culpeper, without the loss of a man. His original plan of the campaign was thus completely thwarted, and he was compelled to abandon the attempt to take Richmond by the land route, after a loss in battle of more men than were in General Lee's whole army, including the reinforcements received at Hanover Junction and Cold Harbor, which latter consisted of two divisions, a brigade, and less than three thousand men under Breckenridge, from the Valley. When we consider the disparity of the forces engaged in this campaign, the advantages of the enemy for reinforcing his army, and the time consumed in actual battle, it must rank as the most remarkable campaign of ancient or modern times. We may read of great victories, settling the fate of nations, gained by small armies of compact, well-trained and thoroughly disciplined troops, over immense and unwieldly hordes of untrained barbarians, or of demoralized soldiers, sunk in effeminacy and luxury; but where shall we find the history of such a prolonged struggle, in which such enormous advantages of numbers, equipped, resources and supplies, were on the side of the defeated party. The proximity of a number of water courses, navigable for steam vessels, and patrolled by Federal gunboats, had enabled Grant to keep open his communications with the sources of his supplies, and to receive constant accessions of troops, so that it was impossible to destroy his army; but if the contest, as in most campaigns of former times, had been confined to the two armies, originally engaged in it, there can be no question but that Grant's would have been, in effect, destroyed. As it was, his whole movement, after the first encounter in the Wilderness, was but a retreat by the flank, the Potomac, the Rappahannock, the York and Pamunkey, and the James, in succession, furnishing him a new base to retire on, for the receipt of supplies and reinforcements, and the resumption of operations. The boldness and fertility of the strategy employed by our glorious Chieftain, during this campaign, was indeed marvellous; and such was the disparity of numbers that it appears like romance, and men are disposed to turn an incredulous ear when the truth is told. In fact, General Lee, himself, was aware of the apparent improbability, which a true statement of the facts would present, and in a letter to me, during the winter of 1865–6, he said:

"It will be difficult to get the world to understand the odds against which we fought."

Notwithstanding the disparity which existed, he was anxious, as I know, to avail himself of every opportunity to strike an offensive blow; and just as Grant was preparing to move across James River with his defeated and dispirited army, General Lee was maturing his plans for taking the offensive; and, in stating his desire for me to take the initiative with the corps I then commanded, he said:

"We must destroy this army of Grant's before he gets to James River. If he gets there, it will become a seige, and then it will be a mere question of time."

He knew well that with the army Grant then had, he could not take Richmond, but he also knew that, if that army could be placed on the South of the James and East of the Appomattox, where it would be out of the reach of ours for offensive operations, it could be reinforced indefinitely, until by the process of attrition, the exhaustion of our resources, and the employment of mechanism and the improved engines of war against them, the brave defenders of our cause would gradually melt away. In fact, he knew that it would then become a contest between mechanical power and physical strength, on the one hand, and the gradually diminishing nerve and sinew of Confederate soldiers, on the other, until the unlimited resources of our enemies must finally prevail over all the genius and chivalric daring, which had so long baffled their mighty efforts in the field. It was from such considerations as these, that he had made his great and successful effort to raise the siege in 1862; his subsequent campaign into Maryland; and his campaign into Pennsylvania in 1863.

Before the contemplated blow against Grant was struck, the startling intelligence of Hunter's operations in the Valley was received, and it became necessary to detach, first Breckenridge's command, and then my corps to meet the new danger threatening all of our communications.

This enabled Grant to reach his new position unmolested, the movement towards which began on the night I received my orders to move by 3 o'clock next morning for the Valley. Finding it necessary to detach my command on a work of pressing urgency, General Lee determined to combine with the movement, a daring expedition across the Potomac, to threaten the enemy's country and capital; about the conduct and results of which, I will merely say, that there has been much misunderstanding and ignorant misrepresentation. After reaching the South bank of the James, Grant made a dash for the purpose of capturing Petersburg, which was thwarted by the good soldier who had already baffled and defeated Butler. The enemy, now having found it impossible to capture the Confederate Capital in a campaign by land, resorted to a combined operation of his army and navy, by the way of the James. The condition of things in the South and Southwest enabled him to still further strengthen Grant's army after its junction with Butler's; and the fall of Atlanta, in September, severed the greater part of Georgia practically from the Confederacy. There were no means of recruiting General Lee's army, to any considerable extent, after its union with Beauregard's small force, which, with the division and brigade of the army of Northern Virginia returned at Hanover Junction, and the division received at Cold Harbor, did not reach twenty thousand men, while my corps had been detached. For nine long months was the unequal contest protracted by the genius of one man, aided by the valor of his little force, occupying a line of more than thirty miles, with scarcely more than a respectable skirmish line. During this time, there were many daring achievements and heroic deeds performed by the constantly diminishing survivors of those who had rendered the Army of Northern Virginia so illustrious; but, finally, constant attrition and lingering starvation did their work. General Lee had been unable to attack Grant in his stronghold, South of the James and East of the Appomattox, where alone such a movement was practicable, because a concentration for that purpose, on the East of the latter river, would have left the way to Richmond open to the enemy. When, by the unsuccessful expedition into Tennessee, the march of Sherman through the centre of Georgia to the Atlantic, his subsequent expedition North through South Carolina into North Carolina, and the consequent fall of army with which to give battle. What he surrendered was the skeleton, the mere ghost of the Army of Northern Virginia, which had been gradually worn down by the combined agencies of numbers, steam-power, railroads, mechanism, and all the resources of physical science. It had, in fact, been engaged in a struggle, not only against the mere brute power of man, but against all the elements of fire, air, earth and water; and even that all-pervading and subtle fluid, whose visible demonstrations the ancients designated "The thunderbolt of the gods," had been led submissive in the path of the opposing army, so as to concentrate with rapidity and make available all the other agencies.

It was by the use of these new adjuncts to the science of war, that McClellan and Pope had escaped destruction in 1862; the Federal Capital been saved, after the terrible chastisement inflicted on their armies; Pennsylvania also saved in 1863, and Meade enabled to fight a drawn battle at Gettysburg; Grant's army preserved from annihilation in 1864, and enabled to reach the welcome shelter of the James and Appomattox; and now, they had finally produced that exhaustion of our army and resources, and that accumulation of numbers on the other side, which wrought the final disaster.

When we come to estimate General Lee's achievements and abilities as a military commander, all these things must be taken into consideration.

I have now given you a condensed sketch of General Lee's military career, and I am aware that what I have said falls short of the real merits of the subject. My estimates of the enemy's strength are taken from their own reports and statements. In the last interview I had with General Lee, since my return to the country, I mentioned to him my estimates of his strength at various times, and he said that they fully covered his force at all times, and in some instances were in excess. They are those I have now given you.

From the facts I have presented, I think you will have no difficulty in discerning that the fall of Richmond, and the surrender of the Army of Northern Virginia, were the consequences of events in the West and Southwest, and not directly of the operations in Virginia. I say this, without intending to cast any reproach, directly or by implication, on the commanders or the rank and file of our armies operating in those quarters. For them I have a profound respect and admiration, and I am ever ready to receive and acknowledge them as worthy coadjutors and comrades of the Army of Northern Virginia. They had, also, the disadvantage of overwhelming numbers, and the other agencies I have mentioned, to contend against, and a truthful history of their deeds will confer upon them imperishable renown. I do not feel that it is necessary or just to attempt to build up the reputation of the Army of Northern Virginia, or its Commander, at the expense of our comrades who battled so gloriously and vigorously on other fields for the same just and holy cause. What I have said is not mentioned with any such purpose, but simply to note what I conceive to be an apparent and indisputable historic fact, that ought not to be overlooked in a review of General Lee's military record.

At the close of the war, the deportment and conduct of our noble and honored leader were worthy of his previous history; and in that dignified and useful retirement to which he devoted the remainder of his days, in your midst, the true grandeur of his soul shone out as conspicuously as had his transcendant military genius in his campaigns; but I leave the duty of illustrating that to others.

There have been efforts to draw parallels between our illustrious Chief and some of the renowned commanders of former times, but these efforts have always proved unsatisfactory to me.

Where shall we turn to find the peer of our great and pure soldier and hero? Certainly, we shall not find one among the mythic heroes of Homer, the wrath of the chief of whom was:

> "—— to Greece the direful spring
> Of woes unnumbered ——"

Nor shall we find one among the Grecian commanders of a later period, though in the devotion of the hero of Thermopylæ, and the daring of the victor of Marathon, may be found similes for the like qualities in our hero. But there is too much of fable and the license of the heroic verse, in the narrations of their deeds, to make them reliable.

Shall we take Alexander, who, at the head of his serried phalanxes, encountered the effeminate masses of Asia and scattered them like sheep before a ravening wolf? While sighing for new worlds to conquer, he could not control himself, but fell a victim to his own excesses.

In the march of Hannibal, the great Carthagenian patriot and hero, over the Alps, and his campaigns in Italy, we might find a similarity to General Lee's bold strategy, but the system of warfare in those days, the implements of war, and the mode of maintaining armies in the field, which had neither baggage nor supply trains, but foraged on the country in which they operated, make such a vast difference, that the parallel ceases at the very beginning. Besides, Carthage and Rome were then nearly equal in power, and Hannibal was enabled to receive reinforcements from Carthage by sea, as the Carthagenians were a great maritime people; and the hostile neighbors to Rome readily furnished him with allies and auxiliaries.

We will not find in Republican Rome a parallel. Certainly not in Julius Cæsar, the greatest of Roman Generals, who, at the head of the legions of "the mistress of the world," overran the countries of barbarians, and then turned his sword against the liberties of his country.

We shall search in vain for one among the Generals of the Roman Empire, either before or after its partition; nor shall we find one among the leaders of the barbaric hordes which overran the territories of the degenerate Romans; nor in the dark ages; nor among the Crusaders, who, under the standard of the Cross, committed such crimes against religion and humanity; nor among the chieftains of the middle ages, to advance whose ambitious projects the nations of Europe were, by turns, torn and ravaged.

Perhaps, in the champion of Protestantism, from the North of Europe, Gustavus Adolphus, there might be found no unworthy parallel for our great Leader, as well in regard to purity and unselfishness of character, as heroic courage and devotion, and the comparison has not inaptly been drawn; but the career of the heroic king of Sweden was cut short, by death in battle, at so early a period, and before he had stood the test of adversity, that the materials for completing the parallel are wanting.

Some have undertaken to draw the parallel between our pure Chieftain and Marlborough, who owed his rise, in the first place, to the dishonor of his family and the patronage of a debauched Court favorite. I utterly repudiate that comparison. Besides, Marlborough commanded the armies of the greatest maritime power in the world, in alliance with all the rest of Europe, against France alone. Shall we compare General Lee to the great Napoleon, or his successful antagonist, Wellington? Napoleon was a captain of most extraordinary genius, but success was always necessary to him. As long as he had what Forest, with such terse vigor, if inelegance, would call "the bulge," he did wondrously, but he could never stand reverses; and the disastrous retreat from Moscow, and the shameful flight from Waterloo, must always be blots on his military escutcheon. He would have been unable to conduct the campaigns of General Lee against the constantly accumulating and ever renewing armies of the enemy, and none of his own campaigns were at all similar to them. He played a bold game for empire and self-aggrandizement, regardless of the lives, liberties or happiness of others, and the first adverse turn of the wheel of fortune ruined him. "The Hundred Days" constituted but the last desperate effort of a ruined gambler.

Wellington was a prudent, good soldier, at the head of the armies of a most powerful nation, "the mistress of the seas," in alliance with all Europe against Napoleon in his waning days. He was emphatically a favorite child of fortune, and won his chief glory in a game against the desperate gambler whose last stake was up, when he had all the odds on his side. "The Iron Duke," though almost worshipped and overwhelmed with honors and riches by the British nation, does not furnish a suitable parallel for the great Confederate Commander.

In regard to all I have mentioned, and all other renowned military chieftains of other days, in the old world, it must be recollected that they did not have to contend against the new elements in the art of war, which were brought to bear against our armies and their commanders.

Coming now to this side of the water, we may draw a parallel between General Lee and our great Washington in many respects; for in their great self-command, in their patriotism, and in their purity and unselfishness of character, there was a great similarity; but the military operations of General Lee were on so much grander a scale than those of Washington, and the physical changes in the character of the country, wrought by the adaptation of steam-power, and the invention of railroads and the telegraph, were so great, that there cease to be any further points of comparison between them as soldiers. It was the physical difficulty of penetrating the country, backed by the material aid, in men, money and ships of war, of a powerful European nation, which enabled the States to win their independence under Washington; while the facilities for rapid communication and concentration, in connection with the aid received by our enemies, in men and money, from all Europe, which was a recruiting ground for them, caused our disasters and lost us our liberties, in a contest in which we stood alone.

There is no occasion to draw a parallel between General Lee and our dead heroes, Sidney Johnston and Jackson. The career of the former, whose dawn gave such bright promise, was, unfortunately, cut off so soon, that the country at large did not have an opportunity of learning all of which those who knew him believed him to be capable.

Whoever shall undertake to draw a parallel between General Lee and his great Lieutenant, for the purpose of depreciating the one or the other, cannot have formed the remotest conception of the true character of either of those illustrious men, and congenial Christian heroes. Let us be thankful that our cause had two such champions, and that, in their characters, we can furnish the world at large with the best assurance of the rightfulness of the principles for which they and we fought. When asked for our vindication, we can triumphantly point to the graves of Lee and Jackson and look the world squarely in the face. Let them, the descendant of the Cavalier from tide-water, and the scion of the Scotch-Irish stock from the mountains of Northwestern Virginia, lie here, in this middle ground, and let their memories be cherished and mingled together in that harmony which characterized them during their glorious companionship in arms.

Nor would it be at all profitable to institute a comparison between General Lee and any of our living commanders. Let us be rejoiced that those still survive who were worthy defenders of our cause, and not unfit comrades of Lee, Sidney Johnston and Stonewall Jackson.

Shall I compare General Lee to his successful antagonist? As well compare the great pyramid which rears its majestic proportions in the valley of the Nile, to a pigmy perched on Mount Atlas.

No, my friends, it is a vain work for us to seek anywhere for a parallel to the great character which has won our admiration and love. Our beloved Chief stands, like some lofty column which rears its head among the highest, in grandeur, simple, pure and sublime, needing no borrowed lustre; and he is all our own.

And now, my friends, I must add that we are often invoked to turn our backs upon the dead past, to forget dead issues and principles—as if true principles ever die—to surrender our cherished traditions, to give up our civilization, and adopt the progressive civilization of the age. We are also told that our ideas are all obsolete, and asked to adopt the spirit of progress from our enemies, in order to restore the prosperity of our country, and start it on a new career of material development and physical power. There are many who are seduced by the flattering visions pictured to them, and it is not to be denied that there exists a feverish desire to emerge from our depressed condition into sudden wealth and prosperity, by the adoption of various fanciful schemes.

This spirit bodes no good to our people or our country. The fortunes of no country can be retrieved from such a depression, as ours have experienced, by any sudden or hot-house process, and all these ideas of doing it by foreign capital or immigrants, are deceptive. Those of us who deprecate the new theories, are said to be behind the age, and called fossils, fogies and Bourbons, who brood over and live in the past, while we take no thought for the future. They very much mistake us who think that, while we do venerate the past, we are not willing to unite in all proper measures for restoring a sound and wholesome prosperity to our beloved country. We do not, however, think it proper to run the ploughshare over the graves of our fathers, in order to conform to the utilitarian spirit of this age; and we do believe that a people who forget or discard their traditions, are unworthy and unfit to be free. We do not like the progressive spirit of this age, because we are not certain from whence it comes, nor whither it tends. We cannot turn our backs on the graves of our fallen heroes, and we will cherish the remembrance of their deeds, and see that justice is done to their memories, believing that when "recording history,"

> "Tells of a few stout hearts, that fought and died,
> Where duty placed them at their country's side;
> The man that is not moved with what he reads,
> That takes not fire at their heroic deeds,

> Unworthy of the blessings of the brave,
> Is base in kind and born to be a slave."

To you, Virginians, I must say, that our ancestors won this country from savage life, and started Virginia on that career which rendered her so prosperous, happy and renowned. That prosperity has not been lost by any fault of ours, but has been torn from us by violence and wrong; and, certainly, in our hands, the glory of the State has suffered no diminution. Have Virginians degenerated so much, that they cannot undertake to restore the prosperity and happiness of their State, without resorting to the maxims and policy of those who have ravaged and desolated their homes, and left their old mother panting and bleeding? Can we not point to the graves of Lee and Jackson, and those who fell fighting under them, and exclaim:

> "And is thy grandeur done?
> Mother of men like these!
> Has not thy outcry gone
> Where justice has an ear to hear?
> Be Holy! God shall guide thy spear."

In you, my fair countrywomen, I have faith. I know that you will continue to honor the brave dead, and strew flowers on their graves. Your sex, in all the South, may be relied on to instil the sentiments of honor and patriotism into the hearts of the rising and future generations, and teach them to venerate the memory, emulate the virtues, and cherish the principles of those who fell fighting for your homes, your all.

In you and your compeers, my young friends, from all the South, must mainly rest the hope of our country, for restoration to prosperity and happiness. You are fortunate in having the opportunity of being prepared for your future career, here, where lie the remains of two such men as Lee and Jackson, and where you can catch inspiration from the hallowed precincts. Profit by the occasion, and go forth into the world with the determination of following their example and battling for the right, leaving the consequences to your Maker.

And to you, my comrades, survivors of that noble army of which I have spoken, followers of Lee and Jackson, I desire to say a few parting words. I trust it is not necessary for me to urge you to remain true to the memory of your venerated leaders, and the principles for which you fought along with them. If there be any, in all the land, who have proved renegade to their comrades and our holy cause, let them go out from among us with the brand of Cain upon them! But while cherishing the memory of our leaders and our fallen comrades, as a sacred trust, it is not proper that we should indulge in vain regrets or cease the battle of life. Let the holy memories connected with our glorious though unsuccessful struggle, afford stronger incentives to renewed efforts to do our duty; but let us discard all deceptive illusions, and rely upon our own energies and the manhood that, I trust, did not make us unworthy comrades of the illustrious dead. We have a mission to perform and we must not prove recreant to it.

We have also a sacred duty to discharge. It is meet and proper that the tomb of our beloved Commander, in this chapel, shall be suitably decorated and honored. Let it be our especial charge to see that the pious work is accomplished; and let us also see that a monument to his glorious memory is erected at the Confederate Capital, in defence of which his wondrous talents and sublime virtues were displayed, which shall proclaim to all the ages, that the soldiers who fought under him remained true to him in death, and were not unworthy to have been the followers of ROBERT E. LEE.

17. "Meeting Between Lee and Jackson" at Cold Harbor in June 1862, a sketch by Adalbert J. Volck, prepared for Emily V. Mason's *Popular Life of Gen. Robert Edward Lee* (Baltimore: John Murphy & Company, 1872), p. 106. A dentist who lived in Baltimore and produced some of the most scathing pro-Confederate etchings and cartoons during the war, Volck drew seventeen illustrations for Mason's biography of Lee. Very simple—even crude—in design, they convey none of the grand military stature for Lee common in later Lost Cause art. This sketch even accords Jackson the dominant position, though by 1872 Lee long had been the most famous Confederate military leader.

18. "Battle of Chancellorsville," Volck's representation of Lee's arrival on the field as the two wings of his army reunite near the blazing Chancellor house on 3 May 1863. Mason, *Popular Life of Lee*, 178.

19. In Volck's "Lee to the Rear," a scarcely identifiable Lee waves a standard to rally troops at the Widow Tapp farm early on 6 May 1864, at the battle of the Wilderness. Mason, *Popular Life of Lee*, 244.

20. "General Lee Entering Richmond After the Surrender," Volck's conception of the welcome Lee received form Richmonders in mid-April 1865. Mason, *Popular Life of Lee*, 317.

21. "Lee and Jackson at Cold Harbor," an illustration by Alfred R. Waud in John Esten Cooke's *A Life of Gen. Robert E. Lee* (New York: D. Appleton and Company, 1871), at pp. 84–85. The ablest Northern field artist during the war, Waud makes Lee the more imposing figure in this sketch, garbing him in a slouch hat and cape that would appear in all his representations of Lee for Cooke's biography.

22. In "Fredericksburg," Waud depicts Lee with James Longstreet and other officers watching Union assaults against Confederate defenders on Marye's Heights on 13 December 1862. Cooke, *Life of Lee*, at pp. 176–77. According to Cooke (p. 184), it was here that Lee turned to Longstreet and said, "It is well this is so terrible! we should grow too fond of it!"

23. Waud's "Chancellorsville," though more detailed than Volck's sketch of the same incident, employs a similar composition and places Lee on a dark horse rather than the gray Traveller. Cooke, *Life of Lee*, at pp. 244–45.

24. For "Lee at Gettysburg," Waud selected the moment when the general rode among the survivors of the Pickett-Pettigrew assault on the afternoon of 3 July 1863. Cooke, *Life of Lee*, at pp. 324–25. "The demeanor of General Lee at this moment," read Cooke's text (p. 325), "remains one of the greatest glories of his memory."

25. "The Wilderness. 'Lee to the Rear,' " Waud's treatment of the incident Volck sketched in plate 19. Cooke, *Life of Lee*, at pp. 444–45.

General Lee

FRANCIS LAWLEY

More than a year has passed away since the death of General Lee. In ordinary times such an event could hardly have happened without reviving, if only for a moment, much of the eager interest with which, between 1861 and 1865, the Old World watched the Titanic Civil War of the New. But during the October of 1870, when General Lee breathed his last, the siege of Paris absorbed the thoughts and engrossed the attention of civilised mankind. Little or no notice has therefore been taken in England of the death of one who, when his career, character, and military genius are better known and understood, will, in spite of his defeat, be pronounced the greatest soldier, with two exceptions, that any English-speaking nation has ever produced. Upon the other side of the Atlantic circumstances have conspired to obscure the great deeds and spotless purity of the noblest son to whom the North American continent has hitherto given birth. A 'Life of General Robert E. Lee' has indeed appeared, from the pen of Mr. John Esten Cooke, upon which we propose to make a few comments; but it can in no sense be regarded as more than an adumbration of the man whom it professes to delineate. Public expectation on the other side of the Atlantic anticipates much from a biography, already too long delayed, of which Colonel Marshall, who for four years served at General Lee's right hand in the position which corresponds in European armies to our Chief of Staff, is to be the author. But in both sections of the reconstructed Union the passions and animosities of the American War are still so much alive that it is a political necessity for General Lee's conquerors to darken his fame and sneer at his achievements. In most of the public papers and utterances which have issued from the victors in the fratricidal strife, the writers and speakers have thought it expedient to brand Lee, Stonewall Jackson, and Jefferson Davis as men worthy to be ranked with Benedict Arnold and Aaron Burr. Thus, for example, the Board of Visitors, to whom was committed the annual supervision of the United States Military Academy at West Point—

of which Board the present American Envoy to England, General Schenck, was president—employ the following language:—

> "Among many improvements"—such are the questionable words of this singular document—"made during the administration of the present superintendent, is one of peculiar and touching interest: it is the device of placing on the walls of the chapel neat marble tablets, or mural monuments, inscribed with the names of those dead army officers who in the past have been made illustrious by rank or gallant deeds of arms, or have fallen in battle. It was a happy thought to be executed at this particular place. It is most fitting that the United States Military Academy should be made to perpetuate such names and histories; thus keeping before the eyes and present in the memories of young men educated here this noble example of faithful service and devotion to our common country.
>
> "The Board recommend that the tasteful and enduring record thus begun shall be continued, and that means be furnished to extend the same mark of respect to all the officers of our army, regulars and volunteers alike, who have suffered and fallen in the war just closed in a glorious and successful struggle to vindicate the honour and maintain the life of the nation. Happy for the recreants who fought to destroy their Government, if, in the light shed from such a brilliant roll of the faithful, their names and treasonable career could be thrown into deeper shadow of oblivion!"

Let us compare with this unseemly and unnecessary passage the following extract from General Badeau's excellent 'Military History of General U. S. Grant.' He tells us that—

> When the first shot was fired at Fort Sumter—the shot which inaugurated the American Civil War—the standing army of the United States numbered 15,433 men, or 10 regiments of infantry, 4 of artillery, and 5 of cavalry. It was officered by Southerners as well as Northerners. Out of 1074 officers 270 were of Southern birth, embracing a fair share of the talent and distinction of the army. Two hundred and two of these espoused the Southern cause. When it became apparent that war was inevitable, they resigned their commissions, and offered their swords to their own section, *holding the authority of a State paramount to that of the Union.* They were followed into secession by fifty others from Northern or border States, most of whom had married Southern wives or acquired Southern property.

Nothing can be fairer than the reasons by which General Badeau explains the secession of General Lee and his Southern fellow-officers. To many of them the struggle to decide whether their State or the Union claimed priority of allegiance was no less painful than the struggle—so beautifully described in Clarendon's 'History of the English Rebellion'—which raged in the breast of Falkland. "When there was any overture or hope of peace," says Lord Clarendon, "Falkland would be exceedingly solicitous to press anything which he thought might promote it; and, sitting among his friends, often, after a deep silence and frequent sighs, would with a shrill and sad accent ingeminate the word *Peace, Peace;* and would passionately profess that the very agony of the war, and the calamities and desolation the kingdom did and must endure, took his sleep from him, and would shortly break his heart." No one who served by General Lee's side during the war, or who had occasional opportunities of conversing with him during the five years of life which remained after his surrender at Appomattox Court-House, can entertain any doubt that he suffered no less agony of heart than the young and accomplished Royalist who died on the field of Newbury. But to brand him with infamy, and call him a traitor and a recreant because he deemed it his duty to fight for the State which sent him to West Point and paid for his education, is unworthy of so brave and sensible a man as General Schenck. Even in the report of Lieutenant-General U. S. Grant upon the armies of the United States in 1864 and 1865, he has but one faint word of approbation to bestow upon the adversary who, having fought with unshaken fortitude and self-denial throughout the war, became the most patient and loyal of citizens when his sword was surrendered. "General Lee's great influence throughout the whole South," says his conqueror, "caused his example to be followed; and today the result is, that the armies lately under his leadership are at their homes, desiring peace and quiet, and their arms are in the hands of our ordnance officers." The patience, humility, and moderation of General Lee during the five closing years of his life extorted frequent admiration from his late antagonists, but have hitherto won from them no concessions to his crushed and oppressed brethren and sisters in the South. The remnant of the armies over which he was supreme "desired peace and quiet" as intensely as their Northern conquerors; but after they had for three years been ruled by the sword, and despoiled by "carpet-baggers" and negroes, it was natural that the discontent of a brave and proud people should here and there break out in a few spasmodic flutterings of disaffection. In one of his speeches to his constituents, Mr. Grant Duff, himself an ardent Northerner, told them that

> Reconstruction is the readmission of the seceding States to political communion with the States, which remained true to the Union, and the restoration to them of those powers of self-government which, forfeited by the war, had been replaced since their defeat by military rule. But how was this to be done? The majority of the United States Legislature decided that each of the States should choose a new constitution for itself, and that in choosing it the old planters, the "mean whites," and the ex-slaves should all have an equal voice; but that all the principal rebels, and the whites

> who would not take a test-oath, should be excluded. The effect of this has been, that constitutions for the Southern States have been prepared in the North, and voted at the South over the heads of white men by negro majorities.

Mr. Anthony Trollope, whose Northern proclivities during the war were not less pronounced than those of Mr. Grant Duff or Professor Goldwin Smith, calls reconstruction, as understood and practised by the Republican party—

> A provision for a war of races, with the express object of keeping down a people, in order that that people may be debarred from all political power in the empire. In Georgia, the black men, on those lines of reconstruction, would have the power of making all laws for the restraint of the white. But it has never been intended to intrust this power to the negroes; the intention is that, through the negroes, all political power, both State and Federal, shall be in the hands of members of Congress from the North—that the North shall have its heel upon the South, and that the conquered shall be subject to the conquerors. *Never has there been a more terrible condition imposed upon a fallen people*. For an Italian to feel an Austrian over him, for a Pole to feel a Russian over him, has been bad indeed; but it has been left for the political animosity of a Republican from the North—a man who himself rejects all contact with the negro—to subject the late Southern slave-owner to dominion from the African who was yesterday his slave.

The oppression of the South, which is to-day far worse than when these words of Mr. Trollope were written, wrung General Lee's affectionate heart as the loss of Calais weighed upon the spirits of our own Queen Mary. Lord Macaulay tells us that "no creature is so revengeful as a proud man who has humbled himself in vain;" but during the concluding years of General Lee's life, no symptoms of passion or vindictiveness were discernible in his daily bearing.[1] He mourned over the abject and oppressed condition of South Carolina until death freed his soul from the suffering which crushed him. Mr. John Esten Cooke makes it abundantly evident that he died from a broken heart. But in order that the virtues of a singularly pure and noble character may not be unrecorded in England, we desire to follow Mr. Cooke through some of the most notable passages of his hero's life, and to do what in us lies to make Robert E. Lee's memory a precious possession wherever the English tongue is spoken.

"The Lees of Virginia," says the volume before us, "spring from an ancient and respectable family of Essex in England," whose ancestor came over to the fast-anchored isle with William the Conqueror. One member of this family, Lionel Lee, accompanied Richard Cœur de Lion to the Holy

Land, and displayed special gallantry at the siege of Acre. The first of the Virginian Lees, Richard by name, was an ardent monarchist, and left the old country in the troubled times of King Charles the First. "It is not certainly known," says Mr. Cooke, "whether he sought refuge in Virginia after the failure of the King's cause, or was tempted to emigrate with a view to better his fortunes in the New World." Whatever may have been his motive in repairing to Virginia, Richard Lee undoubtedly brought with him from England a number of followers and servants, and took up extensive tracts of land in the Old Dominion. Among the manor-houses which he there built or commenced, was one at Stratford, in the Virginian county of Westmoreland—within which county George Washington himself was born. This house having subsequently been destroyed by fire, was rebuilt—Queen Anne herself having been a contributor to the fund subscribed in England and in the colony for its re-creation—and became at a later date the birthplace of Richard Henry Lee, and of his distinguished son, Robert Edward. Richard Henry Lee, the father of the great Confederate general, was one of Washington's best subordinates; and under the *sobriquet* of "Light-Horse Harry," gained conspicuous fame as a cavalry general in the revolutionary war of the American colonies against England. In a letter written in 1789, George Washington conveys his "love and thanks" to Light-Horse Harry, whose admirable qualities as a soldier were always recapitulated with modest pride by his still greater son. In 1869 General R. E. Lee published a new edition of his father's 'Memoirs of the War in the Southern Department,' to which he prefixed an unostentatious life of its author. Richard Henry Lee was twice married; and by his second wife, Anne Hill Carter, he had three sons and two daughters—Charles Carter, *Robert Edward*, Smith, Anne, and Mildred. The old house at Stratford, wherein the great American soldier first saw the light, deserves a few passing words of comment. It is one of those Virginian manor-houses which so warmed the heart and kindled the fancy of William Makepeace Thackeray; for in one of these, he loved to say, that it would delight him to write the history, which he always contemplated but never executed, of the times of good Queen Anne. The bricks, paving-tiles, carvings, window-sashes, furniture, and decorations of these stately old country-houses, were all transported from England to the Old Dominion. English plasterers moulded and spread the ceilings; English masons upraised the Italian mantelpieces which they brought with them across the Atlantic; English carpenters made fast the window-sashes, and set up the lintels of the doors. Their book-shelves were filled with the great English classics who flourished in the Augustan age of Queen Anne. Within the libraries of some of these houses Thackeray passed many hours, enraptured to find himself surrounded by the works of all the

English authors who were most to his taste. There he again familiarised himself with the tender grace of Addison, the rugged force of Smollett; there he forgot the "wild relish and vicious exuberance of the too copious present" by bending over the pages of Swift, Pope, Arbuthnot, Bolingbroke, Walsh, and Granville; and there for the first time he became acquainted with the 'Memoirs of Colonel Byrd of Westover,' the founder, during George II.'s reign, of Virginia's beautiful capital at Richmond. The very bricks, paving-stones, and window-frames of Westover, Brandon, or Stratford, exhaled an atmosphere which was fragrant to his nostrils, and enabled him again to summon into fleshly existence those English worthies of whose literature he was so fond. There he loved to rehearse that Charles II. wore a coronation-robe of Virginia silk when reinstalled upon the throne of Great Britain; and that, in gratitude for her loyalty in the hour of his abasement, he permitted the proud old State to rank thenceforward in the British Empire with England, Scotland, and Ireland, and to bear upon her shield the motto, *En dat Virginia quartam*.

The early influences of the old grange at Stratford, in which he was born, had much to do with shaping the character of General Lee.

> "Critics," says Mr. Cooke, "charged him with family pride. If he possessed that virtue or failing, the fact was not strange. Stratford opened before his childish eyes a memorial of the old splendour of the Lees. He saw around him old portraits, old plate, and old furniture. Old parchments contained histories of the deeds of his race; old genealogical trees traced their line far back into the past; old servants grown grey in the house waited upon the child; and, in a corner of one of the great apartments, an old soldier, grey too, and shattered in health, once the friend of Washington and Greene, was writing the history of the battles in which he had drawn his sword for his native land."

To the last hour of his life, General Lee retained the affection for trees, streams, mountains, and country associations with which his happy childhood at Stratford had imbued him. One of the last letters which he ever wrote contains the following passage:—"My visits to Florida and the White Sulphur have not benefited me much; but it did me good to go to the White House"—a small country seat not far from Richmond, which came into his possession by his marriage with Mary Custis, the daughter of Washington's adopted son—"and to see the mules walking round, and the corn growing." He loved the country, the woods, the birds, and the brooks as fondly as Izaak Walton or Waterton. His favourite talk was about country life; and nothing was so grateful to him as a chat with plain Virginian farmers. The writer of these words well remembers a ride on horseback which he took in company with General Lee upon the morning of the 7th of May 1863. The battle of Chancellorsville—which, regarded militarily, will always bear the same testimony to Lee's tactical ability as did Leuthen to that of Frederick the Great, or Salamanca to that of Wellington—had just been fought. General Hooker, at the head of what he had just called "the finest army of the planet," had retreated, in confusion and discomfiture, across the Rapidan. If ever there was a moment when human vanity would have been pardonable and natural, General Lee might have betrayed it upon the morning of the day which followed Hooker's retreat. With little more than 40,000 men, the great Confederate captain had defeated and utterly routed a host of at least 130,000 Federals. Nevertheless, even at this intoxicating moment, not a particle of self-exaltation or conscious triumph was discoverable on Lee's features, or traceable in his conversation. Cognisant of the enormous superiority of the resources wielded by the enemy with whom he had to do, he felt that Chancellorsville, like Fredericsburg, would produce little effect upon the North, and that "another Union army," magnificently found in every respect, would again take the field before many weeks had passed. Heart-sick at the flow of blood by which he was surrounded—his road lay over ground where the hottest fighting had taken place—and *attendri* by the recent wounds of Stonewall Jackson, from which, however, upon the morning in question, he did not anticipate a fatal result, General Lee said, in weariness and anguish, "All that I want them" (the Federals) "to do is to leave us what we are, plain Virginian farmers." There never was a man who had in him so little of the "politician," as his own countrymen understand that term. "I think," said Mr. Carlisle, the well-known lawyer of Washington, a man of high character, who had known Lee long and intimately, "that he was freer than any man I ever knew from the taint of any passion or party prejudice." He stood apart from the intrigues, schemes, and guile of cities and their denizens, as though unconscious of their existence, but with quiet scorn deep-seated in his heart. He was a fine judge of character; and his diagnosis of men and women was too keen and accurate for him to blind his eyes to the little pettinesses, self-seekings, and intrigues which daily came across him. But although he perceived, and quietly put them aside, he never betrayed his consciousness of their existence, or wounded *amour propre* by anything seeming to convey a reproach. But, after all, the most winning of his traits was the affection and confidence which, without any seeming consciousness, and without an effort, he inspired in little children. Often, in the course of the great Civil War, he would approach a Virginian farmhouse inhabited by a family of whom he knew nothing. Adored as he was throughout the length and breadth of the Old Dominion, the fame of his approach preceded him wherever he went. In response to the cordial welcome always extended to him, he would descend from his horse and sit down for a few minutes upon the porch, accepting, perhaps, a glass of water, and possibly a square inch or two of corn-bread, but never taking anything more. It might have been imagined that the gravity and seriousness of his demeanour would have possessed little attraction for young children. But before many minutes had passed, it was invariably remarked that one or two children would be crowding round his knees, and, finger in mouth, looking up into his kind honest face. He was generally surrounded by younger, more demonstrative, and more talkative officers. But his empire over the hearts of the young, though, like all his other great qualities, unconsciously manifested, was irresistible. If it may be said without irreverence, it was impossible at such moments to forget the affection with which the Master, whom General Lee loved to serve, "suffered little children" to draw near unto His presence, and saw in them an image of that childlike faith which is the shortest and surest path to the kingdom of heaven.

One other advantage was gained by General Lee from the country life and simple tastes of his boyhood. He carried with him into the field a "superb physical health and strength"—to quote Mr. Cooke's words—"which remained unshaken by all the hardships of war." The time has not yet come when the history of the great Civil War in America can be fairly and impartially written. It may reasonably be doubted whether such a history can *ever* be written by any one who took part in, or was an eyewitness of it, upon either side. It is true that some of the greatest military histories of the world—those, for instance, of Thucydides, Xenophon, Sir William Napier, and General Foy—have been written by men who themselves fought in the wars which they have so ably delineated; but, with the exception of the matchless masterpieces of the two Greek historians, narratives of wars by soldiers who fought in them are never free—altogether free—from partisan bias. Traces of it are recognisable in many passages of Sir William Napier; they are of constant recurrence in the pages of his French antitype, General Foy. But whenever the story of the American Civil War is truly and exhaustively told, it will become abundantly apparent, if its chronicler does his duty, that seldom if ever in modern history has there been a struggle, firstly, upon so large a scale; secondly, which was so long maintained; and thirdly, in which the disproportion of the combatants was so great. One of England's greatest soldiers, Sir Charles James Napier, exclaims, "How much more depends upon the chief than upon the numbers of an army! Alexander invaded Persia with only 30,000 foot and 5000 horse; Hannibal entered Italy with 20,000 foot and 6000 horse, having lost 30,000 men in crossing the Alps. What did he attempt with this small army? The conquest of Italy from the Romans, who, with their allies, could bring into the field

800,000 men in arms; and he maintained the war there for fifteen years." Without maintaining that General Lee, who was neither an Alexander nor a Hannibal, had such odds against him as these two great captains of ancient history, we doubt whether any general of modern history ever sustained for four years—a far longer time nowadays that Hannibal's fifteen years in the remote past—a war in which, while disposing of scanty resources himself, he had against him so enormous an aggregate of men, horses, ships, and supplies. It is an under rather than over estimate of the respective strength of the two sections to state that, during the first two years, the odds, all told were ten to one, during the last two twenty to one, against the Confederates. The prolongation of the struggle is in no slight degree attributed to Mr. Jefferson Davis, whose high character and unselfishness are, even now, undervalued by Confederates, and totally denied by his conquerors. The courage of the rank and file of the rebel army is refreshing to contemplate in these days, which have seen a European war between two nations equal in numbers and resources triumphantly closed in seven months, and stained by the three unprecedented capitulations of Sedan, Metz, and Paris. But, after all, the one name which, in connection with the great American Civil War, *posteris narratum atque traditum superstes erit*, is the name of Robert Edward Lee. It is not likely that any biographer or historian will ever portray him as he seemed to those who served by his side and knew him best. It is as impossible to describe as to prove a negative; and the negations of General Lee's character dwell more in the memory than the positive attributes of other men. He was never haughty, never insolent, never vain, never false, never idle, never self-indulgent, never unpoised, never uncharitable, never ungenerous. In no form did he use or touch tobacco; had no taste for liquor of any kind, and seemed never to require a stimulant. Were it possible to give a statistical record of the amount of food which, during his four crucial years of trial, General Lee consumed, it would be found that no great captain was ever so abstemious. Of a truth, his "superb physical health, which remained unshaken by all the hardships of war," counted for much in moulding the shape of his country's history.

The biography from the pen of Mr. J. E. Cooke is more successful in delineating the private and personal traits of General Lee than in tracing his public career. It is well and tastefully written, and its language is altogether free from disfiguring "Americanisms." But Mr. Cooke's descriptions of battles lack fire and force, and he has none of the gifts of a military historian. Reverting to its personal reminiscences, we search in vain for any allusion to one of General Lee's peculiarities, which no one who lived much in his society could have failed to notice. We refer to his rich sense of humour—a quality which Dr. Arnold, in his character of Hannibal, says is rarely wanting in great men. There was a quiet vein of unmalignant fun in 'Uncle Robert'—for thus was he always named by his enthusiastic followers—which was continually cropping to the surface, and the recollection of which often raises a smile on the lips of those who lived by his side, and remember how quaintly he loved to manifest it. The two following anecdotes will serve to illustrate its nature. About a week before the battle of Fredericsburg—that is to say, on or about the 6th of December 1862—the weather was for a few days bitterly cold. General Lee and his Staff were camping out—as usual, in tents—about three miles to the south of the Rappahannock River and the little town of Fredericsburg. There were some members of his Staff who, although young enough to be his sons, were more sensible of the cold than their iron chief. To him, as to Hannibal, cold or heat made no difference; for in both there was, as Livy writes of one of them, *caloris ac frigoris patientia par—nullo labore aut corpus fatigari, aut animus vinci poterat.* Standing round the camp-fire upon the morning in question, and shivering before each blast of a biting wind which came from the frozen north, and reminded the sufferers that the thermometer was below zero, more than one member of General Lee's Staff was heard to mutter an aspiration for a glass of whisky-toddy, or some other alcoholic stimulant. No one noticed that the General took any cognisance, or was even aware of this half-articulate expression of a wish. But presently, emerging from his tent with a stone bottle or demijohn under his arm, he drew near to the camp-fire, and said: "Gentlemen, the morning is very cold—the kindness of a friend enables me to offer you a cordial; pray bring your tin cups and taste what I have here." There were one or two on-lookers who noticed a twinkle in the old soldier's eye, and a lurking smile upon his mouth, which taught them to anticipate "a sell." But the majority of the company hastily fetched their drinking-cups, and stood expectant round their chief. The cork was drawn, and the liquor proved to be butter-milk. Upon another occasion, two members of his Staff sat up late at night discussing a keg of whisky and a problem of algebra. Upon meeting one of them in the morning, General Lee inquired, as usual, after his health, and learned in reply that he was suffering from a headache. "Ah, Colonel," remarked the old man, "I have often observed that when the unknown quantities, x and y, are represented by a keg of whisky and a tin cup, the solution of the equation is usually a headache!"

We are tempted to linger a moment longer over some points of character which caused General Lee to be often misunderstood, and sometimes to be misrepresented. There were many to maintain that, though spotless and irreproachable, he was cold and unsympathetic, and that his immunity from human vices and frailties arose from absence of passion. The truth, however, is, that no one ever had a more human heart than General Lee.

His temper was naturally quick, impetuous, and choleric, but his inexorable and ever-present sense of duty—which, as will presently be seen, he called "the sublimest word in our language"—constrained him to control every passionate impulse. Being in his fifty-fifth year when the Civil War broke out, he had already learned to check his natural tendency to choler; but no one could have seen much of him between 1861 and 1865 without perceiving that passion was by no means extinguished in his heart. There are many who remember how, upon the morning of the 12th of May 1864, a sudden and impetuous onslaught was made, just after the break of dawn, by a picked body of Federal troops, whom General Grant launched against a salient of his adversary's lines in the forests of Spotsylvania. This salient was occupied by Johnson's division of Ewell's Confederate Corps. The Federal onslaught was a complete surprise. The redoubt was stormed at the point of the bayonet; nearly 3000 rebels were taken prisoners, and 18 pieces of artillery fell into the hands of the assailants. General Lee regarded this bit of success as being attributable to want of vigilance and courage in his own men. Instantly throwing himself at the head of a Texan regiment, he waved his hat in the air, and prepared to lead it forward. No man who, at that terrible moment, saw his flashing eyes and sternly-set lips, is ever likely to forget them. But, spurring rapidly to his side, General Gordon—one of Secessia's noblest sons—seized hold of his horse's rein, and exclaimed: "This, General Lee, is no place for you! these are men who never failed yet, and who will not fail now." With unanimous voice the soldiers around them refused to advance until "Uncle Robert" went to the rear. Slowly and reluctantly retiring, General Lee—the light of battle still flaming in his eyes—was dissuaded from his purpose. But it would be idle to tell those who then witnessed him that his nature was cold and passionless, or that his temper, if under better control, was not, *au foud*, as impulsive as that of Washington. Certain it is, that Stonewall Jackson, Longstreet, and Stuart, who all loved Lee with more than filial affection and respect, would never permit him to be called cold in their presence. It is the more necessary to deny the truth of this imputation, since it has been repeated more than once since his death, both by friendly and unfriendly commentators, upon his character. It is rebutted by all that is known of his domestic life and family affections. The following letter could never have been written by one whose heart was not warmed by the living blood of an unusually sympathetic nature. There are few passages in the English language which deserve to be more widely known. The famous lines of advice to his son which Shakespeare puts into the mouth of Polonius may surpass General Lee's letter in the beauty of their language and the worldliness of their wisdom, but they lack the Christian tenderness and purity of the words which follow. The letter was written to his eldest son, then an *alumnus* in the Military Academy at West Point:—

> "You must study," writes the father, "to be frank with the world: frankness is the child of honesty and courage. Say just what you mean to do on every occasion, and take it for granted that you mean to do right. If a friend asks a favour, you should grant it, if reasonable; if not, tell him plainly why you cannot: you will wrong him and wrong yourself by equivocation of any kind. Never do a wrong thing to make a friend or keep one; the man who requires you to do so is dearly purchased at a sacrifice. Deal kindly, but firmly, with all your classmates; you will find it the policy which wears best. Above all, do not appear to others what you are not. If you have any fault to find with any one, tell him, not others, of what you complain; there is no more dangerous experiment than that of undertaking to be one thing before a man's face and another behind his back. We should live so as to say and do nothing to the injury of any one. It is not only best as a matter of principle, but it is the path to peace and honour.
>
> "In regard to duty, let me, in conclusion of this hasty letter, inform you that nearly 100 years ago there was a day of remarkable gloom and darkness—still known as "the dark day"—a day when the light of the sun was slowly extinguished, as if by an eclipse. The Legislature of Connecticut was in session, and as its members saw the unexpected and unaccountable darkness coming on, they shared in the general awe and terror. It was supposed by many that the last day—the day of judgment—had come. Some one, in the consternation of the hour moved an adjournment. Then there arose an old Puritan legislator, Davenport of Stamford, and said that, if the last day had come, he desired to be found at his place doing his duty, and therefore moved that candles be brought in, so that the House could proceed with its duty. There was quietness in that man's mind, the quietness of heavenly wisdom and inflexible willingness to obey present duty. *Duty, then, is the sublimest word in our language*. Do your duty in all things like the old Puritan. You cannot do more, you should never wish to do less. Never let me or your mother wear one grey hair for any lack of duty on your part."

It is always pleasant to know that good seed has not fallen upon barren places. The young man to whom this beautiful letter was addressed, and who has succeeded his father as President of Washington College at Lexington, is, *consensu omniun*, one of the most promising and exemplary men that Virginia now contains.

Within the limits at our command, it would be impossible to rehearse the leading passages of Lee's military career, or to review analytically the constituent elements and characteristics of his genius as a soldier. That he possessed many of the natural aptitudes which go to make up the sum of a great captain, became abundantly evident during the Mexican War of 1846. Many of his comrades in the only two wars wherein Lee ever took part, were of opinion that if he had held supreme command when in his fortieth year, he would have exhibited greater qualities than he possessed when called upon at the age of fifty-four to guide the military destinies of the Southern States. Those who believe that in every field of human endeavour nature occasionally supplies what are called "heaven-born" prodigies, cannot pretend that General Lee belonged to this rare, if not hypothetical, class of beings. He was above all things a painstaking, unempirical, and scientific soldier. By constitution he was a rigid causationist, and knew as well as Napoleon that great ends are unattainable until the means which produce them have been summoned into existence. Mr. Cooke tells us that his hero having thrown up his commission in the United States army, found, upon repairing to Richmond in April 1861, that the South was utterly destitute of the munitions of war essential to her protection:—

> "All," he says, "had to be organised and put at once into operation—the quartermaster, commissary, ordnance, and other departments. Transportation, supplies, arms, ammunition—all had to be collected immediately. The material existed, or could be supplied, as the sequel clearly showed; but as yet there was almost nothing. And it was chiefly to the work of organising these departments that General Lee and the Military Council addressed themselves with the utmost energy. The result was, that Virginia found herself very soon in a condition to offer a determined resistance. The troops at various camps of instruction were sent to the field, others took their places, and the work of drilling the raw material into soldiers went rapidly on; supplies were collected, transportation found, workshops for the construction of arms and ammunition sprung up; small arms, cannon, cartridges, fixed and other ammunition were produced; and in a time which now seems wholly inadequate for such a result, the Commonwealth of Virginia was ready to take the field against the Federal Government."

We hazard little in saying that to this end no one contributed so powerfully as General Lee. He was the first to laugh his countrymen out of their Quixotic notion that discipline was of little or no value, and to teach them that an armed mob full of courage and enthusiasm was not an army. He induced the many hundreds of men whom the South poured into Virginia to submit patiently to daily drill, and to put their faith in the camps of instruction, which owed their existence to him. His resource, ingenuity, and inventiveness were inexhaustible, and while inspiring other men, he allowed them to receive all the credit which they claimed for their activity. If Mr. Jefferson Davis had not found in 1861 such a right hand in Virginia as

General Lee, it is more than doubtful whether the battle of Bull Run could ever have been fought.

There are few more striking evidences of the self-abnegation and modesty of Lee's character than the fact that, for more than a year after the commencement of the great American struggle, he was content to stand unmurmuringly aside to allow inferior men, like Generals Joe Johnston and Beauregard, to "flame in the forehead of the morning sky." Nothing was more common in the winter of 1861 and the spring of 1862 than to hear men say at Richmond that Lee was "of no account," and that Secessia had gained little by his accession to her cause. Such was not the opinion of Mr. Jefferson Davis, who eagerly longed for an opportunity to put him in command of the army of Virginia. At length such an opportunity presented itself, when, on the last day of May 1862, General Joe Johnston was severely wounded at the battle of Seven Pines. Upon the 3d of June, Lee assumed command of the Confederate Army of Northern Virginia. From that day forward until the 9th of April 1865, his life became a term convertible or synonymous with the history for thirty-four months of the North American Continent. Upon both sides, armies of immense magnitude fill the eye of the reader, while generals succeed to generals, strut their hour upon the stage, and then are seen no more. But the American War, as it recedes further and further into the distance, is seen to have derived its shape and form from General Lee more than from any other individual who fought upon either side. It would be difficult to speak or think of the history of Europe betwen 1800 and 1815 without having the tongue and brain occupied exclusively by Napoleon. Similarly, the name of General Lee has blotted out in North America all recollection of those by whom he was supported or opposed. It is very possible that if, at the end of 1862, Stonewall Jackson had been transferred to the command of that Western Confederate Army which, under Bragg, Joe Johnston, or Hood, became familiar with nothing but disaster, Lee's fame might have been shared or diminished by that of another Virginian luminary. But impartial history will eventually pronounce that it is more impossible to regard either Grant or Sherman as Lee's equals, than to maintain that Wellington and Blucher were greater than Napoleon because they defeated him at Waterloo. If in these few pages we endeavour, however inadequately, to draw the attention of English soldiers to Lee's great qualities as a commander, especially when acting upon the defensive, we do so in the conviction that the campaign of 1864 is the finest specimen of resisting strategy that the history of any nation, ancient or modern, supplies. It deserves as well to be studied in this light by professional critics like Colonel Hamley or Colonel Chesney, as the famous campaign of Napoleon in 1796 to be viewed as a model of scientific offensive warfare. And we are but repeating the opinion of the ablest historian that this campaign of 1864 has yet found—we allude to Mr. Swinton, the author of an excellent book called 'The Army of the Potomac'—when we say that, if the issue of the American War had depended solely upon the two rival armies which opposed each other in Virginia, the Stars and Stripes would never have floated above the Capitol of Richmond. Vast as were the resources in men and material of which in 1864 General Grant disposed, it was not by General Grant that Richmond was taken, but by General Sherman. If any American doubts the correctness of this view, we beg to refer him to the passage in Mr. Swinton's book which describes the hopelessness and dejection of General Grant's army after their bloody repulse at Cold Harbour upon the 3d of June 1864. But, in addition to the testimony of Mr. Swinton, who served himself with the Northern army, and was an eyewitness of the deep dejection which he describes, we might easily quote many other facts which irrefragably substantiate this view, and dissipate the sophisms advanced in the case which our cousins have submitted to the Arbitrators at Geneva, that the battle of Gettysburg was the death of the Rebellion. Whenever the private letters of Mr. Stanton, the War Secretary at Washington, shall see the light, it will be conceded, even by the most thoughtless of readers, that if the fate of the contest had depended solely on Lee and Grant, the great Republic would not to-day be one and indivisible.

> "So gloomy," says Mr. Swinton, "was the military outlook after the action at Cold Harbour, and to such a degree by consequence had the moral spring of the public mind become relaxed, that there was at this time great danger of a collapse of the war. The history of this conflict, truthfully written, will show this. The archives of the State Department, when one day made public, will show how deeply the Government was affected by the want of military success, and to what resolutions the Executive had in consequence come. Had not success elsewhere come to brighten the horizon, it would have been difficult to raise new forces to recruit the Army of the Potomac, which, shaken in its structure, its valour quenched in blood, and thousands of its ablest officers killed and wounded, was the Army of the Potomac no more."

In reference to this famous campaign of 1864, which, although Mr. Swinton is its hitherto best historian, still stands much in need of a Jomini or a Napier, we have but space for the following passage from General Lee's last biographer:—

> "The campaign of one month," says Mr. Cooke, "from May 4 to June 4, had cost the Federal commander 60,000 men and 3000 officers, while the loss of Lee did not exceed 18,000 men (*of whom few were officers*).

> The result would seem an unfavourable comment upon the choice of route made by General Grant. General M'Clellan, two years before, had reached Cold Harbour with trifling losses. To attain the same point had cost General Grant a frightful number of lives. Nor could it be said that he had any important successes to offset this loss. He had not defeated his adversary in any of the battle-fields of the campaign, nor did it seem that he had stricken him any serious blow. The army of Northern Virginia, not reinforced until it reached Hanover Junction, and then only by about 9000 men, had repulsed every assault; and in a final trial of strength with a force vastly its superior, had inflicted upon the enemy, in about an hour, a loss of 13,000 men."

When we urge upon military students the importance of giving an attentive study to this campaign of 1864, it may be as well to whet their appetite by stating the comparative numbers of the two rival armies. Lee's numbers upon the 1st of May were, as nearly as possible, 50,000 men. Within the month he was joined at Hanover Junction by 9000 more. General Grant opened the campaign in command of 141,161 men. Within the month, and in fact from the very commencement of the bloody struggle, Grant received reinforcements day by day, which amounted to more than 100,000 additional men before he crossed the James River. "Lee's army," says Mr. Cooke, "small as it was, was wretchedly supplied. Half the men were in rags, and, worse still, were but one-fourth fed. When Lee met his enemy at the commencement of May, the men were gaunt, half-starved, and in no condition to enter into so arduous a campaign." We submit to all military readers that never yet did 59,000 men quit them more gloriously than these tatterdemalion and starving Southern regiments. "Never let me hear," says Sir Walter Scott, "that brave blood has been shed in vain—it sends a roaring voice down through all time." It is not necessary to comment upon the magnificent abundance and variety of food, drink, and munitions of war supplied to the 250,000 men who followed General Grant; but when military epicures, while familiarising themselves with every detail of Wörth and Sedan, profess themselves unable to study the irregular conflicts of two armed American mobs, we venture to tell them that, in all that constitutes true manliness, the Transatlantic Civil War far surpasses the Franco-German conflict. Nothing is easier, says the steward of Molière's miser, than to give a great dinner with plenty of money; the really great cook is he who can set out a banquet with no money at all. General Grant in 1864 drew upon an almost inexhaustible treasury; General Lee's account was heavily overdrawn before the campaign began. Nevertheless, it is every day becoming more and more patent that Mr. Swinton was right in believing that the ragged, famished, and suffering regiments of Secessia, numbering altogether but 59,000 men, would have discomfited their 250,000 pampered and surfeited opponents, if General Sherman and his Western army had not revived the spirits and reanimated the courage of his drooping colleague in Virginia. *Victrix causa Diis placuit, sed victa Catoni.*

Having paid our tribute to Lee's great, if not matchless, qualities as a defensive soldier, we proceed, in conclusion, to offer a few remarks upon the causes of his failure when called upon to assume the offensive, or to turn to advantage the victories which he had gained when acting on the defensive. It cannot be doubted that the two great stains on his military reputation were, first, his omission to "use up" the Federal army of General Burnside before it recrossed the river Rappahannock after the battle of Fredericsburg; and secondly, his handling of the Confederate army in the Gettysburg campaign. Anybody who carefully studies Lee's military genius will come to the conclusion that he was admirably bold when weak, but that he became unduly cautious when he was, comparatively speaking, strong. To our thinking, the unhappiest mistake which he ever made was his rejection of the earnest advice offered on the eve of the battle of Fredericsburg by General J. E. B. Stuart. It was the opinion of this fiery young Confederate general that Burnside's host, huddled together in and about the little city of Fredericsburg, and with a broad and deep river, spanned only by three pontoon-bridges, in its rear, would offer little resistance if vigorously attacked on the night of the 13th or 14th of December—the battle itself, in which not more than 25,000 Confederate soldiers had taken active part, having been fought on the 13th.[2] Unfortunately, Lee cherished the belief that Burnside would renew his attack; and he was satisfied that, in that event, he would have the Federal army at his mercy. But when the morrow of the battle passed without any fresh attack on the part of the Federals, it was a lamentable error on Lee's part not to have attacked shortly before dawn on the 15th. In our opinion, such an attack would have led to the capitulation of at least one-half, if not of two-thirds, of Burnside's army; and it is extremely doubtful whether it would not have ended the war. European recognition of Southern independence could hardly have been withheld if the victory of Fredericsburg had been turned into a Waterloo. No one who is acquainted with the low *morale* of the Federals after their bloody repulse before Marye's Heights, will entertain any doubt that during those three crucial days which intervened between the battle and the Federal retreat across the river, Lee had his enemy in his power. As for the Federal guns on Stafford Heights, of which the fire, according to some critics, would have decimated the Confederates, there is little doubt that their projectiles would have been equally destructive to both armies.

But if Lee's inaction after Fredericsburg was, as we have called it, an unhappy or negative blunder, undoubtedly the greatest positive blunder of which he was ever guilty was the unnecessary onslaught which he gratuitously made against the strong position into which, by accident, General Meade fell back at Gettysburg. We have good reason for saying that, during the five years of calm reflection which General Lee passed at Lexington after the conclusion of the American war, his maladroit manipulation of the Confederate army during the Gettysburg campaign was to him a matter of ceaseless self-reproach. "If," said he on many occasions, "I had taken General Longstreet's advice on the eve of the second day of battle at Gettysburg, and had filed off the left corps of my army behind the right corps, in the direction of Washington and Baltimore, along the Emmetsburg road, the Confederates would to-day be a free people." There can now be no doubt that before Gettysburg, General Lee was, to use a homely expression, "too big for his breeches." Never had the Confederates been so full of fight; and on the first day of battle, the Federals who, under General Reynolds, came into collision with Stonewall Jackson's old corps, then commanded by Ewell, were driven like chaff before the wind. Lee's true policy, after reconnoitring the position into which, by the merest chance, and in no degree by his own deliberate choice, General Meade had been driven, was to have abstained from attacking his enemy. "You are at the head of an invading army," wrote Napoleon to Marmont not long before the battle of Salamanca, "and ought never to fight a battle except on ground of your own choosing. *Il n'y a ni si, ni mais*; choose your own battle-field, force your enemy to attack you upon it, and never yield it so long as one living Frenchman is left." Wise words, which it would have been well if General Lee—who, by the by, was little familiar with any of Napoleon's campaigns or maxims—had known and taken to heart during those three opening days of July which, in 1863, he passed in Pennsylvania. But even after the second day of battle, which had taught him the strength of his enemy's position, there was time for him to have reconsidered his plan, and to have followed General Longstreet's advice. We close the volume of General Lee's life with the conviction that the contemplation of this battle of Gettysburg will for ever prevent his being ranked as a great offensive general. But, *en revanche*, when it became necessary for him to assume the offensive-defensive, he will bear comparison with any general of modern times. His tactical management of the troops which drove M'Clellan away from before Richmond in 1862, and of those which won the battle of Chancellorsville in 1863, is above all praise. But it was in purely defensive strategy that he most shone. We are willing to stand upon the campaign of 1864, and to abide the judgment which enlightened and impartial students will be constrained to pass upon it.

The fame and character of General Lee will hereafter be regarded in Europe and in America under a dual aspect. In Europe, we shall consider him merely as a soldier; and it is more than probable that within the present century we shall have accustomed ourselves to regard him as third upon the list of English-speaking generals, and as having been surpassed in soldierly capacity by Marlborough and Wellington alone. In America, when the passions of the great Civil War shall have died out, Lee will be regarded more as a man than as a soldier. His infinite purity, self-denial, tenderness, and generosity, will make his memory more and more precious to his countrymen when they have purged their minds of the prejudices and animosities which civil war invariably breeds. They will acknowledge before long that Lee took no step in life except in accordance with what he regarded as, and believed to be, his duty; and they will hold up his example, no less than that of Abraham Lincoln, as one of the brightest patterns which they can set before their children. Let us conclude by quoting one final story which ought not to be without influence upon men like General Grant, who, although owing his elevation in life to the magnificent resistance made by the South, seems now to lose no opportunity of demonstrating his vindictive resentment against Southern men:—

> "A still more suggestive exhibition," says Mr. Cooke, "of Lee's freedom from rancour, was presented in an interview which is thus described by a citizen of the North: 'One day last autumn, the writer saw General Lee standing at his gate, in Lexington, talking pleasantly to a humbly-clad man, who seemed very much pleased at the cordial courtesy of the great chieftain, and turned off, evidently delighted, as I and my companions came up. After exchanging salutations, and in answer to my queries, the General said, pointing to the retreating form—"He is one of our old soldiers who is in necessitous circumstances." I took it for granted that it was some Confederate veteran, when the noble-hearted chieftain quietly corrected me by saying—"He fought on the other side; but we must not think of that." I afterwards ascertained—not from General Lee, who never alluded to his charities—that he had not only spoken kindly to the old soldier who had fought on the other side, but had sent him away rejoicing in a liberal contribution to his necessities.' "

NOTES

1. As an evidence of the present state of affairs in South Carolina, we quote the following passage from a letter written in November last by a resident of that State, whose character for truth and honour is unimpeachable. He says—

> One of my brothers has been arrested and thrown into the common jail of the United States soldiers without charge or accusation, without form or warrant of law, without the shadow of right or justice. Before the suspension of the writ of *habeas corpus*, profound quiet prevailed in this section of the country. Men were pursuing their avocations in the most peaceful manner, and a season of prosperity was beginning to dawn upon us; but now words are almost inadequate to describe the reign of terror existing among us. Bands of United States soldiers are riding the country, arresting citizens by wholesale, tearing them from their homes in the night-time, terrifying women and children, hurrying the prisoners off to jail, and cramming them in dungeons and filthy cells. These arrests are made without warrant. Men are ignorant of the offences for which they are thrown into jail. No explanation is given to the prisoner as to the cause of his arrest, no hearing is allowed him. The innocent and guilty fare alike. The fury of the Radicals is levelled against the best of our citizens. Old and young, grey-haired men incapable of committing outrages, mere boys innocent of crime, are arrested indiscriminately. In a time of profound peace, when farmers are engaged in gathering in their corn and cotton, we are declared to be in a state of war. We are suffering for crimes which have never been committed; we are punished for offences of which we are not guilty; we are warred upon by the United States Government on account of a rebellion which has no existence but in the imagination of President Grant, and the vile politicians who have poisoned his ears with false and malicious reports. There is no rebellion—there is no hostility to the United States Government—there is no resistance to lawful authority, either State or Federal; the reports of collisions between armed bands of Ku-Klux and Federal troops are utterly base, false, and slanderous fabrications, invented for a purpose.

2. The following extract from General Lee's official report upon the battle of Fredericsburg will be read with interest:—

> "The attack on the 13th," says he, "had been so easily repulsed, and by so small a part of our army, that it was not supposed the enemy would limit his efforts to one attempt, which, in view of the magnitude of his preparations and the extent of his force, seemed to be comparatively insignificant. Believing, therefore, that he would attack us, it was not deemed expedient to lose the advantages of our position. But we were necessarily ignorant of the extent to which he had suffered, and only became aware of it when, on the morning of the 16th, it was discovered that he had availed himself of the darkness of the night and the prevalence of a violent storm of rain and wind, to recross the river. The town was immediately reoccupied, and our positions on the river-bank resumed."

—Reports of the Operations of the Army of Northern Virginia from June to December 1862, vol. i, p. 43.

General Lee[1]

FIELD MARSHALL VISCOUNT WOLSELEY

The history of the war between the Northern and Southern States of North America is yet to be written. General Long's work on the great Confederate general is a contribution towards the history of that grand but unsuccessful struggle by the seceding States to shake off all political connection with the Union Government. It will be read with interest as coming from the pen of one who was Lee's military secretary, and its straightforward, soldier-like style will commend it to all readers. It is not my intention to enter upon any narrative of the events which led to that fratricidal war. The unprejudiced outsider will generally admit the sovereign right, both historical and legal, which each State possessed under the constitution, to leave the Union when its people thought fit to do so. At the same time, of Englishmen who believe that "union is strength," and who are themselves determined that no dismemberment of their own empire shall be allowed, few will find fault with the men of the north for their manly determination, come what might, to resist every effort of their brothers in the south to break up the Union. It was but natural that all Americans should be proud of the empire which the military genius of General Washington had created, despite the efforts of England to retain her Colonies.

It is my wish to give a short outline of General Lee's life, and to describe him as I saw him in the autumn of 1862, when at the head of proud and victorious troops he smiled at the notion of defeat by any army that could be sent against him. I desire to make known to the reader not only the renowned soldier, whom I believe to have been the greatest of his age, but to give some insight into the character of one whom I have always considered the most perfect man I ever met. Twenty-one years have passed since the great Secession war ended, but even still, angry remembrances of it prevent Americans from taking an impartial view of the contest, and of those who were the leaders in it. Outsiders can best weigh and determine the merits of the chief actors on both sides, but if in this attempt to estimate General Lee's character I offend any one by the outspoken expression of my opinions, I hope I may be forgiven. On one side I can see, in the dogged determination of the North persevered in to the end through years of recurring failure, the spirit for which the men of Britain have always been remarkable. It is a virtue to which the United States owed its birth in the last century, and its preservation in 1865. It is the quality to which the Anglo-Saxon race is most indebted for its great position in the world. On the other hand, I can recognise the chivalrous valour of those gallant men whom Lee led to victory: who fought not only for fatherland and in defence of home but for those rights most prized by free men. Washington's stalwart soldiers were styled rebels by our king and his ministers, and in like manner the men who wore the grey uniform of the Southern Confederacy were denounced as rebels from the banks of the Potomac to the head waters of the St. Lawrence. Lee's soldiers, well versed as all Americans are in the history of their forefathers' struggle against King George the Third, and believing firmly in the justice of their cause, saw the same virtue in one rebellion that was to be found in the other. This was a point upon which, during my stay in Virginia in 1862, I found every Southerner laid the greatest stress. It is a feeling that as yet has not been fully acknowledged by writers on the Northern side.

Rebellion, foul dishonouring word,
Whose wrongful blight so oft hath stained
The holiest cause that tongue or sword
Of mortal ever lost or gained.
How many a spirit born to bless
Hath sunk beneath thy withering name,
Whom but a day's, an hour's success,
Had wafted to eternal fame.

As a looker-on, I feel that both parties in the war have so much to be proud of, that both can afford to hear what impartial Englishmen or foreigners have to say about it. Inflated and bubble reputations were acquired during its progress, few of which will bear the test of time. The idol momentarily set up, often for political reasons, crumbles in time into the dust from which its limbs were perhaps originally moulded. To me, however, two figures stand out in that history towering above all others, both cast in hard metal that will be for ever proof against the belittling efforts of all future detractors. One, General Lee, the great soldier: the other, Mr. Lincoln, the far-seeing statesman of iron will, of unflinching determination. Each is a good representative of the genius that characterised his country. As I study the history of the Secession war, these seem to me the two men who influenced it most, and who will be recognised as its greatest heroes when future generations of American historians record its stirring events with impartiality.

General Lee came from the class of landed gentry that has furnished England at all times with her most able and distinguished leaders. The first of his family who went to America was Richard Lee, who in 1641 became Colonial Secretary to the Governor of Virginia. The family settled in Westmorland, one of the most lovely counties in that historic state, and members of it from time to time held high positions in the government. Several of the family distinguished themselves during the War of Independence, amongst whom was Henry, the father of General Robert Lee. He raised a mounted corps known as "Lee's Legion," in command of which he obtained the reputation of being an able and gallant soldier. He was nicknamed by his comrades, "Light Horse Harry." He was three times governor of his native state. To him is attributed the authorship of the eulogy on General Washington, in which occurs the so-often-quoted sentence, "First in war, first in peace, and first in the hearts of his countrymen," praise that with equal truth might have been subsequently applied to his own distinguished son.

The subject of this slight sketch, Robert Edward Lee, was born January 9th, 1807, at the family place of Stratford, in the county of Westmorland, state of Virginia. When only a few years old his parents moved to the small town of Alexandria, which is on the right bank of the Potomac river, nearly opposite Washington, but a little below it.

He was but a boy of eleven when his father died, leaving his family in straitened circumstances. Like many other great commanders, he was in consequence brought up in comparative poverty, a condition which has been pronounced by the greatest of them as the best training for soldiers. During his early years he attended a day-school near his home in Alexandria. He was thus able in the leisure hours to help his invalid mother in all her household concerns, and to afford her that watchful care which, owing to her very delicate health, she so much needed. She was a clever, highly-gifted woman, and by her fond care his character was formed and stamped with honest truthfulness. By her he was taught never to forget that he was well-born, and that, as a gentleman, honour must be his guiding star through life. It was from her lips he learnt his Bible, from her teaching he drank in the sincere belief in revealed religion which he never lost. It was she who imbued her great son with an ineradicable belief in the efficacy of prayer, and in the reality of God's interposition in the every-day affairs of the true believer. No son ever returned a mother's love with more heartfelt intensity. She was his idol, and he worshipped her with the deep-seated, inborn love which is known only to the son in whom filial affection is strengthened by respect and personal admiration for the woman who bore him. He was her all in all, or, as she described it, he was both son and daughter to her. He watched over her in weary hours of pain, and served her with all that soft tenderness which was such a marked trait in the character of this great, stern leader of men.

He seems to have been throughout his boyhood and early youth perfect in disposition, in bearing, and in conduct—a model of all that was noble, honourable, and manly. Of the early life of very few great men can this be said. Many who have left behind the greatest reputations for usefulness, in whom middle age was a model of virtue and perhaps of noble self-denial, began their career in a whirlwind of wild excess. Often, again, we find that, like Nero, the virtuous youth develops into the middle-aged fiend, who leaves behind him a name to be execrated for all time. It would be difficult to find in history a great man, be he soldier or statesman, with a character so irreproachable throughout his whole life as that which in boyhood, youth, manhood, and to his death, distinguished Robert Lee from all contemporaries.

He entered the military academy of West Point at the age of eighteen, where he worked hard, became adjutant of the cadet corps, and finally graduated at the head of his class. There he mastered the theory of war, and studied the campaigns of the great masters in that most ancient of all sciences. Whatever he did, even as a boy, he did thoroughly with order and method. Even at this early age he was the model Christian gentleman in thought, word, and deed. Careful and exact in the obedience he rendered his superiors, but remarkable for that dignity of deportment which all through his career struck strangers with admiring respect.

He left West Point when twenty-two, having gained its highest honours, and at once obtained a commission in the Engineers. Two years afterwards he married the grand-daughter and heiress of Mrs. Custis, whose second husband had been General Washington, but by whom she left no children. It was a great match for a poor subaltern officer, as his wife was heiress to a very extensive property and to a large number of slaves. She was clever, very well educated, and a general favourite: he was handsome, tall, well made, with a graceful figure, and a good rider: his manners were at once easy and captivating. These young people had long known one another, and each was the other's first love. She brought with her as part of her fortune General Washington's beautiful property of Arlington, situated on the picturesque wooded heights that overhang the Potomac river, opposite the capital to which the great Washington had given his name. In talking to me of the Northern troops, whose conduct in Virginia was then denounced by every local paper, no bitter expression passed his lips, but tears filled his eyes as he referred to the destruction of his place that had been the cherished home of the father of the United States. He could forgive their cutting down his trees, their wanton conversion of his pleasure grounds into a grave-yard; but he could never forget their reckless plunder of all the camp equipment and other relics of General Washington that Arlington House had contained.

Robert Lee first saw active service during the American war with Mexico in 1846, where he was wounded, and evinced a remarkable talent for war that brought himself prominently into notice. He was afterwards engaged in operations against hostile Indians, and obtained the reputation in his army of being an able officer of great promise. General Scott, then the general of greatest repute in the United States, was especially attracted by the zeal and soldierly instinct of the young captain of Engineers, and frequently employed him on distant expeditions that required cool nerve, confidence, and plenty of common sense. It is a curious fact that throughout the Mexican war General Scott in his despatches and reports made frequent mention of three officers—Lee, Beauregard, and McClellan—whose names became household words in America afterwards, during the great Southern struggle for independence. General Scott had the highest opinion of Lee's military genius, and did not hesitate to ascribe much of his success in Mexico as due to Lee's "skill, valour, and undaunted energy." Indeed subsequently, when the day came that these two men should part, each to take a different side in the horrible contest before them, General Scott is said to have urged Mr. Lincoln's Government to secure Lee at any price, alleging he "would be worth fifty thousand men to them." His valuable services were duly recognised at Washington by more than one step of brevet promotion: he obtained the rank of colonel, and was given command of a cavalry regiment shortly afterwards.

I must now pass to the most important epoch of his life, when the Southern States left the Union and set up a government of their own. Mr. Lincoln was in 1860 elected President of the United States in the Abolitionist interest. Both parties were so angry that thoughtful men soon began to see war alone could end this bitter dispute. Shipwreck was before the vessel of state, which General Washington had built and guided with so much care during his long and hard-fought contest. Civil war stared the American citizen in the face, and Lee's heart was well nigh broken at the prospect. Early in 1861 the seven Cotton States passed acts declaring their withdrawal from the Union, and their establishment of an independent republic, under the title of "The Confederate States of America." This declaration of independence was in reality a revolution: war alone could ever again bring all the States together.

Lee viewed this secession with horror. Until the month of April, when Virginia, his own dearly-cherished State, joined the Confederacy, he clung fondly to the hope that the gulf which separated the North from the South might yet be bridged over. He believed the dissolution of the Union to be a dire calamity not only for his own country, but for civilisation and all mankind. "Still," he said, "a Union that can only be maintained by swords and bayonets, and in which strife and civil war are to take the place of brotherly love and kindness, has no charm for me." In common with all Southerners he firmly believed that each of the old States had a legal and indisputable right by its individual constitution, and by its act of Union, to leave at will the Great Union into which each had separately entered as a Sovereign State. This was with him an article of faith of which he was as sure as of any Divine truths he found in the Bible. This fact must be kept always in mind by those who would rightly understand his character, or the course he pursued in 1861. He loved the Union for which his father and family in the previous century had fought so hard and done so much. But he loved his own State still more. She was the Sovereign to whom in the first place he owed allegiance, and whose orders, as expressed through her legally-constituted government, he was, he felt, bound in law, in honour, and in love to obey without doubt or hesitation. This belief was the mainspring that kept the Southern Confederacy going, as it was also the corner-stone of its constitution.

In April, 1861, at Fort Sumter, Charleston Harbour, the first shot was fired in a war that was only ended in April, 1865, by the surrender of General Lee's army at Appomattox Court House in Virginia. In duration it is the longest war waged since the great Napoleon's power was finally crushed at Waterloo. As the heroic struggle of a small population that was cut off from all outside help against a great, populous and very rich Republic, with every market in the world open to it, and to whom all Europe was a recruiting ground, this Secession war stands out prominently in the history of the world. When the vast numbers of men put into the field by the Northern States, and the scale upon which their operations were carried on, are duly considered, it must be regarded as a war fully equal in magnitude to the successful invasion of France by Germany in 1870. If the mind be allowed to speculate on the course that events will take in centuries to come, as they flow surely on with varying swiftness to the ocean of the unknown future, the influence which the result of this Confederate war is bound to exercise upon man's future history will seem very great. Think of what a power the re-United States will be in another century! Of what it will be in the twenty-first century of the Christian era! If, as many believe, China is destined to absorb all Asia and then to overrun Europe, may it not be in the possible future that Armageddon, the final contest between heathendom and Christianity, may be fought out between China and North America?

Had secession been victorious, it is tolerably certain that the United States would have broken up still further, and instead of the present magnificent and English-speaking empire, we should now see in its place a number of small powers with separate interests.

Most certainly it was the existence of slavery in the South that gave rise to the bitter antagonism of feeling which led to secession. But it was not to secure emancipation that the North took up arms, although during the progress of the war Mr. Lincoln proclaimed it, for the purpose of striking his enemy a serious blow. Lee hated slavery, but, as he explained to me, he thought it wicked to give freedom suddenly to some millions of people who were incapable of using it with profit to themselves or the State. He assured me he had long intended to gradually give his slaves their liberty. He believed the institution to be a moral and political evil, and more hurtful to the white than to the black man. He had a strong affection for the negro, but he deprecated any sudden or violent interference on the part of the State between master and slave. Nothing would have induced him to fight for the continuance of slavery: indeed he declared that had he owned every slave in the South, he would willingly give them all up if by so doing he could preserve the Union. He was opposed to secession, and to prevent it he would willingly sacrifice everything except honour and duty, which forbid him to desert his State. When in April, 1861, she formally and by an act of her Legislature left the Union, he resigned his commission in the United States army with the intention of retiring into private life. He endeavoured to choose what was right. Every personal interest bid him throw in his lot with the Union. His property lay so close to Washington that it was certain to be destroyed and swept of every slave, as belonging to a rebel. But the die was cast: he forsook everything for principle and the stern duty it entailed. Then came that final temptation which opened out before him a vista of power and importance greater than that which any man since Washington had held in America. General Long's book proves beyond all further doubt that he was offered the post of commander-in-chief of the Federal army. General Scott, his great friend and leader, whom he loved and respected, then commanding that army, used all his influence to persuade him to throw in his lot with the North, but to no purpose. Nothing would induce him to have any part in the invasion of his own State, much as he abhorred the war into which he felt she was rushing. His love of country, his unselfish patriotism, caused him to relinquish home, fortune, a certain future, in fact everything for her sake.

He was not, however, to remain a spectator of the coming conflict: he was too well known to his countrymen in Virginia as the officer in whom the Federal army had most confidence. The State of Virginia appointed him major-general and commander-in-chief of all her military forces. In open and crowded convention he formally accepted this position, saying, with all that dignity and grace of manner which distinguished him, that he did so "trusting in Almighty God, an approving conscience, and the aid of my fellow-citizens." The scene was most impressive: there were present all the leading men of Virginia, and representatives of all the first families in a State where great store was attached to gentle birth, and where society was very exclusive. General Lee's presence commanded respect, even from strangers, by a calm self-possessed dignity, the like of which I have never seen in other men. Naturally of strong passions, he kept them under perfect control by that iron and determined will, of which his expression and his face gave evidence. As this tall, handsome soldier stood before his countrymen, he was the picture of the ideal patriot, unconscious and self-possessed in his strength: he indulged in no theatrical display of feeling: there was in his face and about him that placid resolve which bespoke great confidence in self, and which in his case—one knows not how—quickly communicated its magnetic influence to others. He was then just fifty-four years old, the age of Marlborough when he destroyed the French army at Blenheim: in many ways and on many points these two great men much resembled each other. Both were of a dignified and commanding exterior: eminently handsome, with a figure tall, graceful, and erect, whilst a muscular, square-built frame bespoke great activity of body. The charm of manner, which I have mentioned as very winning in Lee, was possessed in the highest degree by Marlborough. Both, at the outset of their great career of victory, were regarded as essentially national commanders. Both had married young, and were faithful husbands and devoted fathers. Both had in all their campaigns the same belief in an ever-watchful Providence, in whose help they trusted implicitly, and for whose interposition they prayed at all times. They were gifted with the same military instinct, the same genius for war. The power of fascinating those with whom they were associated, the spell which they cast over their soldiers, who believed almost superstitiously in their certainty of victory, their contempt of danger, their daring courage, constitute a parallel that is difficult to equal between any other two great men of modern times.

From the first Lee anticipated a long and bloody struggle, although from the bombastic oratory of self-elected politicians and patriots the people were led to believe that the whole business would be settled in a few weeks. This folly led to a serious evil, namely, the enlistment of soldiers for only ninety days. Lee, who understood war, pleaded in favour of the engagement being for the term of the war, but he pleaded in vain. To add to his military difficulties, the politician insisted upon the officers being elected by their men. This was a point which, in describing to me the constitution of his army,

Lee most deplored. When war bursts upon a country unused to that ordeal, and therefore unskilled in preparing for it, the frothy babbling of politicians too often forces the nation into silly measures to its serious injury during the ensuing operations. That no great military success can be achieved quickly by an improvised army is a lesson that of all others is made most clear by the narrative of this war on both sides. All through its earlier phases, the press, both Northern and Southern, called loudly, and oftentimes angrily, for quick results. It is this impatience of the people, which the press is able to emphasize so strongly, that drives many weak generals into immature action. Lee, as well as others at this time, had to submit to the sneers which foolish men circulated widely in the daily newspapers. It is quite certain that under the existing condition of things no Fabius would be tolerated, and that the far-seeing military policy which triumphed at Torres Vedras would not be submitted to by the English public of to-day. Lee was not, however, a man whom any amount of irresponsible writing could force beyond the pace he knew to be most conducive to ultimate success.

The formation of an army with the means alone at his disposal was a colossal task. Everything had to be created by this extraordinary man. The South was an agricultural, not a manufacturing country, and the resources of foreign lands were denied it by the blockade of its ports maintained by the fleet of the United States. Lee was a thorough man of business, quick in decision, yet methodical in all he did. He knew what he wanted. He knew what an army should be, and how it should be organised, both in a purely military as well as an administrative sense. In about two months he had created a little army of fifty thousand men, animated by a lofty patriotism and courage that made them unconquerable by any similarly constituted army. In another month, this army at Bull's Run gained a complete victory over the Northern invaders, who were driven back across the Potomac like herds of frightened sheep. As the Federals ran, they threw away their arms, and everything, guns, tents, waggons, &c., was abandoned to the victors. The arms, ammunition, and equipment then taken were real godsends to those engaged in the organisation of the Southern armies. Thenceforward a battle to the Confederates meant a new supply of everything an army required. It may be truthfully said, that practically the Government at Washington had to provide and pay for the arms and equipment of its enemies as well as for all that its own enormous armies required. The day I presented myself in General Lee's camp, as I stood at the door of his tent awaiting admission, I was amused to find it stamped as belonging to a colonel of a New Jersey regiment. I remarked upon this to General Lee, who laughingly said, "Yes, I think you will find that all our tents, guns, and even the men's pouches are similarly marked as having belonged to the United States army." Some time afterwards, when General Pope and his large invading army had been sent back flying across the Maryland frontier, I overheard this conversation between two Confederate soldiers: "Have you heard the news? Lee has resigned!" "Good G——!" was the reply, "What for?" "He has resigned because he says he cannot feed and supply his army any longer, now that his commissary, General Pope, has been removed." Mr. Lincoln had just dismissed General Pope, replacing him by General McClellan.

The Confederates did not follow up their victory at Bull's Run. A rapid and daring advance would have given them possession of Washington, their enemy's capital. Political considerations at Richmond were allowed to outweigh the very evident military expediency of reaping a solid advantage from this their first great success. Often afterwards, when this attempt to allay the angry feelings of the North against the Act of Secession had entirely failed, was this action of their political rulers lamented by the Confederate commanders.

In this article to attempt even a sketch of the subsequent military operations is not to be thought of. Both sides fought well, and both have such true reason to be proud of their achievements that they can now afford to hear the professional criticisms of their English friends in the same spirit that we Britishers have learnt to read of the many defeats inflicted upon our arms by General Washington.

What most strikes the regular soldier in these campaigns of General Lee is the inefficient manner in which both he and his opponents were often served by their subordinate commanders, and how badly the staff and outpost work generally was performed on both sides. It is most difficult to move with any effective precision young armies constituted as these were during this war. The direction and movement of large bodies of newly-raised troops, even when victorious, is never easy, is often impossible. Over and over again was the South apparently "within a stone's throw of independence," as it has been many times remarked, when, from want of a thoroughly good staff to organise pursuit, the occasion was lost, and the enemy allowed to escape. Lee's combinations to secure victory were the conceptions of a truly great strategist, and, when they had been effected, his tactics were also almost always everything that could be desired up to the moment of victory, but there his action seemed to stop abruptly. Was ever an army so hopelessly at the mercy of another as that of McClellan when he began his retreat to Harrison's Landing after the seven days' fighting round Richmond? What commander could wish to have his foe in a "tighter place" than Burnside was in after his disastrous attack upon Lee at Fredericksburg? Yet in both instances the Northern commander got safely away, and other similar instances could be mentioned. The critical military student of this war who knows the power which regular troops, well-officered and well-directed by a thoroughly efficient staff, place in the hands of an able general, and who has acquired an intimate and complete knowledge of what these two contending American armies were really like, will, I think, agree that from first to last the co-operation of even one army corps of regular troops would have given complete victory to whichever side it fought on. I felt this when I visited the South, and during the progress of the war I heard the same opinion expressed by many others who had inspected the contending armies. I say this with no wish to detract in any way from the courage or other fighting qualities of the troops engaged. I yield to none in my admiration of their warlike achievements; but I cannot blind myself to the hyperbole of writers who refer to these armies as the finest that have ever existed.

Those who know how difficult it is to supply our own militia and volunteer forces with efficient officers can appreciate what difficulties General Lee had to overcome in the formation of the army he so often led to victory. He had about him able assistants, who, like himself, had received an excellent military education at West Point. To the experienced soldier it is no matter of surprise, but to the general reader it will be of interest to know that, on either side in this war, almost every general whose name will be remembered in the future had been educated at that military school, and had been trained in the old regular army of the United States. In talking to me of all the Federal generals, Lee mentioned McClellan with most respect and regard. He spoke bitterly of none—a remarkable fact, as at that time men on both sides were wont to heap the most violent terms of abuse upon their respective enemies. He thus reproved a clergyman who had spoken in his sermon very bitterly of their enemies:—"I have fought against the people of the North because I believed they were seeking to wrest from the South her dearest rights; but I have never cherished towards them bitter or vindictive feelings, and I have never seen the day when I did not pray for them." I asked him how many men he had at the battle of Antietam, from which he had then recently returned. He said he had never had, during that whole day, more than about thirty thousand men in line, although he had behind him a small army of tired troops and of shoeless stragglers who never came up during the battle. He estimated McClellan's army at about one hundred thousand men. A friend of mine, who at the same time was at the Federal headquarters, there made similar inquiries. General McClellan's reply corroborated the correctness of Lee's estimate of the Federal numbers at Antietam, but he said he thought the Confederate army was a little stronger than that under his command. I mention this because both those generals were most truthful men, and whatever they stated can be implicitly relied on. I also refer to it because the usual proportion throughout the war between the contending sides in each action ranged from about twice to three times more Federals than there were Confederates engaged. With reference to the relative numbers employed on both sides, the following amusing story was told to me at the time. A deputation from some of the New England States had attended at the White House, and laid their business before the President. As they were leaving Mr. Lincoln's room one of the delegates turned round and said: "Mr. President, I should very much like to know what you reckon to be the number of rebels in arms against us." Mr. Lincoln, without a moment's hesitation, replied: "Sir, I have the best possible reason for knowing the number to be one million of men, for whenever one of our generals engages a rebel army he reports that he has encountered a force twice his strength: now I know we have half a million of soldiers in the field, so I am bound to believe the rebels have twice that number."

As a student of war I would fain linger over the interesting lessons to be learnt from Lee's campaigns: of the same race as both belligerents, I could with the utmost pleasure dwell upon the many brilliant feats of arms on both sides; but I cannot do so here.

The end came at least, when the well-supplied North, rich enough to pay recruits, no matter where they came from, a bounty of over five hundred dollars a head, triumphed over an exhausted South, hemmed in on all sides, and even cut off from all communication with the outside world. The desperate, though drawn battle of Gettysburg was the death-knell of Southern independence; and General Sherman's splendid but almost unopposed march to the sea showed the world that all further resistance on the part of the Confederate States could only be a profitless waste of blood. In the thirty-five days of fighting near Richmond which ended the war of 1865, General Grant's army numbered one hundred and ninety thousand, that of Lee only fifty-one thousand men. Every man lost by the former was easily replaced, but an exhausted South could find no more soldiers. "The right of self-government," which Washington won, and for which Lee fought, was no longer to be a watchword to stir men's blood in the United States. The South was humbled and beaten by its own flesh and blood in the North, and it is difficult to know which to admire most, the good sense with which the result was accepted in the so-called Confederate States, or the wise magnanimity displayed by the victors. The wounds are now healed on both sides: Northerners and Southerners are now once more a united people, with a future before them to which no other nation can aspire. If the English-speaking people of the earth cannot all acknowledge the same Sovereign, they can, and I am sure they will, at least combine to work in the interests of truth and of peace, for the good of mankind. The wise men on both sides of the Atlantic will take care to chase away all passing clouds that may at any time throw even a shadow of dispute or discord between the two great families into which our race is divided.

Like all men, Lee had his faults: like all the greatest of generals, he sometimes made mistakes. His nature shrank with such horror from the dread of wounding the feelings of others, that upon occasions he left men in positions of responsibility to which their abilities were not equal. This softness of heart, amiable as that quality may be, amounts to a crime in the man intrusted with the direction of public affairs at critical moments. Lee's devotion to duty and great respect for obedience seem at times to have made him too subservient to those charged with the civil government of his country. He carried out too literally the orders of those whom the Confederate Constitution made his superiors, although he must have known them to be entirely ignorant of the science of war. He appears to have forgotten that he was the great Revolutionary Chief engaged in a great Revolutionary war: that he was no mere leader in a political struggle of parties carried on within the lines of an old, well-established form of government. It was very clear to many at the time, as it will be commonly acknowledged now, that the South could only hope to win under the rule of a Military Dictator. If General Washington had had a Mr. Davis over him, could he have accomplished what he did? It will, I am sure, be news to many that General Lee was given the command over all the Confederate armies a month or two only before the final collapse; and that the military policy of the South was all throughout the war dictated by Mr. Davis as president of the Confederate States! Lee had no power to reward soldiers or to promote officers. It was Mr. Davis who selected the men to command divisions and armies. Is it to be supposed that Cromwell, King William the Third, Washington, or Napoleon could have succeeded in the revolutions with which their names are identified, had they submitted to the will and authority of a politician as Lee did to Mr. Davis?

Lee was opposed to the final defence of Richmond that was urged upon him for political, not military reasons. It was a great strategic error. General Grant's large army of men was easily fed, and its daily losses easily recruited from a near base; whereas if it had been drawn far into the interior after the little army with which Lee endeavoured to protect Richmond, its fighting strength would have been largely reduced by the detachments required to guard a long line of communications through a hostile country. It is profitless, however, to speculate upon what might have been, and the military student must take these campaigns as they were carried out. No fair estimate of Lee as a general can be made by a simple comparison of what he achieved with that which Napoleon, Wellington, or Von Moltke accomplished, unless due allowance is made for the difference in the nature of the American armies, and of the armies commanded and encountered by those great leaders. They were at the head of perfectly organised, thoroughly trained and well disciplined troops; whilst Lee's soldiers, though gallant and daring to a fault, lacked the military cohesion and efficiency, the trained company leaders, and the educated staff which are only to be found in a regular army of long standing. A trial heat between two jockeys mounted on untrained horses may be interesting, but no one would ever quote the performance as an instance of great racing speed.

Who shall ever fathom the depth of Lee's anguish when the bitter end came, and when, beaten down by sheer force of numbers, and by absolutely nothing else, he found himself obliged to surrender! The handful of starving men remaining with him laid down their arms, and the proud Confederacy ceased to be. Surely the crushing, maddening anguish of awful sorrow is only known to the leader who has so failed to accomplish some lofty, some noble aim for which he has long striven with might and main, with heart and soul—in the interests of king or of country. A smiling face, a cheerful manner, may conceal the sore place from the eyes, possibly even from the knowledge of his friends; but there is no healing for such a wound, which eats into the very heart of him who has once received it.

General Lee survived the destruction of the Confederacy for five years, when, at the age of sixty-three, and surrounded by his family, life ebbed slowly from him. Where else in history is a great man to be found whose whole life was one such blameless record of duty nobly done? It was consistent in all its parts, complete in all its relations. The most perfect gentleman of a State long celebrated for its chivalry, he was just, gentle, and generous, and child-like in the simplicity of his character. Never elated with success, he bore reverse, and at last, complete overthrow, with dignified resignation. Throughout this long and cruel struggle his was all the responsibility, but not the power that should have accompanied it.

The fierce light which beats upon the throne is as that of a rushlight in comparison with the electric glare which our newspapers now focus upon the public man in Lee's position. His character has been subjected to that ordeal, and who can point to any spot upon it? His clear, sound judgment, personal courage, untiring activity, genius for war, and absolute devotion to his State mark him out as a public man, as a patriot to be for ever remembered by all Americans. His amiability of disposition, deep sympathy with those in pain or sorrow, his love for children, nice sense of personal honour and genial courtesy endeared him to all his friends. I shall never forget his sweet winning smile, nor his clear, honest eyes that seemed to look into your heart whilst they searched your brain. I have met many of the great men of my time, but Lee alone impressed me with the feeling that I was in the presence of a man who was cast in a grander mould, and made of different and of finer metal than all other men. He is stamped upon my memory as a being apart and superior to all others in every way: a man with whom none I ever knew, and very few of whom I have read, are worthy to be classed. I have met but two men who realize my ideas of what a true hero should be: my friend Charles Gordon was one, General Lee was the other.

The following lines seem written for him:

> Who is the honest man?
> He who doth still and strongly good pursue,
> To God, his country and himself most true;
> Who when he comes to deal
> With sick folk, women, those whom passions sway,
> Allows for this, and keeps his constant way.

When all the angry feelings roused by Secession are buried with those which existed when the Declaration of Independence was written, when Americans can review the history of their last great rebellion with calm impartiality, I believe all will admit that General Lee towered far above all men on either side in that struggle: I believe he will be regarded not only as the most prominent figure of the Confederacy, but as the great American of the nineteenth century, whose statue is well worthy to stand on an equal pedestal with that of Washington, and whose memory is equally worthy to be enshrined in the hearts of all his countrymen.

WOLSELEY.

NOTE

1. 'Memoirs of Robert E. Lee; his Military and Personal History.' By General A. L. Long and General Marcus J. Wright. London. 1886.

Lee and the Strategy of the Civil War

GEORGE A. BRUCE

It was General Grant who won the first great victory of the war, and, after three years of conflict in which he was never defeated, as Lieutenant-General in command of all the National forces, ended it by the defeat and surrender of the Army of Northern Virginia. One of the three greatest Confederate soldiers said of him, "As the world continues to look at and study the grand combinations and strategy of General Grant, the higher will be his award as a great soldier." There is but one among the Confederate leaders that the most partial of Southern writers has ever thought of as his rival in ability and achievement as a soldier,—he who so long commanded the Army of Northern Virginia, General Robert E. Lee.

Lord Rosebery, in his Napoleon, the Last Phase, rightly says that no one man would be capable of writing the career of the great Emperor. His dual capacity as statesman and warrior would require a historian of the first ability to adequately present his influence on the world as a legislator and a specialist in the art and science of war—like Captain A. T. Mahan for illustration—to fitly write his military career and determine his rank as a soldier. Here we are more self-confident. A Virginia novelist, with no doubt of his ability to decide, says that Lee is the greatest soldier of the English-speaking race, and a Northern occasional writer of discursive essays tells his readers that, in a certain view, he must be considered the greatest defender of democracy the world has seen! As in his career Confederate strategy and methods of waging the war are seen at their best, a short sketch of it may not be out of place. In 1861, Lee, with the full rank of General, the highest in the Confederate service, was placed in command of all the forces in Virginia, and with President Davis and General S. H. Cooper acting together as a war council, decided the numerous military problems the crisis presented. Later he was assigned to the command in West Virginia, where, with Generals

Wise, Floyd and some others of like character under him, he failed in a way so marked, and suffered thereby so much in reputation without the least fault on his part, that when later he was sent to command the Department of South Carolina, Georgia, and Florida, President Davis felt called upon to write a letter to the Governor of South Carolina to tell him his opinion of the general he had sent on so important a command.[1]

General Johnston, having been wounded at Fair Oaks, General Lee succeeded him in the command of the Army of Northern Virginia on the 1st day of June, 1862. It was then an army finely organized and, for its numbers, equal, either for offensive or defensive warfare, to any of which we have record. It was composed entirely of the earliest volunteers who came forward in 1861. The flower of Southern manhood and Southern valor were in its ranks. More than one fourth of its infantry and three fourths of its cavalry were from Virginia. As the service it was destined to perform was almost entirely within the limits of this State, the fact above mentioned was of inestimable value. Wherever it went and whenever it was called upon to meet the enemy, there were hundreds in the ranks to point out the way and give information of every road, by-path, stream, wood, hill, or, in short, of every local feature that could be of value to a commander to know.

Those only who campaigned in Virginia can fully understand the value of such aid, and the disability which the Army of the Potomac suffered for want of such assistance. When Lee came to the army he found in command of its various divisions and brigades the best military talent the South possessed or that was to be developed during the war. To command its right and left wings were Longstreet and Jackson, superior to any corps commanders in any of our armies. What Davoust was to Napoleon, Longstreet was to Lee, and Jackson certainly filled the place of Ney. With Stuart at the head of his cavalry, and such officers as Hood, Early, Ewell, the two Hills, Mahone, Pickett, Heth, Rodes, Field, Gordon, Kershaw, and others to lead his brigades and divisions, there was nothing wanting to make up as perfect and powerful a military machine as was ever constructed. Even its lack of transportation and equipment enabled it to get ready for a movement quicker and move along the road with less liability to delay than its opponent, generally over-supplied with everything. Soon after the 1st of June, Lee found the Army of the Potomac in his front, with the Fifth Corps on the left bank of the Chickahominy and four corps on the right.

Thus far the Confederate army had been encamped near the inner circle of detached forts that had been constructed around Richmond. Lee at once commenced a line of fortifications for infantry and artillery from the right bank of the Chickahominy to Chaffin's Bluff, and, when completed, moved forward his army to occupy them. With that spirit of aggression, which remained permanently his most prominent characteristic as a soldier, he decided upon a plan to attack the isolated Fifth Corps, consisting of 17,330 men, the object being to cut McClellan off from his base of supplies at White House on the Pamunkey River, and drive him from his position, with such other damage as might fall within his power to inflict. He first brought Jackson to him from the Valley of Virginia and other reinforcements in numbers sufficient to swell his army to nearly 100,000 men, consisting of 181 regiments of infantry, the largest force he was ever destined to command. Mr. Davis says, in his Rise and Fall of the Confederate Government, that the recall of Jackson was due to a suggestion of his to Lee. Jackson, having arrived at Ashland with his army, came to Richmond, and in a conference with Lee, Longstreet, and Hill, designated the 26th of June as the day when he would be ready to begin the attack on the right of the Fifth Corps. At this time McCall's division of Porter's command (the Fifth Corps) was entrenched on the left bank of Beaver Dam Creek, the other two divisions about a mile to the rear. Jackson not having kept his own appointment, Hill commenced the battle by an attack on McCall, which was kept up with such tenacity of purpose as to cause a loss of between 2000 and 3000 men in his division. McCall held his line with a killed and wounded list of only 361. It was not until three o'clock the following morning that Porter received an order from McClellan to take up a new line east of Powhite Creek, where he fought the next day with his nine brigades against the twenty-five under Lee, being reinforced by Slocum between three and four in the afternoon. The line was broken at about dusk by Longstreet, after which Porter withdrew to the other side of the Chickahominy. The victory was with Lee, but his killed and wounded numbered 8335 in comparison with 4261 in the Fifth Corps and Slocum's division, to which, however, is to be added a list of 2941 prisoners. This clearly is the strongest fight put up during the war by a corps, slightly reinforced, against an army, and suggests a comparison of Porter at Gaines' Mill with Thomas at Chickamauga. General Alexander, the ablest and fairest of Southern military writers, who was present with Lee, says that a corps sent in aid of the Fifth would have resulted in a defeat of the Confederates. Lee, having planned the battle in expectation that McClellan, if defeated, would endeavor to secure his base, for twenty-four hours was in doubt as to what had happened, and sent Jackson forward down the river to find out. As at Gettysburg, he had deprived himself of all use of the cavalry by sending Stuart to the White House to harry the Federal retreat in that direction. On the 29th, he set the whole army in prompt pursuit, having at length gained correct information of the enemy's intentions. Magruder made two attacks on Sumner at Allen's Farm and Savage's Station, which were easily thrown off with an admitted loss to the Confederates of 4000 and about 3000 to the Federals. To intercept the retreat was Lee's aim, and for this purpose he ordered Longstreet with his own and Hill's division to break in on the line by the Derbytown road, giving him Huger's division, who was directed to open the attack on Longstreet's right. Longstreet was in such close proximity to Sumner when he reached Glendale that he was obliged to halt the Second Corps, and the other troops over whom he had control as senior officer, to fight a battle.

General Lee and President Davis were with Longstreet and together indulged in pleasing anticipations of the decisive results expected from a strategic combination thought to have been effected around the Union army, Huger on its right flank, Jackson expected on the left or rear, and the two divisions of Longstreet and Hill in the centre.[2] They waited long to hear the opening guns of Huger or Jackson, each of whom failed to perform any part in the assigned programme, and the battle was bravely fought by the two centre divisions, through the twilight and up into the darkness of night, when the pleasing anticipations referred to were dispelled by the steady bravery of our troops, who later continued their interrupted march, and the next day the Army of the Potomac was again together in position on Malvern Hill.

The same day, but a few hours later, all the divisions of Lee's army were united in front and the next day was to see the last conflict in what is now called the "Seven Days' Battle," in which the Confederates met with a most decisive and bloody repulse. General Longstreet says that the Confederates lost here about 5000 and puts the Union loss at one third of that number.[3] The following remarkable order was issued for this battle:—

> Batteries have been established to take the enemy's line. If it is broken, as is probable, Armistead, who can witness the effect of the fire, has been ordered to charge with a yell. Do the same.
>
> By order General Lee.
>
> R. H. CHILTON,
> ASSISTANT ADJUTANT-GENERAL.

Malvern Hill was the precursor of Fredericksburg on a scale of about one to two, and whether better conducted is a doubtful question. The campaign, as a whole, resulted in a loss to the Confederate army, by official reports, of 3478 killed, 16,261 wounded, and 895 missing; and in a Union loss of 1734 killed, 8062 wounded, and 6053 missing.[4] That Lee defeated McClellan is clear enough, but can it be claimed that in any sense, except technically, the Army of the Potomac was defeated by him during these seven bloody days, a continuous battle in six separate but related actions, in four of which parts of his army were repulsed by parts of the opposing army, and on the sole occasion when all of the forces of each were opposed, the Army of Northern Virginia met with a decisive defeat?

There was a diarist in Richmond, who, seeing the city crowded with fifteen thousand wounded soldiers and only a few square miles of barren territory regained, asked of himself whether, after all, Lee had not been fighting a battle like that of Pyrrhus that was likely to bring ruin to the cause for which it was fought.

For the reason, probably, of knowledge gained during the events just described, many changes took place in the organization of the Army of Northern Virginia. The names of four of its division commanders never again appear on its rolls—Magruder, Holmes, Huger, and Whiting. Longstreet became the commander of the right wing, and Jackson, though falling below his reputation and what was expected of him on every occasion during the Seven Days, was given the left wing. Leaving McClellan at Harrison's Landing on the James, Lee withdrew his army back near Richmond, and on the 13th of July sent Jackson with two divisions to Gordonsville to keep a watch on General Pope, who was operating in that vicinity, and two days later ordered Longstreet with twelve brigades to the same place. Learning soon after of the intention to withdraw the Army of the Potomac from the James, he called to him the divisions of D. H. Hill, R. H. Anderson, McLaws, and Walker. Holding the opinion of General Pope that was common to military men of both armies, he formed a plan to crush him before the Army of the Potomac could be brought to his assistance. He sent Jackson by a circuitous route to get in between Pope and Washington, a movement only justified on the ground that he had formed a correct estimate of his opponent, which brought on the second battle of Manassas, resulting in Pope's defeat and retreat behind the fortifications of the Capital. After the battle, and before the cannon had had time to cool, Lee ordered Jackson to start in the early morning by the Little River Turnpike and endeavor to pass with his corps for a second time between Pope's army and Washington, or to attack his flank during his retreat. Pope had neglected to picket the roads leading to the Capital, and was at Centreville in total ignorance of a movement that had already progressed far enough to endanger his army, when it was discovered by two roving cavalrymen who hastened to make report of their discovery. It was by the quick thought and heroic action of General Isaac I. Stevens, aided later by General Philip Kearny, that Jackson's purpose was defeated and a large part of his corps roughly handled. In this conflict at Chantilly, both of these distinguished officers lost their lives. The next day Lee turned his face northward and set his army in motion toward Leesburg. Having before, or soon thereafter, formed a plan for crossing into Maryland, as soon as he received the approval of Mr. Davis by letter, he promptly, entered upon the campaign that terminated with the battle of Antietam, which has always been acknowledged as a Union victory, though the fruits gathered from the battlefield were not great. An indecisive battle was, however, quickly followed by a decisive political action, for Mr. Lincoln used it as a fitting occasion to issue his Proclamation of Emancipation.

The campaign had been undertaken by Lee and sanctioned by Davis, under a delusion, common to both, that the people of Maryland and Delaware were only waiting for the encouragement that the presence of a Confederate army would give them to throw off their allegiance to the Government and rush by thousands to enlist under their banner. He had prepared, and, soon after crossing the Potomac, caused to be published a proclamation in which he made known to the people of Maryland the sympathy of the Southern people for the tyranny and oppression under which they were living and their willingness to aid them to throw off a foreign yoke and again enjoy the inalienable rights of freemen. He found, what General Johnston found, when at an earlier date he invaded Kentucky, that he had come among a people who were unconscious of living under a foreign yoke and did not require the extended sympathy for assumed suffering and wrongs. Even among those originally sympathizing strongly with the South, time had cooled their ardor, for it was then generally known that those fiery spirits from Baltimore and other parts of Maryland who enlisted to serve for one year in the Confederate army in the spring of 1861, and formed what was known as the Maryland Line, at the expiration of their terms of service had been refused their discharge under the Conscription Act, which Mr. Davis, who construed constitutions and contracts in a way to help along his ambition and purposes, held applied to all citizens of the Confederacy, and as these men had served for a year, they were no longer entitled to claim any rights as citizens of Maryland. Lee had crossed the Potomac in expectation of a complete overthrow of the Union army, and had made arrangements for Mr. Davis to meet him to make a treaty with the Government recognizing the independence of the Confederate States on what they considered was Southern soil. With these lost illusions he retired into Virginia, changing position from time to time in accordance with the tardy and slow advance of the army under McClellan, until December, when on the heights in the rear of Fredericksburg, in a defensive line, he fought successfully in the fourth great battle of the year, the opposing army under General Burnside, its new commander. It was Malvern Hill on a larger scale, with the parts of the actors reversed. Confederate writers take especial delight in recording that General Grant lost 39,000 men in getting his army to the James River, when he might have reached the same point by the use of transports with his army intact, but they never mention the fact that Lee in five months of 1862 had lost nearly 60,000 men in four battles, and still found Jackson's part of his army one hundred miles south and the remainder only sixty miles north of their starting-points, Grant, in 1864, moving forward toward final victory; Lee, in 1862, by his general policy, toward a sure defeat.

During the winter the two armies remained in sight of each other on opposite sides of the Rappahannock, getting, rather than enjoying, a much-needed rest. On the 3d of May was fought the battle of Chancellorsville, the army of the Potomac being under Hooker, its third commander, on which occasion, for the last time, Lee and his army saw their long-time opponents turn their backs to them in retreat from a battle-field.

The impulsive nature of Lee, his audacity as described by General Alexander, his "up and-at-'em" courage as noted by Longstreet, would not let him rest, and just thirty days from Chancellorsville he entered upon the Gettysburg campaign by sending a part of Longstreet's corps on march for Culpeper Court-House. No campaign during the war, or the battle that terminated it, has been discussed by so many writers both here and in Europe. Every order and act of Lee has been defended by his staff officers and eulogists with a fervency that excites suspicion that, even in their own minds, there was need of defence to make good the position they claim for him among the world's great commanders. Some points have been omitted in this discussion, apparently not yet ended, to be presented in this paper, which, I think, have a bearing on it.

General Lee in his report says, that, not deeming it wise to move against Hooker in his position, he thought by transferring his army to the north he would draw him away from the Rappahannock for the defence of Washington, and in northern territory might so manœuvre his army as to place his opponent in a position where he could gain a decisive victory over him. This discloses a piece of strategy with no definite objective, but one resting on a contingency. There is certainly something quixotic in the idea of moving an army two hundred miles for the purpose of finding a battlefield, leaving his base of supplies one hundred miles or more at the end of the railroad at Winchester, when able to carry along only ammunition enough for a single battle, as was necessarily the case. The first campaign the year before across the Potomac had a definite objective, to aid the people of Maryland to throw off the yoke of a tyrant and enjoy the freedom and happiness that would come from a union with the Confederate Government, and is, therefore, free from this criticism. The memories of their experience in Maryland, if recalled, were not such as to encourage any over-sanguine expectations. There stands out the fact in Confederate despatches and reports that about 20,000 fell out from the ranks by exhaustion before reaching Sharpsburg on the 15th of September, and a battle fought with depleted numbers. There was no reason to suppose that something of the same kind would not happen in 1863. We heard Professor Johnston, of Harvard

University, designate Lee, at our last meeting but one, as the psychological general, with slight reason, as it seemed to me. With more propriety he should be classed as a temperamental general. It was his temperament that was in conspicuous display from the day he took command of the Army of Northern Virginia until the Wilderness, in 1864, enforced caution and restraint.

It was not until the evening of the 28th of June that he learned of the presence of the Army of the Potomac at Frederick City, at which time Ewell was at Carlisle, Early at York, and the two corps of Longstreet and Hill at Chambersburg in the Cumberland Valley. General Lee at once sent orders for the concentration of his army, directing Ewell and Early to return to Cashtown at the eastern foot of the mountains, to which place Hill moved on the following day. During the 30th of June, Lee learned that General Meade had relieved Hooker and was then at Middletown, thirty miles southwest from Gettysburg. Early in the morning of the 1st of July, General Heth started with his division, Hill consenting, for the sole purpose of supplying his men with shoes supposed to be found in the stores of the village of Gettysburg. This fact has been denied. While sitting with General Heth on the piazza of the Vaden Mansion in Manchester, Virginia, in June, 1865, he told me the story with great particularity of detail, and the fact is recorded in his official report. This brought on the battle which during the forenoon was waged between the First Corps and two divisions under Hill, the lines facing east and west. Ewell, hearing the sounds of battle, at once changed direction, and moved towards Gettysburg with Rodes' division, sending directions for Early to take the Carlisle Road farther to the east. Rodes formed his division in double lines on Oak Hill, just about the time that Howard was bringing to the field two small divisions of the Eleventh Corps which he drew out across the plain facing to the north. Rodes came on directly against the right flank of the First Corps, which compelled Doubleday to change front with part of his corps, so that the two wings were nearly at right angles to each other. The Eleventh Corps' position was in line with the right wing of the First, but a wide gap was left between them. Rodes waged a fierce battle for three hours or more along his front, and Early, coming in on his left, prolonged it from the Seminary Ridge to the Carlisle Turnpike. General Gordon, of Early's division, overlapping Barlow on the extreme right, broke down the defence in that quarter, and very soon the Eleventh Corps gave way, later the First Corps, each retiring, with heavy loss in prisoners, to Cemetery Hill, where they were re-formed and placed in position for defence. This battle was brought on by a division commander, taken up and carried through by two corps commanders, in the absence of and without the knowledge of General Lee, who arrived at Seminary Ridge after the last shot had been fired, but in time to see the defeated Federals in process of re-forming on the opposite heights. If the concentration of the scattered divisions of the Confederate army had been ordered to take place at the very time and points as above described that they did take place, it would have been considered as one of the finest pieces of strategical or tactical concentration of forces on a battle-field of which there is record, and yet it all took place without design, or, as the saying is, by accident! One day of perfect battle, with Lee absent, followed by two days with Lee present, marked by unnecessary delays, disobedience of orders, failure of coöperation, the machinery of the army out of joint, faultless direction on the part of the commander-in-chief, and a disastrous defeat! Such is the picture of these great days drawn by the friends of Lee *after his death*, a cult including most of his staff officers, a few novel writers, mostly Virginians, with here and there an associate member in the North. John Esten Cooke published a highly eulogistic life of General Lee a few months after his death, in which a full account of the Gettysburg campaign and battle is given, and there is in it no allusion to failure on the part of any officer to put forth his best efforts to secure the victory. Cooke was a gallant officer, a member of General Stuart's staff, an accomplished writer, endowed with attractive personal qualities that gained for him a friendly reception everywhere in the army. It is likely, if the views later so widely circulated had then been formed, that he would have heard of them and given them a place in his book.

General Pendleton, a member of Lee's staff, in a lecturing tour in 1872 through the South in aid of a memorial church to General Lee, to be erected at Lexington, first made the charge that General Lee had ordered Longstreet to attack the left flank of the Union army at sunrise July 2, and said to him (Pendleton), "I want you to be up long before sunrise so as to reëxamine and save time." When this statement was published in the Southern papers, in reply to a letter of inquiry from Longstreet, four of Lee's staff officers, those nearest to him, including his adjutant-general, informed him that they had never heard of such an order. It is not to be supposed that General Pendleton made a wilful misstatement, but out of the private discussion that went on after the end of the war to explain their failure, and particularly after Longstreet wrote a letter in 1867 on the politics of the day that was displeasing to the extreme Southern sentiment, the belief became an honest and settled conviction that such an order was given. Pendleton's own official report, not then published, and, probably forgotten, is quite inconsistent with what he told the Southern people as a historic fact of his own knowledge. It illustrates the danger of resting historic writings on memory alone. Notwithstanding its denial and refutation, Pendleton's story is still doing duty in upholding a groundless charge. In a milder form, the charge that the commander of the First Corps was unreasonably dilatory, and that, if he had commenced the battle as early as Lee expected, a great victory would probably have been won, has been made by every Confederate writer. This flattering conclusion is based on information, at the time unknown, that little Round Top was not occupied in the early day except by signal officers, and the Fifth Corps did not arrive on the field until noon, and the Sixth until three hours later. The situation in the evening of the 1st of July was as follows: Cemetery Hill was occupied by the First Corps and three divisions of the Eleventh, one of which had not been engaged, and Buford's cavalry was drawn up in an imposing array west of the town covering the Emmettsburg Road. At half-past five the Twelfth Corps came up, at dusk the Third Corps, and the Second, resting for the night near Round Top, came into position along the ridge a little after daylight the next morning. The Confederates were strengthened by Anderson's and Johnson's divisions at about dusk. Two divisions of the First Corps, less one brigade, were on the march early in the morning of the 1st from the Cumberland Valley for Gettysburg, but were ordered to halt and permit Johnson's division to file in front with a wagon-train several miles long. The leading division went into camp at nine o'clock in the evening four miles from Gettysburg, and Hood's division at midnight. Longstreet rode up to Seminary Ridge in the afternoon and conversed with his chief about the situation and what should be done the next day. Longstreet, after an examination of the position in front, filled as it then was by the troops that had come up, near to Little Round Top, advised a movement to the right rather than attack so formidable a line. Lee told him that he should attack the enemy in the morning without indicating when or where. This is Longstreet's version, and besides his own word to support it,—the word of a man of as high standing in every particular as any one in the army,—it was in accordance with the requirements of the situation. There was no information in regard to the location of the remainder of Meade's army, but it was clear enough that a decision had been made to accept battle at Gettysburg, and the whole army might well be expected on the field before morning. How long its line would be, where its flanks would rest, and what would be the weak spot, if any, to assail, no one could then tell, for no examination for the purpose had been made. From the only point where observations had or could then be made, the whole line appeared strong and the position formidable. It is doing Lee an injustice to think that he would order his army into battle blindly, or any part of it even, as his over-zealous friends assert. It was thought from partial observations made by a few officers that Culp's Hill was the key to the position and that its possession would compel our army to retire. There was an ill-defined impression that the first efforts the following day would be made in that direction. About sunrise General Lee sent Colonel Venable, one of his staff, to Ewell to ask him what he thought were the advantages of an attack on the enemy from his position.[5] General Ewell made him ride with him from point to point, that he might see with him the exact position of things, and before they were through, Lee joined them. General Lee was explicit in saying that the question in his mind was whether he should move all the troops round on the right and attack on that side. This is entirely inconsistent with an order to commence a battle on the right at sunrise or at any other hour or place. Longstreet started, before light, his two divisions, less Law's brigade, which had been marching all night to join its division (Hood's), and rode to Lee's headquarters for orders. Soon after, Hood and McLaws, having turned their troops off the road to the right, where they rested ready to be called into action, joined him. It was probably in a field just west of Willoughby Run, where the troops were left, a convenient point for any movement to the right or left. The artillery under General Alexander did not come up with the infantry until nine o'clock in the forenoon. About this hour Lee rode over to see Ewell, as stated by his staff officer, Colonel Venable, and returned at ten o'clock, having in the mean time decided upon the right attack. His battle order was issued at eleven o'clock. There was a five-mile stretch of unknown territory for the First Corps to pass over before reaching its position, and at three o'clock, the artillery, in place, opened fire. With a necessary wait, when on the battle line, of half an hour for Law's brigade to join, which had marched twenty-eight miles since three o'clock in the morning, there is not much ground for charging such troops as being laggards. For the battle of the second day four brigades of the Third Corps were assigned to Longstreet in addition to his own, and the orders required that the other corps should give active support and follow up with vigorous attack whenever opportunity occurred. From about three o'clock of a long summer's day one of the fiercest of battles was waged between the men of the North and South until darkness brought it to a close. The Third Corps under Sickles was forced from the field across the Emmettsburg Road, but the onward march of the enemy was stopped by reinforcements sent from the Second and Fifth Corps. During the battle no advance was made by Hill or Ewell, and nothing done to aid the fierce and persistent efforts of the 17,000 men under Longstreet, in whose hands alone the fortunes of the Confederacy were allowed to rest. We owe to John Esten Cooke, in his Life of Lee, information of the fact that General Lee was sitting on a log on Seminary Ridge, near the centre of Hill's corps, watching the battle through his glasses; that he sent but one order, of an unknown purport; that having given the orders for battle, as was his custom he trusted to his lieutenants to execute them in their own way. If there was ever an occasion where, on the part of the commander of an army, there was need to do more than issue an order to begin a battle, it was here and now. The critics of Longstreet confine their charge to his slowness in beginning the battle, not to his manner of carrying it on. Not content with charging the loss of a battle to the chief of the First Corps for commencing it at too late an hour, on the 2d of July, the same writers assert, that, by disobedience of orders that required him to use the whole of his own corps and other troops assigned him on the 3d of July, again the opportunity of breaking through the centre of the Union line held by the Second Corps under Hancock, and the overthrow of the army was lost, the prestige of the Army of Northern Virginia lowered, and the field strewn with thousands of its bravest soldiers in vain.

It so happened that Lee's orders at Gettysburg were verbal, or, if in writing, have not been preserved. During the forenoon of the 3d, he went with Longstreet over the field, pointed out to him the direction of the attacking column, wisely consented, after learning of the conditions existing in front of Hood's and McLaws' divisions, occupying the extreme right, that they should remain on their present line,—the danger being great that his line of retreat would be seized in case of their removal to the left,—and then assigned to him parts of two divisions of Hill's corps, amounting with Pickett's division to 15,000 muskets, with which to attack and overthrow an army in a strong position. The Fifth corps was in line on Round Top in front of the two divisions of Longstreet, and just in rear the Sixth Corps, which had not been engaged. Any movement of these two divisions to the left for use as part of the assaulting column would have been instantly seen, and would have presented such an opportunity for a flank attack that no prudent commander would for a moment have offered to his opponent. In making these assertions in regard to these orders and intentions of General Lee, they are unconsciously laying the foundation for a just and severer criticism of his conduct of this battle than any one has ever presumed to make, and they cannot be accepted as true. It was promised, as on the day before, that Pickett should be supported by the whole army, and as on the day before no support was given. Not a regiment moved to within effective rifle distance of the enemy outside the devoted column of 15,000 men. For two days, Gettysburg presents the spectacle of two desperately fought and bloody battles by less than one third of the army on each occasion, the other two thirds looking on, for the conflict was visible from nearly every point on the Confederate lines. Does not all this present another question to solve, then, whether a corps commander was quick or slow? Was the commander-in-chief justified in assigning such a task to such a force?

I confess that for years I had been of the opinion that the fighting qualities of the Army of Northern Virginia were superior to those of the Army of the

Potomac. A few years ago, I expressed to a distinguished Confederate officer belonging to that army the opinion that Pickett's Charge would become historic as the most heroic effort made by any equal number of men during the war. Without replying yes or no, he at once said, "I was with Lee's army from the beginning and surrendered at Appomattox, and am free to say that I never saw anything that surpassed the charge made by Hancock and Humphreys at Fredericksburg." I was led by this remark to make anew the study of every battle, for the purpose of verifying or re-forming my opinion. The task was not long or difficult. I found that Lee in his first battle took 60,000 muskets across the Chickahominy, and for two days pressed his attack against the Fifth Corps with 17,300 men, which was reinforced with only one division of 8000 late on the second day; that just before dusk he sent an aide, from his position on the left with Jackson, to the commander on the right with the message "that all efforts have failed and if something cannot be done on the right the day is lost,"[6] and the day was barely saved with the loss of over 8000 men; that in three subsequent attacks all were repulsed and in a general battle at Malvern Hill he met with a disastrous defeat; that at the Second Manassas the victory was gained, not by superior fighting by his battalions, but for the reason that, while the army under Pope was pressing Jackson so strongly that he was sending for aid, Longstreet, whose whereabouts Pope knew nothing of, swept down with his 30,000 men in double lines on his left flank and drove him from the field; that after Antietam he retired into Virginia; of Fredericksburg nothing need be added to what has already been expressed; the lesson of Chancellorsville is not different from that of the Second Manassas, a line broken by a flank attack and a victory won over a disabled general. In all the hundreds of reports by Confederate officers of the various engagements, there is constant mention of the heroic fighting of the enemy, and never a suggestion of cowardly conduct, or abandoning a position except under circumstances such as would compel any troops to retire. In every instance of Confederate victory, it came about by the superior generalship on the part of the commander and the superior leadership of the divisions of the army.

Had General Lee, who had fought for two days with 60,000 or more men against 25,300 at Gaines' Mill, where every one of his 60,000 or more was on the firing-line and forced to their utmost exertion to win a dearly bought victory, any right to expect, a year later, to overthrow 80,000 with a column of 15,000 or 17,000? Had there been any occasion since where he had seen less heroism, less willingness to fight, less power of resistance by the men composing those parts of the Army of the Potomac over which he had gained victories? Was it not lack of judgment, the act of an over-excited mind, that sent Longstreet twice to perform an impossible task? There was nothing of generosity or magnanimity on the part of Lee when he said the loss of the battle "is all my fault," but a simple statement of a fact. By the winning of a series of victories over McClellan, Pope, Burnside, and Hooker, with a lesser army than theirs, there had grown up, gradually at first, a feeling of confidence and superiority, which, after Chancellorsville, reached a point where officers and men alike considered their army invincible. Lee shared with them this feeling and belief. He repeatedly said that with his army he felt that he could go anywhere. He wrote to Longstreet in 1863, when in front of Suffolk, that with his corps he was able to go anywhere. He assumed for his army the same superiority over its opponent that is by everybody admitted he had proved himself to possess over the four commanders of the Army of the Potomac he had successively defeated. It is clear that he had never analyzed his victories for the purpose of finding out the one sole fact to which the yielding up of four battlefields to him by the Federal army was due.

From Gaines' Mill to Gettysburg, the Confederate army had been divided into two corps or wings under Longstreet and Jackson with thirty to forty thousand under each. After the death of Jackson, it was organized into three corps with new commanders for the Second and Third. Gettysburg was the first battle to be fought under the new arrangement. The old arrangement, with two such men as Longstreet and Jackson competent to command large forces, was simpler and much the best. The weight and force of such numbers, accustomed to act together, with confidence in their chief, when thrown into battle, had been felt on more than one occasion, notably at Chancellorsville and Manassas. The machine that had worked so well for a year, at Gettysburg was out of joint, and little was done to put it into working order. Colonel William Allan, one of Lee's staff officers, in his article published in the third volume of the Society's series, on the Strategy of the Gettysburg Campaign, though claiming that the failure was primarily due to Longstreet for dilatory movements on the second day and failure in not using two of his battered divisions on the third, seems to have been fully conscious of Lee's inactivity, for he says "it will probably remain a question" how far he could have prevented the miscarriage. The more thoroughly the battle is studied, the stronger will be the conviction that the Confederate failure was not due in any way to delay, neglect of orders, the want of concerted action on the second day by the neglect of Ewell to attack the right when the guns opened on the left,—an attempted combination contrary to one of the established rules of war,—but to the fact that Lee gave to his army a task beyond its power to accomplish.

That the campaign was wrong in its conception and should not have been entered upon is now universally admitted. Its effect upon Southern sentiment is well put by Mr. Dargan, a doughty member of Congress from Mobile, in a letter to the Secretary of War, in which he says: "The disastrous movement of Lee into Pennsylvania and the fall of Vicksburg, the latter especially, will end in the ruin of the South without foreign aid in some shape. Mississippi is nearly subdued and Alabama is nearly exhausted. The failure of the Government to reinforce Vicksburg, but allowing the strength and flower of our army to go North, when there could be but one fate attending them, has so broken down the hopes of our people that even the little strength yet remaining can only be exerted in despair, and a slight change in the policy of Lincoln would end our revolution and hopes."[7]

What will be the final ranking of Lee, whatever followed, rather than Gettysburg, and what preceded it, will surely contribute most to its upbuilding and support. Though twice appointed commander-in-chief of the Confederate armies, his fame will ever rest upon what he did as the leader of the Army of Northern Virginia. He can never be placed in the ranks of those great captains who have affected the fortunes of nations, for good or ill, as commander of the national forces. In this respect be falls far below Washington and Grant. He was in close council with President Davis when the first Confederate war policy was adopted. Mr. Davis, in his address at the Memorial Meeting of the Army of Northern Virginia, after his death, declared Lee always agreed with him. In his printed address he put in italics the words, "*I repeat, we never disagreed.*" It well may be thought that these words cannot be considered as giving value to his eulogy. The first Confederate war policy was a defensive one, right in principle, but fatal in execution. On the 31st of December, 1861, the Confederate armies numbered 326,768, of which number only 258,688 were present.[8] At the time of establishing the first general policy the forces were much less. The aim was to guard every foot of their territory and prevent an invasion at any point. To effect this object the territory bordering on the Atlantic and Gulf was divided into eight military departments, each department subdivided into two or more districts. Troops were stationed along the coast from Cape Henry to Galveston, necessarily in small detachments. In October, 1861, there were present in Georgia 5497, at twenty-one different stations, the largest aggregation at Tybee Island numbering 1086 officers and men. There were fifteen positions along the coast of South Carolina and only 5341 soldiers to hold them. Practically the water-line of each State was guarded in the same way with a distribution of forces similar to those already mentioned. Early in 1862 there were about 17,000 troops in Florida, a State with little over one inhabitant to the square mile scattered through its pine barrens, the occupation of which by Union troops would have been of no value.

It was General Bragg, later derided by Southern writers as a mere drill-master, who first called attention of his Government to their weak and faulty strategy in a letter to the Secretary of War, advising the abandoning of all but a few posts along the coast, the whole of Florida and Texas, and the concentration of their forces.[9] Whether on this advice or by the sterner lesson that came with the fall of Fort Henry, Donelson, Roanoke Island, and Port Royal, the President, in his address on the 22d of February, on his inauguration as the first President of the Confederacy under what was called the permanent constitution, confessed that he had undertaken a task beyond his means to accomplish and promised a new policy better adapted to their resources. This was followed by the policy of concentration of the scattered forces into large armies which remained a constant feature throughout the war.

On the 2d of March, 1862, the President sent a telegram to Lee, saying, "I wish to see you here with the least delay." He was immediately appointed to the command of the Confederate armies to carry out the new policy, which he approved, as he had, also, the previous one, its opposite. It was a few days after the fall at Fort Donelson and Nashville that this appointment was made, and when it was known that an advance southward of the Western armies would soon begin. After the defeat of the Confederate army at Shiloh, it fell back to the entrenched position at Corinth, in front of which was gathered an immense army under Halleck, and at the same time General Butler was at Ship Island with an army of 12,000 men, or more, and Admiral Farragut with his powerful fleet was preparing to enter the Mississippi River. That the concentration of these two forces at opposite ends of the line was with the intention of taking New Orleans and controlling the great river was taken for granted. The question before the new commander-in-chief was from which force was the immediate and great danger to be apprehended. It was decided that New Orleans should be "defended from above," as the expression was in the orders from Richmond, to send the great guns, the fleet, the army, nearly everything gathered for defence of the city, up the river to Columbus and Corinth.[10] Halleck had not even commenced his march of thirty miles from the Tennessee River to Corinth, before the news was flashed to Richmond of the fall of their chief city. The attempt, five or six hundred miles up the river, to defend New Orleans, was a costly failure. A month and a few days later Lee assumed command of the Army of Northern Virginia and remained with it until the surrender at Appomattox. He supplemented the second general war policy, above referred to, with the principle of aggressive warfare which was congenial to his impulsive nature. In the short period of one year and seven days he fought six of the greatest battles of the war. In history there is no record that equals it. In this short time there had fallen, killed and wounded, of his men 82,208, not counting losses in skirmishes, minor engagements, and the hardships of forced marches and exposure, which would probably swell these figures to a full 100,000; the Union loss, figured in the same way, during the same period, was 74,720. If the people of the North were weak, volatile, lacking in purpose and resolution, he might well expect that, after such quick and powerful demonstrations, with trembling knees we would come suing for peace and ready to acknowledge the South their independence. On no other supposition were his methods justifiable. General Lee has been considered as a great judge of men from the correct estimate made by him of McClellan, Pope, Burnside, and Hooker, whose characteristics as soldiers were not difficult to read. His psychological powers or insight stopped at the individual, and did not enable him to penetrate to the mind and purpose of a people. The population of the Confederate States was little less than half that of the Northern States. If the resolution of the one was equal to that of the other, it would be easy to calculate the end of a war where the losses on each side in every contest were equal. To illustrate, if a manufacturer or merchant worth a million dollars should enter into a trade warfare with a competitor worth two millions, and so aggressively carry it on as to entail a loss to each of $250,000 a year, the result would be that at the end of four years one would be bankrupt and the other still rich. This was the kind of war inaugurated by General Lee, and followed, with the encouragement of the Government, by all their principal generals. On our side the war was necessarily offensive and, on the other, logically defensive. For nearly three years these parts were practically reversed. Of the seven great battles fought in the Eastern zone including the Wilderness, only one was fought by the Army of the Potomac offensively during an offensive campaign, and one, Antietam, to repel an invasion. The Wilderness was partly offensive on each side, the last battle of the kind begun by Lee. The logic of their methods of warfare had resulted so near a bankruptcy of men that henceforth Lee was compelled, against his instincts and nature, to resort to the defensive with the aid of breastworks. In Virginia, Lee is compared to Washington and placed on an equal pedestal. There is some but only slight grounds for such comparison. In character each was high and equally noble. Washington was gifted with a far higher and broader intelligence. If the art of war consists in using the forces of a nation in a way to secure the end for which it is waged, and not in a succession of great battles that tend to defeat it, then Washington, though commanding a much smaller army, as a soldier reaches a higher plane than Lee. With his broad intelligence and unrivalled judgment he looked at the war as a whole, estimated correctly all the advantages and disadvantages on either side, what would be the relative strength of forces, and adopted a method of warfare, generally defensive, but sometimes offensive when the chances were enough in his favor. In strategy he never made a mistake. He had courage to do and dare, and, what is more rare, the courage to refrain from doing and suffer criticism when doing would injure the cause in his keeping. He had a correct insight into the minds of his own people and that of the enemy, the strength of resolution of each to endure heavy burdens, looking forward with certainty to the time when the public sentiment of England, led by Chatham and Burke, would be ready to acknowledge the Colonies as an independent nation. With these views he carried on the war for seven years, all the way from Boston to Yorktown, on a generally defensive plan, the only one pointing to the final goal of independence.

I heard an ex-President of the United States a short time ago state from this platform that the offensive was the only true theory of war, whether a nation was defending its own rights or seeking to enforce its claims against another. He expressed his contempt for the defensive not only in words, but in tone of voice, with facial expressions that were unmistakable. He, too, if a general would be classed as a temperamental one. In the same way, in the olden days, thought Sempronius, Flaminius, and Terentius Varro, with the result that one was killed, the other two disgraced, and the army of each overthrown and scattered. So thought Davis, who sent into retirement his wisest general who thought differently. So thought Hood, who destroyed an army of 60,000 men in four or five months, illustrating his mental weakness and the folly of his method. Notwithstanding the eminent authority of an ex-President, it is more than possible, perhaps certain, that military men will continue to look upon war problems in the future as in the past, adopting one system or the other as all the circumstances surrounding each particular case may require.

In the fall of 1863, after retiring from Pennsylvania, General Lee attempted from his position south of the Rapidan, what Jackson accomplished a year earlier, to interpose his army between Meade and Washington, and was foiled in his enterprise. In November Meade made a counter move, what is known as the Mine Run campaign, but, finding the enemy strongly entrenched, thought it unwise to attack and retired to his camps. The two armies passed the winter on either side of the Rapidan River.

With the loss of nearly 30,000 men during the campaign in Pennsylvania and 40,000 in and about Vicksburg, the decisive defeat of Bragg at Chattanooga, the occupation of East Tennessee by a Union Army, with only a single line of railway remaining between Virginia and the Gulf States, the situation was such as to create alarm in the mind of the most hopeful. Mr. Davis sent a request to General Lee, General Johnston, and General Longstreet for suggestions or plans to restore the declining fortunes of the

State. General Johnston had nothing to offer, nor had General Lee, save as hereafter related. General Longstreet, then at Greenville with his corps, devised a plan which he submitted to Lee, who approved it, and urged strongly its adoption by the President.[11] In a few words the plan was to draw a force of 20,000 men from the coast under Beauregard to Abingdon, Virginia, and as soon as the roads were passable, cross the mountains into Kentucky, followed by Longstreet, the whole to march against the railway running south from Louisville, and when this should uncover General Johnston's front at Dalton, the latter to advance through Tennessee and Kentucky, the three armies to join somewhere, if they could, near the Ohio River. This plan has the appearance of being adventurous, complicated, and difficult of execution, without even the excuse or justification offered by Hood for his ill-starred venture in the fall of the same year,—the absence of a large army in his front,—and is referred to, as it confirms in a striking manner what has heretofore been said, that Lee never looked at the war in abroad, general way, his mind being absorbed upon a single campaign with slight reference to its bearings upon or relation to other operations. Assume for a moment that this campaign, which he so strongly approved, had been put in execution. If those columns had been given the right of way and met no opposition they could not have made half the distance to the Louisville railway before the middle of May, and would then be beyond recall, Lee would have been left in Virginia with two corps of about 40,000 men, and Richmond would have been at the mercy of Butler. Under such conditions, it is easy to see that he would have found an Appomattox somewhere many months before the real one was brought to his view. One may search the records, with greatest care, read all of Lee's reports, his voluminous correspondence with the President, the Secretary of War, Adjutant-General, governors of states and many officers, and he will find little, if anything, to disprove, and much to confirm the opinion of one of Virginia's brilliant writers, that, outside of the limits of the Army of Northern Virginia, Lee's influence with reference to the general affairs of the Confederacy was negative and accomplished absolutely nothing.[12] Neither the campaign suggested by Longstreet and approved by Lee, nor one of similar character devised by Davis and Bragg were put to the test of actual experience for the reason that General Johnston, who was to take the principal part in it, with better judgment and clearer vision foresaw the impossibility of success, the extent of the disaster likely to follow from failure, and refused his sanction to it. So after three years of offensive warfare the Confederacy returned again to the defensive, not by the wish of the Government, but as it would seem by compulsion. It was forced to adopt a sane policy by the refusal of their most far-sighted general to hasten its downfall by adopting the plan so urgently pressed upon him by

Mr. Davis. What would have been the result of the contest if such a policy had been adopted at an earlier date and reasonably adhered to will not be considered here.

On account of the disagreement between the President and General Johnston, Longstreet with his corps was ordered East the last of April, and again became a part of the Army of Northern Virginia. The Union armies in 1864 took up and maintained thereafter their logical position in the war, and forced the Confederates to adopt their logical position as well, though the impulsive temperament of Lee sought relief from the restraint that oppressed him by sending Early on his threatening raid against Washington, which resulted in the destruction of his army; and Davis, who for two months had nursed his wrath against General Johnston for not carrying out the plan which his genius had prepared, removed him and sent Hood and his army to meet their fate at Franklin and Nashville. Excepting these two episodes, in a general way it is true that the Northern armies dominated the military situation throughout 1864–5 and determined all the movements of the enemy's forces.

As from the signal station on Clark's Mountain the camps of the Army of the Potomac could be seen, the three corps of the army commenced their march for the fords of the Rapidan at midnight on the 3rd and 4th of May, the desire being to pass through the Wilderness before joining in battle with Lee's army. This was not to be. The arrival of the heads of columns at the fords was duly reported on the morning of the 4th, and Lee at once set the corps of Hill and Ewell in motion with the view of making an attack before the enemy could reach the open country near Spotsylvania Court House. Hill took the plankroad on the right and Ewell the turnpike about three miles to the north. Lee, riding with Hill's corps, ordered Ewell to keep the head of his column even with that of Hill, and not to bring on a general battle until the arrival of Longstreet, who would be nearly a day behind, with a longer march from about Gordonsville. As at Gettysburg, the battle was brought on contrary to orders, and was waged with great persistency during the 5th of May, and continued during the 6th, Longstreet having arrived in the morning. It is remarkable what independence of action the corps commanders of that army assumed throughout the war. During the last day of the battle at Manassas, General Lee, then being with Jackson, whose corps behind the railroad enbankment was so pressed that there was fear of his ability to hold his position, sent an order to Longstreet to send one of his divisions to support him. Longstreet, having his corps of 30,000 men nearly formed at right angles to the Groveton Pike, and being in a position to gain a more correct idea of what the situation required, completed his formation, neglected Lee's order, and moved down the pike with his whole force, struck the flank of the enemy and swept them from the entire front of Jackson and decided the action. Lee's staff officers, in their writings, make no mention here of his disobedience of orders when it resulted in victory, but complacently credit it to the masterly troop handling of their chief.

It is no part of my purpose to attempt to give the details of this wonderful and unprecedented campaign, which reflects so great credit upon the heroic army that endured its burdens. Upon it, more than any other part of his career, will rest the rank of General Lee as a commander. There has never been but one opinion as to this part of his military career. His quick detection of every movement by the enemy, his rapid sending of the whole or the necessary part of his army to meet it, have always commanded the admiration of all who have made a study of the campaign. It takes rank above the contemporaneous campaign of General Johnston chiefly by reason of the more aggressive character imparted to it by General Grant, who saw more clearly than Sherman the relation of public opinion at the North to the possible length of its duration, and the necessity of bringing it to a close before public sentiment should drop from its high resolve and unnerve the arm of the Government. If for three days, while the Army of the Potomac was crossing the James and moving to Petersburg, Lee was in doubt as to the intention of the enemy and his movements, he quickly recovered from an apparent fault and hesitation but suffered no loss thereby.

During nine months and a half Lee defended Richmond and Petersburg against every attempt to take it, amid difficulties sufficient to bring discouragement to a less heroic soul. To the indomitable will and resolution of Grant he opposed a will and resolution not less firm. During the fall and winter of '64 and '65, while the lines of the besieging army were being pushed to the right and left, it was met and opposed with a resourceful skill that exacted at times heavy penalties for successes gained. While this prolonged contest was going on there came nothing to cheer but much to dishearten the heroic defenders of the Confederate Capital. At not infrequent intervals they heard the salute of a hundred shotted guns that made known to them the fall of Atlanta; the defeat of Early at Winchester, Fisher Hill, and Cedar Creek; the failure of Hood at Franklin and the loss of his army at Nashville; and, before these echoes had died away, the fall of Savannah and the loss of Fort Fisher and Wilmington. In September the Army of the James had captured Fort Harrison and held a line six miles south of Richmond, extending from the James River east of the Derbytown road and then bending back until it again reached the river at Deep Bottom. The Army of the Potomac had gained control of the Weldon Railroad and extended its lines westward as far as Hatcher's Run. The Confederates had been compelled to extend, also, until their breastworks stretched from the Chickahominy to Gravelly Run, forty miles in extent, an unbroken line save where the James and the Appomattox flowed through them. Between the Alleghanies and the Mississippi there was no longer an army, and barely troops enough to furnish a skirmish line to oppose the forces that were being organized to sweep through the country with the coming of early spring. The Trans-Mississippi was now only a fallen limb from a decaying trunk, and to the appeals of President Davis for aid from that quarter Kirby Smith made no reply, well knowing that if he attempted to move his army to the East his men would desert him long before he could reach the western bank of the river. In January, Sherman started on his long march from Savannah to the North, and there were only the scattered remnants of defeated armies that could be gathered in his front for a feeble resistance. A little later, Sheridan with his ten thousand horsemen was on his way from the Valley to Petersburg, meeting with more obstacles to a rapid march from the elements than from the enemy, as he went from town to town, destroying Confederate property of every description—foundries, manufactories, workshops, depots of supplies, railroads, bridges and canals. Only one railroad, with rails worn nearly to the rotting sleepers on which they rested, was open for such service as it could render to bring supplies into the city of Richmond from the South. The last port had been closed and all chance of relief from abroad was at an end. The Confederacy was a beleaguered state, surrounded on every side, shut up within itself, dependent upon its own exhausted resources to sustain its future life. In the midst of this scene of desolation and despair the great army of Northern Virginia still threw its protecting arms about it, and nightly set its guards, ill-fed and thinly clad, through tangled swamps and over bleak and storm-swept hills around its beleagured Capital. At length, though too late, the Confederate Congress awoke to the weakness and inefficiency of their President and passed what was intended as a revolutionary measure, a bill giving to General Lee the absolute control of the war, but he accepted the position as coming from the President and not from the Congress. As the spring approached, each commander was filled with anxious fear,—Grant, lest the enemy should escape; Lee, lest he should not be able to move away. On the 25th of March, Lee, with his old aggressive spirit, made an attack on the right of the Petersburg lines, thinking he might loose the hold of the enemy on the city and thus assist his plans to retreat. His early success was soon ended, and, with 4000 fewer men to meet the impending conflict, he recalled his shattered columns back to their camps. Two days later, Grant sent out his orders for the commencement of his last campaign. On the 1st of April, Sheridan with his cavalry and the Fifth Corps struck and utterly routed Lee's isolated right wing at Five Forks, which was followed by the grand attack along the Petersburg lines at daylight on the morning of the 2d.

The Ninth Corps broke through near the Appomattox and the Sixth Corps west of the Jerusalem Plankroad, when, turning to the left, it swept the line of its defenders, in cooperation with the 24th Corps, as far as Hatcher's Run. During the night Richmond and Petersburg were evacuated, and Lee ordered the scattered fragments of his shattered army to unite at Amelia Court House, which was accomplished on the 5th near midday. Besides the killed and wounded Lee had thus far lost at least 12,000 prisoners and his army had been reduced from 60,000 to 40,000 in the last four days. The next day at Sailor's Creek, Ewell's command, the naval contingent, and the Second Corps were surrounded and 6000 of the 10,000 composing the three commands were captured; at the same time, and not far away to the right, Gordon's corps was attacked by General Humphreys at Perkinson's Mills, who took 13 battle-flags, 1700 prisoners and the larger part of the main trains of Lee's army. The total losses for the day were between 8000 and 10,000, not including the large number who had dropped from the ranks for different reasons on the march. Lee found on the morning of the 9th of April that the Army of the James was in his front, the Army of the Potomac ready to attack in his rear and flank, and, being in a position from which escape was impossible, terms for the surrender of the Army of Northern Virginia were entered into and the great war was ended.

There has been much written in high eulogy of General Lee in regard to his conduct and bearing during the trying period of the last few days of the Appomattox campaign. That there should have been much sympathy expressed for him by both officers and men is natural and in every way commendable. But the spirit of eulogy has at times taken so wild a flight as to lose all point and value by its extravagance and folly. General Richard Taylor, brother-in-law of Jefferson Davis, in his book published under the fantastic title of Destruction and Reconstruction, says that the dignity and grandeur of General Lee during the last scene of all at Appomattox made of General Grant a mere accessory or insignificant figure. In the same way the Russian officers spoke and wrote of another great historic event,—the meeting of Alexander and Napoleon on the raft at Tilsit. In their eyes the little Emperor was a mere accessory and insignificant figure in the presence of the majestic person of their Czar. To such absurdity of opinion and expression does an overwrought patriotic zeal lead ill-balanced and unreflecting minds. If there had been nothing more than a simple meeting of Grant and Lee at the McLean house and of Napoleon and Alexander on the raft at Tilsit to the physical eye, there would be much to relieve the extravagance of expression on the part of the perfervid Southron and the perfervid Russian. But to the eye of the mind those historic scenes take on a different aspect. History regards the pageantry as a mere accessory and the submission of the will of Alexander to Napoleon and of Lee to the generous terms of Grant as the essential point.

At Appomattox, without exultation at final victory over a fallen foe, with that subdued and almost solemn feeling that great men experience in the presence of the epochs of history which they have made, Grant dropped the rôle of the soldier and rose to the height of the great statesman, saw with clear prevision the nation again united in peace, looked upon the former enemies of the country as again his fellow-citizens and treated them as such. When his exultant and triumphant soldiers were preparing to fire a salute of a hundred guns over their victory, he bade them stop. Who else, save Lincoln, could have risen to the height of this great act and foreseen its significance? In the beginning of the war he electrified the North with the words, "No terms except an immediate and unconditional surrender can be accepted"; and at its close he surprised and cheered the South with his order "to let every man who claims a horse or mule take one, for they will be needed in cultivating their farms."

I do not think that General Lee appears in an attractive light during the days now in review. On the 6th of April he lost one half of his army with arms in their hands, and there remained only 7500 effective infantry according to his own statement.[13] There were, however, some 20,000 men who had thrown their muskets away, who were, of course, a burden rather than a help for future operations. General Ewell, a sturdy old fighter, said, after the capture of his corps at Sailor's Creek, that for every man that should be killed from that time some one would be responsible and that it would be but very little better than murder.[14] General Henry A. Wise, one of the extreme Southern men, went to General Lee that day and said to him in his impassioned way that it was his duty to surrender his army and that he would be personally responsible for every life that should thereafter be sacrificed. In the evening of the same day there was a meeting called of the principal officers of the army, and the unanimous opinion was that further resistance was not justifiable, and General Pendleton, the Chief of Artillery, was deputized to present to Lee the result of their deliberations. In accordance with the Confederate Articles of War each one of these officers had committed an offence punishable with death. General Lee replied to general Pendleton after he had made his report, "Oh, no, I trust it has not come to that"; and added, "General, we have yet too many bold men to think of laying down our arms. The enemy do not fight with spirit, while our boys do."[15] It is not easy to understand what could have been his state of mind when making such a statement. General Lee had seen personally but little of the fighting which had taken place during the campaign, and, if such a report had been made to him by those who did, the results, which were certainly known, ought to have been sufficient to have discredited them. He was well aware that on the 1st of April two divisions of the Fifth Corps assaulted the line of entrenchments held by his best troops, ran over them, captured half of his right wing and put the rest to flight. He knew, but did not see, that a division of the Sixth Corps broke through his lines at Petersburg, and, with the other divisions, aided by the Twenty-fourth Corps, swept westward to Hatcher's Run and took prisoners by thousands. Later in the same day he saw a part of the Twenty-fourth Corps assault Fort Gregg, an enclosed work with a deep ditch filled with water, saw the men move up with alacrity to its very edge and swarm around until they discovered an entrance over a disused breastwork wide enough for two or three to march abreast, from which they leaped inside and overpowered its garrison, leaving 715 of their comrades strewing the ground, dead and wounded. He came up to a hill overlooking Sailor's Creek just as two divisions of the Sixth Corps and the cavalry had routed the corps of Ewell and Anderson, and, as the sight burst upon his view, exclaimed, "My God! has the army dissolved?" Was it sights such as these and reports from others just as disastrous that justified the conclusion that the enemy did not fight with alacrity and our boys do? The statement was not true and there was no reason for making it. The unanimous opinion of all Federal officers was that the army had recovered its best form and fought with a valor never before excelled. It is not intended to intimate that General Lee intentionally would make a misstatement of an important fact, but simply to show that, under the pressure of adversity, he was in such a state of mind, when these words were uttered, that he did not fully weigh their meaning.

It is a singular coincidence that the very day General Pendleton had the interview referred to, General Grant was writing his first letter to Lee, giving him the same opinion that he had received from his own officers of the hopelessness of further resistance on the part of the Army of Northern Virginia, and asking for its surrender. There was in it, too, the same motive that had actuated the Confederate officers—a desire to avoid the useless sacrifice of more lives, as also the feeling that it would be easier for Lee to act on a suggestion thus made than for him to be the first to propose a surrender. However, the advice, coming from two such opposite sources, was disregarded, and in the early morning of the second day thereafter, Lee was urging his advance column under Gordon to force their way to Lynchburg. Gordon soon sent back word by Colonel Venable that he was confronted by infantry as well as cavalry, and that, unless heavily reinforced from Longstreet's corps, he could not break through the lines confronting him. Then it was that Lee saw the necessity of meeting General Grant. Three letters had previously passed between the two commanders in reference to the surrender of the Confederate army. After having received notice of the liberal terms offered, Lee, the day before, had written Grant that "*to be frank*, I do not think the emergency has arisen to call for the surrender of this Army." Lee now expressed his fears lest Grant should impose different terms from those offered the day before, which he rejected, since his army was at length surrounded and unable to escape. When in 1862 he was informed that General McClellan was removed from the command of the Army of the Potomac, he said, "I am sorry to part with General McClellan, for we have come to understand each other so well, I am afraid, if they continue to make these changes, they will find some one whom I don't understand." What he feared in 1862 came to pass and he found in General Grant the man he did not understand. The real terms granted on the 9th were in fact more liberal than those offered on the 8th, and were carried into effect with a delicate consideration not to wound the most sensitive nature. While discussing with his staff officers the subject of going to meet General Grant, Lee said to them, "Is it right to surrender this army? If it is right, then *I* will take *all* the responsibility." Looking at the situation as it then was, there does not appear to have been any question of right or wrong: it was simply a matter of necessity.

He went to meet General Grant, with a mental reservation as to the surrender of his army. Before sending his last letter, or immediately after, he gave orders for his army to be in readiness for immediate action, having resolved, that, in case Grant demanded the surrender of his army as prisoners of war, he would not consent to such terms, but make a desperate attempt to break through at all hazards and escape.[16] Is there an American citizen North or South who would not wish that his over-zealous eulogist had suppressed this fact? Does it not reveal something in General Lee's character that is not entirely pleasant to contemplate? So far as concerned the cause which he had thus far so valiantly upheld, there could be no difference upon what terms the surrender took place; the support of his army was lost to it whether they became prisoners of war unconditionally or on parole. Thus it became a mere matter of personal pride with him, for when his officers advised him to take the initiative and surrender, they expressed their readiness to accept the position as prisoners of war. General Lee's son, General Custis Lee, and 19,132 officers and men of the Army of Northern Virginia had been captured between the 29th of March and the 8th of April and were then being held as prisoners of war, and under the worst circumstances they would only be sharing the fate of their equally valiant comrades. Besides General Lee, throughout his career, had taken many prisoners and always on conditions to which he declared he would never submit. For a moment let us consider the situation in which he was placed, and what would have been the result if circumstances had been such as to lead him to carry out his resolution.

With only 7500 men with muskets in their hands, about 2000 cavalry and 20,000 unarmed, in the open country of the Appomattox Valley, General Lee was surrounded by at least 75,000 as good soldiers as he had ever commanded. In his front was the Army of the James, the Fifth Corps, and Sheridan with 10,000 cavalry, not less than 45,000 men. Fronting them was Gordon's corps, now reduced to 2000,[17] and a cavalry force a little less numerous. Two miles to the rear was Longstreet with 5000 muskets, against whom the Second and Sixth Corps were drawn up in battle line, with little space between, 30,000 men, eager and ready to spring forward the very moment the truce was ended. With two hundred cannon in place on the hills in front and every commanding position in the rear and on the flanks covering the narrow valley with their direct and converging fire, into which were crowded 20,000 defenceless men, the mind shudders to think of the scenes of horror that might have followed on a mere question of punctilio. The subject is too appalling in its possibilities for further speculation. It is fortunate for General Lee's reputation that he went to meet at the McLean house the one man he did not understand, and was relieved by him from attempting the rash resolution which he had formed, that would inevitably have resulted in the death, wounding, and capture of the remnant of that heroic army. It only remains to contrast this with the noble sentiment expressed by another great soldier of Virginia, General Johnston, who a few days later wrote to Mr. Davis: "I have surrendered this army to avoid the *crime* of waging a hopeless war."

NOTES

1. Jefferson Davis, *The Rise and Fall of the Confederate Government*, 2 vols. (New York: D. Appleton and Company, 1881), 1:437.

2. James Longstreet, *From Manassas to Appomattox: Memoirs of the Civil War in America* (Philadelphia: J. B. Lippincott Company, 1896), 134.

3. Longstreet, *Manassas to Appomattox*, 151.

4. All figures and number of troops cited in this article are taken from Thomas L. Livermore, *Numbers and Losses in the Civil War in America, 1861–65* (Boston: Houghton, Mifflin and Company, 1901).

5. Venable's letter quoted in Longstreet, *Manassas to Appomattox*, 380.

6. Longstreet, *Manassas to Appomattox*, 127.

7. U.S. War Department, *The War of the Rebellion: A Compilation of the Official Records of the Union and Confederate Armies*, 127 vols., index, and atlas (Washington DC: GPO, 1880–1901), ser. 4, vol. 2, pp. 664–65.

8. *Official Records*, ser. 4, vol. 1, p. 822.

9. *Official Records*, ser. 1, vol. 6, pp. 826–27.

10. *Official Records*, ser. 1, vol. 6, pp. 841, 878, 881.

11. Longstreet, *Manassas to Appomattox*.

12. Edward A. Pollard, *The Lost Cause: A New Southern History of the War of the Confederates* (New York: E. B. Treat & Company, 1866).

13. J. William Jones, comp., *Army of Northern Virginia Memorial Volume* (Richmond: J. W. Randolph & English, 1880), 47.

14. Ulysses S. Grant, *Personal Memoirs of U. S. Grant*, 2 vols. (New York: C. L. Webster & Company, 1885), 2:477–78.

15. Longstreet, *Manassas to Appomattox*, 620–21.

16. Jones, *Army of Northern Virginia*, 47.

17. Armistead Lindsay Long, *Memoirs of Robert E. Lee* (New York: J. M. Stoddart & Company, 1886), 420.

The Sword of Robert E. Lee

DOUGLAS SOUTHALL FREEMAN

Amid the deep shadows of some of the old tombs in European cathedrals the observant traveller occasionally sees a sword that bears the marks of actual combat. Hacks and gaps there still remain, not made, like Falstaff's, to adorn a tale of pretended valor, but won in war when furious blade met challenging steel. No scratch was on the sword that General Lee laid away that April day in Richmond on his return from Appomattox. His weapon had never been raised except in salute. Rarely had it been even drawn from its scabbard. Yet it was the symbol of a four-year war, the symbol of an army and of a cause. Where it had been, the red banners of the South had flown. About it all the battles of the Army of Northern Virginia had surged. As he puts it down, to wear it no more, the time has come, not to fix his final place as a soldier, but to give an accounting of his service to the state in whose behalf alone, as he had written on another April day, back in 1861, he would ever have drawn his blade in fratricidal strife.

Had his sense of duty held him to the Union, as it held Winfield Scott and George H. Thomas, how much easier his course would have been! Never, then, after the first mobilization, would he have lacked for troops or been compelled to count the cost of any move. He would not have agonized over men who shivered in their nakedness or dyed the road with shoeless, bleeding feet. Well clad they would have been, and well fed, too. They would not have been brought down to the uncertain ration of a pint of meal and a quarter of a pound of Nassau bacon. The superior artillery would have been his, not his adversary's. On his order new locomotives and stout cars would have rolled to the front, swiftly to carry his army where the feeble engines and the groaning trains of the Confederacy could not deliver men. He would have enjoyed the command of the sea; so that he could have advanced his base a hundred miles, or two hundred, without the anguish of a single, choking march. If one jaded horse succumbed on a raid, the teeming prairies would have supplied two. His simplicity, his tact, his ability, and his self-abnegation would have won the confidence of Lincoln that McClellan lost and neither Pope, Burnside, nor Hooker ever possessed. He would, in all human probability, have won the war, and now he would be preparing to ride up Pennsylvania Avenue, as was Grant, at the head of a victorious army, on his way to the White House.

But, after the manner of the Lees, he had held unhesitatingly to the older allegiance, and had found it the way of difficulty. Always the odds had been against him, three to two in this campaign, two to one in that. Not once, in a major engagement, had he met the Federals on even terms; not once, after a victory, had his army been strong enough to follow it up. To extemporize when time was against him, to improvise when supplies failed him, to reorganize when death claimed his best lieutenants—that had been his constant lot. From the moment he undertook to mobilize Virginia until the last volley rolled across the red hills of Appomattox, there had been no single day when he had enjoyed an advantage he had not won with the blood of men he could not replace. His guns had been as much outranged as his men had been outnumbered. He had marched as often to find food as to confound his foe. His transportation had progressively declined as his dependence upon it had increased. The revolutionary government that he espoused in 1861 had been created as a protest against an alleged violation of the rights of the states, and it made those rights its fetish. When it required an executive dictatorship to live, it chose to die by constitutionalism. Fighting in the apex of a triangle, one side of which was constantly exposed to naval attack by an enemy that had controlled the waterways, he had been forced from the first to accept a dispersion of forces that weakened his front without protecting his communications. Always, within this exposed territory, his prime mission had been that of defending a capital close to the frontier. With poverty he had faced abundance; with individualism his people had opposed nationalism.

Desperate as his country's disadvantage had been, it had been darkened by mistakes, financial, political, and military. Of some of these he had not been cognizant, and of others he had not spoken because they lay beyond a line his sense of a soldier's duty forbade his passing. Against other errors he had protested to no purpose. From the first shot at Sumter he had realized that the South could only hope to win its independence by exerting itself to the utmost; yet he had not been able to arouse the people from the overconfidence born at Bull Run. Vainly he had pleaded for the strict enforcement of the conscription laws, exempting no able-bodied man. Times unnumbered he had pointed out that concentration could only be met by like concentration, and that the less important points must be exposed that the more important might be saved. On the strategy of particular campaigns he had been heard and heeded often; on the larger strategy of full preparation, his influence had not been great, except as respected the first conscription act. Regarding the commissary he might as well not have spoken at all, because Mr. Davis held to Northrop until it was too late to save the army from the despair that hunger always breeds.

Lee had himself made mistakes. Perhaps no one could have saved Western Virginia in 1861, but he had failed to recover it. With it the Confederacy had lost the shortest road to the Union railway communications between East and West. In his operations on that front and during the Seven Days, he had demanded professional efficiency of an amateur staff and had essayed a strategy his subordinates had been incapable of executing tactically. After Second Manassas he had overestimated the endurance of his men, and in Maryland he had miscalculated the time required for the reduction of Harpers Ferry. Longstreet had been permitted to idle away in front of Suffolk the days that might have been spent in bringing his two divisions back to Chancellorsville to crush the baffled Hooker. In reorganizing the army after the death of Jackson, Lee had erred in giving corps command to Ewell. Apart from the blunders of that officer and the sulking of Longstreet at Gettysburg, he had lost the Pennsylvania campaign because his confidence in his troops had led him to assume the offensive in the enemy's country before his remodelled machine had been adjusted to his direction. At Rappahannock Bridge he had misread the movements of the Federals, and in the Wilderness, on the night of May 5–6, 1864, he had left Wilcox and Heth in a position too exposed for their weary divisions to hold. Wrongly he had acquiesced in the occupation of the Bloody Angle at Spotsylvania. Incautiously, that blusterous 11th of May he had withdrawn his artillery from Johnson's position. The detachment of Hampton and of Early, however necessary, had crippled him in coping with Grant when the Army of the Potomac crossed the James. He had strongly underestimated Sheridan's strength in the Shenandoah Valley, and he had failed to escape from Petersburg. Until the final retreat, none of these errors or failures, unless it was that of invading Pennsylvania so soon after the reorganization of the army, affected the outcome of the war, but together they exacted of the South some of its bravest blood.

Deeper still had been the defect of Lee's excessive amiability. When every hour of an uneven struggle had called for stern decision, he had kept all his contention for the field of battle. The action opened, he was calm but terse and pugnacious; the fighting ended, he conceded too much in kind words or kinder silence to the excuses of commanders and to the arguments of politicians. Humble in spirit, he had sometimes submitted to mental bullying. Capable always of devising the best plan, he had, on occasion, been compelled by the blundering of others to accept the second best. He had not always been able to control men of contrary mind. His consideration for others, the virtue of the gentleman, had been his vice as a soldier.

Perhaps to this defect may be added a mistaken theory of the function of the high command. As he explained to Scheibert, he believed that the general-in-chief should strive to bring his troops together at the right time and place and that he should leave combat to the generals of brigade and division. To this theory, which he had learned from Scott, Lee steadfastly held from his opening campaign through the battle of the Wilderness. It was for this reason, almost as much as because of his consideration for the feelings of another, that he deferred to Longstreet at Second Manassas and did not himself direct the attacks of the Confederate right on July 2 and 3 at Gettysburg. Who may say whether, when his campaigns are viewed as a whole, adherence to this theory of his function cost the army more than it won for the South? If this policy failed with Longstreet, it was gloriously successful with Jackson. If the failure at Gettysburg was partly chargeable to it, the victory at Chancellorsville was in large measure the result of its application. Not properly applicable to a small army or in an open country, this theory of command may have justified itself when Lee's troops were too numerous to be directed by one man in the tangled terrain where Lee usually fought. Once adopted where woods obscured operations, Lee's method could not easily be recast for employment in the fields of Pennsylvania.

When Lee's inordinate consideration for his subordinates is given its gloomiest appraisal, when his theory of command is disputed, when his mistakes are written red, when the remorseless audit of history discounts the odds he faced in men and resources, and when the court of time writes up the advantage he enjoyed in fighting on inner lines in his own country, the balance to the credit of his generalship is clear and absolute.

In three fast-moving months he mobilized Virginia and so secured her defense that the war had been in progress a year before the Unionists were within fifty miles of Richmond. Finding the Federals, when he took command of the Army of Northern Virginia on June 1, 1862, almost under the shadow of the city's steeples, he saved the capital from almost certain capture and the Confederate cause from probable collapse. He repulsed four major offensives against Richmond and by his invasion of Pennsylvania he delayed the fifth for ten months. Ere the Federals were back on the Richmond line again—two years to the day from the time he had succeeded Johnston—Lee had fought ten major battles: Gaines's Mill, Frayser's Farm, Malvern

Hill, Second Manassas, Sharpsburg, Fredericksburg, Chancellorsville, Gettysburg, the Wilderness, and Spotsylvania. Six of these he had indisputably won. At Frayser's Farm he had gained the field but had not enveloped the enemy as he had planned. Success had not been his at Malvern Hill and at Sharpsburg, but only at Gettysburg had he met with definite defeat, and even there he clouded the title of his adversary to a clear-cut victory.[1] During the twenty-four months when he had been free to employ open manœuver, a period that had ended with Cold Harbor, he had sustained approximately 103,000 casualties and had inflicted 145,000. Holding, as he usually had, to the offensive, his combat losses had been greater in proportion to his numbers than those of the Federals, but he had demonstrated how strategy may increase an opponent's casualties, for his losses included only 16,000 prisoners, whereas he had taken 38,000.[2] Chained at length to the Richmond defenses, he had saved the capital from capture for ten months. All this he had done in the face of repeated defeats for the Southern troops in nearly every other part of the Confederacy. In explanation of the inability of the South to capitalize its successes, one British visitor quoted Lee as saying: "The more [the Confederates] followed up the victory against one portion of the enemy's line the more did they lay themselves open to be surrounded by the remainder of the enemy." Lee "likened the operation to a man breasting a wave of sea, who, as rapidly as he clears a way before him, is enveloped by the very water he has displaced." These difficulties of the South would have been even worse had not the Army of Northern Virginia occupied so much of the thought and armed strength of the North. Lee is to be judged, in fact, not merely by what he accomplished with his own troops but by what he prevented the hosts of the Union from doing sooner elsewhere.[3]

The accurate reasoning of a trained and precise mind is the prime explanation of all these achievements. Lee was preeminently a strategist, and a strategist because he was a sound military logician. It is well enough to speak of his splendid presence on the field of battle, his poise, his cheer, and his manner with his men, but essentially he was an intellect, with a developed aptitude for the difficult synthesis of war. The incidental never obscured the fundamental. The trivial never distracted. He had the ability—who can say how or why?—to visualize his fundamental problem as though it had been worked out in a model and set before his eyes. In Richmond, during May, 1862, to cite but one instance, he saw clearly where others saw but dimly, if at all, that Jackson's little army in the Valley was the pawn with which to save the castle of Richmond.

Once his problem was thus made graphic, he projected himself mentally across the lines to the position of his adversary. What was the logical thing—

not the desirable thing from the Confederate point of view—for his opponent to do? Assuming that the Federals had intelligent leadership, he said, "It is proper for us to expect [the enemy] to do what he ought to do."[4] After he had studied the probabilities, he would turn to his intelligence reports. Prisoners' statements, captured correspondence, newspapers, information from his spies, dispatches from the cavalry outposts—all these he studied carefully, and often at first hand. Every stir of his enemy along the line he canvassed both for its direct meaning and for its relation to other movements.

In assembling this information he was not more adept than many another capable general, and in studying it he was not more diligent, but in interpreting it he excelled. Always critical of the news that came from spies, few of whom he trusted, he was cautious in accepting newspaper reports until he learned which correspondents were close-mouthed or ill-informed and which were reckless or well-furnished with fact. When he discovered that the representative of *The Philadelphia Inquirer,* for example, knew what he reported and reported what he knew, he attached high importance to his statements. A credulous outpost commander received scant attention when he forwarded countryside rumor; but Stuart's "sixth sense" Lee soon learned to appreciate, and when that tireless officer affirmed that the enemy was marching toward an objective he named, Lee rarely questioned it. The infantry were apt to move quickly in the hoof-prints made by Stuart's returning courier. If Lee's strategy was built, in large part, on his interpretation of his intelligence reports, that interpretation was facilitated more by Stuart and Stuart's scouts than by anything else.

Lee did not rely so much as has been supposed upon his knowledge of his adversaries. He knew that McClellan would be meticulous in preparation, and that Meade, making few mistakes himself, would be quick to take advantage of those of which he might be guilty. But these were the only Federal generals-in-chief with whom he had been closely associated before the war. The others, save Grant, were in command for periods so brief that he scarcely knew them before they were gone. Grant's bludgeoning tactics and flank shifts he quickly fathomed, but he was progressively less able to combat them as his own strength declined.

Whether it was the cooking of rations in the Federal camps, coupled with verified troop movements on the Baltimore and Ohio; whether it was the ascent of transports on the James and a knowledge that McClellan would not renew his attack on Richmond until he felt himself strong enough to sustain the offensive; whether it was the gabble of deserters and a careful report of what Stuart himself had seen of dust clouds and covered wagons—whatever the information on which Lee acted, it was almost always cumulative. In nothing was he more successful, as an analyst of intelligence reports, than in weighing probabilities, discarding the irrelevant, and adding bit by bit to the first essential fact until his conclusion was sure. The movement from the Wilderness to Spotsylvania was perhaps the most dramatic example of this method, but it was only one of many where Lee built up his strategy from information steadily accumulated and critically examined.

Having decided what the enemy most reasonably would attempt, Lee's strategy was postulated, in most instances, on a speedy offensive. "We can only act upon probabilities," he said, "and endeavor to avoid greater evils,"[5] but he voiced his theory of war even more fully when he wrote, ". . . we must decide between the positive loss of inactivity and the risk of action."[6] His larger strategy, from the very nature of the war, was offensive-defensive, but his policy was to seize the initiative wherever practicable and to force his adversary to adapt his plans thereto. If a "fog of war" was to exist, he chose to create it and to leave his opponent to fathom it or to dissipate it.

Once he determined upon an offensive, Lee took unbounded pains to execute it from the most favorable position he could occupy. As far as the records show, he never read Bourcet, but no soldier more fully exemplified what that master taught of the importance of position. The student can well picture Lee in his tent, his map spread on his table before him, tracing every road, studying the location of every town and hamlet in relation to every other and choosing at last the line of march that would facilitate the initial offensive and prepare the way for another. A monograph of high military value might be based entirely on his use of the roads of Piedmont Virginia and the gaps of the Blue Ridge, now to further his own strategic plan, now to block that of the enemy. All this might be termed the "grand strategy of position." Of his great aptitude for reconnaissance and of the wise strategic employment, in combat, of ground that had been previously selected, or occupied from necessity, enough has already been said in comment on particular campaigns. Lee's career does not prove that a soldier must be a great military engineer to be a great strategist, but it does demonstrate that if a strategist is an engineer as well he is doubly advantaged.

If Lee on occasion seemed "slow" to his restless and nervous subordinates, it was because some unvoiced doubt as to the enemy's plan or his own best position still vexed his mind. For when his military judgment was convinced, he begrudged every lost hour. Herein was displayed the fourth quality that distinguished his strategy, namely, the precision of his troop movements, the precision, let it be emphasized, and not the speed nor always the promptness of the march. The army as a whole, under Lee's direction, could never cover as much ground in a given time as the Second Corps under Jackson or under Ewell. It was very rarely that the whole force completed, under pressure, what "Old Jack" would have regarded as an average day's march. Usually Lee had to ride with Longstreet to accomplish even as much as was credited to the slow-moving commander of the First Corps. Lee, however, could calculate with surprising accuracy the hours that would be required to bring his troops to a given position. This was true, also, of the various units in a converging movement unless the units were Longstreet's and were not operating under Lee's own eye. After the Seven Days' campaign had acquainted him with his men and their leaders, Lee made only three serious mistakes in logistics. One of these was in the time required to occupy Harpers Ferry and to reconcentrate the army at Sharpsburg. The next was in calculating when the First Corps would arrive at Gettysburg, and the third was in estimating the hour at which that same corps would overtake A. P. Hill in the Wilderness. In two of these three instances, Lee based his advance on Longstreet's assurances, which were not fulfilled. Against these three cases of the failure of Lee's logistics are to be set his transfer of the Army of Northern Virginia to meet Pope; the movement down the Rappahannock to confront Burnside at Fredericksburg; the quick and sure detachment of Anderson and then of Jackson at Chancellorsville; the convergence of Hill's and of Ewell's corps at Gettysburg; the march from the Wilderness to Spotsylvania; the shift to the North Anna, and thence to the Totopotomoy and to Cold Harbor, and the careful balancing of force north and south of the James during the operations against Petersburg—the list is almost that of his battles. Had his mastery of this difficult branch of the art of war been his only claim to distinction as a soldier, it would of itself justify the closest scrutiny of his campaigns by those who would excel in strategy.

His patient synthesis of military intelligence, his understanding employment of the offensive, his sense of position and his logistics were supplemented in the making of his strategy by his audacity. Superficial critics, puzzled by his success and unwilling to examine the reasons for it, have sometimes assumed that he frequently defied the rules of war, yet rarely sustained disaster in doing so because he was confronted by mediocrity. Without raising the disputable question of the capacity of certain of his opponents, it may be said that respect for the strength of his adversaries, rather than contempt for their abilities, made him daring. Necessity, not choice, explains this quality. More than once, in these pages, certain of his movements have been explained with the statement that a desperate cause demanded desperate risks. That might well be written on the title-page of his military biography, for nothing more surely explains Lee, the commander. Yet if "daring" is an adjective that has to be applied to him again and again, "reckless" is not. Always in his strategy, daring was measured in terms of probable success, measured coldly, measured carefully. If the reward did not seem worth the risk, nothing could move him—except the knowledge that he had no alternative. In detaching Jackson for the march against Pope's communications, and in dividing his forces at Chancellorsville, examination of the circumstances will show that daring was prudence. In ordering Pickett's charge at Gettysburg, he felt that he had a fair chance of success if he attacked, and ran worse risks if he did not. The same thing may be said of the assault on Fort Stedman. From the Seven Days to Gettysburg, his daring increased, to be sure, as well it might, with his army performing every task he set before it; but the period after Gettysburg affords proof, almost incontrovertible, that he never permitted his daring to become recklessness. Throughout the spring and early summer of 1864, he felt, as he said on the North Anna, that he must "strike a blow"; but each time, save on May 5–6, his judgment vetoed what his impulse prompted.

These five qualities, then, gave eminence to his strategy—his interpretation of military intelligence, his wise devotion to the offensive, his careful choice of position, the exactness of his logistics, and his well-considered daring. Midway between strategy and tactics stood four other qualities of generalship that no student of war can disdain. The first was his sharpened sense of the power of resistance and of attack of a given body of men; the second was his ability to effect adequate concentration at the point of attack, even when his force was inferior; the third was his careful choice of commanders and of troops for specific duties; the fourth was his employment of field fortification.

Once he learned the fighting power of his army, he always disposed it economically for defense, choosing his position and fortifying it with the utmost care, so as to maintain adequate reserves—witness Fredericksburg. Only when his line was extended by the superior force of the enemy, as at Sharpsburg and after the Wilderness, did he employ his whole army as a frontline defense. In receiving attack, he seemed to be testing, almost with some instrument of precision, the resistance of every part of his line, and if he found it weakening, he was instant with his reserves. Over and again, in the account of some critical turn of action, it is stated that the reserves came up—rather accidentally than opportunely—and restored the front. Behind this, almost always, was the most careful planning by Lee. On the offensive it was different. "It is only by the concentration of our troops," he said in November, 1863, "that we can hope to win any decisive advantage."[7] He was writing then of the general strategy of the South, but he applied the same principle to every offensive. At Gaines's Mill and at Malvern Hill he early learned the wastefulness of isolated attacks, and thereafter, confident of the *élan* of his troops, it was his custom to hurl forward in his assaults every man he could muster, on the principle that if enough weight were thrown against the enemy, there would be no need of reserves. The final attack at Second Manassas and the operations of May 3 at Chancellorsville illustrate this. Only when he was doubtful of the success of an assault, as on the third day at Gettysburg, did he deliberately maintain a reserve. In partial attacks he somehow learned precisely what number of men would be required, with such artillery preparation as he could make, and he rarely failed until the odds against him became overwhelming.

For swift marches and for desperate flank movements, Lee relied on the Second Corps as long as Jackson lived; to receive the attack of the enemy he felt he could count equally on the First. Within the corps he came to know the distinctive qualities of the different divisions, and even among the divisions he graded the brigades. He was guided less in this, perhaps, by the prowess of the men than by the skill and resourcefulness of the different general officers. If danger developed unexpectedly in some quarter, his first question usually was, "Who is in command there?"[8] and he shaped his course according to his knowledge of the type of leadership he could anticipate.

Whether that leadership was good or bad, Lee gradually developed fortifications to support it. The earthworks he threw up in South Carolina were to protect the railroad he had to employ in bringing up his army. Those built around Richmond, in June, 1862, were designed in part to protect the approaches from siege tactics and in part to permit of a heavy concentration north of the Chickahominy. The works were too light to withstand the continued hammering of siege guns, but, quickly constructed, they served admirably to cover his men and to discourage assault. They thus were midway between permanent fortifications of the old type and the field fortifications he subsequently employed. The same might be said of the works he constructed at Fredericksburg. His digging of trenches in the open field, while actively manœuvering, began with the first stage of the Chancellorsville campaign and was expanded at Mine Run. After May, 1864, when increasing odds forced him unwillingly to the defensive, he made the construction of field fortifications a routine of operations. The trenches, well laid, well sighted, and supplied where possible with abatis, served both a strategical and tactical object. They were strategical in that they made it possible for him to detach troops for manœuver; they were tactical in that they enable him successfully to resist a superior force with a steadily diminishing army. General Sir Frederick Maurice has held this to be Lee's major contribution to the art of war.

As a tactician, Lee exhibited at the beginning of hostilities the weaknesses that might be expected of one who had been a staff officer for the greater part of his military career. Until he lost many of his most capable officers he held strictly to his theory of the function of the high command—that of bringing the troops together in necessary numbers at the proper time and place. Yet he continued to learn the military art as the war progressed, and of nothing did he learn more than of tactics. He overcame his lack of skill in the employment of his cavalry. In the end he was deterred from elaborate tactical methods only because, as he confided to Hill in their conversation at Snell's Bridge,[9] he did not believe the brigade commanders could execute them. He was often desirous of delivering an attack perpendicular to the line of the enemy and of sweeping down the front. This was his plan for the Confederate right on the second day at Gettysburg, and it was often suggested to his mind thereafter, but it was never successfully executed on a large scale. His subordinates could not get their troops in position for such a manœuver. Almost invariably the attack became frontal.

Predominant as was strategy in the generalship of Lee from the outset, and noteworthy as was his later tactical handling of his troops on the field of battle, it was not to these qualities alone that he owed the record he closed that day when he unbelted his sword after Appomattox. It had been as difficult to administer the army as to use it successfully in combat. Never equipped adequately, or consistently well-fed after the early autumn of 1862, the Army of Northern Virginia had few easy marches or ready victories. Lee had to demand of his inferior forces—as he always affirmed the administration had to exact of the entire population—the absolute best they could give him. The army's hard-won battles left its ranks depleted, its command shattered by death or wounds, its personnel exhausted, its horses scarcely able to walk, its transportation broken down, its ammunition and its commissary low. That was why its victories could not be pressed. Earnestly, almost stubbornly, he had to assert, "The lives of our soldiers are too precious to be sacrificed in the attainment of successes that inflict no loss upon the enemy beyond the actual loss in battle."[10]

On him fell the burden of an endless reorganization that is as much a part of his biography as it is of his title to fame. Out of the wreckage of battle, time after time, he contrived to build a better machine. He did not work by any set formula in administering the army, but by the most painstaking attention to the most minute details. Hungry men had to be restored by better rations: if the commissary could not provide them, he would seek them by raids or by purchases in the surrounding country, even if he had to send out details to thresh wheat and to grind it at the country mills. Rest was imperative: he would choose a strategically sound position, where the troops could have repose without uncovering the approaches to Richmond. To select men to succeed the general officers who fell in action, he would confer with those who knew the colonels of the regiments and he would examine each officer's record for diligence, for capacity, and for sobriety. Had the men worn out more shoes than they had been able to capture from the enemy? Then he would present their plight to the administration and would continue writing till the footgear was forthcoming, or else he would organize his own cobblers, save and tan the skins of the animals the commissaries had slaughtered, and out of them would seek to make shoes that would keep his men, at least, from having to march barefooted over snowy roads. If state pride demanded that troops from the same area be brigaded together and commanded by a "native son," he might disapprove the policy, but he would shift regiments and weigh capabilities and balance fighting strength until the most grumbling congressman and the most jealous governor were satisfied. The very soap his dirty men required in the muck of the Petersburg trenches was the subject of a patient letter to the President. His mobilization of Virginia, though it was among his most remarkable achievements and afforded sure evidence of his rating as an administrator, was equaled by the speed and success of his reorganization of the army after the Seven Days, after Sharpsburg, and after Gettysburg.

One aspect of his skill in administration deserves separate treatment as a major reason for his long-continued resistance. That was his almost uniform success in dealing with the civil government, a sometimes difficult business that every military commander must learn. Although the front of his army may be where the general-in-chief can direct every move, its rear stretches back far beyond the most remote bureau of the War Department. Few generals are ever much stronger than their communications with the authorities that sustain them, and few are greater, in the long view, than the confidence they beget. Often and tragically, both North and South illustrated this maxim during the War between the States. It was by the good fortune of former association that Lee had the esteem of President Davis; it was by merit that he preserved that good opinion, by merit plus tact and candor and care. During the war, General Lee received a few sharp messages from Mr. Davis, and he must have known him to be nervous, sensitive, and jealous of his prerogatives; yet it cannot be said that Lee found Davis a difficult man with whom to deal. This was because Lee dominated the mind of his superior, yet applied literally and loyally his conviction that the President was the commander-in-chief and that the military arm was subordinate to the civil. He reported as regularly to the President as Stuart or Jackson, those model lieutenants, reported to him. Reticent toward his own staff about military matters, he rarely made a move without explaining his full purpose to the President in advance. In judgment he always deferred to Mr. Davis. The detachment of troops frequently diminished the army's power of resistance, and sometimes threatened its very life, but Lee usually closed his reasoned protest with the statement that if the executive thought it necessary to reduce the forces under his command, he would of course acquiesce. Although he was entrusted with the defense of the capital of the Confederacy, and had constantly to seek replacements, Lee never put the needs of his army above those of the Confederacy. Steadfastly he worked on the principle he thus stated; "If it is left to the decision of each general whether he will spare any troops when they are needed elsewhere, our armies will be scattered instead of concentrated, and we will be at the mercy of the enemy at all points."[11] He never vexed a troubled superior by magnifying his difficulties. If, to the unsympathetic eye, there frequently is a suggestion of the courtier in the tone of Lee's letters to the President, it was because of Lee's respect for constituted authority.

Dealing with four Secretaries of War in order—Walker, Benjamin, Seddon, and Breckinridge—Lee encountered little or no friction. Benjamin was reputed to be the most exacting of them all in that he was charged with desiring to dictate the strategy as well as to administer the department. Johnston's friends have said if that officer had not forced the issue with Benjamin, no other general in the field would have been free to command his army. Lee had no occasion to fear this would be so. His relations with Benjamin, though never close, were consistently pleasant. To each of the secretaries Lee reported and before each of them he laid his difficulties. Usually he was candid with them as to his plans, so much so, indeed, that often if a letter were not addressed to the "Hon. Secretary of War," one would think it were intended for the confidence of the President. Only when important moves were afoot and secrecy was imperative was Lee ever restrained in addressing the war office.

Increasingly as the emergencies demanded, Lee addressed directly the administrative heads of the bureaus of the War Department, without reference to the secretary, but in so doing he escaped clashes with their superior. Colonel Northrop, of course, was a thorn in his flesh. In correspondence with him Lee was always courteous and always restrained. In a long controversy over the impressment of food from farmers,[12] Lee simply held his ground in the face of all the arguments of Colonel Northrop. Sometimes, when the commissary general insisted that rations be reduced, Lee ignored the suggestion and, from available supplies, fed his men what he considered necessary to restore their vitality or to maintain their health. This provoked complaining endorsements by Northrop on papers meant for the President's eye, but it brought Lee no rebuke from Mr. Davis. Northrop was Lee's one outspoken critic in the administration. Most of the others were his open admirers.

With Congress, Lee had little directly to do. Perhaps it was fortunately so. He often captivated politicians, and at one time, it will be remembered, he virtually acted for the administration in dealing with that difficult and positive individual, Governor Zebulon Vance of North Carolina; but Lee had seen too much of Congress in Washington to cherish any illusions regarding it in Richmond. He had, in fact, an ineradicable distrust of politicians. Although he rarely broke the bounds of his self-imposed restraint, he was convinced that Congress was more interested in the exemptions than in the inclusions of the conscript laws. In the winter of 1864–65, he thought the lawmakers were playing politics when the existence of the Confederacy depended upon the enlistment of every able-bodied man. His outburst in his conversation with Custis Lee, after his conference with the Virginia delegation in Congress, revealed many things that he had long felt but had not said.

Next in order, among the reasons for Lee's success as a soldier, is probably to be ranked his ability to make the best both of the excellencies and of the limitations of his subordinate officers. Thanks to the President's understanding of the need of professional training for command, and thanks, also, to the wisdom of his own early selections, Lee had some of the best graduates of West Point among his officers. He saw to it that such men held the posts of largest responsibility. At one period of his warring, a council of his corps and divisional commanders would almost have been a reunion of alumni of the Military Academy. Yet these officers were not all of them outstanding in ability, nor were they sufficient in number to command the divisions, much less the brigades. Even when he availed himself of the well-schooled former students of the Virginia Military Institute, and of like schools in other states, he had to entrust the lives of many thousands of his men to those who had received no advanced training in arms prior to 1861. Along with the individual jealousies, ambitions, and eccentricities that have to be encountered in every army, he had to cope with political generals and with those who had a measure of class antagonism to the professional soldier. Perhaps Lee's most difficult labor was that of taking a miscellaneous group of Southern individualists, ranging in capacity from dullness to genius, and of welding them into an efficient instrument of command.

No commander ever put a higher valuation on the innate qualities of leadership. "It is," he wrote, "to men . . . of high integrity and commanding intellect that the country must look to give character to her councils.[13] He was not quick to praise but he was sparing in criticism. When he offended the *amour propre* of any officer, he made amends. Unless a man was grossly incapable, he was slow to relieve him of command. He preferred to suffer the mediocrity he knew than to fly to that of which he was not cognizant. If a general was disqualified by slowness, by bad habits, or by obtuseness, Lee sought quietly to transfer him to a post where his shortcomings would be less costly. In some instances, perhaps, officers did not know that they owed their change of command to the fact that Lee had weighed them and had found them wanting. Indecision, notorious ill-temper, intemperance, and a pessimistic, demoralizing outlook were the qualities he most abhorred in a soldier. "I cannot trust a man to control others who cannot control himself," he said, and, in the saying, explained why some men of capacity, even of brilliance, never rose high in his army or remained long with it. For personal cowardice he had a soldierly scorn, but he rarely encountered it. There was only one brigadier general in his army, and none above that grade, concerning whose personal courage in the presence of the enemy there ever was serious question.

Lee would listen patiently to suggestions from any quarter, even when they were given by those who seemed disposed to usurp his function as commanding general; and he was always patient in dealing with personal idiosyncrasies, unless they touched his sense of honor and of fair play. Whatever the station of an officer, Lee endeavored to see that full justice was done him, though he avoided personal dealings, if he could, with those who had no merit with which to sustain their grievances.

Except perhaps in the case of Longstreet, the more a soldier was capable of doing, the more Lee demanded of him. Never brusque unless with extreme provocation, Lee was least suave and most exacting in dealing with those whose conception of duty he knew to be as high as his own. Once he got the true measure of Jackson, he would have considered it a reflection upon that officer's patriotism to bestow soft words or to make ingratiating gestures. He had a personal affection for the praise-loving Stuart, but he rarely put flattery or flourishes into his letters to that remarkable man. Yet when a dull brigadier or a stupid colonel came to his quarters, Lee did his utmost to hearten him. For young officers he always had kind words and friendly, considerate attention, except when it was manifest that they needed a rebuke. If he had nothing else to give an exhausted lieutenant who brought dispatches through the burning dust of a July day, he would proffer him a glass of water in the same tones he would have employed in addressing the President. Although he realized that a trained and disciplined officers' corps was the greatest need of the army, he was almost alone among the higher commanders of the Confederacy in realizing that the volunteer leaders of a revolutionary force could not be given the stern, impersonal treatment that can be meted out to the professional soldiers of an established government. How different might have been the fate of Bragg and perhaps of the Confederacy if that officer had learned this lesson from Lee!

Lee's social impulses aided him in dealing with his officers. He kept a frugal table, as an example to the army, and he entertained little, but he was an ingratiating host and a flawless guest. Mindful of the amenities, he never failed to show captivating courtesies to the wife of any officer of his acquaintance when she visited the army. His calls were always prompt and cordial, and in talking to the wife he usually had more kind things to say of the husband than he ever voiced to the soldier in person. If grief came in the loss of a child, he was among the mourners. When a general was wounded, his were the most encouraging words to the alarmed wife. At every review held in the season when the "ladies of the army" might visit it, he personally arranged that they should witness the ceremonies from a point of vantage, and usually he rode over to speak to them. His subordinates respected him for his ability and his rectitude; their wives made them love him.

All that can be said of Lee's dealings with his officers as one of the reasons for his success can be said in even warmer tones of his relations with the men in the ranks. They were his chief pride, his first obligation. Their distress was his deepest concern, their well-being his constant aim. His manner with them was said by his lieutenants to be perfect. Never ostentatious or consciously dramatic, his bearing, his record of victories, his manifest interest in the individual, and his conversation with the humblest private he met in the road combined to create in the minds of his troops a reverence, a confidence, and an affection that built up the morale of the army. And that morale was one of the elements that contributed most to his achievements. The men came to believe that whatever he did was right—that whatever he assigned them they could accomplish. Once that belief became fixed, the Army of Northern Virginia was well-nigh invincible. There is, perhaps, no more impressive example in modern war of the power of personality in creating morale. More than one writer has intimated that Lee's forbearance in dealing with Longstreet showed him too much of a gentleman to be a commander of the very first rank. It would be well for these critics to remember that the qualities of a gentleman, displayed to those in the ranks, contributed to far more victories than Longstreet ever cost Lee.

The final major reason for Lee's successes in the face of bewildering odds is akin to the two just considered. It was his ability to maintain the hope and the fighting spirit of the South. The confidence aroused by the first victory at Manassas sustained the South until the disasters at Fort Henry and Fort Donelson. Thereafter, for a season, the belief was strong that Europe's need of cotton would bring recognition and intervention. As months passed with no hopeful news from France or from England, while the Union forces tightened their noose on the Confederacy, the Southern people looked to their own armies, and to them alone, to win independence. Vicksburg fell;

the Confederacy was cut in twain. The expectations raised by the victory at Chickamauga were not realized. The Army of Tennessee failed to halt the slow partition of the seceded states. Gradually the South came to fix its faith on the Army of Northern Virginia and on its commander. Elsewhere there was bickering and division; in Virginia there was harmony and united resistance. The unconquered territory was daily reduced in area, but on the Rapidan and the Rappahannock there was still defiance in the flapping of each battle flag. The Southern people remembered that Washington had lost New York and New England, Georgia and South Carolina, and still had triumphed. Lee, they believed, would do no less than the great American he most resembled. As long as he could keep the field, the South could keep its heart. So, when the despairing were ready to make peace and the cowardly hid in the swamps or the mountains to escape the conscript officer, the loyal Confederate took his last horse from the stable for his trooper-son, and emptied his barn of corn in order that "Lee's army" might not starve. Morale behind the line, not less than on the front of action, was sustained by Lee. Conversely, he could count upon a measure of popular support that neither the President, the Congress nor any other field commander could elicit.

The qualities that created this confidence were essentially those that assured Lee the unflagging aid of the President, the loyalty of his lieutenants and the enthusiastic devotion of his men. But the order in which these qualities were esteeemed by the civil population was somewhat different. Mr. Davis and the corps commanders knew that Lee was better able than any other Southern soldier to anticipate and to overthrow the plans of the enemy; the men in the ranks were satisfied he would shape his strategy to defeat the enemy with the least loss to them. The people in the Southern towns and on the farms of the Confederate states saw, in contrast, a series of military successes they were not capable of interpreting in terms of strategy or of tactics. They understood little of all the subtle factors that entered into army administration and into the relations of commander with President and with soldiers. But for them the war had taken on a deeper spiritual significance than it had for some of those who faced the bloody realities of slaughter. In the eyes of the evangelicals of the South, theirs was a contest of righteousness against greed, a struggle to be won by prayers not less than by combat. They saw in Lee the embodiment of the faith and piety they believed a just Heaven would favor. A war that would make a partisan of God works other changes no less amazing to the religious concepts of a nation, and among the Southern people, during the last year of the struggle, it lacked little of lifting Lee to be the mediator for his nation. The army, seeing him in battle, put his ability first and his character second. The civilian population, observing him from afar, rated his character even above his ability.

These, then, would seem to be the signal reasons why Lee so long was able to maintain the unequal struggle of a Confederacy that may have been foredoomed to defeat and extinction. To recapitulate, the foundation stone of his military career was intellect of a very high order, with a developed aptitude for war. On that foundation his strategy was built in comprehensive courses. Visualizing a military problem with clarity, he studied every report that would aid in its absolution. If it were possible, he put his solution in terms of the offensive. With care he would select his position; with skill he would reconnoiter it; with precision of logistics he would bring his troops to it, and with daring he would engage them. For every action he sought to concentrate adequately, and for every task he endeavored to utilize the lieutenant best suited. In combat, however excellent his constantly improving tactics, he begrudged the life of each soldier he had to expose, yet he hurled his whole army into the charge, sparing not a man, when his daring gave him an opening for a major blow. As his numbers diminished and he was forced to the defensive, he perfected a system of field fortification that had a strategic no less than a protective value. A diligent army administrator, self-controlled and disciplined in his dealings with his superiors, he chose his subordinates wisely and treated them with a justice that Washington himself could not have excelled. He had, besides, a personality and a probity that combined with his repeated victories to gain for him the unshakable confidence of his troops and of the civil population. The tactics he employed in the 1860's belong to the yesterday of war, but the reasons for his success remain valid for any soldier who must bear a like burden of responsibility, whether in a cause as desperate or where the limitless resources of a puissant government are his to command.

When the story of a solider is completed, and the biographer is about to leave the last camp-fire of a man he has learned to respect and to love, he is tempted to a last word of admiring estimate. May he not, by some fine phrase, fan into enduring flame the spark of greatness he thinks he has discovered in the leader whose councils he has in spirit shared? May he not claim for him a place in the company of the mighty captains of the past? Yet who that reverences historical verities can presume to say of any soldier who rises above the low shoulders of mediocrity, "In this he outshone or in that he rivaled another who fought under dissimilar conditions for a different cause in another age?" Circumstance is incommensurable: let none essay to measure men who are its creatures. Lee's record is written in positive terms; why invoke comparatives? The reader who can appraise the conditions under which he fought can appraise the man. Others need not linger at the door or watch him take off his sword, or strain to hear the words he spoke to Mrs. Lee in the first moment of their meeting.

NOTES

1. See Douglas Southall Freeman, *R. E. Lee: A Biography,* 4 vols. (New York: Charles Scribner's Sons, 1934–36), 3:154, n. 101.

2. Prisoners are reckoned in the total estimates, which, compiled from a variety of sources, cover roughly the period 1 June 1862 to 31 May 1864.

3. Herbert C. Saunders, 1866, quoted in R. E. Lee Jr., *Recollections and Letters of General Robert E. Lee* (New York: Doubleday, Page & Company, 1904), 232–33.

4. U. S. War Department, *The War of the Rebellion: A Compilation of the Official Records of the Union and Confederate Armies*, 127 vols., index, and atlas (Washington DC: GPO, 1880–1901), ser. 1, vol. 25, pt. 2, p. 624 [set hereafter cited as *Official Records;* all references to series 1].

5. *Official Records*, vol. 19, pt. 2, p. 715.

6. *Official Records*, vol. 27, pt. 3, p. 868.

7. *Official Records*, vol. 29, pt. 2, p. 819.

8. John Esten Cooke, *A Life of Gen. Robert E. Lee* (New York: D. Appleton and Company, 1871), 368.

9. See Freeman, *Lee*, 3:331.

10. *Official Records*, vol. 21, p. 1086.

11. *Official Records*, vol. 29, pt. 2, p. 820.

12. See Freeman, *Lee*, 3:251.

13. *Official Records*, vol. 21, p. 1067.

The Generalship of Robert E. Lee

CHARLES P. ROLAND

Machiavelli wrote that victory is the final test of skill in war. "If a general wins a battle," he said, "it cancels all other errors and miscarriages." Conversely, one may infer, if a general loses a battle, it cancels all other brilliance and daring. Experience in two world wars, followed by a growing insecurity in the modern age, heightens the American sense of nationalism today. Supreme excellence in all things (whether economic, intellectual, or military) must come of our peculiar political and social institutions, Americans are accustomed to believe. Rudely upset in the field of science by Sputnik, Gagarin, and Titov, this happy theme yet pervades much of the literature of American history, and especially many recent treatises on the Civil War. Provincialism and conservatism restricted the Confederate military mind, say our nationalistic scholars, and assured victory to the Union. Here are the major problems in expounding the talents of Robert E. Lee: for he fought against the Union; and he is the only American general who has ever lost a war.

Fortunately, insofar as Lee's reputation is concerned, history sometimes flouts the inference from Machiavelli's rule: occasionally a great genius in war—a Hannibal, a Charles XII, or a Napoleon—falls in defeat. These exceptions to such a law of success and failure in war demonstrate that generalship alone does not always prevail, however good it may be. Victory requires that one side overmatch the opposite in the sum of its generalship plus all other capabilities for waging war. Hence, judged fairly, a general's record must be weighed against the resources at his command.

Lee and the Confederacy opposed awesome superiority in the means of making war. "All else equal," said Clausewitz, "numbers will determine victory in combat. . . . In ordinary cases an important superiority of numbers, but which need not be over two to one, will be sufficient to ensure victory, however disadvantageous other circumstances may be." Early in the war Southern troops were outnumbered 2 to 1; before war's end they were outnumbered 3 to 1.[1] In industrial strength, the decisive weapon of modern war, the Confederacy was hopelessly overmatched: in 1860, for example, the North produced 20 times as much pig iron as did the South, and 24 times as many locomotive engines. At like disadvantage today, the United States would be pitted against an adversary manufacturing annually one billion tons of steel, along with comparable quantities of automotive and other industrial wares. The United States census-taker in 1865 wrote with candor that the Confederacy fell for want of material resources, and not for lack of will, skill, or courage. Forge and lathe, plow and reaper, rail and piston: all weighed in the balance against Lee and his associates.[2]

Since the South must be invaded and conquered before Federal authority could reassert itself, the Confederacy held the strategic advantage of interior, or shorter, lines of communication. Theoretically, she was able more rapidly to concentrate troops upon points of decision than could the Union. Actually, this was seldom true. Possessing less than half the railway mileage that the North had, and virtually no facilities for manufacturing or repairing locomotives and rolling stock, the Confederacy was unable to profit significantly from interior lines. Early in the war she lost the railroads of western and central Tennessee, including a long stretch of the vital Memphis and Charleston track. Command of these roads and of the upper Mississippi River and the lower Tennessee River gave to the Union forces the interior lines of communication within the broad western theater of the Confederacy. Unable to control the seas, the Confederacy fought with flank and rear continuously threatened with invasion.

Lee and the Confederate government had also to contend with the powerful influence of localism within the Confederacy. Asserting the rights of state sovereignty, many Southern governors withheld large numbers of men from the Confederate armies, and demanded protection of all territory within their states. The institution of slavery aggravated this tendency; even the temporary appearance of Northern troops in any part of the South so disrupted the labor force and the economy that they could never be returned to normal. Hence, Confederate authorities were obliged to scatter many thousands of troops at scores of points having little strategic importance, if any.

Though Lee was not responsible for the general strategy of the defensive adopted by Jefferson Davis early in the war, Lee tacitly endorsed it. Some Confederate leaders urged a prompt invasion of the North; they called for a lightning stroke against the people of the Union, before her vast resources could be mobilized. Certain historians today support this strategy by pointing out that in a prolonged war of attrition the South was foredoomed to defeat.

Critics speak with authority in disparaging Confederate strategy; they speak with uncertain voices in saying what it ought to have been. Offensive war against the North would seem to have been futile. Four years were required for the immensely more powerful Union to conquer the Confederacy; that the South could have conquered the North is inconceivable. Through the defensive, the South could conserve her lesser strength and exact of the North a heavier toll in blood and treasure. Doubtless unwittingly, Southern leaders followed Clausewitz's dictum, "Defense is the stronger form of war." Even that implacable critic of Confederate leadership, General J. F. C. Fuller, acknowledges that the defensive was the only sound policy for the South.[3]

Exigencies of Southern politics, society, and logistics caused Davis to adopt, and Lee to second, a strategy of territorial defense. Accordingly, the Confederacy was split into departments (or theaters), each with its own army, and each to be defended against invasion, with no territory to be yielded voluntarily to the enemy. Such a design fell short of the military rule, "Unity of plan, concentration of force." Lee was aware that this strategy failed to achieve maximum concentration of force; that it thus violated the fundamental principle of war as set forth by the military theorist Henri Jomini, whom Lee is nowadays accused of following slavishly. But in fashioning this plan, Confederate leaders anticipated a principle of modern warfare not then generally recognized; they sought to provide what Cyril Falls describes as ". . . that vital factor of the most recent times, the defence of the home base and civil population."[4]

In condemning this failure to concentrate, General Fuller says that the Confederacy ought to have yielded temporarily the state of Virginia and other areas of the upper South in order to mass her forces at the key rail center Chattanooga. By harassing Union communications and drawing Union armies away from base, he opines, the Confederacy may then have struck a decisive blow with her entire *grande armée.* As military science in the narrow sense, this may be sound, though it tempts the speculation that such an initial Confederate concentration would merely have caused a like Union concentration, but in far greater strength. "Concentration *a priori* and without regard to enemy dispositions invites disaster," writes General de Gaulle in a perceptive comment on French operations in World War I. As strategy in the highest sense, strategy that blends military science with political science, social psychology, and economics, General Fuller's plan is folly. Abandonment of the upper South to the Shermans and Sheridans of the Northern army would have undone the Confederacy without a battle.

"There is nothing in [Lee's] generalship," says Sir Frederic Maurice, "which is more striking than the manner in which he grasped the problems of the Confederacy and . . . adapted his strategy both to the cause for which the South was fighting and to the major political conditions of the time." Considering the circumstances of Southern life, territorial defense was probably the only strategy open to the leaders of the Confederacy.[5]

As advisor to President Davis early in the war, Lee did not decide strategy; he was in no sense general-in-chief of Confederate armies. "Broadly speaking," says biographer Douglas Southall Freeman, "Davis entrusted to [Lee] the minor, vexatious matters of detail and the counselling of commanders in charge of the smaller armies. On the larger strategic issues the President usually consulted with him and was often guided by his advice, but in no single instance was Lee given a free hand to initiate and direct to full completion any plan of magnitude."[6]

Restricted as he was by the character of his assignment, Lee nevertheless at this time showed deep insight into the nature of the war, and urged certain measures that would greatly strengthen the South for the struggle ahead. In the early days after Fort Sumter, when many people of the South still predicted that there would be no war, and that, if it should come, it would be quickly won by Southern arms, Lee said that war was inevitable, and that it would be long and bloody. In the fall, 1861, when many thought that England was about to enter the war against the North because of the *Trent* affair, Lee warned against such hope. "We must make up our minds to fight our battles and win independence alone," he wrote prophetically. "No one will help us."[7]

When in the spring, 1862, Forts Henry and Donelson fell, and the Confederate Army in the west was threatened with destruction, Lee wisely advised stripping the Gulf Coast of troops in order to reinforce Albert Sidney Johnston and Beauregard at Corinth, Mississippi. To Johnston, Lee gave sound strategic counsel: concentrate, said Lee, and strike the enemy at your front before the two wings of his army can be joined. The battle of Shiloh, fought according to this plan, came within an inch of destroying the Union army there: neither side would again come so close to a total victory until exhaustion had overtaken the Confederacy at war's end.[8]

Lee's support of conscription to muster the manpower of the South indicated advanced military thinking and willingness to break with American precedent. As early as December, 1861, Lee recommended state conscription by the government of Virginia: after Confederate losses at Shiloh and New Orleans the following spring, Lee's endorsement of Confederate conscription helped to secure passage of the act by the Southern Congress. Lee's ideas on conscription offer proof of how far beyond Jomini he had gone during the first year of the Civil War. Jomini considered war an affair to be settled by professional armies; he refused to contemplate a people's war, and wrote, "[It] would be so terrible that, for the sake of humanity, we ought never to see it." Lee said, "Since the whole duty of the nation [will] be war until independence [is] secured, the whole nation should for a time be converted into an army, the producers to feed and the soldiers to fight." Not until the outbreak of World War I would the governments of the world grasp fully this principle of total mobilization laid down by Lee almost threescore years before.[9]

In the spring, 1862, as McClellan's powerful army moved to the Virginia Peninsula and threatened Richmond at close quarters, Davis leaned heavily upon Lee for support. Lee's talent as a strategist now began to emerge in his daring shift of Confederate troops to oppose McClellan's advance. But Lee saw the futility of meeting the Federal concentration with like concentration; he realized that the smaller Southern force must ultimately be overwhelmed if this were done. Instead, Lee adopted the more resourceful technique of weakening McClellan's army by threatening a blow at the North. "As to dividing the enemy's strength," wrote Machiavelli, "there can be no better way . . . than by making incursions into their country. . . ." From relatively unexposed points in the Carolinas and Georgia, Lee drew reinforcements piecemeal for the Confederate army on the Peninsula: meantime, Lee urged General Jackson in the Shenandoah Valley to strike the enemy there in order to divert Northern troops from McClellan. This was the genesis of Lee's later strategy for the entire Confederacy.[10]

On May 31, 1862, Confederate General Joseph E. Johnston fell wounded in the fighting on the Peninsula, and Davis named Lee to command the Army of Northern Virginia. Lee's mission was to defend Virginia, and especially the Confederate capital, Richmond. He opposed the strongest of Union concentrations, which outnumbered his own force by 2 to 1. For three years Lee would fulfill his mission against the heaviest odds ever faced by an American commander.

The wisdom of defending Richmond, to the relative neglect of other points in the South, has been seriously questioned. Defense of the capital to the bitter end cannot be justified; but there was reason for holding it as long as possible without sacrificing the army. Even if Richmond had possessed no intrinsic military value, as the capital it had great symbolic value. One may lightly disparage both Davis and Lincoln for waging long and bitter campaigns for the capture or protection of idle cities; yet both men sensed the psychological importance of being able to retain the seat of government. Winston Churchill recognized this principle when late in World War II he urged that Berlin was still an objective of great strategic importance; that nothing else would blight German morale so much as would the fall of Berlin. Moreover, Richmond was by no means an idle city: she contained the great parent-arsenal of the South, the Tredegar Works, besides many other armories and factories. To the Confederacy, Richmond was Washington and Pittsburgh in one. Aside from symbolic and material values, northern Virginia possessed great strategic value for the Confederacy. It was a dagger pointed toward the heart of the enemy, a potential base for strikes against the Northern capital and the great northeastern centers of population, industry, and communication. A powerful, mobile Southern army in northern Virginia was the most effective instrument of the Confederacy for paralyzing the mind of President Lincoln and the will of the Northern people.

Lee preferred this command to all others, since it would keep him in his beloved Virginia. Though Davis made the decision to defend Richmond, Lee unquestionably approved of it.

Once in command, Lee instantly did what he would always do as long as he had the strength for it; he seized the initiative in the campaign. His strategy for weakening McClellan's force had already borne fruit; Jackson's spectacular demonstration in the Valley (April 30–June 9) caused President Lincoln to divert McDowell's corps there. Ordering Jackson to Richmond by rail, Lee now attempted a concerted blow against McClellan. Faulty staff work and the derelictions of subordinates may have cost Lee a decisive victory. Nevertheless, in a series of fierce engagements (June 26–July 2) Lee persuaded McClellan to abandon the drive for Richmond.[11]

Blunting of McClellan's thrust enabled Lee to open what Davis called an offensive-defensive against the Union armies in Virginia. From the beginning, Lee knew that his army could not withstand a siege by the vastly stronger Northern numbers opposing it. Lee must keep the enemy forces divided; he could not afford for them to concentrate upon him. In order to prevent such concentration, he must constantly maneuver and confound his opponents with threats against Washington and with lightning blows against exposed fractions of their strength. Second Manassas was a brilliant demonstration of this technique.

In mid-July Lee learned that Federal troops were concentrating under General John Pope on the Rapidan River in northern Virginia. Lee had to decide quickly whether the next Union main effort was to be from the north or from the Peninsula. Sensing that it would be made by Pope, Lee started Jackson's corps north by rail; when on August 13 Lee learned that the Union force on the James was being reduced, he reasoned that these troops were being sent to Pope. Lee then rushed the remainder of his army up to strike Pope before McClellan's reinforcements could reach him. By dividing the Confederate army and sending Jackson around Pope's flank to threaten communications with Washington, Lee unsettled his adversary and forced him out of position. Reuniting Longstreet and Jackson on the battlefield, Lee then defeated Pope (August 29–30, 1862) and drove him back to the Washington earthworks.

Lee's decision to move his army from the James to the Rapidan showed seeming uncanny ability to anticipate the enemy; it has been called a supreme example of the manner in which judgment and boldness must supplement available information in shaping strategy. Lee's shift of force was a lesson in the use of interior lines of communication and the strategic employment of railroads. Dividing the Confederate army in the face of superior numbers violated the rules of warfare; Jomini warned against it; Lee was criticized for doing it. But Clausewitz says, "What genius does must be the best of all rules, and theory cannot do better than to show how and why it is so." Lee himself gave the explanation. "The disparity . . . between the contending forces rendered the risks unavoidable," he said.[12]

With the Federal army reeling under defeat, and his own troops flushed with victory, Lee now determined to carry the war to the enemy. He proposed to invade Maryland and Pennsylvania. Invasion of the North would extend Lee's war of maneuver; it would find provisions for his troops; and it would free Virginia of molestation during the harvest. A successful campaign across the Potomac might do much more than this; it might add Maryland to the Confederacy; it might sever communications between northeast and northwest; it might place the great cities of the east at Lee's command; and it might bring foreign recognition. It might even end the war, thought Lee; and he proposed that Davis offer peace with honor to the North at this time.

In early September Lee crossed the Potomac. Segments of his army were spread wide to cut the railroads and isolate McClellan from reinforcements. Here the fates deserted Lee. His appeal to the people of Maryland fell on deaf ears. Far worse, McClellan moved against him with disconcerting assurance. One of the traits of a great general is his insight into the character of the opposing general: the ability, as Colonel G. F. R. Henderson phrases it, "to penetrate the adversary's brain." In this faculty, Lee has had few peers. On the eve of marching into Maryland, he said, "McClellan's army will not be prepared for offensive operations—or he will not think it so—for three or four weeks. Before that time I hope to be on the Susquehanna." Ordinarily, Lee would have been right about McClellan; but something extraordinary happened on this occasion. Providentially supplied with a copy of Lee's plan of campaign, found wrapped around three cigars on the ground, McClellan struck Lee's divided army and came near destroying it at Sharpsburg on September 16–17. Lee held McClellan off and won tactical victory; but Lee was obliged to return to Virginia and abandon the campaign.[13]

In striking at the North and her capital, say some scholars today, Lee again was simply obeying the stale rules of warfare as set forth by Jomini, or by his chief American disciple, Professor Dennis Hart Mahan of West Point. Actually, Lee was using a strategy as old as war itself; and as modern, too. "If the defender has gained an important advantage," says Clausewitz, "then the defensive form has done its part, and under the protection of this success he must give back the blow. . . . Common sense points out that iron should be struck while it is hot. . . . A swift and vigorous assumption of the offensive—the flashing sword of vengeance—is the most brilliant point in the defensive." This principle was alike sound for Scipio Africanus, or Frederick the Great, or George Catlett Marshall. It was also sound for Lee.[14]

In retrospect, the grander aims of Lee's campaigns into the North seem visionary. Probably England and France would have remained neutral even if Lee had won a victory on Northern soil; that the Lincoln administration would have accepted a peace offer is unlikely. But Lee did not have the advantage of hindsight. The true goal in war, says Clausewitz, is to subject the enemy to one's will. Often this can be done only through destroying the enemy's armed forces. But this is not the sole method for accomplishing the object of war, continues Clausewitz: moreover, when one lacks the resources to destroy the enemy's armed forces, he must resort to other means; he must then attempt to destroy the enemy's will through measures short of the destruction of his military power. Among such, says the German theorist, are the seizure of the enemy's capital, or the inflicting of casualties beyond the enemy's expectations. Here was just Lee's situation.[15]

Lee knew that the South could not possibly destroy the war strength of the North, however successful in battle the South might be; that, ironically, Southern victories in the field weakened the South in men and material resources relatively more than they weakened the North. Shortly after his greatest triumph (Chancellorsville), Lee wrote to Davis, "We should not . . . conceal from ourselves that our resources in men are constantly diminishing, and the disproportion in this respect between us and our enemies . . . is steadily augmenting."[16] Only by paralyzing the Northern will to victory could the South hope to achieve her war aims. Lee was aware that Washington had no intrinsic military value. But he knew also that President Lincoln and the Northern people had invested the city with great symbolic value; and he knew that defeat at home shakes a population more than defeat in a distant land. He believed that a successful invasion of the North by a victorious Confederate army was most likely to exalt his own people and to blight the morale of the enemy. Considered in this light, his decisions to invade the North are reasonable.

In Virginia again after the fruitless Maryland campaign, Lee dispersed his army, recruited his strength, and braced for another Federal assault. It came in mid-December against the impregnable heights of Fredericksburg. Reconcentrating quickly, Lee met the attack pointblank. Bloodily repulsed, the Northern army fell back across the Rapidan to await a new commander and a new occasion.

Spring of 1863 found the lines of the Confederacy holding fast in the east but deeply pierced in the west. New Orleans was lost; Grant pressed upon Vicksburg; and Rosecrans was lodged in central Tennessee, threatening Chattanooga. Davis and his counselors sought desperately for a strategy that would restore the balance in the west. Many plans were offered. Most of them called for a shift of troops from relatively secure points elsewhere to the faltering armies of the west in the hope of concentrating sufficient strength there to win decisively over Grant or Rosecrans, or both. In early March, Lee told Davis that for some time he had hoped that the situation in Virginia would enable him to detach an entire corps of his army to the support of the west. Secretary of War Seddon strongly urged this move; and Generals Longstreet and Beauregard set forth variations of it. But the strength and activity of the Army of the Potomac, now commanded by General Joseph Hooker, prevented such an operation at this time, thought Lee. A month later, as affairs in the west grew worse, Secretary of War Seddon called upon Lee to consider sending one division there. Seddon's request for Lee's views on this measure caused Lee to formulate a general strategy for meeting the crisis.

In principle, the strategy now expounded by Lee was not new to him; rather, it was an elaboration of his ingrained philosophy of war, as adapted to the peculiar needs of the Confederacy. Lee agreed with Davis and Seddon that the situation required boldness; that the Confederate armies in the west ought at once to take the initiative. Let Joseph E. Johnston concentrate and attack Grant in Mississippi, recommended Lee; let Bragg strike into Kentucky and threaten Ohio. But Lee cautioned against weakening the Army of Northern Virginia; Hooker would not stand idle, predicted Lee, but soon would strike a powerful blow against Virginia. An advocate of the maximum concentration of force against isolated segments of the enemy, Lee nevertheless felt that, in this instance, the distances were too great and the transport facilities of the South too feeble to justify such a move. The Confederacy could not match the Union in shifting troops from one department to another, he said; to rely on that method might render Confederate reserves always too late.

To prevent the North from transferring troops in order to concentrate at a given point, Lee said that all Southern commanders ought to take the offensive upon any weakening of the enemy on their fronts. Let Confederate armies in the major departments be reinforced from the less exposed departments of the deep South, he advised—from the vicinity of Charleston, Savannah, Mobile, and Vicksburg. Lee's curious listing of Vicksburg came of an erroneous notion that Federal operations there would soon have to quit because of the pestilential Mississippi summer. Apparently Davis, whose home was but a few miles from Vicksburg, never disabused Lee of this idea.

Lee's prime recommendation was that he again strike at the North with his own army. "The readiest method of relieving pressure upon General Joseph E. Johnston," said Lee, "is for the [Army of Northern Virginia] to cross into Maryland. . . . Greater relief would in this way be afforded to the armies in middle Tennessee." To penetrate the enemy's vitals, or if this were impossible, to threaten them with Clausewitz's "flashing sword of vengeance"—this was the key to Lee's strategy.

True to Lee's prediction, in late April Hooker advanced in Virginia. Again Lee seized the initiative with great audacity. Splitting the Confederate force, Lee occupied the bulk of Hooker's powerful army with slightly above one-third of his own; at the same time Lee sent the remainder of his troops under the indomitable Jackson to fall upon Hooker's vulnerable flank and rear. Lee's victory at Chancellorsville (May 2–3), says Colonel Henderson, was one of the supreme instances in history of a great general's ability to outwit his adversary and direct the attack where it is least expected. The Army of the Potomac once more fell back across the Rapidan; Confederate leaders again took inventory of strategic resources.[17]

Anxious over the security of Vicksburg, Secretary of War Seddon again proposed the shift of troops from Lee's army to support Pemberton on the Mississippi. If necessary, replied Lee, order Pickett's division to the west. But Lee warned anew that the great distance required by the move, plus the uncertainty of employment of Pickett's troops in Mississippi, made the venture inadvisable. Weakening of the Army of Northern Virginia, he felt, might force it to retire into the Richmond defenses, where it would cease to be a formidable instrument of Confederate strategy. Davis and his cabinet met with Lee on June 16 and, with Postmaster General Reagan possibly dissenting, approved Lee's plan to invade the North again. This meant that Confederate armies in the west must fend for themselves.

Already a part of Lee's army was on the move toward Pennsylvania. As he put his troops in motion, Lee searched the Confederacy for reinforcements and pondered other measures that would strengthen his blow. Earlier he had called upon Davis to bring idle troops from the Carolinas, Georgia, and Florida to the Army of Northern Virginia; if necessary, Lee had advised, strip the coastal garrisons except for enough men to operate the water batteries. He now repeated this plea and added another recommendation.

Let General Beauregard come with these reserves to northern Virginia, Lee said, and there create a diversion in favor of the advance into Pennsylvania. Anxiety of the Northern government over the safety of Washington would cause a large force to be left for protection of the capital, Lee believed. Beauregard ought to command the diversionary column in person, said Lee. "His presence would give magnitude to even a small demonstration and tend greatly to perplex and confound the enemy." A mere "army in effigy" under Beauregard would have good effect, thought Lee, if no more troops than this were available.

Thinking the North shaken by Chancellorsville and the threat of Confederate invasion, Lee again advised a Southern peace overture. The South ought not to demand peace unconditionally, he said; rather, she ought to encourage the peace party of the North to believe that the Union could be restored by negotiation. "Should the belief that peace will bring back the Union become general, the war would no longer be supported. . . ." he observed. Once hostilities ended, he believed that they would not be resumed, and that Southern independence would thus be achieved.

Gettysburg was Lee's debacle. Again fortune turned upon him; at Brandy Station, on the eve of the march into Pennsylvania, Federal cavalry seized Confederate correspondence indicating a northward move by Lee. Davis made no effort to bring up reinforcements or to create the army in effigy requested by Lee. Exceeding Lee's orders, Jeb Stuart rode amiss and deprived Lee of his "eyes," the cavalry, so that he groped his way into Pennsylvania without knowing the whereabouts of the Union army. General Ewell, recently elevated to corps commander as a result of Jackson's death, proved unequal to his responsibilities and failed to seize the key position, Cemetery Hill, early in the battle, when it probably could have been taken. Longstreet sulked and was sluggish in attacking Cemetery Ridge on the second day. Lee erred gravely in ordering the frontal assault against Cemetery Ridge on the third day, when it was impregnably held. After three days of carnage, Lee retreated into Virginia. The tide of the Confederacy was spent.[18]

That in the Gettysburg campaign Lee was below his best goes without saying. His more severe critics see in the Gettysburg decision a narrow provincialism that blinded Lee to the war as a whole. In contrast to Lee's strategy, which the critics say was primarily a defense of Virginia, they see in the plan urged by Seddon, Longstreet, and Beauregard a truly comprehensive Confederate military design. It would have been a Jominian stroke on the grand scale, they say, taking advantage of the Confederacy's interior lines of communication, and concentrating a maximum of Confederate strength for the destruction of Rosecrans' isolated army in Tennessee. Thus

Lee becomes the culprit who squandered the Confederacy's one opportunity to win the war.[19]

This criticism is highly problematical. It rests upon the present knowledge that Lee's plan was tried, at least in part, and that it failed. The critics assume what cannot be known: that western concentration was more likely to succeed than was Lee's eastern offensive. Exponents of western concentration do not take into account the logistical weaknesses of the South, which Lee felt made the western venture impractical. After the war, Confederate General E. P. Alexander had a vision of a powerful Confederate "army on wheels" using the interior lines of the South to shuttle rapidly back and forth between engagements east and west. Alas for the Confederacy, this could be but a vision. Southern troops could, of course, move somewhat more quickly from Virginia to Tennessee than could Northern troops, who had more than twice as far to go. But continued shifting of a large army to and fro across the South, as Alexander contemplated, was roughly the equivalent in time and effort of a like movement across Siberia today. Lee well knew the military significance of railroads; many of his campaigns had been skillful demonstrations in the strategic and logistical use of them. But he accurately sensed that Northern railroad superiority largely nullified the Confederacy's theoretical advantage of interior lines on a grand scale. General Alexander's plan was beyond the capacity of Southern transport and industry; it probably would have exhausted the Confederacy without a battle.[20]

Supporters of the western plan exaggerate the probability of decisive victory over Rosecrans and minimize the effect of weakening Lee's army as a major strategic weapon of the Confederacy. To achieve the purpose of the western effort, Confederate forces there had to do more than win a battle; they must win so prodigiously as to cause the North to quit the war. That a western Confederate victory of any degree would have done this is questionable. Complete defeat or capture of Rosecrans' army would not have destroyed the war capacity of the Union; her major striking force was elsewhere. One may further question that a total victory over Rosecrans was likely, even granting the maximum Confederate concentration. Walter Millis has pointed out that the advent of railroad, steamboat, and telegraph ended the great battlefield decisions of finality.[21] No such victory was won by either side in the Civil War, regardless of numerical advantage, until the last stages of weakness and demoralization had come upon the Confederacy. If the South could, in any event, have won a western victory of such magnitude as to end the war, she could have done it probably only through three conditions: Rosecrans must obligingly remain exposed to destruction until the Confederacy could mass her strength against him; Hooker with the most powerful of Union armies must sit idle in the east all the while; and the western Confederate force, hastily assembled from all over the South, must operate free of the very kind of miscarriage that plagued Lee's veteran army—the varsity team—in its Pennsylvania offensive. That any of these circumstances would have prevailed seems doubtful; that all of them would have prevailed seems incredible.

Nevertheless, everything ought to have been hazarded for the west, it is said; the war was lost in the west. This would appear to be only half truth; it obscures that the war was lost in east and west, and through a long process of exhaustion. The west was not intrinsically more valuable to the Confederacy than was the east; once the east was taken, the west would surely fall. The Confederacy could not live without both east and west.

Close examination of Lee's strategy refutes the accusation that it was merely a defense of Virginia. It was a comprehensive strategy for the Confederacy, however faulty it may have been. Interestingly, it was in some ways quite like Grant's later strategy for the Union: it employed Lee's seemingly invincible army, greatly strengthened, as the major Confederate striking force; and it called for simultaneous offensives by all major Confederate armies to prevent Northern concentration upon any one of them. It was designed, in part, to nullify the Northern advantages in transportation that enabled her to shift troops swiftly from one department to another. Lee's plan for an army in effigy under Beauregard was a superbly ingenious stratagem that might well have upset a nervous foe. It anticipated by almost a century General Patton's mock invasion of the Pas de Calais coast in World War II, which helped to deceive the German high command and to free the Normandy beachheads from heavy counterattack for many precious days.[22] Lee's request was worthy of strenuous effort to fulfill it.

Finally, Lee's plan would have cured the major ill in the deployment of Southern manpower; it would have drawn strategic reserves from the minor departments of the Confederacy to the main effort. Throughout most of the war, excessive numbers of Confederate troops were scattered at relatively idle stations about the South. In early 1863, total Confederate armies were outnumbered 2 to 1: but the major Confederate armies at this time faced odds of 2.5 to 1, while Confederate garrisons along the Atlantic Coast actually outnumbered the opposing Union armies. In the departments of the Carolinas, Georgia, and Florida, 45,000 Confederates opposed 27,000 Federals. From these troops, and others at various places in Virginia, Lee could have added an entire corps to his army, with enough left over to guard the coast and form Beauregard's army in effigy as well.[23]

In a word, Lee proposed to apply to the entire Confederacy the strategy that he had successfully employed within his own department. With offensives throughout the South he would keep the total enemy force divided; with diversions in northern Virginia he would confound and divide the local enemy force; then, with the strongest, the most skillful, and the most cohesive army of the Confederacy, he would direct his main effort against the vital center of the North.

Lee asked for a diversionary force too late for Davis to create it, under the circumstances, even if he had attempted it. Lee proposed this ruse on June 23, only a week before Gettysburg. By now many of the troops from the Atlantic Coast had been sent, without Lee's certain knowledge, to Mississippi, where they would accomplish nothing. This suggests a further thought in weighing Lee's role in the Gettysburg decision. Lee was not general-in-chief of Confederate armies; he was still merely commander of the Army of Northern Virginia, with the primary mission of defending Virginia against invasion. He lacked the authority, the information, the point of vantage, and the breadth of mission for putting into effect such a plan as he expounded. The supreme weakness of Confederate operations in the summer of 1863 was not the offensive into Pennsylvania: it was the want of a unified command and strategy. As a result, no adequate strategic reserve was ever created out of the minor departments: the weak reserve that was formed was sent to Mississippi, while the main effort of the Confederacy was made in Pennsylvania. The right hand knew not what the left hand was about.

Let us deal the cards in Lee's favor, as they are often dealt in favor of the hypothetical plans that he opposed, and for a moment speculate on what might have been, had he been authentic general-in-chief in early 1863. Lee would have stripped the minor departments of troops, save for minimum defensive garrisons, and from this source would have strengthened the main effort of the Confederacy. He would have given Joseph E. Johnston full authority in Mississippi, and would have ordered a concentrated effort against Grant there. Lee would have ordered Bragg to strike again into Kentucky in order to draw Rosecrans out of Tennessee and alarm the authorities and people of the North. Lee would have placed Beauregard with an army in effigy to threaten Washington from the South and paralyze his opponent. Lee would have led the Army of Northern Virginia, powerfully reinforced, into Pennsylvania. Lee would have kept his cavalry in hand, and would have discovered and destroyed Meade's two advance corps at Gettysburg on July 1, before the rest of the Northern army could reach the battlefield. With his opponents scattered, confused, and demoralized, Lee would have struck the final psychological blow at the Northern will: he would have offered a negotiated peace with a hint that the Union might thus be preserved. Given all of these conditions, the Gettysburg campaign was perhaps as likely to end the war successfully for the South as was any other strategy.

But enough of make-believe: campaigns are seldom waged as critics afterward would have them waged.

During the months after Gettysburg, Lee continued to believe that even yet he might be able to invade the North successfully. But defeat in Pennsylvania left its mark on him: when, upon Meade's failing to press Lee, Davis again desired to send a part of Lee's troops west, Lee consented. In early September he dispatched Longstreet with 12,000 men to strengthen Bragg's army before Chattanooga. Victory at Chickamauga in mid-September was followed by disaster at Chattanooga in November. Weakened by Longstreet's absence, Lee made one unsuccessful offensive effort against Meade (Bristoe Station, October 14), then fell back on the defensive.

Lee now knew that the South was too weak to invade the North. Loss of Chattanooga moved him again to write Davis concerning the general Confederate military situation. The Union army at Chattanooga now threatens Georgia with her factories and provisions, Lee said; it must be stopped if the Confederacy is to survive. Place Beauregard in command of the Confederate army in Georgia, and reinforce him with troops from Mississippi, Mobile, and Charleston, urged Lee. To defeat the coming Federal move, he explained, "the safety of points practically less important than those endangered by [it] must be hazarded. Upon the defense of the country threatened by [the enemy march] depends the safety of the points now held by us on the Atlantic, and they are in as great danger from [a] successful advance as by the attacks to which they are at present subjected." Written four months before Sherman set forth to destroy the war support of the lower South, these words show profound insight into the deficiencies of Confederate strategy. They were a prophecy of total war uttered out of season.[24]

Spring of 1864 brought face to face the military giants of the Civil War, Lee and Grant. Now came the heaviest sustained fighting that American troops have ever experienced. True to their natures and to their philosophies of war, both men attempted to seize the initiative in order to destroy the other. As Grant advanced below the Rapidan, Lee attacked fiercely. Had the two forces been equal in numbers, Lee may have achieved his aim, for he took Grant at disadvantage on the march in a country of woods and bramble. But the forces were not equal. For two days in the battle of the Wilderness (May 5–6) the result trembled in the balance as both forces fought desperately for survival. Then the armies broke off action, neither of them victorious. Sensing his opponent's tenacity and purpose, Lee now moved unerringly to block Grant's circling advance against the flank and rear of the Army of Northern Virginia.

Failure to destroy or stop Grant in the Wilderness marked the beginning of a new phase in Lee's career. He continued to seek favorable opportunity to strike Grant, for Lee had long said that his army would be lost if ever it should be pinned down in the Richmond defenses. But the Wilderness was Lee's last general offensive action; the Army of Northern Virginia no longer had the power to attack. Hoping yet to demoralize the people of the North and place the peace party there in the ascendancy, Lee husbanded his waning strength and sought to exact of Grant the maximum toll in blood and energy. When one lacks the strength to destroy the enemy, says Clausewitz, then one ought, by skillful conservation of his own resources, to seek to exhaust the enemy's will by showing him that the cost of victory far exceeds his anticipation.[25] Lee's strategy was now the strategy of conservation.

For more than a week of fierce but intermittent fighting at Spotsylvania Courthouse (May 8–18) Grant hammered at Lee's line. Unable to break it, Grant moved again. Repeatedly he sideslipped to the left and inched forward in an effort to encircle Lee's flank, force him out of position, and destroy him. Repeatedly Lee anticipated his opponent's move and shifted athwart the flanking column. From Spotsylvania Courthouse to the North Anna River, and from there to Cold Harbor veered the deadly grapple. Earthworks went up at every position. At Cold Harbor (June 3) Grant again drove his battering-ram against the Southern line. Reinforced with troops rushed from minor Confederate victories in the Shenandoah Valley and on the James River below Richmond, Lee repulsed the Northern assault with fearful punishment. Voices of censure began to rise against Grant "the butcher" among the civil and military population of the North. After a month of bloodshed such as the American people had never seen, the Army of the Potomac was still farther from Richmond than McClellan had been in the summer of 1862: Lee's gaunt army was still apparently invincible.[26]

Lee used his great talents to the utmost during this month of remorseless combat. His ability to foresee and counteract enemy strategy has become a part of universal military tradition. Carefully fitting together the shards of information collected from the battlefield, from prisoners, and from scouts and spies, Lee supplied the gaps from his own intellect and intuition: out of the whole he created a true mosaic of enemy intentions. Then he was bold enough to trust his judgment and to act accordingly. Lee must be a great strategist, wrote a Michigan soldier; for everywhere the Northern army goes, it finds the Rebels already there. To friend and foe alike, Lee's skill seemed miraculous.[27]

With remarkable effectiveness, Lee made capital of the advantages inherent in the defense. His tactical employment of interior lines enabled him to move more quickly than did his opponent from one position to another. On a larger scale, he used interior lines to draw reinforcements from the Shenandoah Valley and the Peninsula; thus he partially offset the unavoidable handicap of fighting with flank and rear exposed to a sea controlled by the enemy. Relying upon the increased firepower of Civil War weapons, and ignoring Jomini's contempt for prepared positions, Lee developed the science of field fortification to a degree that significantly altered modern defensive tactics; he elevated axe and spade to near-equality with musket and howitzer.

Lee's choice of position was unimpeachable; his eye for ground unerring. "When his eye swept a countryside it never betrayed him," says Cyril Falls. "From the ground or the map, or both in combination, [Lee] realized how to make the best use of every feature of the country, and the trace of every defensive position from his hand was masterly." Sound position, strengthened by field fortification, enabled Lee at critical moments to flout the tactical rule that one must always keep a reserve in being; he achieved maximum firepower by placing every regiment on the line. "If I shorten my lines to provide a reserve he will turn me," Lee told an observer at Cold Harbor. "If I weaken them to provide a reserve, he will break me." Audacity thus met the summons of necessity.[28]

Students of Lee's conduct in this campaign find it a brilliant lesson in defensive warfare. "[It] is a classical example in military history of how these objects [conserving one's own strength and taxing that of the enemy] ought to be sought," says Sir Frederic Maurice. "In method it was fifty years ahead of the times, and I believe that if the allies in August, 1914, had applied Lee's tactical methods to the situation . . . the course of the World War [I] would have been changed."[29]

Having failed to break Lee at Cold Harbor, Grant on June 12–16 marched around Richmond on the east and struck at Lee's communications by attacking the Petersburg rail junction below Richmond. As Grant half-circled Richmond, Lee warily moved along an inner half circle that kept his army between Grant and the city. This enabled Grant to pass south of the James River and fall with overwhelming force upon the defenders of Petersburg under Beauregard. Grant's move was daring in concept and skillful in execution. For several days Lee lost touch with the Army of the Potomac. But Grant's attack at Petersburg wanted the skill of his march. Beauregard held the Northern army at bay, and on June 18 Lee hastened the Army of Northern Virginia into the Petersburg trenches where the great siege of the war began.

Lee shrewdly anticipated Grant's move south of the James; before Grant left Cold Harbor, Lee predicted such an attempt. Aware that he could not indefinitely withstand the full weight of Grant's numbers, which would grow with time, Lee sought again to weaken Grant's main body by creating a diversion elsewhere. Should he succeed in this, Lee hoped to be able to strike a telling blow at the force still opposing him. He hoped to repeat the maneuver that had caused a diversion of troops from McClellan's Peninsula army in the summer of 1862. Lee knew that Grant would not be shaken by this ruse. Lee's strategy was aimed above Grant's head; it was aimed at Lincoln himself. On June 13, the day on which Lee learned that Grant's army was no longer before him at Cold Harbor, Lee sent General Jubal Early with 13,000 men to threaten Washington from the Shenandoah Valley.

Notwithstanding Lee's foresight, and in spite of General Beauregard's many warnings and pleas for reinforcement, Lee responded slowly to Grant's move away from Cold Harbor. Lee's tardiness has some justification; it was the result of a narrow mission and of his want of information on the whereabouts of Grant's army. Lee's primary mission was to protect the capital; without accurate knowledge of Grant's location, Lee thought it hazardous to uncover the direct route to the city. Confederate cavalry was absent, defending the Virginia Central Railroad against a massive Union cavalry raid. Beauregard's cries for help gave Lee no accurate information about the enemy; not until June 17 did Beauregard report that the Army of the Potomac was south of the James. Nevertheless, Lee did permit Grant to make the maneuver to Petersburg without striking him while on the march and vulnerable; and Lee did fail to checkmate the move at Petersburg until almost too late. Beauregard's determined resistance there saved the vital rail junction from capture. One must conclude that Grant was at his best in the passage of the James, while Lee's performance here was below that of the Wilderness-to-Cold Harbor campaign.[30]

The siege of Petersburg lasted almost nine months. It was so long and costly that it seriously blighted Northern morale; it brought to the South a false hope of ultimate success. Sherman was now halted before Atlanta, and the end of the war appeared nowhere in sight. The peace movement in the North was growing. President Lincoln himself believed his re-election to the presidency unlikely; if his Democratic opponent, General McClellan, should be victorious on a peace platform, said Lincoln, the Union probably could not be restored. Lee now learned that Davis was about to relieve Joseph E. Johnston from command of the Confederate army at Atlanta. Again Lee offered advice on general Confederate strategy. If Davis felt it necessary to remove Johnston, said Lee, then it must be done; but Lee made clear his own aversion to the decision. "It is a grievous thing to change the commander of an army situated as [the Army of Tennessee is]," he said.

He had hoped that Johnston was strong enough to fight for Atlanta, wrote Lee; which was his way of saying that battle ought to be risked in an effort to save the city. If not, he counseled, concentrate all cavalry in the west on Sherman's communications, and let the Confederate army fall back upon Augusta. This was probably as wise a move as the Confederacy was capable of making at this time.[31]

Lee's demonstration against Washington failed to break Grant's hold at Petersburg. Response of the Union authorities showed that Lee's instinct was sound. As General Early crossed the Potomac and threatened Washington during the first week of July, General Halleck called upon Grant for troops; and on July 10, President Lincoln recommended, though he did not order it, that Grant himself come to the capital with a portion of the Army of the Potomac. But Lee wanted the strength to take advantage of his opponent's dispersals. Ultimately, Grant sent into the Valley enough troops to defeat Early; but Grant kept in the Petersburg entrenchments enough men to render an attack there by Lee impossible. Either Lee must hold his lines at Petersburg to the bitter end, or he must abandon Richmond altogether.

Doubtless Richmond ought now, at all hazard, to have been given up. Atlanta was lost on September 2; its fall assured Lincoln's re-election to the presidency and doomed the Northern peace movement. Lee could not hope to destroy or seriously cripple Grant's army: Hood's effort to stop Sherman had ended in disaster. Perhaps the only remote chance of Confederate survival was for Lee to break away from Grant and attempt junction with Hood somewhere in the lower South for alternate blows, first against Sherman and then against Grant. That this would have brought deliverance to the stricken Confederacy is, of course, well-nigh inconceivable: it would have meant the immediate loss of the entire east; and Sherman's army could have been promptly reinforced to a strength that would have rendered him secure even against such combined attack. Lee saw the futility of trying to hold Richmond any longer. He had long said that a siege would destroy his army; that it must remain free to maneuver and strike if it were to live in the presence of so powerful a foe. In October, probably after the final defeat of Early in the Valley, Lee told his staff officers that Richmond was a millstone to his army. But the decision to abandon Richmond was not Lee's to make. Only Davis could make it: and Lee's exaggerated deference to the President and Commander-in-Chief would not permit him to suggest it as long as the city's defense was the first mission of his army.[32]

Hunger, cold, disease, and heartache over the plight of distant loved ones: these immeasurably assisted Grant's shells during the winter of 1864–65 to break Lee's army in flesh and spirit. Still his troops held grimly to the Petersburg defenses. In early February, under heavy public pressure, the Confederate Congress created the position of general-in-chief: though Davis rightly interpreted this as a vote of censure against his leadership, he appointed Lee to the post.

As general-in-chief, Lee held dubious rank. President Davis had once written to Lee, "I have neither the [constitutional] power nor the will to delegate" to someone else the supreme command. In appointing Grant to command all Union forces, President Lincoln said to him, "The particulars of your plan I neither know nor seek to know. . . . I wish not to obtrude any constraints or restraints upon you. . . ." Such a letter as Lincoln's is unimaginable from Davis. When General Joseph E. Johnston heard of Lee's appointment as general-in-chief, Johnston wrote perceptively, "Do not expect much of Lee in this capacity. He cannot give up the command of the Army of Northern Virginia without becoming merely a minor official. . . ." No man could with impunity trespass upon Davis' authority; for Lee to attempt it would have been futile. Through tact and suggestion Lee accomplished far more with Davis than he could have accomplished in any other way. Lee thus saved his talents, though circumscribed, for the Confederacy: others, such as Beauregard and Joseph E. Johnston, who sought through sharper methods to influence Davis, wasted their faculties during most of the war in idleness and frustration. As long as Davis was president of the Confederacy he would be commander-in-chief in fact as in law.[33]

Only by the most drastic means could Lee have made his new authority tell. Only by a passionate appeal, in his own name, to the spirit of the South; only by commandeering railroads and provisions; only by abandoning Richmond, if possible, in order to concentrate against fractions of the enemy: in sum, only by making himself dictator in the manner of ancient Rome could Lee possibly have prolonged the life of the dying Confederacy. Prolonged it for a brief season, that is; for at this stage nothing could have postponed the final outcome for very long. Lee knew what measures were required: he discussed them with his staff and others. Doubtless the Congress and people of the South would have supported him in these moves. But Lee would not take them.

In accepting the appointment as general-in-chief, Lee made clear that he would continue to operate under Davis' authority. Lee is often censured for this subordination to Davis. Lee's adjutant general admitted that this deference robbed Lee of the qualities of a revolutionary leader.[34] But it is one thing to criticize Lee as a revolutionary: it is quite another thing to disparage Lee's generalship. Subordination of the military to the civil authorities is usually deemed a virtue among Americans: George Washington shunned the temptation to grasp the reins of government at dark moments during the

War for Independence: nothing in Grant's career indicates that he would have led a coup d'état against President Lincoln if he had thought Lincoln a bungler. Indeed, Grant probably was as submissive to Lincoln as was Lee to Davis. To Grant's admirers, Lee's submissiveness was servility, while Grant's submissiveness was military statesmanship. Modern scholars who condemn Lee for his subordination to Davis look with indignation upon an American general who dared defy his President and Commander-in-Chief in a recent war. Lee was too American to play Napoleon.

Nevertheless, rather through suggestion than through command, Lee as general-in-chief attempted certain broad, coordinated strategic measures. He brought Joseph E. Johnston out of idleness and sent him to North Carolina to oppose Sherman; Lee ordered Johnston to collect for this effort all the scattered troops of the Confederacy, except the Army of Northern Virginia. Lee advised the War Department that he must now unite his own force with that of Johnston, though this would forfeit the capital. Hoping to strike a concerted blow against Sherman, then one against Grant, Lee began to prepare supply depots for a march to the south.[35]

But such a move was impossible through the mud of winter and with horses near starvation: Lee must wait for the roads to dry and for his livestock to regain strength. Lee must also win Davis to the desperate plan. The President blew hot and cold on it: previously he had hinted that all of the cities of the South might have to be given up in the waging of the war; now in early March he approved Lee's strategy of joining forces with Johnston. But Davis never gave unqualified consent to the abandonment of the capital; he never fully prepared himself to leave. On April 1, the day before Lee was driven from the Petersburg line, someone asked Davis whether Richmond would be held. "[Yes] If we can," replied the indomitable Mississippian.[36]

As commander of the Army of Northern Virginia, Lee strove mightily during these last days just to keep his army alive: hunger, exposure, demoralization, and constant attack by Grant's well-fed and well-clad army rendered this a burden beyond description. That, under these conditions, Lee was able to maintain a cohesive fighting force through the winter of 1864–65 is an enduring tribute to his leadership.

As general-in-chief, Lee devoted his thought to disengaging his army from Grant's tentacles and moving south to join Johnston. To combine the armies against Sherman would be a prodigious feat. It required far more than simply moving the Army of Northern Virginia from Petersburg to North Carolina, though this alone would have taxed grievously the waning resources of the Confederacy. To accomplish the junction, Lee must free himself from Grant; then Lee's famished and exhausted troops must outmarch Grant's vigorous army. Moreover, since Grant's line enveloped

Lee on the south, and the direct route to North Carolina (the Weldon Railroad) was in Grant's control, Lee had to move farther to escape than did Grant to block the escape. Lee must march west and then turn south, describing two sides of a triangle, while to intercept this movement, Grant need only proceed along the third side of the triangle. Lee intended to do all in his power to make the junction; but he rightly sensed that it was well-nigh impossible. Since the coming of winter, quite likely no man or measure could have freed the Army of Northern Virginia from the Army of the Potomac, competently led.

On March 25, Lee made his move to escape and join Johnston. In an effort to force Grant to withdraw his encircling troops from the southern end of the line, Lee attacked Fort Stedman east of Petersburg. Lee planned then to slip away and gain a march on his adversary in the deadly race. Probably no better strategy could have been devised. But the attempt failed; Lee's army was too weak to break Grant's fortified line. Grant countered instantly with a successful thrust at Five Forks on the Southside Railroad (April 1): Lee's last line of supply was severed. The next day he abandoned Petersburg and marched west for the Danville Railroad, which would carry him roundabout to junction with Johnston's army. Lee gained the railroad at Amelia Courthouse, only to lose a precious day there because his order for rations had gone awry. Before he could move south, Grant blocked the railroad at Burkeville. Lee then pushed west again, hoping somewhere to be able to turn the corner and get south of Grant's army. All was futile: outpaced and surrounded, Lee ended the terrible drama on April 9 in the surrender of his army.[37]

At last Lee's sword was sheathed.

For near a century, most students of the art of war have looked with unqualified admiration upon the generalship of Lee. Early Northern historians of the Civil War lavished praise upon him: James Ford Rhodes attributed chiefly to Lee's talents the South's unsurpassed power of resistance; John C. Ropes said of Lee, "No army commander on either side was so universally believed in, so absolutely trusted. Nor was there ever a commander who better deserved the support of his Government and the affection and confidence of his soldiers." General Viscount Wolseley of England believed that Lee was the most skillful of American generals. Colonel G. F. R. Henderson, one of the nineteenth century's most perceptive military analysts, called Lee "one of the greatest, if not the greatest, soldier who ever spoke the English tongue." Sir Frederic Maurice, critic of strategy both ancient and modern, placed Lee among the most illustrious commanders of the ages. After studying the careers of the most renowned generals of the last hundred years, Cyril Falls concludes that Lee is the greatest of them all. "Lee alone in a century of warfare deserves to be ranked with Hannibal and Napoleon," says Falls. Dennis W. Brogan, keenest of present European students of American history, says that Lee was the supreme military leader of the Civil War. Grant's solutions were adequate but seldom elegant, says Brogan; Lee's solutions were frequently elegant. The man who is perhaps today's greatest living scholar-warrior and surest connoisseur of military leadership seconds these exalted estimates of Lee. Winston Churchill writes, "Lee was one of the greatest captains known to the annals of war."[38]

Critics arise from time to time to challenge the grounds of Lee's fame. They have found human failings in him; but frequently their complaints against his generalship cancel one another out. Lee was too rash and combative, says one: Lee was excessively slow and cautious, says another. Lee did not take advantage of the South's interior lines, says one: Lee clung to the obsolete concept of interior lines, says another. Lee failed to concentrate the forces of the Confederacy, says one: Lee was preoccupied with the outworn principle of concentration, says another. Lee was a slave to Jomini, says one: Lee violated Jomini's fundamental principle of war, says another. Criticism of Lee thus often ends in a confusion of tongues.

Certainly Lee was mortal: notwithstanding remarkable accomplishments, his military leadership fell short of the abstract yardstick of perfection. Major criticisms of Lee as a strategist have already been considered in this essay: that he was too provincial to see the war as a whole, and too conservative to break the fetters of the past. Without laboring all of the minor criticisms of Lee, a few may be scrutinized here.[39]

It has been said that Lee did not see the relationship between strategy and statecraft in modern war. This is true in that Lee deferred excessively to Davis and refused to seize dictatorial authority in a belated effort to save the Confederacy. But on a higher plane the criticism is not true. Lee's foresight regarding the nature and magnitude of the war; his prescience in urging total mobilization; his prediction that Europe would remain aloof from the war; his adaptation of abstract military theory to the exigencies of Southern politics, economics, and logistics; his strategies aimed as well at President Lincoln's fears as at the weaknesses of opposing generals; his suggestions of peace overtures to encourage the Northern peace movement and split the mind of the enemy; and his advocacy of the employment of Negro troops and their subsequent emancipation: all argue that Lee saw far beyond the battlefield in waging war. Lee seasoned military strategy with a rich wisdom and insight into human affairs that transcended statecraft in its primal sense to become true statesmanship.

Lee is sometimes disparaged for the slack discipline of his command;

certainly, by professional standards, or by twentieth-century standards in citizen armies, discipline in the Army of Northern Virginia was easy. Yet one may question whether any other method of managing the army would have accomplished as much. To be of value, discipline must be suited to the character of the men, says Sir Frederic Maurice. "Lee knew well that the discipline of Frederick [the Great's] grenadiers" would destroy his army of highly individualistic Southern planters and farmers. "The object of discipline in an army is to give bodies of men both cohesion and the instinct to suffer all for duty in circumstances of great stress and danger," explains Maurice. Few armies, if any, have ever endured more steadfastly the stress of privation and the danger of combat than did the Army of Northern Virginia.[40]

Lee's most unsparing critic, General J. F. C. Fuller, heaps scorn upon Lee as being a poor provider for his army. But General Fuller offers no promising remedy for the ills of the Confederate quartermaster and commissary. Lee kept every wheel turning, and the wires hot with dispatches; he scattered his troops among the fields and flocks of the Southern countryside, often at the expense of combat efficiency; and he sometimes launched invasions of the well-stocked North: all in a ceaseless effort to feed and clothe his men. How, under the circumstances, anyone else in Lee's position could have done better is beyond convincing explanation.

Lee is sometimes taken to task for his extreme combativeness, his lust for battle for its own sake. "It is well that war is so terrible," said Lee while surveying the carnage before his position at Fredericksburg, "else we should grow too fond of it." This trait perhaps unsettled Lee's judgment on the third day of Gettysburg and caused him to attempt the impossible. But the will to fight is a fault easily forgiven in a warrior. Too often the critics believe that wars are won in some manner other than that by which they must be won, says Cyril Falls, which is by fighting. "Happy the army in which an untimely boldness frequently manifests itself," wrote Clausewitz. Lee's "fighting blood" (as Freeman calls it) was one of the qualities that made him formidable. If, on occasion, it betrayed him into unwise combat, on many others it saved him. It helped to make him, in the words of an opponent, "a very thunderbolt in war."

General Fuller believes that Lee failed to stamp his mind upon his military operations. Oddly, if Lee did not stamp his mind upon his own operations, he stamped it powerfully upon the operations of his enemy. "Among the many achievements of this remarkable man [Lee]," writes Bruce Catton, "nothing is more striking than his ability to dominate the minds of the men who were fighting against him." Lee's campaigns were the very product of his mind. One had as well say that the frescoes of the

Sistine Chapel want the stamp of Michelangelo's mind as that the operations of the Army of Northern Virginia want the stamp of Lee's mind.[41]

Under the travail of his command, Lee sometimes made unaccountable errors of judgment regarding enemy capabilities outside his own department. His belief that the summer climate of Mississippi would stop Grant at Vicksburg; and his doubt that Sherman could march through the Carolinas: these were wide of the mark. But they were offered as mere opinions. Significantly, they did not alter Lee's strategy: notwithstanding his notions, Lee urged that Joseph E. Johnston concentrate and attack Grant in Mississippi without delay; and later Lee ordered Johnston to oppose Sherman's drive in North Carolina with every man available to the embattled Confederacy.

Perhaps the chief flaw in Lee's generalship came of his boundless courtesy and humility. These traits heightened his deference to President Davis; sometimes they weakened Lee's supremacy over his army. Lee chose rather to lead through tact and orders of discretion than through iron discipline and positive commands. Freeman believes that at times Lee even permitted himself to be browbeaten by a stubborn subordinate. Yet the critic must be careful in scoring Lee on this count; some of Lee's most spectacular victories were the result of discretionary instructions to resourceful corps commanders. Ideally, Lee ought to have known to give Jackson his head, but to keep tight rein on Stuart and Ewell; to stir Gordon with quiet suggestion, but to impel Longstreet with sharp command. Here Lee made the mistake of attributing to all of his lieutenants his own great tactical insight and high code of gentlemanly attitude.[42]

Lee's theory of battlefield command did not always measure up to his other qualities of leadership. To fashion strategy and so manage his army as to bring it with maximum efficiency to the point of decision: this, felt Lee, was his primary function. Once the missions were assigned and the battle joined, he sometimes permitted control to drift. He was most guilty of this on the second day of Gettysburg: here, for a time, says Freeman, the Army of Northern Virginia was virtually without a commander. Lee remedied this mistake during the later campaigns of the war.[43]

In dwelling upon Lee's particular weaknesses and misjudgments, both real and imagined, critics obscure his achievements as a whole. As commander of the Army of Northern Virginia, Lee's sole responsibility throughout most of the war, he earned the acclaim of history. Circumscribed in command, opposing overwhelming numbers, and fighting under every material disadvantage known to the science of war, Lee through his generalship largely sustained the Confederacy in one of the most prodigious military efforts of the modern age. What he could have accomplished as untrammeled general-in-chief must remain conjecture. His actual accomplishments, all things considered, were second to none in the American military experience. His virtues as a general transcended his faults.

Lee's prime quality, according to Freeman, was intellect; it was "the accurate reasoning of a trained and precise mind"; it was a "developed aptitude for the difficult synthesis of war." Intellect of the highest order enabled Lee to look into his opponents' minds and read their intentions, doubts, and fears; then with maximum efficiency to capitalize upon this knowledge.[44]

Audacity enhanced intellect to make Lee the general. Boldness is the noblest of military virtues, says Clausewitz; it is the "true steel which gives the weapon its edge and brilliancy. . . . Boldness, directed by an overruling intelligence, is the stamp of the hero." Audacity enabled Lee repeatedly to seize the initiative from opponents commanding twice his strength; audacity moved him time and again to flout the established rules of warfare in order to strike the foe at the least expected times and places. "We must decide between the positive loss of inactivity and the risk of action," Lee once wrote in a terse but profound exposition of his theory of war. Lee's prowess came largely of a readiness to accept the risk of action.[45]

Character exalted intellect and audacity to make Lee one of the greatest leaders of men the world has known. "Alexander, Hannibal, Caesar . . . and Napoleon [had] the highest faculties of mind," says F. E. Adcock in a study on the outstanding generals of antiquity. "But . . . they possessed character in a still greater degree. To this list," continues Adcock, "I would add . . . Robert E. Lee." Character lights the moral flame of leadership, a quality indefinable and mysterious, one that Clausewitz says can be spoken of only in words vague and rhapsodical. Deep religious conviction united with the chivalric tradition of Virginia aristocracy to endow Lee with remarkable serenity and nobility of nature. "I have met many of the great men of my time," said General Viscount Wolseley, "but Lee alone impressed me with the feeling that I was in the presence of a man who was cast in a grander mould, and made of different and finer metal than all other men. He is stamped upon my memory as a being apart and superior to all others in every way: a man with whom none I ever knew, a very few of whom I have ever read, are worthy to be classed." Lee's sharpest critic eloquently tells the effect of Lee's leadership through character. "Few generals," writes General Fuller, "have been able to animate an army as [Lee's] self-sacrificing idealism animated the Army of Northern Virginia. . . . What this bootless, ragged, half-starved army accomplished is one of the miracles of history."[46]

Times are perilously late for Americans to permit the zeal of nationalism to blind them to excellence, no matter whence it may come. Lee's career teaches certain lessons for the military leadership of today. Jet airplanes, intercontinental missiles, and thermonuclear bombs make the weapons of Lee's era as obsolete as the tomahawk; they bring war to hypertrophy. But if today's "balance of terror" should continue to prevail, and mankind be spared the fiery bolts of extinction, then Lee's strategic and tactical concepts will again prove useful in the employment of conventional military forces. Victory through attrition, which has been the key to American strategy in the Civil War and the two world wars, is no longer possible for this nation; nor can she hope to destroy the war strength of her opponents without resort to thermonuclear weapons. She must again learn the skills of swift maneuver and the delivery of paralyzing blows by highly mobile forces upon lines of communication and points of decision. Armies of the future must be composed of semi-independent, self-contained units, says General Matthew Ridgway, units capable of operating over great distances on a fluid battlefield, and with a minimum of control from higher headquarters.[47] These words remind one of Lee's discretionary orders to the virtually independent commanders, Jackson, Stuart, Early, and at the end, Joseph E. Johnston. In darker extremity, this nation must again learn to wage cunning defensive war for the conservation of weaker resources: war that destroys the enemy's resolve by taxing him beyond his anticipation.

Finally, if this people must fight again, either with conventional arms or in the holocaust of thermonuclear war, then the nobler qualities of Lee's generalship will offer an even brighter example than his techniques of combat. Intellect to divine and cope with enemy capabilities and intentions; boldness to strike when the occasion demands, however grave the risk; and above all, character to inspire purpose and sacrifice in the midst of supreme stress, hardship, and danger: these will be the imperatives of leadership for national survival. The art and science of war can yet profit from the genius of Lee.

NOTES

1. Carl von Clausewitz, *On War*, 3 vols. (London and New York: E. P. Dutton and Company, 1940), 1:194–95, 3:170–71.

2. Charles P. Roland, *The Confederacy* (Chicago: University of Chicago Press, 1960), 34–41.

3. J. F. C. Fuller, *Grant & Lee: A Study in Personality and Generalship* (1933; reprint, Bloomington: Indiana University Press, 1957), 262.

4. Cyril Falls, *A Hundred Years of War* (London: Duckworth, 1953), 18; Archer Jones, *Confederate Strategy from Shiloh to Vicksburg* (Baton Rouge: Louisiana State University Press, 1961), 16–32.

5. Fuller, *Grant & Lee*, 39–40; Charles de Gaulle, *The Edge of the Sword* (New York: Criterion Books, 1960), 93–94; Sir Fredrick Maurice, *Robert E. Lee, The Soldier* (Boston and New York: Houghton Mifflin Company, 1925), 76.

6. Douglas Southall Freeman, *R. E. Lee: A Biography,* 4 vols, (New York: Charles Scribner's Sons, 1934–36), 2:6–7.

7. Freeman, *Lee*, 1:621.

8. R. E. Lee to Albert Sidney Johnston, 26 March 1862, in Mrs. Mason Barret Collection of Albert Sidney and William Preston Johnston Papers, Tulane University Archives, New Orleans.

9. Freeman, *Lee*, 2:28.

10. Niccolo Machiavelli, *The Art of War* (Albany NY: H. C. Southwick, 1815), 233; Freeman, *Lee*, 2:39–50, 53–57.

11. Freeman, *Lee*, 2:199.

12. Clausewitz, *On War*, 1:100; Freeman, *Lee*, 2:302, 256–349.

13. G. F. R. Henderson, *The Science of War* (London and New York: Longmans, Green, and Company, 1905), 175; R. Ernest Dupuy and Trevor N. Dupuy, *The Compact History of the Civil War* (New York: Hawthorn Books, 1960), 156–57.

14. David Donald, *Lincoln Reconsidered: Essays on the Civil War Era* (New York: Alfred A. Knopf, 1956), 94; T. Harry Williams "The Military Leadership of North and South," in *Why the North Won the Civil War*, ed. David Donald (Baton Rouge: Louisiana State University Press, 1960), 32; Clausewitz, *On War*, 2:154–55.

15. Clausewitz, *On War*, 1:35, 174.

16. Freeman, *Lee*, 3:34.

17. Henderson, *The Science of War*, 35.

18. Jones, *Confederate Strategy from Shiloh to Vicksburg*, 211–13; Freeman, *Lee*, 3:29–161.

19. Williams, "The Military Leadership of North and South," 40–46.

20. E. P. Alexander, *Military Memoirs of a Confederate: A Critical Narrative* (New York: Charles Scribner's Sons, 1907), 364–65.

21. Walter Millis, *Arms and Men: A Study in American Military History* (New York: Putnam, 1956), 111.

22. Gordon A. Harrison, *Cross Channel Attack* (Washington DC: GPO, 1951), 76; Forrest C. Poague, *The Supreme Command* (Washington DC: GPO, 1954), 182–83. Both of these volumes are in the *United States Army in World War II* series, prepared by the Office of the Chief of Military History, Department of the Army.

23. Jones, *Confederate Strategy from Shiloh to Vicksburg*, 24–25.

24. Freeman, *Lee*, 3:206–7.

25. Clausewitz, *On War*, 1:35.

26. Freeman, *Lee*, 3:275–391; Bruce Catton, *A Stillness at Appomattox* (New York: Doubleday, 1953), 63–187.

27. Catton, *A Stillness at Appomattox*, 152.

28. Falls, *A Hundred Years of War*, 59–60; Alfred H. Burne, *Lee, Grant and Sherman: A Study in Leadership in the 1864–65 Campaign* (New York: Charles Scribner's Sons, 1939), 49.

29. Maurice, *Robert E. Lee, The Soldier*, 85.

30. Burne, *Lee, Grant and Sherman*, 55–61; Freeman, *Lee*, 3:392–447.

31. Freeman, *Lee*, 3:461–62.

32. Freeman, *Lee*, 3:441, 496n.; Walter H. Taylor, *Four Years with General Lee* (New York: D. Appleton and Company, 1878), 145.

33. Jones, *Confederate Strategy from Shiloh to Vicksburg*, 232; Dupuy and Dupuy, *Compact History of the Civil War*, 281; Gilbert E. Govan and James W. Livingood, *A Different Valor: The Story of General Joseph E. Johnston, C. S. A.* (New York: Bobbs-Merrill, 1956), 343.

34. Taylor, *Four Years with General Lee*, 148.

35. Govan and Livingood, *A Different Valor*, 347.

36. Varina Howell Davis, *Jefferson Davis, Ex-President of the United States: A Memoir by His Wife*, 2 vols. (New York: Belford Company, 1890), 2:579.

37. Freeman, *Lee*, 4:1–143.

38. Burne, *Lee, Grant and Sherman*, 207; John C. Ropes, *The Story of the Civil War: A Concise Account of the War in the United States of America between 1861 and 1865*, 3 vols. in 4 (New York: Putnam's Sons, 1894–1913), 2:157–58; Garnot J. Wolseley, *General Lee* (Rochester NY: Press of C. Mann Printing Company, 1906), 62; Henderson, *The Science of War*, 314; Maurice, *Robert E. Lee, The Soldier*, 293–94; Falls, *A Hundred Years of War*, 48; D. W. Brogan, "A Fresh Appraisal of the Civil War," *Harper's Magazine* (April 1960), 136; Winston Churchill, *A History of the English-Speaking Peoples*, 4 vols. (New York: Dodd, Mead, 1956–58), 4:169.

39. The most sweeping criticisms of Lee's generalship are in Fuller, *Grant & Lee*. Other sharp criticisms are in Donald, *Lincoln Reconsidered*, 82–102, and Williams, "The Military Leadership of North and South," in *Why the North Won the Civil War*, ed. David Donald, 23–47.

40. Maurice, *Robert E. Lee, The Soldier*, 162–63.

41. Catton, *A Stillness at Appomattox*, 48.

42. Freeman, *Lee*, 4:168.

43. Freeman, *Lee*, 4:168–69.

44. Freeman, *Lee*, 4:170–73.

45. Clausewitz, *On War*, 1:188–91; Freeman, *Lee*, 4:172.

46. F. E. Adcock, *The Greek and Macedonian Art of War* (Berkeley: University of California Press, 1957), 83; Clausewitz, *On War*, 1:178–79; Wolseley, *General Lee*, 60–61; Fuller, *Grant & Lee*, 280, 117.

47. Quoted in Millis, *Arms and Men*, 318.

Robert E. Lee and the Western Confederacy: A Criticism of Lee's Strategic Ability

THOMAS L. CONNELLY

In a recent essay on Robert E. Lee's generalship, a historian referred to his Army of Northern Virginia as the "varsity team." Such a statement might be expected from an eastern historian. That the comment originated with the biographer of one of the Army of Tennessee's first commanders, however, only reiterates the colonial status of the western Confederate army in both Civil War writing and thinking. The dominance of the eastern theater in Civil War historiography is well known. Beginning with such early works as the *Southern Historical Society Papers*, the stress has been on the East. Despite recent biographies of western leaders such as P. G. T. Beauregard and Leonidas K. Polk, the overemphasis of eastern matters apparently has not been curbed.[1]

Many reasons might be given for this imbalance. The proximity of Virginia battlefields to large population centers, the eastern success in battle, the relative isolation of western military areas, and the glamor associated with a Stonewall Jackson or a J. E. B. Stuart certainly are contributing factors. So, too, was the unified nature of the eastern army, both in command structure and later in historiography. Geographically, post-war sentiment and archival materials in the Confederate West were less unified. That eight generals commanded the western army also prevented a later idolization of a single leader as was the case in Virginia.

Yet the most enduring reason for the eastern emphasis has been the character of Robert E. Lee. Writings on Lee are voluminous, so much so that the Bibliographical Society of the University of Virginia in 1951 issued a preliminary checklist. Since then three additional major biographies and two compilations of Lee's papers have appeared. In this morass of over thirty biographies and hundreds of other monographs and articles, the image of Lee has been that of the Christian knight-soldier, magnificent in victory and in defeat.

No single war figure stands in greater need of re-evaluation than Lee. On at least three major counts, personality, field success, and strategy, he may have been the beneficiary of special pleading. Lee's personality has been amplified in every biography. His traits of kindness, patience, generosity, and others have become stereotyped. However, has anyone depicted Lee as he actually was? In the post-war writings of his former generals and staff officers, how much of the adulation of his personal qualities was the human tendency to prove one's closeness and accessibility to a popular hero? Too, in the stress on his virtues noted in late nineteenth-century writings, Lee perhaps has been shaped into a semi-religious symbol of suffering and resignation for a disillusioned, distraught South. There may be some correlation in the obituary in the *Halifax Chronicle* which declared Lee's life had seen no wrong doing, in Gamaliel Bradford's lengthy portrayal in 1912 of Lee's patience, love for animals, and Christian spirit, and in Douglas Freeman's later account of the young mother who brought her child to Lee "to be blessed." Also, in the many writings on Lee which appeared at the turn of the century, perhaps he was amplified above other Confederate leaders because he allegedly possessed traits which fitted well into the trend of nationalistic historical writing, such as his love for the Union, his generosity, and his single-minded concern with duty. Perhaps not by accident did Bradford label his biography, *Lee the American.* Later, how much were Lee's personality and reputation enhanced by the literary ability of Douglas Freeman? A balanced treatment of his personality may have been lost in the aura and glamor of the Virginia segment of the war as treated by Freeman, Clifford Dowdey, and others.[2]

One wonders as well if the depiction of his personal habits has not been a matter of special pleading. For Lee, unlike other Confederate generals, personality faults have become virtues. His weakness in handling subordinate officers, his seemingly submissive approach in dealing with Jefferson Davis, and his disinterest in political matters have been praised as evidence of his great kindness, his respect, and his sole interest in the military. Such a measuring stick has not been applied equally to other officers. By this same standard, Bragg should have been praised for his harshness and his martinet attitude, which molded what Arthur Fremantle termed the best disciplined army in the Confederacy.[3]

Lee's strategic and tactical success in Virginia perhaps needs reexamination as well. Was Lee actually as successful as his admirers have maintained? His penchant for the offensive, at least until the spring of 1864, leaves much open to question. Aside from the repercussions on overall war strategy to be mentioned later, there are other considerations. Was the Confederacy able to afford Lee? From the summer of 1862 until mid-1864, Lee utilized an operational strategy designed to keep the enemy away from Virginia, particularly the Richmond area, by offensive maneuvers. Thus the South's largest field army, contained in the smallest war theater, was bled to death by Lee's offensive tactics. In the Seven Days' campaign, Lee lost more men in his defense of Richmond than Albert Sidney Johnston's Army of Tennessee possessed the previous fall. In the Gettysburg campaign, Lee lost more men in his avowed purpose to prevent an advance on Richmond than Bragg's western army possessed in October of 1862. Lee lost more men at Chancellorsville than the Confederates surrendered at Forts Henry and Donelson combined in 1862. In the first three months of his command in Virginia in 1862, Lee lost 50,000 men.[4]

This manpower drain, seemingly inconsistent with both the general Confederate strategy of a defensive war and southern manpower shortages, is seldom criticized. Historians have measured Lee's success in terms of his holding territory in Virginia at whatever the cost. In contrast, P. G. T. Beauregard was judged a failure by his government for his skillful retreat into Mississippi in the spring of 1862 in the face of an enemy of over three times his strength. Likewise, Braxton Bragg was considered a failure because he lost the battle of Perryville in 1862, although by his maneuver he disrupted Federal plans to take Chattanooga, and recovered North Alabama and much of Middle Tennessee.

In other respects, Lee's reputation as a field general needs a second look. What would Lee have done had he faced the Federal command structure of the West? Lee gained his most spectacular field victories against weaker links in the Union command—John Pope, Joseph Hooker, and Ambrose Burnside. In contrast, Federal commanders generally considered more able fought in the West either until 1864 or for the war's duration. Grant and Philip Sheridan did not go eastward until 1864; William Sherman and George Thomas remained in the West until 1865. One wonders, too, how Lee's army would have fared if confronted with the problems of its western counterpart, the Army of Tennessee. Lee's activities were confined to a relatively small area of 22,000 square miles; the western army had to defend a territory of 225,000 square miles, eventually embracing seven states. This difference in the matter of maneuver, which placed an obvious strain on western logistics, was evident on several occasions. The Army of Northern Virginia never traveled more than some sixty miles north of the Virginia border. In contrast, Bragg's 1862 campaign from Tupelo to Lexington, via Chattanooga, required an 800-mile trek and a consequent strain on his army's transportation.

There were unusual problems of geography, as well as area, in the western theater. No Potomac, Rappahannock or Rapidan Rivers offered defensive lines; instead, the Tennessee, Mississippi and Cumberland offered excellent avenues of penetration deep into the West. Too, the primitive western rail system imposed special problems of maneuver on western commanders. After early 1862, the western Confederates possessed only one east-west line, via Vicksburg, Mobile, Montgomery, and Atlanta. Thus, to traverse the east-west limits of his command, Bragg would cover fully ten times the distance Lee marched from Virginia into Pennsylvania. This problem of maneuvering in the West was complicated by the need to defend the South's great single production area of foodstuffs, iron, raw materials and munitions, which dotted Tennessee, North-Central Georgia, and North-Central Alabama.[5]

Nor did Lee have to deal with the difficulties of the western command situation. The western army's high command never gelled around a single leader. The close dependency upon corps leaders, as in the case of Lee and Jackson, was impossible in the West. Eight different men held the post of commander-in-chief of the Army of Tennessee during the war; four either were removed by the government or resigned to avoid removal. Twenty-five different men held the post of corps command in the Army of Tennessee. During the single campaign from June, 1863, to November, 1863, eight men held corps or wing commands. In no two consecutive western campaigns was the make-up of corps commanders and commanding generals the same. Lee was aware of this flux, and sought to avoid it. In December of 1863, when offered the western command, he declined for the reason that he would not receive cooperation from his subordinates.[6]

One also wonders how Lee's field reputation as a successful offensive general would have fared if he had faced the numerical inferiorities of the western command. At almost every point in the war, the difference between Union and Confederate strength was far greater in the West than in the East. By November of 1862, the entire Union effective force on the Atlantic, from North Carolina to Delaware, even including the Washington and Philadelphia garrisons, numbered only some 216,000 men. Lee had available 97,000 effectives, including the defenses in southern Virginia. In the West, the Departments of the Ohio, Tennessee and Cumberland had amassed over 180,000 effectives against only 55,000 effectives in Bragg's army and that in Mississippi. In August of 1863, some 230,000 Federal effectives faced 67,000 in the Army of Tennessee and Joseph E. Johnston's defunct Mississippi army. In the East, the total Federal force on the Atlantic coast, from the coastal forts of New England to North Carolina, could amass only 172,000 effectives against 60,000 men under Lee and his allied Departments of South Virginia and North Carolina. When the Sherman-Grant campaign began in May, 1864, the Federal command on the Atlantic had 148,000 effectives available against over 82,000 effectives for Lee. In contrast, the Federal Military Division of the West had amassed over 198,000 men listed as effective to confront 74,000 effectives in Joseph E. Johnston's army and the smaller department in Mississippi and Alabama. By the spring of 1865, Sherman had accessible a total of over 207,000 effectives to oppose less than 40,000 Confederates stretched from the Carolinas to Mississippi. On the Atlantic, from Maine to Virginia, the Federals had available less than 200,000 effectives against Lee's potential strength of almost 75,000.[7]

Lee stands most in need of reappraisal in regard to his ideas of grand strategy. Only a few historians have ventured to comment on this aspect of his policy. Again, Lee seems to have benefited from special pleading. Either his chroniclers admit that he fostered no over-all strategic design or else they remain silent on the subject.

Two reasons, both debatable, have been given for Lee's not taking a more apparent interest in over-all strategy. It has been argued that his rightful concern was the Army of Northern Virginia; thus, Lee had neither the time nor the right to suggest policy. Yet many other commanders and subordinates found such opportunities. Beauregard in 1862, 1863, and 1864 presented several detailed plans. Joseph E. Johnston and James Longstreet suggested policies in 1863 and 1864. Even General Dabney Maury of the Department of the Gulf suggested an over-all strategy plan in the spring of 1863, as did General Leonidas Polk in 1863 and 1864. Lee, however, leading the South's largest army and possessing probably more influence than most others on the civil authorities, seemed almost aloof from the subject.[8]

A stronger reason given for this aloofness was that Lee did not possess the power to suggest strategy. Consistently, Lee scholars speculate on what Lee might have done had he had genuine authority. The inference is always the same—that he lacked real authority to aid the entire Confederate effort, East and West. His defenders argue that when he was advisor to Davis in the spring of 1862, he lacked any real power, that his position as army commander further dimmed his chances of any broad direction, and that when in 1865 he was appointed commander, Lee's hands were tied by the jealous machinations of Davis and by the over-all war. Thus Lee is absolved of any responsibility and is stereotyped as the brilliant but powerless war leader in Virginia.[9]

That Lee had little power is one of the great bits of mythology of the entire Civil War. Throughout the war, he exerted powerful influence, both official and unofficial. When the government was moved to Richmond in 1861, Lee already occupied a position described by his son as Davis' "constant and trusted adviser." In March, 1862, Lee was summoned to be what his biographers have labeled as a weak military advisor to the President. Many of these writers use as evidence Lee's own letter to his wife on March 14, in which he stated that he could see no advantage or pleasure in his duties. But Lee did not deny there—or elsewhere—that he had influence. His orders stated that he was to have charge of the armies of the Confederacy, under Davis' direction. Later, when General John Magruder congratulated him on being advanced to "Commander-in-Chief of the Confederate forces," Lee in his reply made no correction. In fact, Douglas Freeman himself admits that during Lee's three-month official duties in this particular office, he was called upon to pass on operations in every southern state, and that Davis consulted him on larger issues of strategy. However, Freeman argues that Lee was allowed no free hand on any plan of "magnitude." What plan of magnitude did Lee propose? The question was not a lack of power as much as a matter of selection. His correspondence as advisor largely concerned matters on the Atlantic slope with scant mention of the West. That Lee possessed great influence was indicated by his well-known role in Davis' decision of May, 1862, to order Joseph E. Johnston's army to assemble on the Peninsula and oppose that of General McClellan.[10]

Also, many historians have assumed that when Lee took command of the Army of Northern Virginia on June 1, he relinquished his position as military advisor. But his orders said nothing of abolishing his former office. In fact, on June 1, Davis told Lee that the new command "renders it necessary to interfere temporarily with the duties to which you were assigned in connection with the general service, but only so far as to make you available for command in the field of a particular army." Lee's son recalled later that "at all times" Lee continued to advise Davis and the War Department as to the disposition of other Confederate armies. Even Clifford Dowdey admits that in November, 1863, Lee was acting in the capacity of an unofficial advisor.[11]

The question of whether Lee officially or unofficially retained his formal position as advisor is academic. What is important is that, beginning in the summer of 1862, Lee exerted an advisory influence on Confederate matters which contradicts assertions that he lacked a position of power. Officially or not, Lee advised the government on general strategy and command problems from the summer of 1862 until 1865.

Examples of Lee's advisory capacity are many and far-reaching. In June,

1862, he suggested stripping Georgia and the Carolinas to inaugurate a second front in Virginia under Thomas Jackson. In July, 1862, he suggested an invasion of Kentucky. In September, 1862, Lee suggested that the Army of Tennessee be sent to hold Richmond while he invaded Maryland. In December, he again suggested the reinforcement of Virginia by Bragg's army, and suggested the reinforcement of North Carolina from South Carolina.[12]

In January and February, 1863, Lee offered advice regarding the reinforcement of Wilmington from the Georgia-South Carolina area. He conferred with Davis in March, 1863, in regard to what Bragg and Pemberton should do in the West. Throughout April and May he was consulted on western problems. In May he suggested how Johnston should fight Grant in Mississippi; the following month he advised Davis on how and why Bragg should take the offensive against Rosecrans. After Gettysburg, Lee advised Davis that Beauregard's army should be transferred from the Carolinas to Virginia. In August and early September, 1863, Lee closely conferred with Davis on the western situation. In September and October, Lee repeatedly offered advice as to how Bragg should deal with Rosecrans. After Missionary Ridge, he was consulted about the matter of Bragg's successor. In fact, on four occasions, Lee was consulted on the subject of naming a new commander of the Army of Tennessee.[13]

Lee's continual offering of advice continued in 1864. Throughout the early spring, he repeatedly made suggestions as to how Johnston should deal with Sherman in Georgia, and he even produced a plan for combined operations between Johnston and Longstreet. He continued to consult with Davis regarding the North Georgia campaign until Johnston was removed, and then was consulted about Johnston's replacement. In fact, prior to this removal, Davis even asked Lee who should be placed in command of Leonidas Polk's corps after that general was killed. Meanwhile, in May, 1864, he advised Davis to send all organized forces from the Department of South Carolina, Georgia and Florida to Virginia. In early 1865, he suggested bringing Hood's Army of Tennessee to Virginia. In January, 1865, he also recommended bringing Kirby Smith's trans-Mississippi force to Virginia, and offered counsel on how Beauregard should deal with Sherman in the Carolinas.[14]

If Lee so often advised on over-all matters, what did he propose? Though he never formulated a comprehensive plan, three factors are evident in his views, and generally comprise his strategic thinking. First, Lee possessed an almost startling lack of knowledge of the West. He seemed somewhat naive concerning both Federal purposes and strength in the West. Lee seemed not to appreciate that the Federals were maintaining a two-front war between the Appalachians and the Mississippi. Lee seemed to believe that only the seizure of Richmond and the control of the Mississippi River were prime Federal objectives. The long-existing Federal plan to seize Chattanooga and eventually Atlanta, initiated in May, 1862, went almost unnoticed in Lee's correspondence.

Too, Lee seemed uninformed as to both Federal strength and Confederate weakness, and thus sometimes assumed that the southerners could do more than they were able. The Federals maintained three large field armies in the West from early 1862 until 1865, the Departments of the Ohio, Tennessee, and Cumberland. Any one of these outnumbered the only genuine Confederate army between the Appalachians and the Mississippi, the Army of Tennessee. There was an additional army in the Mississippi-Alabama department, but this satellite element sustained itself only by reinforcement from the Army of Tennessee. The only time the Mississippi army achieved any respectable strength was after it had been reinforced by the Army of Tennessee three times between December, 1862, and May, 1863.

Lee's response to the Federal power in the West was a long series of suggestions which indicated that he hardly believed a serious front existed there. For example, in September, 1862, he argued that the overwhelming Yankee concentration in Virginia necessitated bringing Bragg's army to protect Richmond. At that time, the western Federals had available 124,000 men, mainly in Tennessee, to oppose Bragg's 35,000 effectives and an additional small force in Mississippi. Moreover, one Federal arm, the Army of the Ohio, was maneuvering to within twenty miles of the critical Chattanooga rail junction and defensive barrier. Again, in December, 1862, his request for Bragg's army in Virginia grossly underrated Federal power on the Tennessee front, which consisted of 125,000 effective troops. In June, 1863, after maintaining that "Virginia is to be the theater of action," Lee urged that Bragg operate in Ohio. Lee overlooked the fact that Federal strength in the West had been boosted to 214,000 effectives and present for duty, and that Bragg, after reinforcing Pemberton, possessed barely 50,000 men. Again, in the autumn of 1863, Lee's lengthy September-October correspondence with Davis and Longstreet indicated that he expected short work could be made of Rosecrans' army. Repeatedly in the spring of 1864, Lee urged that Joseph E. Johnston take the offensive against Sherman because "the great effort of the enemy in this campaign will be made in Virginia." Thus, Lee argued, such a great force in Virginia must have come from the Federals in the West. Lee even suggested that same spring that part of Johnston's cavalry be given to him for operations in Virginia, although the cavalry shortage in the Army of Tennessee was well-known. To the end, Lee grossly short-changed the western threat. In March, 1865, he reported innocently that Johnston's North Carolina army "is believed . . .

to be inferior to that of the enemy." At that time Johnston possessed barely 20,000 effectives arrayed against over 100,000 effectives under Sherman and Schofield, not to mention an additional 87,000 back-up troops in Kentucky and Tennessee.[15]

One senses this unrealistic, if not impatient, tone in Lee's letters concerning why western commanders could not take the offensive as he did in Virginia. This attitude was also due to his lack of understanding of geography. Lee himself admitted to Davis that he knew little of the West. Some of his errors are well-known, such as his statement that the summer weather in Mississippi would force a withdrawal of Grant from Mississippi in June, 1863, and his belief in 1865 that Sherman could not march across the Carolinas.[16]

Other miscalculations run much deeper than these two misjudgments. Lee's correspondence indicates that he never fully grasped the importance of the southern munitions-supply area of Georgia, Alabama, and Tennessee, at least not until 1864. Twice in 1862 he recommended an almost wholesale withdrawal from that area in order to garrison Virginia. In the early summer crisis of 1863, Lee interpreted the problem as merely being which of two areas, the Mississippi River or Virginia, was more endangered. In the fall of 1863, after Bragg had lost Chattanooga to Rosecrans and the Federals threatened to seize the Atlanta railroad, Lee bemoaned the fact that he had allowed Longstreet to reinforce Bragg. Lee admitted that his real purpose in detaching Longstreet was not to protect the Georgia-Alabama munitions area, but to save Knoxville, lest western Virginia be affected. In fact, Lee also admitted that had he known of the fall of Knoxville, he would not even have allowed Longstreet to go to Georgia. Instead, he would have sent him to operate from western Virginia.[17]

Too, Lee may have underrated the logistical problems of maneuver in the West. The presence of the single west-east rail line between Georgia and Mississippi placed the western Confederates on a long exterior line. Federal control of the three main river arteries, the Mississippi, Cumberland, and Tennessee, always interposed the threat of a flanking force. Also, with innumerable vital installations to be protected, ranging from the broad belt of Alabama iron works and rail junctions to the manufactories of Atlanta, Selma, Columbus, Augusta, and other towns, the Lee style of offensive maneuvering against the enemy was not easy.

Above all, the immense depth and width of the western theater, which strained Confederate logistics, made Lee's concept of offensives almost impossible. Lee stressed the concept of maneuvering so as to threaten directly an enemy base, such as in the Peninsula and Second Manassas campaigns. In the West, Federal bases were sometimes 400 miles to the rear, and the increasingly deteriorating condition of western cavalry and the constant improvement of Federal engineering made such threats difficult. The western army usually did not have the logistical strength to take the offensive. Basic Confederate commissary policy from late 1862 until at least 1864 imposed a special burden on the western army, which crippled the chances of effective maneuvers such as Lee often suggested. Supplies gathered in the rich Tennessee grain lands and elsewhere were usually sorted at Chattanooga, Atlanta, and other depots for the use of Lee's army alone. Commissary General Lucius Northrop insisted that the Army of Tennessee could live off the country instead. This hand-to-mouth existence wrecked the army's transportation system. By the spring of 1863, Bragg was almost immobilized because of the strain imposed on his wagon transportation in obtaining forage from as far away as 250 miles.[18]

Suggestions made by Lee would seem to indicate that he did not understand the western logistical problem. In January, 1863, he urged that Bragg drive back Rosecrans to the Ohio River. In the spring of 1864, Lee made two strategy proposals for the West which further indicated his lack of understanding of logistics. Though he admitted to Longstreet that "I am not sufficiently acquainted with the country to do more than indicate the general plan," he suggested in March an unrealistic joint offensive by Johnston and Longstreet. Johnston was to move up the Tennessee Valley around Sherman at Chattanooga, then join Longstreet, who was to move down from East Tennessee around Burnside at Knoxville. The two columns were then to cross the wide Cumberland Plateau to Middle Tennessee. It was not merely that this move was geographically impossible, since Sherman blocked the valley at Chattanooga; Johnston simply could not move his army almost 400 miles across the well-foraged East Tennessee valley and the barren Cumberland Mountains. A month earlier, Lee had proposed that Longstreet mount his corps on mules and raid Kentucky, a suggestion which took little cognizance of either transportation shortages in the West or the barrenness of east Kentucky's mountains.[19]

Lee's strategic policies were colored by a second principle that may explain much of his attitude toward the West. Lee was convinced that the main war zone was in Virginia, and shaped his strategy accordingly. In September and December of 1862, he seemed sure the main Federal concentration was in Virginia. Even with Grant and Rosecrans preparing for operations in the West, Lee in May, 1863, declared that "Virginia is to be the theater of action. . . ." Though Sherman had amassed three departmental armies against Johnston in the spring of 1864, Lee in April contended that "the great effort of the enemy in this campaign will be made in Virginia." He proposed that such large reinforcements could come only from the West and other areas. Therefore, Johnston must take the offensive to relieve Lee. Again in April, Lee urged that the approaching storm would "burst on Virginia," unless it could be diverted by Johnston's taking the offensive. On another occasion, Lee argued that the main concentration was being made in Virginia, and that Johnston must take the offensive to halt it. Even in the fall of 1863, when his own scouts had reported that the eastern Federals had sent two corps to Rosecrans in addition to Burnside's corps which was previously sent, Lee was adamant. He labeled the reinforcements as small, and warned that Meade was ready to overrun Virginia in force.[20]

Thus Lee's strategy essentially was based on defending Virginia. From the summer of 1862 until the spring of 1864. Lee practiced his well-known policy of maneuver and the offensive—break up the enemy's campaigns and keep him away from the heart of Virginia, above all away from Richmond. When failing manpower and logistics made this impossible in 1864, Lee reverted to a defensive which was still designed to keep the Federals away from the capital.

This was basically Lee's strategy not only for Virginia but for the entire South. During both of these periods, his interest seemed limited to what the West could do to help Virginia: either the West should contribute troops to the East or take the offensive to improve conditions in the East. In the fall and winter of 1862, his recommendations were for the wholesale reinforcement of Virginia. In the spring of 1863, the plea was for strong Virginia reinforcement. In the autumn of 1863, Lee maintained that a quick thrust should be made against Rosecrans so that Longstreet could be returned. In the spring of 1864, Johnston was urged to take the offensive to curtail reinforcement of Virginia.

Always this matter of reinforcement was a one-way policy. It sometimes led Lee into inconsistent reasoning, so much so that it seems Lee's basic policy was either to reinforce Virginia or to let each man shift for himself. In the spring of 1863, hard pressed by Davis, Seddon, and Cooper to reinforce the West, Lee seemed to grope for practically any reason why he could not do so. Thus, Lee was inconsistent. He argued that it was not wise to transfer troops between departments; that whenever shifts were made by the Federals, it did no good for the Confederates to make corresponding shifts. Yet his pleas for having the western army sent to Virginia in September and December of 1862 had been based upon the reverse principle—that a heavy concentration was building up in Virginia and that a corresponding shift should be made. Later, in July, 1863, Lee requested a major shift of troops from Beauregard's South Carolina Department to meet a Virginia concentration. In May, 1864, Lee argued again that, since two Federal corps had been removed from the Carolinas to Virginia, the Confederates should make a corresponding shift. Again, in April, 1864, Lee completely reversed the reasoning by which he had opposed sending Johnston troops in 1863. Noting a heavy Federal concentration in Virginia, he argued that troops from less threatened departments should be sent to Richmond.[21]

Several factors emerge here. Lee never voiced a consistent policy of concentration. Though he sometimes spoke of a need to concentrate men at needed areas, he would never admit that Virginia should not receive the highest priority. Thus he did not reverse his many pleas for troops from the West and did not offer assistance from Virginia. He sometimes spoke of the need for western reinforcement, but this was conditional, in that such reinforcement must not be taken from him.

Only on one occasion did Lee consent to a reinforcement of the West. This move, Longstreet's reinforcement of Bragg, has been magnified out of proportion as to both aim and extent. As mentioned, Lee's purpose was not to bolster Bragg's strength against Rosecrans, but to save Knoxville lest western Virginia be endangered. He was unenthusiastic at the move. Even while conferring with Davis in late August and early September, he wanted to keep his troops in order to take the offensive against Meade. As late as August 31, he told Longstreet to ready the army for an offensive and spoke of crushing Meade. When Davis prevailed, the reinforcement was weak and halfhearted. Only two divisions were sent, and the slowness in determining this reinforcement was a factor in the lateness of their arrival for the campaign. Less than five thousand men from Lee's army were engaged at Chickamauga. Also, even before the last of Longstreet's men had arrived in Georgia, Lee had written Davis twice asking that they be returned. By September 25, Lee had already penned four suggestions for their return.[22]

The Longstreet reinforcement indicated, too, the double standard Lee used in his reinforcement policy. Later in 1864, he continually badgered Davis to have Johnston take the offensive because Lee believed a heavy force had been sent from Sherman to Grant. Lee thus argued that Johnston could hold back further reinforcement. Yet Lee made little effort to do the same on his front, though he knew two corps had been sent to the West. He considered moving against Meade to prevent further reinforcement, but nothing was done.[23]

Lee's apparent obsession that the main Federal front was in the East indicated a third element in his strategic thinking. Historians have speculated what Lee might have done had he held the powers of a generalissimo, or had he possessed even stronger powers in his positions of military advisor, army commander, and commander-in-chief in 1865. Usually the conclusion is rhetorical—that Lee possessed an overall strategic mind but no power. Yet this explanation overlooks the key element of localism in his thinking.

What qualities of a master strategist did Lee possess? Some historians have spoken of his weakness in logistical matters on the Virginia front. As mentioned, his unfamiliarity with the West indicated a lack of understanding of western supply. Nor did Lee seem aware of the closeness of political and military matters. His offensive tactics, which cost the South 50,000 men in his first three months, did not harmonize well with the basic Confederate defensive posture. His Maryland invasion seemed ill-suited to diplomatic and political considerations. That he even refused to comment to Senator Ben Hill on the strategic value of moving the capital further south because it was a political question seems strange, since Lee commanded the South's largest army committed to the capital's defense. Too, his asking the government in 1863 to choose between the Mississippi River and Virginia seemed to show a failure to grasp the political implications of the river's loss, whereas his Virginia reasoning was based solely on the military merits of an offensive.[24]

One might also debate whether Lee possessed a sufficiently broad military mind to deal with over-all Confederate matters. Keeping the enemy away from Richmond seemed to dominate his strategic thinking from the time of his emotional plea in Richmond council in May, 1862, that Richmond must not be given up. Dedicated to the task of maneuvering in Virginia to keep the Federals out, Lee seemed to choose the short gain. When he proposed the Maryland campaign, and later in his report of that invasion, his emphasis was on what such a campaign would do locally in Virginia. Even Lee's sympathetic biographer, Clifford Dowdey, conceded that in his Sharpsburg planning Lee was willing to settle for the short-range goal of clearing Virginia of Federals even if it meant defeat. The planning for the Pennsylvania invasion also demonstrated Lee's short-range thinking. As one writer has recently noted, Lee's decision to invade the North probably had little if anything to do with the western situation. Lee's June 8 explanation for wanting such a move was based not on national considerations but on the fear that the Federals would soon advance on Richmond. Lee added that "it is worth a trial" to prevent such a move. On June 25, he spoke of his plans as designed to embarrass General Joseph Hooker's plans to invade Virginia.

Then, after the campaign had failed, Lee, on July 12, explained to Davis that had it not been for an unexpected rise in the Potomac during the retreat everything would have been accomplished that could be expected. What did he consider his accomplishments—that the Army of the Potomac had been thrown north of the Potomac, and that the lower Virginia-North Carolina coast had been cleared? Thus Lee, on July 31, labeled his campaign a general success—three weeks after the South had lost Middle Tennessee,

47,000 men in the campaign at Vicksburg, the last link in the control of the Mississippi, over 27,000 at Gettysburg, and great political prestige in the Northwest.[25]

Finally, one wonders whether Lee could have shed his local prejudices for Virginia sufficiently to give a dispassionate appraisal of war matters in other areas of the Confederate states. Lee seemed to evince a more localistic, provincial outlook than did other major Confederate leaders, so much so that one perhaps might infer that Lee was fighting for Virginia and not for the South. He said this, in effect, in the spring of 1861. To his brother and sister he confided that he had no desire to fight save for the defense of his state. To the Virginia convention he declared his allegiance solely to the service of Virginia. Perhaps there is much truth in the reminiscence by Lee's comrade at Washington College, William Jones. In his biography of the general, Jones remarked that "Robert Edward Lee regarded his allegiance to the sovereign state of Virginia as paramount to all others."[26]

This obsession with Virginia was seen even in the make-up of his own army. Intentionally or not, Lee surrounded himself with Virginia-bred officers who led an army composed of troops from the entire South. Perhaps there is something to be said for the comment of one Lee biographer that in the post-Sharpsburg reorganization, the sending of Mississippi-bred Chase Whiting to North Carolina eliminated the "last unwanted legacy" of the older army, and that henceforth the army reflected Lee totally. In July, 1862, seven of Lee's twelve infantry corps and division commanders were Virginians. At Gettysburg, four of Lee's five infantry and artillery and cavalry leaders were from Virginia. By the beginning of the May, 1864, campaign, Lee possessed fifteen corps and division commanders in his infantry and cavalry. Nine were Virginians, including two of Lee's sons and a nephew.[27]

With a mention of Lee's Virginia ties, one comes full circle in any discussion of Lee's strategy. For Lee, who misunderstood the West, who was convinced that the war would be won or lost in Virginia, and who had unusually strong family ties in his state, Confederate strategy was essentially the salvation of Virginia. Lee never espoused a consistent philosophy of concentration, and did not present a stable plan for operating on a single line of the enemy's advance. Though he freely offered advice on the West, it always was given in the context of his strategy for Virginia, and thus lacked scope.

By no means did the government accept all of Lee's suggestions. But with his prestige as a winner and his unusual capacity to advise, Lee often succeeded even when he failed. Even when he could not persuade the government to implement a stronger eastern concentration, he almost always managed to maintain the *status quo* and keep his army intact in

Virginia. Also, by his prestige, Lee may have influenced the government to take a less broad strategic view, and to go for the short gain in Virginia where victory seemed more possible.

The metahistorical speculation of what the Confederacy might have done without Lee is an old one. Almost always it is assumed that had Lee not cast his lot with the South, the Confederacy would have died quickly on the Virginia field in 1861–1862. Yet, when all the glamor of the war in Virginia is laid aside, was the South, poor in men and logistics, able to afford Lee? The need to conserve manpower and logistical strength, and the need to maintain a defensive status that used well the great area of Southern territory somehow never fitted well with his strategic ideas. When these things are considered, one ponders whether the South may not have fared better had it possessed no Robert E. Lee.

NOTES

1. Charles P. Roland, "The Generalship of Robert E. Lee," in *Grant, Lee, Lincoln and the Radicals: Essays on Civil War Leadership*, ed. Grady McWhiney (New York, 1964), 48.

2. See J. William Jones, *Personal Reminiscences, Anecdotes and Letters of General Robert E. Lee* (New York, 1876), 66–67, 44, 49, 51, 53, 58; Gamaliel Bradford, *Lee the American* (Boston and New York, 1912), 196–246; Douglas Southall Freeman, *R. E. Lee: A Biography* (New York, 1935–36) 4:505; see also pp. 490–504.

3. For sympathetic accounts of Lee's personality, see Henry E. Shepherd, *Life of Robert Edward Lee* (New York and Washington, 1906), 436–73; A. L. Long, *Memoirs of Robert E. Lee* (New York, 1886), 433–35, 460–64; Sir Frederick Maurice, *Robert E. Lee the Soldier* (Boston and New York, 1925), 274–84; Clifford Dowdey, *Lee* (Boston and Toronto, 1965), 638–39.

4. Louis H. Manarin, "Lee in Command: Strategical and Tactical Policies," (Ph.D. dissertation, Duke University, 1965), 574; T. Harry Williams, "The Military Leadership of North and South," in *Why the North Won the Civil War*, ed. David Donald (New York, 1962), 47; J. F. C. Fuller, *Grant and Lee: A Study in Personality and Generalship* (Bloomington, 1957), 260–65, 286–87.

5. Frank E. Vandiver (ed.), *Civil War Diary of General Josiah Gorgas* (Tuscaloosa, 1947), 3; J. W. Mallet, "Work of the Ordnance Bureau of the War Department of the Confederate States, 1861–1865," *Southern Historical Society Papers* 37 (1909): 4–6, 10–11; Josiah Gorgas, "Ordnance of the Confederacy: Notes of Brig. Gen. Josiah Gorgas, Chief of Ordnance, C. S. A." *Army Ordnance* 16 (Jan.–Feb. 1936): 213–14, 285–97; Richard Steuart, "How Johnny Got His Gun," *Confederate Veteran* 32 (May 1924): 166–67; A. L. Conger, "Fort Donelson," *Military Historian and Economist* 1 (Jan. 1916): 56–59; United States Bureau of Census, *Agriculture*

of the United States in 1860: Compiled from the Original Returns of the Eighth Census (Washington DC, 1864), 2, 6, 18, 62, 66, 84, 92, 108, 128, 136, 148, 162; J. B. Killebrew, *Middle Tennessee as an Iron Centre* (Nashville, 1879), 9–15; J. P. Lesley, *Iron Manufacturer's Guide to the Furnaces, Forges and Rolling Mills of the United States* (New York, 1859), 130–36; Frank Vandiver, *Ploughshares into Swords: Josiah Gorgas and Confederate Ordnance* (Austin, 1952), 122, 148–76.

6. The Army of Tennessee was at one time or another commanded by Generals Leonidas Polk, Albert Sidney Johnston, P. G. T. Beauregard, Braxton Bragg, William J. Hardee, Joseph E. Johnston, John Bell Hood, and Richard Taylor. For Lee's refusal to go West, see U.S. War Department, *The War of Rebellion: A Compilation of the Official Records of the Union and the Confederate Armies*, 127 vols., index, and atlas (Washington DC: 1880–1901), series 1, vol. 29, pt. 2, p. 861 [all references hereafter are to series 1]. See also Lee to Davis, 6 Sept. 1863, in Clifford Dowdey and Louis H. Manarin (eds.), *The Wartime Papers of R. E. Lee* (Boston, 1961), 596.

7. *Official Records*, vol. 37, pt. 2, pp. 543, 547, 552–53, 555; vol. 27, pt. 3, pp. 806, 809, 811, 814, 815, 818, 1065, 1067, 1068; vol. 29, pt. 2, pp. 374, 660; vol. 18, pt. 2, pp. 750–51, 441; vol. 47, pt. 3, pp. 73–74, 748–49; vol. 49, pt. 1, pp. 792, 798, 801; vol. 46, pt. 3, pp. 389–92; vol. 38, pt. 4, pp. 374, 376; vol. 36, pt. 3, pp. 326–27; vol. 23, pt. 2, pp. 606–7; vol. 24, pt. 3, p. 568.

8. See Roland, "The Generalship of Robert E. Lee," 35; Otto Eisenchiml, *The Hidden Face of the Civil War* (Indianapolis and New York, 1961), 216. For evidence of other general strategic plans, see Beauregard to Pierre Soule, 8 Dec. 1863, P. G. T. Beauregard Papers, Confederate Records, Record Group 109, National Archives; Beauregard to Bragg, 2 Sept. 1862, 7 July 1863, in Braxton Bragg Papers, Western Reserve Historical Society; Beauregard to Louis Wigfall, 16 May 1863, in Wigfall Family Papers, Library of Congress; Beauregard to Bragg, 7 Oct. 1863, Beauregard Papers; Beauregard to Charles Villere, 26 May 1863, *Official Records*, vol. 14, p. 955. By December 1863, Beauregard had presented six general plans to the government; see *Official Records*, vol. 31, pt. 3, p. 812. See also Polk to Hardee, 30 July 1863, Leonidas Polk Papers, University of the South Library; Polk to Jefferson Davis, 9 Aug. 1863, Leonidas Polk Papers, Duke University Library; Polk to Davis, 26 July 1863, *Official Records*, vol. 23, pt. 2, p. 932; James Seddon to James Longstreet, 3 May 1875, James Longstreet Papers, Emory University Library; Archer Jones, *Confederate Strategy from Shiloh to Vicksburg* (Baton Rouge, 1961), 206–10; Longstreet to Thomas Jordan, 27 March 1864, Longstreet to Beauregard, 15 March 1864, *Official Records*, vol. 22, pt. 3, pp. 627, 679; H. J. Eckenrode and Bryan Conrad, *James Longstreet, Lee's Warhorse* (Chapel Hill, 1936), 285–87; Longstreet to Lee, 5 Sept. 1863, *Official Records*, vol. 19, pt. 2, p. 699.

9. Dowdey, *Lee*, 181, 519; Freeman, *Lee*, vol. 2, pp. 4–7; Walter Taylor, *Four Years with General Lee* (New York, 1878), 37–38; Long, *Memoirs of Robert E. Lee*, 391–92, 401; Roland, "The Generalship of Robert E. Lee," 35, 58–59.

10. Robert E. Lee, *Recollections and Letters of General Robert E. Lee* (New York, 1904), 103; Freeman, *Lee*, vol. 2, pp. 6–7; Lee to wife, 14 March 1862,

in Dowdey and Manarin, *Wartime Papers*, 127–28; Fuller, *Grant and Lee*, 114; Dowdey, *Lee*, 181, 189–90; Magruder to Lee, 14 March 1862, *Official Records*, vol. 9, p. 66; Lee to Magruder, 17 March 1862, *Official Records*, vol. 9, pp. 70–71.

11. Davis to Lee, 1 June 1862, *Official Records*, vol. 11, pt. 3, pp. 568–69; Lee, *Recollections and Letters*, 103; Dowdey, *Lee*, 409.

12. Lee to Davis, 3 Sept 1862, in Dowdey and Manarin (eds.), *Wartime Papers*, 182–84; Lee to Davis, 3 Sept. 1862, *Wartime Papers*, 292–94; Lee to Davis, 6 Dec. 1862, *Wartime Papers*, 352–53; Lee to Davis, 26 July 1862, in *Lee's Dispatches: Unpublished Letters of General Robert E. Lee, C. S. A. to Jefferson Davis and the War Department of the Confederate States of America 1862–65*, ed. Grady McWhiney (New York, 1957), 38–40; Seddon to Beauregard, 13 Dec. 1862, *Official Records*, vol. 14, p. 714.

13. Lee to Davis, 6 Jan. 1863, in McWhiney (ed.), *Lee's Dispatches*, 68–70; Jones, *Confederate Strategy*, 199–214; Lee to Seddon, 9 April 1863, and Lee to Cooper, 16 April 1863, in Jefferson Davis Papers, Louisiana Historical Association Collection, Howard-Tilton Library, Tulane University; Lee to Davis, 28 May 1863, in McWhiney (ed.), *Lee's Dispatches*, 96–98; Lee to Davis, 8 July 1863, in Dowdey and Manarin (eds.), *Wartime Papers*, 543–44; Douglas Southall Freeman, *Lee's Lieutenants: A Study in Command* (New York, 1942–44) 3:220–22; Lee to Davis, 11 Sept. 1863, *Wartime Papers*, 599; Lee to Davis, 30 Sept. 1863, *Wartime Papers*, 606–7; Lee to Davis, 9 Sept. 1863, *Official Records*, vol. 19, pt. 2, p. 706; Lee to Davis, 11 Sept. 1862, *Official Records*, vol. 19, p. 712; Lee to Davis, 14 Sept. 1863, *Official Records*, vol. 19, pp. 720–21; Lee to Davis, 18 Sept. 1863, *Official Records*, vol. 19, pp. 730–31; Lee to Davis, 29 Sept. 1863, *Official Records*, vol. 19, p. 756; Lee to Davis, 18 Sept. 1863, *Official Records*, vol. 19, p. 766; Lee to Davis, 23 Sept. 1863, in Georgia Portfolio, vol. 2, Duke University Library; Lee to Longstreet, 25 Sept. 1863, in Jackson-Dabney Papers, Southern Historical Collection, University of North Carolina Library; Lee to Davis, 3 Dec. 1863, *Official Records*, vol. 21, pt. 3, p. 779; Lee to Davis, 7 Dec. 1863, *Official Records*, vol. 19, p. 792.

14. Lee to Longstreet, 16 Jan. and 17 Feb. 1864, in James Longstreet Papers, Emory University Library; Lee to Davis, 5 April 1864, in Robert E. Lee Papers, Emory University Library; Lee to Davis, 21 June 1864, in McWhiney (ed.), *Lee's Dispatches*, 255–56; Lee to Davis 3 Feb. 1864, in Dowdey and Manarin (eds.), *Wartime Papers*; Lee to Davis, 25 March 1864, *Wartime Papers*, 682–83; Lee to Longstreet, 28 March 1864, *Wartime Papers*, 684–85; Lee to Davis, 30 March 1864, *Wartime Papers*, 687–88; Lee to Braxton Bragg, 7 April 1864, *Wartime Papers*, 692; Lee to Davis, 8 April 1864, *Wartime Papers*, 693–94; Lee to Bragg, 16 April 1864, *Wartime Papers*, 701; Lee to Davis, 30 April 1864, *Wartime Papers*, 798–99; Lee to Davis, 12 July 1864, *Wartime Papers*, 821–22; Lee to Davis, 12 July 1864, *Wartime Papers*, 821; Lee to Davis, 15 June 1864, *Wartime Papers*, 783; Lee to Longstreet, 8 March 1864, *Official Records*, vol. 32, pt. 3, p. 594; Lee to Longstreet, 19 March 1864, *Official Records*, vol. 32, pt. 3, p. 656; Lee to Longstreet, 28 March 1864 *Official Records*, 648; Lee to Davis, 2 April 1864, *Official Records*, vol. 32, pt. 3, p. 736.

15. Lee to Davis, 3 Sept. 1862, in Dowdey and Manarin (eds.), *Wartime Papers*, 292–94; Lee to Davis, 6 Dec. 1862, *Wartime Papers*, 352–53; Lee to Davis, 11 May 1863, *Wartime Papers*, 483; Lee to Davis, 5 April 1864, *Wartime Papers*, 690–91; Lee to Davis, 5 July 1864, *Wartime Papers*, 814–15; Lee to John C. Breckinridge, 9 March 1865, *Wartime Papers*, 913; *Official Records*, vol. 23, pt. 2, pp. 378–80; vol. 24, pt. 3, p. 249; vol. 47, pt. 3, pp. 73–74, 748; vol. 49, pt. 1, pp. 792, 798, 801; vol. 23, pt. 2, p. 806; see also Lee to Davis, 11 Sept. 1864, *Official Records*, vol. 29, pt. 2, p. 712.

16. Lee to Davis, 18 Feb. 1864, in Dowdey and Manarin (eds.), *Wartime Papers*, 674–75; Lee to Seddon, 9 April 1863, Lee to Cooper, 16 April 1863, in Davis Papers, Tulane; Jones, *Confederate Strategy*, 204; Lee to Breckinridge, 19 Feb. 1865, in Dowdey and Manarin, *Wartime Papers*, 904–5; Lee to Davis, 23 Feb. 1865, *Wartime Papers*, 909; Lee to Seddon, 10 May 1863, *Wartime Papers*, 482.

17. Lee on 10 May told Seddon that the government must decide whether the line of Virginia was more in danger than the line of the Mississippi. Lee to Seddon, 10 May 1863, *Wartime Papers*, 482. In a telegram the previous day, Lee had contended that any question of reinforcing the West became a question between Virginia and Mississippi. Jones, *Confederate Strategy*, 211–12. On 14 September 1863, Lee wrote Davis that "Had I been aware that Knoxville was the destination of Gen. Burnside, I should have recommended that Gen. Longstreet be sent to oppose him, instead of to Atlanta," *Official Records*, vol. 29, pt. 2, pp. 720–21.

18. Bragg to B. S. Ewell, 18 March 1863, in Bragg Papers, Western Reserve; John Walker to Maj. Cummings, 20 Dec. 1862, in Bragg Papers, Western Reserve; W. L. Callaway et al. to Bragg, 13 Oct. 1863, in Carter Stevenson Papers, National Archives; see also *Official Records*, vol. 23, pt. 2, pp. 647, 648–49, 657, 662, 688, 695, 700, 702, 708, 718. On 4 February Northrop insisted that the supplies in Georgia depots were for Lee's army "and it alone," *Official Records*, vol. 23, pt. 2, p. 624. See also: *Chattanooga Daily Rebel*, 20 Dec. 1862; Johnston to Seddon, 4, 21 March, 25 Feb. 1863, Johnson to Northrop, 25 Feb. 1863, in Joseph E. Johnston Papers, College of William and Mary Library.

19. Lee to Davis, 6 Jan. 1863, in McWhiney (ed.) *Lee's Dispatches*, 68–70; Lee to Longstreet, 17 Feb. 1864, in Longstreet Papers, Emory University Library; Lee to Davis, 3 Feb. 1864, in J. William Jones, *Life and Letters of Robert Edward Lee;* Lee to Longstreet, 8 March 1864, *Life and Letters of Robert Edward Lee*, 327–28. Lee admitted to Longstreet that "I am not sufficiently acquainted with the country to do more than indicate the general plan."

20. Lee to Davis, 11 May 1863, in Dowdey and Manarin (eds.), *Wartime Papers*, 483–84; Lee to Bragg, 7 April 1864, *Wartime Papers*, 692; Lee to Davis, 5 April 1864, in Jefferson Davis Papers, Emory University Library; Lee to G. W. C. Lee, 29 March 1864, in Jones, *Life and Letters*, 303.

21. Lee to Seddon, 9 April 1863, Lee to Cooper, 16 April 1863, in Davis Papers, Tulane; Jones, *Confederate Strategy*, 203–4; Lee to Davis, 8 July 1863, in Dowdey and Manarin (eds.), *Wartime Papers*, 544; Lee to Davis, 4 May 1863, *Wartime*

Papers, 719–20; Lee to Davis, 11 May 1863, *Wartime Papers*, 483; Lee to Davis, 5 April 1863, Davis Papers, Emory University Library.

22. Lee to Longstreet, 24 Aug. 1863, in Dowdey and Manarin (eds.), *Wartime Papers*, 593–94; Longstreet to Lee, 3 Sept. 1863, *Official Records*, vol. 29, pt. 2, pp. 693–94; Lee to Davis, 11 Sept. 1863, in *Wartime Papers*, 712; Lee to Davis. 14 Sept. 1863, *Wartime Papers*, 720–21. Lee to Davis, 23 Sept. 1863, in Georgia Portfolio, Duke University Library; Lee to Longstreet, 25 Sept. 1863, in Jackson-Dabney Papers, University of North Carolina.

23. Lee to Davis, 11 Sept. 1863, *Official Records*, vol. 23, pt. 2, p. 712; Lee to Davis, 14 Sept. 1863, *Official Records*, vol. 23, pt. 2, pp. 20–21; Lee to Longstreet, 26 Oct. 1863, *Official Records*, vol. 52, pt. 2, p. 549.

24. Fuller, *Grant and Lee*, 123–24; Williams, "Military Leadership of North and South," 48–49; Long, *Memoirs of Robert E. Lee*, 401, 454.

25. Lee to W. P. Miles, 19 Jan. 1864, in Dowdey and Manarin (eds.), *Wartime Papers*, 885–86; Lee to Davis, 3 Sept. 1862, *Wartime Papers*, 291; Lee's Sharpsburg Report, 19 Aug. 1863, *Wartime Papers*, 313; Dowdey, *Lee*, 299–300, 393; Fuller, *Grant and Lee*, pp. 286–87; Lee to Seddon, 8 June 1863, *Wartime Papers*, 505; Lee to Davis, 12 July 1863, *Wartime Papers*, 548; Lee to Davis, 31 July 1863, *Wartime Papers*, 568.

26. Lee to Sydney Smith Lee, 20 April 1861, in Fitzhugh Lee, *General Lee*, 88–89; see also Lee to wife, 9 June 1861, *General Lee*, 98; also *General Lee*, 92; Lee to sister, 20 April 1861, Lee, *Recollections of General Lee*, 26; Jones, *Life and Letters of Robert Edward Lee*, 126.

27. Dowdey, *Lee*, 325.

The Historian and the General: Thomas L. Connelly versus Robert E. Lee

ALBERT CASTEL

The June 1969 issue of *Civil War History* contains an article by Thomas L. Connelly entitled "Robert E. Lee and the Western Confederacy: A Criticism of Lee's Strategic Ability." In it Connelly, the author of an ongoing study of the Confederate Army of Tennessee,[1] contends (among other things) that Lee is overrated both as a man and a soldier, that his selfish preoccupation with Virginia was an important factor in causing the Confederacy to devote a disproportionate share of its limited military resources to the East at the expense of the strategically more important West, and that his ill-conceived and wasteful offensives hastened Confederate defeat if in fact they did not cause it. Connelly concludes with the assertion that "one ponders whether the South may not have fared better had it possessed no Robert E. Lee."[2]

It is at once apparent that Connelly set out to do a job on Bobby Lee. Now there is nothing wrong with this as such. Scholars should be critical, reassessments are always in order, and Lee need not be regarded as some sort of sacrosanct saint on horseback. Personally I find it instructive to compare him with some of those German generals of World War II, such as Von Manstein, who by all accounts possessed admirable characters, but who gave their military talents to the service of an evil cause—in their case Naziism, in Lee's case slavery.[3] And being myself a native of Kansas and having studied somewhat the South's struggle in the West, I can understand Connelly's resentment against what he terms "the colonial status of the western Confederate army in both Civil War writing and thinking."[4]

Nevertheless I find that most of Connelly's criticisms of Lee are either unfounded, excessive, or pointless. Furthermore I regard his article in general as constituting an example of a type of pseudohistory that has always existed, but which in recent times seems to be flourishing. It is a type most notoriously represented by such works as Charles C. Tansill's *Backdoor to War* and D. F. Fleming's *The Cold War and Its Origins.*[5] In them the authors, like Connelly in his article, disparage previous writers on their subject as being biased, guilty of superficial research and analysis, and as being members of some ill-defined scholarly establishment with a vested interest in perpetuating an historical myth. Also they, like Connelly, ignore obvious and fundamental truths while marshaling a massive array of carefully selected and one-sided data, all impressively buttressed by footnotes, in order to "prove" that the orthodox view is false and their own supposedly original interpretation is true. Thus Tansill "proves" that Roosevelt, and not the Japanese government, "got us into" World War II, and Fleming "proves" that Truman, and not Stalin, is mainly to blame for the Cold War. Similarly, Connelly "proves" that Lee was a poor strategist who hurt more than he helped the Confederate cause.

Connelly begins his indictment of Lee by stating that in spite of the "morass" of biographies and monographs written about him, no Civil War figure "stands in greater need of re-evaluation than Lee," who on "at least three major counts, personality, field success and strategy . . . may have been the beneficiary of special pleading." With respect to the first count, Connelly suggests that Lee's awesome personal reputation may be undeserved, that perhaps it is really the product of the adulatory postwar writings of his former generals and staff officers, the South's need for a "symbol of suffering and resignation," and the "literary ability of Douglas Freeman."[6]

This is not without an element of truth—but the element of falseness is greater. For it is apparent that even before Lee became the South's hero he consistently impressed all who came in contact with him as a man of superior parts and potential greatness. Thus, to cite merely one example, early in 1860 a Texan who met the then lieutenant colonel wrote to Sam Houston that "he is a 'Preux chevalier, sans peur et sans reproche,' he is very careful to do nothing that may cast a slur on his name . . . [and] is well informed in matters of state, honest, modest, brave and skillful. . . ."[7]

In further downgrading Lee, Connelly commits another exaggeration, to put it mildly, when he charges that Lee's biographers have transformed his personality faults, such as "weakness in handling subordinate officers," into virtues.[8] Freeman, for instance, makes it very clear that this particular fault was one of Lee's most serious defects as a general and that as much as anything else it caused his defeat at Gettysburg.[9] And Connelly is simply being peevish when he asserts that since historians have praised Lee for his faults, by the same standard "Bragg should have been praised for his harshness and his martinet attitude, which moulded what Arthur Fremantle termed the best disciplined army in the Confederacy."[10] Bragg's army may or may not have been the "best disciplined," but it definitely was the least successful, army in the Confederacy. Which is the reason, not historical favoritism for Lee, why Bragg has never been praised for his "harshness and martinet attitude."

Moving on to the second major count on which he believes Lee should be reevaluated, Connelly states that "Lee's strategic and tactical success in Virginia perhaps needs re-examination as well." It does so, he argues, for the following reasons, each of which I will present and then criticize:

(1) Lee's "penchant for the offensive" up to 1864 cost the Confederacy more men than it could afford, caused "the South's largest field army" to bleed to death, and was "inconsistent with both the general Confederate strategy of a defensive war and Southern manpower shortage."[11]

Criticism: Yes, Lee's army did suffer heavy losses and it did ultimately bleed to death—otherwise it would never have been defeated. But, as Freeman points out, between June, 1862, when Lee took command of the Virginia army, and June, 1864, when he was forced into the trenches of Petersburg, he fought ten major battles, in every one of which he was outnumbered, sometimes as much as two to one. Nonetheless, he indisputably won six of these engagements, gained a tactical victory in two (Frayser's Farm and Antietam), and definitely lost only two—Malvern Hill and Gettysburg—both in large measure because of the failures of subordinates. In the process he suffered 103,000 casualties while inflicting 145,000 on a much stronger enemy who usually fought on the tactical defensive.[12] These figures are much more meaningful than the ones Connelly employs to back his contention, e.g., "Lee lost more men at Chancellorsville than the Confederates surrendered at Forts Henry and Donelson combined in 1862."[13] On this basis of comparison McClellan would have to be rated a better general than Grant because he lost hardly any men during the period February-April, 1862, whereas Grant lost over 15,000 men at Donelson and Shiloh. Moreover, it was precisely because Lee assumed the offensive whenever possible that he won so many battles, inflicted such heavy casualties on the enemy, and prevented for so long the fall of Richmond, an event which, Connelly notwithstanding, would have been a major blow to the Confederacy as a whole. Finally, it should be noted that even J. F. C. Fuller, who is very critical of Lee on most counts, states that the best chance the Confederacy had to win the war was to wage a successful offensive, whereas to "stand on a passive defensive . . . in the end was likely to spell ruin . . . ."[14]

(2) "Lee gained his most spectacular field victories against weaker links in the Union command, whereas the Confederate commanders in the West were up against the more able Federal generals—Grant, Sherman, Sheridan, Thomas."[15]

Criticism: This is meaningless. Could not one also say that Napoleon won his most spectacular victories against the weaker links in the Austrian, Russian, and Prussian commands? And, to turn things around, how well would have Grant, Sherman *et al.* fared against Lee and Jackson in Virginia in 1862? Certainly Grant did not exactly outshine Lee in 1864; he merely outnumbered him.

(3) Lee had an easier strategic problem than the Confederate generals in the West. Not only did they have a much larger area to defend and a poorer transportation system to support them, but "No Potomac, Rappahannock, or Rapidan offered defensive lines; instead, the Tennessee, Mississippi and Cumberland offered excellent avenues of penetration into the West."[16]

Criticism: The size of a theater of operations in itself means little. However, often an extensive area is an asset to defenders, a liability to invaders (e.g., Russia). In Lee's case the close and almost constant proximity of the Federals to Richmond reduced substantially his possibilities of maneuver. In contrast, Bragg's Kentucky invasion and Hood's Tennessee campaign demonstrated the great possibilities for strategic maneuver in the West. As for the West's poor transportation system, was this not at least as much a problem for the northern armies as for the southern, as for instance when Van Dorn's capture of Holly Springs and Forrest's raid into Kentucky forced Grant to abandon his first drive on Vicksburg? And with respect to the rivers in the two theaters, Connelly seems to forget both Federal sea power and the fact that the Rappahannock, York, and James all "offered excellent avenues of penetration" into the very heart of Virginia. In 1862 and again in 1864 the Federals used these approaches with some success, and it was chiefly Lee's generalship that prevented them from achieving greater success. (Incidentally, the Potomac no more served as a defensive barrier for Virginia than the Ohio did for Tennessee.)

(4) Lee did not have the difficult command problem of the western generals, because the "western army's high command never gelled around a single leader."[17]

Criticism: Frankly, this borders on the ludicrous. What caused the high command of the Army of Northern Virginia to gell around a single leader, if not the character and leadership of Lee? In other words, the advantage Lee had of a "gelled" high command was one of his own making, just as the disadvantage of an un-gelled high command from which the Army of Tennessee suffered was mainly the product of Bragg's abrasive personality and chronic incompetency.

(5) The western commanders faced far greater numerical odds than Lee. Thus (to cite only one of several similar examples given by Connelly as evidence for this contention) in November, 1862, effective Union strength along the Atlantic seaboard from North Carolina to Delaware was "only some 216,000 as opposed to 97,000 effectives under Lee. In contrast the Federals in the Departments of Ohio, Tennessee, and Cumberland "had amassed over 180,000 effectives against only 55,000 effectives in Bragg's army and that in Mississippi."[18]

Criticism: These figures, the accuracy of which I would not think of questioning, are in themselves practically meaningless. What is significant is the relative strength of the main field armies actively engaged in major operations. And here we find a radically different picture than the one painted by Connelly. Thus at the end of December, 1862, Bragg attacked 45,000 Federals at Murfreesboro with 38,000 men and was defeated. Earlier that same month Lee with 58,500 effectives faced 113,000 Federals at Fredericksburg and inflicted a crushing defeat on them. Moreover, not once in actual combat did Lee have numbers equal to the enemy's, yet much more than once he achieved victory. On the other hand, in the West, the Confederates at Ft. Donelson initially had more men than did Grant; Albert Sidney Johnston assaulted Grant's 37,000 at Shiloh with 40,000 and failed; Bragg suffered strategic defeat at Perryville although his army was equal in manpower and superior in experience to Buell's; Van Dorn had more men at Pea Ridge and equal strength at Corinth and was defeated at both places; during the early phases of the Vicksburg campaign, Pemberton and Joe Johnston had available a force stronger than Grant's 43,000 and yet failed to prevent the investment of that fortress; and at Franklin 30,000 Rebels under Hood vainly assaulted 28,000 Federals. As a matter of fact, the western Confederates won only one major battle during the entire war—Chickamauga—and there they held a 65,000 to 57,000 advantage.[19] Clearly the numerical odds against the southern generals in the West were not as overwhelming as Connelly would have us believe, and their lack of success was due mostly to their own lack of skill, and not lack of numbers. For although the North did deploy immense numbers of troops in the western theater, a higher proportion of them than in the East were engaged in occupation duties and in guarding the West's longer and more exposed supply lines.[20] As a result the Union armies in the West frequently were, as indicated, little if any stronger than the Confederates on the battlefield—quite the reverse of the situation in Virginia.

It is on the third count, ability as a strategist, that Connelly considers Lee "most in need of reappraisal," and to it he devotes the bulk of his article. He begins this "reappraisal"—actually it is an attack—by spending four pages proving something that no one has ever denied; namely, that Lee had an important role in the formulation of Confederate military policy while serving as Davis' chief of staff in early 1862, and that "Lee advised the [Confederate] government on general strategy and command problems" after assuming command of the Army of Northern Virginia.[21] Connelly's real purpose in this otherwise pointless exercise is to convey the impression that Lee had a decisive or determining influence on the South's conduct of the war as a whole. However he does not dare openly and explicitly state this, for he no doubt knows that one of the most firmly established facts of the Civil War is that Lee never had, not even after he received the title of commanding general in 1865, the power to determine Confederate grand strategy and to control the operations of all the southern armies. From beginning to end this power lay solely with Davis, who was no more prepared to share it than was Lee to seek it.[22] That Lee had, in Connelly's words, a "powerful influence" with Davis is obvious. But just how powerful this influence was—as Alexander Hamilton once remarked, influence is not power—is not so obvious.[23] Therefore Connelly fails in his attempt-by-implication to pin a major if not main share of the blame for alleged mistakes in Confederate war-planning on Lee. As Archer Jones noted, "Though he [Davis] had five secretaries of war and two nominal commanders-in-chief, all decisions and policies were those of the President."[24]

Next Connelly proceeds to build a case to the effect that Lee's advice on overall strategy matters was invariably bad, particularly with respect to the West. In so doing he advances three propositions: One, that Lee was ignorant, "naive," and "unrealistic" in his thinking about the West; two, that he "was convinced that the main war zone was in Virginia" and so subordinated all else to the defense of that state; and three, that because of his parochial obsession with Virginia he was not a "master strategist," that indeed it is questionable "whether Lee possessed a sufficiently broad military mind to deal with overall Confederate matters."[25]

Unfortunately, a thorough and systematic analysis of these propositions and their supporting evidence would require an article at least twice as long as Connelly's. Therefore I shall have to confine my detailed criticism of Connelly's case against Lee as a strategist to his treatment of the transfer of Longstreet's corps to Bragg's army in 1863. In taking this approach I can only affirm that the errors and distortions which I shall point out are not at all untypical—that in fact they are merely a sample of those to be found throughout the article.[26]

Connelly realized that in trying to demonstrate that Lee knew little and cared less about the West he must somehow account for the fact that the only major instance of Confederate forces being sent from one department to another occurred in September, 1863, when most of Longstreet's corps—nearly 12,000 crack troops—went from Lee's army in Virginia to the Army of Tennessee in Georgia. His solution to this problem is not merely to disparage the importance of Longstreet's transfer, but actually to find in it proof—additional proof, as he sees it—of Lee's alleged selfish preoccupation with Virginia. However, the data and arguments he presents in support of this point of view, although superficially impressive, do not stand up under close examination.

Item: Connelly states that Lee "was unenthusiastic at the move."[27] To be sure. But what general ever was enthusiastic about being deprived of a large portion of his best troops while faced with an enemy that already is considerably stronger? Especially if these troops were to be sent to a general as inept as Bragg? Connelly's statement is pointless.

Item: "Only two divisions were sent . . . ."[28] Correct. But Connelly does not mention the reason for this, namely, that Pickett's division (the only one not sent) had not recovered from its charge at Gettysburg, and that the Confederate authorities hesitated to send the Georgia units in Longstreet's corps for fear they would desert on reaching their home state. Neither does Connelly refer to the fact that two of Lee's brigades were also sent at this time to bolster the defense of beleagured Charleston.[29] Indeed, Connelly, who is so critical of Lee for allegedly being unaware of the importance of the Mississippi River and Tennessee fronts, himself appears to be oblivious even to the existence of yet another vital area of operations, the Atlantic coast. From time to time throughout the war, sizable numbers of troops were detached from Lee's army for service along the coast, as for instance when the bulk of Longstreet's corps went to the Suffolk area early in 1863, leaving Lee to fight at Chancellorsville outnumbered two to one.[30]

Item: " . . . and the slowness in determining this reinforcement was a factor in the lateness of their [Longstreet's troops] arrival for the [Chickamauga] campaign."[31] By implication at least, this seems to blame Lee for preventing more decisive results at Chickamauga by not quickly and enthusiastically agreeing to the dispatch of Longstreet to Bragg. But what are the facts on this matter? On August 24, 1863, Davis summoned Lee to Richmond to consult him and other top commanders on overall strategy. On September 6, Davis, with Lee's acquiescence, made (in Freeman's words) "the swift, final decision . . . to send the greater part of Longstreet's Corps to reinforce Bragg." That night Lee ordered his quartermaster general to prepare transportation for Longstreet's troops, and two days later these troops began moving southward from Lee's camps on the Rapidan.[32] If there was any "slowness in determining this reinforcement," it was on the part of Davis, not Lee. And in the absence of any positive evidence to the contrary, Davis' slowness—if such it was—cannot be attributed to the influence of Lee, who moved to execute Davis' decision, once it was made, with exemplary promptness.

Item: "Also, even before the last of Longstreet's men had arrived in Georgia, Lee had written Davis twice that they be returned. By September 25, Lee had already penned four suggestions for their return."[33] This would appear to show that Lee was obstinately uncooperative with regard to Longstreet's employment in the West. However, in the first of the two letters mentioned by Connelly, one written September 11 while Longstreet still was on the way to Georgia, Lee began by stating that if he were a "little stronger" he might be able to "drive Meade's army under cover of the fortifications of Washington before he gathers more reinforcements," then went on to say that "the blow at Rosecrans [by Bragg reinforced by Longstreet] should be made promptly and Longstreet be returned."[34] This, I submit, is not the same as asking that Longstreet be returned even before he joins Bragg, which is the meaning Connelly attempts to convey. Examination of the other letters cited by Connelly will reveal a similar twisting of Lee's actual views on this matter.[35]

Item: Even the sending of Longstreet to the West, Connelly claims, was prompted by Lee's obsession with Virginia, for Lee's purpose in agreeing to the move "was not to bolster Bragg's strength against Rosecrans, but to save Knoxville lest western Virginia be endangered."[36] Connelly's source for this allegation is Lee's letter of September 14, 1863, to Davis, written five days before the start of the battle of Chickamauga:

> Everything looks like a concentration of their [the Army of the Potomac's] forces, and it is stated by our scouts that they have learned of the large reduction of this army. I begin to fear that we lost the use of troops here where they are much needed, and that they have gone where they will do no good. I learn by the papers of today that Genl Rosecrans' army entered Chattanooga on the 9th, and that Genl Bragg has retired still farther into the interior. It also appears that Genl Burnside did not move to make a junction with Rosecrans, but marched upon Knoxville. Genl Bragg must therefore either have been misinformed of his movements, or he subsequently changed them. Had I been aware that Knoxville was the destination of Genl Burnside, I should have recommended that Genl Longstreet be sent to oppose him instead of to Atlanta. If Genl Bragg is unable to bring Genl Rosecrans to battle, I think it would be better to return

> Genl Longstreet to this army to enable me to oppose the advance of Genl Meade with a greater prospect of success. . . . Should Genl Longstreet reach Genl Bragg in time to aid him in winning a victory and return to this army, it will be well, but should he be detained there without being able to do any good, it will result in evil.[37]

This makes it self-evident that Connelly's assertion that Lee's purpose in agreeing to Longstreet's going west was not to aid Bragg against Rosecrans, but to protect Knoxville is a complete misreading of the evidence, an utter reversal of the facts. For only when it appeared to Lee on the basis of the information available to him that Longstreet's reinforcing Bragg would not be likely to accomplish anything worthwhile did Lee suggest that Longstreet might be used to defend Knoxville, the threat to which from Burnside he did not know about until long after Longstreet's men were on the way to Georgia. And, needless to say, Lee's misgivings about Longstreet being detained in the West "without being able to do any good" proved fully justified. For although Longstreet did reach Bragg in time to aid in winning the Battle of Chickamauga, the victory, thanks to Bragg's incompetence, was strategically barren.

Item: Connelly refuses even to give Longstreet much credit for the help he did render at Chickamauga. Seeking as always to minimize the importance of Longstreet's transfer, he points out that only 5,000 of his men participated in the battle of Chickamauga.[38] True enough. But did not these 5,000 men make an appreciable difference during the battle? And will Connelly deny the vital, in fact decisive, part played in the fighting by the superb combat leadership of Longstreet, who ignored Bragg's orders and struck the crushing blow that routed half the Union army? I look forward with interest to the second volume of his history of the Army of Tennessee to see if he will do so.

Item:

> The Longstreet reinforcement indicated, too, the double standard Lee used in his reinforcement policy. Later in 1864, he continually badgered Davis to have Johnston take the offensive because Lee believed a heavy force had been sent from Sherman to Grant. Lee thus argued that Johnston could hold back further reinforcement. Yet Lee made little effort to do the same on his front, though he knew two corps had been sent to the West.[39]

Frankly, I find this entire passage incomprehensible. First of all, in the paragraph preceding it Connelly discusses events in 1863, and the first sentence of this paragraph has to do with Longstreet's move to Georgia, which also occurred in 1863. Yet Connelly begins the second sentence with "Later in 1864"! But perhaps there has been a typographical error—maybe it should read "Later in 1863." But, no—the references to Grant, Sherman, and Johnston seem to indicate 1864. So perchance there has been a little oversight in punctuation, and hence these three words should read "Later, in 1864," etc. However the footnote in which Connelly documents his allegation that Lee "badgered" Davis in 1864, cites two letters written by Lee to Davis in September, 1863, plus one by Lee to Longstreet on October 26, 1863![40] But no doubt this is merely another unfortunate error. Probably Connelly meant to cite Lee's letter of March 25, 1864, to Davis as evidence of Lee having "continually badgered" (in just one letter?) Davis to have Johnston take the offensive in Georgia in order to relieve the pressure on Lee in Virginia. In it Lee states that the Confederates, in anticipation of the 1864 Union offensive, should hold themselves "in constant readiness to concentrate as rapidly as possible wherever it may be necessary," that is, either in Virginia or Georgia. The Federals, he believes, most likely will strike first against Johnston, but in case they move in large force against Richmond they "no doubt" will indicate their intention by withdrawing troops from the Atlantic coast and the West. In that case, "Should Genl Johnston or Genl Longstreet [who was still in Tennessee] find the forces opposed to them reduced sufficiently to justify attacking them, they might entirely frustrate the enemy's plans by defeating him."[41]

If you are determined to build a case against Lee, you can label the above badgering and cite it as an example of Lee's "double standard" when it came to reinforcements. But I doubt if any objective-minded historian would do so. The only real ground on which Lee can be criticized is for failing to appreciate the enormous strength the North had arrayed against the South by 1864, a strength which would enable Grant to send superior armies against Lee and Johnston simultaneously and so prevent either from helping the other.[42]

All in all, Connelly, in attempting to show that Longstreet's transfer was just another example of Lee's "localism," merely reveals his own lack of fairness and balance in writing about Lee. And if there can be any lingering doubt that Connelly is practically blinded by his prejudice against Lee, consider these two final items which appear near the end of the article, both of which have to do with Lee's alleged "obsession with Virginia:" (1) "To the Virginia convention he [Lee] declared his allegiance solely to the service of Virginia," and (2) Lee "surrounded himself with Virginia-bred officers," nine of his fifteen corps and division commanders in May, 1864, being Virginians, among them "two of Lee's sons and a nephew."[43]

With respect to (1), Connelly conveniently neglects to mention that Lee declared "his allegiance solely to the service of Virginia" on April

23, 1861, at a time when Virginia was not yet officially a member of the Confederacy. Hence it would have been inappropriate, not to say illegal, for Lee to have declared his allegiance to anything except Virginia.[44] And as for (2), Freeman's *Lee's Lieutenants* provides three volumes of proof that Lee selected his officers on the basis of ability and that nativity played no part in his choices except to the degree that he had to take into account the state pride of the men comprising his army. Connelly, on the other hand, offers not one shred of evidence to the contrary, only an innuendo.[45]

To repeat, the errors and distortions specified above are not untypical of the article as a whole. As a consequence, Connelly's attack on Lee is about as successful as Burnside's at Fredericksburg. Moreover, there is little if anything in it that is original. Back in 1932 J. F. C. Fuller, whom Connelly frequently cites, argued that Lee has been overrated as a general, criticized him for his offensive tactics, and declared that since "his thoughts were always concentrated on Virginia . . . he never fully realized the importance of Tennessee . . . . Not until Sherman was hammering at the back door of Richmond did he begin to see the importance of the Western areas. . . ."[46] And in 1960 T. Harry Williams, obviously inspired by Fuller's criticisms, expressed doubt "that Lee, who was a product of his culture and obsessed with the war in his native Virginia, could have adjusted his strategic thinking to the problems of national strategy on many fronts."[47] Actually, all that Connelly has done is attempt—with what success, we have seen—a detailed and systematic documentation of what might be termed the Fuller-Williams thesis.[48]

In addition to flimsy data and dubious analysis, Connelly's case against Lee rests on two tacit but fundamental assumptions: That the West and not the East was the decisive arena of the Civil War; and (the other side of the same coin) that if the Army of Tennessee and the other Confederate forces in the West had received appreciably more and the Army of Northern Virginia appreciably less in the way of manpower and materiel, the war would have gone better for the South.

Now it is probably true that the North won the war and the South lost it in the West. But was not this in large part because Lee, against battlefield odds greater than those usually faced by the southern generals in the West, was able to hold back the North so long and so well in the East? Moreover, as Charles Roland points out, the "west was not intrinsically more valuable to the Confederacy than was the east; once the east was taken, the west would surely fall. The Confederacy could not live without both east and west."[49] And, lastly, irrespective of the comparative strategic importance of the East and West in objective terms, the plain fact is that the vast majority of northerners and southerners alike *thought* of Virginia as the paramount war zone and that their leaders shared this view. Or, in other words, Lee the Virginian was not alone in his "obsession" with Virginia. Davis the Mississippian and Lincoln the Illinoisian kept him company.[50]

As for the second assumption, one can only say that there is absolutely nothing in the military records of Bragg, Kirby Smith, the Johnstons, Pemberton, Van Dorn, Price, *et al.* to inspire confidence that they would have suffered fewer defeats had they commanded more men. Probably all that would have resulted from switching large numbers of troops from the East to the armies of these generals would have been to deny Lee any chance at all of keeping the Union hosts at bay and preventing the capture of Richmond, symbol of southern independence. Hence, to Connelly's closing question, Would not the South "have fared better had it possessed no Robert E. Lee?" the answer is this: Of course it would have! For without Lee, without his military genius, and without the inspiration his victories and character provided, Confederate resistance would have crumbled much sooner [than] it did, with the result that tens of thousands of southern lives would have been spared and an incalculable amount of human suffering in the South prevented. Indeed, looked at this way, it is remarkable that more southerners have not joined with Tennessee-born Thomas L. Connelly in condemning the costly generalship of Robert E. Lee.

NOTES

1. Thomas L. Connelly, *Army of the Heartland: The Army of Tennessee, 1861–1862* (Baton Rouge, 1967).

2. Thomas L. Connelly, "Robert E. Lee and the Western Confederacy: A Criticism of Lee's Strategic Ability," *Civil War History* 15 (June, 1969): 132.

3. To be sure, Lee in his own mind was fighting for his country. But the same was true of Hitler's generals.

4. Connelly, "Lee and the Western Confederacy," 116.

5. Charles C. Tansill, *Backdoor to War: The Roosevelt Foreign Policy, 1933–1941* (Chicago, 1952); D. F. Fleming, *The Cold War and Its Origins, 1917–1960* (Garden City, 1961). Works of a similar type are Howard Zinn (ed.), *New Deal Social Thought* (New York, 1966), and W. A. Williams, *The Tragedy of American Diplomacy* (New York, 1962).

6. Connelly, "Lee and the Western Confederacy," 116–17.

7. A. M. Lea to Sam Houston, Feb. 23, 1860, Sam Houston Papers, Texas Historical Collection, University of Texas Library. In addition, Winfield Scott, prior to the war, referred to Lee as "the greatest military genius in America," J. F. C. Fuller, *Grant and Lee* (Bloomington, Ind., 1957), 107. The *Richmond Dispatch* of April 26, 1861, declared that "A more heroic Christian, noble soldier and gentleman, could not be found." Quoted in Douglas Southall Freeman, *R. E. Lee: A Biography* (New York, 1933–36), 1:469.

8. Connelly, "Lee and the Western Confederacy," 117.

9. Freeman, *R. E. Lee*, 4:168–9. See also Charles P. Roland, "The Generalship of Robert E. Lee," in Grady McWhiney (ed.), *Grant, Lee, Lincoln and the Radicals: Essays on Civil War Leadership* (New York, 1964), 65–6.

10. Connelly, "Lee and the Western Confederacy," 117. Connelly does not cite the passage in Fremantle's diary where this is asserted. Presumably, however, he refers to the May 31, 1863, entry, where Fremantle states, "I imagine that the discipline in this [Bragg's] army is the strictest in the Confederacy. . . ." Walter Lord (ed.), *The Fremantle Diary* (Boston, 1954), 125. Note, however, that Fremantle qualifies this statement with the word "imagine," and that he does not say that Bragg's army was the *best* disciplined but that its discipline was the *strictest.* Furthermore, Fremantle had not yet visited Lee's army when he wrote this.

11. Connelly, "Lee and the Western Confederacy," 117–8.

12. Freeman, *R. E. Lee*, 4:169–70.

13. Connelly, "Lee and the Western Confederacy," 118.

14. Fuller, *Grant and Lee*, 139.

15. Connelly, "Lee and the Western Confederacy," 118.

16. Connelly, "Lee and the Western Confederacy," 118–9.

17. Connelly, "Lee and the Western Confederacy," 119.

18. Connelly, "Lee and the Western Confederacy," 120.

19. It is very difficult to establish definitely and precisely the troop strength of opposing armies in the Civil War. My figures are derived mainly from the pertinent sections of Robert U. Johnson and C. C. Buel (eds.), *Battles and Leaders of the Civil War* (New York, 1884–87), which I consider to be most useful and reliable in these matters. The statement regarding the comparative size of Bragg's and Buell's armies at Perryville is derived from Kenneth P. Williams, *Lincoln Finds a General* (New York, 1949–59) 4:121–3, 497–8. Williams makes a good case to the effect that Buel and Bragg both had about 60,000 men, with most of Bragg's being veterans whereas the bulk of Buel's were raw troops.

20. For example, in 1864 Sherman had 100,000 men employed in guarding depots and supply lines, the same number as in his field army (Johnson and Buel [eds.], *Battles and Leaders* 4:294). In fact, if we are to accept one estimate, not even in 1864 did the Army of Tennessee face as great odds as the Army of Northern Virginia. Thus, according to this estimate, at the Battle of New Hope Church, Johnston was outnumbered by Sherman only 5 to 4, whereas at the same time Grant outnumbered Lee 2 to 1. Johnson and Buel (eds.), *Battles and Leaders* 4:281–2.

21. Connelly, "Lee and the Western Confederacy," 120–3.

22. Freeman, *R. E. Lee*, 1:6–7 and 3:534–5.

23. Frank Vandiver states in *Rebel Brass* (Baton Rouge, 1956), p. 30, that Davis recognized the importance of the West and did not neglect it in his strategical thinking. Either Connelly, who studied under Vandiver, does not agree, or else he would have to admit that Lee's "powerful influence" was not so powerful after all.

24. Archer Jones, *Confederate Strategy from Shiloh to Vicksburg* (Baton Rouge, 1961), 17.

25. Connelly, "Lee and the Western Confederacy," 124–31.

26. The reader will find it quite revealing to do as I have done—namely, go through Connelly's entire article comparing his statements about Lee with the sources he cites as evidence for these statements.

27. Connelly, "Lee and the Western Confederacy," 129.

28. Connelly, "Lee and the Western Confederacy," 129.

29. Lee to Davis, Sept. 9, 1863, in Clifford Dowdey and Louis H. Manarin (eds.), *Wartime Papers of R. E. Lee* (Boston, 1961), 597; Douglas Southall Freeman, *Lee's Lieutenants, A Study in Command* (New York, 1942–44), 3:223–4.

30. In early 1863 the Confederates had 45,000 troops in the Carolinas, Georgia, and Florida as opposed to 27,000 Federals (Roland, "Generalship of Lee,"p. 49). This could be used and usually is used as an example of the bad deployment of Confederate manpower. But it is also indicative of the importance assigned the Atlantic coast front by the Confederate government. The role of that front in the Civil War has yet to receive adequate historical treatment.

31. Connelly, "Lee and the Western Confederacy," 129.

32. Freeman, *Lee's Lieutenants*, 3:220–3; Freeman, *R. E. Lee*, 3:65–6.

33. Connelly, "Lee and the Western Confederacy," 129.

34. Lee to Davis, Sept. 11, 1863, in Dowdey and Manarin (eds.), *Wartime Papers*, 599. See also the actual words of Lee's letter of Sept. 14, 1863, to Davis, in Dowdey and Manarin (eds.), *Wartime Papers*, 600–601.

35. Lee to Davis, Sept. 23 and Sept. 25, 1863, in Dowdey and Manarin (eds.), *Wartime Papers*, 602–3, 665–6.

36. Connelly, "Lee and the Western Confederacy," 125–6, 129.

37. Dowdey and Manarin (eds.), *Wartime Papers*, 600–601.

38. Connelly, "Lee and the Western Confederacy," 129.

39. Connelly, "Lee and the Western Confederacy," 129.

40. Connelly, "Lee and the Western Confederacy," 129 fn. 23. In the letter to Longstreet Lee mentions how he attempted early in October to prevent Meade from detaching troops from Rosecrans (the Mine Run campaign). Yet Connelly not only cites this as evidence of Lee's selfish attitude in 1864, he uses it as support for his statement that Lee made "little effort" to prevent the Federals in the East from sending reinforcements to the West! See Lee to Longstreet, Oct. 26, 1863, in *The War of the Rebellion: A Compilation of the Official Records of the Union and Confederate Armies* (Washington DC, 1881–1901), vol. 52, pt. 2, p. 549.

41. Dowdey and Manarin (eds.), *Wartime Papers*, 682–4.

42. Lee's lack of precise, reliable information about not only Union but Confederate armies outside of Virginia, which Connelly cites as proof that he was a poor strategist, merely reflects the lack of an adequate staff and intelligence system in the Confederate high command in Richmond. One is struck, as one reads Lee's military correspondence, by how dependent Lee was for information about the West on what he read in Northern and Southern newspapers, and by how little intelligence on that theater he received from official sources. But this does not prevent Connelly from condemning Lee for being ignorant, "naive," and "unrealistic" about the West.

43. Connelly, "Lee and the Western Confederacy," 131.

44. Freeman, *R. E. Lee*, 1:468–71.

45. States Connelly, "Lee and the Western Confederacy," 131: "Perhaps there is something to be said for the comment of one Lee biographer [Clifford Dowdey] that in the post-Sharpsburg reorganization, the sending of Mississippi-bred Chase Whiting to North Carolina eliminated the 'last unwanted legacy' of the older army and that henceforth the army reflected Lee totally." There is something to be said for this comment—but not what Connelly would like to have said.

46. Fuller, *Grant and Lee*, 242–75.

47. T. Harry Williams, *Americans at War* (Baton Rouge, 1960), 64. See also T. Harry Williams, "The Military Leadership of North and South," in David Donald (ed.), *Why the North Won the Civil War* (Baton Rouge, 1960), 39–40, where Williams, quoting Fuller with approval, also casts doubts on Lee's ability in the field of grand strategy.

48. Pro-Lee historians have held that if Lee had been given the power to conduct overall Confederate military operations, he would have displayed, in all probability, a high degree of competence in so doing. I consider this a more reasonable assumption than the contrary view argued by Fuller, Williams, and now Connelly. For instance, I see no reason to doubt that if Lee had been placed in command of all Confederate armed forces, his sense of duty if nothing else would have caused him to obtain full and accurate intelligence about other war zones besides Virginia and then on the basis of this intelligence to make strategic decisions in the overall interests of the Confederacy. Also, in criticizing Lee for not being more interested in being better informed about the West, Fuller, Williams, and Connelly forget that, in the words of Williams himself, commanding a field army "alone is usually important enough to occupy fully the energies of one man" (Williams, *Americans at War*, 13).

49. Roland, "Generalship of Lee," 48.

50. Vandiver, *Rebel Brass*, 26, states that "after a while he [Davis] could see little beyond the confines of Richmond and Lee's military department." As for Lincoln, it is significant that while he several times visited the Army of the Potomac, not once did he inspect Union forces in the West. Davis, on the other hand, made at least three trips to his western armies.

General Lee

ALAN T. NOLAN

The 1989 edition of the *Encyclopedia Americana* states that Lee was "one of the truly gifted commanders of all time," "one of the greatest, if not the greatest, soldier who ever spoke the English language." The entry for Lee in the 1989 *Encyclopaedia Britannica* reflects a similar judgment. According to the 1988 revised edition of the *Civil War Dictionary,* Lee "earned rank with history's most distinguished generals." These evaluations reflect the consensus of standard reference sources. Those sources also agree that Lee's lieutenants, not Lee, were responsible for his army's failures.

The standard reference books do not stand alone. The excellence of his generalship is a Lee dogma and is widely asserted. In 1963, Marshall W. Fishwick wrote, "In his field he was a genius—probably the greatest one the American nation has produced." *Lee Takes Command,* volume 7 of the popular Time-Life Civil War series, published in 1984, reports that as of the Confederate victory at Second Bull Run, "Lee was well on his way to becoming the greatest soldier of the Civil War." In 1985 the respected popular journal *Civil War Times Illustrated* devoted an entire monthly issue to Lee under the title "Robert E. Lee: The Life and Career of the Master General." A juvenile biography of the general published in 1988 starts a new generation out with the classic, simple message: Lee was "a military genius," a "nearly invincible general." In this same biography, James Longstreet, Richard S. Ewell, and Jeb Stuart are characterized as "defective." Only Stonewall Jackson is seen as a worthy lieutenant. Indeed, the perennial question of why the South lost the war is finally disposed of: readers are told that Jackson's death at Chancellorsville "would unravel the entire Southern cause."[1] With only occasional and essentially unheeded dissent, a belief in Lee's paramount greatness as a general is the most intense and enduring aspect of the Lee tradition.[2]

Douglas Southall Freeman has stated the case for the tradition. He recounts the situation before Richmond when Lee took command of the

Army of Northern Virginia on June 1, 1862, and his saving of the capital at that time. Noting the repulse of four major Federal offensives against Richmond and the delay of a fifth such effort by means of the Pennsylvania campaign, Freeman recites Lee's ten major battles—Gaines's Mill through Spotsylvania—explaining that six of these he won "but only at Gettysburg had he met with definite defeat, and even there he clouded the title of his adversary to a clear-cut victory." Freeman continues:

> During the twenty-four months when he had been free to employ open manoeuver, a period that had ended with Cold Harbor, he had sustained approximately 103,000 casualties and had inflicted 145,000. Holding, as he usually had, to the offensive, his combat losses had been greater in proportion to his numbers than those of the Federals, but he had demonstrated how strategy may increase an opponent's casualties, for his losses included only 16,000 prisoners, whereas he had taken 38,000. Chained at length to the Richmond defenses, he had saved the capital from capture for ten months. All this he had done in the face of repeated defeats for the Southern troops in nearly every other part of the Confederacy. . . . These difficulties of the South would have been even worse had not the Army of Northern Virginia occupied so much of the thought and armed strength of the North. Lee is to be judged, in fact, not merely by what he accomplished with his own troops but by what he prevented the hosts of the Union from doing sooner elsewhere.[3]

In view of these facts—and, except for the argumentative statement suggesting that Gettysburg was not a clear-cut victory for the Union, they are facts—one questions the traditional view of Lee's generalship at his peril. At the outset, therefore, it is appropriate to define the scope of the inquiry undertaken here, to set forth what the issue is *not* as well as what the issue is.

In the first place, this book [*Lee Considered*] accepts the fact that Lee's campaign and battle strategy and his tactical performance were largely, although not invariably, brilliant. Granting this brilliance, there nevertheless are grounds for questioning his generalship. The questions are in reference to the grand strategy of the war from the Confederacy's standpoint. In order to evaluate Lee's performance as a general, it is imperative that we distinguish between military *tactics* and military *strategy,* including some refinements of the latter term. Definitions are therefore required.

To paraphrase Clausewitz, tactics concern the use of armed forces in battle. Gen. Henry W. Halleck's *Elements of Military Art and Science* states the same thing more elaborately: "We have defined tactics to be the art of bringing troops into action, or of moving them in the presence of the enemy." A contemporary military dictionary states that tactics are the "techniques of deploying and directing military forces . . . in coordinated combat activities . . . in order to attain the objectives designated by strategy."

In contrast, the term "strategy" is used in two ways. It has, in effect, two different definitions. On the one hand, within the context of a particular campaign or battle, it refers to the plan or idea of that campaign or battle, as distinguished from the tactical factor of employing and directing military forces in the combat activities of that campaign or battle. Thus, Halleck says that strategy in this sense "regards the theatre of war" and "forms the plan and arranges the general operations of a campaign."

But strategy has a more profound meaning in the context of war as a whole, as distinguished from the context of a campaign or battle. In this larger sense, Clausewitz defines it as "the use of engagements to attain the objects of war." An expanded modern version of this definition says that strategy is "the art and science of developing and employing in war military resources and forces for the purpose of providing maximum support for national policy."[4]

An understanding of this distinction between the two meanings of strategy is critical to this book [*Lee Considered*]. In order to minimize the risk of their being confused, different terms will be used. Strategy in the context of a campaign or battle will be called "operational strategy." Strategy in the more profound sense as related to the "objects of war" and the employment of military forces to carry out national policy will be identified as "grand strategy."

This book makes an additional distinction that the reader should bear in mind. It is the distinction between the *true* grand strategy of the sectional protagonists, North and South, and the *official* grand strategy of the sections. The true grand strategy is that which, in view of the circumstances of the section, would have maximized that section's chances of achieving its war objective. The official grand strategy is that which the government of the section authorized and directed its military establishment to carry out.

Much, perhaps most, of the writing about Lee's generalship never asks what seems to be the critical question in any military analysis of his generalship, that is, how his direction of military forces related to the national policy of the Confederacy and its object in the war. His campaigns and battles are typically considered almost as disembodied, abstract events, unrelated to the necessities and objectives of the war from the standpoint of the South, and without regard to whether they advanced or retarded those necessities and objectives. It is as if a surgeon were to be judged on the basis of his skillful, dexterous, and imaginative procedures, incisions, and sutures, without regard to whether the operation actually improved the patient's chances for survival. This is another way of saying that Lee is traditionally viewed as a performer, like the surgeon, or like an athlete participating in a competition or an exercise. The critical purposes and issues of warfare are not even acknowledged. Freeman and the other previously quoted sources are simply representative of this general phenomenon.

In evaluating Lee or any army commander, however, the key consideration is not the brilliance or boldness of his performance in a tactical or operationally strategic sense. These are surely matters of interest and importance, but the key consideration must be whether the general's actions helped or hurt the cause of his government in view of that government's grand strategy. In short, the appropriate inquiry is to ask whether the general's actions related positively or negatively to the war objectives and national policy of his government.

The issue addressed is not, therefore, Lee's tactics and operational strategy in any given campaign or battle. His brilliant direction of his forces during the fighting at Antietam and what happened at Gettysburg are not the point. At Gettysburg he suffered a decisive defeat, a defeat that did not alone decide the war but in which his losses, on the heels of other casualties, were so great that his army's subsequent ability to maneuver was severely restricted. The reference-book evaluations of Lee include the traditional view that this defeat was the fault of his subordinates. Contemporary students of the battle disagree on this point. Some persuasively contend that Lee's subordinates, especially Longstreet, are unfairly blamed for the Gettysburg loss. But, whatever may be said about the factors that determined the outcome of this or any battle, the issue here is more profound than explaining Lee's campaign or battle failures or successes. The issue is to understand the grand strategy of the Confederacy and to appreciate Lee's contribution to the larger success or failure of that strategy.

Lee's role as commander of the Army of Northern Virginia, a role he assumed on June 1, 1862, and retained for the duration of the war, is the critical area of inquiry in evaluating his generalship. It is true, of course, that he was military adviser to President Davis beginning on March 13, 1862, and continuing until February 6, 1865, on which date he became the Confederacy's general-in-chief.[5] But the relevant consideration of his generalship is concerned with his army command. Among other things, this statement of the issue means that the inquiry does not involve the familiar contention that Lee concentrated too much on his own army and the Virginia theater and paid insufficient attention to other parts of the country.

It is necessary to acknowledge an underlying factor that is bound up with any consideration of Lee's generalship. For almost one hundred years after the war, the conventional view was that the defeat of the South was inevitable. Part of the romance of the Lost Cause was the assumption that it literally could not have been a successful cause. It was, in short, the impossible dream. One of the premises of this inevitable-loss tradition was that the South was fatally handicapped from the beginning because of the relative manpower and material resources of the two sections. The North, and historians generally, seemed to accept an oft-quoted and probably apocryphal statement by a former Confederate: "They never whipped us, Sir, unless they were four to one. If we had anything like a fair chance, or less disparity of numbers, we should have won our cause."

More recent scholarship concedes the North's advantage in population and the capacity to make war but rejects the inevitable-loss tradition and its premise in regard to men and material wealth. It is generally believed today that the South could indeed have won the Civil War. In 1956 Southern historian Bell I. Wiley suggested:

> In the years since Appomattox millions of Southerners have attributed Confederate defeat to the North's overpowering strength. This is a comforting conclusion and it is not without a substantial basis of fact. For the North unquestionably had an immense superiority of material and human resources. But the North also faced a greater task. In order to win the war the North had to subdue a vast country of nine million inhabitants, while the South could prevail by maintaining a successful resistance. To put it another way, the North had to conquer the South while the South could win by outlasting its adversary, by convincing the North that coercion was impossible or not worth the effort. The South had reason to believe that it could achieve independence. That it did not was due as much, if not more, to its own failings as to the superior strength of the foe.[6]

In a 1960 volume edited by David Donald, a number of distinguished professional historians also argued that the defeat of the South was not a foregone conclusion; the South could have won.[7] More recently, in 1986, historians Richard E. Beringer, Herman Hattaway, Archer Jones, and William N. Still, Jr., expressed the same view. Noting that "no Confederate army lost a major engagement because of the lack of arms, munitions, or other essential supplies," these authors summarized the case as follows:

> By remarkable and effective efforts the agrarian South did exploit and create an industrial base that proved adequate, with the aid of imports, to maintain suitably equipped forces in the field. Since the Confederate armies suffered no crippling deficiencies in weapons or supply, their principal handicap would be their numerical inferiority. But to offset this lack, Confederates, fighting the first major war in which both sides armed themselves with rifles, had the advantage of a temporary but very significant surge in the power of the tactical defensive. In addition, the

> difficulties of supply in a very large and relatively thinly settled region proved a powerful aid to strengthening the strategic defensive. Other things being equal, if Confederate military leadership were competent and the Union did not display Napoleonic genius, the tactical and strategic power of the defense could offset northern numerical superiority and presumably give the Confederacy a measure of military victory adequate to maintain its independence.[8]

In his book *Ordeal By Fire,* James M. McPherson lays out the facts that set up the grand strategic situation, including the necessity on the part of the North "to invade, conquer, and destroy the South's capacity and will to resist." McPherson also observes that "invasion and conquest are logistically far more difficult than defense of one's territory." He notes that, at the beginning of the war, British military experts, recalling their nation's experience in America one hundred years before, believed that a country as large as the Confederacy could not be conquered. It was expected that the North would ultimately have to give up the effort.[9]

The task of the North was to conquer and occupy an area as large as the Northern states themselves, if faraway California and Oregon are disregarded. This area was crossed by rivers and streams, mountains and valleys, and wooded, unimproved roads. These natural circumstances impeded an invader who sought to penetrate or hold the area. The South could work on interior lines, in friendly country, and with maximum terrain advantages. The North, with the constant necessity to advance, had to fight on extended lines of communication in hostile country. This required the availability of large numbers of men stationed in the rear to protect these extended lines. And the North could have been defeated in any one of three ways, each inextricably mixed with the other two. It could have been defeated militarily, by actual combat in the field, although given its resources in men and material this was unlikely. It could have been defeated politically, by discouragement of the Northern people, who had the power simply to vote a defeat for the North. And it could have been defeated diplomatically, that is, by European intervention.

Much has been casually written about the risk of British or French recognition of the Confederacy. Such a diplomatic act, not an unlikely prospect—at least until the issuance of the Emancipation Proclamation—would surely have changed the nature of the war in terms of international law and custom. Whether this change of status would have led to European military intervention is quite another question. Although those who discuss recognition seem sometimes to assume military intervention as a consequence of recognition, this is simply an assumption and is speculative at best. Naval activity at the expense of the North might have occurred.

But given the distances and their logistical implications, and in view of the always fractious state of relations among the European powers, it is far from certain that either Great Britain or France would have committed naval forces, let alone ground forces, to the contest. As pointed out in Chapter 6 [*Lee Considered*], Lee himself did not expect European assistance to the Confederacy, and he was a realist in this respect. The unlikelihood of such assistance should be borne in mind in considering the appropriate Confederate grand strategy and the discussion later in this chapter of the reasons offered to justify Lee's aggressive military leadership.

In any event, the point is that the task of the North was literally gigantic. It was the task of organizing and harnessing its superior resources and committing them to warfare on a geographic and financial scale that was historically unprecedented. The South, too, had a similar organizing job to do, but inertia was on its side and would have been fatal to the North. In short, disregarding for the moment the concepts of military science and drawing instead on a legal metaphor, one side, the North, was the plaintiff. It had the burden of proof, the necessity to conquer. The South was the defendant; it could win the war simply by not being conquered. It did not have to seize or occupy a foot of ground outside its borders.

It seems plain that the traditional premise—that the South simply could not have won the war—has had much to do with establishing Lee's reputation as an almost perfect general. Indeed, the entire direction of one's inquiry into Lee's generalship depends on whether one accepts the tradition of the inevitable loss of the Lost Cause or alternatively sees the success of that cause as a possibility. If the cause was from the beginning simply a forlorn hope, the criteria in the evaluation of its military leadership are immediately lowered because advancing the objective of victory is read out of the case. As in the situation of the hypothetical surgeon or the athlete, the war is reduced to a forum in which the performance of the general is considered outside of the context of his government's war objective. The criteria of evaluation then pose such questions as, did the general put up a good fight? did he inflict significant losses on the enemy? did he win battles? On the other hand, if the evaluator believes that the war could have been won, a sterner test arises: did the general maximize the chance for victory?

Lee's task as commander of the Army of Northern Virginia was not to put on a martial show, a performance; it was to make the maximum contribution toward the South's chances of winning the war. Meaningful consideration of his generalship must refer to this task. Evaluating Lee's generalship in this context is not to say that the South would necessarily have won the war had Lee conducted himself differently. Had Lee been fully effective in the Virginia theater, the Union's military victories and inexorable advance in the West, and then from the West to the East, might ultimately have caused the collapse of the Confederacy. It is nevertheless fair to examine Lee's generalship with reference to his contribution to the South's chances of winning the war.

Before proceeding, it is necessary to say a quick word about the problem of counting casualties during the Civil War. As any student of the war knows, this is a difficult task because strength and casualty returns were frequently not made and when made were frequently carelessly done. In citing strength and casualty data in this chapter, no attempt is made to question or rationalize the numbers used by the authorities cited even when they are in disagreement, because a choice of numbers does not affect the analysis. Disagreements concerning numbers and losses are not material in terms of the issues with which this chapter is concerned.

What has been said about the physical situation and the tasks of the North and South suggests an identification of their respective military circumstances and true grand strategy in a military sense. Kenneth P. Williams, in a work entitled *Lincoln Finds a General* (the general being, of course, U.S. Grant), credits Grant with having recognized and executed as general-in-chief what had from the beginning of the war been the true Federal grand strategy. Essentially, as distinguished from the piecemeal and episodic engagements followed by withdrawal that had marked the war in the East before Grant, this true Federal grand strategy was to destroy the South's capacity to carry on the war. As characterized by the English general J. F. C. Fuller, Grant's "central idea was concentration of force from which he intended to develop a ceaseless offensive against the enemy's armies, and the resources and *moral* [*sic*] of the Confederacy" (emphasis added). Grant's plan for dealing with the Confederate field armies called for the Army of the Potomac to operate against Lee's Army of Northern Virginia, while William Tecumseh Sherman's Army of the Tennessee engaged Gen. Joseph E. Johnston's army in the West. Gen. Franz Sigel was to occupy the Confederates' attention in western Virginia and the Shenandoah Valley, and Gen. Benjamin F. Butler's Army of the James was to move south of Richmond. As stated by Fuller, "All four armies were to attack simultaneously. . . . This continued movement Grant hoped would prevent any one Confederate army reinforcing the other."[10] In addition, Gen. Nathaniel P. Banks, commanding the Department of the Gulf, was to be active. At the time of Grant's appointment as general-in-chief, Banks was embarked on the Red River expedition. Under Grant's plan, Banks was promptly to complete that mission and then lead an assault against Mobile, a fifth front on which simultaneously to challenge the Confederacy.[11]

Grant's intention for each army was very plain. It was to destroy the opposing Confederate military force. In a communication dated March 15, 1864, to General Banks, Grant wrote: "I look upon the conquering of the organized armies of the enemy as being of vastly more importance than the mere acquisition of territory." A similar message went to Gen. George Meade: "Lee's army will be your objective point. Wherever Lee goes, there you will go also."[12] And, as noted by Fuller, "Meade's attack . . . was to be an attack in such overwhelming force that Lee would suffer so heavily that the Confederate Government would be unable to reinforce any other army. . . . It was also to be a continuous attack, in order to prevent Lee's army recuperating." As further interpreted by Fuller: "Grant's grand tactics were . . . to lead to such an attenuation of [Lee's] strength that he would be compelled to use his entire force on the defensive."[13]

It is widely conceded that Grant's grand strategy was the true grand strategy of the Union. Grant was the general-in-chief; Lincoln had literally turned the military aspect of the war over to him. As of the advent of Grant, the true grand strategy and the official grand strategy of the Union coincided. General Fuller explains the logic of this grand strategy: "Grant was right in deciding that both his tactics and strategy must be offensive; for it was obvious to him that the longer the war lasted the less likely would the North hold out." And this, of course, was the risk for the Union—that the human, emotional, and financial cost of subduing the South would become so burdensome that the Northern people would abandon their support of the war. This was a genuine risk. In the 1862 elections, the Republicans had suffered losses as a result of Northern discouragement. According to Massachusetts senator Charles Sumner, in 1863 Lincoln feared " 'the fire in the rear'—meaning the Democracy, especially in the Northwest—more than our military chances." And in August 1864, before the fall of Atlanta, Lincoln had written his private prediction: "It seems exceedingly probable that this Administration will not be re-elected."[14] A politician of unusual insight, Lincoln was personally aware of the mounting sense of frustration in the North and was in close touch with party leaders in the Northern states. War-weariness was growing, as was the belief that the conquest of the South was an impossibility. From the beginning, the true grand strategy of the North was to destroy the South's capacity to resist, and this required the destruction of its armies, before the Northern people gave up the contest.

If the true grand strategy of the North was offensive, as indeed it was, what grand strategy was most likely to contribute to the South's chances of winning the war? The South's goal was to be released from the Union. It neither desired to conquer the North nor had the need or resources to do so. Accordingly, the true grand strategy for the Confederacy, the only grand strategy that afforded a chance to win the war, was defensive. Edward Porter Alexander, chief of ordnance of the Army of Northern Virginia and later chief of artillery of Longstreet's corps, identified the premises of this policy:

> When the South entered upon war with a power so immensely her superior in men & money, & all the wealth of modern resources in machinery and transportation appliances by land & sea, she could entertain but one single hope of final success. That was, that the desperation of her resistance would finally exact from her adversary such a price in blood & treasure as to exhaust the enthusiasm of its population for the objects of the war. We could not hope to *conquer* her. Our one chance was to wear her out. (Emphasis in original.)[15]

McPherson is correct in stating that "to 'win,' the Confederates did not need to invade the North or to destroy its armies; they needed only to stand on the defensive and to prevent the North from destroying Southern armies."[16] As stated earlier, the South as well as the North had the rifled gun, and that ordnance created the relative power of the strategic, as well as the tactical, defensive. William Garrett Piston confirms the power of the defense for the same reason.[17]

The feasibility of the grand strategy of the defensive was sensed by British observers as the war began. As has been said, harking back to their own experience in America, they did not see how the South could be conquered. The War of Independence analogy is not perfect, but it is illustrative of the circumstances. Military historian Col. George A. Bruce made the point. Washington, he writes, "had a correct insight into the minds of his own people and that of the enemy, *the strength of resolution of each to endure heavy burdens,* looking forward with certainty to the time when the public sentiment of England, led by Chatham and Burke, would be ready to acknowledge the Colonies as an independent nation. With these views he carried on the war for seven years, all the way from Boston to Yorktown, on a generally defensive plan, the only one pointing to the final goal of independence" (emphasis added).[18] The Americans, on the grand strategic defensive, lost many battles and retreated many times, but they kept forces in the field so as not to be ultimately defeated, and they won because the British decided that the struggle was either hopeless or too burdensome to pursue. General Fuller describes this grand strategy with another historical reference: "In truth, Lee's one and only chance was to imitate the great Fabius, and plot to win the war, even if in the winning of it he lost every battle fought."[19]

In short, as suggested by its status as the defendant, the Souths' true grand strategy of the defensive could have kept its armies in the field long enough to wear down the North's willingness to carry on the war. And despite the Southern armies' manpower disadvantages, this grand strategy was at the outset feasible because of the North's logistical task and the relative power that the rifled gun afforded the defense.

The grand strategy of defense would not have required Southern armies always to be on the strategic operational or tactical defense. As Fuller points out, "It is possible to develop an offensive tactics from a defensive strategy."[20] Thus, if Lee's grand strategic sense of the war had been defensive, he could nevertheless on appropriate occasions have pursued offensive campaigns and offensive tactics in the context of that defensive grand strategy. The Revolutionary War again provides an illustration. Although pursuing a grand strategy of defense, the Americans were sometimes aggressive and offensive, as exemplified in their conduct of the battles of Trenton, Saratoga, and Yorktown.

This is not to say that the South should have adopted a perimeter or frontier defense. The Confederacy did not have the manpower or other resources to engage exclusively in a war of position. It is also conceded that Southern home front morale and political pressure would, on occasion, have dictated offensive thrusts. Because General Johnston was removed, history does not tell us at what point he would have been the aggressor in a battle for Atlanta, how successful he would have been, or whether he could have protected Atlanta against a siege. But there are significant degrees between Johnston's backward movement toward Atlanta and Lee's direction of his army. Identifying the South's true grand strategy as defensive, is not, therefore, the same as embracing Johnston's apparently exclusively defensive operational strategy and tactics in Georgia. Nor is it contended that offensive thrusts would have been wholly proscribed by the grand strategy of defense.

Identifying the Confederacy's official grand strategy, that is, the grand strategy that the Confederate government ordained, is a complex task about which much has been written. McPherson observes that "no one ever defined this strategy in a systematic, comprehensive fashion."[21] Commentators have therefore fashioned interpretations from selected official correspondence and reports and from particular military actions. These interpretations contain significant variations and disagreements. General Fuller writes that "President Davis . . . had no grand strategy beyond a rigid defensive."[22] Louis H. Manarin agrees, maintaining that the South adopted "a strictly defensive policy."[23] A second school of thought—to which Russell F. Weigley, Emory M. Thomas, and Frank E. Vandiver all belong—holds that Davis and the Confederate government emphasized a grand strategy of defense, but with a significant modification that contemplated attacking invading armies on appropriate occasions. These authors accordingly deny that the official grand strategy was entirely defensive. In their analyses, Thomas and Vandiver acknowledge Davis's concept of the "offensive defensive." Vandiver interprets this "offensive defensive" as premised on the Confederacy's maintaining its armies but also undertaking counterthrusts when the chance of victory and the availability of supply existed. In this way, according to Vandiver, the South was to prolong the war until the North desisted.[24] A third view of the South's official grand strategy is that, in effect, there was none. Thus, in evaluating Davis as a commander-in-chief, Wiley asserts that "a basic shortcoming . . . was his failure to map an overall strategy." And in *The Politics of Command,* Thomas L. Connelly and Archer Jones trace in detail the erratic and makeshift course of the government's grand strategy, suggesting that a meaningful Confederate grand strategy may never have existed.[25]

In the absence of a systematic official statement from the Confederate authorities, and in view of the conflicts in the evidence and among the writers who have studied the matter, McPherson's conclusion must be accepted. The Souths' grand strategy was never really defined. In any event, it is unnecessary to pursue the point here. The correctness of the government's policy is not at issue, and it is not contended that Lee was responsible for the Confederacy's grand strategy in the war as a whole. At issue here is the correctness of Lee's sense of grand strategy in regard to his own army.

As will be discussed in Chapter 6 [*Lee Considered*], Lee fully accepted civilian control, reported regularly to Richmond, and did not act without the authority of President Davis and his administration. But he was unquestionably the author of his own sense of the grand strategy pursued by the Army of Northern Virginia. Connelly and Jones correctly state that although President Davis asserted "unity of control over the Confederate war effort," there was "a large measure of autonomy for department commanders." The notion that "Lee had little power" they describe as "one of the great myths of the Civil War."[26] In point of fact, it was Lee, not Davis, who proposed and initiated the movements of Lee's army, movements that brought on its battles, including the Maryland campaign and Gettysburg, and he had complete tactical control of that army.[27] Davis and the administration were drawn into the grand strategy that Lee pursued with his army, and therefore share responsibility for Lee's generalship, but the grand strategy was Lee's. He was not acting out a grand strategy formulated or directed by his civilian superiors.

What, then, was Lee's grand strategic sense of the war? How did he understand "the use of engagements to attain the objects of war" as it related to his and the Confederacy's situation? It is not surprising that Lee at no time sat down and made a detailed and comprehensive statement of his view of the grand strategy for securing Southern independence. And since there were no War Department, Security Council, or staff minutes in which his views were recorded, one must resort to indirect sources to identify Lee's grand strategic thinking. Three such sources are available: his occasional communications indicating how he thought the war was to be won, the military movements and actions that he planned and advocated, and the campaigns and battles of the Army of Northern Virginia.

The first of Lee's occasional communications setting forth his sense of the appropriate grand strategy for the Confederacy appears in a letter dated June 25, 1863, to President Davis, from Williamsport, Maryland. This letter states: "It seems to me that we cannot afford to keep our troops awaiting possible movements of the enemy, but that our true policy is, as far as we can, so to employ our own forces as to give occupation to his at points of our selection." The letter argues that "our concentration at any point compels that of the enemy."[28] It is important to note that this letter was concerned with Confederate military forces on a wide range of fronts, including Virginia, North Carolina, and Kentucky. Since it contemplates the drawing of Federal armies to Confederate points of concentration to "give occupation" to the Federals, the letter is a prescription for military confrontation. It is therefore a statement of an offensive grand strategy, whether the confrontation at the "point of concentration" was to take the form of the offensive or defensive on the part of the South. A later letter to Davis on July 6, 1864, shortly after the siege of Petersburg began, was quite plain in its statement of Lee's grand strategic sense. Lee wrote: "If we can defeat or drive the armies of the enemy from the field, we shall have peace. All our efforts and energies should be devoted to that object."[29] Such was Lee's view of the way in which the South could achieve its war aims.

How did this grand strategic view translate into the specific movements that Lee planned and advocated? On May 30, 1863, shortly before starting for Pennsylvania, Lee wrote Davis from Fredericksburg, Virginia, lamenting his inability to take the offensive: "I have for nearly a month been endeavoring to get this army in a condition to move, to anticipate an expected blow from the enemy. I fear I shall have to receive it here at a disadvantage, or to retreat. . . . If I was stronger, I think I could . . . force him back . . . There may be nothing left for me to do but fall back."[30] A curious letter went to Secretary Seddon on June 8, 1863. Although Lee had actually begun the movement that would end at Gettysburg, he seemed both to be anxious to begin offensive action and to want to shame Seddon into agreeing with him:

> As far as I can judge, there is nothing to be gained by this army remaining quietly on the defensive, which it must do unless it is reenforced. I am aware that there is difficulty and hazard in taking the aggressive with so large an army in its front, entrenched behind a river, where it cannot be advantageously attacked. Unless it can be drawn out in a position to be assailed, it will take its own time to prepare and strengthen itself to renew its advance upon Richmond. . . . Still, if the Department thinks it better to remain on the defensive, and guard as far as possible all the avenues of approach, and await the time of the enemy, I am ready to adopt this course.[31]

As is well known, Lee initiated and carried forward the Gettysburg campaign and did, indeed, "assail" the Army of the Potomac on that ground. After Gettysburg, on August 31, 1863, from Richmond where he was meeting with Davis, Lee posted a dispatch to Longstreet who was at army headquarters in the field. He instructed Longstreet to "use every exertion to prepare the army for offensive operations. . . . I can see nothing better to be done than to endeavor to bring General Meade out and use our efforts to crush his army while in its present condition."[32] Later, in September, he filed his report of the Chancellorsville campaign and spoke in these approving terms of the Army of Northern Virginia: "Attacking largely superior numbers in strongly entrenched positions their heroic courage overcame every obstacle of nature and art, and achieved a triumph most honorable to our arms." This, of course, was the good news. The bad news was candidly reported: "The returns of the Medical Director will show the extent of our loss, which from the nature of the circumstances attending the engagements could not be otherwise than severe. Many valuable officers and men were killed or wounded in the faithful discharge of duty."[33]

The Chancellorsville report of September was followed on October 11, 1863, by a report to Seddon from near Madison Court House, Virginia, in which Lee announced, "Yesterday I moved the army to this position with the hope of getting an opportunity to strike a blow at the enemy."[34] Less than a week later, he informed Davis from Bristoe Station:

> I have the honor to inform you that with the view of bringing on an engagement with the army of Gen. Meade, which lay around Culpeper Court House, extending thence to the Rapidan, this army marched on the 9th instant by way of Madison Court House and arrived near Culpeper on the 11th. The enemy retired toward the Rappahannock at the railroad bridge declining battle, and removing all his stores. I determined to make another effort to reach him, and moved through Warrenton towards the railroad north of the Rappahannock.

Lee then described Meade's continued retreat, skirmishing with his rear guard, and the ultimate decision not to pursue the Federals further. Toward the end of the communication he reported, "Our own loss was slight, except in the action at this place, where it was quite severe."[35]

Later in 1863, the Army of the Potomac moved south to Mine Run but Meade decided against an attack when he found Lee in what seemed a strong position. On December 3, 1863, Lee reported to Adjutant and Inspector General Samuel Cooper: "This movement of General Meade, and all reports received as to his intention, led me to believe that he would attack, and I desired to have the advantage that such an attempt on his part would afford. After waiting his advance until Tuesday evening, preparations were made to attack him on Wednesday morning. This was prevented by his retreat. The dense forest which covers the scene of operations prevented our discovering his withdrawal until he was beyond pursuit."[36] Frustrated in his hope for a battle at Mine Run, Lee turned in February, 1864, to thoughts of a spring offensive, writing to Davis: "I can do nothing for want of proper supplies. With these & effective horses I think I could disturb the quiet of the enemy & drive him to the Potomac."[37] On April 15, 1864, he wrote again to Davis: "If Richmond could be held secure against the attack from the east, I would propose that I draw Longstreet to me & move right against the enemy on the Rappahannock."[38] Even after Grant's campaign had begun—after the Wilderness and Spotsylvania—Lee proposed to Davis on May 23, 1864, "It seems to me our best policy to unite upon it [Grant's army] and endeavor to crush it."[39]

Lee's sense of the offensive was not confined to his own army. Having dispatched Longstreet and certain divisions of the Army of Northern Virginia to Gen. Braxton Bragg's Army of Tennessee, Lee wrote Davis from Orange Court House, Virginia, on September 9, 1863, regarding the Chattanooga situation. "I think," he stated, "Rosecrans is maneuvering to cause the evacuation of Chattanooga, & for Burnside to form a junction with him. He ought to be attacked as soon as possible."[40] And writing to General Early in the Shenandoah Valley on July 11, 1864, he declared, "None of the forces . . . will be able in my opinion to resist you, provided that you can strike them before they are strengthened by others."[41]

It may be argued that these examples of Lee's military thinking concern his concepts of operational strategy or his tactical views, having in mind, as stated earlier, that a defensive grand strategy can involve offensive operational strategy or the tactical offensive. However, it is impossible to read the documents in *The Wartime Papers of R. E. Lee,* the dispatches from Lee to Davis and the War Department, and Lee's communications in the *Official Records* without being struck by the fact that they bristle with offensive rhetoric and planning: striking a blow, driving the enemy, crushing the enemy. In short, they are consistent with Lee's expressed theory that peace would come when the Confederates "defeat or drive the armies of the enemy from the field." This was an idée fixe with Lee. Porter Alexander was witness to the ultimate flash of Lee's predilection for the attack. He writes of April 5, 1865, and the Army of Northern Virginia's "last mile" en route to Appomattox. Elements of the army had stopped at Amelia Court House that morning. As reported by Alexander:

> About 1 P.M. . . . we took the road for Jetersville, where it was understood that Sheridan with his cavalry was across our path, & Gen. Lee intended to attack him. I rode with him & his staff & Gen. Longstreet, & we were not long in coming to where our skirmish line was already engaged. I never saw Gen. Lee seem so anxious to bring on a battle in my life as he seemed that afternoon, but a conference with Gen. W. H. F. Lee in command of the cavalry in our front seemed to disappoint him greatly.
>
> [W. H. F.] Lee reported that Sheridan had been reinforced by two infantry corps who were entrenching, & that force was more than we could venture to attack.[42]

Any doubt that Lee was committed to the offensive as the South's appropriate grand strategy is presumably eliminated when one considers the third source for identifying his grand strategic thinking, the campaigns and battles of the Army of Northern Virginia. Consistent with the grand strategy that he said he believed in and repeatedly planned and advocated, Lee from the beginning embraced the offensive. Appointed to command the Army of Northern Virginia on June 1, 1862, he turned at once to the offensive, beginning with major engagements on the Peninsula—Mechanicsville, Gaines's Mill, Frayser's Farm, and Malvern Hill.[43] Following on the heels of the Seven Days, the Second Bull run campaign was strategically offensive in an operational sense, although except for Longstreet's August 30 counterattack it may be classified as defensive from a tactical standpoint. At Antietam Lee stood on the defensive, but the Maryland campaign was strategically offensive. His moving into Maryland assured a major battle in that state. At Chancellorsville, he chose not to retreat when confronted by the Federals' pincer movement. Instead, he repeatedly attacked, and the Federals retreated back across the river.[44]

Gettysburg was, of course, the most daring of Lee's operationally strategic offensives, and he attacked repeatedly there all along the admirable Federal defensive line. As indicated by his communications set forth above, he maneuvered so as to attack after Gettysburg and failed to attack only because Meade would not accept battle. And in the Wilderness, although Grant was initiating the final Federal offensive, Lee again attacked. Even during the final days of the war, Lee attempted the offensive. On March 25, 1865, he ordered an attack on Fort Stedman, a Federal stronghold in the Richmond-Petersburg line. Having described the overwhelming odds that faced the attackers, Alexander rationalizes the effort as "worth all it cost merely as an illustration of the sublime audacity of our commander." It was, he writes, "very characteristic of Gen. Lee . . . one of the greatest instances of audacity which the war produced." He comments further, however, that "the few who got back, of all those sent forward to execute the plan, had to run a gauntlet of terrible fire."[45]

The point is not that each of these campaigns and battles represented an error by Lee. As has been said, the grand strategic defensive may at times translate into the operational or tactical offensive. Thus, driving the Federals away from Richmond in 1862 may have been required in view of Southern morale and the practical consequences of the loss of the capital. Going on the offensive in Wilderness may have been strategically or tactically justified. The point is that the offensive *pattern* is plain. Lee believed that the South's grand strategic role was offensive. He had consistently planned and advocated the offensive. He had told President Davis that the way to peace was to drive the opposing army from the field, and this is what he sought to accomplish. Thus, Manarin asserts that "Lee never seems to have forgotten that although on the defensive the only way to win was by attacking and driving the enemy."[46] And Connelly and Jones conclude that "Lee's frequent offensive thrusts and his almost invariable assumption of the offensive in battle" suggest that he believed the war was to be won by "annihilation of the enemy army."[47]

There was a profound problem with Lee's grand strategy of the offensive: it was not feasible to defeat the North militarily as distinguished from prolonging the contest until the North gave it up. And indeed to attempt an outright defeat of the Federal army was counterproductive in terms of the Confederacy's "objects of war." Curiously, that Lee's attack grand strategy was misplaced is suggested by his own awareness of factors that argued against it.

The primary factor that made the attack grand strategy counterproductive was numbers, and Lee was sensitive to the South's manpower disadvantage and the implications of that disadvantage. A letter of January 10, 1863, to Secretary of War Seddon, written between Lee's victory at Fredericksburg and Burnsides's abortive Mud March, reflects this. He wrote:

> I have the honor to represent to you the absolute necessity that exists . . . to increase our armies, if we desire to oppose effectual resistance to the vast numbers that the enemy is now precipitating upon us. . . .

> The success with which our efforts have been crowned . . . should not betray our people into the dangerous delusion that the armies now in the field are sufficient to bring the war to a successful and speedy termination.
>
> . . . The great increase in the enemy's forces will augment the disparity of numbers to such a degree that victory, if attained, can only be achieved by a terrible expenditure of the most precious blood of the country. . . .
>
> The country has yet to learn how often advantages, secured at the expense of many valuable lives, have failed to produce their legitimate results by reason of our inability to prosecute them against the reinforcements which the superior numbers of the enemy enabled him to interpose between the defeat of an army and its ruin.
>
> More than once have most promising opportunities been lost for want of men to take advantage of them, and victory itself has been made to put on the appearance of defeat, because our diminished and exhausted troops have been unable to renew a successful struggle against fresh numbers of the enemy.[48]

Further awareness of the numbers problem appears in Lee's letter of June 10, 1863, to Davis, after Chancellorsville and at the outset of the Gettysburg campaign:

> While making the most we can of the means of resistance we possess . . . it is nevertheless the part of wisdom to carefully measure and husband our strength, and not to expect from it more than in the ordinary course of affairs it is capable of accomplishing. We should not therefore conceal from ourselves that our resources in men are constantly diminishing, and the disproportion in this respect between us and our enemies, if they continue united in their effort to subjugate us, is steadily augmenting. The decrease of the aggregate of this army as disclosed by returns affords an illustration of this fact. Its effective strength varies from time to time, but the falling off in its aggregate shows that its ranks are growing weaker and that its losses are not supplied by recruits.[49]

On July 8, 1863, immediately after the defeat at Gettysburg, Lee again discussed the strength issue in a letter to Davis, remarking that "though conscious that the enemy has been much shattered in the recent battle, I am aware that he can be easily reinforced, while no addition can be made to our numbers."[50]

Again in regard to his army's strength problem, Lee wrote to Seddon on August 23, 1864, after the siege of Petersburg had begun. He observed, "Unless some measures can be devised to replace our losses, the consequences may be disastrous. . . . Without some increase of our strength, I cannot see how we are to escape the natural military consequences of the enemy's numerical superiority." On September 2, 1864, he wrote in a similar vein to the president, remarking, "As matters now stand, we have no troops disposable to meet movements of the enemy or strike where opportunity presents, without taking them from the trenches and exposing some important point. . . . Our ranks are constantly diminishing by battle and disease, and few recruits are received. The consequences are inevitable."[51]

Consciousness of his numerical disadvantage, of the ever-increasing Federal disproportion, did not mute Lee's commitment to the grand strategic offensive. Nor did that grand strategy permit his army to husband its strength. During the Seven Days battles on the Peninsula, George McClellan lost approximately 9,796 soldiers killed and wounded, 10.7 percent of his forces; Lee's casualties were 19,739 men, 20.7 percent of his army. Although Federal casualties in killed and wounded at Second Bull Run exceeded Lee's by approximately 1,000, the Army of Northern Virginia lost more than 9,000 men, which represented almost 19 percent of the army, as compared to the Federals' 13.3 percent. In spite of McClellan's ineptitude, Lee lost 10,000 men, 31 percent of his force, at Antietam, including missing, immediately following losses in excess of 2,500 at South Mountain on September 14. At Chancellorsville, a victory, Lee lost 13,000 of 61,000 effectives, more than 21 percent, a much higher percentage loss than that suffered by the Federals. Lee's admirer Clifford Dowdey has remarked that "this was the high cost of performing miracles with an undermanned army, to which no significant replacements were coming." In the defeat at Gettysburg, according to a conservative estimate, 21,000 men, one-third of Lee's army, went down, again a higher percentage than the Federal losses. In 1914, before he had decided that Gettysburg was not a "clearcut victory" for the Federals, Freeman wrote that Lee's "army . . . had been wrecked at Gettysburg." As is well-known, Grant lost heavily in the Wilderness, but Lee's casualties, again by a conservative count, exceeded 7,000 men.[52]

Battle casualties were not, however, the only source of attrition for Lee's army. On September 21, 1862, Lee reported to President Davis, describing his first three and a half months of command—a period of aggressive warfare that included the Seven Days, Second Bull Run, and the Antietam campaign—and acknowledged that the army "has had hard work to perform, long and laborious marches, and large odds to encounter in every conflict." Porter Alexander's comment about September 17, 1862, at Antietam is consistent with his description: "When at last night put a welcome end to the bloody day the Confederate army was worn & fought to a perfect frazzle."[53] As one would expect, a price was paid for this kind of service. In regard to Antietam, Piston states, "Desertions reached nightmare proportions during and after the Campaign. Perhaps as many as 20,000 men left the army either before it crossed the Potomac, or prior to the fight at Antietam. Significantly, desertions *increased* after the Confederates returned to Virginia" (emphasis added).[54]

Lee's communications confirm these morale problems. Writing to Davis from Hagerstown, Maryland, on September 13, before the battle at Sharpsburg, Lee stated: "One great embarrassment is the reduction of our ranks by straggling, which it seems impossible to prevent with our present regimental officers. Our ranks are very much diminished—I fear from a third to one-half of the original numbers." In the above-quoted letter of September 21, after the battle, he described the state of the army:

> Its present efficiency is greatly paralyzed by the loss to its ranks of the numerous stragglers. I have taken every means in my power from the beginning to correct this evil, which has increased instead of diminished. A great many men belonging to the army never entered Maryland at all; many returned after getting there, while others who crossed the river kept aloof. The stream has not lessened since crossing the Potomac, though the cavalry has been constantly employed in endeavoring to arrest it. . . . Some immediate legislation, in my opinion, is required, and the most summary punishment should be authorized. It ought to be construed into desertion in face of the enemy, and thus brought under the Rules and Articles of War. To give you an idea of its extent in some brigades, I will mention that, on the morning of the battle for the 17th, General Evans reported to me on the field, where he was holding the front position, that he had but 120 of his brigade present, and that the next brigade to his, that of General Garnett, consisted of but 100 men.

On September 22, 1862, Lee again addressed Davis on the subject: "In connection with the subject of straggling, about which I had the honor to write to you again yesterday, the destruction of private property by the army has occupied much of my attention. A great deal of damage to citizens is done by stragglers, who consume all they can get from the charitable and all they can take from the defenseless, in many cases wantonly destroying stock and other property." With this letter of September 22 Lee enclosed an earlier letter dated September 7, 1862, in which he stated that the "greater number" of stragglers were "the cowards of the army, [who] desert their comrades in times of danger" and recommended that a military commission accompany the army to provide punishment for these offenders. On September 25 he advised Davis that after withdrawing from Sharpsburg into Virginia, he had intended to cross the Potomac again "to advance on Hagerstown and endeavor to defeat the enemy at that point," but he changed his mind, deciding this would be too hazardous because the army did not "exhibit its former temper and condition."[55]

Lee apparently appraised his army correctly, according to a letter of September 27, 1863, from Brig. Gen. J. R. Jones. In charge of one of the cavalry commands trying to "arrest" the "stream" of stragglers referred to in Lee's letter of September 21, Jones reported from Winchester, Virginia, that he had sent 5,000 or 6,000 men back to the army. Significantly, he stated that "The number of officers back here is astonishing. . . . There are about 1,200 barefooted men here. I am satisfied that a large number throw away their shoes in order to remain. If barefooted men are permitted to remain here, the number will continue to increase."[56]

In view of the casualties from death and wounds and the Confederate morale problems after Antietam, Piston comments that "Lee's offensive tactics were bleeding the army white, and many of those who remained with him during the Maryland excursion took 'French leave' as soon as they returned."[57] Piston's judgment is supported by the conclusions of Manarin, a staunch champion of Lee's generalship: Antietam, he states, "momentarily paralyzed" the army. In another passage he revises this characterization and states that "Lee's army never fully recovered" from that battle.[58]

What Freeman calls "mass desertion" was a source of losses to Lee's army after Gettysburg as well.[59] Reporting to President Davis on July 27, 1863, Lee stated, "There are many thousand men improperly absent from this army." On the same day, he advised Davis that on July 4, before his army had quit the battlefield, "on sending back the train with the wounded, it was reported that about 5,000 well men started back at night to overtake it. I fear most of these were captured by the enemy's cavalry and armed citizens, who beset their route." Desertion after Gettysburg extended to distinguished fighting regiments, such as the Twenty-second and Thirty-eighth North Carolina, from which fifty men deserted on July 29, 1863.[60]

Immediately prior to the North Carolina incident Lee had requested Davis to issue a general amnesty for deserters who would return to duty. On August 11, 1863, Adjutant and Inspector General Cooper issued General Orders No. 109 to this effect.[61] Desertions nevertheless continued. Lee advised Davis on August 17, 1863, that "immediately on the publication of the amnesty . . . many presumed on it, and absented themselves from their commands. . . . In one corps, the desertions of North Carolinians, and, to some extent, Virginians, has grown to be a very serious matter. . . . General [John Daniel] Imboden writes that there are great numbers of deserters in the valley, who conceal themselves successfully from the small squads sent to arrest them." On the same day, Imboden was ordered to collect and send back deserters from the Valley and northwest Virginia. Lee was further troubled by reports from North Carolina of an "organization of deserters . . . a formidable and growing evil" there. These men, according to Secretary of War Seddon, were engaged in "dangerous combinations and violent proceedings."[62]

Colonel Bruce, basing his observations on a particular interval of time—apparently Gaines's Mill through Gettysburg—and entirely disregarding desertions, sums up the attrition problem. He cites Lee's "principle of aggressive warfare which was congenial to his impulsive nature" and states:

> In the short period of one year and seven days he fought six of the greatest battles of the war. In history there is no record that equals it. In this short time there had fallen, killed and wounded, of his men 82,208, not counting losses in skirmishes, minor engagements, and the hardships of forced marches and exposure, which would probably swell these figures to a full hundred thousand; the Union loss, figured in the same way, during the same period, was 74,720.[63]

The Confederacy faced a constant dilemma concerning the deployment of its limited manpower between its eastern and western armies. Connelly and Jones provide casualty statistics that graphically address this tension: "Lee's losses in the Seven Days' exceeded the number of effectives in the Army of Tennessee the previous autumn. In the Gettysburg campaign, Lee lost more men . . . than Braxton Bragg had in his Army of Tennessee in October of 1862. At Chancellorsville, Lee's casualties almost equaled those of the combined Confederate surrenders of Forts Henry and Donelson. In fact, during his first four months as commander of the Army of Northern Virginia, . . . Lee lost almost fifty thousand troops. Such a number far exceeded the total troop strength of the Army of Tennessee . . . during the same time span."[64]

Because Lee's biographers seem to overlook the point, it is necessary to emphasize that there was a profound difference between Federal casualties and Lee's casualties. Federal casualties could be, and were in fact, made up with additional manpower. Lee's were irreplaceable, including the severe losses, even prior to Gettysburg, in field-grade officers and other mid-level commanders. As Robert K. Krick has noted, these leadership casualties were especially crippling for the Army of Northern Virginia.[65] Writers like Freeman would impress us with statements of Federal losses that on occasion exceeded Lee's in absolute numbers. They miss the point that the losses were of very different significance for the two antagonists because of the replacement factor. As his own correspondence indicates, Lee realized this difference and said so. His advocates disregard it.

Lee was conscious of another problem related to numbers as well, namely, the consequences to his army of a siege. He consistently expressed the view that his army's being besieged in the Richmond defenses was bound to result in its defeat. Writing in the Southern Historical Society Papers, General Henry Heth quoted Lee as having said this regarding his 1863 situation: "I considered the problem in every possible phase, and to my mind it resolved itself into a choice of one of two things—either to retire on Richmond and stand a siege, which must ultimately have ended in surrender, or to invade Pennsylvania." On June 8, 1863, he wrote to Secretary of War Seddon that the siege eventuality would be a "catastrophe." In June 1864, in a letter to A. P. Hill, he said that if he was "obliged to take refuge behind the works of Richmond and stand a siege, [his defeat] would be but a work of time." General Jubal A. Early reported that Lee had said to him in 1864, "We must destroy this army of Grant's before he gets to the James River. If he gets there, it will become a siege, and then it will be a mere question of time."[66]

There are two possible defenses to a siege: the availability of sufficient military power to break the siege, or protection of the supply routes of the besieged site, so that the siege fails. Both require numbers, that is, sufficient personnel to attack the enemy and drive it away by force or to protect lines of communication and supply, which in Lee's case meant such avenues as the Weldon and Petersburg Railroad and the Southside Railroad at Petersburg. Lee knew this. Knowing also that the ratio of his manpower relative to the Federals' was constantly decreasing, he accurately foresaw the catastrophic character of a siege. Accordingly, he hoped to avoid being caught in a siege in the first place. But in order for an army to avoid being fixed, to avoid a siege, that army must be mobile. And mobility, the ability of an army to maneuver, also requires numbers in some reasonable proportion to the enemy's. In Lee's phraseology, the risk of being besieged was a "natural military consequence" of the increasing disproportion of the size of his army.

According to Dowdey, referring to the day the siege of Petersburg began, "June 18th [1864] marked the end of Grant's campaign against Richmond, and it also marked the end of Lee's capacity to maintain maneuver. In achieving a stalemate against Grant's hosts, Lee had been forced into static fortifications, the one eventuality he most dreaded."[67] Freeman addresses the same issue of mobility in a part of the statement quoted at the outset of this chapter and concludes that mobility was lost at Cold Harbor. He entirely disregards Lee's concern about disproportionate numbers. And in boasting of Lee's prowess, he unwittingly makes the same case concerning the relationship between Lee's casualties and his loss of mobility that is presented here. As previously noted, Freeman states: "During the twenty-four months when he had been free to employ open manoeuvre, a period that had ended with Cold Harbor, he had sustained approximately 103,000 casualties and had inflicted 145,000. Holding, as he usually had, to the offensive, his combat losses had been greater in proportion to his numbers than those of the Federals."[68] Referring to the final Virginia campaign, McPherson remarks that "Lee could no longer risk his limited manpower outside his trenches,"[69] another way of expressing the loss of mobility. In short, it is apparent that Lee's heavy and disproportionate losses had contributed to the disparity in manpower that led to the siege. Contrary to Dowdey's implication, these losses long preceded Grant's Virginia campaign. They had in fact occurred throughout the period of Lee's command and were a consequence of his attack grand strategy. His grim anticipation of a siege did not, however, moderate that grand strategy.

A third consideration that might have suggested to Lee that his grand strategy of the attack was mistaken was his understanding that it was critical for the South to maintain the existence of its armies. As has been noted, on the eve of Gettysburg, which suggests an irony, he had written to Davis that "it is the part of wisdom to carefully measure and husband our strength." In a letter to General Samuel Jones, the commander of the Department of Western Virginia, Lee on January 21, 1864, addressed the supply aspect of his situation. After thanking Jones for cattle and beef that had been forwarded to the Army of Northern Virginia, Lee pointed out, "It is necessary to make every exertion to procure supplies in order to keep our armies in the field." Lee's appreciation of the necessity that the armies be maintained was later expressed in a letter of March 14, 1865, to Davis, in which he discouraged a "general engagement" in North Carolina by Gen. Joseph E. Johnston. "The greatest calamity that can befall us," he wrote, "is the destruction of our armies. If they can be maintained, we may recover from our reverses, but if lost we have no resource."[70] The extent of the casualties that were inherent in his offensive approach risked Lee's capacity to maintain his own army as a viable force.

Finally, Lee also seems to have had intimations that the outcome of the war depended on the North's political reaction and will rather than on military defeat of the North. A letter to his son Custis on February 28, 1863, expresses the view that a "revolution" among the Northern people was the only check on the intent of the "present administration" vigorously to prosecute the war against the South.[71] A more comprehensive statement of this thinking appears in a letter to Mrs. Lee written on April 19, 1863:

> I do not think our enemies are so confident of success as they used to be. If we can baffle them in their various designs this year & our people are true to our cause & not so devoted to themselves & their own aggrandisement, I think our success will be certain. We will have to suffer & must suffer to the end. But it will all come right. This year I hope will establish our supplies on a firm basis. On every other point we are strong. If successful

> this year, next fall there will be a great change in public opinion at the North. The Republicans will be destroyed & I think the friends of peace will become so strong as that the next administration will go in on that basis. We have only therefore to resist manfully.[72]

On June 10, 1863, after Chancellorsville but before Gettysburg, Lee raised the same point in a letter to President Davis that was quoted in the preceding chapter [of *Lee Considered*]. In that letter he said, "We should neglect no honorable means of dividing and weakening our enemies . . . the most effectual mode of accomplishing this object, now within our reach, is to give all the encouragement we can, consistently with truth, to the rising peace party of the North." In this letter, Lee also discussed specific political and diplomatic strategies that he believed would divide and weaken the Northerners who were interested in prosecuting the war. Among these was permitting the North to believe that the South would accept peace on the basis of returning to the Union. In this regard he wrote, "Should the belief that peace will bring back the Union become general, the war would no longer be supported, and that, after all, is what we are interested in bringing about."[73]

In the above-quoted letter to his wife, Lee shows that he relied especially on the defeat of the Lincoln administration in the 1864 election. That letter was written before Chancellorsville and Gettysburg. In the former battle, Lee engaged in a brilliant series of slashing attacks and took heavy losses accordingly. The entire thrust of the Pennsylvania campaign was offensive, strategically and tactically. He punished the Federals heavily in both battles but lost 34,000 of his own men. As has been said, these losses, combined with losses previously suffered, limited his mobility and increased the risk of a siege. And, in fact, by the time of the 1864 election, he was locked in the defenses of Richmond and was in the process of being surrounded by an overwhelming force.

In sum, there were at least four aspects of Lee's own assessment of his army's situation that ran counter to the logic of his grand strategy of the offensive. He was aware of his numerical disadvantage, believed a siege would assure his defeat, and thought it critical for the South to keep its armies in the field. Yet his offensives consistently produced high casualty rates, and these casualties exacerbated the manpower differential, made a siege more likely, and reduced the Confederacy's ability to maintain an effective fighting force. In addition, he saw the loss of Northern support for the war as "what we are interested in bringing about." He nevertheless did not abandon his offensive campaigns until 1864, by which time they were practically impossible. Lee pursued the war with what Colonel Bruce calls "that spirit of aggression, which remained permanently his most prominent characteristic as a soldier."[74]

Rationalizations of Lee's offensives and the resultant prohibitive casualties abound. In the first place, we are told that Lee did not intend for his most daring offensive thrusts to result in major battles. A few examples of this rationalization will suffice. Freeman writes that Lee did not intend to give battle at Manassas in 1862. Manarin and Col. Charles Marshall, an aide-de-camp of Lee, argue that it was Jackson's attack on the Iron Brigade on August 28, 1862, at the Brawner Farm on the Warrenton Turnpike that committed Lee to the battle there. And in a letter to Davis dated August 30, 1862, in the midst of the battle of Second Bull Run, Lee himself stated, "My desire has been to avoid a general engagement."[75] But having destroyed Gen. John Pope's depot at Manassas Junction and interdicted his communications, and having moved his own army a scant twenty-five miles from Washington, it was inevitable that the Federals would have to try to find him. Lee did not like to avoid a fight; thus battle was inherent in Lee's Manassas maneuver.

In September 1862, Lee entered Maryland with the intention of proceeding on to Pennsylvania, a plan that ended at Antietam on September 17. Dowdey contends that "Lee definitely did not cross the Potomac to seek battles."[76] In his justification of this campaign, Freeman draws a picture that would be more at home in a novel by Sir Walter Scott: "Secure in western Maryland or in Pennsylvania, the Army of Northern Virginia would be able to harass if it might not destroy the Federals, and while the farmers of Virginia harvested their crops, untroubled by the enemy, Lee could wait with equanimity the arrival of cold weather."[77] An analysis of Lee's communications with Richmond, which has been ably set forth by Stephen W. Sears, persuasively contradicts the assertion that Lee did not intend a battle.[78] After the war, as Sears notes, Lee himself said that he went into Maryland to give battle. Indeed, he told William Allan that he "intended then to attack McClellan."[79] But whatever his intent, it is apparent that, contrary to Freeman's idyllic anticipation, the Union could not let Lee invade a loyal state and move north of the capital with impunity. In short, when Lee crossed the Potomac in September, he was pursuing the grand strategic offensive. He was on his way to a battle that Sir Frederick Maurice, one of his admirers, says "must be numbered among the unnecessary battles."[80]

And there is also Gettysburg, Lee's most dramatic offensive move and the most costly in its result. Recent military writers have substituted the word "raid" for the word "invasion" in reference to the Pennsylvania campaign. It is frequently suggested that Lee intended simply to forage in Pennsylvania, not to become involved in a battle. This is the argument, for example, of

Hattaway and Jones in *How the North Won.* On the other hand, Maurice justifies the campaign on the ground that "Lee was still convinced that the one way for the Confederacy to obtain the peace which it sought was to convince the public opinion of the North that the attempt to keep the South within the Union was not worth its cost, and that the surest way to bring that about was to win a victory on Northern territory." Alternatively, Krick, also conscious of Lee's foraging intent, states that Pennsylvania "offered Lee wider chances to maneuver" whether or not a battle was intended.[81] But in his letter to Seddon on June 8, 1863, Lee referred to his move as "taking the aggressive" and adverted to the possibility of drawing out the enemy into "a position to be assailed." In addition, in his outline report of the campaign, dated July 31, 1863, Lee at first refers to the "valuable results [that] might be attained by military success." Later in the same communication he asserts, "It had not been intended to fight a general battle at such a distance from our base, unless attacked by the enemy," but recites the circumstances that in his view meant that "a battle thus became, in a measure, unavoidable." These comments by Lee mesh with another of Hattaway and Jones's conclusions: "Lee could have been under no illusion that he could bring off such a protracted campaign without a battle. . . . If he raided enemy territory, it would be politically if not strategically imperative for the Union army to take the offensive." As had been true for McClellan in Maryland in 1862, they remark, "Meade would have been under irresistible political pressure to attack any Confederate army in Pennsylvania."[82]

Another explanation of Lee's pursuit of the offensive in the North is the contention that "there was no alternative." This argument is most pronounced with respect to the Maryland campaign. We are to believe that the only thing Lee could do after Second Bull Run was move into Maryland and perhaps Pennsylvania. Colonel Marshall argues this point, as follows:

> It follows therefore that as General Lee could not remain in Virginia near enough to Washington to detain the enemy's army there, and could not retire without the loss of the moral effect of a successful campaign, and without encouraging the enemy to return to his former position near Richmond, or at least without affording him such an opportunity to return as it cannot be supposed that the enemy would have neglected, General Lee had nothing left to do after the battle except to enter Maryland.[83]

Accepting this conclusion, Freeman states the thesis in detail. He attempts to foreclose all other options: Lee could not have moved eastward because that would have placed his army "under the very shadow of the Washington defenses"; not southward because that would have taken his army into the "ravaged land" of Virginia and "bring the war back toward

Richmond"; not westward because that would have put the army in the Shenandoah Valley, from which a retreat would have moved the army "steadily back toward the line of the Virginia Central Railroad." Freeman also refers ambiguously to the possibility of Lee's moving the army a "slight distance southward" from Manassas, "to Warrenton, for instance. . . . That would put the Army of Northern Virginia on the flank of any force advancing to Richmond, and would give it the advantage of direct rail communication with the capital." He does not say why this "slight distance southward" move was not feasible, but the thrust of his argument is plain: crossing the Potomac was the only practical thing for Lee to do.[84]

In regard to Marshall's statement, it appears that the "moral effect" argument cuts the other way. Having won a victory at Manassas, having driven the Federals into the defenses of Washington, Lee was from a standpoint of morale in an ideal position to desist from a prompt offensive move. Marshall's other contentions are presented more elaborately by Freeman and may be dealt with by considering Freeman's thesis. Disregarding his failure to foreclose the "slight distance southward" option, which was surely an available alternative, it seems on analysis that Freeman has constructed a series of straw men. As noted later in this chapter, after the retreat from Maryland, Lee supplied his army in the "ravaged land" until the Gettysburg campaign. Avoiding moving the war back "toward Richmond" surely did not mean that Lee *had* to go into Maryland. His army's being in the Shenandoah Valley would not have led necessarily to a retreat, let alone a steady retreat, for any distance. And as for the move toward Washington, Kent Masterson Brown has argued that advancing to the defenses of Washington, a feint to confront the defeated and disorganized Federal armies in their own capital, even for a time, was action most likely to move the British politicians toward recognition. Lee could have demonstrated the military and political viability of the Confederacy by even a brief "strategic checkmate" at the gates of Washington, and avoided Antietam and its losses.[85]

The rational that there was no alternative also overlooks the time between Lee's crossing into Maryland, September 4 through September 7, 1862, and the onset of the battle of Antietam on September 16 and 17. Alexander makes the point that whether or not Lee should have entered Maryland, he should not have accepted battle on September 17 along Antietam Creek. He writes: "News of the surrender at Harpers Ferry reached Gen. Lee that night [September 15]. That was the time for him to have . . . recrossed into Va. & saved the blood shed for no possible good on the 17th." Alexander went further with this point. Remarking that the Confederates "could have been easily retired across the river," he states that "we would, indeed have left Maryland without a great battle, but we would nevertheless have come off with good prestige & a very fair lot of prisoners & guns & lucky on the whole to do this, considering the accident of the 'lost order' "[86] There was, in short, an alternative to a battle at Antietam. Even Manarin seems to concede that accepting battle there was a mistake. Having recited the disadvantages that Lee faced, Manarin tries to find a reason for his having "invited attack." His analysis contains a conventional, Lee-as-a-performer conclusion: "To stand and fight was a gamble and Lee gambled."[87]

The no-alternative rationale for the Gettysburg campaign is not as vigorous as it is for Antietam, but it has been elaborately presented by Colonel Marshall.[88] His analysis is worthy of close examination because it is typical of much of the argumentative advocacy in Lee's behalf.

During the period following Chancellorsville, Lee's army remained near Fredericksburg on the Rappahannock, facing Gen. Joseph Hooker's Army of the Potomac situated on the north side of that river. Marshall begins his argument by reasoning that "after the battle of Chancellorsville, . . . the questions presented to General Lee were not only how to avert the manifest danger to which his army was always exposed but also how to use his army so as to bring the enemy's plans to naught." He then posits three options available to Lee: attacking Hooker in his position opposite Fredericksburg, remaining where he was awaiting the enemy's advance, or crossing the Potomac and marching into Pennsylvania. Persuasively disposing of the option of attacking across the river, Marshall turns to the option of waiting for the enemy's advance, which he evaluates in relation to the remaining option, the Pennsylvania move.

Marshall begins his discussion of the option of waiting for the Federals' move by declaring that Lee "was bound to *assume* . . . the enemy would abandon his effort to dislodge him from his position at Fredericksburg, and would move his army to Richmond by water" (emphasis added). This, he says, would have required Lee to withdraw to defend Richmond and:

> During the retreat . . . accident *might* bring on an engagement on ground unfavourable to the Confederates, . . . but even if that eventually [*sic*] were avoided nothing could justify the *deliberate adoption* of a policy the *immediate* and *unavoidable result* of which would be to impose upon the Confederate army the burden of such a defense. Better far to risk the battlefield which chance might bring us during a movement northward than *deliberately* to accept *what we knew* to be altogether favourable to the enemy, and altogether unfavourable to us. (Emphasis added.)

This argument is too clever by far. It depends in the first place on the assertion that there were only three available options. This was not necessarily so. Lee could have fallen back to favorable defensive ground in northern Virginia with the reasonable expectation that Hooker would have followed him. In the second place, the argument rests on the assumption, for which no proof is offered, that instead of moving against Lee by land the Federals would necessarily have proceeded directly to Richmond by water. In fact, the evidence since the 1862 withdrawal from the Peninsula pointed to the fact that the North was committed to the overland route.[89] In any event, having set forth his assumption, Marshall then treats it as an established fact, which effectively eliminates the option of Lee's defending at the Rappahannock: he would have to rush toward Richmond.

After converting his hypotheses of the water route and the necessity for Lee's retiring to Richmond into categorical facts, Marshall proceeds to set up the possibility of catastrophic events during that retreat. Lee "might" have had to fight on unfavorable ground, which speculation is also immediately converted into a certainty: "the immediate and unavoidable result of which . . . we knew to be altogether favourable to the enemy, and altogether unfavourable to us." Thus Marshall destroys the option of Lee's waiting to defend against a Federal move at Fredericksburg by the argumentative device of disparaging it with gratuitous assumptions and unfounded factual assertions.

Marshall's ultimate comparison of the relative merits of Lee's defending in northern Virginia or moving into Pennsylvania is classic. Having characterized these options in his own freewheeling way, he is able to conclude as he wants to: "Better far to *risk* the battlefield which *chance* might bring us during a movement northward than deliberately to accept *what we knew* to be altogether favourable to the enemy, and altogether unfavourable to us" (emphasis added). This conclusion is entirely logical, but it rests on Marshall's tendentious analysis, including the assumptions that Lee would have had to fight on unfavorable terms during a retreat to Richmond, which he treats as objective facts. Having set up only three options for Lee and eliminated two of them, the third—marching into Pennsylvania—is all that is left.

A more convincing scenario than Marshall's would anticipate the Federals' again undertaking an overland offensive and Lee's having an opportunity to defend against it, as he had done at Fredericksburg and was to do again in 1864, by which time his numbers were much reduced as a result of Gettysburg. There may have been a theoretical risk of the Union's resorting again to the water route, but this was unlikely in view of the Federal requirement that the task of Northern forces in the theater was to remain between Lee and Washington. Further, the mounting of the armada would have taken time and would have been open for all to see. If the Federals had undertaken to organize the fleet and move the army to a staging area,

Lee would at that time have had options other than simply retreating to Richmond. These would have included crossing the Potomac so as to deter the Federal embarkation. In any event, to convert the theoretical risk of the water route into a certainty as the premise for justifying the objective risk of Lee's extending his communications in a move into Pennsylvania is casuistry.

Lee himself was quoted after the war on the issue of his options after Chancellorsville. In what seems a shorthand version of Marshall's argument, Lee, as has been previously noted, is alleged to have said that his alternatives were to "retire on Richmond and stand a siege . . . or to invade Pennsylvania." Although there are those who accept this statement as justification for Gettysburg, it is unsupported with any data and seems on its face unreasonable. There were many miles and many places between these alternatives.

As noted above, Lee's outline report argues that having stumbled onto the Federals at Gettysburg, "A battle thus became, in a measure, unavoidable." Although not presented as a rationale for the campaign as a whole, this statement does raise the question of alternatives in regard to the Confederate offensive thrusts of July 2 and 3. In other words, whether or not there was an alternative to the campaign, were there alternatives to Lee's actions on the latter two days of the battle? Alexander has also addressed this point:

> Now when it is remembered that we stayed for three days longer on that very ground, two of them days of desperate battle, ending in the discouragement of a bloody repulse, & then successfully withdrew all our trains & most of the wounded through the mountains; and, finding the Potomac too high to ford, protected them all & foraged successfully for over a week in a very restricted territory along the river, until we could build a bridge, it does not seem improbable that we could have faced Meade safely on the 2nd at Gettysburg without assaulting him in his wonderfully strong position. We had the prestige of victory with us, having chased him off the field & through the town. We had a fine defensive position on Seminary Ridge ready at our hand to occupy. It was not such a really *wonderful* position as the enemy happened to fall into, but it was no bad one, & it could never have been successfully assaulted. . . . The onus of attack was on Meade anyhow. We could even have fallen back to Cashtown & held the mountain passes with all the prestige of victory, & popular sentiment would have forced Meade to take the aggressive.
>
> I cannot believe that military critics will find any real difficulties in our abstaining from further assault on the following day, or in pointing out more than one alternative far more prudent than an assault upon a position of such evident & peculiar strength. (Emphasis in original.)

According to Alexander, "I think it must be frankly admitted that there was no real difficulty, whatever, in our taking the defensive the next day [July 2]; & in our so manouvring afterward as to have finally forced Meade to attack us . . . 60 per cent of our chances for a great victory were lost by our continuing the aggressive." Concluding, he remarks:

> Now the gods had flung to Meade . . . a position unique among all the battlefields of the war, certainly adding fifty percent to his already superior force, and an adversary stimulated by success to an utter disregard of all physical disadvantages & ready to face for nearly three quarters of a mile the very worst that all his artillery & infantry could do. For I am impressed by the fact that the strength of the enemy's position seems to have cut no figure in the consideration [of] the question of the aggressive.[90]

Historians have also rationalized Lee's Antietam and Gettysburg campaigns on other grounds. In the case of Antietam, the political advantage of a victory on Northern soil, which might have carried with it British recognition of the Confederacy, is said to justify the obvious risk of the campaign. The potential effect of the campaign on the Northern election later in 1862 is also seen as justification. These are credible contentions, although, as has been said, the recognition prospect was not the panacea that some writers suggest. Even so, there is still the problem of the irreplaceable losses that would result from a victory as well as from a defeat In addition, although such a victory would have had great value, to try for it was to risk the negative consequences of falling short of victory, consequences which Lee's army, of course, came to realize. Porter Alexander is again worth consulting. Regarding Antietam, he writes:

> And this, I think will be pronounced by military critics to be the greatest military blunder that Gen. Lee ever made. . . .
>
> In the first place Lee's inferiority of force was too great to hope to do more than to fight a sort of drawn battle. Hard & incessant marching, & camp diseases aggravated by irregular diet, had greatly reduced his ranks, & I don't think he mustered much if any over 40,000 men. McClellan had over 87,000, with more & better guns & ammunition, &, besides that, fresh troops were coming to Washington & being organized & sent him almost every day. A drawn battle, such as we did actually fight, was the best *possible* outcome one could hope for. Even that we only accomplished by the Good Lord's putting it into McClellan's heart to keep Fitz John Porter's corps entirely out of the battle, & Franklin's nearly all out. (Emphasis in original.)

Alexander states flatly that Lee "gave battle unnecessarily at Sharpsburg Sept. 17th, 1862. . . . He fought where he could have avoided it, & where he had nothing to make & everything to lose—which a general should not do."[91]

Antietam is further justified by some of Lee's admirers because of the general's need for food supplies and forage, expected to be available north of the Potomac and scarce in northern Virginia. There are at least two logical flaws in this justification. In the first place, Lee recrossed the Potomac on the night of September 18, and his army subsisted in Virginia until the Gettysburg campaign. Accordingly, it was not in fact necessary for him to go to Maryland for commissary supplies. Indeed, as Hattaway and Jones note, "Having left Maryland . . . [Lee] adhered to his original military objective by remaining close to the south side of the Potomac. Here he found abundant forage and subsistence."[92] The rationale is further flawed because it was surely unnecessary to send an entire army to obtain these supplies. On the eve of Chancellorsville, Longstreet and two of his divisions engaged in what Freeman calls a "commissary campaign" in southern Virginia in which they collected provisions.[93] This could have been done in Maryland in 1862, and such a raid would not have drawn the entire Federal army into pursuit and thereby set up a battle.

The Gettysburg justifications include the necessity to upset Federal offensive plans, avoidance of a siege, alleviation of supply problems in unforaged country, encouragement of the peace movement in the North, drawing the Federal army north of the Potomac, and even the relief of Vicksburg. Again, these were worthwhile goals, but the risks were plain to Lee—and, win or lose, significant casualties inhered in the campaign. Citing Gettysburg as an occasion on which Lee's celebrated audacity was "overdone," Alexander makes this comment: "Then perhaps in taking the aggressive at all at Gettysburg in 1863 & certainly in the place & dispositions for the assault on the 3rd day, I think, it will undoubtedly be held that he unnecessarily took the most desperate chances & the bloodiest road." Indeed, referring to the third day, Alexander states, "I thought it madness to send a storming column out in the face of [the Federal artillery], for so long a charge under a mid-day July sun."[94]

When all is said and done, the commentators' rationalizations of Lee's most daring offensive thrusts seem contrived. Although these commentators are aware that Lee's efforts were unsuccessful, costly, and destructive to the South's chances of victory in the war, they are committed to the Lee tradition and seem to strain to absolve him. If simple logic rather than complicated and contradictory rationalization prevails, these offensives can be seen to fall readily into the pattern of Lee's mistaken grand strategy, the grand strategy of attack.

Still other arguments have been put forward in behalf of Lee's leadership.

Some who admire his performance argue that he in fact pursued a defensive grand strategy but did so in the form of the previously noted "offensive defensive," at a distance from Richmond. Freeman, among others, presents this argument. As has been emphasized, a defensive grand strategy may involve reasonable offensive operational strategy and tactics. But regardless of the general validity of this strategic concept, as applied to Lee the "offensive defensive" is a sham. The facts at hand reveal a general who specifically stated that military defeat of the Federals to "drive the armies of the enemy from the field" was what the South had to achieve in order to win the war, who consistently advocated the attack and undertook movements that were designed for giving battle or foreseeably led to battle, and who until his army was decimated and penned up in the Richmond defenses persisted in using his forces offensively. The contention that Lee's strategy entailed an "offensive defensive" is not credible in the face of the facts: the facts identify a general who believed that the offense was the appropriate grand strategy.

Perhaps the most thoughtful rationalization of Lee's generalship was that presented after the war by aide-de-camp Col. Charles Marshall. Marshall underscored the critical importance of the safety of Richmond and then summarized what he called "Lee's military policy":

> In these circumstances there was but one course left for General Lee to pursue, if he would save Richmond from the peril which he knew would attend its investment by the large army of the enemy. He must give occupation to that army, and such occupation as would compel the largest concentration of its forces. By this means he might even induce the enemy to withdraw troops from other parts of the Confederacy, and thus obtain additional reinforcements for himself.

Marshall argued that, consistent with this course, Lee sought "to employ the enemy at a distance and prevent his near approach to the city." The Maryland and Pennsylvania campaigns and the entire war in Virginia had this purpose, according to Marshall.

Marshall's rationale is plausible, but it fails because it is built on false premises. Thus Marshall states that Lee was "unwilling to incur the risks and losses of an aggressive war having for its object the destruction of the enemy." According to Marshall, mindful of his strength problem,

> General Lee thought that to expose our armies to the sacrifices of great battles the object of which was only to disperse or destroy those of the enemy would soon bring the Confederacy to the verge of exhaustion. Even victory in such engagements might prove disastrous. The North could readily raise new armies, while the means of the South were so

> limited that a few bloody victories might leave it powerless to continue the struggle.[95]

But Lee did in fact incur the risks and losses that Marshall abjured. He advised President Davis that military victory was the way to peace. In his efforts to defeat or drive the Federal armies from the field he did expose the Army of Northern Virginia to the "sacrifices of great battles," some of which were "bloody victories" that did bring the Confederacy to the "verge of exhaustion." In short, the policy that Marshall described is not the policy that Lee carried out.

The no-alternative thesis regarding Antietam and Gettysburg has been previously discussed above. In more general terms, the same contention underlies much of the traditional Lee literature: especially in view of the constant necessity of protecting Richmond, there was no practical alternative to the entire conduct of Lee's army command, conduct that was dominated for two years by the grand strategy of the offensive. Lee's admirers do not ask whether he could reasonably have carried out his leadership in a different way. Indeed, many of them do not acknowledge that the question of alternatives exits. This traditional assumption leads to anomalous conclusions. A recent fervently admiring commentary is marked by unusually graphic, unintended irony. The author notes that Lee went "from one victory that led nowhere to another" and refers to Lee's "glorious . . . campaign filled with victories that resulted in total defeat."[96]

Was there an alternative to Lee's glorious campaign leading to total defeat? A perimeter defense or war of position was not feasible. Johnston's apparently entirely defensive policy in Georgia did not have promise. But there was another option: a defensive grand strategy, within the context of which Lee could on occasion have undertaken offensive thrusts, appropriate operationally strategic and tactical offensives, while avoiding the costly pattern of offensive warfare that he pursued in 1862 and 1863.[97]

Of course, there is no guarantee that a defensive grand strategy would necessarily have succeeded. In terms of negatives, it could have involved the loss of Confederate territory, but so did the offensive grand strategy that Lee adopted. It could have risked dampening home front morale among a civilian population that craved victorious offensives, but so did Lee's offensive grand strategy. When he was ultimately forced to resort to the defensive in 1864, that strategy was effective even though his army and its leadership by that time had been grievously reduced by the casualties that resulted from his prior offenses. Had Lee adopted this defensive approach during the two years that he spent on the offensive, he could have had available a fair proportion of the more than 100,000 of his soldiers and officers who went down during the offensive years. With these additional numbers, he could have maintained mobility and avoided a siege. Maneuvers like Early's 1864 movement down the Valley could have been undertaken with sufficient numbers. The Union, on the offensive, could have suffered for an earlier or longer period the ceaseless Federal casualties that began in May 1864. The war could have been prolonged and the Northern people could have abandoned their political support of the war.[98] All of these things are conjectural, but they arise reasonably from the fact that there was an alternative. The truth is that in 1864, Lee himself demonstrated the alternative to his earlier offensive strategy and tactics. In the process he demonstrated the feasibility of the grand strategy of the defense.

When compared to the defensive, Lee's offensive grand strategy, because of the losses entailed, led inexorably, to use his words, to the "natural military consequences of the enemy's numerical superiority," that is, surrender. That superiority was enhanced by Federal reinforcements, but it was also heightened by Lee's heavy and irreplaceable losses. The grand strategy of defense would have muted these "natural military consequences" because it would have slowed the increase in the enemy's numerical superiority insofar as that numerical superiority arose from Lee's heavy and disproportionate losses. Further, because of the strategic and tactical advantages of the defense, that numerical superiority would have been less significant had Lee assumed the defensive in 1862–63. Lee proved this when massively outnumbered on the defensive in 1864–65. In 1864, Lee's defense, in Porter Alexander's words, exacted "a price in blood" that significantly threatened "the enthusiasm of [the North's] population." Adopted earlier, this defensive policy might have worn the North out. The grand strategy of the defense was therefore not only a feasible alternative; it was also more likely to have led to victory.

The views of historians who have recently examined Lee's generalship are worth consulting. In 1984, Hill Junior College at Hillsboro, Texas, presented a Confederate history symposium. The subject was Lee. Five professional historians appeared on the program. One of the Hillsboro participants, Grady McWhiney, discussed Lee's preoccupation with the offensive: "From the outset of the South's struggle for independence," he said, "Lee suggested offensives to President Jefferson Davis and urged other generals to be aggressive." McWhiney also stated that "though Lee was at his best on defense, he adopted defensive tactics only after attrition had deprived him of the power to attack." Ending his remarks, McWhiney concluded: "The aggressiveness of Robert E. Lee, the greatest Yankee killer of all time, cost the Confederacy dearly. His average losses in his first six battles were six percent greater than his opponents' losses; his total casualties exceeded 120,000."[99]

Another distinguished military historian, Frank E. Vandiver, provided a survey account of Lee's leadership at the Hillsboro symposium that is worth describing at length. Beginning with Lee's assumption of command in 1862 on the Peninsula, Vandiver remarked that "the plan for the Seven Days showed that Lee had a sound grasp of what I call 'grand tactics'—tactics elevated almost to the level of strategy. But the casualty ratio was extremely high. In this kind of attack, the attackers are at risk; the Confederates coming up against strongly fortified Federal positions paid heavily for an advance." Turning to Antietam, Vandiver stated,

> One of the most uncomfortable concerns for Jackson and Longstreet and the other Confederate commanders is that Lee, his army weakened and wearied after the second day of Antietam, . . . wants to stay another day, is even thinking of attacking. With what? He has put into action every man he can get on the field, even A. P. Hill's Division coming up from Harpers Ferry. McClellan has a whole Federal Corps he has not committed. Lee's generals know this and they don't want to stay around much longer. But it is clearly in Lee's mind; he does not want to relinquish the offensive. He does not want to cease to be audacious. He won't retreat if he can help it.

At Gettysburg, according to Vandiver, Lee "failed to accept reality. . . . He simply wanted to go on and attack because he wanted to attack." Referring to the situation later in 1863, mindful of Lee's correspondence with subordinates and Krick's thesis in regard to the loss of officers, Vandiver asserted that Lee could not undertake a particular maneuver because "attrition was cutting away the high command. Lee was unable to find division and corps commanders, even brigade commanders with the kind of ability that he had come to expect during the past two years." Proceeding into 1864 and referring to the Wilderness, Vandiver noted that "attrition is affecting [Lee's] thinking and limiting his options. For the first time he is forced seriously to consider yielding the strategic offensive." Finally, with Lee besieged at Petersburg, according to Vandiver, "The strategic and tactical and permanent defensive he cannot accept and keeps looking for a way to break through the lines and get back to audacity."

In an ambiguous characterization of his prior comments, Vandiver also remarked: "I would emphasize though, that again by pushing audacity, always audacity, Lee practiced the high art of grand tactics. He also lost a lot of men by attacking and attacking and attacking." Ultimately, conceding "some trepidation" in doing so, Vandiver ventured this conclusion: "Lee may have been too addicted to the offensive, even against outstanding firepower. Now,

I'm not sure about that assertion. I think you have to balance the fact that he lost a lot of men and stuck to the offensive against *what he considered to be the strategic necessities of attack.* So I would level the charge that he might have been too addicted to the offensive" (emphasis added).

In the statement just quoted, Vandiver abandons an objective analysis of the casualty problem in midstream and begins to speak in terms of what *Lee* considered his necessities to be. Vandiver's analysis is provocative in another way as well. In charging that Lee was "too addicted to the offensive," Vandiver was clearly stating a criticism. It is also plain that Vandiver believed that the problem with Lee's addiction to the offensive was the losses it entailed. But addiction to the offensive and the taking of losses are not in and of themselves negative. They become negative with reference to some strategic criterion. It seems that Vandiver had in mind but did not express such a criterion, the same one that has formed the basis for criticism of Lee's attack grand strategy in this chapter, namely, that Lee's addiction and his losses limited the South's chances of winning the war. But having implicitly acknowledged this criticism, and in spite of it, Vandiver returned to the Lee tradition: "I think he will forever stand among the world's great captains."[100]

Vandiver missed the point in his admiration of Lee's audacity. However much one admires audacity, Lee was not engaged in a theatrical event. He was an army commander charged with using his army so as to maximize the South's chances of achieving independence. The aggressiveness that Vandiver and McWhiney point out was not an incidental flaw; it reflected a fundamental misconception of the proper Southern grand strategy.

Believing that Lee's job was to fight the war so as to make a maximum contribution to victory, General Fuller states that Lee "never seems to have realized the uselessness of squandering strength in offensive actions as long as the policy of the Richmond government remained a defensive one." And he pronounces this judgment: "[Lee] did not create a strategy in spite of his government; in place, by his restless audacity, he ruined such strategy as his government created." Indeed, he "rushed forth to find a battlefield, to challenge a contest between himself and the North." This characteristic is also proclaimed in substance by Lee admirers. Fishwick notes that Lee "never defended when he could attack." Dowdey, referring to Antietam, states that for Lee "it went against the grain to quit the field without battle."[101] To insist on the offensive, regardless of a defensive opportunity, is simply not strategically sound. Whether or not to commit an army to battle is not appropriately a question of the commander's "grain."

As acknowledged by General Fuller in describing the Virginia campaign of 1864–65,

> The fight [Lee] put up exceeded in courage and grandeur anything he had yet accomplished. . . . Hitherto his strategy and tactics had been offensive, now they were defensive; and by combining rapidity of movement with earthworks he blocked Grant's advance at every turn, holding Richmond and Petersburg for nine months against every attack. . . . With his back against the wall, he parried every thrust, until Sherman's advancing columns and Grant's unceasing pressure brought the Confederacy to collapse.

No one would deny that this defense, characterized by Fuller as "skilful, masterful and heroic," was a remarkable one.[102]

But the point is that it was too late for this masterful defense. During the two years prior to the Virginia campaign of 1864, lacking a real understanding of the practical circumstances of the antagonists, or lacking the capacity to relate his grand strategy to those circumstances, Lee had pursued the counterproductive grand strategy of the offensive. Although the Federal military establishment prior to Grant's advent as general-in-chief had not recognized or carried out the true Federal grand strategy of relentless offensive, Lee's direction of his army had unilaterally accomplished the destruction of his force that was the objective of the true Federal grand strategy. Although he had recognized in June 1863 that being besieged in the Richmond defenses would predict the surrender of his army, Lee thereafter initiated the risky and costly Gettysburg offensive and then went on the offensive again, also at great cost, in the Wilderness. These losses helped to seal him up in the trenches around Richmond. Maurice states that "Lee's great weapon was manoeuvre, and Grant had taken it from him," but Lee's attack grand strategy, prior to Grant's Virginia campaign, was also a large factor in Lee's loss of this great weapon.[103]

Writing in 1913, Colonel Bruce offered this characterization of Lee's grand strategy:

> The population of the Confederate States was little less than half that of the Northern States. If the resolution of one was equal to that of the other, it would be easy to calculate the end of a war where the losses on each side in every contest were equal. To illustrate, if a manufacturer or merchant worth a million dollars should enter into a trade warfare with a competitor worth two millions, and so aggressively carry it on as to entail a loss to each of $250,000 a year, the result would be that at the end of four years one would be bankrupt and the other still rich. This was the kind of war inaugurated by General Lee.[104]

In sum, Lee's "kind of war," the grand strategy of the offensive, contradicted the South's true grand strategy. It therefore contributed to the loss of the Lost Cause.

Douglas Southall Freeman, Lee's unquestioning and devoted biographer, sets forth the qualities that he believes to have been responsible for Lee's strategic eminence: "his interpretation of military intelligence, his wise devotion to the offensive, his careful choice of position, the exactness of his logistics, and his well-considered daring." Later, after characterizing Lee's repeated offensives, he describes the circumstances of the army, without relating the offensives to that condition: "The army's hard-won battles left its ranks depleted, its command shattered by death or wounds, its personnel exhausted, its horses scarcely able to walk, its transportation broken down, its ammunition and its commissary low."[105] The loss of mid-level officers as described by Krick is presumably included in the shattering of command that Freeman notes. According to Krick, "The heart of the Confederate army was starting to feel this difficulty . . . just *before Gettysburg*" (emphasis added).[106] These conditions were not inevitable. They did not fall from the sky. They were in significant part the consequences of Lee's "devotion to the offensive" and his "daring."

Porter Alexander writes of Lee: "He had the combative instinct in him as strongly developed as any man living." Admiration for this attribute underlies a 1984 characterization of the general, a classic statement of Lee's greatness, appearing in volume 7 of the above-noted Time-Life Civil War series: "Perhaps his greatest asset was pure audacity—his willingness to run risks, his eagerness to attack, his instinct of taking the initiative at just the right moment."[107]

These, then, are the martial qualities of the Lee of tradition: devotion to the offensive, daring, combativeness, audacity, eagerness to attack, taking the initiative. Whether these qualities were wise or unwise, well considered or ill considered, assets or liabilities, would seem to depend on one's criterion. If one covets the haunting romance of the Lost Cause, then the inflicting of casualties on the enemy, tactical victory in great battles, and audacity are enough. On the other hand, in the words of Colonel Bruce, "If the art of war consists in using the forces of a nation in a way to secure the end for which it is waged, and not in a succession of great battles that tend to defeat it," a very different assessment of Lee's martial qualities is required.[108]

NOTES

1. *Encyclopedia Americana*, 1989 ed., s.v. "Lee, Robert Edward"; *Encyclopaedia Britannica*, 15th ed., s.v. "Lee, Robert Edward"; Mark M. Boatner, *The Civil War Dictionary* (New York: David McKay Company, 1959), 476–77; Marshall W.

Fishwick, *Lee After the War* (New York: Dodd, Mead, 1963), 178; Editors of Time-Life Books, *Lee Takes Command: From Seven Days to Second Bull Run* (Alexandria VA: Time-Life Books, 1984), 8; Manfred Weidhorn, *Robert E. Lee* (New York: Atheneum, 1988), 50, 106, 76.

The *Americana* alludes to Lee's habit of discretionary orders, one of the well-known issues concerning his leadership. The issue divides the commentators. Louis H. Manarin, a vigorous defender of Lee, says this: "Doubtless Lee's use of discretionary orders led to some confusion, but they were a necessary part of his tactics and strategy: to baffle his opponent by maneuvering to advantage, striking when opportunity presented, always with the objective of destroying the enemy's army or disrupting his campaigns. Weakness required vigilence. Subordinate commanders had to be able to assume the initiative when the opportunity occurred, or execute the correct move as the situation developed. Lee could not be everywhere at the same time. He related to his subordinates, through discretionary orders, his ideas, often outlining necessary moves to counter specific moves by the enemy. A war of movement necessitated the issuance of such discretionary orders" (Louis H. Manarin, "Lee in Command: Strategical and Tactical Policies," Ph.D. dissertation, Duke University, 1965, 596).

Edward Porter Alexander had quite a different view: "No commander of any army does his whole duty who simply gives orders, however well considered. He should *supervise their execution*, in person or by staff officers, constantly, day & night, so that if the machine balks at any point he may be most promptly informed & may most promptly start it to work" (Edward Porter Alexander, *Fighting for the Confederacy: The Personal Recollections of General Edward Porter Alexander*, ed. Gary W. Gallagher [Chapel Hill: University of North Carolina Press, 1989], 110; emphasis in original). Referring to the second day at Gettysburg and Longstreet's route to the Confederate right, Alexander wrote: "That is just one illustration of how time may be lost in handling troops, and of the need of an abundance of competent staff officers by the generals in command. Scarcely any of our generals had half of what they needed to keep a *constant & close supervision on the execution of important orders.* And that ought always to be done. An army is like a great machine, and in putting it into battle it is not enough for its commander to merely issue the necessary orders. He should have a staff ample to supervise the execution of each step, & to promptly report any difficulty or misunderstanding. There is no telling the value of the hours which were lost by that division that morning" (*Fighting for the Confederacy*, 236; emphasis in original).

Manarin seems entirely to overlook the use of staff officers in regard to the supervision of orders. I am persuaded by Alexander, who is critical of Lee's lack of control, and unpersuaded by Manarin's thesis.

2. Prominent critics of Lee's generalship, none of whom has significantly affected the tradition, have appeared in three generations of Civil War writing. They are Lt. Col. George A. Bruce; Maj. Gen. J. F. C. Fuller, the English military historian; and Prof. Thomas L. Connelly.

Bruce's "The Strategy of the Civil War" was published in 1913 in *Papers of the*

Military Historical Society of Massachusetts (Boston: published by the Society). Faulting Lee in a number of specific campaigns, Bruce was especially concerned with Lee's aggressiveness and his unacceptable casualties. His analysis is suggestive of my own thesis. General Fuller wrote *The Generalship of Ulysses S. Grant*, published in 1929 (New York: Dodd, Mead). This was followed by *Grant & Lee: A Study in Personality and Generalship*, published in 1933 (London: Eyre and Spottiswoods). In both books he examined critically the then-prominent stereotype of Grant, the inept "butcher," and Lee, the great strategist. Like Colonel Bruce, Fuller criticized Lee's addiction to the offensive and the casualties that it entailed.

Thomas L. Connelly, historian of the Confederate Army of Tennessee, is a well-identified modern critic of Lee. He has made several efforts to reevaluate Lee. In 1969, *Civil War History* (15:2 [June], 116–32) published his "Robert E. Lee and the Western Confederacy: A Criticism of Lee's Strategic Ability." Although concentrating on Lee's neglect of the war in the West, his lack of understanding of its significance, and his alleged Virginia parochialism, Connelly was also critical of Lee's "penchant for the offensive." Connelly was again heard from in 1973. "The Image and the General: Robert E. Lee in American Historiography" appeared in *Civil War History* (19:1 [March], 50–64). As suggested by its title, this article was less concerned with the pros and cons of Lee's generalship. Remarking that the "sensitivity of Lee partisans to any criticism of the General has enshrouded him in a protective mantel enjoyed by no other Confederate figure," Connelly concentrated on "the process by which his image has developed in American letters since the Civil War." The same year brought still another of Connelly's reevaluations; he and Archer Jones of North Dakota State University published *The Politics of Command* (Baton Rouge: Louisiana State University Press, 1973), which returned to and considerably amplified the thesis of the 1969 *Civil War History* article in the context of a thoughtful discussion of the Confederacy's endemic dilemma: in view of limited manpower and resources, how was it to balance their deployment between Virginia and the West?

Connelly's earlier attention to Lee both predicted and culminated in his 1977 book, *The Marble Man: Robert E. Lee and His Image in American Society* (New York: Alfred A. Knopf). This book had two principal components: an intellectual history of the development of the Lee tradition and a psychological inquiry into the man. In both cases, Lee's aggressiveness and casualties were seen as relevant by Connelly. A recent discussion of Connelly's concerns can be found in Richard M. McMurry's *Two Great Rebel Armies: An Essay in Confederate Military History* (Chapel Hill: University of North Carolina Press, 1989).

3. Douglas Southall Freeman, *R. E. Lee: A Biography*, 4 vols. (New York: Charles Scribner's Sons, 1934–36), 4:169–70.

4. An interesting discussion of the misplaced offensive tactics of both armies and an analysis of Lee's casualty percentages can be found in Grady McWhiney and Perry D. Jamieson, *Attack and Die* (Tuscaloosa: University of Alabama Press, 1982). I do not embrace the authors' racial-ethnic theories, but the book is nevertheless useful. Henry W. Halleck, *Elements of Military Art and Science* (New York:

D. Appleton, 1846), 114, 38; Trevor N. Dupuy, Curt Johnson, and Grace P. Hayes, comps., *Dictionary of Military Terms* (New York: H. W. Wilson, 1986), 214, 209. See also Carl von Clausewitz, *On War*, trans. J. J. Graham and ed. Anatol Rapaport (Baltimore: Penguin Books, 1968), 173.

5. U.S. War Department, *The War of the Rebellion: A Compilation of the Official Records of the Union and Confederate Armies*, 127 vols., index, and atlas (Washington DC: GPO, 1880–1901), vol. 46, pt. 2, p. 1205 [set hereafter cited as *Official Records*; all references are to series 1].

6. Bell I. Wiley, *The Road to Appomattox* (Memphis: Memphis State College Press, 1956), 77.

7. David Donald, ed., *Why the North Won the Civil War* (Baton Rouge: Louisiana State University Press, 1960). This book contains essays by Richard N. Current, T. Harry Williams, Norman A. Graebner, David Donald, and David M. Potter.

8. Richard E. Beringer, Herman M. Hattaway, Archer Jones, and William N. Still, *Why the South Lost the Civil War* (Athens: University of Georgia Press, 1986), 9, 16.

9. James M. McPherson, *Ordeal by Fire* (New York: Alfred A. Knopf, 1982), 184.

10. Fuller, *Generalship of Ulysses S. Grant*, 210, 223.

11. *Official Records*, vol. 34, pt. 2, pp. 610–11, vol. 33, p. 729, vol. 34, pt. 1, p. 11.

12. *Official Records*, vol. 34, pt. 2, p. 611, vol. 33, p. 828.

13. Fuller, *Generalship of Ulysses S. Grant*, 222–23, 336.

14. Edward L. Pierce, *Memoir and Letters of Charles Sumner*, 4 vols. (Boston: Roberts Brothers, 1893), 4:114 (letter of 17 January 1863 to Francis Lieber); Abraham Lincoln, *The Collected Works of Abraham Lincoln*, ed. Roy P. Basler, 9 vols. (New Brunswick NJ: Rutgers University Press, 1953–55), 7:514.

15. Alexander, *Fighting for the Confederacy*, 415. Quoting William Swinton, Alexander also writes: "War is sustained quite as much by the moral energy of a people as by its material resources, and the former must be active to bring out and make available the latter. It has not unfrequently occurred that, with abundant resources, a nation has failed in war by the sapping of the animating principle in the minds of its citizens. For armies are things visible and formal, circumscribed by time and space; but the soul of war is a power unseen, bound up with the interests, convictions, passions of men" (416).

16. McPherson, *Ordeal by Fire*, 183.

17. William Garrett Piston, *Lee's Tarnished Lieutenant: James Longstreet and His Place in Southern History* (Athens: University of Georgia Press, 1987), 31–32.

18. Bruce, "Strategy of the Civil War," 469.

19. Fuller, *Generalship of Ulysses S. Grant*, 376. See also Frank E. Vandiver, *Rebel Brass* (Baton Rouge: Louisiana State University Press, 1956), 16–17.

20. Fuller, *Generalship of Ulysses S. Grant*, 365.

21. James M. McPherson, *Battle Cry of Freedom* (New York: Oxford University Press, 1988), 338.

22. Fuller, *Generalship of Ulysses S. Grant*, 29.

23. Manarin, "Lee in Command," 274. It should be noted that Manarin's distinction between offensive and defensive is ambiguous, both with respect to the Confederacy's official policy and Lee's grand strategy. On balance, he seems to conclude that the official policy was defensive but that Lee's was offensive.

24. Russell F. Weigley, *The American Way of War* (New York: Macmillan, 1973), 101–2; Emory M. Thomas, *The Confederate Nation, 1861–1865* (New York: Harper & Row, 1979), 104–8; Frank E. Vandiver, *Their Tattered Flags* (New York: Harper's Magazine Press, 1970), 93–94, 121.

25. Wiley, *Road to Appomattox*, 39; Connelly and Jones, *Politics of Command.*

26. Connelly and Jones, *Politics of Command*, 126, 35.

27. *Official Records*, vol. 19, pt. 2, pp. 590–94; Edwin B. Coddington, *The Gettysburg Campaign* (New York: Charles Scribner's Sons, 1968), 5–9.

28. Dowdey and Manarin (eds.), *The Wartime Papers of R. E. Lee* (Boston: Little, Brown, 1961), 532–33.

29. Dowdey and Manarin, *Wartime Papers*, 816.

30. Dowdey and Manarin, *Wartime Papers*, 496.

31. *Official Records*, vol. 27, pt. 3, pp. 868–69.

32. *Official Records*, vol. 51, pt. 2, p. 761.

33. Dowdey and Manarin, *Wartime Papers*, 469.

34. *Official Records*, vol. 29, pt. 1, p. 405.

35. Dowdey and Manarin, *Wartime Papers*, 609

36. Dowdey and Manarin, *Wartime Papers*, 631.

37. Dowdey and Manarin, *Wartime Papers*, 675.

38. Dowdey and Manarin, *Wartime Papers*, 700.

39. Dowdey and Manarin, *Wartime Papers*, 747.

40. Dowdey and Manarin, *Wartime Papers*, 597.

41. Dowdey and Manarin, *Wartime Papers*, 820.

42. Alexander, *Fighting for the Confederacy*, 521.

43. Alexander makes several interesting and relevant observations about the Seven Days. Thus, he writes: "Very few of the reports distinguish between the casualties of different battles, of which there were four, beside a sharp affair of Magruder's at Savage Station on Sunday the 29th, about which I have never known the particulars except that it was an isolated attack on a strong rear guard by 2 1/2 brigades & it was repulsed, as might have been expected. No *small* force of ours could have hoped for any real success, & all such inadequate attacks were mistakes.

"Of the other four actions, three were assaults by main force right where the enemy wanted us to make them. The first, Ellison's Mill, was an entire failure & very bloody—but fortunately was in a small scale. The second, Cold Harbor or Gaines's Mill, was also a bloody failure at first—being made piecemeal. Finally made in force it was a success. The third, Malvern Hill, was an utter & bloody failure. Ellison's Mill & Malvern Hill could both have been turned, & Gen. D. H. Hill asserts that the enemy's right at Cold Harbor could have [been] better assaulted than the centre or left where our attack was made" (*Fighting for the Confederacy*, 120; emphasis in original).

Alexander was especially critical of the Confederates' costly and unsuccessful attack at Malvern Hill: "I don't think any military engineer can read this description of this ground without asking in surprise, & almost in indignation, how on God's earth it happened that our army was put to assault such a position. The whole country was but a gently rolling one with no great natural obstacles anywhere, fairly well cultivated & with farm roads going in every direction. Why was not half our army simply turned to the left & marched by the nearest roads out of the enemy's view & fire to strike his road of retreat, & his long, slow & cumbersome trains, a few miles below, while the rest in front could threaten & hold his battle array but without attacking it" (*Fighting for the Confederacy*, 111).

44. Alexander also discusses the Confederate attacks at Chancellorsville. At the time of Lee's appointment to command the Army of Northern Virginia, Alexander's friend Capt. Joseph C. Ives had told Alexander that Lee was the most audacious man in either army. Alexander writes this about Chancellorsville: "There was still another occasion when I recalled ruefully Ives's prophecy that I would see all the audacity I wanted to see, & felt that it was already overfulfilled: but when, to my intense delight, the enemy crossed the river in retreat during the night, & thus saved us from what would have been probably the bloodiest defeat of the war. It was on the 6th of May 1863 at the end of Chancellorsville. . . . Hooker's entire army, some 90,000 infantry, were in the Wilderness, backed against the Rapidan, & had had nearly three days to fortify a short front, from the river above to the river below. And, in that dense forest of all wood, a timber slashing in front of a line of breastworks could in a few hours make a position absolutely impregnable to assault. But on the afternoon of the 5th Gen. Lee gave orders for a grand assault the next morning by his whole force of about 40,000 infantry, & I was all night getting my artillery in position for it. And how I did thank God when in the morning the enemy were gone!" (*Fighting for the Confederacy*, 92).

45. Alexander, *Fighting for the Confederacy*, 92, 506, 507. Lt. Col. Alfred H. Burne comments on Lee's aggressiveness and his sense of casualties as the Federals moved to the west at Petersburg, immediately prior to Five Forks on 1 April 1865 that "in spite of the great loss he had just sustained at Fort Stedman, and the resulting lowering of the morale of the troops, Lee instantly decided on a counter-offensive, *cost what it might*" (Alfred H. Burne, *Lee, Grant and Sherman* [New York: Charles Scribner's Sons, 1939], 186; emphasis added).

46. Manarin, "Lee in Command," 260.

47. Connelly and Jones, *Politics of Command*, 33.

48. Dowdey and Manarin, *Wartime Papers*, 388–89.

49. *Official Records*, vol. 27, pt. 3, p.881.

50. Dowdey and Manarin, *Wartime Papers*, 544.

51. Dowdey and Manarin, *Wartime Papers*, 843–44, 847–48.

52. Thomas L. Livermore, *Numbers and Losses in the Civil War in America, 1861–65* (1901; reprint, Dayton OH: Morningside House, 1986), 86, 140, 88–89,

140, 91, 111; Stephen W. Sears, *Landscape Turned Red* (New York: Ticknor & Fields, 1983), 296; John Bigelow Jr., *The Campaign of Chancellorsville* (New Haven: Yale University Press, 1910), 475; Coddington, *Gettysburg Campaign*, 536. Dowdey's quote appears in Dowdey and Manarin, *Wartime Papers*, 426. Freeman is quoted from Douglas Southall Freeman, ed., *Lee's Dispatches: Unpublished Letters of General Robert E. Lee, C.S.A., to Jefferson Davis and the War Department of the Confederate States of America, 1862–65* (1915; revised ed., New York: G. P. Putnam's Sons, 1957), xxxvii.

53. *Official Records*, vol. 19, pt. 1, p. 143; Alexander, *Fighting for the Confederacy*, 153.

54. Piston, *Lee's Tarnished Lieutenant*, 174.

55. *Official Records*, vol. 19, pt. 2, p. 606, vol. 19, pt. 1, p. 143, vol. 19, pt. 2, pp. 617–18, 597, 626–27.

56. *Official Records*, vol. 19, pt. 2, pp. 629–30.

57. Piston, *Lee's Tarnished Lieutenant*, 176. Manarin, "Lee in Command," 374–75, 378, acknowledges these morale problems.

58. Manarin, "Lee in Command," 413, 578.

59. Douglas Southall Freeman, *Lee's Lieutenants: A Study in Command*, 3 vols. (New York: Charles Scribner's Sons, 1942–44), 3:217.

60. *Official Records*, vol. 27, pt. 3, pp. 1041, 1048, 1052.

61. *Official Records*, vol. 27, pt. 3, p. 1041; vol. 29, pt. 2, pp. 641–42.

62. *Official Records*, vol. 29, pt. 2, pp. 650, 650–51, 692, 768–69.

63. Bruce, "Strategy of the Civil War," 467.

64. Connelly and Jones, *Politics of Command*, 33.

65. Robert K. Krick, "Why Lee Went North," in *Morningside Bookshop Catalogue Number 24* (Dayton OH: Morningside Bookshop, 1988), 11. On 21 May 1863, Lee wrote General Hood about the need for "proper commanders," suggesting that they were not available (Dowdey and Manarin, *Wartime Papers*, 490).

66. Henry Heth, "Causes of Lee's Defeat at Gettysburg," in *Southern Historical Society Papers* 4 (October 1877):154; *Official Records*, vol. 27, pt. 3, pp. 868–69; vol. 40, pt. 2, p. 703; J. William Jones, *Personal Reminiscences, Anecdotes, and Letters of Gen. Robert E. Lee* (New York: D. Appleton, 1875), 40.

67. Dowdey and Manarin, *Wartime Papers*, 744.

68. Freeman, *Lee*, 4:170.

69. McPherson, *Ordeal By Fire*, 422–23.

70. Dowdey and Manarin, *Wartime Papers*, 858, 915.

71. Dowdey and Manarin, *Wartime Papers*, 411.

72. Dowdey and Manarin, *Wartime Papers*, 437–38.

73. *Official Records*, vol. 27, pt. 3, p. 881. Lee also wrote Davis on this subject on 25 June 1863. See Dowdey and Manarin, *Wartime Papers*, 530.

74. Bruce, "Strategy of the Civil War," 447.

75. Freeman, *Lee*, 2:301–2; Sir Frederick Maurice, ed. *An Aide-de-Camp of Lee: Being the Papers of Colonel Charles Marshall* (Boston: Little, Brown, 1927),

133; Manarin, "Lee in Command," 351; Dowdey and Manarin, *Wartime Papers*, 267.

76. Dowdey and Manarin (eds.), *Wartime Papers*, 287.

77. Freeman, *Lee*, 2:351.

78. Sears, *Landscape Turned Red*, 66–67.

79. Col. William Allan, "Conversations with Gen. R. E. Lee," 3, Southern Historical Collection, Wilson Library, University of North Carolina at Chapel Hill. See also page 26.

80. Sir Frederick Maurice, *Robert E. Lee, The Soldier* (Boston: Houghton Mifflin, 1925), 152.

81. Herman Hattaway and Archer Jones, *How the North Won* (Urbana: University of Illinois Press, 1983), 397–98; Maurice, *Robert E. Lee*, 189; Krick, "Why Lee Went North," 10.

82. Dowdey and Manarin, *Wartime Papers*, 505; *Official Records*, vol. 27, pt. 2, pp. 305, 308; Hattaway and Jones, *How the North Won*, 319, 414.

83. Sir Frederick Maurice, ed., *An Aide-de-Camp of Lee: Being the Papers of Colonel Charles Marshall* (Boston: Little, Brown, 1927), 148.

84. Freeman, *Lee*, 2:350–51.

85. Kent Masterson Brown, "The Antietam Tapes," Video Cassette 7, Panel Discussion at Antietam Seminar, Virginia Country Civil War Society, Harpers Ferry, West Virginia, 19 April 1987.

86. Alexander, *Fighting for the Confederacy*, 149–50, 145.

87. Manarin, "Lee in Command," 369. Manarin's defense of Lee at Antietam extends to such statements as "Lee was not dividing his army in the face of a superior enemy" (383) and "The movements as Lee planned them seemed simple" (388).

88. Maurice, *An Aide-de-Camp of Lee*, 190–93.

89. Although concerned with the overland campaign of 1864–65, Andrew A. Humphreys's discussion of the water route alternative illuminates the considerations affecting the choice of routes toward Richmond. Andrew A. Humphreys, *The Virginia Campaign of '64 and '65* (New York: Charles Scribner's Sons, 1883), 6–9.

90. Alexander, *Fighting for the Confederacy*, 233–34, 277–78.

91. Alexander, *Fighting for the Confederacy*, 145–46.

92. Hattaway and Jones, *How the North Won*, 244.

93. Freeman, *Lee*, 2:499–501; *Official Records*, vol. 18, pp. 906–7.

94. Alexander, *Fighting for the Confederacy*, 92, 258. Alexander states an additional stricture regarding the third day, as follows: "And, as a student of such technical questions, I think that all military engineers, who will study that field, will agree that the point selected for Pickett's attack was very badly chosen—almost as badly chosen as it was possible to be. I have no idea by whom it was done—whether by a general or staff officer, or a consultation of officers. There was a rumor, in our corps, that Ewell & Hill each reported against assault in his front, & so, by a process of exhaustion, it came to Longstreet's" (*Fighting for the Confederacy*, 252). On this point, Alexander also refers to "the very great mistake made, in my judgement, in

the selection of the point of attack" (278). Related to Lee's control and supervision of his army, Alexander states, "Here again, as when the question of the aggressive or the defensive was up, on the night of the first day, there seems a lack of appreciation of the immense figure which the character of the ground may cut in the results of an aggressive fight. Not only was the selection about as bad as possible, but there does not seem to have been any special thought given to the matter. It seems to have been allowed almost to select itself as if it was a matter of no consequence." (278).

Fitzhugh Lee attempted to rationalize the charge of the third day on the grounds that his uncle intended for additional infantry to participate, at least in support, but that orders to this effect somehow went awry. At one time this was a commonplace defense of Lee's acts, but Lee's later defenders abandoned it, perhaps because, if accepted, it says too much about Lee's lack of control and the fact that he was present as the charge began so that, if the charge was improperly undertaken, he could have done something about it. Fitzhugh Lee's argument, which unintentionally resembles Alexander's "madness" characterization, has an ironic ring today: "A consummate master of war such as Lee would not drive *en masse* a column of fourteen thousand men across an open terrene [sic] thirteen or fourteen hundred yards, nearly every foot of it under a concentrated and converging fire of artillery, to attack an army, on fortified heights, of one hundred thousand, less its two days' losses, and give his entering wedge no support! Why, if every man in that assault had been bullet proof, and if the whole of those fourteen thousand splendid troops had arrived unharmed on Cemetery Ridge, what would have been accomplished? Not being able to kill them, there would have been time for the Federals to have seized, tied, and taken them off in wagons, before their supports could have reached them" (Fitzhugh Lee, *General Lee* [New York: D. Appleton, 1894], 289).

95. Maurice, *An Aide-de-Camp of Lee*, 72, 73, 68–69.

96. Weidhorn, *Robert E. Lee*, 105, 120.

97. Compare Fredericksburg, Lee's defensive battle, to his other 1862–63 battles. According to Livermore, at Fredericksburg Lee lost 4,656 men, 6.4 percent of his force. Burnside's losses were 10,884, 10.3 percent. Livermore, *Numbers and Losses*, 96.

98. Burne, *Lee, Grant and Sherman*, 51–52, 65, 67. Burne writes at length about the Federal casualties from the Wilderness to Cold Harbor, noting that "the national will for war was impaired, and a strong move for peace . . . began to make itself felt" (65). He also says about 1864, "Lee was content to stand on the defensive, trusting that the heavy casualties he could inflict . . . would make the Northern people war-weary, and thus bring about the defeat of Lincoln" (67). William Swinton speaks to this point as well, stating that "had not success elsewhere come to brighten the horizon . . . there was at this time great danger of a collapse of the war" (William Swinton, *Campaigns of the Army of the Potomac* [New York: Charles Scribner's Sons, 1882], 494–95). My point is that Lee should have undertaken this kind of defensive much earlier in the war.

99. Grady McWhiney, "Robert E. Lee: The Man and the Soldier, 1830–1855," in *Confederate History Symposium*, D. B. Patterson, ed. (Hillsboro TX: Hill Junior College, 1984), 66, 67, 68.

100. Frank E. Vandiver, "Lee During the War," in Patterson, *Confederate History Symposium*, 12, 14, 19, 20–21, 23, 24–25. Freeman's treatment of Lee's decision to remain facing McClellan at Antietam on the day following 17 September 1862, represents the classic traditional reaction to his conduct: Having described the desperate condition of the army and McClellan's superior numbers and uncommitted divisions, rhetorically Freeman asks, "What manner of man was he who would elect after that doubtful battle against vast odds to stand for another day with his back to the river?" (Freeman, *Lee*, 2:404). Conditioned by the tradition, including the inevitability of the loss of the Lost Cause, readers are supposed to respond as they would to a quarterback who runs the ball on fourth down and impossible yardage. But Lee was not an athlete or a performer of any kind; he was an army commander responsible for advancing the political cause of his government. The realistic answer to Freeman's question, an answer that I embrace, is that of Gary W. Gallagher: "The answer is that the R. E. Lee of September 18, 1862, was a man who irresponsibly placed at peril his entire army" (Gary W. Gallagher, "The Campaign in Perspective," in *Antietam: Essays on the 1862 Maryland Campaign*, ed. Gary W. Gallagher [Kent, Ohio: Kent State University Press, 1989], 89).

101. Fuller, *Generalship of Ulysses S. Grant*, 375, 377; Fishwick, *Lee After the War*, 96; Dowdey, *Lee*, 308.

102. Fuller, *Generalship of Ulysses S. Grant*, 381.

103. Maurice, *Robert E. Lee*, 261–62. With respect to Lee's having accomplished the attrition of his army, Bruce makes this observation: "On our side the war was necessarily offensive and, on the other, defensive. For nearly three years these parts were practically reversed. Of the seven great battles fought in the Eastern zone including the Wilderness, only one was fought by the Army of the Potomac offensively during an offensive campaign, and one, Antietam, to repel an invasion" (Bruce, "Strategy of the Civil War," 468).

104. Bruce, "Strategy of the Civil War," 468. Bruce made an interesting comparison between the attitudes of Lee and Gen. Joseph E. Johnston; he perceived the perspective of the latter in these terms: "He came to the sane and correct conclusion that the passion of the Southern people for headlong fighting and great battles with a mortality list of Napoleonic proportions, about equal on each side, and little else to show for them save the deceptive glare of Victory, could have but one ending,—the ultimate defeat of the cause for which they were fought" (440).

105. Freeman, *Lee*, 4:175, 178.

106. Krick, "Why Lee Went North," 11.

107. Alexander, *Fighting for the Confederacy*, 365; Editors of Time-Life Books, *Lee Takes Command*, 8.

108. Bruce, "Strategy of the Civil War," 468–69. Bruce is quite plain in his

statement of the criteria for judging any particular military campaign, and they are the criteria on which this chapter is premised: "Each separate campaign is to be examined and judged successful or unsuccessful in accordance with the aid, and to the extent of the aid, which it contributes towards the final result of the war" (408).

Another Look at the Generalship of R. E. Lee

GARY W. GALLAGHER

Americans have embraced Abraham Lincoln and R. E. Lee as the two great figures of the Civil War. In one of the many ironies associated with the conflict, the principal rebel chieftain overshadows Ulysses S. Grant, William Tecumseh Sherman, and all other Federal generals who helped to save the Union. Although Lee's transcendent reputation as a great captain remains firmly ensconced in the popular mind and virtually no one challenges his brilliance as a field commander, scholars increasingly have questioned his larger contribution to the Confederate war effort.[1] Did he fail to see beyond his beloved Virginia, crippling Confederate strategic planning through a stubborn refusal to release troops badly needed elsewhere? Did his strategic and tactical choices lengthen the conflict, thereby increasing the odds that Northern civilian morale would falter? Or did his penchant for the offensive unnecessarily bleed Confederate manpower when a defensive strategy punctuated by limited counteroffensives would have conserved Southern resources? Did his celebrated victories improve the odds for Confederate nationhood, or were they nothing but gaudy sideshows that diverted attention from more significant military events elsewhere? In short, what was Lee's impact on the outcome of the war?

One of the most common criticisms of Lee alleges a lack of appreciation for the problems and importance of the trans-Appalachian Confederacy. J. F. C. Fuller frequently alluded to Lee's inability to see the war as a whole. The British author stated in one characteristic passage that Lee "was so obsessed by Virginia that he considered it the most important area of the Confederacy. . . . To him the Confederacy was but the base of Virginia."[2] A number of subsequent historians expanded upon the idea that Lee failed to take in the entire strategic situation. Especially strident in this regard was Thomas L. Connelly, who wondered "whether Lee possessed a sufficiently broad military mind to deal with over-all Confederate matters." Connelly saw Lee as intensely parochial, blinded by a desire to protect Richmond, and unwilling, or unable, to look beyond each immediate threat to his native state and its capital. When Lee did turn his attention to the West, averred Connelly, he invariably made suggestions "in the context of his strategy for Virginia." Connelly and Archer Jones reiterated many of these points in their study of Confederate command and strategy. They questioned Lee's knowledge about the geography of the West and deplored his habit of requesting reinforcements for the Army of Northern Virginia at the expense of other Confederate armies. Even Lee's grudging deployment of two-thirds of James Longstreet's First Corps to Georgia in September 1863 had a Virginia twist—he hoped that the movement might save Knoxville and shield Virginia's western flank.

Connelly and Jones admitted that all theater commanders tended to see their own region as most important but asserted that Lee's viewing Virginia in this way proved especially harmful. He had been Jefferson Davis's military adviser in the early days of the war and remained close to the president throughout the conflict; moreover, his reputation exceeded that of any other Confederate army commander. The result was as predictable as it was pernicious for the Confederacy: "His prestige as a winner and his unusual opportunity to advise undoubtedly to some degree influenced the government to take a narrower view on strategy and to go for the short gain in Virginia where victory seemed more possible." In the opinion of Connelly and Jones, Lee's influence was such that a powerful "Western Concentration Bloc," the roster of which included Joseph E. Johnston, P. G. T. Beauregard, James Longstreet, and John C. Breckinridge, could not counter his lone voice. The consequent failure to shift forces to threatened areas west of Virginia hindered the Southern cause.[3]

Lee's aggressive style of generalship, with its attendant high casualties, also has generated much criticism. Grady McWhiney and Perry D. Jamieson propounded the thesis that a reckless devotion to offensive tactics bled the South "nearly to death in the first three years of the war" and sealed the fate of the Confederacy. Lee fit this pattern perfectly, they observed, sustaining losses approaching 20 percent in his first half-dozen battles compared to fewer than 15 percent for the Federals. A controversial aspect of McWhiney and Jamieson's book ascribed the South's love of direct assaults to a common Celtic ancestry. Whether or not readers accept the proposition that a cultural imperative prompted Lee to order attacks, McWhiney and Jamieson succeeded in accentuating his heavy losses throughout the war.

Elsewhere, McWhiney bluntly claimed that the "aggressiveness of Robert E. Lee, the greatest Yankee killer of all time, cost the Confederacy dearly."[4]

A number of other historians agreed with McWhiney. The Army of Northern Virginia suffered more than fifty thousand casualties in the three months after Lee assumed command, claimed Thomas L. Connelly, and overall "the South's largest field army, contained in the smallest war theater, was bled to death by Lee's offensive tactics." Russell F. Weigley asserted that Lee shared Napoleon's "passion for the strategy of annihilation and the climactic, decisive battle" and "destroyed in the end not the enemy armies, but his own." J. F. C. Fuller believed that Lee's only hope for success lay in emulating "the great Fabius," who often retreated to avoid costly battles. Instead, time and again Lee "rushed forth to find a battlefield" and "by his restless audacity, he ruined such strategy as his government created." Alan T. Nolan's reasoned analysis of Lee explored the question of "whether the general's actions related positively or negatively to the war objectives and national policy of his government." Nolan thought that Lee came up far short when measured against this standard. His strategy and tactics won specific contests and made headlines but traded irreplaceable manpower for only fleeting advantage. "If one covets the haunting romance of the Lost Cause," wrote Nolan, "then the inflicting of casualties on the enemy, tactical victory in great battles, and audacity are enough." But such accomplishments did not bring the Confederacy closer to independence. Lee's relentless pursuit of the offensive contravened the strategy best calculated to win Southern independence and thus "contributed to the loss of the Lost Cause."[5]

One last piece of testimony on this point typifies a common tension between admiration for Lee's generalship and a sense that his aggressive actions might have hurt the Confederacy. In a lecture delivered at a symposium on Lee in 1984, Frank E. Vandiver commented that his subject "lost a lot of men by attacking and attacking and attacking" and "may have been too addicted to the offensive, even against outstanding firepower." Vandiver then quickly hedged his conclusion:" "I think that you have to balance the fact that he lost a lot of men and stuck to the offensive against what he considered to be the strategic necessities of attack. So I would level the charge that he might have been too addicted to the offensive with some trepidation."[6]

These historians raise serious questions about the relationship between Lee's generalship and Confederate chances for independence. A different reading of the evidence, however, suggests that Lee pursued a strategy attuned to the expectations of most Confederate citizens and calculated to exert maximum influence on those who made policy in the North and in Europe. Far from being innocent of the importance of the West and the psychological dimension of his operations, he might have seen more clearly than any of his peers the best road to Confederate independence. His victories buoyed Southern hopes when defeat lay in all other directions, dampened spirits in the North, and impressed European political leaders. They also propelled him to a position where, long before the end of the war, he stood unchallenged as a military hero and his Army of Northern Virginia had become synonymous with the Confederacy in the minds of many Southern whites.[7] While his army remained in the field there was hope for victory; his capitulation extinguished such hope and in effect ended the war. Lee had selected a strategy that paradoxically enabled the Confederacy to resist for four years *and* guaranteed that it would not survive the surrender of his army at Appomattox.

Modern historians usually attribute Confederate military defeat to failure in the West, where vast chunks of territory and crucial cities fell to the Federals. They often add that Lee's unwillingness to send part of his own army to bolster forces beyond the Appalachians may have hastened Confederate defeat. Is this belief in the primacy of western campaigns a modern misreading of the actual situation? Certainly it was the Virginia theater that captivated foreign observers. For example, Lee's victories at the Seven Days and Second Manassas in the summer of 1862 conveyed to London and Paris a sense of impending Confederate success. Apparently unimpressed by the string of Union triumphs in the West that extended from Fort Henry through the fall of New Orleans, Prime Minister Viscount Palmerston and Emperor Napoleon III leaned toward some type of intervention by the first week in September. Northern public opinion also seemed to give greater weight to the Seven Days than to events in Tennessee, prompting Lincoln's famous complaint to French Count Agénor-Etienne de Gasparin in early August: "Yet it seems unreasonable that a series of successes, extending through half-a-year, and clearing more than a hundred thousand square miles of country, should help us so little, while a single half-defeat should hurt us so much."[8]

Other evidence of a Northern preoccupation with the East abounds. Albert Castel has noted that Lincoln himself, who beyond doubt believed the West to be more important, visited the Army of the Potomac several times but never favored a western army with his presence. (Jefferson Davis joined his western armies on three occasions.) Senator Charles Sumner revealed a good deal about attitudes among powerful Northern politicians when he wrote during the winter of 1865 that Secretary of War Edwin M. Stanton thought "peace can be had only when Lee's army is beaten, captured or dispersed." Sumner had "for a long time been sanguine that, when Lee's army is out of the way, the whole rebellion will disappear." So long as Lee remained active, " there is still hope for the rebels, & the unionists of the South are afraid to show themselves."[9] Among the most telling indications of the public mood was a demand that Grant go east when he became general-in-chief of the Union armies in March 1864. He could have run the war as efficiently from Tennessee or Georgia, but the North wanted its best general to bring his talents to bear on the frustrating Virginia theater.

If anything, the South exhibited a more pronounced interest in the East. Following reverses in Tennessee and along the Mississippi River during the winter and spring of 1862, Confederates looked increasingly to Virginia for good news from the battlefield. Stonewall Jackson supplied it in the spring of 1862 with his Shenandoah Valley campaign—after that, Lee and the Army of Northern Virginia provided the only reliable counterpoint to Northern gains in other theaters and consequently earned a special position in the minds of their fellow Confederates. William M. Blackford of Lynchburg, an antislavery man who nonetheless supported the Confederacy and sent five sons into Southern service, applauded the cumulative effect of Lee's 1862 campaigns: "The defeats of the enemy in the Valley, in the Peninsular, in the Piedmont, the invasion of Maryland, the capture of Harper's Ferry and lastly the victory at Fredericksburg," he remarked, "taken all together, are achievements which do not often crown one year." Lamenting the fall of Vicksburg in late July 1863, Kate Stone, a young refugee in Texas, added that "[o]ur only hope is in Lee the Invincible." Ten months and the reverse at Gettysburg did not alter Stone's thinking about Lee. "A great battle is rumored in Virginia," she wrote in May 1864. "Grant's first fight in his 'On to Richmond.' He is opposed by the Invincible Lee and so we are satisfied we won the victory." A Louisiana officer serving in the West echoed Stone's opinion on 27 May 1864, dismissing talk of a setback in Virginia with an expression of "complete faith in General Lee, who has never been known to suffer defeat, and probably never will."[10]

No one better illustrated the tendency to focus on Lee than Catherine Ann Devereux Edmondston of North Carolina. "What a position does he occupy," she recorded in her diary on 11 June 1864, "the idol, the point of trust, of confidence & repose of thousands! How nobly has he won the confidence, the admiration of the nation." Shifting to a comparison between Lee and officers who had failed in other theaters, Edmondston remarked: "God grant that he may long be spared to us. He nullifies Bragg, Ransom, & a host of other incapables." The *Charleston Daily Courier* implicitly contrasted Lee with Confederate generals in the West when it noted that "Grant is now opposed to a General who stands in the foremost rank of Captains, and his army is confronted with men accustomed to victory." More explicit was a Georgian who after the fall of Atlanta gazed longingly at the commander in Virginia: "Oh, for a General Lee at the head of every *corps d' armee*!"[11]

Well before the close of the war, Lee's position in the Confederacy approximated that held by Washington during the American Revolution. "It is impossible for me to describe the emotions of my heart. . . . I felt proud that the Southern Confederacy could boast of such a man," a North Carolina lieutenant wrote after Lee had reviewed his unit in May 1863. "In fact, I was almost too proud for the occasion for I could not open my mouth to give vent to the emotions that were struggling within." The *Lynchburg Virginian* affirmed after Chancellorsville that the "central figure of this war is, beyond all question, that of Robert E. Lee." Alluding to the phenomenon of Lee's offsetting Confederate reverses in the West, the *Virginian* admired his "calm, broad military intellect that reduced the chaos after Donelson to form and order." "He should certainly have entire control of all military operations through-out the Confederate States," stated one of the general's artillerists in mid-1864. "In fact I should like to see him as King or Dictator. He is one of the few great men who ever lived, who could be trusted." Lee's belated elevation to general-in-chief of the Confederate armies in February 1865 prompted Edward O. Guerrant, an officer serving in southwest Virginia, to observe that "[this] has inspired our country with more hope, courage, & confidence than it has had for a year or two. . . . It puts us all in good humor, & good spirits, and for myself—I feel more confident of our final triumph than for several months past." Gen. Henry A. Wise told Lee on 6 April 1865 that there "has been no country, general, for a year or more. You are the country to these men. They have fought for you."[12]

Testimony from soldiers lends powerful support to Wise's statements. A Georgian in the Army of Northern Virginia wrote shortly after Gettysburg that "[i]t looks like it does not do any good to whip them here in this state, and out West they are tearing everything to pieces. . . . But I am willing to fight them as long as General Lee says fight." When Lee reviewed the First Corps after its return to Virginia from East Tennessee in April 1864, a South Carolinian described an emotional scene: "[T]he men caught sight of his well known figure, [and] a wild and prolonged cheer . . . ran along the lines and rose to the heavens. Hats were thrown high, and many persons became almost frantic with emotion. . . . One heard on all sides such expressions as: 'What a splendid figure!' 'What a noble face and head!' 'Our destiny is in his hands!' 'He is the best and greatest man on this continent!' " A perceptive foreign observer picked up on this attitude when he described Lee in March 1865 as the "idol of his soldiers & the Hope of His country" and spoke of "the prestige which surrounds his person & the almost fanatical belief in his judgment & capacity wh[ich] is the one idea of an entire people."[13]

Many Confederates tied Lee directly to the sainted Washington. During the fall of 1862, the *Columbus* (Georgia) *Times* spoke of his winning "everybody's confidence" and noted that he "has much of the Washingtonian dignity about him, and is much respected by all with whom he is thrown." Peter W. Alexander, perhaps the most widely read Confederate war correspondent, assessed Lee just before the battle of Fredericksburg in December 1862: "Like Washington, he is a wise man, and a good man, and possesses in an eminent degree those qualities which are indispensable in the great leader and champion upon whom the country rests its hope." Alexander added that the Confederacy "should feel grateful that Heaven has raised up one in our midst so worthy of our confidence and so capable to lead"—the "grand-son of Washington, so to speak. . . . the wise and modest chief who commands the Army of Northern Virginia." In the wake of Lee's triumph at Fredericksburg in December 1862, Georgian Mary Jones expressed thanks "that in this great struggle the head of our army is a noble son of Virginia, and worthy of the intimate relation in which he stands connected with our immortal Washington. What confidence his wisdom, integrity, and valor and undoubted piety inspire!" Eliza Frances Andrews, another resident of Georgia, called Lee simply "that star of light before which even Washington's glory pales."[14]

In line with such sentiment inside and outside his army, Lee's surrender understandably signaled the end of the war to most Confederates (as it did to most Northerners). President Davis might speak bravely of the war's simply moving into a new phase after Appomattox, but a trio of women voiced far more common sentiments. "How can I write it?" asked Catherine Edmondston. "How find words to tell what has befallen us? *Gen Lee has surrendered*! . . . We stand appalled at our disaster! . . . [That] *Lee*, Lee upon whom hung the hopes of the whole country, should be a prisoner seems almost too dreadful to be realized!" The first report of Lee's capitulation reached Eliza Andrews on 18 April 1865: "No one seems to doubt it," she wrote sadly, "and everybody feels ready to give up hope. 'It is useless to struggle longer,' seems to be the common cry, and the poor wounded men go hobbling about the streets with despair on their faces." From Florida, a young woman reacted with the "wish we were all dead. It is as if the very earth had crumbled beneath our feet." A North Carolinian in the Army of Northern Virginia spoke for many soldiers and civilians in a single succinct sentence written the day Lee agreed to Grant's terms: "The life of the 'C.S.' is gon' when Gen Lee and his army surrendered."[15]

The foregoing testimony indicates a widespread tendency *during the war* to concentrate attention on Lee and Virginia. Lee himself discerned the centrality of his military operations to Confederate morale (after Gettysburg he commented on the "unreasonable expectations of the public" concerning the Army of Northern Virginia),[16] as well as to perceptions in the North and Europe. A man of far more than ordinary intelligence, he read Northern and Southern newspapers assiduously, corresponded widely, and discussed the political and civilian dimensions of the conflict with a broad range of persons. He appreciated the incalculable industrial and emotional value of Richmond as well as the profound concern for Washington among Northern leaders. He knew the records and personalities of officers who led Confederate armies in the West. He watched the dreary procession of defeats from Fort Donelson and Pea Ridge through Shiloh, Perryville, Stones River, Vicksburg, and Chattanooga. Robustly aware of his own ability and the superior quality of his army, he faced successive opponents with high expectations of success. A combination of these factors likely persuaded him that victories in Virginia were both more probable and calculated to yield larger results than whatever might transpire in the West.

Within this context, it followed that the Confederacy should augment his army to the greatest degree possible. Lee's official restraint prevented his questioning overtly the competence of fellow army commanders; however, in opposing the transfer of George E. Pickett's division to the West in May 1863, he mentioned the "uncertainty of its application" under John C. Pemberton.[17] That guarded phrase came from the pen of a man who quite simply believed he was the best the Confederacy had and thus should be given adequate resources to do his job. Braxton Bragg's sheer waste of two divisions under James Longstreet in the fall of 1863 demonstrated the soundness of Lee's reluctance to reinforce western armies at the expense of the Army of Northern Virginia. As Richard M. McMurry has suggested, the "Rebels' dilemma was that they did not have either the leadership or the manpower and materiel" to hang on to both Virginia and the West. That being the case, perhaps they should have sent available resources to Virginia: "Such a strategy would have employed their best army under their best general at the point where conditions were most favorable to them. . . . If the Confederates could not have won their independence under such circumstances, they could not have won it anywhere under any possible circumstances."[18] To put it another way, the Confederacy could lose the war in either the West or the East, but it could win the war only in the East.

What about Lee's supposed overreliance on the offensive? His periodic use of highly questionable and costly assaults is beyond debate. Natural audacity overcame the dictates of reason when he ordered frontal attacks at Malvern Hill, on the third day at Gettysburg, and elsewhere, and when he elected to give battle north of the Potomac after 15 September 1862. But these unfortunate decisions should not unduly influence interpretations of his larger military record. After all, Grant and Sherman also resorted to unimaginative direct attacks at various times in their careers. Many critics fail to give Lee credit for what he accomplished through aggressive generalship. At the Seven Days he blunted a Federal offensive that seemed destined to pin defending Confederates in Richmond; his counterpunch in the campaign of Second Manassas pushed the eastern military frontier back to the Potomac and confronted Lincoln with a major crisis at home and abroad. The tactical masterpiece at Chancellorsville, coming as it did on the heels of a defensive win at Fredericksburg, again sent tremors through the North. Lee failed to follow up either pair of victories with a third win at Antietam or Gettysburg; however, in September 1862 and June 1863 it was not at all clear that the Army of Northern Virginia would suffer defeat in Maryland and Pennsylvania. A victory in either circumstance might have altered the course of the conflict.

Too many critics of Lee's offensive movements neglect to place them within the context of what the Confederate people would tolerate. It is easy from a late-twentieth-century perspective to study maps, point to the defensive power of the rifle-musket, speculate about the potential of wide-scale guerrilla warfare, and reach a conclusion that Lee's aggressive strategic and tactical decisions shortened the life of the Confederacy. From the opening of the war, however, Southern civilians, newspaper editors, and political leaders clamored for decisive action on the battlefield and berated generals who shunned confrontations with the Federals.

As early as the winter of 1861–62, the *Richmond Dispatch* described a "public mind . . . restless and anxious to be relieved by some decisive action that shall have a positive influence in the progress of the war." In mid-June 1862, shortly after Lee assumed command of the Army of Northern Virginia, the *Richmond Enquirer* conceded the value of entrenchments but stressed the need for offensive moves. "To attack the enemy at every opportunity, to harass him, cut him up, and draw him into general engagements," insisted the *Enquirer*, "is the policy of every commander who has confidence in the strength and spirit of his army. . . . [L]et activity, aggression, attack, stand recorded and declared as our line of policy." Three months later the Macon (Georgia) *Journal & Messenger* greeted news of Lee's raid into Maryland in typically bellicose fashion: "Having in this war exercised Christian forbearance to its utmost extent, by acting on the defensive, it will now be gratifying to all to see . . . the war carried upon the soil of those barbarians who have so long been robbing and murdering our quiet and unoffending citizens."[19] Confederate writings, both public and private, bristle with innumerable sentiments of this type.

Although Confederates often linked Lee and George Washington, they really craved a type of generalship different from that of their Revolutionary hero. Joseph E. Johnston retreated often, fought only when absolutely necessary, and otherwise fit Washington's military mold quite closely. Such behavior created an impression in the Confederacy that he gave up too much territory far too easily. A young lieutenant in Savannah complained to his father on 12 May 1862 about the Peninsula campaign: "General Joseph Johnston, from whom we were led to expect so much, has done little else than *evacuate*, until the very mention of the word sickens one *usque ad nauseam*." Twelve days later Virginia planter William Bulware excoriated Johnston in a conversation with Edmund Ruffin. The general had avoided battle for days and given up twenty miles of ground, facts that demonstrated his "incompetency and mismanagement." Bulware predicted that Johnston would continue to withdraw, causing the "surrender of Richmond, & evacuation of all lower Virginia." Criticism intensified during Johnston's retreat toward Atlanta in 1864. "I don't think he will suit the emergency," complained Josiah Gorgas long before Johnston reached Atlanta. "He is falling back just as fast as his legs can carry him. . . . Where he will stop Heaven only knows."[20] Long since disenchanted with Johnston's tendency to retreat (together with many other facets of his behavior), Jefferson Davis finally replaced him with John Bell Hood, an officer who understood Southern expectations and immediately went on the offensive.

Lee's style of generalship suited the temperament of his people—though many fellow Confederates initially harbored doubts about his competency to succeed Joseph Johnston in field command. Known as "Granny Lee" or the "King of Spades" early in the war, he seemed more devoted to fortifications than to smiting the enemy. Edward Porter Alexander recalled that John M. Daniel, editor of the *Richmond Examiner*, bitterly attacked Lee in June 1862 as one who would misuse the army: "It would only be allowed to dig, that being the West Point idea of war, & West Point now being in command; that guns & ammunition would now only be in the way, spades & shovels being the only implements Gen. Lee knew anything about, &c., &c." The correspondent for the *Enquirer* remarked at this same time that "you have only to go into the army, amongst the men in the ranks, to hear curses heaped upon West Point and the spade."[21]

Questions about Lee's aggressiveness disappeared rapidly after his victory in the Seven Days. His admittedly bloody battles in 1862–63 created an aura of invincibility that offset gloomy events in the West, and that aura clung to him and his army through the defensive struggles of 1864–65. Lee's initial eighteen months as commander of the Army of Northern Virginia built credibility on which he drew for the rest of the war to sustain civilian morale.

Confidence in his army as it lay pinned in the trenches at Petersburg during the summer of 1864 remained high, while Northerners experienced their darkest period of doubt. Far from hastening the demise of the Confederacy, Lee's generalship provided hope that probably carried the South beyond the point at which its citizens otherwise would have abandoned their quest for nationhood.

Nor was Lee's generalship hopelessly "old-fashioned." The simplistic notion that Grant was among the first modern generals and Lee one of the last of the old school withers under the slightest scrutiny. Lee differed in many respects from Grant and Sherman—most notably in his rejection of war against civilians—but had come to terms with many facets of a modern struggle between societies. He predicted from the beginning a long war that would demand tremendous sacrifice in the Confederacy. A member of the Virginia secession convention recounted how Lee warned the delegates shortly after Fort Sumter fell that "they were just on the threshold of a long and bloody war." He knew the Northern people well and believed "they never would yield . . . except at the conclusion of a long and desperate struggle." "The war may last 10 years," he predicted to his wife on 30 April 1861, and no part of Virginia would offer safe refuge from the armies. Clear-eyed about the chances for European intervention at the time of the *Trent* affair, Lee insisted that Confederates "must make up our minds to fight our battles & win our independence alone. No one will help us." He believed in the subordination of "every other consideration . . . to the great end of the public safety," testified Colonel Charles Marshall of his staff, "and that since the whole duty of the nation would be war until independence should be secured, the whole nation should for the time be converted into an army, the producers to feed and the soldiers to fight."[22]

Lee's actions underscored this attitude. Although wearing the uniform of a republic fond of rhetoric praising state and individual rights, he demanded that the national interest come first. He issued an order in March 1862, for example, calling for more unified control of Southern railroad traffic to better satisfy the "exigencies of the service." As early as December 1861, he urged extending the terms of service for soldiers then under arms who originally had signed on for just twelve months: "The troops, in my opinion, should be organized for the war," he wrote. "We cannot stop short of its termination, be it long or short."[23] A staunch supporter of national conscription, Lee played a key role in the process that resulted in the Confederate conscription law of April 1862.[24] Beyond coercing military service, Lee supported the concentration of manpower in the principal Southern field armies, the central government's right to procure needed war material through impressment, and other measures strikingly at odds with the doctrine of state rights.

Late in the war Lee publicly endorsed arming black men and granting them freedom in return for Confederate service. He thus undercut the institution of slavery (with state rights one of the twin pillars on which the Confederacy had been founded), proclaiming openly what he long had urged confidentially. Loath to disagree with his government or intrude in the political sphere during the conflict, Lee had waited to express himself officially on this question until too late to affect Confederate fortunes. He later spoke privately of telling Jefferson Davis "often and early in the war that the slaves should be emancipated, that it was the only way to remove a weakness at home and to get sympathy abroad." A presidential "proclamation of gradual emancipation and the use of the negroes as soldiers" would have furthered the Confederate cause, but Davis resisted taking this step because of the political firestorm it would ignite.[25]

Contrary to what critics such as John Keegan say, Lee was not a man of "limited imagination" whose "essentially conventional outlook" helped undo the Confederacy.[26] He formulated a national strategy predicated on the probability of success in Virginia and the value of battlefield victories. The ultimate failure of his strategy neither proves that it was wrongheaded nor diminishes Lee's pivotal part in keeping Confederate resistance alive through four brutally destructive years. That continued resistance held the key to potential victory—Southern armies almost certainly lacked the capacity to defeat decisively their Northern counterparts, but a protracted conflict marked by periodic Confederate successes on the battlefield more than once threatened to destroy the North's will to continue the war. Indeed, the greatest single obstacle to Northern victory after June 1862 was R. E. Lee and his Army of Northern Virginia. Without Lee and that famous field command, the Confederate experiment in rebellion almost certainly would have ended much sooner.

NOTES

1. For a discussion of Lee's lofty image as a soldier, see Alan T. Nolan, *Lee Considered: General Robert E. Lee and Civil War History* (Chapel Hill: University of North Carolina Press, 1991), 3–8, 59–60.

2. J. F. C. Fuller, *Grant and Lee: A Study in Personality and Generalship* (1933; reprint, Bloomington: Indiana University Press, 1957), 254.

3. Thomas L. Connelly, "Robert E. Lee and the Western Confederacy: A Criticism of Lee's Strategic Ability," *Civil War History* 15 (June 1969): 130–31; Thomas L. Connelly and Archer Jones, *The Politics of Command: Factions and Ideas in Confederate Strategy* (Baton Rouge: Louisiana State University Press, 1973), 47–48.

4. Grady McWhiney and Perry D. Jamieson, *Attack and Die: Civil War Military Tactics and the Southern Heritage* (University: University of Alabama Press, 1982), xv, 19–23; Grady McWhiney, "Robert E. Lee: The Man and the Soldier, 1830–1855," in *1984 Confederate History Symposium*, [ed., D. B. Patterson] (Hillsboro TX: Hill Junior College, 1984), 68.

5. Connelly, "Lee and the Western Confederacy," 118; Russell F. Weigley, *The American Way of War: A History of United States Military Strategy and Policy* (New York: Macmillan, 1973), 127; J. F. C. Fuller, *The Generalship of Ulysses S. Grant* (1929; reprint, Bloomington: Indiana University Press, 1958), 375–77; Nolan, *Lee Considered*, 62–63, 71, 105–6.

6. Frank E. Vandiver, "Lee, During the War," in *1984 Confederate History Symposium*, [ed. D. B. Patterson] (Hillsboro TX: Hill Junior College, 1984), 23, 24–25.

7. Thomas L. Connelly's *The Marble Man: Robert E. Lee and His Image in American Society* (New York: Knopf, 1977) maintains that Lee became the most celebrated Confederate hero only after the war—an interpretation that overlooks a mass of wartime evidence to the contrary.

8. Abraham Lincoln, *The Collected Works of Abraham Lincoln*, ed. Roy P. Basler et al., 9 vols. (New Brunswick NJ: Rutgers University Press, 1953–55), 5:355–56.

9. Albert Castel, "The Historian and the General: Thomas L. Connelly versus Robert E. Lee," *Civil War History* 16 (March 1970): 62, note 50; Charles Sumner, *The Selected Letters of Charles Sumner*, ed. Beverly Wilson Palmer, 2 vols. (Boston: Northeastern University Press, 1990), 2:268.

10. William M. Blackford diary, 31 December 1862, quoted in L. Minor Blackford, *Mine Eyes Have Seen the Glory* (Cambridge, Mass.: Harvard University Press, 1954), 152–53; Kate Stone, *Brokenburn: The Journal of Kate Stone, 1861–1868*, ed. John Q. Anderson (Baton Rouge: Louisiana State University Press, 1955), 230, 284; Felix Pierre Poché, *A Louisiana Confederate: Diary of Felix Pierre Poché*, ed. Edwin C. Bearss (Natchitoches: Louisiana Studies Institute of Northwestern State University of Louisiana, 1972), 126.

11. Catherine Ann Devereux Edmondston, *"Journal of a Secesh Lady": The Diary of Catherine Ann Devereux Edmondston, 1860–1866*, ed. Beth Gilbert Crabtree and James W. Patton (Raleigh: North Carolina Division of Archives and History, 1979), 576–77; *Charleston Daily Courier*, 10 May 1864; John Jones to Mrs. Mary Jones, 23 September 1864, in Robert Manson Myers, ed., *The Children of Pride: A True Story of Georgia and the Civil War* (New Haven: Yale University Press, 1972), 1203.

12. Lewis Battle to his brother, 29 May 1863, Battle Family Papers, Southern Historical Collection, Wilson Library, University of North Carolina, Chapel Hill; *Lynchburg Virginian*, 12 May 1863; William Ransom Johnson Pegram to Mary Evans (Pegram) Anderson, 21 July 1864, Pegram-Johnson-McIntosh Papers, Virginia Historical Society, Richmond; Edward O. Guerrant diary, 23 February 1865, Southern Historical Collection; John Sergeant Wise, *The End of an Era* (1899; reprint, New York: Thomas Yoseloff, 1965), 434.

13. Sidney Richardson to his parents, 13 August 1863, in Mills Lane, ed., *"Dear Mother: Don't grieve about me. If I get killed, I'll only be dead.": Letters from Georgia Soldiers in the Civil War* (Savannah: Beehive Press, 1977), 258–59; letter from "R" dated 1 May 1864, printed in the *Daily South Carolinian*, 10 May 1864; Thomas Conolly, *An Irishman in Dixie: Thomas Conolly's Diary of the Fall of the Confederacy*, ed. Nelson D. Lankford (Columbia: University of South Carolina Press, 1988), 52.

14. *Columbus* (Georgia) *Times*, undated clipping [sometime in the fall of 1862]; Atlanta *Southern Confederacy*, 5 December 1862; Mary Jones to Col. Charles C. Jones Jr., 19 December 1862, in Myers, ed., *Children of Pride*, 1001; Eliza Francis Andrews, *The War-Time Journal of a Georgia Girl 1864–1865*, ed. Spencer Birdwell King Jr. (1908; reprint, Atlanta: Cherokee Publishing Company, 1976), 371.

15. Edmondston, *Journal of a Secesh Lady*, 694–95; Andrews, *War-Time Journal*, 154–55; Susan Bradford Eppes, *Through Some Eventful Years* (Macon, Ga.: Press of the J. W. Burke Company, 1926), 270; William D. Alexander diary, 9 April 1865, quoted in J. Tracy Power, "From the Wilderness to Appomattox: Life in the Army of Northern Virginia, May 1864–April 1865," 561 [unpublished manuscript, 1994].

16. R. E. Lee to Jefferson Davis, 31 July 1863, in R. E. Lee, *The Wartime Papers of R. E. Lee*, ed. Clifford Dowdey and Louis H. Manarin (Boston: Little, Brown, 1961), 565.

17. R. E. Lee to James A. Seddon, 10 May 1863, in R. E. Lee, *Wartime Papers*, 482.

18. Richard M. McMurry, *Two Great Rebel Armies: An Essay in Confederate Military History* (Chapel Hill: University of North Carolina Press, 1989), 155.

19. *Richmond Dispatch*, 3 January 1862; *Richmond Enquirer*, 17 June 1862; Macon (Georgia) *Journal & Messenger*, 10 September 1862.

20. Lt. Charles C. Jones Jr., to Rev. C. C. Jones, 12 May 1862, in Myers, ed., *Children of Pride*, 893; Edmund Ruffin, *The Diary of Edmund Ruffin*, ed. William Kauffman Scarborough, 3 vols. (Baton Rouge: Louisiana State University Press, 1972–89), 2:313; Josiah Gorgas, *The Civil War Diary of General Josiah Gorgas*, ed. Frank E. Vandiver (University: University of Alabama Press, 1947), 55.

21. Edward Porter Alexander, *Fighting for the Confederacy: The Personal Recollections of General Edward Porter Alexander*, ed. Gary W. Gallagher (Chapel Hill: University of North Carolina Press, 1989), 90; *Richmond Enquirer*, 20 June 1862.

22. John Echols to Thomas W. Bullitt, 1 July 1883, printed in Thomas W. Bullitt, "Lee and Scott," in J. William Jones et al., eds., *Southern Historical Society Papers*, 52 vols. (1876–1959; reprint with 3-vol. index, Wilmington, NC: Broadfoot Publishing Company, 1990–92), 11:452; R. E. Lee to Mary Custis Lee, 30 April 1861, in Lee, *Wartime Papers*, 15; Sir Frederick Maurice, ed., *An Aide-De-Camp of Lee: Being the Papers of Colonel Charles Marshall, Sometime Aide-De-Camp, Military Secretary, and Assistant Adjutant General on the Staff of Robert E. Lee 1862–1865* (Boston: Little, Brown, 1927), 32.

23. U.S. War Department, *War of the Rebellion: A Compilation of the Official Records of the Union and Confederate Armies*, 127 vols., index, and atlas (Washington DC: GPO, 1880–1901), series 4, vol. 1, pp. 1010–11; R. E. Lee to [Magrath], 24 December 1861, in *Official Records*, series 1, vol. 6, p. 350.

24. On Lee's role regarding the conscription act, see Douglas Southall Freeman, *R. E. Lee: A Biography*, 4 vols. (New York: Charles Scribner's Sons, 1934–35), 2:25–29.

25. Lee's comments about arming and freeing slaves were recorded by William Allan and William Preston Johnston on 10 March and 7 May 1868, respectively. On the roles of Lee and Davis in the public debate over these issues, see Robert F. Durden, *The Gray and the Black: The Confederate Debate on Emancipation* (Baton Rouge: Louisiana State University Press, 1972).

26. John Keegan, *The Mask of Command* (New York: Viking, 1987), 197.

Lee and Jefferson Davis

WILLIAM C. DAVIS

In 1861, as the new Confederacy rushed to arms, President Jefferson Davis faced a crisis at every turn. Just one of those crises was the creation of his army and the choice of the men to lead his field commands. Seniority in the old United States Army, and the inevitable logic of giving high command to the men with the most experience and highest Old Army rank, almost tied his hands. Not that he minded. Jefferson Davis believed in seniority, both as a West Point graduate himself, and from his perspective as one-time secretary of war.

Nevertheless, this system of ranking did not serve him well. With the one shining exception of Robert E. Lee, it might have been difficult to assemble a greater collection of mediocre talents and insufficient personalities than those to be found in the other seven full-rank generals of the Confederacy. Samuel Cooper could not take the field. Albert Sidney Johnston, in his brief time in command, did little to justify his exalted reputation. Of Braxton Bragg little needs to be said, though it is significant that of all the commanders, he stands second to Lee as the most aggressive. Edmund Kirby Smith repeatedly politicked for command, then ran away from its responsibility, while John Bell Hood, brave though he was, simply was not capable of commanding more than a division. That leaves P. G. T. Beauregard and Joseph E. Johnston. Beauregard could not see beyond his own ego to the greater obligation before him. Johnston, though a man of limitless personal courage, repeatedly showed himself a moral coward when it came to making a decision and taking responsibility for committing himself and his army to any effort in which failure might diminish his reputation.

Anyone seeking the reasons for the failures of the Confederate field armies need not look much further than these men. Collectively, they went a long way toward justifying the cries of politicians like Robert Toombs and Louis T. Wigfall against the policy of giving command to West Pointers. Yet Davis saw few serious alternatives to this sad cast of characters, and circumstances, seniority, logic, and Davis's own choices forced him to try to find commanders from them for his armies. The one shining exception was the eighth full-rank general of the Confederacy, Robert Edward Lee. And even when not glistening by comparison with the rest, he stood out as what a general in a civil democracy ought to be.

Davis and Lee first met in 1825 at the U.S. Military Academy at West Point, when Lee entered as a fourth classman. Davis stood a year ahead of him, yet it was Lee who would come to stand as the ideal of all cadets. Davis, one given at that time of his youth to hero worship, probably looked up to the younger Lee, but only from afar. Lee, after all, came from the bluest of bloods, with a name known in almost every literate household in America. Moreover, Lee would be the exemplary cadet, finally graduating second in the class of 1829. Davis, on the other hand, was almost the typical fraternity boy, court martialled and dismissed once for being caught at an off-limits tavern, reinstated, and then nearly killed when he fell down a steep slope while sneaking back to the post drunk after a visit to the same tavern, and finally narrowly averting irrevocable dismissal and disgrace during the famous "egg nog" riot of 1826. He escaped after getting too drunk too early; he was back in his room sick while his fellow classmen rioted and threatened to kill a professor. Lee, in contrast, took no part in such revels, earning but a single demerit in his entire four years at the academy. It would not be hard to imagine that Davis, then a fun-loving and irresponsible man whom his later contemporaries would hardly recognize, mixed a bit of resentment for the better-than-the-good Lee with his almost certain admiration.

When Davis—almost miraculously—graduated in 1828 in the bottom third of his class, he would not see Lee for at least two decades. When war came with Mexico, Davis joined Zachary Taylor's army at Saltillo in January 1847 as colonel of the First Mississippi Rifles. Lee was there at the same time, but if they saw each other, neither ever mentioned it. Nevertheless, Davis did not remain unaware of Lee during the war or the years that followed. Both emerged from the war as heroes, though Davis's notoriety outstripped Lee's. In 1850, now a senator from Mississippi, Davis was approached by Gen. Narciso Lopez, a Cuban patriot trying to raise an army and mount an invasion of his homeland to free it from its Spanish overlords. He came to Davis, the war hero, to offer him command of the army and the expedition. Davis declined but then suggested Lee for the post. Lee also declined, but it is apparent that he already enjoyed both Davis's respect as a man, and regard for him as a potential commander.[1] A few years later, in 1855, when now-Secretary of War Davis created the Second U.S. Cavalry, he gave Lee its choice lieutenant colonelcy, just one grade behind its commander, Davis's lifelong hero and idol Albert Sidney Johnston.

For his part, Lee left little to attest to his pre-Civil War opinion of Davis, other than to comment after that war that he had regarded Davis as one of the extremist Southern rights politicians, which only showed that Lee either did not pay that much attention to politics, or else did not have a very sophisticated grasp of men and affairs in the 1850s. Davis, in fact, was one of the more moderate leaders, slow to come to secession, and widely suspected of being a reconstructionist even after he was elected and inaugurated president of the Confederacy.[2]

Davis continued to pay careful attention to Lee. From the new Confederate capital in Montgomery, Alabama, he tried to build his infant army. Just five days after the secession of Virginia, Davis wired Governor John Letcher to ask Lee's whereabouts, though he had been kept informed of Lee's activities for some days beforehand. There was never a question in Davis's mind that he wanted Lee with him. When Davis and the government moved to Richmond in late May 1861, Lee was one of those he first sought out. Indeed, well before then he had tried to get Lee to come to Montgomery to confer with him, but the growing emergency on Virginia's Potomac front kept Lee in place. Even so, Lee's very first wartime communication to Davis exposed part of the bedrock of their future relationship. Along with other questions in a prior communication from the president, Davis had asked Lee if he felt any unease about the fact that his commission as a major general was in the Virginia state forces, whereas once Virginia was in the Confederacy, he would be superseded by brigadiers commissioned in the regular national army, such as Joseph E. Johnston. If the question had been asked of Johnston he would have turned apoplectic. Lee simply replied that "my commission in Virginia [is] satisfactory to me."[3] When Davis was already starting to have problems with ambitious men seemingly more interested in rank and reputation than in serving their new nation, such modesty and subordination made Lee a man of mark before he had yet heard a gun fired.

During the ensuing months the president and Lee, now made a full-rank general in the national forces second only to Samuel Cooper and Sidney Johnston, conferred constantly on the defense of northern Virginia. In the last stages of planning and movement prior to the battle of First Manassas, Davis discovered that he and Lee thought alike strategically; both were inclined to reject the grandiose and risky plans submitted by Beauregard. At this stage Davis seems not to have thought of Lee as a field commander. Perhaps this was because the seat of war was in Virginia at the moment, and Lee, with his intimate knowledge of the state and its soldiers, could best serve in Richmond in an advisory capacity. Furthermore, Lee had spent much of his Old Army career as an engineer, not a field commander.

Lee received his first posting to the field in late July 1861, taking command in western Virginia. His initial campaign of the war soon ended with little if anything to his credit. Davis sent him next to South Carolina, not to lead an army but to see to its defenses. Lee did well there, even finally pleasing Gov. Francis W. Pickens, who had earlier thought that Lee was not at heart with the cause but merely a man with a fine family name, good looks, but "too cautious for practical revolution."[4]

Davis retained his regard for Lee throughout these months. The president called his general back to Richmond in March 1862, once more making him his chief adviser and appointing him to the then largely meaningless title of general in chief. During the frustrating spring of 1862, as Joseph E. Johnston, commanding in Virginia, gave increasing evidences of his incapacity for command and his unwillingness either to fight, or even to communicate with his commander in chief, Davis turned often to Lee for counsel. He also used him as a conduit of communication with Johnston, hoping that the two Virginians and old friends enjoyed a rapport that Davis and Johnston certainly did not. It was a vain effort but revealed Davis's steadily growing trust in Lee as a man. As a commander, however, there was still precious little from which to judge, though as a strategist Lee continued to voice opinions in accord with Davis's own. While Johnston repeatedly argued in favor of retreat and abandonment—his two favorite words—Lee and Davis were as one in their determination that the Virginia Peninsula be held in the face of George B. McClellan's landing and advance toward Richmond.

The situation became more desperate in mid-May, with Johnston repeatedly pulling back without authorization, or without even notifying the government of what he was doing. Davis began to include Lee in cabinet meetings in which strategy was discussed. Lee emphatically argued that Richmond should not be abandoned in the face of McClellan. But then he did something that Johnston would never have done. Lee asked the president what *he* thought they should do.[5] Of course Davis was never hesitant to voice an opinion—which with him was the same as a certitude—but it is significant that Lee was one of the few high-ranking generals in the war who would repeatedly *ask* the president what he thought. Davis was a vain man in many ways, and his military vanity was particularly well developed. Contrary to popular myth, he did not interfere very much with his commanders in the field in their conduct of operations, so long as they were *doing* something. But Lee's apparent humility in asking Davis's opinion touched the president now, and would for the rest of the war. It endeared Lee to him, and no doubt Lee—a much better judge of men and character than Davis—knew that Davis would be flattered.

Of course, one of the most propitious Yankee bullets of the war finally relieved Johnston of command on May 29. (Arguably, the only more propitious Union projectile from a Confederate point of view was the shell that did in Leonidas Polk two years later.) Davis may not at first have intended to turn the army over to Lee, but after only a few hours of having Gen. Gustavus Woodson Smith in command, Davis put Lee in charge. It would be the single best decision of his presidency.

Prior to June 1862, Lee and Davis still had little more than a formal and professional relationship. Very possibly the proud Mississippian may even have resented the Virginian at one time, especially because Lee had been the leading protegé of Winfield Scott, a man with whom Davis had a long-running feud dating back to the Mexican War, when Scott politically outmaneuvered Davis's personal favorite and former father-in-law Zachary Taylor. Then, when Davis was secretary of war, he carried on a celebrated—and utterly childish—letter-writing feud with Scott that did no credit to either of them, but found its way into the nation's press. Being Scott's favorite was no recommendation in Davis's eyes.

Familiarity during the first year of the war bridged whatever gap may have existed between Davis and Lee. Davis did not love Lee as he had the now-dead Sidney Johnston, but he respected Lee's ability and believed that he could rely upon and work with him. For his part, Lee judged his commander-in-chief brilliantly. He had seen the correspondence with Scott. He knew of Davis's feuds with other officers during the Pierce administration. He observed firsthand the breakdown in relations between the president and both Joseph Johnston and Beauregard, as well as others. In none of these disagreements did Davis hold exclusive title to blame, but he owned a good share of it in all of them, and for a man with Lee's keen insight into character, lessons were drawn. A man could get along with Jefferson Davis if he observed a few simple rules: Do not question him unless he invited criticism. Do not challenge him. Keep him fully informed at all times. Do not assail his friends or cronies. Have nothing to do with the press, and eschew all public controversy. Avoid politicians, especially those in the growing anti-Davis camp. Most of all, remain loyal. These were requirements of anyone who expected to get along with him, but especially of subordinates. No man on earth who enjoyed Davis's friendship would ever have a more loyal friend, but Davis expected that loyalty to be returned in kind. Happily, in almost every respect, these requirements accorded with Lee's own notions of the proper deportment of a general to his commander-in-chief.

As a result, Robert E. Lee was ideally suited to be Davis's commanding general in the days before Johnston was wounded, and now Lee was better equipped than any other man in the Confederacy to manage both the army and the president. In short, though he may not have realized it, Lee was a better politician and statesman than Davis. He knew how to subordinate his own pride to the greater goal of getting what he needed from men, whether his lieutenants or his superiors. He would even show that he knew how to be a sycophant at times, giving Davis more flattery than did most other generals of the war, and on Davis's most prideful topic, his military judgment.

Lee started off in exactly the right way on 2 June as he took over the command and finished a strategy meeting with Davis and his other generals. Beauregard would have told the president in the boldest terms what he intended to do. Johnston would have told him nothing at all. Gustavus Smith would have proposed some great and impractical maneuver. But Robert E. Lee asked the President what *he* would do. That made all the difference, and Davis's aide, William Preston Johnston, almost immediately felt some stirrings of hope. "The trouble is we have no *Generals*," he complained to his wife that same day, but now he hoped for much from Lee. "I believe he has more capacity," wrote the colonel, and in answering the general's questions, Davis had revealed that he felt the same.[6] He agree with and approved all of Lee's suggestions for turning McClellan back, and then wrote to his wife Varina that "General Lee rises with the occasion, and seems to be equal to its conception."[7] There had been constant talk of Davis himself taking the field to lead Johnston's army. A week after Lee assumed command, almost all such talk ceased. "You need have no fears that the President will take the field in person," wrote the aide Johnston. "He has perfect confidence in Genl. Lee and sees no good that could arise from assuming the nominal command, especially as Genl. Lee acts in accord with him."[8] By the end of the Peninsula campaign, with McClellan safely quivering at Harrison's Landing and Richmond secure, Davis knew he had his man. When Lee asked for more troops, Davis sent them, even though it weakened the capital defenses, something he would not have done for Johnston. "Confidence in you," said Davis to his general, "overcomes the view which would otherwise be taken of the exposed condition of Richmond."[9] Lee rewarded his trust.

The way in which Lee nurtured his relationship with Davis is worth considering in some detail. Better than anyone else, Lee knew that Joseph E. Johnston's greatest failing was his refusal to communicate with Davis. Johnston's feeble excuse was the fear that if he suggested anything to Davis, he would then be committed to carrying it out whether he wished to or not. Moreover, when it came to fighting or responsibility, Johnston, like Bartleby the scrivener, generally "preferred not to." On 5 June, just four days after assuming command of what he would soon style the Army of Northern Virginia, Lee wrote Davis a very full letter outlining all of his thoughts and closing with the comforting expression that "our position requires you should know everything."[10] Better yet, Lee then *apologized* for troubling Davis with more information than he might want, a brilliant touch. A few days later, as he struggled to reinforce Thomas J. Jackson in the Shenandoah Valley, Lee "proposed" such a movement to Davis, yet asked the president to decide.[11] Henceforward, expressions such as "I need not tell you," or "do you think anything can be done," or "what do you think of the propriety of," and most humble and flattering of all, "I shall feel obliged to you for any directions you may think proper to give," appeared in many of Lee's letters.[12] These and similar expressions may have been nothing more than sincerely felt questions, but it cannot be denied that by their wording and use they also, whether by chance or premeditation, consistently reinforced Lee's attitude of respect and subordination to the president. At the same time they salved Davis's ego and helped, in part, to ease the president's frustration over not being at the front, where of all places he would have preferred to be.

Thanks to this attitude of rapidly growing trust, Davis lent an interested and willing ear to Lee's proposal for the fall invasion of Maryland. And once it was underway, for all of the other considerations confronting him, Lee never lost sight of the president's need to know what was happening. Lee wrote him at least one full letter every day, giving details of his positions and movements, and his intentions for movements to come. "When you do not hear from me," Lee had told Davis, "you may feel sure that I do not think it necessary to trouble you." On the other hand, Lee would also apologize for writing too often. "I beg you will excuse my troubling you with my opinions," he wrote Davis in August 1862, "but your kindness had led you to receive them without objection so often that I know I am tempted to trespass."[13]

Yet Lee would also speak his mind, however diplomatically, in dealing with Davis. The president earnestly wanted to be with the army as it invaded Maryland. Just as earnestly, Lee did not want him along. Certainly, the general believed, as he told Davis, that it would be too arduous and dangerous for Davis to make the trip, even risking capture. But it is hard not to see a subtext in which Lee also did not want his independence to be fettered by having the president looking directly over his shoulder. Exercising considerable powers of persuasion, Lee even sent a special aide back to Richmond, charged to lay out in detail for the president all the hazards at every point along the route, though Lee at the same time covered himself by saying that "I should feel the greatest satisfaction in having an interview with you and consulting upon all subjects of interest."[14] In the end, Lee's persuasions worked and Davis stayed in Richmond. Significantly, too, while Lee was away on his campaign, and daily communicating with the president, Davis from Richmond declined to bombard the general with letters and telegrams as he did other generals. He issued no orders, nor even suggestions. By keeping Davis steadily informed, Lee also kept him off his own back. Indeed, so well was Lee's demeanor suiting itself to Davis's psychological needs that when Lee overstepped his military bounds and proposed to Davis that the time was right to propose peace terms and Confederate independence to Lincoln, Davis did not bristle at such a suggestion touching on his own civil authority, as he would have from almost any other commander in his army.[15] From *this* general Davis would accept much because this general gave him much. It was also a sign of how well Davis could work with a man on the rare occasion when he found one who suited him.

Again during the Fredericksburg campaign, Lee wrote to Davis daily keep him fully advised of affairs, even when there was nothing to tell. Davis craved information and had a right to it. Lee's openness proved to be a double blessing now. It relieved much of Davis's natural anxiety, and it gave him renewed confidence in his general, which always meant that the president interfered less, and in this campaign not at all. Indeed, so completely did Davis trust Lee's judgment, and his plans as outlined in detail in Lee's correspondence, that during the ensuing campaign, leading up to the largest land battle ever fought on the American continent in terms of numbers engaged, the President only wrote to his commanding general twice, and then only to offer more men and guns. Lee, in turn, rewarded Davis with a victory.

Lee did the same during the Chancellorsville operations, and Davis, in turn, complimented him upon "this addition to an unprecedented series of great victories which your army has achieved."[16] And then when the two met in Richmond late in May 1863, and Lee proposed another invasion of the North, Davis, after some early trepidation, gave his approval. Better yet, he was entirely out of the planning and left it all up to Lee.

Another facet of Lee's character, and of his perfect alignment with Davis's personality, became evident. When Lee failed to achieve complete success in any of his campaigns, as he failed to bag McClellan completely at the end of the Peninsula fighting, he took the responsibility squarely onto his own shoulders. "I fear all was not done that might have been done to harass and destroy our enemies," he told Davis, "but I blame nobody but myself." Now following upon the crushing defeat at Gettysburg, Lee took all of the responsibility upon himself and asked to be allowed to resign.

Nothing was better calculated to win Davis's undying regard. Lee's letter touched him deeply. It reminded him of his dead hero Sidney Johnston, and how he had always said that "success is the test of merit," and how he had borne in silence the clamor of uncomprehending critics such as those now blaming Lee for the defeat. "My dear friend," Davis responded, "there is nothing which I have found to require a greater effort of patience than to bear the criticisms of the ignorant." From his greater experience at being the object of calumny, he advised Lee to ignore it. As for resignation and replacement, Lee had no equal, he told him, much less a superior. "To ask me to substitute you by someone in my judgment more fit to command," said Davis, "is to demand an impossibility."[17]

Instead of having his confidence in Lee diminished by defeat, Davis only felt it increase. More and more now he thought of Lee when he looked to other theaters of the war where his confidence was sorely tested, if not eradicated. The Army of Tennessee was a trouble spot almost from the beginning of the conflict, thanks chiefly to Braxton Bragg's peculiar unfitness for command. With that army practically in rebellion against its commander by August 1863, and with a campaign against Rosecrans underway, Davis thought of sending Lee west to assume the command. Lee declined on several grounds, and the president accepted. But then later in August he called Lee to Richmond to discuss the matter again, and again Lee declined. Davis was a man who knew what he wanted, but this general held a special place in his affections and had his respect, and he resisted exercising his raw authority to compel his best commander to do something against his wishes. Davis did, however, finally send James Longstreet and most of his First Corps to Tennessee, even though Lee asked that it not be done, and when the president once again expressed a desire that Lee go along with Longstreet, he took Lee's refusal as final. As Lee remained in Virginia, sparring with Meade in the months of relative inactivity following Gettysburg, Davis visited the army frequently to confer with the general. While there, they were often seen going to church together. The professional relationship was blossoming into a warm friendship, at least on Davis's part. Interestingly, one searches almost in vain in Lee's wartime correspondence to find evidence of his personal feelings toward, or opinion of, the president.

Again in December, after Bragg's disastrous defeat at Chattanooga, Davis asked Lee to take the western command, and again Lee declined, showing his own perception of the condition of affairs in that troubled command by saying he feared he would not get cooperation from its officers. Davis spent a full week putting Lee on the spot in meeting after meeting, sometimes with the secretary of war or other cabinet members present, but Lee held firm. Not only did Davis yield in the end to Lee's firm resolve, but he also listened to other advice from Lee, even when it ran against every fiber of judgment he possessed. With Beauregard in such poor stead with the president that he was lucky even to have a uniform, Lee suggested that the only available and logical commander for the Army of Tennessee was Joseph E. Johnston. This, for a change, reveals that Lee, too, was occasionally capable of abominable judgment of men, but in the Confederate system of high command at the moment, alternatives were few, or nil. What is significant is that Davis listened to him. Of course, for the good of the cause, perhaps Davis should have ordered Lee to take the command, and that would have been that. Lee's sense of duty would not have allowed him to do anything but accept. We may conjecture another time about what changes, if any, to the outcome of the war in Georgia might have ensued. What matters here is that the relationship between this commander and this commander-in-chief had developed to such an extent that Davis was unwilling to order Lee to do that which he did not wish to do.

The following spring, Davis tried everything but bombs and levers to get Johnston to move; he found himself fighting an action in his rear with journalists and politicians by whom the naive Johnston allowed himself to be used as a tool in their own vendetta against the president. Meanwhile, Lee continued to be the one bright spot in Davis's high command. He did not complain. He did not plot. He did not talk to newspapermen. And even when he did not bring Davis victories, still Davis found it impossible to fault the conduct of his campaigns. Often they met daily as the spring of 1864 wore on toward the inevitable opening of the campaign with U. S. Grant and George G. Meade. As he had for almost two years, Davis found himself leaving things almost entirely in Lee's hands. As he had for two years, Lee told everything, whether there was anything to tell or not. Even while the Army of the Potomac slowly pushed Lee back during May, Davis felt unbounded confidence in his general and repeatedly expressed that confidence to his cabinet. Secretary of the Navy Stephen R. Mallory recalled that Davis regarded Lee as "standing alone among the confederate soldiers in military capacity." When Davis spoke of Lee, said Mallory, "all others were, in comparison to him, beginners."[18] This was the only general in the army whom Davis addressed repeatedly as "my dear friend" in his letters. Remembering the loss of other friends and great leaders like Sidney Johnston, "Jeb" Stuart, "Stonewall" Jackson, and more, Davis also began to worry more and more for this most invaluable of generals. "Don't expose yourself," he told Lee repeatedly.

By the end of 1864, when even Lee had not been able to hold back the legions of the Union and as Richmond lay besieged, Davis's popularity within the Confederate hierarchy fell to an all-time low. There were calls for his removal, by impeachment if possible, by extralegal means if necessary. Rumors surfaced suggesting that Lee should take office in Davis's place, even become dictator, in the emergency. Lee refused to countenance such nonsense, nor even to give evidence that he knew of such thoughts. He remained loyal to Davis in the dark days just as Davis had always been loyal to him, though now, for the first and only time in the war, their relationship appears to have suffered a severe strain. It started with that perennial running sore, Joseph E. Johnston. Davis had removed him after it became evident that he would not try to hold Atlanta. His replacement, John Bell Hood, failed as well, and then almost lost his army in Tennessee. When he had to be replaced, once more, like a recurring nightmare, there was only Johnston. General-in-chief again by February 1865, Lee tried his best to make it easier for Davis to swallow Johnston. On his own authority, he asked to have Johnston assigned to the command, but pointedly added that Johnston would be reporting directly to him. Davis saw some hope in this. It relieved him from the odium of acting on his own to reinstate Johnston—he was simply granting his general-in-chief's request on a matter quite within that general's area of responsibility. He also continued to hope that where he and Johnston had failed to be able to work together, perhaps Johnston and Lee would be able, a vain hope as it proved.

Still it cost Davis much inwardly to see his old nemesis given the honor of another army command, and this left him testy a few days later when he asked Lee to come into Richmond to confer with him on a matter of secondary import. Probably frustrated at Davis's frequent calls for hand-holding conferences and increasing unwillingness to address the realities of the Confederacy's dreadful situation, Lee failed for once to respond as he always had in the past. If sources can be believed, the general replied that he could not spare the time. The response hurt and angered Davis, who shot back a reply that the general might "rest assured I will not ask your views in answer to measures. Your counsels are no longer wanted in this matter." It smacks of nothing so much as the response of a hurt child. Lee immediately sensed that he had hurt the president's feelings. He went to see him after all, and though their correspondence temporarily took on a cooler tone—Davis ceased addressing him as "my dear friend" for a while—the injury was soon forgotten. Davis just needed to talk to Lee for security and support. He needed to have his friend with him for comfort in those darkening hours.[19]

Lee realized long before Davis that the cause was lost. Indeed, as 1865 wore on he almost marveled at the president's continuing optimism that somehow a victory would be wrested from the Yankees and freedom achieved. "The President is very pertinacious in opinion and purpose," Lee told an associate then, showing a "remarkable faith in the possibility of still winning our independence."[20] He might better have called it obstinacy, if not a retreat from reality. Yet when Davis seized a new potential weapon for winning that independence—the idea of enlisting blacks to fight in Confederate armies—Lee enthusiastically supported him. Indeed, three years later Lee would claim that he told Davis often and repeatedly as early as 1862 that the slaves should be emancipated. He believed it would strengthen Confederate hopes abroad and weaken the moral arguments advanced by the Union, but Davis "would not hear of it." Perhaps so. Certainly Lee embraced the idea of raising Negro regiments, but for all of them it was too little, too late.[21]

Finally came the fateful loss of Five Forks and the evacuation of Richmond. Davis and Lee spent some of that last day together, as they had met occasionally during the last of March, often at the home of the Rev. Charles Minnegerode. The minister could not but note that at the dinner table "it was sad to see these two men with their terrible responsibilities upon them and the hopeless outlook." When Lee arrived during one dinner, all the other diners left the room and closed the door behind them, leaving Lee and the president "to consult in lonely conference." That 1 April was the last time Lee and Davis saw one another for the next year and one-half.

We all know what followed for the two of them. For Davis, an attempt to reach the western Confederacy, his capture, and two years of imprisonment leading to a trial that was never completed, and finally his release, to wander England and Europe, and then the South for years before finally he settled in Mississippi once more. For Lee, a quiet surrender at Appomattox, a return first to his Richmond home, and then a measure of peace in Lexington before his early death in 1870, worn out by the war and its strains on a weakened heart. Never during those years or afterward did Davis utter a single reproachful word about Lee for Appomattox, nor for any other episode of his career. Rather, Davis became an enthusiastic contributor to the Lee legend, and one of his most ardent defenders. Lee, on the other hand, as he had during the war, largely kept his views of the president to himself. He did speak critically, and in confidence, only twice that we know of. In 1869 he told a painter that, while he admired Davis's sterling qualities of character, he believed that the president was, "of course, one of the extremist politicians." A year earlier, speaking to a confidant, Lee observed that despite his high regard for Davis, he still blamed him for being so confrontational with opponents like Johnston and Beauregard and thereby failing to unite everyone to the single purpose of the cause. "Mr. Davis' enemies became so many," said Lee, "as to destroy his power and to paralyze the country."[22]

Nothing was said of this at their first meeting after the war—and what would prove to be their last. Lee was called to testify in Davis's trial, in the hope that his testimony would help to place the full responsibility for all Confederate activities on its former president. Lee refused to play the game. "I am responsible for what I did," he said on the witness stand, "and I cannot now recall any important movement I made which I would not have made had I acted entirely on my own responsibility."[23] That ended any usefulness Lee might have had for the prosecution. This straightforward, manly acceptance of his own responsibility was to be the last thing Davis ever heard from his beloved general's lips.

In 1863 Davis had written to his brother Joseph that "a *General* in the full acceptation of the word is a rare product, scarcely more than one can be expected in a generation, but in this mighty war in which we are engaged there is need for half a dozen."[24] In the end, Davis really got only one, Robert Edward Lee. And for whatever he may be blamed for shortening the war in the decisive Western Theater by his adherence first to Bragg and then his deadly dance of command with Joseph E. Johnston, it is inarguable that in the Eastern Theater, Davis prolonged the war if by no other single fact than his unwavering and unyielding support for Lee. It is often forgotten that Lee came to command with an unenviable war record behind him. Many thought him too timid, others believed him not entirely committed to the cause, and in Virginia and South Carolina especially he had been dubbed derisively "Granny" and "Spades" Lee. Davis was not obliged to give him command of the Army of Northern Virginia, and might not have but for his disillusionment with G. W. Smith, and Smith's own psychosomatic ailments whenever under pressure. But once Lee was in command, Davis quickly realized his worth and stood by him, even when he confided to Varina that on the Peninsula, Lee had not achieved all that the president had hoped for. Through the near loss of most of his army at Antietam and the crushing defeat at Gettysburg, the president never once wavered in his attachment to Lee. Furthermore, by resisting the clamor to send Lee to the troubled Army of Tennessee—and his own desire to do so—Davis kept in place the one man who knew his army and countryside better than any other. Moreover, Davis listened to Lee, in time taking his counsel almost as if it had come from the lips of Sidney Johnston himself, whom he always believed might have been an even greater general had he lived. Davis did not interfere with Lee's army, gave him the generals he wanted for his corps and divisions, and bent every effort to send him the regiments he needed.

For his part, Lee read his commander-in-chief brilliantly, and showed a maturity and a devotion to cause above self that would have shamed most other high-ranking commanders. While Johnston would whimper over his rank and spend most of the war complaining, and while Beauregard preened and blustered and took every opportunity to politick behind the back of a president who had the audacity to think he outranked the great Beauregard, Lee consistently subordinated himself to his goals. He realized that his mission was not to pamper his own ego or advance his reputation. He had a job to get done with his army, and the best way to achieve it was to have the full support and confidence of his commander-in-chief. If that meant flattering the president, he would do it. If that meant allowing Davis to think that Lee's ideas were sometimes his own, so be it. If it meant taking precious time while on an arduous campaign to write the president a letter when there was nothing to say, Lee would do it. If it meant simply being a friend and helping a man deal with a crushing burden even greater than Lee's, then the general knew what he had to do. Sycophantic at times? Yes. Fawning, even, now and then? Yes. Counterproductive or wasteful of time? Never. Lee's eye was on his mission, and he knew better than anyone else how much stronger was his steel if he had the president behind his weapons rather than in front of them.

And thus, these two very different men, who in another time or under different circumstances probably would not—could not—have been friends, achieved a synergy that helped to keep the Confederacy afloat in the East far longer than could have been expected with any of the other full-rank generals of the South in command. In the understanding and rapport they achieved, and in the way they cooperated, Davis and Lee formed a model civil-military team surpassing any other of the war, even Lincoln and Grant, and matched in our national history only by that between Franklin D. Roosevelt and George C. Marshall in World War II.

Lee, alas, lived too short a life. Davis, for the benefit of his own memory, lived too long. Following his release from prison and his European wanderings, his very first public address in the South came on the sad occasion of Lee's death at a memorial service. Weeks earlier, just as he returned from Europe, Davis first got the news of Lee's death. It struck him almost like the loss of his brother, who had died a few days before. The one-time president could not fully express what or how he felt when he learned of Lee's passing. "He was my friend," Davis wrote in his anguish, "and in that word is included all that I could say of any man."[25]

NOTES

1. William C. Davis, *Jefferson Davis, The Man and His Hour* (New York: Harper/Collins, 1992), 197.

2. Charles Bracelyn Flood, *Lee: The Last Years* (Boston: Little, Brown, 1981), 220.

3. Robert E. Lee, *The Wartime Papers of R. E. Lee*, ed. Clifford Dowdey and Louis H. Manarin (Boston: Little, Brown, 1961), 21.

4. Francis W. Pickens to Milledge L. Bonham, 7 July 1861, Milledge L. Bonham Papers, South Caroliniana Collection, University of South Carolina, Columbia.

5. William C. Davis, *Jefferson Davis*, 425.

6. William Preston Johnston to Rosa Johnston, 1–2 June 1862, Mason Barret Collection, Howard-Tilton Memorial Library, Tulane University, New Orleans, Louisiana.

7. Jefferson Davis, *Jefferson Davis, Constitutionalist: His Letters, Papers and Speeches*, ed. Dunbar Rowland, 10 vols. (Jackson: Mississippi Department of Archives and History, 1923), 5:264.

8. William Preston Johnston to Rosa Johnston, 9 June 1862, Mason Barret Collection.

9. U.S. War Department, *The War of the Rebellion: The Official Records of the Union and Confederate Armies*, 127 vols, index, and atlas (Washington DC: GPO, 1880–1901), series 1, vol. 12, pt. 3, p. 945.

10. Lee, *Wartime Papers*, 184.

11. Lee, *Wartime Papers*, 188.

12. Lee, *Wartime Papers*, 233, 238, 254.

13. Lee, *Wartime Papers*, 254, 259.

14. Lee, *Wartime Papers*, 303.

15. Lee, *Wartime Papers*, 301.

16. William C. Davis, *Jefferson Davis*, 500.

17. William C. Davis, *Jefferson Davis*, 508.

18. Stephen R. Mallory Diary, n.d., Stephen R. Mallory Papers, Southern Historical Collection, Wilson Library, University of North Carolina, Chapel Hill.

19. William C. Davis, *Jefferson Davis*, 588–89.

20. John B. Gordon, *Reminiscences of the Civil War* (New York: Charles Scribner's Sons, 1903), 393.

21. Douglas Southall Freeman, *R. E. Lee: A Biography*, 4 vols. (New York: Charles Scribner's Sons, 1934–35), 3:544.

22. Flood, *Lee*, 287n.

23. Flood, *Lee*, 171.

24. Jefferson Davis to Joseph E. Davis, 1863, copy in files of Jefferson Davis Association, Rice University, Houston, Texas.

25. Jefferson Davis, *Jefferson Davis, Constitutionalist*, 7:284.

★ III ★

THE GREAT CAMPAIGNS

From "King of Spades" to "First Captain of the Confederacy": R. E. Lee's First Six Weeks with the Army of Northern Virginia

CAROL REARDON

Well before Appomattox, both Northern and Southern observers of military affairs agreed on at least one point. Joel Cook, a special correspondent from Philadelphia accompanying the Army of the Potomac in 1862, wrote soon after the battle of Fair Oaks that the shell that wounded Confederate General Joseph E. Johnston "changed the entire Southern tactics. It took away incompetency, indecision, and dissatisfaction, and gave skillful generalship, excellent plans, and good discipline. It removed the first commander of the Confederate army . . . and replaced him by a most eminent leader, General Robert E. Lee," whose troops "went to battle with shouts, and without being urged, and when in it, fought like tigers. The wounding of General Johnston was one of the best things for the enemy which had ever happened." Similarly, in Richmond, John Beauchamp Jones, the "rebel war clerk" and diarist, declared that Lee's appointment to army command "may be hailed as the harbinger of bright fortune."[1]

To modern Civil War enthusiasts, such commentaries on Robert E. Lee's capacity for leadership seem entirely unexceptional, even predictable. Lee remains, after all, larger than life in the national memory. He was the Confederacy's flawless "marble man," its most successful commander, apparently the South's best hope for victory. We appreciate even today those elements of his professional and personal character that made him great. He was ferocious in battle but careful to take care of his men's needs. He showed great compassion for his foe, to whom he sometimes referred as "those people" rather than choosing harsher epithets. Almost never outgeneraled, he surrendered in 1865 only when the press of Union resources rendered further resistance futile. Once vanquished, the victor of so many battlefields became a model citizen who promoted the cause of national reunion. If character were the measure, even in defeat Lee was a winner.

This familiar image of Lee did not exist in the spring of 1862. While a string of victories soon put the Confederate chieftain on the path to lasting renown, he had not yet won the laurels that made him one of the great military leaders in American history. Nor was that path without obstacles. All students of the Civil War are familiar with the controversy that surrounds his performance at Gettysburg; however, well before those three days in Pennsylvania, Lee revealed during the Seven Days battles another important—and considerably less well-understood—instance when he did not live up to his carefully crafted postwar image.

History has been generous to Lee and his failure to notch a decisive win on his first try. Perhaps this stems from a respect for the accomplishments that follow. Perhaps it comes from understanding that for the general and his revitalized Army of Northern Virginia, the clashes through the woods and swamps east of Richmond in June and early July 1862 were a series of "first battles." Such fights allow soldiers and their leaders to learn about each other's capabilities and expectations. They test the mettle of the combatants and their commanders, and they reveal hidden flaws in organization, administration, strategy, and tactics that must be improved to better guarantee success.[2] Perhaps history's relative silence on Lee's performance in the Seven Days comes from another source as well. "First battles" also commonly generate controversy in their wake. This is not true for the Seven Days, and in this case, Alan T. Nolan's contention is essentially correct. "[A]lmost all of those who have written about Lee have accepted him entirely on his own terms; whatever he has said about events or about himself, his actions and his reasons, is taken as fact."[3] If ever evidence of the strength of the "Lee mystique" were needed, the impact of the general's own pronouncements on the literature of the Seven Days campaign offers incontrovertible proof. Lee's own after-action report even today continues to circumscribe the parameters of discussion. Indeed, Lee seems to have succeeded so admirably in foreclosing objective or imaginative investigation of his failure to win more decisively that students of the campaign invariably have chosen instead to delve into the reasons why McClellan lost.

In any case, the Seven Days campaign heralded the military "rebirth" of Robert E. Lee. His Civil War service before June 1862 suggested little of his future stature. He had yet to live up to the South's high expectations for him after he had turned down command of the Union armies in the

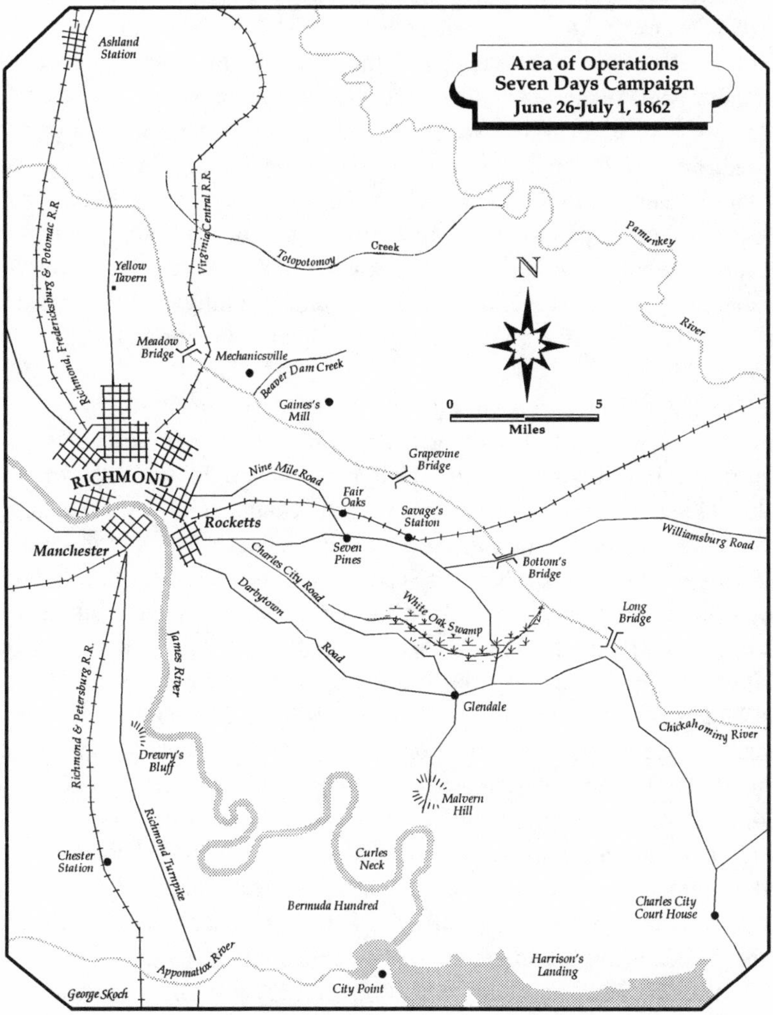

spring of 1861 to follow his state. While Southern armies won on the battlefields of Manassas and Ball's Bluff in eastern Virginia in 1861, Lee failed signally to stop Union forces from penetrating deeply into the western mountain counties of his home state that fall. Transferred south to oversee coastal defenses in the Department of Georgia, South Carolina, and East Florida, Lee could do little to prevent the Union from strengthening their foothold at Port Royal or to counter their threats against other key ports in his district without giving up valuable Southern territory. When Lee was named Jefferson Davis's military adviser in March 1862, Southerners greeted the news with only guarded optimism. Thomas Nelson Page, in later years, recalled that Lee's "prestige at this time was far from being what it soon afterward became, or even what it had been previous to the war. . . . [T]he proof of a general is victories, and that proof he had not given."[4] Indeed, among those most enthusiastic about Lee's joining Davis's staff was George B. McClellan. In a letter to Abraham Lincoln, "Little Mac" wrote that in the field he would much prefer to face Lee than Joseph E. Johnston because "the former is TOO cautious & weak under grave responsibility—personally brave & energetic to a fault, he yet is wanting in moral firmness when pressed by heavy responsibility & is likely to be timid & irresolute in action."[5]

McClellan made many mistakes in his military career, and his assessment of Lee was among his worst. But for a while, many of Lee's own men would have agreed with the Union general's opinion. Early on, Lee ordered the digging of earthworks around the Confederate capital, seeming to provide evidence of just the sort of caution McClellan had described. Lee's men called him "the King of Spades." We know now that his directive did not reflect any special penchant for the defensive. As he explained in his campaign report for the Seven Days battles, he only constructed the earthworks "to enable a part of the army to defend the city" while leaving "the other part free to cross the Chickahominy and operate on the north bank."[6] But few understood that side of Lee just yet. Even the perspicacious artilleryman E. Porter Alexander had wondered to a friend who had served with the new commander, "Has General Lee the audacity that is going to be required for our inferior force to meet the enemy . . . to take the aggressive, and to run risks and stand chances?" The answer had surprised Alexander: "If there is one man in either army . . . head and shoulders above every other in audacity, it is General Lee! His name might be Audacity."[7]

Lee destroyed most doubts about his military personality in late June 1862. From the first of the major Seven Days battles at Mechanicsville on 26 June until McClellan pulled back into strong defenses on the James River on 2 July, Lee took the offensive and struck hard. Violent frontal attacks at Mechanicsville, Gaines's Mill, and Malvern Hill surely disabused the survivors of any notion of Lee's commitment to the defensive. And to many, this was a relief. On the evening of 27 June, at the end of the fighting at Gaines's Mill, war clerk Jones exalted: "What genius! what audacity in Lee!"[8]

Audacity did not necessarily equate to victory. Not every Confederate charge succeeded. Nor had every day brought another stunning victory. Lee unsuccessfully attempted several times to disrupt McClellan's safe passage to his new base on the James River, but opportunities for crushing blows slipped away at White Oak Swamp and again at Frayser's Farm. To many Southerners, however, Lee's very aggressiveness had breathed life back into their cause. He certainly won more accolades for attacking than Johnston had for his Fabian defense of Richmond, regardless of the skill of its execution. Some of Lee's early biographers became so enamored of his offensive tactics that even the great Confederate bloodletting at Malvern Hill could be claimed as a victory. Lee's command style in that fight may have seemed artless—"mostly frontal assault" and "costing needless waste of life," recalled Thomas Nelson Page later—but he accomplished his most important objective: saving Richmond. That night, McClellan retreated to his new base of operations on the James, "his great army shattered and his prestige destroyed."[9]

In time, unrestrained praise such as this came in great profusion. Immediately after the Seven Days battles, however, Lee had not convinced all his critics of his skill as an army commander. Indeed, public opinion remained mixed. His contemporaries tended to view his performance in one (or more) of three ways. Critics, even those who admitted their delight with Richmond's salvation, openly attacked specific elements of Lee's efforts to save the capital. Others cautioned against exaggerating the importance of this series of local battles; the strategic implications of the campaign—well beyond Lee's reach—were more important. Finally, some also embraced Lee then and there—imperfections and all—as "the first captain of the Confederacy" and the South's best hope for final victory.

In any case, both supporters and critics quickly made known their opinions. Perhaps most vocal was *Richmond Examiner* editor Edward A. Pollard, an enemy of Jefferson Davis and, unfortunately for Lee, a foe of anyone closely associated with the Confederate president. As McClellan's forces boarded ships for the return to their Washington encampments, Pollard wrote: "A great deal was claimed for 'generalship' in the battles around Richmond," but the glory belonged to "the hardy valor of our troops," not to "the genius of the strategist." Claiming that only the "vulgar and unintelligent mind worships success" alone, Pollard argued that most Southerners could not begin to comprehend the long-term implications of the recent "extraordinary and happy train of victories." Too many people, he believed, looked upon the recent successes as a suitable "contribution to the personal fame of General Lee, who, by no fault of his own, was followed by toadies, flatterers and newspaper sneaks in epaulets, who made him ridiculous by their servile obeisances and excess of praise."[10] The editor of the *Charleston Mercury*, also critical of much administration policy, declared that the "desultory manner in which he [McClellan] has been pursued by divisions instead of our whole force, enabling him to repulse our attacks, to carry off his artillery, and, finally, to make a fresh stand with an army reinforced are facts, we fear, not very flattering to the practical generalship of General Lee."[11]

Lee's later victories did little to dilute the vehemence in these partisan diatribes. Pollard continued his invective even into his *Second Year of the War,* published in New York in 1864. Perhaps to influence political affairs in this election year, Pollard insisted that anyone seeking evidence of genuine military skill in the Seven Days campaign should look not to the actions of Lee but to those of his rival, and now Democratic presidential candidate, George McClellan. The Confederate leader had not forced the Union troops into a headlong retreat. On the contrary, the "skill and spirit with which McClellan had managed the retreat was, indeed, remarkable, and afforded no mean proofs of his generalship."[12]

Lee's Southern critics in 1862 extended beyond the journalistic community. Some of his own subordinates could be counted among them. General John B. Magruder, for one, believed that those military commentators who believed Lee to be too passive had misread the man entirely. Indeed, "Prince John" felt certain that the new commander had been far too aggressive. He accused Lee of leaving Richmond at risk, placing Magruder with only twenty-five thousand men to block McClellan from entering the city while the rest of his force moved north of the Chickahominy River.[13] Catastrophe beckoned, in Magruder's view, had Lee been unable to recross the river if needed. For his part, Lee believed that Magruder exaggerated the danger and explained as much in his official report.[14] Magruder was not alone among cautious Southerners who continued to believe that all the good Lee had accomplished might have been rendered moot if the capital had fallen. Most of Lee's other subordinates kept their silence, but some, such as Gen. Robert Toombs of Georgia, a hater of West Point and West Pointers, decried the loss of so many soldiers in a less than total victory.[15]

Interestingly, such contemporary criticisms by Confederate soldiers, whether inspired by personal pique or intellectual quibbling, found a measure of objective professional confirmation. Officers in the English army, who watched with considerable detached professional interest, reached similar conclusions without encumbering them with personal invective. In 1863, Capt. Charles C. Chesney, professor of military history at Sandhurst, believed that while Lee's "later doings show him to be a strategist of high order," the general had to be blamed for "an incompleteness in the result of his successes on the actual fields of strife" during the Seven Days. He concluded that "Lee wants to some extent the swift *coup d'oeil* and vigorous will attributed to Johnston by both friends and foe."[16]

Despite the criticism of some, many in Richmond were entirely satisfied that Lee had accomplished his most important goals. The *Richmond Dispatch* described Lee's operations as "those of a master. No captain that ever lived could have planned or executed a better plan."[17] The editor of the *Dispatch* knew what Lee and his men had achieved, and it was considerable. As Lee himself wrote, "The siege of Richmond was raised, and the object of a campaign, which had been prosecuted after months of preparation at an enormous expenditure of men and money, completely frustrated. More than 10,000 prisoners, including offers of rank, 52 pieces of artillery, and upward of 35,000 stands of small arms were captured. The stores and supplies of every description which fell into our hands were great in amount and value, but small in comparison with those destroyed by the enemy." Incorrectly, Lee believed that the enemy's losses "exceeded our own, as attested by the thousands of dead and wounded left on every field." He had lost about 20,000 men to only 16,000 Union casualties, but he took satisfaction from the "subsequent inaction" of the Union troops, which "shows in what condition the survivors reached the protection to which they fled."[18] War clerk Jones certainly could be counted among Lee's firm supporters. He condemned the general's critics, certain that Lee "knows that the fatal blow has been dealt this 'grand army' of the North. The serpent has been killed, though its tail still exhibits some spasmodic motion," Jones wrote, but "It will die."[19]

Such diversity of opinion about Lee's conduct during the Seven Days disappeared shortly after the war as Lee's image-builders took control of much Southern history. Flaws had to disappear or be portrayed as insignificant to preserve unsullied the reputation of the "marble man." Still, one troublesome concern remained unresolved: the Army of the Potomac had not been eliminated as a threat to the South. The victory was hollow, as Lee himself admitted. Indeed, much postwar discussion about what was, or what might have been, accomplished during the Seven Days battles stems from Lee's own frank—and frequently cited—observation in his campaign report: "Under ordinary circumstances the Federal Army should have been destroyed."[20] If Lee had believed that more could have been done to defeat McClellan, what had happened to prevent it? And to what extent should Lee be held accountable for the incompleteness of the results?

The general offered two answers of his own, and in so doing carved out the paths that historians have followed in lock step. First, Lee believed that McClellan had not been destroyed for "the want of correct and timely information." The Southern army's poor maps and "the character of the country" had permitted the Army of the Potomac to conceal its retreat "and to add much to the obstructions with which nature had beset the way of our pursuing columns."[21] The failure of Confederate troops to intercept or split the Union army around White Oak Swamp on its way to the James represented just one promising opportunity lost because of poor information about roads or troop dispositions. Similarly, lack of knowledge about the local network stymied Confederate leaders in attempts to mass their troops quickly for a strong blow against the Union troops who safely withdrew from Malvern Hill to the protection of artillery and gunboats on the river.

These were important instances where Lee very well might have done more. Early on, however, Lee's first biographers took care to show why the acknowledged absence of accurate information about terrain or roads should not reflect poorly on "Marse Robert." To John Esten Cooke, Lee's conduct of the Seven Days battles clearly "indicated the possession of a nerve approaching audacity," a spirit of daring made even more impressive by Lee's willingness to fight in the forests and fields east of Richmond, cut frequently by creeks, swamps, and rivers. Any attack in such compartmentalized terrain required coordination and cooperation, making accurate maps on all levels of command an absolute must. But, as Cooke now made clear, any lack of timely information was "justly attributable to the War Department at Richmond, rather than to an officer who had been assigned to command only three or four weeks before."[22]

This notion quickly became accepted truth. In his 1887 memoir, Lee's former military secretary, Armistead L. Long, criticized Richard Taylor, who in *Destruction and Reconstruction* had blamed Lee for planning overly complex operations in a region where his subordinates "knew no more about the topography of the country than they did about Central Africa." Long also believed Jefferson Davis's *The Rise and Fall of the Confederate Government* blamed Lee unfairly for poor intelligence and cartographic work, and he concluded, much as Cooke had in 1866, that the fault "should be placed where it properly belongs—with the war-directing authorities at Richmond."[23] Lee himself knew the region well, Long argued. He often had traveled between Richmond and the family estate at White House on the Pamunkey River, and he also knew the James River plantations of family friends. Moreover, Confederate cavalryman J. E. B. Stuart brought back useful information from his ride around McClellan's army. Whoever was at fault, the cost of not providing Southern officers with accurate maps cost many lives. According to General Daniel Harvey Hill, "Our engineers seem to have had little knowledge of the country, and none of the fortifications on the creek. The maps furnished the division commanders were worthless. . . . The result was, as might have been foreseen, a bloody and disastrous repulse."[24] But Lee's friends always argued the point strongly that this reverse did not stem from any inattention to duty on the general's part.

For a brief time just after the war, narratives of the battles used the challenging terrain in another way to suggest a more startling explanation for Lee's incomplete success. While Lee's men struggled through the maze of swamps and confusing roads, rival George McClellan had shown uncommon skill in using those same elements to make good his army's escape. Indeed, present-day Civil War scholars might well be surprised by the accolades Southerners offered up in praise of the military talents of "Little Mac." For one, James Dabney McCabe, who admired Lee very much, believed that the Union army's safe arrival on the James was due mostly "to the great skill of their general." In retreating from the Chickahominy, "General McClellan exhibited high qualities" even though "his movements were greatly favored by the country he marched through."[25] Implicity indicted, of course, were those War Department functionaries who had not given Lee the information he needed to defeat his foe.

In addition to his complaints about "the want of correct and timely information," Lee offered a second reason to explain why his victory over McClellan had not been complete. "It was deemed inexpedient to attack" the Union forces as they retreated from Malvern Hill to their new base on the James River "in view of the condition of our troops, who had been marching and fighting almost incessantly for seven days under the most trying circumstances." Lee withdrew "in order to afford them the repose of which they stood so much in need."[26]

In some ways, Lee meant exactly what he wrote in his report. The Army of Northern Virginia after Malvern Hill was, in many respects, an entirely different force than that which had retreated up the Peninsula under Johnston's leadership just six weeks earlier. When Lee took it into battle, he had not yet finished the forging of the army that would become his greatest weapon. In his essay on "General Robert *Edmund* Lee," William Parker Snow praised Lee's immediate efforts to improve his men's food and camp sanitation and to remedy soldier complaints about officers, pay, and mail. "Mutiny and dissatisfaction almost universally disappeared," Snow wrote, and the payoff came quickly. Discipline improved. During the Seven Days, the men "went into battle with shouts, and without being urged, and, when in it, fought like tigers. A more marked change for the better never was made in any body of men than that wrought in his army by General Lee."[27] The reorganization of Lee's army was far from complete, however, and the week-long fight offered the first test to see how far the process had progressed.

Always the soul of courtesy, Lee hid a variety of problems in the phrase "condition of his army." Determining what he really meant, or what he might have meant, has provided one of the few opportunities for scholars to step beyond the lines of discussion that Lee sketched out.

When the general died in 1870, the momentum for his elevation to heroic stature picked up immediately. This new "marble man" image of Lee allowed for no flaw, but if he were guilty of any shortcoming, it lay in his toleration of the mistakes of others. Therefore, any criticism of Confederate efforts in the Seven Days battles—or of any other fight the Army of Northern Virginia did not win decisively, for that matter—had to cast primary blame for failure on someone or something other than Lee. No shadow could fall on Lee.

The influence of the "Lee cult" must have been almost irresistibly strong. No one did so complete an about-face as Edward Pollard. By the early 1870s, the editor, who during the war condemned as hapless the general's leadership in western Virginia, had come to sympathize with Lee. After all, he had found himself "in the midst of a hostile population" and faced "wild ranges . . . known only to the most experienced woods men and hunters frequenting them." Pollard now believed that Lee had not deserved his "sadly diminished reputation" after his early service in western Virginia.[28]

Joining Lee in his increasingly secure place in Southern (and later, national) history was his Army of Northern Virginia, approaching legendary status in its own right. When the general began the task of molding his force, he enjoyed the benefits of many recent legislative enactments, including the culling of ineffective officers through reelection, longer periods of enlistment, and conscription. In the hands of Lee's partisans, however, these administrative imperatives paled to insignificance when compared to the general's energy in using them to temper his new weapon. He had faced a daunting task. The "new" Pollard described the Confederate army taken over by Lee outside Richmond in early June 1862 as "raw; there was not time to season the new recruits. . . . [N]early two-thirds were new conscripts, who had never been under fire, and were only half-instructed." Moreover, that army on 1 June had not exceeded 50,000 men. Yet one month later, it was 80,000 strong. Lee proved able to motivate even this imperfectly organized force to take the offensive and to "force his adversary, notwithstanding his superiority of numbers and the finely-appointed state of his army, to abandon a base of operations that had occupied almost the exclusive attention of his Government for over a year."[29]

The miraculous transformation of the army under Lee's guiding hand became quite a seductive notion. In 1897, Henry Alexander White proclaimed that after the Seven Days battles, "General Lee now possessed the full confidence of his soldiers." Much of his success came from his willingness to share his men's risks. As White explained, "Under heavy fire from the enemy's guns, he rode in person to direct the assaults. Reconnaissance to points of danger he made alone in person." Lee had become a "tower of strength . . . by one month's service in the field with this army of heroes," who looked "with devotion upon a leader who dared to give battle against heavy odds, and who showed, also, the generous daring to shoulder the responsibility for every movement."[30] In the words of George Cary Eggleston, Lee had "made of the Virginia army such a fighting machine as has rarely been known in the history of the world."[31]

After the early 1870s, all who dared challenge the new views of Lee and the army molded in his image usually met loud opposition and faced growing frustration at their inability to right wrongs in the historical record. Depicting Lee as the architect of the Army of Northern Virginia certainly did not please everybody. Joseph E. Johnston felt the pain of injustice especially keenly. Again and again, he pointed out that he had "repeatedly suggested to the Administration the formation of a great army to repel McClellan's invasion," but Davis and his associates had ignored him. Johnston complained bitterly, "As soon as I had lost the command of the Army of Virginia by wounds in battle, my suggestion was adopted." Long after the war ended, he continued to believe that if he had been heeded and the army properly and timely strengthened, the results of the Seven Days "might and ought to have been decisive." Johnston railed against those writers who "represent, to my disparagement, that the army with which General Lee fought in 'the seven days' was only that which I had commanded."[32] But in defending his own actions on the retreat up the Peninsula, he also backhandedly saluted Lee's talents for organization, a trait more often associated with his Union rival in the Seven Days battles. Indeed, Johnston asserted that his army had changed so much in just a single month that he discounted as very far from the truth any suggestion that he could have done on the Peninsula what Lee did in the Seven Days battles.

Still, Lee's was not a perfected military organization. In what ways did "the condition of his army" contribute to a less-than-decisive Confederate performance at the Seven Days? As Robert L. Dabney described it, "The army was not sufficiently instructed, either in its officers or its men, for its great work. The capacity for command, the practical skill and tact, the professional knowledge, the devotion to duty, which make the efficient officer, do not come in a day," and when "the Confederate Government attempted to produce *extempore* officers of all grades for armies so great, out of a people who had been reared in the pursuits of peace, it could only be partially successful."[33]

The indecisiveness of the Confederate effort in the Seven Days fight—once attributed to the exhaustion of Lee's army—stemmed, then, from many factors the general had little time to correct during his first days in command. He had inherited a group of subordinates who ranged from the superb, to the disappointing, to the downright dangerous, and, although he made the attempt, he had little time to take their measure. Longstanding administrative and operational flaws in staff work, organization, intelligence gathering, and myriad other details had to wait until he contained the Union threat to the capital. The flaws in Lee's "new" force did not lead to catastrophic defeat, but we still have much to learn about how his army "deprived him of more than half the expected fruits of his own consummate generalship" in the Seven Days.[34] This is why students of the military art study "first battles."

Acknowledging the growing pains of the army and its high command also relieves Lee personally of much of the blame for a less-than-complete victory. Others must bear the burden. Pollard, for one, argued that Lee's army "was not as mobile as he expected; there was an evident disarray throughout it; some of the division commanders were utterly incompetent." The situation was so bad that Pollard considered it a "wonder and admiration" that Lee "accomplished what he did under circumstances so exceptional and injurious."[35] Even to the present, most analysts of the Seven Days campaign still agree that one or more of Lee's subordinates bore responsibility for throwing away opportunities for a more decisive victory. If further proof be needed, the reassignment (some would argue for "banishment") of three of the hardest cases to new commands in the West or Trans-Mississippi seems to offer all that is needed. Or does it?

Initially, at least, apportioning the blame appeared without much venom behind it. Early on, John Esten Cooke explained Lee's campaign plan as a design that "his able subordinates translated detail by detail, with unimportant modification, into action, under his eyes in the field." But that left no room to explain how the Southern army squandered so many opportunities for crushing blows. It did not take long for even Cooke to hedge. To those who criticized Lee's failure to interdict the Union forces near White Oak Swamp, Cooke explained without pointing a finger that "putting an end to nearly or quite one hundred thousand men is a difficult undertaking, and that in one instance, at least, the failure of one of his subordinates in arriving promptly, reversed his plans at the most critical moment."[36]

It took little time for Lee's friends to disclose the weak links in the Confederate army's chain of command. As Armistead L. Long wrote in *The Memoirs of Robert E. Lee,* on 28 June, John B. Magruder had been sent orders "to keep a vigilant watch on the Federals and without delay report any movement that might be discovered." These instructions "were not as faithfully executed as they should have been"; the Union forces marched away unmolested, and their absence remained unnoticed for nearly twenty-four hours.[37] The list of Magruder's faults did not stop there. Likewise, General Benjamin Huger had failed in ways that were both too obvious and, as Douglas Southall Freeman later would write, too "irredeemable" to ignore.[38] Charged with assailing McClellan's retreating columns near Frayser's Farm, Magruder and Huger "failed Lee at the crisis," wrote George Cary Eggleston. In so doing, they denied their army the "capture of McClellan's army upon which Lee had reckoned as the crowning achievement of this Seven Days' campaign."[39] General Theophilus Holmes also disappeared from Lee's army, following his lack of aggressiveness on several fields. The shortcomings of some of Lee's chief subordinates provided ready scapegoats. As General Jubal A. Early wrote soon after the war, "Notwithstanding the favorable nature of the country for his escape, McClellan's army would have been annihilated, had General Lee's orders been promptly and rigidly carried out by his subordinates."[40] It seems almost easy to agree with one observer who noted that because Lee's lieutenants failed "to do their proper part at the critical time the Federal commander was spared the humiliation of a surrender."[41]

But what about Lee's greatest lieutenant, Thomas J. "Stonewall" Jackson? " 'Even great Homer sometimes nods,' and even Stonewall Jackson was not infallible," wrote J. William Jones in 1881.[42] Jackson's failure to launch a timely flank attack at Mechanicsville forced A. P. Hill's men to attempt a costly frontal assault against a well-placed and protected foe. At Gaines's Mill, Lee again waited for Jackson's men to join in the assault. "Ah, General," Lee is supposed to have said in mild chastisement to his dust-covered subordinate, whom he found sitting astride his horse and sucking on a lemon. "I am very glad to see you. I had hoped to be with you before."[43] Jackson's inaction at White Oak Swamp made him "an idle spectator of the gallant fight by which Hill and Longstreet finally drove the enemy from this field to the much stronger position of Malvern Hill," where the Confederate casualty list was excessively long.[44]

What does Jackson's retention, and the departure of other generals who disappointed, say about Lee as an army-builder? Finding an answer is no simple matter. From the spring of 1862 until immediately after his tragic death, Jackson was the South's greatest military hero. His partisans, of course, admitted no wrongdoing. John Esten Cooke, a Lee biographer who also wrote one of the first Jackson biographies to appear after Chancellorsville, did not so much as hint at controversy. At Gaines's Mill, "the general and decisive charge was made all along the line, in obedience to Jackson's brief, stern order—'Press them with the bayonet.' " In this volume, at least, Cooke concluded that "Jackson's appearance decided all."[45] Robert L. Dabney similarly argued that "the arrival of General Jackson brought a strength to the Confederates beyond that of his numbers. . . . His assault was regarded by friends and foes as the stroke of doom, and his presence gave assurance of victory."[46] Even if there had been a delay on the march to Gaines's Mill, according to Mary Anna Jackson's approved version of her husband's biography, the general merely said "with his customary patience, 'Let us trust that the providence of God will so overrule it, that no mischief shall result.' "[47] If no fault is apportioned to Jackson for his performance at the Seven Days, it nevertheless remains a great overstatement to assert, as has one modern scholar, that the "notion of a Lee-Jackson merger" had been in Lee's mind "for at least a month—even before he replaced Johnston—and now was the time to move from intuitive collaboration to active participation."[48]

More objective observers nearly always have agreed that Lee had a right to be concerned about his unexpectedly passive subordinate. As Maj. Matthew Forney Steele, whose *American Campaigns* remained a standard in U.S. Army classrooms from its publication in 1909 until the 1950s, concluded about the South's failure of win decisively in the Seven Days, "The chief blame rests upon Stonewall Jackson. In all these operations the 'Jackson of the Chickahominy,' . . . was a different man from 'the Jackson of the Valley.' "[49] If Jackson was retained while other generals departed, Lee appreciated the fact that his subordinate possessed other useful army-building tools—the ability to inspire high morale, great popular appeal, a knack for instilling discipline, and an absolute steeliness once in battle.

Other flaws—all part of "the condition of the army"—also have surfaced in the historical record from time to time. The poor employment of the Confederate artillery came in for special attention. On several occasions, most notably at Malvern Hill, Southern gunners found themselves outnumbered and outweighed by the massed Union artillery. Because Lee continued Johnston's earlier practice of parcelling out a single battery to each infantry brigade, it was not surprising that, on one occasion, "Six guns in the presence of thirty were quickly put out of action" and "there was nowhere any authority to bring these scattered batteries together and make them effective by massing them."[50] Lee's artillery chief, Gen. William Nelson Pendleton, belonged on the list of those who disappointed his chief, but he, like Jackson, stayed on.

As Lee's stature grew, his accomplishments, not only during his first five weeks in army command but also during his term as Davis's military adviser, took on all the more grandeur. Lee became the power directing the actions of others; from behind the scenes, he had helped to set the stage for victory around Richmond. It was no longer just Stonewall Jackson's Shenandoah Campaign: now Lee "had sent Jackson at work in the Valley" and "managed to detain 65,000 Federals in the Valley, and 20,000 or 30,000 more in and around Washington." Then, "he had managed to have Jackson suddenly and secretly quit the Valley," and thus derailed McClellan's plans "by his masterful strategy."[51] Even so influential an authority as British military writer G. F. R. Henderson, a Jackson biographer, admitted "[i]t is, perhaps, true that Johnston and Lee had a larger share in Jackson's success than has been generally recognised." Of the two, Lee deserved special credit because "[f]rom the moment he assumed command we find the Confederate operations directed on a definite and well-considered plan: a defensive attitude around Richmond, a vigorous offensive in the Valley, leading to the dispersion of the enemy, and a Confederate concentration on the Chickahominy. His operations were very bold."[52] Henderson's fellow British officer, Lt. Col. H. M. E. Brunker, agreed that Lee had demonstrated the strength of "acting on 'interior lines' " by using Jackson to hold back reinforcements from McClellan while concentrating "the whole of his available force on the decisive point, thus acting up to the first principle of strategy."[53]

Indeed, for the first fifty years after the war, it was rare to find assessments that strayed from these various conclusions. John Codman Ropes shocked some Civil War students with his opinion that "[i]n intellect it may be doubted whether he [Lee] was superior to the able soldier whom he succeeded; indeed, Joseph E. Johnston possessed as good a military mind as any leader on either side." Maj. Gen. Sir Frederick Maurice expressed his surprise at such a view, especially because he considered Ropes a historian deserving "the very greatest respect." Still, Maurice was not willing to whitewash Lee's performance. If the fruits of victory were not fully garnered, "Lee must bear a share of responsibility." Lee's plans were too intricate, his orders too vague, his staff unequal to the challenge, too many of his troops too green to be entirely effective.[54] British Maj. Gen. J. F. C. Fuller stands out for his determination that Lee's command style, first revealed at the Seven Days and repeated elsewhere, stemmed primarily from "two cardinal defects" in military leadership: "his dislike to interfere with his subordinates once battle was engaged, and his reliance on verbal orders."[55]

All these factors, both good and bad, with shadings of gray and nuances in between, remain even today the standard elements in any evaluation of Lee's performance at the Seven Days. In his masterful *R. E. Lee*, published in the 1930s, Douglas Southall Freeman practically codified all that went before and continued to provide the framework for campaign histories that would follow. Freeman attributed Lee's incomplete victory to four shortcomings: (1) the lack of information about the terrain, due to bad maps, inexperienced staff officers, and absent cavalry; (2) poor Confederate artillery employment; (3) Lee's faith in untrustworthy, if not incompetent, subordinates; and (4) Lee's lack of tactical genius in fighting the Union army.[56] Freeman's analysis changed no prevailing historical interpretation of the Seven Days, following instead comfortable, well-worn paths.

Freeman did contribute examples of the ways in which Lee dealt with these concerns after fighting ended outside Richmond. Interestingly, Freeman noted that Lee took few immediate steps to correct most of the problems. He continued to rely almost exclusively on his cavalry—especially on Jeb Stuart—for the collection of battlefield and theater intelligence, and he would pay the price for overreliance on that one source when Stuart failed him in Pennsylvania in 1863. He hoped for better cartographic service. Still, two years later, when he ordered troops to rush to Spotsylvania to block Grant's advance in May 1864, he had to make his dispositions from "only a poor sketch that showed none of the elevations."[57] He delayed the reorganization of his artillery until after Second Manassas and Antietam, when he created battalions of four batteries each, most of them refitted with captured Union ordnance and organized to operate in massed formations when terrain and opportunity permitted.[58] No system for the professional development of staff officers existed in either army, and Lee cannot be faulted for doing little about that. Each general would continue to cull the inefficient from his personal staff and seek out soldiers to help handle all the required tasks. How much Lee had learned about the folly of his tactics is a bit more problematic. Freeman insists that "[f]lank attacks, quick marches to the rear, and better tactics took the place of great designs of destruction."[59] But for every Chancellorsville in the army's future, there was also a Gettysburg and a Pickett's Charge.

At the same time Freeman offered his criticisms, he also suggested three reasons to explain why Lee won anyway: (1) the fundamental soundness of his strategy, irrespective of his tactical decisions or those of his subordinates; (2) the valor of his infantry "neither shaken by losses nor impaired by long campaigning"; and (3) reversing some early chronicles that spoke well of "Little Mac," the "singular temperament of McClellan."[60] By the 1930s, these findings, too, were not strikingly new conceptions. Nearly all students of the fight would have agreed with Jubal Early's postwar assessment that "[t]he movement of General Lee against McClellan was a strategic enterprise of the most brilliant character."[61] So too would they have accepted Captain Steele's professional comments on the strategic excellence of the Seven Days battles contained in *American Campaigns:* the effort was "on the part of the Confederates, a campaign of good plans and bad execution."[62]

Since the 1930s, when Freeman reinforced the parameters for evaluating Lee's performance in the Seven Days battles first determined by the general himself, little has changed on the historigraphical front. Lee still enjoys the unusual luxury of a honeymoon period during which, as a newcomer to high command, he could mishandle the imperfectly organized force he inherited and still win praise for achieving a notable, if incomplete, victory.

Three major histories of the Seven Days battles have appeared since Freeman's account. Despite significantly greater research efforts, including some attempts to delve into the manuscript resources of the campaign's participants, the final products reveal a sameness with one another and with the works that preceded them. The differences are those of nuance, not substance.

In *The Seven Days: The Emergence of Lee,* Clifford Dowdey noted early on that Lee "did not assume command completely developed as 'sprung for the forehead of Jove.' " Lee was "a novice, inexperienced in the tactical arrangements necessary for moving in battle the separate masses of men whose action must be coordinated over miles of obscuring terrain." Still, in abandoning the static defense of Richmond for a more active counteroffensive, "Lee brought to the war in Virginia the first instance in which the military objective perfectly expressed the political purposes." He learned much from his experience during the Seven Days. Most important, perhaps, "his character made it necessary for Lee to work with men who wanted responsibility and were capable of assuming it." More critical of Jeb Stuart's performance than most previous students of the fight, Dowdey still noted that from watching his subordinates in action, Lee could forge the Army of Northern Virginia's winning team—Lee and Jackson and Longstreet—as well as make the army's Magruders disappear.[63]

A second modern work that considered Lee's leadership in the Seven Days battles was Joseph P. Cullen's *The Peninsula Campaign, 1862.* It, too, tread over well-worn ground. Interested more in "McClellan's Failure" than in Lee's success, Cullen reached conclusions about the South's military efforts that were entirely predictable. Noting Lee's statement that "[u]nder ordinary circumstances the Federal Army should have been destroyed," Cullen wondered exactly what the general had meant by "ordinary circumstances." Because Lee wrote his report long after the end of the campaign, he may have been thinking "in terms of what he and his commanders and the Army of Northern Virginia would have done *then* under the same conditions." If so, Lee's assessment becomes "a meaningless statement, because two years later the Federal army and its commanders had also changed and developed from experience." The Seven Days, Cullen concluded, was primarily "a shake-down cruise" for Lee and his army—in other words, a "first battle"—and an affirmation of the military principle that "the defensive should never be assumed except as a means of shifting to the offensive under more favorable conditions." Lee made mistakes at Malvern Hill, But he "had proved himself a competent and daring field commander who would learn from experience." Cullen missed the mark, however, in asserting that "Lee's reputation was now an established fact, and the war in the east would be entrusted to his direction."[64] The real test, as John Hennessy argues persuasively, came in northern Virginia in August, when Lee led his army in a campaign and battle of his own design and won a smashing victory at Second Manassas.[65]

The most recent study of the Seven Days campaign is *To the Gates of Richmond* by McClellan biographer Stephen W. Sears. While steeped in the kinds of manuscript sources that enlighten our understanding of the common soldier's point of view, this work offers little new about Lee's first campaign with the Army of Northern Virginia. "For Lee's part, never again would he attempt such elegant chessboard maneuvers as the converging movements of Mechanicsville and Glendale," Sears argues, understating the effectiveness of the general's tactical combinations at Second Manassas and Chancellorsville. Sears also contends that "never again would he command with the indirection and deference he showed during this week of battle," perhaps forgetting that Lee himself often said that he saw his greatest duty as getting his troops to the battlefield in a timely way and then trusting to God and the initiative of his subordinates to accomplish the mission. "As by an annealing process, Lee—and Jackson—emerged from the Seven Days stronger generals than before," Sears comments, ignoring Longstreet, to whom Lee entrusted the bulk of his forces in the post-campaign army reorganization.[66]

Recent work on Lee's key subordinates, however, has offered modern students of the Seven Days something more to think about. Longstreet's biographers, in particular, agree strongly that emphasis on the Lee-Jackson tandem disguises Lee's most important revelation about his chain of command in the Seven Days battles. William Garrett Piston notes that "Lee called Longstreet 'the Staff of my right hand' and magnamiously gave Longstreet much credit for the South's victories when he spoke in public" after the Seven Days.[67] Jeffry D. Wert gives an even more blunt assessment: "Longstreet emerged from the campaign as Lee's most reliable subordinate commander."[68] Taking a fresh look at questions that seemed to be dead issues can help to recast our perceptions about the Confederate high command at the Seven Days and afterward.

Finally, modern reassessments of Lee himself offer yet more grist for the intellectual mill. Perhaps Thomas L. Connelly was correct in asserting that we cannot understand the general's true role in the Seven Days because the Richmond press and the Southern people obsessed on even the smallest action of Stonewall Jackson and thus overlooked Lee's real contributions.[69] Perhaps John Morgan Dederer is right to credit Light Horse Harry Lee, the Confederate general's father, as the inspiration for the Army of Northern Virginia's offensive spirit in the Seven Days; perhaps neither an overreliance on Jominian theory nor resentment toward unflattering nicknames such as "Granny Lee" should suffice as the explanation for ordering Gaines's Mill or Malvern Hill.[70] Perhaps scholars need to admit that we just do not know very much about the professional growing pains of generals who never had led a mass army into battle before; this was, after all, a "first battle" for Robert E. Lee, the military engineer.

Most of all, in this case at least, Alan T. Nolan is right. Robert E. Lee indeed has held an unprecedented degree of control over the way history has evaluated his actions. More than 130 years later, Lee still commands the gates to Richmond.

NOTES

1. Joel Cook, *The Siege of Richmond: A Narrative of the Military Operations of George B. McClellan during the Months of May and June, 1862* (Philadelphia: George W. Childs, 1862), 246–47; J. B. Jones, *A Rebel War Clerk's Diary at the Confederate States Capital*, 2 vols. (Philadelphia: J. B. Lippincott & Company, 1866), 1:133

2. The importance of the "first battle" concept as an analytical tool is best developed in William A. Stofft and Charles E. Heller, *America's First Battles, 1776–1965* (Lawrence: University Press of Kansas, 1986).

3. Alan T. Nolan, *Lee Considered: General Robert E. Lee and Civil War History* (Chapel Hill: University of North Carolina Press, 1991), 6.

4. Thomas Nelson Page, *Robert E. Lee: Man and Soldier* (New York: Charles Scribner's Sons, 1911), 144.

5. George B. McClellan, *The Civil War Papers of George B. McClellan: Selected Correspondence, 1860–1865*, ed. Stephen W. Sears (New York: Ticknor & Fields, 1989), 244–45.

6. U.S. War Department, *The War of the Rebellion: The Official Records of the Union and Confederate Armies*, 127 vols., index, and atlas (Washington DC: GPO, 1880–1901), series *1*, vol. 11, pt. 2, p. 490 [hereafter cited as *Official Records;* all references can be found in volume 11, part 2].

7. Edward Porter Alexander, *Military Memoirs of a Confederate: A Critical Narrative* (New York: Charles Scribner's Sons, 1907), 110–11.

8. J. B. Jones, *Diary*, 1:138.

9. Thomas Nelson Page, *Robert E. Lee, The Southerner* (New York: Charles Scribner's Sons, 1908), 97.

10. Quoted in Stanley F. Horn, ed., *The Robert E. Lee Reader* (Indianapolis: Bobbs-Merrill, 1949), 204.

11. *Charleston Mercury*, 8 July 1862.

12. Edward A. Pollard, *The Second Year of the War* (New York: Charles B. Richardson, 1864), 73.

13. *Official Records*, p. 662.

14. *Official Records*, p. 490.

15. Ulrich Bonnell Phillips, ed., *The Correspondence of Robert Toombs, Alexander H. Stephens, and Howell Cobb* (Washington DC: GPO, 1913), 601.

16. Capt. C. C. Chesney, *A Military View of Recent Campaigns in Virginia and Maryland* (London: Smith, Elder and Co., 1863), 50.

17. The *Richmond Dispatch*, 9 July 1862.

18. *Official Records*, p. 497–8.

19. J. B. Jones, *Diary*, 1:141.

20. *Official Records*, p. 497.

21. *Official Records*, p. 497.

22. John Esten Cooke, *A Life of Gen. Robert E. Lee* (New York: D. Appleton and Company, 1871), 91–92.

23. Armistead Lindsay Long, *Memoirs of Robert E. Lee* (New York: J. M. Stoddart & Company, 1886), 179–80.

24. Daniel H. Hill, "Lee Attacks North of the Chickahominy," in *Battles and Leaders of the Civil War*, 4 vols., ed. Robert Underwood Johnson and Clarence Clough Buel (1887; reprint, New York: Thomas Yoseloff, 1956), 2:352.

25. James D. McCabe, *Life and Campaigns of General Robert E. Lee* (Atlanta: National Publishing Company, 1866), 165.

26. *Official Records*, p. 497.

27. William Parker Snow, *Southern Generals, Who They Are, and What They Have Done* (New York: Charles B. Richardson, 1865), 57–58.

28. Edward A. Pollard, *The Early Life, Campaigns, and Public Services of Robert E. Lee; With a Record of the Campaigns and Heroic Deeds of His Companions in Arms* (New York: E. B. Treat & Co., 1871), 62–63.

29. Pollard, *Early Life, Campaigns, and Public Services of Lee*, 70.

30. Henry Alexander White, *Robert E. Lee and the Southern Confederacy, 1807–1870* (1897; reprint, New York: Haskell House Publishers, 1969), 169–70.

31. George Cary Eggleston, *The History of the Confederate War, Its Causes and Its Conduct, A Narrative and Critical History*, 2 vols. (New York: Sturgis & Walton Company, 1910), 1:362.

32. Joseph E. Johnston, *Narrative of Military Operations* (New York: D. Appleton and Company, 1874), 142, 145.

33. Robert Lewis Dabney, *Life and Campaigns of Lieut. Gen. Thomas J. Jackson* (New York: Blalock & Co., 1866) 479.

34. Pollard, *Early Life, Campaigns, and Public Services of Lee*, 70.

35. Pollard, *Early Life, Campaigns, and Public Services of Lee*, 77.

36. Cooke, *Life of Lee*, 76, 91.

37. Long, *Memoirs of Lee*, p. 174.

38. Douglas Southall Freeman, *R. E. Lee: A Biography*, 4 vols. (New York: Charles Scribner's Sons, 1934–35), 2:246.

39. Eggleston, *History of the Confederate War*, 1:408.

40. Jubal A. Early, *The Campaigns of Gen. Robert E. Lee: An Address by Lt. Gen. Jubal A. Early, before Washington and Lee University, January 19th, 1872* (Baltimore: John Murphy and Co., 1872), 10.

41. Eggleston, *The History of the Confederate War*, 1:410.

42. J. William Jones, "Seven Days around Richmond," in *Southern Historical Society Papers*, J. William Jones et al., 52 vols. and 3-vol. index (1876–1959; reprint, Wilmington, NC: Broadfoot Publishing Company, 1990–92), 9:564.

43. Cooke, *Life of Lee*, 84.

44. J. William Jones, "Seven Days around Richmond," 565.

45. A Virginian [John Esten Cooke], *The Life of Stonewall Jackson* (New York: Charles B. Richardson, 1863), 120–21.

46. Dabney, *Life of Jackson*, 484–85.

47. William C. Chase, *Story of Stonewall Jackson . . . Approved by His Widow, Mary Anna Jackson* (Atlanta: D. E. Luther Publishing Company, 1901), 400.

48. Paul D. Casdorph, *Lee and Jackson: Confederate Chieftains* (New York: Paragon House, 1992), 256.

49. Matthew Forney Steele, *American Campaigns*, 2 vols. (Washington DC: Byron S. Adams, 1909), 1:215.

50. Eggleston, *History of the Confederate War*, 1:411. For a complete discussion of this question, see Jennings Cropper Wise, *The Long Arm of Lee: The History of the Artillery of the Army of Northern Virginia*, 2 vols. (1915; 1-vol. reprint, New York: Oxford University Press, 1959), 197–233.

51. Eggleston, *History of the Confederate War*, 1:397–98.

52. G. F. R. Henderson, *Stonewall Jackson and the American Civil War*, 2 vols. (1898; 1-vol. American edition, New York: Longmans, Green and Company, 1949), 312.

53. H. M. E. Brunker, *Story of the Campaign in Eastern Virginia, April 1861 to May, 1863* (London: Forster Groom & Company, Ltd., 1910), 67.

54. Sir Frederick Maurice, *Robert E. Lee, The Soldier* (Boston: Houghton Mifflin Company, 1925), 116.

55. J. F. C. Fuller, *Grant & Lee: A Study in Personality and Generalship* (1933; reprint, Bloomington: Indiana University Press, 1957), 162.

56. Freeman, *Lee*, 2:241.

57. Freeman, *Lee*, 3:431.

58. Wise, *Long Arm of Lee*, 327–56; Freeman, *Lee*, 2:413–14.

59. Freeman, *Lee*, 2:249.

60. Freeman, *Lee*, 2:241–42.

61. Jubal Anderson Early, *War Memoirs: Autobiographical Sketch and Narrative of the War Between the States* (1912; reprint, Wilmington NC: Broadfoot Publishing Company, 1989), 90.

62. Steele, *American Campaigns*, 1:215.

63. Clifford Dowdey, *The Seven Days: The Emergence of Lee* (Boston: Little, Brown, 1964), 6–7, 349–51.

64. Joseph P. Cullen, *The Peninsula Campaign*, 1862 (Harrisburg PA: Stackpole Books, 1973), 165–69.

65. This theme is developed throughout John Hennessy, *Return to Bull Run: The Campaign and Battle of Second Manassas* (New York: Simon and Schuster, 1992).

66. Stephen W. Sears, *To the Gates of Richmond: The Peninsula Campaign* (New York: Ticknor and Fields, 1992), 343–44.

67. William Garrett Piston, *Lee's Tarnished Lieutenant: James Longstreet and His Place in Southern History* (Athens: University of Georgia Press, 1987), 22.

68. Jeffry D. Wert, *James Longstreet: The Confederacy's Most Controversial Soldier—A Biography* (New York: Simon & Schuster, 1993), 151.

69. Thomas L. Connelly, *The Marble Man: Robert E. Lee and His Image in American Society* (New York: Alfred A. Knopf, 1977), 18.

70. For the development of this theme, see John Morgan Dederer, "The Origins of Robert E. Lee's Bold Generalship: A Reinterpretation," *Military Affairs* 49 (July 1985): 117–23.

26. "The Last Meeting of Lee and Jackson," an engraving after the painting by E. B. D. Julio. This famous Lost Cause image leaves no doubt that Lee is the superior and "Stonewall" Jackson the loyal subordinate. Collection of the editor.

27. H. A. Ogden's late-nineteenth-century depiction of Lee at Fredericksburg gives the general a more benign expression than Waud's earlier treatment in plate 22. This reflects the Lost Cause conception of Lee as a reluctant Christian warrior. Collection of the editor.

28. Although titled "Jefferson Davis and His Generals," this 1890 engraving features Lee as the dominant figure. A popular Lost Cause print, it also appeared in versions without Jubal A. Early (at far right) or Robert Toombs (in the framed portrait next to the Confederate flag). Collection of the editor.

29. "Gen. Robert E. Lee" by Charles Shober, published in 1891, offers a combative Lee astride Traveller amid the chaos of battle. Courtesy of the Library of Congress.

30. Warren B. Davis's "General Lee Leading the Troops at Chancellorsville," an 1896 treatment of the subject, presents Lee almost as a statue among his cheering soldiers. *Frank Leslie's Popular Magazine*, June 1896.

31. "Robert Edward Lee, 1807–1870," an engraving based on the Brady photograph in plate 6 and published for the Confederate Memorial Literary Society in 1906. Collection of the editor.

32. “Lee and His Generals,” which rivals Julio’s “The Last Meeting of Lee and Jackson” as a ubiquitous Lost Cause print. Published in the early twentieth century, it makes Lee (an almost direct copy of the Brady photograph in plate 6) slightly taller than the other Confederate generals, all of whom appear to be almost identical in height. Collection of the editor.

33. "Summer," one of four murals completed shortly after World War I by the French artist Charles Hoffbauer that represent the "Seasons of the Confederacy." Few Lost Cause images match the power of this depiction of Lee on Traveller at the forefront of an assemblage of the most prominent Confederate generals (a group never together except in the artist's imagination). Courtesy of the Virginia Historical Society, Richmond.

Robert E. Lee and the Maryland Campaign

D. SCOTT HARTWIG

On 5 September 1862 Captain Henry L. P. King of Maj. Gen. Lafayette McLaws's staff wrote in his diary: "Finally Gen. McLaws gave us the order—we are to cross White's Ford into Maryland in the morning at daylight. Hurrah! We go indeed at last to Maryland!" The Army of Northern Virginia was riding a tide of summer victories over the Union armies of Virginia and the Potomac. With these Federal forces now huddled within the powerful fortifications of Washington, Robert E. Lee positioned his army to strike northward into Maryland. "The present seems to be the most propitious time since the commencement of the war for the Confederate Army to enter Maryland," he had written Confederate President Jefferson Davis, in his well-known communication of 3 September. An opportunist, Lee sensed fresh possibilities for the Confederacy north of the Potomac River.[1]

Two principal strategic options lay open to Lee following his victory at Second Manassas. He could assume the strategic defensive, falling back to the vicinity of Warrenton, Virginia, where he would have rail communication with Richmond and some opportunity for maneuver should the Federals attempt an overland advance against the capital. He also could cross the Potomac into Maryland. Lee chose Maryland. This course seemingly held far more risk than withdrawing into the security of Virginia, but the latter option offered a delusive security—passing the initiative to the Union army at a time when its ranks swelled with the first arrivals of Lincoln's July call for 300,000 volunteers. It also allowed the Federals leisure to select the time and place to strike; they might even employ their ability to transport an army by water to outflank Lee's position and transfer the war back to the gates of Richmond.[2]

Lee sensed that by entering Maryland he could control events. There was sound logic in trying to keep the Federals dancing to the beat of his drum. The Union war effort in the East had been thrown off balance. Only by moving north of the Potomac could Lee maintain this situation and perhaps draw the Federal army out of its fortifications before it could be substantially reinforced, reequipped, and reorganized. Lee understood the sensitivity among Federal authorities about Maryland, where they had jailed dissidents and suspended the writ of habeus corpus. A Confederate army in Maryland could provoke an immediate reaction from the Lincoln government, which is precisely what Lee desired.

What strategic objectives did Lee hope to secure by marching north? In a conversation after the war with William Allan, a former ordnance officer in the Army of Northern Virginia, Lee explained that he entered Maryland to draw the Union army above the Potomac and to subsist his army on Maryland's abundant supplies. In *Lee Considered,* Alan T. Nolan challenged the validity of the second objective, observing that "Lee recrossed the Potomac on the night of September 18 and his army subsisted in Virginia until the Gettysburg Campaign. Accordingly, it was not in fact necessary for him to go into Maryland for commissary supplies." Although Nolan's point is valid, Lee likely considered it better to draw his army's sustenance from Maryland's fertile fields while husbanding Virginia's food and forage for the time when his army returned to the Old Dominion. The army, Lee knew, could not remain north of the Potomac indefinitely. As Edward Porter Alexander, Lee's chief ordnance officer, pointed out, the absence of rail communications from Virginia into Maryland meant the army was as certain to recross the Potomac into Virginia "as a stone thrown upward is certain to come down."[3]

Lee hoped that invading the North would accomplish more than merely subsisting his army and keeping the Federal army out of Virginia. "Should the results of the expedition justify it," he wrote Jefferson Davis on 4 September, "I propose to enter Pennsylvania." According to John G. Walker, a division commander with the army, Lee hoped to carry his soldiers as far as the banks of the Susquehanna River at Harrisburg, where he might destroy the Pennsylvania Railroad bridge over that river and inflict a heavy blow to the Union's east-west communications. Beyond these goals lurked a higher objective revealed in a conversation between Lee and William Allan in 1868. "I went into Maryland to give battle," Lee said with eyes flashing. He sought battle on his own terms, when and where he chose. Time favored the Federals, but by positioning his army in Maryland or Pennsylvania, where its presence, politically and militarily, could not be tolerated by the Northern government, Lee could force the Federals to give battle before they recovered from their defeat at Second Manassas. "He probably never would find the Federal army in poorer condition for a great struggle (at

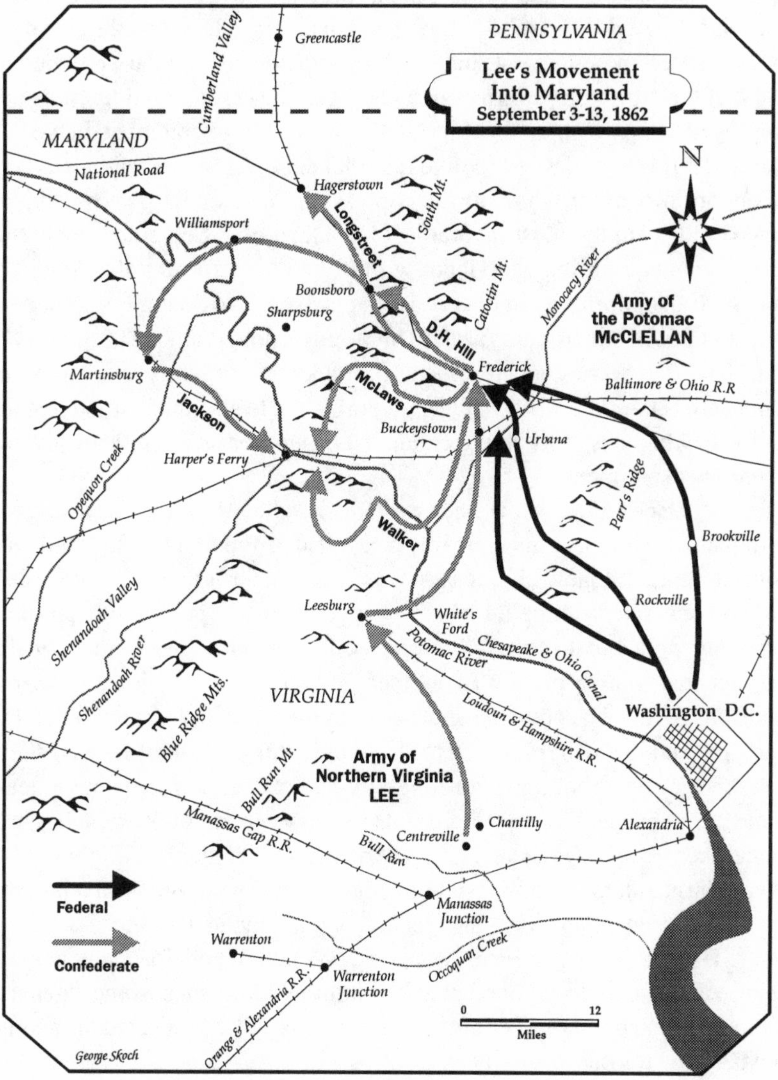

least so he thought) than at that time," wrote historian John Ropes. There was far greater chance of profit from an engagement on these terms than if Lee withdrew to Virginia and awaited the advance of a reorganized and reinforced enemy. Far from the reasoning of a general blindly devoted to the offensive, Lee's decision to venture north rested on sound strategic logic.[4]

How Lee expected Maryland to react to his army's presence generally has been misunderstood. This confusion stems partly from the apparent optimism Lee evidenced about the subject in letters to Davis on the eve of the invasion. Lee knew elements in the state sympathized with the Confederacy and that the Northern government had suspended certain civil liberties and employed troops to maintain Maryland's loyalty. On 3 September, Lee wrote Davis: "If it is ever desired to give material aid to Maryland and afford her an opportunity of throwing off the oppression to which she is now subject, this would seem the most favorable." He added on 5 September that "this army is about entering Maryland, with a view of affording the people of that State an opportunity of liberating themselves." No doubt, Lee hoped his invasion might stir trouble for the Union government among dissenters in Maryland, but he was not so naive as to think the brief entry and exit of his army across the state would trigger an uprising. He also understood that the region in which his army would conduct its operations rivaled Pennsylvania in unionist sentiment.

Lee grasped these facts because Col. Bradley T. Johnson, a brigade commander with the army and prewar resident of Frederick, Maryland, met with him and "Stonewall" Jackson on 4 September, giving the generals a full and accurate briefing on what to expect from the portion of Maryland the army prepared to enter. "I impressed upon him [Lee] emphatically the fact that a large portion of the people were ardent Unionists," wrote Johnson. As for the secessionist element in the state, Johnson explained to Lee, "they could not be expected to afford us material aid until we gave them assurance of an opportunity for relief, by an occupation promising at least some permanence." Lee heeded Johnson's assessment of Maryland. On 7 September he sent Davis an appraisal of what Confederates might expect from Marylanders: "Notwithstanding individual expressions of kindness that have been given, and the general sympathy in the success of the Confederate States, situated as Maryland is, I do not anticipate any general rising of the people in our behalf." Nothing more than some "general sympathy" and perhaps a handful of recruits was all Lee expected the people of Maryland to offer his army.[5]

The condition of the Army of Northern Virginia left much to be desired in September 1862. "The army is not properly equipped for an invasion of an enemy's territory," Lee wrote on 3 September. Battle casualties, hard campaigning, bad or nonexistent food, disease, straggling, and desertions had reduced its strength to approximately fifty-one thousand on the eve of the campaign. This figure includes the divisions of D. H. Hill, Lafayette McLaws, and John G. Walker, as well as Wade Hampton's cavalry brigade, all of which joined the army from the defenses of Richmond after Second Manassas. A woman in Shepherdstown, Virginia, who observed armies pass back and forth through her town throughout the war, wrote of Lee's army in September 1862: "[N]ever before or after did I see anything comparable to the demoralized state of the Confederates at this time." But Lee expected to afford the army a brief respite, allowing it to recover strength before calling upon it to do battle with the Federals in Maryland or Pennsylvania. According to General Walker, Lee anticipated concentrating his army at Hagerstown, Maryland, for "a few days' rest." Lee believed this period of repose would allow him to recover many of the numerous stragglers from the Second Manassas campaign, whose number he estimated at between eight thousand and ten thousand. A sizeable number of new conscripts, raised by the 1862 Conscription Act, had arrived in Richmond for assignment to regiments in the field, and Lee also hoped to have these men join his army.[6] Had Lee been able to remain stationary long enough to receive these reinforcements, the army would have obtained a respectable paper strength. The moment Lee began to maneuver, however, the drain on his "present for duty" strength by straggling would begin again. Even amid Maryland's rich farmland, his quartermaster and commissary systems could not keep the army adequately supplied. Heavy losses to brigade, regimental, and company officers in the summer's battles also left the army critically short of officers with the rank and experience demanded to maintain the discipline necessary to prevent straggling. The physical condition of the army lengthened the odds against Lee's accomplishing anything substantial in his Northern invasion. But as Army of Northern Virginia historian Robert K. Krick noted: "The difficulties that his shrunken army faced could not deter him from grasping the moment."[7]

Although physically run down that September, the Army of Northern Virginia possessed strengths that afforded it key advantages over the numerically superior Army of the Potomac. Much of the army enjoyed splendid morale and confidence. Porter Alexander wrote that by the time of the Maryland campaign, Lee's "army had acquired that magnificent morale which made them equal to twice their numbers . . . and his confidence in them, & theirs in him, were so equal that no man can yet say which is the greatest." With the exception of a sprinkling of conscripts who had reached the army before it entered Maryland, the soldiers were veterans. They "were as hard and tough as troops ever have been, for the process of elimination had dropped out all the inferior material," wrote Bradley Johnson. This contrasted sharply with the Army of the Potomac, which carried nearly 20,000 new recruits into Maryland. Nor could the Federals match the command combination of Lee-Jackson-Longstreet that had worked so well at Second Manassas. Lee counted on these strengths, and perhaps some luck, to offset his weaknesses and bring success in Maryland and Pennsylvania.[8]

At Leesburg, Virginia, Lee ordered his men to strip to the barest essentials for the invasion of Maryland. Only wagons needed to transport cooking utensils and the "absolute necessaries of a regiment" would accompany the army. Batteries with horses too exhausted for service were broken up or directed to transfer their serviceable horses and personnel to other batteries. To prevent stragglers from committing depredations that would alienate Marylanders, Lee organized a provost guard under a tough brigadier general named Lewis A. Armistead, investing him with the authority to "arrest stragglers, and punish severely all depredators and keep men with their commands." As an added precaution, each brigade commander would post a rear guard to prevent any soldier from leaving the ranks.[9]

While at Leesburg, Lee learned that the Union garrison at Winchester, Virginia, had withdrawn down the Valley. This freed him to break up his vulnerable line of communication by way of Manassas and Culpeper and establish a more secure path that ran from Culpeper to Luray, then down the excellent Valley turnpike to Winchester. Lee ordered a depot to be established at Winchester that would support his invasion of Pennsylvania. Union garrisons at Harpers Ferry and Martinsburg posed threats to this new line of communications, but Lee believed the two posts would be abandoned once his army entered Maryland.[10]

The army began crossing the Potomac at the fords near Leesburg on 4 September. Lee had decided to negotiate the river east of the Blue Ridge Mountains for several reasons. First, he would threaten both Baltimore and Washington, compelling the Federals to shift their army to the north bank of the Potomac and thus removing a threat to his communications. With the enemy north of the river, salvage operations at Manassas also could continue uninterrupted. Second, this invasion route almost certainly would elicit a more immediate reaction from the Union army. According to John G. Walker, Lee did not believe the Army of the Potomac would take the field for three to four weeks. Walker's account has gone unchallenged in nearly every study of the Maryland campaign, but his memory probably failed him on this point. Lee's actions and invasion route indicate he hoped to force the Federals to field an army before they were ready to do so. He had rejected the Shenandoah Valley invasion axis, which Jackson favored, because he feared this might not cause the Union army to leave the fortifications of Washington. It defies reason to think that if Lee expected the Army of the Potomac to remain in Washington for three to four weeks he would select the more exposed invasion route east of the Blue Ridge.[11]

Lee intended to move his army to the vicinity of Frederick, Maryland, where he would rest the troops and observe developments. Once the Army of the Potomac emerged from its fortifications and Federals abandoned

Harpers Ferry and Martinsburg, he planned to shift his army west of South Mountain to Hagerstown, then north into Pennsylvania, drawing the Federals after him.[12]

Between 4 and 7 September, the Army of Northern Virginia completed its crossing of the Potomac unhindered and tramped north on dusty roads to Frederick. By 7 September, the infantry formations bivouacked in the vicinity of Frederick, except for Walker's division at Buckeystown, while Stuart's cavalry brigades picketed the eastern front to observe any activity on the part of the Army of the Potomac. Frederick's reception conformed to Bradley Johnson's gloomy prediction. Confederate invaders received cool treatment, and Marylanders proved reluctant to accept Confederate money or script for supplies. Lee had hoped to avert the problem of Marylanders' nonacceptance of Confederate money by having former Maryland governor, and Southern sympathizer, Enoch Lowe, join his army at Frederick. Lowe's presence, Lee believed, could calm the fears of Marylanders and ease their suspicion of accepting Confederate currency, but Lowe never made an appearance, and tapping the abundant supplies of Maryland remained a problem for Lee to the end of the campaign. He could not force Marylanders to supply his army without earning their enmity. To solve this problem, Lee determined to draw his supplies by way of the Shenandoah Valley. The continued presence of the Union garrisons at Harpers Ferry and Martinsburg, together with the brevity of the campaign, frustrated this plan, and Lee's soldiers remained poorly fed despite the plenitude of Maryland's lush farmland.[13]

When ex-Governor Lowe failed to show, Lee believed it necessary to address the people of Maryland concerning the purpose of his army's presence on their soil. On 8 September, he issued his famous proclamation to Marylanders, the significance of which has been neglected by nearly every historian of the campaign. Most scholars have dwelled on the failure of the declaration to arouse any feeling among Marylanders, but their aloof response came as no surprise to Lee. He issued the proclamation more to assuage fears about the intentions of his army than to flame a revolt. There are several sections of the proclamation that bear repeating here: "Believing that the people of Maryland possessed a spirit too lofty to submit to such a government, the people of the South have long wished to aid you in throwing off this foreign yoke, to enable you again to enjoy the inalienable rights of freemen, and restore independence and sovereignty to your State. In obedience to this wish, our army has come among you, and is prepared to assist you with the power of its arms in regaining the rights of which you have been despoiled. This citizens of Maryland, is our mission, so far as you are concerned." With this statement, Lee pledged his army to assist Marylanders to regain freedoms lost during Lincoln's crackdown on secessionist activities in the state. On 8 September the words echoed harmlessly through Frederick, but on 15 September, when Lee had to choose between abandoning Maryland without offering McClellan battle or standing to fight and thereby honoring his pledge, they would loom very large.[14]

By 8 September, Lee had received two important pieces of military intelligence. One indicated that Union garrisons at Harpers Ferry and Martinsburg had not been withdrawn as expected. Those Federal troops continued as threats to the army's line of communications down the Valley. The second piece of news came from Stuart, whose cavalry reported that the commands of Edwin V. Sumner, Franz Sigel, Ambrose E. Burnside, and Joseph Hooker had left Washington and were marching toward Frederick by way of Rockville, Darnestown, and Seneca Mills. This, Lee would have known, represented at least four Union corps. He could take satisfaction that his strategy to pull the enemy after him had worked. The Union garrisons in the Valley, however, posed a problem to the planned invasion of Pennsylvania and would have to be removed.[15]

Lee summoned Jackson to his headquarters on 8 September and outlined an operation calling for five of the army's nine divisions to descend on Harpers Ferry from three directions and capture the garrison and all its war material. Of the four remaining divisions, D. H. Hill's would be halted at Boonsboro, where it could intercept any forces that might escape from Harpers Ferry. Longstreet's command, consisting of three divisions and one independent brigade, would march to Hagerstown. Stuart's cavalry would screen the Army of the Potomac. The movement would commence on 10 September; the timetable called for all forces directed against Harpers Ferry to be in place by 12 September. Jackson's force, numbering three divisions, was to seal off the western escape route from Harpers Ferry. Granted discretion in his selection of routes to accomplish this mission, Jackson could cross at Sharpsburg, or at Williamsport if he wished to drive the Union garrison at Martinsburg into Harpers Ferry. Should Jackson select the Williamsport route, which he did, his march would be sixty-two miles. McLaws's division, numbering slightly less than five thousand men, faced a march of twenty-four miles to capture Maryland Heights, the most commanding of the heights surrounding Harpers Ferry. Walker's division of about four thousand effectives had to recross the Potomac, march twenty miles, and seize Loudoun Heights, situated on the south bank of the junction of the Potomac and Shenandoah Rivers.

When Lee submitted this plan, Jackson, according to his biographer Robert L. Dabney, balked at its audacity. He recommended instead that Lee deal first with McClellan, then with Harpers Ferry. Lee's confidence and Jackson's loyalty evidently changed the latter's thinking, and he soon had his mind "settled firmly upon the enterprise." Longstreet was not so easily persuaded. He earlier had suggested to Lee that dividing the army in front of the Army of the Potomac while in Northern territory courted trouble. "The Federal army, though beaten at the Second Manassas, was not disorganized, and it would certainly come out to look for us, and we should guard against being caught in such a condition," Longstreet claimed to have told Lee. Finding Lee and Jackson settled upon the operation, Longstreet suggested only that the entire army should be used in the movement. Lee apparently disapproved this, for Longstreet next asked that McLaws's division at least be reinforced by the three brigades of Richard H. Anderson's division, and that the remainder of Longstreet's command be halted at Boonsboro with D. H. Hill. Lee agreed to the latter of Longstreet's suggestions but withheld judgment on the former until he had discussed the operation with McLaws.[16]

Lee's plan generally has been applauded as a standout example of his daring generalship. William Allan considered it in "every way worthy of the famous commander of the army of Northern Virginia." Perhaps so, but its original form contained certain weaknesses. Longstreet, who dared to point some of them out, has suffered harshly under the pens of historians. Clifford Dowdey portrayed Longstreet as "outraged at finding Lee and Jackson cozily preparing an action he had advised against." Douglas Southall Freeman, in *R. E. Lee,* wrote: "Longstreet was not sympathetic with the project, and sulked at the decision." In their effort to tarnish Longstreet's reputation at every opportunity, such writers failed to appreciate both the soundness of several of "Old Pete's" suggestions and the fact that Jackson had been of similar mind regarding keeping the army concentrated. Longstreet recognized that Lee underestimated the difficulty of Lafayette McLaws's part of the operation. Lee expected McLaws with four brigades to march twenty-four miles, crossing South Mountain en route, capture Maryland Heights, block escape exits into Pleasant Valley, and leave detachments in his rear to garrison the gaps through South Mountain. The enemy at Harpers Ferry, according to Lee's information, numbered 7,000 to 8,000 men. Given his familiarity with the topography of Harpers Ferry, Lee must have known that a considerable portion of this force would be dedicated to defending Maryland Heights. How Lee expected McLaws to execute his mission by 12 September with the force provided is difficult to fathom. Longstreet's suggestion, buttressed by McLaws's opinion, caused Lee to reinforce the Georgian with six brigades under Richard H. Anderson, raising his force to nearly 10,800. Subsequent events in Pleasant Valley proved the wisdom of Longstreet's recommendation.[17]

Two other potential problems weakened the plan in its final form. One was the timetable. Jackson's three divisions, arguably the most physically exhausted troops in the army, were expected to execute a march of nearly sixty-two miles in two days. Jackson met the spirit of his orders by grueling marches, but the cost in nonbattle casualties, which never have been calculated, was certainly high. Lee's certainty that McClellan would move slowly enough to permit the operation to be carried out and the army safely reunited at Hagerstown constituted a second problem. He believed this risk acceptable, and given McClellan's record on the Peninsula, his confidence was understandable. Bad luck would undermine this element of Lee's calculations, and we can never know whether he would have been able to reassemble his army at Hagerstown, rest it, and enter Pennsylvania unhindered by McClellan.[18]

The Harpers Ferry operation commenced on 10 September as the entire army, save Walker's division, marched west on the broad, smooth surfaced National Road. Jackson's command, with the most difficult task ahead, led the way. McLaws marched in rear of Longstreet's command, whose two divisions and independent brigade followed Jackson. This placement caused McLaws's two divisions to spend most of 10 September waiting for Jackson and Longstreet to pass, and his soldiers did not reach Middletown, Maryland, a distance of fourteen miles, until midnight. Staff work, never a strength of the Army of Northern Virginia in 1862, clearly suffered here and exposed McLaws's soldiers to unnecessary fatigue and delay. It also led to the famous loss of Special Orders No. 191—the operational plan for the Harpers Ferry operation. The details of the story are too well known to repeat here, but as E. P. Alexander observed, "the incident occurred from our unsettled organization. D. H. Hill's division had been attached to Jackson's command upon its crossing the Potomac. No order should have issued from Lee's office for Hill. Jackson so understood it, and, with his usual cautious habit, on receipt of the order, with his own hand made a copy for Hill, and sent it." Hill received and kept Jackson's copy. The copy from army headquarters never reached Hill and, incredibly, Lee's staff was unaware of this.[19]

On the march west from Frederick, Lee learned of a rumored concentration of Union forces in Pennsylvania's Cumberland Valley that threatened to seize Hagerstown. He could not ignore the rumor both because of the importance of Hagerstown to his strategic goals and because of reported supplies of flour and other badly needed military stores in the town. Modifying the army's operational plan, Lee ordered Longstreet to continue his march to Hagerstown on 11 September, while D. H. Hill stayed at Boonsboro to watch for escapees from Harpers Ferry and provide infantry support to

Stuart's cavalry screen east of South Mountain. This weighting of forces, with the larger at Hagerstown and the smaller at Boonsboro, underscores Lee's confidence that McClellan would act predictably.[20]

The Union commander, in fact, had acted with atypical celerity. By 12 September, his army had pressed back Stuart's cavalry screen and occupied Frederick. Lee's army remained dangerously divided. The Harpers Ferry operation, originally scheduled for completion by the twelfth, dragged on. Through no fault of their own, Walker and McLaws lagged a full day behind the demanding timetable, and Confederates had taken neither Loudoun Heights nor Maryland Heights. On the thirteenth, unusually aggressive Federal cavalry pushed Stuart's cavalry back along the National Turnpike to South Mountain, compelling D. H. Hill to occupy Turner's Gap, where the pike crosses the mountain, with an infantry brigade. Although the delay at Harpers Ferry did not concern Lee unduly, the Union army's unusual activity in the Middletown Valley presented a potential crisis. Lee's concern deepened after nightfall when he received an "alarming dispatch" from D. H. Hill. Stuart had assured Hill that no more than two brigades of Union infantry supported the Federal cavalry in his front. But when night fell, Col. Alfred H. Colquitt, the brigade commander occupying Turner's Pass, observed campfires in the Middletown Valley of an enemy force far in excess of Alfred Pleasonton's cavalry and the alleged two infantry brigades. The approaching troops in reality consisted of Pleasonton's cavalry and three divisions of the Ninth Corps! Colquitt immediately passed this information on to Hill, who in turn sent it to Lee.[21]

More worrisome news soon arrived, the precise substance of which has inspired speculation since publication in *Lee's Lieutenants* of William Allan's and E. C. Gordon's memoranda of conversations with Lee at Washington College in 1868. According to both Gordon's and Allan's memoranda, Lee stated that following Hill's dispatch that reported a large Union force in Middletown Valley, he received a report from Stuart. As Lee remembered it six years later, a Confederate sympathizer had been present at Federal headquarters when McClellan was handed a copy of Special Orders No. 191 that had been discovered by two soldiers of the Twelfth Corps. He had observed McClellan's reaction to the discovery, then galloped out of Frederick until he caught up with Stuart at South Mountain. Stuart listened to the man's story, then quickly communicated the news to Lee. The discovery of Allan's and Gordon's memorandum caused Douglas Southall Freeman to revise his conclusion, stated in *R. E. Lee,* that Lee did not know McClellan had discovered a copy of Special Orders No. 191. When he published the second volume of *Lee's Lieutenants* in 1943, Freeman asserted that Lee *did* know by the night of the thirteenth that McClellan held a copy of the order.[22]

But on this point either Lee's memory failed him or hindsight crept into his recollections. Substantial evidence suggests Lee did not know a copy of his orders had fallen into McClellan's hands. First, Lee's correspondence to President Davis during the campaign never mentions a lost order. Second, in an 1867 letter to D. H. Hill, Lee's military secretary, Charles Marshall, wrote that until Lee read McClellan's report, which was published in August 1863, the general "frequently expressed his inability to understand the sudden change in McClellan's tactics which took place after we left Frederick." Third, Ezra A. Carman, a Union veteran of the campaign and afterwards its most careful historian, wrote in an unpublished manuscript that the civilian may have been present when McClellan received the order but did not know its contents. The man observed unusual activity at Federal headquarters that indicated a forward movement, stated Carman, and passed this information but nothing more on to Stuart. Apart from this evidence, Lee's actions on the night of 13 September, as we shall see, were not those of a general who had learned the enemy possessed the operational plan of his entire army. Most likely, Lee learned nothing from the unknown Maryland civilian beyond the fact that the Army of the Potomac was advancing from Frederick—news that merely confirmed the picture already in place based on Stuart's and Hill's earlier reports.[23]

Lee reacted to the threat in his rear with a dispatch to McLaws at 10 P.M. warning that the Union army was marching to relieve Harpers Ferry and stressing the need to expedite the capture of the Union garrison. Lee informed Jackson of the Union army's advance as well, urging him to press matters on his front. To buy the time necessary to capture Harpers Ferry, Lee took steps to defend the mountain gaps through South Mountain. D. H. Hill would go to Turner's Gap in the morning to oversee its defense, and Longstreet would march to Beaver Creek, three miles northwest of Boonsboro, early on the fourteenth. Lee's orders on the night of the thirteenth reveal that although he perceived some danger to his army, he did not believe McClellan would strike a blow on the fourteenth. Had he considered the situation more menacing, he would have instructed Longstreet to march the ten miles from Hagerstown on the night of the thirteenth rather than the following morning. Moreover, Longstreet's orders specified that his column start not at dawn but after 8:00 A.M. "The hallucination that McClellan was not capable of serious work seemed to pervade our army, even to this moment of dreadful threatening," Longstreet later observed. By counting on McClellan to act with predictable caution, Lee offered the Federal a splendid opportunity to defeat his army in detail.[24]

Fortunately for Lee, McClellan did not seize the beckoning opportunity on the fourteenth with enough energy to achieve great results. He engaged

D. H. Hill, but by displaying a bold front the North Carolinian managed to hang on. Longstreet's command rose early on the fourteenth and prepared for the march to Beaver Creek in leisurely fashion. Soon after sunrise the faint sound of artillery could be heard from the direction of Boonsboro. The troops completed their preparations and were ordered to remain in camp, ready to march at a moment's notice. For reasons neither Lee nor Longstreet ever explained, the main body of Old Pete's command did not march until after 11:00 A.M. By then Lee knew of Hill's desperate situation in the gaps, and Longstreet had to push his men at a blistering pace. A member of Richard B. Garnett's brigade recalled the march "was very rapid and at times a double quick step was kept up for two or three miles together. Men exhausted by the rapid march and overcome by the dust and heat, fell out of ranks and were left along the roadside by dozens." Sgt. David Johnston, of James L. Kemper's brigade, noted with pride that "this army made fourteen miles to the immediate vicinity of the battleground in three and a half hours—good time for a Hamiltonian horse." Good time indeed, but no one ever questioned why Longstreet's command was subjected to a grueling forced march during the hottest time of the day. If begun at daylight, the march could have been accomplished without haste and minus the dreadful straggling. The hard march bore bitter fruit; Longstreet's brigades arrived piecemeal and completely worn out. The state of exhaustion in some brigades caused Longstreet to observe that the men "dropped along the road, as rapidly as if under severe skirmish." Those who stood the march and went into action fought splendidly, but they failed to retrieve the situation on the mountaintop. By nightfall the Army of the Potomac held the high ground on both flanks, although Turner's Pass remained in Confederate hands.[25]

In evaluating the battle of South Mountain afterward, most Southern writers emphasized the prowess of Confederate soldiers battling against overwhelming Yankee numbers. In his official report, D. H. Hill set the tone for a familiar theme. "This small force (Hill's division) successfully resisted, without support, for eight hours, the whole Yankee army," he stated. Seaton Gales, writing after the war in *Our Living and Our Dead,* declared, "It may safely be said that in its consequences, in the accomplishment of pre-determined objects, and in the skillful disposition of small numbers to oppose overwhelming odds, it is without a parallel during the war." A careful examination of the forces engaged gives the Federals sixteen brigades totaling about 20,165 men against thirteen Confederate brigades with approximately 11,950 men. This disparity in numbers, by no means "overwhelming," does not explain the Confederate defeat at South Mountain. William Allan, who examined the battle more objectively than most, pronounced it "poorly managed by the Confederates"—a judgment

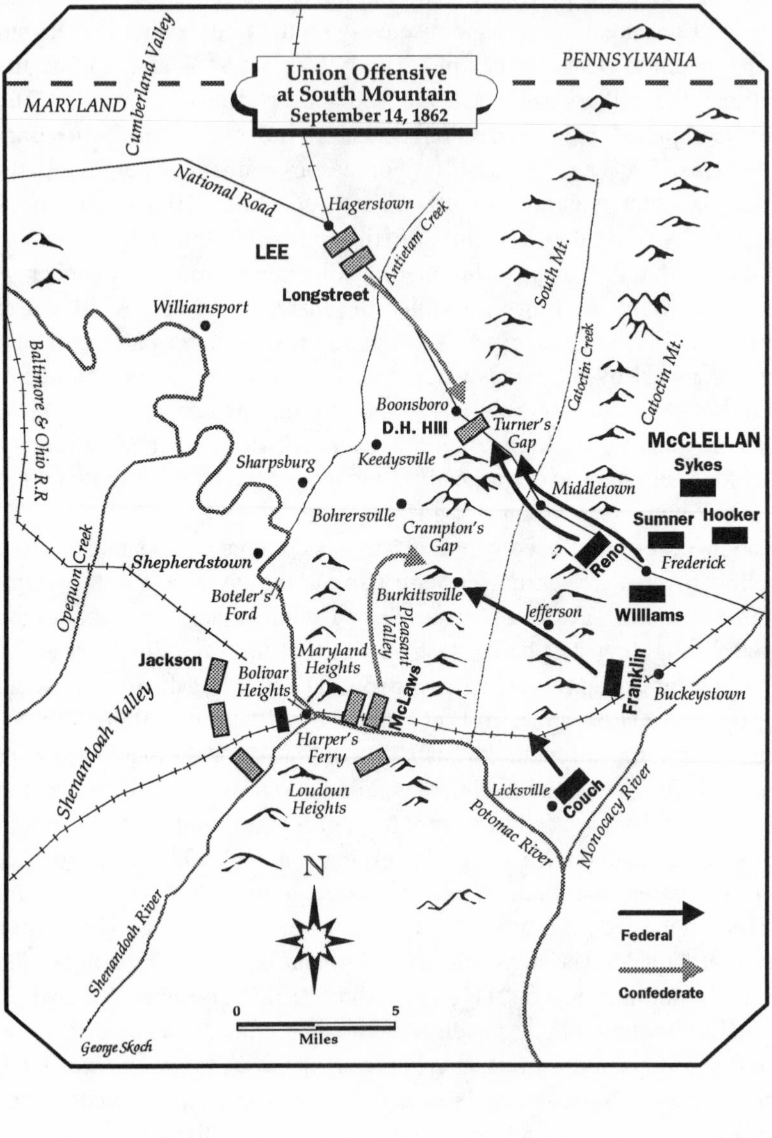

sustained by the fact that at every contested point on the battlefield, save one, Union leaders managed to mass superior numbers. Thirteen of the Union brigades fought on 14 September; only six Confederate brigades saw substantial action. In the area of tactical leadership, the Confederates performed below par. They had been surprised by McClellan's offensive, from D. H. Hill to Lee himself, and mounted a helter-skelter defense that staved off disaster largely because of luck and the tenacity of individual Confederate soldiers.[26]

"If the battle of South Mountain was fought to prevent the advance of McClellan, it was a failure on the part of the Confederates," wrote D. H. Hill after the war. "If it was fought to save Lee's trains and artillery, and to reunite his scattered forces, it was a Confederate success." Lee probably fought the battle with the former object in mind, but McClellan's failure to mount an aggressive pursuit allowed him to accomplish the latter. On the night of 14 September, however, Lee correctly interpreted the battle of South Mountain as both a tactical and strategic defeat. At 8:00 P.M. he sent a now well-known order to Lafayette McLaws in Pleasant Valley: "The day has gone against us and this army will go by Sharpsburg and cross the river. It is necessary to abandon your position tonight." A dispatch also went to Jackson ordering him to disengage at Harpers Ferry and march his command to Shepherdstown, where he would support the withdrawal of Longstreet's and Hill's men. The messages to McLaws and Jackson preceded Lee's knowledge of a debacle that had befallen Confederate forces at Crampton's Gap, where William B. Franklin's Sixth Corps smashed through a slim force of infantry and cavalry and descended into Pleasant Valley across McLaws's rear.[27]

News of the disaster at Crampton's Gap reached Lee at around 10:00 P.M. and dramatically altered the strategic picture. If Lee withdrew with Longstreet and Hill by way of Sharpsburg on the fifteenth, he would render McLaws, with mountains on his flanks and a river to his rear, exposed and ripe for destruction. In order to support the Georgian while extricating himself from a perilous position, Lee modified Longstreet's and Hill's orders. Instead of immediately departing Maryland, they would halt at Keedysville, a village approximately two and one-half miles west of Boonsboro. At 10:15 P.M., Lee dictated a dispatch to Thomas T. Munford, whose cavalry had withdrawn from Crampton's Gap to Rohrersville, ordering him to hold his position and attempt to reconnoiter a route for McLaws to follow over Elk Mountain, the land mass bordering the western side of Pleasant Valley. An hour later, Lee sent another message to McLaws informing him that Longstreet and Hill would halt at Keedysville and asking whether the Georgian could exit Pleasant Valley by one of two routes and reach Sharpsburg. If McLaws could not do so, Lee offered the option of retreat across the Potomac to Virginia.[28]

The reasoning behind Lee's decision to halt Longstreet's and Hill's commands at Keedysville and his orders to McLaws eluded two of the general's most famous biographers. Both Douglas Southall Freeman and Clifford Dowdey believed Lee had experienced a change of heart regarding the retreat from Maryland upon receipt of news from Stonewall Jackson late on the fourteenth that Harpers Ferry likely would surrender the next day. But Ezra Craman discovered that Lee, while resting in a meadow near the Pry house (later to be McClellan's headquarters) outside Keedysville, did not receive Jackson's dispatch until after 8:00 A.M. on 15 September. Unaware of this important piece of information in Carman's unpublished work on the campaign, Freeman and Dowdey, together with many other writers, erred in interpreting Lee's actions on the night of the fourteenth. He had not changed his mind about withdrawing to Virginia, and he intended for the stand at Keedysville to distract the Union army to cover McLaws's withdrawal. As for McLaws's orders, they reflected Lee's desire to have that command rejoin Longstreet and Hill if possible.[29]

It was after 11:00 P.M. when Longstreet's and Hill's units began to leave South Mountain and take up the march to Keedysville. Lee arrived at that village approximately one hour before daybreak. A note from Munford reached army headquarters at Keedysville with the news that McLaws could negotiate his way over Elk Mountain only with great difficulty. The position at Keedysville thus became a less attractive point from which to provide support for McLaws. Sharpsburg now appeared to offer a better opportunity to accomplish that purpose. At Sharpsburg, Confederates would threaten the flank of any Union force attempting to move south from Boonsboro, while also enjoying a better defensive position because of Antietam Creek and high ground west of that stream. For these reasons, Lee changed Longstreet's and Hill's orders, directing them to continue their march to Sharpsburg.[30]

Lee remained near Keedysville until 8:00 A.M. hoping to hear from McLaws. Soon after that hour he heard instead from Jackson that Harpers Ferry almost certainly would fall on the fifteenth. This added yet another twist to the strategic picture. Lee might not have to flee ignominiously from Maryland. If he could bluff McClellan on the fifteenth, he might purchase enough time to concentrate his army and give battle. Many students of the campaign delight in extolling the daring of Lee's decision to face down McClellan's powerful army with only the fifteen thousand men of Longstreet and Hill, but this interpretation overstates the Confederate chief's audacity. Lee knew it would take McClellan's army the whole of the fifteenth, marching on one road, to cross South Mountain and mass for battle once they found the Confederates in position. Beyond this one-day period of grace, there were no guarantees—though Lee knew he faced the normally lethargic McClellan.[31]

The defensive position Lee selected possessed moderate advantages. Antietam Creek covered the front, its level high enough to force enemy infantry to seek fords or use one of four bridges in the vicinity of the battlefield. Wheeled vehicles could only cross by bridge. Lee's paucity of men and vagaries of the ground caused him to defend directly only one span—the Rohrbach Bridge (or Burnside Bridge). Federals could use the Middle Bridge, which carried the Boonsboro Pike over Antietam Creek, but once on the west bank they faced Confederates on dominating ground. The terrain around the Lower Bridge, at the mouth of Antietam Creek, allowed McClellan little room for maneuver, and Lee left only a light cavalry force to observe this point. The Upper Bridge stood about two miles above the Middle Bridge and lay beyond the means of Lee's force to dispute its passage. West of the creek, Lee's soldiers held high ground abounding with good artillery positions blessed with excellent fields of fire. The defenders derived additional advantage from the undulating terrain, which offered them cover and concealment while limiting the enemy's knowledge of their strength and position.

Three factors did much to offset these advantages. First, Lee held a relatively shallow position, the average depth between Antietam Creek and the Potomac River being approximately three miles. Second, nearly the entire Confederate front fell within range of Union twenty-pounder Parrott batteries on the east bank of the creek, where they might fire with impunity from beyond the effective range of Lee's guns. Porter Alexander, Lee's chief of ordnance, illuminated a third factor "which should have been conclusive against giving battle there. That feature was the Potomac River. We were backed up against it, within two miles, and but a single ford accessible, and that a bad one, rocky and deep. This single feature of the field should have been conclusive against giving battle there. I believe Lee would never have done so, had he ever before crossed the ford in person."[32]

Yet Lee determined to give battle if he could assemble his army. "This decision," wrote the eminent Northern historian John C. Ropes, "is beyond controversy one of the boldest and most hazardous decisions in his whole military career. It is in truth so bold and so hazardous that one is bewildered that he should have even thought seriously of making it." Certainly no decision Lee made during the war, save the third day at Gettysburg, has been subjected to as much criticism. "The moral effect of our movement into Maryland had been lost by our discomfiture at South Mountain, and it was then evident that we could not hope to concentrate in time to do more than make a respectable retreat," opined Longstreet in *Century Magazine* after the war. Porter Alexander, in a private memoir published many years after he wrote it, predicted bluntly that the decision to fight at Sharpsburg "will be pronounced by military critics to be the greatest military blunder that Gen. Lee ever made. . . . In the first place Lee's inferiority of force was too great to hope to do more than to fight a sort of drawn battle." A

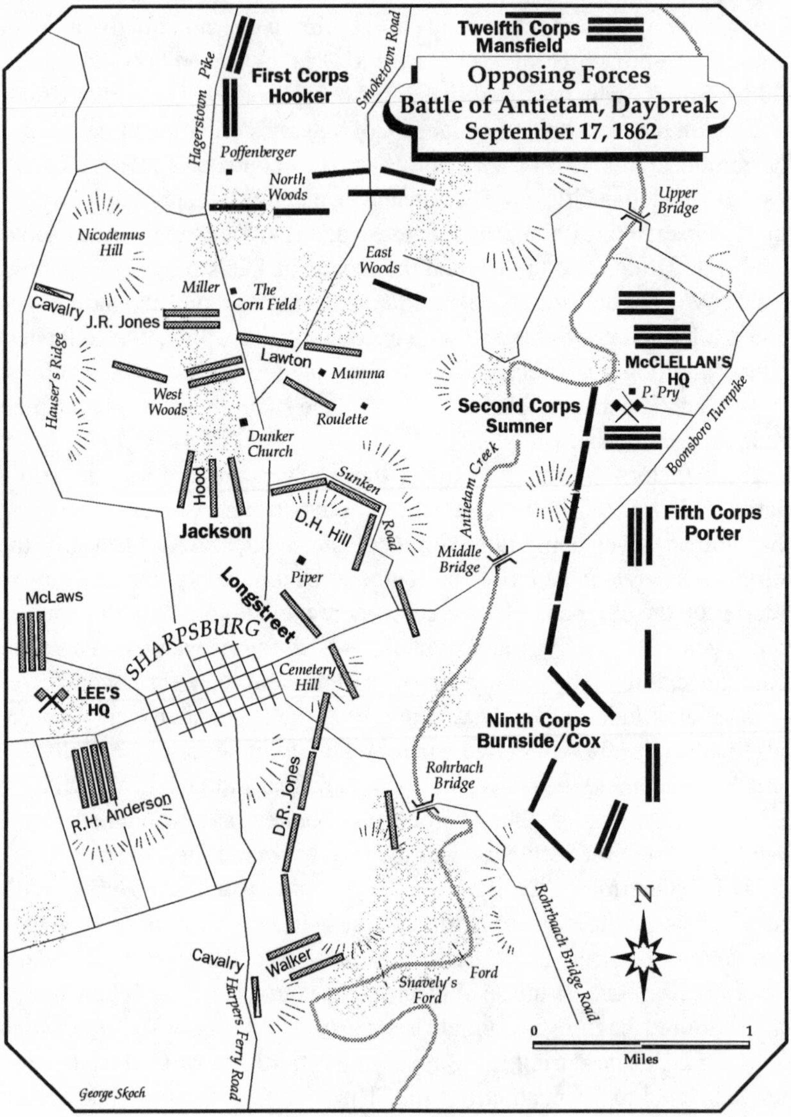

drawn battle, Alexander believed, "was the best *possible* outcome one could hope for." Even Clifford Dowdey admitted that "with the critical reduction of his army, it would not seem that he could have reasonably expected to do more than repulse McClellan's army." Dowdey added that Lee "never sought battles in which he could do no more than repulse the enemy."[33]

Why then, did he remain at Sharpsburg? Bruce Catton wrote in *Terrible Swift Sword* that Lee was not out of his mind and therefore must have "believed he could win."[34] Win what? With a broken-down army opposed by an enemy nearly double his own numbers, it seems improbable that he could have accomplished more that Alexander's drawn battle. But McClellan's presence opened possibilities to achieve more than a tactical stalemate. If McClellan were repulsed and withdrew, Lee, with his line of communications secure down the Valley, could replenish his army from depots at Winchester and strike north to resume his campaign of maneuver. Long odds militated against such an outcome, however, and Lee's decision, considered in hindsight from a strictly military standpoint, was probably an error.

It is important to remember that Lee did not fight at Sharpsburg for purely military reasons. The influence of his 8 September proclamation to the people of Maryland has been neglected in attempts to understand why he would offer battle at Sharpsburg. "Our army has come among you, and is prepared to assist you with the power of its arms in regaining the rights of which you have been despoiled," stated the proclamation. To abandon the campaign after South Mountain, when chance remained to fight the enemy on Maryland soil, would have mocked every word of the proclamation and probably guaranteed the loss of future support in the state. It also might have tarnished the prestige won in Europe by Lee's summer victories. Among former officers in the Army of Northern Virginia who later wrote about the Maryland campaign, perhaps only Porter Alexander divined the true importance of the proclamation to Lee: "I think the only real effect of the proclamation was subjective, or upon Gen. Lee himself," wrote Alexander in his military memoir. "Necessarily, in it he was compelled to appear as a deliverer who had come to free the Marylanders from a yoke. In his decision to stand his ground and fight, his attitude as a deliverer probably had a large share." Lee's decision merits praise for its determination to stand by strong words, but it courted potential crises that far outweighed likely returns. "Lee took a great risk for no chance of gain except the killing of some thousands of the enemy with the loss of, perhaps, two-thirds as many of his own men," wrote Alexander. "That was a losing game for the Confederacy."[35]

Lee anticipated on 15 September that McClellan's elaborate preparations for battle would forestall any attack until the seventeenth. He proved, as he would throughout the war, to have an uncanny ability to assess accurately his opponent's intentions. On the afternoon of the sixteenth, Jackson arrived at the head of two divisions, followed by Walker's division. By nightfall, McLaws's, Anderson's, and A. P. Hill's divisions, consisting of one third of the army, were still absent. A severe night march brought

McLaws and Anderson to the field by daylight on the seventeenth; Hill's soldiers completed their trek about midday. Lee initially had six divisions on hand, perhaps 25,000 effectives, which he placed along a front that stretched nearly three miles. His deployment reflected uncertainty about where McClellan would strike. Because McClellan moved Hooker's corps against Lee's left late on the sixteenth, historians have presumed that this telegraphed to Lee where the main effort on the seventeenth would fall. Lee's dispositions suggest otherwise. McClellan's testing the left on the sixteenth in no way guaranteed a major blow at that point on the seventeenth. For all Lee knew, Union activity on his left represented a diversion to cause him to redeploy. Although Lee placed his only reserve, John Bell Hood's division, in support of Jackson on the left, he maintained an overall posture calculated to meet an attack at any likely axis of advance along the three-mile front. And when McLaws arrived, Lee did not rush his troops off to reinforce the left but held them in a central reserve. An important oversight in the deployment and preparation for battle, for which Lee has been rightly criticized, was his failure to entrench at any point—a curious omission for a general earlier nicknamed the "King of Spades." Lee would not repeat this mistake.

Although Chancellorsville often has been hailed as Lee's greatest battle, Antietam stands as a worthy competitor. The desperate nature of the fighting forced Lee to assume a tactical role he would not repeat until the 1864 campaign. By then the loss of capable officers compelled him to become more directly involved in the tactical direction of his battles. He filled a comparable tactical role, as well as that of army commander, with sublime skill on 17 September. "It would be difficult for us now," wrote Colonel William Allan in 1888, "with all the facts before us, to correct his dispositions. . . . Lee handled his forces with a judgment so cool and clear as to leave nothing for criticism." This evaluation of Lee's generalship on the field at Antietam remains unchallenged. He fought magnificently under pressure that would have overwhelmed a lesser man. With an outnumbered, exhausted army, he conducted a defense so aggressive and violent that Federal officers not prone to exaggerate credited the Confederates with numbers far greater than actually engaged. His timing in releasing precious reserves could not have been improved. Even the most skillful general must have some luck, and Lee enjoyed his share of it at Antietam. McClellan's sequential attacks allowed time to shift reserves to each threatened sector, preventing the Federals from gaining the superiority in numbers requisite to assure success. Moreover, had A. P. Hill's division not arrived at precisely the right time and place, all the brilliant maneuvering and stubborn fighting would have gone for nothing. Burnside's Ninth Corps could not have been checked.

With uncommon confidence, skill, and a liberal dose of luck, Lee and his men stood the Federals off all day on 17 September. Their performance helped build a legend—but at a cost of more than ten thousand men, fully a quarter of the Army of Northern Virginia's effective strength.[36]

In light of his immense casualties and narrow escape from disaster, Lee seemingly should have retreated during the night after Antietam. Yet after hearing the reports of is commanders, he chose to remain on the eighteenth. It was a bold, but not a foolhardy, decision. Lee's provost guard rounded up thousands of stragglers during the night, who together with recovered convalescents, recruits, and others who had assembled at Winchester, hastened forward to the army. Capt. H. L. P. King noted in his diary that McLaws's division on 18 September "had a larger force than when we went into action" on the seventeenth. Similarly, Lt. William W. Wood of the Nineteenth Virginia wrote that during the night of the seventeenth so many stragglers and others joined his brigade that it counted "nearly double" the number of men on the eighteenth as on the preceding day. Many other units experienced the same phenomenon, and this infusion of strength gave Lee confidence to offer battle again on the 18th.[37]

Practical considerations also influenced Lee's decision to remain on the battlefield another day. The wounded could be transported south of the Potomac and stores captured at Harpers Ferry removed. But Lee was not content to maintain the defensive. He ordered Jackson to explore the possibilities of mounting an attack against the Union right. Wishful thinking on Lee's part, the search for an offensive opening reflected his indomitable will for victory. Fortunately for the army, Lee recognized that remaining on the nineteenth could accomplish nothing. His army would grow no stronger, while intelligence indicated the Federal army expected reinforcements. Lee ordered a withdrawal during the night, which the army executed flawlessly. By the morning of 19 September, the Army of Northern Virginia stood on the Virginia shore, its excursion into Maryland at an end.[38]

"General Lee was not satisfied with the results of the Maryland Campaign," recalled James Longstreet after the war. Lee's comments about the campaign to E. C. Gordon and William Allan at Washington College in 1868 support Longstreet's statement. He saw the campaign as a failure when measured against his strategic goals. Confederates could point to some high points: the Union war effort had been kept off balance, and Harpers Ferry with its abundant and useful military stores had fallen to Jackson. But these successes proved fleeting. Lee had hoped for far-reaching and decisive results, which an invasion of Pennsylvania might have achieved. Long-term consequences favored the Union. Lincoln issued his preliminary proclamation of emancipation, and ardor for the Confederate cause cooled in England and France, never to be rekindled in the wake of Lincoln's proclamation. For these failures, Lee had spent heavily from the Confederacy's limited manpower. The army's 13,964 battle casualties told only part of the story. Many deserters, the sick, and stragglers also had been lost. Had Lee withdrawn from Maryland after South Mountain, as he first intended, the campaign would have suffered the same strategic failures but avoided the 10,000 casualties at Antietam while preserving the prestige of taking Harpers Ferry.[39]

Because the campaign ended in disappointment, historians have been tempted to pronounce it doomed from the start. They argue that Lee's army, exhausted and understrength, lacked the means to accomplish anything decisive. Lee took a different view when he reflected on the campaign in 1868. His confidence that the decision to enter Maryland was correct remained undiminished. Had Special Orders No. 191 not fallen into Union hands, he "did not doubt" that a united Army of Northern Virginia "could have crushed the army of McClellan." McClellan's host may not have been "crushed," but there can be little question that without Special Orders No. 191 the Federal commander would not have moved rapidly or aggressively enough to prevent Lee's reuniting his army after Harpers Ferry surrendered. Any subsequent battle likely would have occurred on ground selected by Lee. The result of such a contest lies in the realm of pure speculation. It is not speculative, however, to say that Lee's decision to invade Maryland represented his best play. As Longstreet wrote in his memoirs, following Second Manassas "[t]here was but one opening—across the Potomac." Forbidding risks balanced against even greater potential gains. Lee reached for those gains. That he did so and failed does not tarnish but rather adds luster to his reputation as a general.[40]

NOTES

1. H. L. P. King Diary, 5 September 1862, Southern Historical Collection, Wilson Library, University of North Carolina, Chapel Hill; U. S. War Department, *The War of the Rebellion: A Compilation of the Official Records of the Union and Confederate Armies*, 127 vols., index, and atlas (Washington DC: GPO, 1880–1901), series 1, vol. 19, pt. 2, p. 590 [hereafter cited as *Official Records;* all references are to series 1].

2. *Official Records*, vol. 19, pt. 2, p. 593.

3. Douglas Southall Freeman, *Lee's Lieutenants: A Study in Command*, 3 vols. (New York: Charles Scribner's Sons, 1942–44), 2:720; Alan T. Nolan, *Lee Considered: General Robert E. Lee and Civil War History* (Chapel Hill: University of North Carolina Press, 1991), 97; Edward Porter Alexander, *Military Memoirs of*

a Confederate: A Critical Narrative (New York: Charles Scribner's Sons, 1907), 222.

4. *Official Records*, vol. 9, pt. 2, p. 592; John G. Walker, "Jackson's Capture of Harper's Ferry," in *Battles and Leaders of the Civil War*, 4 vols., ed. Robert Underwood Johnson and Clarence Clough Buel (New York: Century, 1887), 2:605–6 [set hereafter cited as *Battles and Leaders*]; Freeman, *Lee's Lieutenants*, 2:717; John Ropes, *The Story of the Civil War* (New York: G. P. Putnam Sons, 1898), 328. For a criticism of Lee's strategy, see Nolan, *Lee Considered*, 91–92, 96–98.

5. *Official Records*, vol. 19, pt. 2, pp. 590, 593, 596; Bradley T. Johnson, "Address on the First Maryland Campaign," in *Southern Historical Society Papers*, 52 vols. and 3-vol. index, ed. J. William Jones et al. (1876–1959; reprint, Wilmington, N. C.: Broadfoot Publishing Company, 1990–92), 12:503–4.

6. *Official Records*, vol. 19, pt. 2, pp. 590–91; Mary B. Mitchell, "A Woman's Recollections of Antietam," in *Battles and Leaders*, 2:688; Walker, "Jackson's Capture of Harper's Ferry," 605.

7. Robert K. Krick, "The Army of Northern Virginia in September 1862: Its Circumstances, Its Opportunities, and Why It Should Not Have Been at Sharpsburg," in *Antietam: Essays on the 1862 Maryland Campaign*, ed. Gary W. Gallagher (Kent, Ohio: Kent State University Press, 1989), 36–37. The figure fifty-one thousand for the strength of the army is based on the author's statistical study that draws on numerous sources.

8. Edward Porter Alexander, *Fighting for the Confederacy: The Personal Recollections of General Edward Porter Alexander*, ed. Gary W. Gallagher (Chapel Hill: University of North Carolina Press, 1989), 139; Johnson, "Address on the First Maryland Campaign," 507.

9. *Official Records*, vol. 19, pt. 2, pp. 592–93.

10. *Official Records*, vol. 19, pt. 2, pp. 593–94.

11. *Official Records*, vol. 19, pt. 2, p. 145; Walker, "Jackson's Capture of Harper's Ferry," 606; Lenoir Chambers, *Stonewall Jackson*, 2 vols. (New York: William Morrow, 1959), 2:180.

12. *Official Records*, vol. 19, pt. 1, p. 145.

13. *Official Records*, vol. 19, pt. 2, pp. 596, 602.

14. *Official Records*, vol. 19, pt. 2, p. 602.

15. *Official Records*, vol. 19, pt. 2, p. 602; vol. 19, pt. 1, p. 145. Sigel was not in the field. His corps had been left in the defenses of Washington.

16. *Official Records*, vol. 19, pt. 1, p. 839; James Longstreet, *From Manassas to Appomattox: Memoirs of the Civil War in America* (Philadelphia: J. B. Lippincott, 1896), 202–4; Longstreet, "The Invasion of Maryland," in *Battles and Leaders*, 2:663. At this time, Anderson's division consisted of only three brigades. Three other brigades, which had operated as a division at Second Manassas under Cadmus Wilcox, were placed at Longstreet's suggestion under Anderson during the Harpers Ferry operation, bringing his division to six brigades. Lafayette McLaws, "The Capture of Harper's Ferry," Philadelphia *Weekly Press*, 5 September 1888.

17. Jedediah Hotchkiss, *Virginia*, in *Confederate Military History*, 12 vols., ed.

Clement A. Evans (1899; reprint, New York: Thomas Yoseloff, 1962), 3:339; Clifford Dowdey, *Lee* (Boston: Little, Brown, 1965), 303; Douglas Southall Freeman, *R. E. Lee: A Biography*, 4 vols. (New York: Charles Scribner's Sons, 1934–35), 2:361; McLaws, "The Capture of Harpers Ferry."

18. Observing the effects of the march to Harpers Ferry, Greenlee Davidson, a battery commander in Jackson's wing, wrote that when the troops reached Martinsburg "every house in town was crowded with the broken down and weary soldiers" and that "hundreds of men are perfectly barefoot." Greenlee Davidson, *Captain Greenlee Davidson, C. S. A.: Diary and Letters, 1851–1863*, ed. Charles W. Turner (Verona, Va.: McClure Press, 1975), 49–50.

19. McLaws, "The Capture of Harper's Ferry;" Alexander, *Military Memoirs*, 229. The literature on the "Lost Order" is voluminous. One of the better examinations is Stephen W. Sears, *Landscape Turned Red: The Battle of Antietam* (New Haven and New York: Ticknor and Fields, 1983), 349–52.

20. *Official Records*, vol. 19, pt. 1, p. 145; vol. 19, pt. 2, p. 605.

21. George D. Grattan, "The Battle of Boonsboro," in *Southern Historical Society Papers*, 52 vols. and 3-vol. index, ed. J. William Jones et al. (1876–1959; reprint, Wilmington, N. C.: Broadfoot Publishing Company, 1990–92), 39:36.

22. Freeman *Lee*, 2:367; Freeman, *Lee's Lieutenants*, 2:173, 718, 721.

23. Charles Marshall to D. H. Hill, 11 November 1867, D. H. Hill Papers, Virginia State Library, Richmond, Virginia. Although Lee's report of the Maryland campaign mentions the lost order, it was prepared in August 1863 after the publication of McClellan's report in which the Federal commander disclosed the discovery of the order. See *Official Records*, vol. 19, pt. 1, p. 146, and Ezra A. Carman, "History of the Antietam Campaign," p. 393, Ezra A. Carman Papers, Library of Congress, Washington DC. Carman had numerous contacts with Confederate veterans who provided him detailed information about the Maryland campaign.

24. Ezra A. Carman, "History of the Antietam Campaign," p. 396; *Official Records*, vol. 19, pt. 1, pp. 606, 607; D. H. Hill, "The Battle of South Mountain, or Boonsboro," in *Battles and Leaders*, 2:560; Longstreet, *Manassas to Appomattox*, 220.

25. William T. Owen, "The Battle of South Mountain" [manuscript account], pp. 3–4, William T. Owen Papers, Virginia Historical Society, Richmond, Virginia; David Johnston, *The Story of a Confederate Boy in the Civil War* (1914; reprint, Radford, Va.: Commonwealth Press, Inc., 1980), 139. The evidence does not support Longstreet's claim that his command marched at daylight. See Longstreet, *Manassas to Appomattox*, 220, 225.

26. *Official Records*, vol. 19, pt. 1, p. 1022; Seaton Gales, "Gen. George Burgwyn Anderson," in *Our Living and Our Dead* 3 (September 1875): 327; William Allan, "Strategy of the Campaign of Sharpsburg or Antietam" (typescript), Ezra A. Carman Papers, New York Historical Society, New York City, 17.

27. Hill, "Battle of South Mountain," 580; *Official Records*, vol. 51, pt. 2, pp. 618–19; Carman "History of the Antietam Campaign," 508, 509.

28. *Official Records*, vol. 19, pt. 1, p. 855. Lee received word of Crampton's

Gap via Munford, who wrote in his memorandum diary that a Capt. W. K. Martin reported the news in person. Munford diary, 13 September 1862 [entry covers 13–15 September; Munford may have prepared this document after the fact], in Thomas T. Munford Papers, Perkins Library, Duke University, Durham, North Carolina. The time that Lee would have received this news is inferred from the timing of his orders to Munford. *Official Records*, vol. 19, pt. 2, pp. 608–9; Carman, "History of the Antietam Campaign," 507.

29. Dowdey, *Lee*, 306–7; Freeman *Lee*, 2:375–76; Carman, "History of the Antietam Campaign," 518–19.

30. Carman, "History of the Antietam Campaign," 518.

31. Carman, "History of the Antietam Campaign," 518.

32. Alexander, *Military Memoirs*, 247.

33. John C. Ropes, *The Story of the Civil War: A Concise Account of the War in the United States of America between 1861 and 1865*, 4 vols. (New York: G. P. Putnam's Sons, 1894–1913), 2:349; James Longstreet, "The Invasion of Maryland," in *Battles and Leaders*, 2:666–67; Alexander, *Fighting for the Confederacy*, 146; Dowdey, *Lee*, 308.

34. Bruce Catton, *Terrible Swift Sword*, (Garden City, N.Y.: Doubleday & Company, 1963), 452.

35. Alexander, *Military Memoirs*, 225, 249.

36. William Allan, "Strategy of the Campaign of Sharpsburg or Antietam. September, 1862," in *Campaigns in Virginia, Maryland and Pennsylvania 1862–1863*, in *Papers of the Military Historical Society of Massachusetts*, 14 vols. and index (1895–1918; reprint, Wilmington, N.C.: Broadfoot Publishing Company, 1989–90), 3:102–3.

37. King Diary, 18 September 1862, Southern Historical Collection, Wilson Library, University of North Carolina, Chapel Hill; William N. Wood, *Reminiscences of Big I* (Jackson, Tenn.: McCowat-Mercer Press, 1956), 40.

38. *Official Records*, vol. 19, pt. 1, p. 820; Chambers, *Jackson*, 2:229–30.

39. Longstreet, *Manassas To Appomattox*, 200; Freeman, *Lee's Lieutenants*, 2:716–21.

40. Freeman, *Lee's Lieutenants*, 2:718.

Lee at Chancellorsville

ROBERT K. KRICK

A Pennsylvanian much distinguished at Chancellorsville wrote two decades later: "It is probable that there has been more said and written about the battle . . . than any other engagement that took place during the war." The flood of words that he remarked upon continued unabated through a series of good books that culminated in John Bigelow's epic *Campaign of Chancellorsville* in 1910, a study frequently and aptly described as the best book ever written on any American campaign. Most Chancellorsville analyses reach conclusions akin to that of R. E. Lee's artillery officer who wrote: "The Chancellorsville campaign was altogether the most remarkable conducted by General Lee."[1] The purpose of this essay is to examine Lee's options and decisions at the several turning points that determined the results of the engagement.

On the eve of Chancellorsville, Lee's Army of Northern Virginia stood at the height of its powers in large part because of the flowering of a fabulously successful collaboration between Lee and the able executor of his plans, Thomas J. "Stonewall" Jackson. The army had imbibed success so often that it expected victory as a matter of course, and consequently fulfilled its own prophecy on a regular basis. A Northerner who studied the battle described the rebel army as "a remarkable and powerful body of men, led by one of the ablest soldiers of the age." General Joseph Hooker, who ineptly led the army opposing Lee at Chancellorsville, paid his foemen grudging tribute mixed with regional chauvinism. Despite "a rank and file vastly inferior to our own, intellectually and physically," Hooker grumbled, the Army of Northern Virginia somehow had "acquired a character for steadiness and efficiency unsurpassed, in my judgment, in ancient or modern times."[2]

Hooker's putative intellectual inferiors could count on calm, strong leadership from Lee and dazzling flair from Jackson. The mutual confidence and trust the two men shared, which was crucial to their success, existed remarkably infrequently between other tandems in Civil War armies—and throughout military history. The oft-quoted tribute by Jackson to Lee, "that he would be willing to follow him blindfolded," was both figuratively, and no doubt literally, true for the literal-minded Stonewall. Most Confederates still revered Jackson more than Lee at this stage of the war. In late 1862 a Georgian thought, Lee "will do very well; but the idol of the army, as well as of the people, is the gallant Stonewall Jackson." Two days after Jackson's death, another Georgian attempted to shift gears vis-à-vis the two famed leaders. Jackson "was thought more of then are nother general that we have got, but old general Lee is a might good general."[3]

Lee approached the onset of campaigning just having recovered from a bout of chronic illness, disdainful of his foe, and full of the droll wit often overlooked in sketches of his persona. Col. A. L. Long of the general's staff returned from compassionate leave to the headquarters camp along Mine Road south of Fredericksburg that spring, exultant over the birth of a daughter. Long visited Surgeon Lafayette Guild's tent for some medicinal brandy "& was correspondingly elated" when he reached the general's table with his announcement. "General Lee looked very grave," an eyewitness recalled, and said "Colonel, do I understand you right, is it a daughter?" When Long responded with a cheerful affirmation, Lee, "with the gravest countenance, said, 'Colonel Long, I wonder that you should try to evade the conscript laws in this way. You must try it again.' "[4]

Military stirrings among Federals across the Rappahannock River put Lee in a characteristically aggressive mood. In the peaceful setting of a Sunday church service on 19 April, Lee told Gen. Joseph B. Kershaw that he was eager to "run those *people* [his favorite locution for Yankees] from over there." In a letter to his wife, Lee disdained his enemy's feints and posturing. "The enemy is making various demonstrations either to amuse themselves or deceive us," he wrote on the twenty-fourth. "I suppose they thought we were frightened out of all propriety." The general sardonically suggested that a Unionist sally across the river to loot civilian property would "serve for texts to the writers for the [New York papers] for brilliant accounts of grand Union victories & great rejoicings of the saints of the party."[5]

The first and most basic question that Lee faced on the eve of Chancellorsville was whether to remain on the line of the Rappahannock. Even before Hooker's clever and well-executed initiative upstream in late April put Lee at a tactical disadvantage, the Confederate leader contemplated the edge to be gained by retiring to the protection of another stream system farther south. The North Anna offered the next substantial obstacle to an invader headed toward Richmond, and "greater scope to manœuver" for the

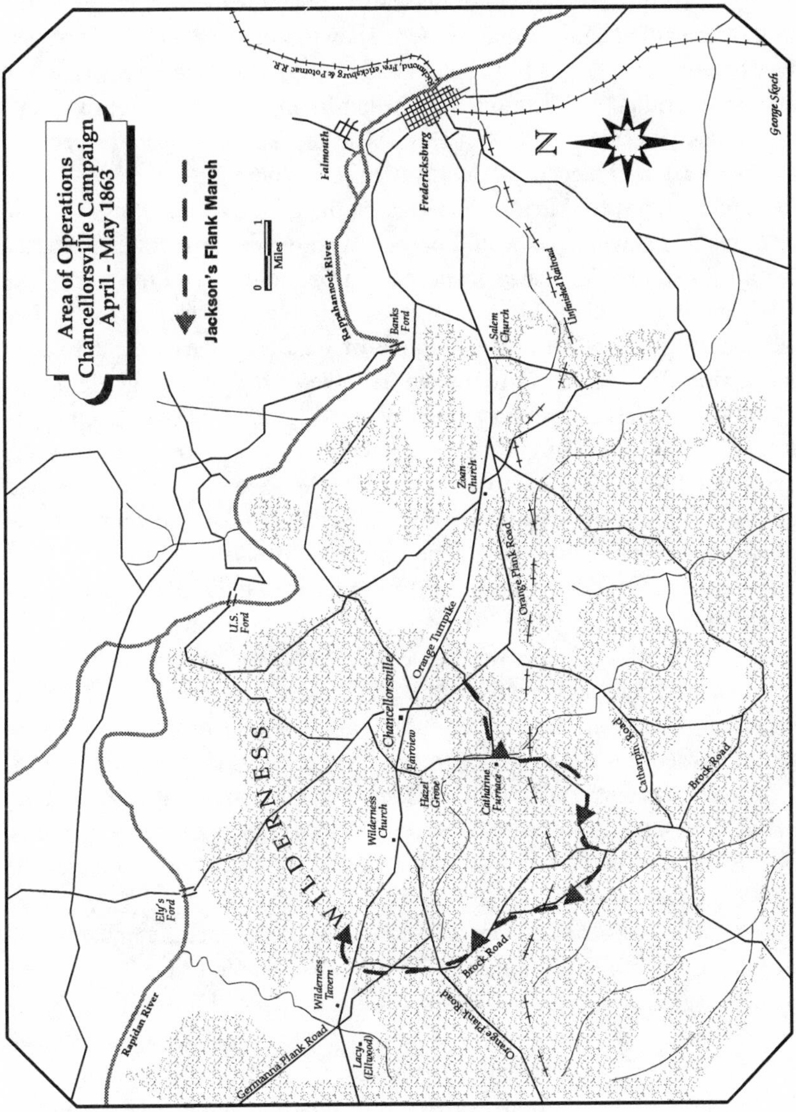
Area of Operations
Chancellorsville Campaign
April - May 1863
Jackson's Flank March
0
1
Miles
Richmond, Fredericksburg & Potomac R.R.
Falmouth
Fredericksburg
Rappahannock River
Banks Ford
Salem Church
Unfinished Railroad
N
George Skoch
Zoan Church
Orange Plank Road
Orange Turnpike
U.S. Ford
Chancellorsville
Fairview
Hazel Grove
Catharine Furnace
Catharpin Road
Brock Road
Wilderness Church
WILDERNESS
Ely's Ford
Wilderness Tavern
Rapidan River
Germanna Plank Road
Lacy (Ellwood)
Orange Plank Road
Brock Road

defending army. Lee sent two of his staff to examine the south bank of the North Anna along a thirty-mile stretch. They found no considerable advantages that outstripped the Rappahannock. In any case, the administration in Richmond bridled at Lee's intimation that he might need to retire to that point unless President Jefferson Davis sent up reinforcements (especially cavalry) wasted in piecemeal detachments elsewhere.[6]

R. E. Lee's invariable interest in taking the initiative, and thus selecting the terms under which he would operate, uncovered no acceptable means to "run those people" away from their stronghold across the river. The fiery Marylander, Gen. Isaac Ridgeway Trimble, had forwarded to Lee a visionary plan spun from a pastiche of trestle bridges, secret raiders, and derring-do. Lee gently reminded Trimble of the "powerful elements" affecting logistics and noted pointedly (in language P. G. T. Beauregard and James Longstreet might have heeded with merit), "I know the pleasure experienced in shaping campaigns [and] battles, according to our wishes, and have enjoyed the ease with which obstacles to their accomplishment (in effigy) can be overcome."[7] The greatest obstacle Lee would have to overcome at Chancellorsville was the most basic of military disadvantages: a huge disparity in numbers. He could only oppose some 60,000 men to Hooker's host of 130,000. At no time during the war, except in its closing weeks, did Lee face odds nearly so steep. He was accustomed to disagreeable numerical odds from long experience. This worse disproportion resulted from the absence of James Longstreet with two strong divisions of his First Corps on a foraging expedition to Tidewater Virginia. Longstreet eagerly extended his operations with fond (but forlorn) hopes of an independent coup. Even after Hooker had opened the campaign, Lee cherished the vain hope that Longstreet might reach him in time to help.[8]

Longstreet's absence changed the entire personality of the campaign, and not just because it kept thousands of men unavailable to Lee. Longstreet by this stage of the war had fallen upon a military philosophy perfectly suited to his stolid personality and narrow grasp: he would spend the rest of the war longing pathetically for someone of Ambrose E. Burnside's caliber who would hurl troops hopelessly against an impregnable position of Longstreet's choosing. Disappointed in that impossible yearning for a battle of Fredericksburg Redux, Longstreet would stubbornly seek circumstances that might yield his cherished vision. The battle of Chancellorsville unfolded as Lee's most imaginative gamble, built upon a series of risks impossible to imagine with Longstreet anywhere near the council fires.

One of Lee's nagging concerns was for the railroad-junction village of Gordonsville, forty miles southwest of his center of gravity at Fredericksburg. The crossroads there made Gordonsville the third most important military location in the state, behind Richmond and Petersburg. Confederates denied the logistical network beyond Gordonsville would have faced fatal shortages. Even though a succession of Federal commanders remained nonchalantly indifferent to the junction's value through four years of war, Lee could not presume upon their sloth. Expecting his enemy to do what he should do, the Southern leader remained worried about Gordonsville through the opening phases of the Chancellorsville campaign. To Lee's chagrin the first Federal moves, beginning in mid-April, involved cavalry threats at about Gordonsville's longitude. He could not ignore that delicate southwestern flank until the campaign was several days old.[9]

General Lee faced his first Chancellorsville decisions on 29 April when Federals pushed bridges across the Rappahannock below Fredericksburg at about 5:30 A.M. Soon after gunfire began, prompted as it was by the crossing, Lee rode up to Gen. Jubal A. Early near the front and guyed his subordinate: "Gen. Early, what are you making all this racket about?" When Early explained the Yankee initiative, Lee responded, "Oh the troublesome fellows." He knew that the depth of the riverbed provided such thorough defilade to the enemy that Southern artillery could not harass the bridges effectively. Lee had been through precisely the same situation during the December battle on the same ground and quickly recognized the need "to select positions with a view to resist the advance of the enemy, rather than incur the heavy loss that would attend any attempt to prevent his crossing."[10]

Throughout the day on Wednesday the twenty-ninth, Lee accumulated and analyzed intelligence from several sources. Before noon word reached him from cavalry chief J. E. B. Stuart that the enemy had moved in force across the Rappahannock far upstream. Later news from other cavalry told of Federal columns near fords on the Rapidan River closer to the Confederate rear. Lee told Jefferson Davis by telegram late on the twenty-ninth that he presumed the enemy's intention was "to turn our left, and probably to get into our rear." Lee's first major move was to dispatch Gen. Richard H. Anderson and his division toward Chancellorsville as an initial bulwark against the Northern tide. Because of Anderson's propensity toward lassitude, the army commander felt obliged to remind him pointedly: "I wish you to go forward *yourself* and attend to this matter." (emphasis added) Gordonsville remained on his mind. If Federals sought to cut Lee off from Richmond, he must stay ahead of them.[11]

For much of 30 April, Lee remained undecided about abandoning his position near Fredericksburg or fighting for it. Anderson retired from Chancellorsville to a position near Zoan Church early that morning and began to intrench. Lee spurred the effort with a message exhorting Anderson to "Set all your spades to work as vigorously as possible." Sizable field fortifications remained a novelty on battlefields grown from meeting engagements, but Lee was in the process of revolutionizing that aspect of warfare.[12]

In the face of growing evidence that Hooker had swung many men upstream, while crossing others right at Fredericksburg, Lee faced the obligation to move against one force or the other, or to retire. He never seriously considered backing down. As a perceptive Confederate participant later wrote: "By all the rules of war, one-half or the other should be at once attacked." Gen. John Sedgwick's force in the bridgehead near Fredericksburg was the closer and smaller of the enemy lodgments and seemed like the obvious target for an assault. Stonewall Jackson proposed to attack, at once and vigorously. Lee thought that it would be "hard to get at the enemy and harder to get away if we drove him into the river." After Jackson carefully examined the terrain, he agreed with his chief that an attack was impracticable. Lee then ordered him to "move in the morning up to Anderson."[13]

The decision to move west to counter Hooker's turning movement was a bold one, based in part on Lee's conviction that Hooker could never uncover Washington. The enemy objective, therefore, must be the vicinity of Chancellorsville, not Gordonsville or some point farther south. As Lee said in retrospect, "Everything was risky in our war. . . . [A] very bold game . . . was the only *possible* one." By Thursday evening the thirtieth, he had determined that Hooker's intentions were sufficiently developed to warrant decisive action. Orders crackled through the army. Gen. Lafayette McLaws was to move his division "as soon as possible" to Zoan Church; he marched at midnight. Jackson, of course, needed no special prompting. At midnight Lee wired to the War Department in Richmond: "I determined to hold our lines in rear of Fredericksburg with part of the force and endeavor with the rest to drive the enemy back to the Rapidan." Three days of battle would accomplish that end.[14]

McLaws reached Anderson near Zoan Church at daylight and occupied intrenchments north of the Orange Turnpike. Stonewall Jackson arrived on the scene at 8:00 A.M. and immediately, as was his wont, prepared to advance; he moved westward an hour before noon. Lee accompanied Jackson but did not participate in the tactical arrangements. The presence of the two eminently successful leaders, an artillery colonel wrote, elated the army. "We were not going to wait for the enemy to come & attack us in those lines, we were going out on the warpath after him. And the conjunction of Lee & Jackson at the head of the column meant that it was to be a supreme effort, a union of audacity & desperation. . . . How splendidly the pair of them looked to us, & how the happy confidence of the men in them shone in everyone's face, & rang in the cheers which everywhere greeted them."[15]

Lee's own happy confidence might have been dampened had he been aware of how completely his calls for reinforcement were being ignored in Richmond and elsewhere. On 1 May he optimistically wired the War Department concerning his estimate that a brigade from North Carolina should reach him that night, and that Longstreet's two divisions might arrive by "to-morrow evening." In the event, Longstreet would chase chimeras long enough to avoid helping Lee at all, and no other reinforcements arrived during the battle.[16]

With his army concentrating around Zoan Church, Lee had in a single stroke wrested the operational advantage—and the initiative—from Joe Hooker. The Confederate rearguard at Fredericksburg (Early's division with an appended brigade) could be expected to hold off the Federals there under Gen. Sedgwick. Hooker's legions were in the toils of a vast brushy region known as the Wilderness of Spotsylvania. Their immense advantage in numbers would be neutralized to some extent by the inability to use them in places other than along the few roads and in the occasional clearings. Furthermore, Lee had achieved the textbook goal of interior lines. Hooker still had Sedgwick demonstrating at Fredericksburg to divert Lee, after Lee had moved west. The concentration of Confederate strength near Zoan surprised Hooker as thoroughly as he had surprised Lee on the preceding days. A Federal general analyzed the situation after the war: "Lee from his central position was closer to every part of Hooker's army than Hooker's extreme . . . corps were to each other. . . . While Lee could operate from his central position on the radii of the circle, Hooker was compelled to operate on the circumference."[17]

Lee's battle would benefit substantially from the inadequacies of General Hooker. The degree to which Lee counted on those shortcomings is beyond knowing, but he certainly behaved in a fashion he would not have attempted against sterner opposition. Hooker's stunning success at reaching Chancellorsville and turning the Confederate flank clearly gratified him—as well it might—but it also left him bewildered when his foe did not react as though stunned. A Federal student of the battle suggested that had Hooker been killed on 1 May, "his successful crossing of the Rappahannock, and complete out-generalling of Lee . . . would have justified the country in claiming that it had produced a great commander."[18] The live Joe Hooker, however, thoroughly disabused the country of that notion by his demeanor on 1–3 May, to Lee's great advantage.

The brilliant Confederate commentator E. Porter Alexander summarized what most others have concluded about Hooker's moral status on 1 May:

"He had confidently expected Lee to retreat without a battle, and finding him, instead, so quick to take the aggressive, he lost his nerve and wished himself back on the line he had taken around Chancellorsville, where he would enjoy the great advantage of acting upon the defensive." In the same vein, Hooker's subordinate and bête noire, Gen. O. O. Howard, declared: "[O]ur commander could not cope with the situation in that blind-wilderness country after the action had gone beyond his original anticipation." The Federal commander's own apologia for his 1 May shriveling of purpose, given before the Jacobin Committee on the Conduct of the War, blamed the Wilderness terrain: "[A]s the passage-way through the forest was narrow, I was satisfied that I could not throw troops through it fast enough . . . and was apprehensive of being whipped in detail."[19] A sympathetic audience of fellow Radicals forbore asking Hooker why he did not simply move out of the Wilderness, as he could readily have done, instead of succumbing impotently to its clutches.

Not only was Hooker's advance near Zoan Church on 1 May out of the Wilderness, a column on his extreme left also had moved far east of the eastern edge of the tangled thickets and approached Banks's Ford. Suggestions that Lee determined to hold that crucial ford, which divided Hooker's army and forced him to use deeply exterior lines, are not borne out by Lee's actions. He may have benefitted from good fortune on the front. In any event, Hooker pulled in the Banks's Ford column when he collapsed the rest of his front. General Lee's interest in the Federal left was more offensive than defensive. During the afternoon he rode toward that flank of the enemy's army to reconnoiter in person, reprising the personal scouting role that had won him brevets and fame in Mexico two decades earlier. Lee "wanted to attack on his [own] right," he said five years later, "to cut Hooker off from the river, and rode down & examined [the] Yankee lines all [the] way to the river, but found no place fit for attack."[20]

Jackson's aggressive measures easily pushed the quiescent Hooker back along both the Orange Plank Road and the Orange Turnpike from Zoan Church. The finishing touch was use of an unfinished railroad grade as a secret conduit for moving a Georgia brigade through the Wilderness to bend back the Union right flank. The twisted configuration of Hooker's line that resulted presented Lee and Jackson with a great opportunity for the morrow's operations. So complete had been Hooker's moral collapse, and so zealous Jackson's pursuit, that a subordinate Federal general feared calamity that evening. "The rebels followed up our army closely," Abner Doubleday wrote, "and it is quite possible that a [further] sudden attack, when it was heaped up around Chancellorsville, might have been disastrous to us."[21]

Lee and Jackson met on the evening of 1 May at the intersection of the Orange Plank Road and the Catharine Furnace Road to consider their options. Yankee sharpshooters firing at long range from perches in tall trees forced the generals to retire into a copse of woods in the intersection's northwest corner. Lee opened with the obvious question, "How can we get at these people?" He already knew from personal observation that the Federal left was impregnable. Jackson, in an egregious miscalculation, had convinced himself that Hooker was so supine that he would recross the river overnight. Lee rejected that analysis. The threat of an advance from the rear by Sedgwick's Federals hovered over the meeting. Lee expected Hooker to resume operations somehow, if given the chance, and hoped to beat him to the punch. The stakes were obvious, as he told Jefferson Davis in a telegram: "It is plain that if the enemy is too strong for me here, I shall have to fall back, and Fredericksburg must be abandoned. If successful here, Fredericksburg will be saved and our communications retained."[22]

The obvious first step was to ascertain whether Hooker might be attacked head on, up the Orange Plank Road. Maj. T. M. R. Talcott of Lee's staff and Capt. J. Keith Boswell of Jackson's headed north through the moonlit woods to find out. They returned with a decidedly unfavorable report. Lee also dispatched Lt. James Power Smith (of Jackson's staff) to inquire of Generals Anderson and McLaws about the practicability of attacking in front. Smith brought back a pessimistic response. On the basis of what they had learned, the two generals easily rejected any thought of a frontal assault. In his report Lee described the strength of the fortified Federal center and concluded that "a direct attack upon the enemy would be attended with great difficulty and loss." Hooker well knew that his center was strong and presumed that Lee had no remaining option but inglorious flight. Lee did not agree.[23]

In the face of evidence that his right and center offered no opportunities, Lee turned to consideration of his left. The location of that Federal flank was only vaguely known. Wright had been spectacularly successful on 1 May by lunging down the unfinished railroad in that direction, which gave impetus to the hope that more could be accomplished. Soon after Talcott, Boswell, and Smith arrived with their reports ruling out an attack in front, Lee gestured across a crude map toward the Federal right and ordered Jackson to move in that direction early the next morning.[24]

Credit for originating the daring movement to the left quickly became, and to some degree remains, one of the most mooted of Civil War tactical matters. Based on primary sources, however, it is clear that Lee initiated the concept and Jackson perfected and executed it. Some of Jackson's staff and intimates, but by no means all of them, insisted that their chief conceived the idea. Lieutenant Smith concluded that the "superb strategy was General Lee's, with all its audacity" while the "execution was General Jackson's." Kyd Douglas, who had been on Jackson's staff and was still a line subordinate, wrote that "Jackson *was selected* to make the movement" (emphasis added). On the other hand, Jackson's brother-in-law and aide, Joseph Morrison, claimed that Stonewall "formed his plan of attack Friday evening; proposed it to Gen. L. Friday night, and that Gen. L. did not consent to it at first, but finally yielded."[25]

The leading proponent of Jackson as originator of the movement was his former chief of staff, the Rev. Robert L. Dabney. Dabney was earnest and pious—just to Jackson's taste—but had been fabulously maladroit during the few months in 1862 that he spent on the staff. His early (and generally good) biography of his hero understandably never painted Stonewall in muted hues. By Dabney's account, Jackson "proposed to throw his command entirely into Hooker's rear." Lee only acquiesced to his lieutenant's daring suggestion "after profound reflection," Dabney declared.[26] A great many narrators followed Dabney's lead during the early postwar years.

Lee's staff uniformly attributed the initiative to their chief. Armistead Long stated "from personal knowledge . . . gained on the ground at the time" that "Lee determined to turn the Federal position" and then "the execution of a movement so much in accordance with his genius and inclination was assigned to General Jackson." Long quoted Jackson as saying, "You know best. Show me what to do." Charles Marshall reported that Lee gave Jackson general directions toward the left before the two consulted on details. Writing soon after the war, Walter H. Taylor described the collaboration as illustrating "the peculiar talent and individual excellence of Lee and Jackson. For quickness of perception, boldness in planning, and skill in directing, General Lee had no superior: for celerity in his movements, audacity in the execution of bold designs and impetuosity in attacking, General Jackson had not his peer."[27]

R. E. Lee's own testimony is unequivocal—and uncharacteristic. Jubal Early, James Longstreet, and a dozen other immodest Confederates leaders tooted their own horns regularly enough to prompt caution in accepting what they claimed. Lee's customary quiet modesty leaves us wondering about his perspective in almost every instance. Often the best clue about responsibility comes from a passive construction in his reports. About this decision Lee reported, "It was, therefore, resolved to endeavor to turn his right flank and gain his rear."

Lee used active construction of sentences, attributing credit where due, except when describing his own behavior. "It was . . . resolved" means that Lee designed the movement.[28]

The commanding general wrote far more incisively on the subject in two letters. He told a Southern author fairly bluntly that, despite having "the greatest reluctance to . . . [detract from Jackson's] well-deserved fame," the responsibility had been his own. In an unusually frank letter to Jackson's widow, answering her specific inquiry on the matter, Lee gracefully lauded her husband and Dr. Dabney. He then pointedly explained: "I am misrepresented at . . . Chancellorsville in proposing an attack in front. . . . On the contrary, I decided against it, and stated to Gen. Jackson, we must attack on our left as soon as practicable." There is no equilvalent declaration by Lee on any event from the war.[29]

One of the first public allusions to the fact that Lee, rather than Jackson, inaugurated the flank march came in 1875 in a reunion address by John Warwick Daniel. Even so, some late-nineteenth-century narrators, unaware of Lee's quiet comments to the contrary, painted Jackson as the originator. The careful T. A. Dodge, for instance, said that "Jackson, with characteristic restless energy, suggested a movement with his entire corps around Hooker's right flank." Confederate artillery colonel John J. Garnett wrote in 1896 more accurately that "General Lee determined to . . . turn the enemy's right flank and gain his rear." Bigelow's judicious study dodged the issue, stating that "Lee and Jackson in consultation projected a turning movement against Hooker's rear."[30]

The slightly variant accounts by contemporaries resulted, as so often was the case, from witnessing different fragments of a long and complex transaction. No one summarized the situation better than Major Talcott: "It is evident that what occurred in the presence of each of us was at different times during a conference which lasted several hours." Jimmie Smith awakened once during the night and saw the two generals bending alone over a scant fire of twigs—a period for which no one could offer testimony, conflicting or otherwise. A. P. Hill participated at one point, though his presence usually has been overlooked. The initial conception forwarded by Lee required considerable refinement through the night. Cavalrymen brought new intelligence; so did staff officers, local citizen guides, and, according to a suspicious Federal, even women from the Dowdall's Tavern residence.[31]

Evolution of the plan continued as word about route options came into the general's bivouac. Jackson kept looking for a shorter route, keeping in mind the necessity of good cover for so dangerous an undertaking. Once a means of reaching the Brock Road had been ascertained, Jackson tenaciously pressed for further cover and deception on woods roads beyond and parallel to the Brock Road. With the final results in, Stonewall was ready to lead his greatest (and last) march. The two generals engaged in an oft-quoted formal colloquy, restating the plan. "General Jackson, what do you propose to do?" "Go around here," while tracing a route on a map. "What do you propose to make the movement with?" "With my whole corps." "What will you leave me?" "The divisions of Anderson and McLaws." "Well, go on!"[32]

The question remains whether the decision to find and flatten Hooker's right flank was a good one. The sweeping success that resulted supplied empirical validation, but was the immense risk worth taking by comparison to the other alternatives? Lee's aide, Walter Taylor, stated the patently obvious when he wrote, "Bold it certainly was!" What alternatives to such boldness existed? No other Federal sector was susceptible to approach. Porter Alexander described the "very desperate" situation as leading to "the audacious strategy." Since Hooker had maneuvered Lee out of his Fredericksburg position without a battle, "there was now nothing left but to attack . . . or to attempt a retreat already dangerously delayed." The distasteful consequences of a retreat made Lee's decision easy. The flank movement was all that was left. "Only a very sanguine man could even hope" to achieve what Lee essayed, Alexander thought: "But no risks appalled the heart of Lee, either of odds, or position, or of both combined. His supreme faith in his army was only equalled by the faith of his army in him."[33]

Northern writers pontificating about Lee's strategy often took the easy high ground: Lee had violated basic rules of warfare by taking such a gamble. One Federal officer marveled, "It should be remembered that . . . not an officer or a soldier of Lee's had seen the right flank of Hooker's army." A Pennsylvanian narrator cited Jomini and called the flank march "particularly faulty." Theodore A. Dodge, an evenhanded and thoughtful commentator, blistered Lee, whom he thought "not entitled to commendation" for the decision. "Had it resulted disastrously, as it ought to have done," Dodge declared, "it would have been a serious blow to Lee's military prestige." Dodge was right about the consequences, of course: even more, it would probably have destroyed Lee's country.[34]

Federals familiar with General Hooker's frailties imagined that Lee behaved so daringly because he recognized his foe's inadequacy. A Northern officer thought: "If Gen. Lee's experience with our . . . army commanders had not led him to . . . hold our army commanders in such utter contempt, he would never have consented to have thus divided his army in the face of this powerful enemy." Dodge believed that a critical factor was that "Hooker had shown clear intention of fighting a defensive battle; and perhaps Lee measured his man better than the Army of the Potomac had done. . . . In the presence of a more active foe, Lee would never have hazarded so much."[35]

John Bigelow's last word in his magisterial study reminded readers of the basic premises affecting the force with operational initiative: "The defensive has to be strong at every point, the offensive has to be strong at but one point. A commander who attacks when and where his opponent expects him to suffers all the disadvantages of the offensive without realizing its characteristic advantage." Lee's chosen point was anything but where his opponent expected him.[36]

On Saturday morning the second of May, Lee bade his trusted lieutenant farewell near the intersection where they had hatched their remarkable plan. Lee sat mounted beneath a big oak tree and leaned over to listen to Stonewall Jackson, who stood beside him with one arm on the neck of Lee's horse and the other "gesticulating while he talked very earnestly and rapidly." Once Jackson disappeared on his risky endeavor, Lee waited calmly and resolutely for its results. He had told a German military observer that, after forging "plans as good as my human skill allows . . . I lay the fate of my army in the hands of God; it is my generals' turn to perform their duty."[37] Jackson was wonderfully adept at taking his turn, as this day would prove anew.

Lee found time during his wait to worry about other military opportunities. He communicated with Jefferson Davis about the cavalry raids far away in the mountains of western Virginia led by Generals John D. Imboden and William E. "Grumble" Jones. Closer to Chancellorsville, one of Lee's staff, far less capable than Jackson of taking his turn, complicated the campaign during 2 May. Col. Robert H. Chilton, Lee's awkward chief of staff, took a discretionary verbal order back to Jubal Early and the rearguard near Fredericksburg. Lee prudently gave Early the choice of falling back if pressure from Sedgwick mounted too high. Chilton garbled the discretionary message into peremptory orders that Early grudgingly obeyed, creating a situation that would result in trouble the next morning. The deadly potential for confusion of verbal orders has bedeviled military leaders over the centuries—but they are so much more convenient to prepare![38]

General Lee's personal role in the operations of his rearguard on 2 May was far greater than normal because he had no corps commander at hand to direct McLaws and Anderson as they feinted with their divisions against Hooker's masses. The colonel of one of Anderson's regiments commented that on this day "I saw more of Gen. Lee than during any battle of the war. . . . [He] sat on his horse a great deal of the time immediately in the rear of our regiment, and you could see a shade of anxiety . . . on his face." The general gave no indication that he noticed shells exploding around him as he ordered brigade commander William Mahone "to feel the enemy, to feel them 'pretty heavily, pretty heavily.'" Hooker was eager to be fooled into quiescence and succumbed to the subterfuge. Lee doubtless echoed Mahone's sentiments when at last the sound of Jackson's attack reverberated across the countryside that evening: "Thank God! There are

Jackson's guns!" Mahone exclaimed. Lee promptly ordered McLaws and Anderson to press the enemy strongly to keep them from concentrating on Jackson's new front.[39]

The worst crisis Lee faced at Chancellorsville reached his attention at three o'clock the next morning and was all but beyond his power to control. Capt. R. E. Wilbourn reached Lee at that hour with the alarming news that Stonewall Jackson had been seriously wounded late on 2 May while reconnoitering beyond his lines. Wilbourn found Lee asleep under an oil cloth in a copse of pines, sat down on his pallet, and described the battle. Lee said of Stonewall's injuries, "[A]h: don't talk about it. Thank God it is no worse." An hour later Jedediah Hotchkiss arrived with a similar report. Lee also deflected Hotchkiss away from the painful details of Jackson's wounding.[40]

The fatal effect upon the army of the permanent loss of Jackson must have crossed Lee's mind instantly. For the short term, though, he must pull victory out of the chaos resulting from Jackson's long march, successful attack, and eventual wounding. J. E. B. Stuart, who had assumed command in Stonewall's stead, must press the enemy in conjunction with Anderson and McLaws from the other side until the two halves of Lee's army were reunited. No greater danger confronted Lee during the campaign than this of being divided in the face of a much larger foe—after the excitement and momentum of Jackson's attack had abated. He sent both Hotchkiss and Wilbourn back around to Stuart with ardent messages that "we must press these people right away." A written injunction at once went to Stuart: the advantage must be "prosecuted with the utmost vigor, and the enemy given no time to rally. . . . They must be pressed, so that we can unite the two wings of the army." To be sure that the message got through, Lee indited a second urgent note that began, "I repeat what I have said half an hour since."[41]

Lee could not afford the luxury of going in person across the gap to Stuart's end of the line because he had to direct McLaws's and Anderson's divisions as they fought to reunite the army from their side. He accompanied the troops in their attacks. Soldiers of Gen. Carnot Posey's brigade were lying inactive between the Plank Road and Catharine Furnace, under a heavy fire, when Lee rode up to them and asked what their unit was. He encouraged them with a verbal salute, "Ah, my brave Mississippians!" and then rode on down the line.[42]

The general next moved toward the narrowing gap between Posey's left and the right of Jackson's troops under Stuart. There he watched the fighting through a field glass in company with a foreign officer as the Confederate lines came together. In an unmilitary aside, Lee waxed philosophical to the observer about the future of the boys and men fighting so hard for him.

"You have before you the elite of our people from sixteen to forty-five years of age. The state is to be made up of them in the future. . . . War is a savage business, and one must accustom the men as well as possible to self-control"[43]

Lee's desperate efforts to reunite the army before Hooker could take advantage of its dreadfully vulnerable state included no tincture of military art. Bigelow aptly criticized the Confederate efforts on 3 May: "A general who should think of adopting the tactics that Lee and Stuart employed . . . should be sure, before doing so, that he realizes the conditions under which these tactics succeeded—the mental collapse of the enemy's commanding general. . . . To try them on a commander in his senses . . . would be to court defeat and invite disaster." On the other hand, the exigencies of the moment, with Jackson's leadership beacon extinguished and the army still divided, called for stern measures. No option existed but to reunite the army by main force.[44]

By 10:00 A.M. the costly job was done and Lee rode into the Chancellorsville clearing amidst his triumphant army. Lee's men realized that they were participants in "the most spectacular episode of the war," as a member of Gen. E. A. Perry's staff wrote, and "the most characteristic and masterful of all [Lee's] battles." Artillery Maj. David Gregg McIntosh wrote: "The troops were wild with excitement and success. The past with its horrors was forgotten, and they knew only the delirium of victory. The welkin rang with shouts and cheers, and the war-worn veterans almost wept for joy." Lee's aide, Walter Taylor, described that when the foot soldiers "caught sight of their general [they] rent the air with their cheers . . . and pushed forward more rapidly, waving their hats on high and calling his name." Charles Marshall's frequently quoted description of the scene presents the most vivid picture of the moment:

> The fierce soldiers with their faces blackened with the smoke of battle, the wounded crawling with feeble limbs from the fury of the devouring flames, all seemed possessed with a common impulse. One long, unbroken cheer, in which the feeble cry of those who lay helpless on the earth blended with the strong voices of those who still fought, rose high above the roar of battle, and hailed the presence of the victorious chief. . . . and as I looked upon him in the complete fruition of the success which his genius, courage, and confidence in his army had won, I thought that it must have been from such a scene that men in ancient days rose to the dignity of gods.[45]

Lee promptly and characteristically set about exploiting the momentum generated by his stirring victory. Hooker's regiments had disappeared in disarray into the woods north of Chancellorsville. The substantial barrier of the Rappahannock behind them might provide an anvil against which Lee could hammer his enemy. Hopes for a more comprehensive victory drained away in reaction to startling news from the rearguard near Fredericksburg: Sedgwick had broken through Early's force and was headed toward Chancellorsville. Lee struggled for a time with the notion of storming Hooker's apparently demoralized army before Sedgwick could reach him but quickly reached the conclusion that he could not expect success enough to warrant the danger. The army commander disappointedly started four brigades in the direction of Fredericksburg under General McLaws's command.[46] A casual examination of the campaign might suggest that Lee confronted his greatest crisis at this moment; but in fact his options were limited. The bitter fruits of Chilton's malfeasance were unpalatable but unavoidable.

The commanding general's demeanor showed little of his frustration over the unexpected development. An English correspondent saw Lee shortly after he received the bad news and found him "calm, unruffled, evenly balanced, but not, even at that time, wholly devoid of that quaint humor of which so rich a vein runs through his composition." As the general galloped past the army's Florida brigade, the troops yelled in tribute, their band hailed him—and enemy artillery fired at the target delineated by the noise. The best gauge of Lee's chagrin at the turn of events that denied him the chance to snap at Hooker's heels shows through a message he sent to Early that evening: "I very much regret the possession of Fredericksburg by the enemy." Early expected Lee's regret, and every Confederate shared it. The mild restatement of the obvious was a typical Lee emphasis by calm iteration.[47]

A sturdy stand by Gen. Cadmus M. Wilcox's brigade of Alabamians against Sedgwick around Salem Church, four miles west of Fredericksburg, stabilized the situation in that quarter. When McLaws's reinforcements closed on Salem Church, the midday crisis of 3 May ended. The next morning Lee reconnoitered Hooker's position north of Chancellorsville again, recognized his inability to affect it, and determined to concentrate instead on Sedgwick. To that end he directed General Anderson and the rest of his division to join McLaws and Wilcox around Salem Church. Before the day was much advanced Lee followed their route eastward in person. Bigelow defined the sequential attack on Hooker on 2–3 May and Sedgwick on the fourth as "a brilliant use of interior lines." Lee deserves credit for bold and efficient execution of his options, but the measure was hardly brilliant. Since the moment word reached Chancellorsville of Sedgwick's success, Lee had had no real choice in the matter (other than to abandon the entire theater, which some lesser men might have done).[48]

Operations on the fourth did not meet Lee's expectations. General

McLaws had wasted no energy preparing to press Sedgwick. Jubal Early had proposed, from the far side of the Federal salient, that he and McLaws cooperate to drive the enemy back to the river. At midnight on the third, Lee sent a message to McLaws approving Early's plan and said, apparently resignedly, that McLaws ought at least to do enough "so as to prevent their concentrating on General Early." When the army commander reached McLaws the next morning, he was disgusted to find that officer calmly doing nothing, when a great deal needed attention. "Probably no man ever commanded an army and, at the same time," attested the sometimes critical Porter Alexander, "so entirely commanded himself, as Lee. This morning was almost the only occasion on which I ever saw him out of humor." The rest of the army heard about the general's display of temper, which reportedly included expressions of "his displeasure in words which bore no uncertain sound."[49]

The lassitude that irritated Lee resulted in delays so lengthy that it was 6:00 P.M. before the combined attack against Sedgwick began. The troops involved did not trust their leaders and Lee had to invigorate them with a personal appearance. Capt. Richard Watson York of the Sixth North Carolina wrote a few years later:

> Rumor had it that Anderson, McLaws, & so on were commanding. I never saw officers & men so utterly and so generally demoralized. I confess I myself to some extent participated. Suddenly we saw passing through the thin woods on the little hill in our rear, Gen. Lee. As soon as his face was well seen, and known to be certainly he, every man instantly commenced getting ready. The word soon went down the line, "All is right, Uncle Robert is here, we will whip them." There was no cheering, the men leaned on their muskets and looked at him, as he rode along his lines, as tho' a God were passing by.[50]

Pressure from Early, Anderson, and McLaws was ample (even though tardily applied) to push Sedgwick back to the Rappahannock and across the river overnight on 4–5 May. Having achieved the objective of clearing the threat from his rear, Lee returned his attention to Hooker's main body waiting "listlessly expectant at Chancellorsville," in the apt phrase of a Northern historian. Lest Sedgwick reprise his role of the previous days, Lee again left Early behind when he led Anderson and McLaws back to Chancellorsville on 5 May through a violent storm. Once back at the battlefield, the commanding general spent the rainy night preparing to assail Hooker anew.[51]

Lee's last decision at Chancellorsville probably was his worst of the campaign. Hooker had enjoyed nearly three days of rest, during which his men had entrenched avidly while Lee's marched and fought. The Federal preponderance in numbers had not been abated by the operations of 1–3 May. Porter Alexander declared that Lee "never in his life took a more audacious resolve than when he determined to assault Hooker's intrenchments." Alexander and many other Confederates viewed the prospect with dismay, but the artillerist admitted that two critically important individuals did believe that, "in spite of all the odds, it would have been victorious. These two persons were Gens. Lee and Hooker."[52]

Hooker destroyed the potential for empirical testing of Lee's final decision at Chancellorsville by retreating under cover of the stormy night. When word reached Confederate headquarters the next morning, Lee "manifested much disappointment at the announcement." Colonel Alexander, on the other hand, thought the news very good indeed: "The enemy had gone! . . . There was to be no bloody assault on those strong entrenchments!" John Bigelow agreed with the analysis from the opposite perspective of a Northerner. "No greater mistake was made during the campaign than Hooker's final one of recrossing the Rappahannock," he wrote in indictment. "Lee was about to play into his hands by attacking him on his own ground."[53]

Alexander and Bigelow may well have been right in their conclusions; each had an excellent track record in military commentary. On the other hand, most of what Lee perpetrated upon poor Hooker that week in the Wilderness went at least as sharply against the grain of military wisdom. The move west to face a triumphant Hooker on 1 May, if not proved apt by success in the field, would have been susceptible to easy, unctuous criticism. Jackson's flank march and attack would have been an even easier mark had it been suspended unfulfilled—to say nothing of how it would have looked if unsuccessful.

Chancellorsville's most important result unfolded four days after Hooker scurried back across the Rappahannock, in an arena beyond Lee's power to control. Stonewall Jackson, the incomparable executive officer and a literally invaluable component of the army's successes, lay in extremis at Guiney Station on 10 May. General Lee told a chaplain that morning that he did not believe God "would take [Jackson] away from his country." With tears in his eyes, Lee told the preacher to tell Stonewall that "he prayed for him last night as he had never prayed for his [own] soul." Jackson died before the message could be delivered, and Lee faced the daunting task of attempting to replace an irreplaceable asset. He never came close to succeeding.[54]

Among the long-term results of Lee's success, despite being outnumbered and hard-pressed at Chancellorsville, was reinforcement of Federal dread of what he might do next. An educated Massachusetts soldier, writing two weeks after Appomattox, characterized the disturbingly ubiquitous Lee as "like a ghost to children, something that haunted us so long." Family members had expressed astonishment at his "want of enthusiasm for Lee's surrender," but the Yankee explained: "It will take me some months to be conscious of this fact,"[55] The establishment of this theaterwide momentum extended the fruits of Chancellorsville across many months and many battlefields.

Confederates contemplating what they had wrought at Chancellorsville considered the results fantastic. Having weathered crisis after crisis against heavy odds, both in numbers and circumstances, they knew they had participated in a remarkable military event. A captain in J. B. Kershaw's brigade was not a voice crying in the wilderness when he wrote simply, "General Robert E. Lee is the greatest living general." Lee himself, of course, said nothing of where the battle fit in his own catalogue of successes. His general orders announcing the victory praised God and the troops and regretted Jackson's fall, all in platitudinous terms. Lee showed his distaste for public utterance on army business by ranking officers when Jubal Early indulged in a newspaper controversy about a small aspect of his Chancellorsville operations. Early wrote in 1868 that Lee issued him "a mild rebuke for that, and I never repeated the offence."[56]

Postwar Confederate writing, free from such constraints, understandably denominated Chancellorsville Lee's greatest victory. Walter H. Taylor wrote in 1878, "Of all the battles fought by the Army . . . Chancellorsville stands first." In a later book he declared, "Chancellorsville perhaps adds greatest luster to [Lee's] fame as a strategist." Col. J. J. Garnett called it "without doubt, the most brilliant of all General Lee's battles." Jed Hotchkiss identified the outcome as the highest point achieved by the Confederates in Virginia. Col. D. G. McIntosh believed that Chancellorsville "proved [Lee] to be a master in the art of war, and [was] his greatest triumph."[57]

Northern military writers played to the same refrain in the decades after the war. Theodore Dodge pointed out the deadly impact of Jackson's loss on Southern fortunes but concluded that even more important to the Confederacy was the performance of Lee—"the greatest in adversity of the soldiers of our civil war." A. C. Hamlin admitted that "the campaign was Lee's masterpiece in audacity and celerity," and "the culminating point" of the Confederate army's attainments. John Bigelow's acclaimed study of the campaign concluded that the victory at Chancellorsville resulted in "the brightest period of the Civil War" for the South. In Lee at Chancellorsville, Bigelow wrote, the Confederacy relied upon "one of the world's great military leaders" and the Civil War's best: "No other commander, North or South, at this or any later stage of the war, had such a creditable military record as his."[58]

Lee opened the campaign with a potentially deadly mistake: he let his foe steal a long march on him, with potentially dire consequences. Once Hooker had achieved his initial success, however, Lee befuddled his opponent with a series of daring decisions. Some of them involved risks of outlandish proportions; all of them succeeded. With too few men to operate in comfort, and an alarmingly narrow range of choices as a result, Lee did things that Hooker could not imagine his doing. In the process he won his greatest victory. "In all history," a British military writer declared near the turn of the century, "[T]here is not recorded a campaign which exemplifies more fully the preponderance of skilful direction over superior numbers than this week's fighting in the forest of Virginia."[59] All of history covers several recorded millennia past, but that writer's judgment may well deserve consideration through centuries to come.

NOTES

1. Pennock Huey, *A True History of the Charge of the Eighth Pennsylvania Cavalry at Chancellorsville* (Philadelphia: Porter & Coates, 1883), 5; John Bigelow Jr., *The Campaign of Chancellorsville* (New Haven, Conn.: Yale University Press, 1910); David Gregg McIntosh, *The Campaign of Chancellorsville* (Richmond, Va.: William Ellis Jones Sons, 1915), 3.

2. Augustus Choate Hamlin, *The Battle of Chancellorsville* (Bangor, Maine: printed by the author, 1896), 6; Hooker testimony in *Report of the Joint Committee on the Conduct of the War at the Second Session Thirty-Eight Congress* (Washington DC: 1865), 5:113 (first collation). The confusing arrangement of the Joint Committee publications includes various designations for volumes and multiple collations within each. This reference is to the volume fifth in the collected series.

3. John S. Mosby, *The Letters of John S. Mosby*, comp. Adele H. Mitchell (n.p.: Stuart-Mosby Historical Society, 1986), 78–79; *Columbus* (Georgia) *Weekly Sun*, 2 September 1862; Sidney Jackson Richardson to parents, 12 May 1863, Georgia Department of Archives and History, Atlanta. Mosby had the Jackson comment on Lee at close secondhand from J. E. B. Stuart.

4. Charles Marshall to Jubal A. Early, 2 March 1883, Jubal A. Early Papers, Library of Congress, Washington, DC.

5. William O. Fleming letter, 20 April 1863, Fleming Papers, Southern Historical Collection, Wilson Library, University of North Carolina, Chapel Hill; Lee to Mary Lee, 24 April 1863, in Robert E. Lee, *The Wartime Papers of R. E. Lee*, ed. Clifford Dowdey and Louis H. Manarin (Boston: Little, Brown, 1961), 439–40.

6. Armistead Lindsay Long, *Memoirs of Robert E. Lee* (New York and Philadelphia: J. M. Stoddart & Company, 1886), 247–48; McIntosh, *Chancellorsville*, 54.

7. U. S. War Department, *The War of the Rebellion: A Compilation of the Official Records of the Union and Confederate Armies*, 127 vols., index, and atlas (Washington DC: GPO, 1880–1901), series 1, vol. 25, pt. 2, p. 658. This work is hereafter cited as *Official Records*, with all references to series 1, vol. 25.

8. McIntosh, *Chancellorsville*, 3; Robert E. Lee, *Lee's Dispatches: Unpublished Letters of General Robert E. Lee, C. S. A., to Jefferson Davis and the War Department of the Confederate States of America, 1862–65*, ed. Douglas Southall Freeman (New York: G. P. Putnam's Sons, 1915), 84–85.

9. Lee, *Wartime Papers*, 441–42; Lee, *Lee's Dispatches*, 84.

10. Sgt. David E. Moore (Rockbridge Artillery) to John W. Daniel, undated, Box 22, folder headed "1907" and "Chancellorsville," John Warwick Daniel Papers, University of Virginia, Charlottesville; *Official Records*, pt. 1, p. 796.

11. *Official Records*, pt. 1, p. 796, and pt. 2, pp. 756–57, 759; Bigelow, *Chancellorsville*, 208–9.

12. *Official Records*, pt. 1, p. 796, and pt. 2, p. 761; Bigelow, *Chancellorsville*, 232.

13. Edward Porter Alexander, *Military Memoirs of a Confederate: A Critical Narrative* (New York: Charles Scribner's Sons, 1907), 324; "Conversations with Gen. R. E. Lee," recorded by William Allan on 15 February 1868 and 19 February 1870, pp. 3–4 and 21 of typescript in William Allan Papers, Southern Historical Collection.

14. McIntosh, *Chancellorsville*, 23; Allan, "Conversations," 20 (19 Feb. 1870); Theodore A. Dodge, *The Campaign of Chancellorsville* (Boston: J. R. Osgood and Company, 1881), 41–42; *Official Records*, pt. 2, p. 762; Lee, *Wartime Papers*, 448–49. The last source also offers an example of the guidance Lee sometimes had to supply to subordinates, as he was reduced to asking wearily if Jackson would help McLaws figure out "who is to relieve his pickets." Dodge's good book has been outstripped by Bigelow's work and by new scholarship, but it remains a solid analytical source, written by the author of a massive and reputable set on Napoleonic military affairs.

15. *Official Records*, pt. 1, p. 797; Dodge, *Chancellorsville*, 43; Edward Porter Alexander, *Fighting for the Confederacy: The Personal Recollections of General Edward Porter Alexander*, ed. Gary W. Gallagher (Chapel Hill: University of North Carolina Press, 1989), 196.

16. *Official Records*, pt. 2, p. 763.

17. McIntosh, *Chancellorsville*, 24; James H. Wilson, *The Campaign of Chancellorsville [April 27–May 5, 1863], by Major John Bigelow Jr., U. S. A.: A Critical Review* (Wilmington, Del.: Chas. L. Story, 1911), 26. Wilson was not yet a general, nor did he participate at Chancellorsville. His analysis of the situation on 1 May, however, is precisely apt.

18. Samuel P. Bates, *The Battle of Chancellorsville* (Meadville, Pa.: Edward T. Bates, 1882), 162.

19. Alexander, *Military Memoirs*, 327; O. O. Howard, "General Robert E. Lee," *Frank Leslie's Popular Magazine* 42 (December 1896): 646; *Report of the Joint Committee*, 5:125 (first collation).

20. Dodge, *Chancellorsville*, 40; Allan, "Conversations," 4 (15 February 1868).

21. *Official Records*, pt. 1, p. 797; Abner Doubleday, *Chancellorsville and Gettysburg* (New York: Charles Scribner's Sons, 1882), 15.

22. Thomas Mann Randolph Talcott, *General Lee's Strategy at the Battle of Chancellorsville* (Richmond, Va.: Wm. Ellis Jones, 1906), 19–20; Fitzhugh Lee, citing Charles Marshall, in J. William Jones, ed., *Army of Northern Virginia Memorial Volume* (Richmond: J. W. Randolph & English, 1880), 315; Bigelow, *Chancellorsville*, 262; *Official Records*, pt. 2, p. 765. The Talcott essay, which also was published under the same title as a pamphlet in Richmond in 1906, is among the most important sources for Lee at Chancellorsville and deserves more attention than it has received. It provides an especially thoughtful appraisal of the various claims about the origination of Jackson's flank march and attack on 2 May.

23. Talcott, *Lee's Strategy*, 19; memorandum by Jedediah Hotchkiss based on conversation with James Power Smith, Roll 36, Hotchkiss Papers, Library of Congress; Henry Kyd Douglas, *I Rode With Stonewall* (Chapel Hill: University of North Carolina Press, 1940), 220; Long, *Memoirs*, 252; *Official Records*, pt. 1, pp. 797–8; Bigelow, *Chancellorsville*, 263. Smith noted that when he reported, Lee, in the fashion he often used to tease young staff officers, demanded to know why Smith and his comrades "had allowed Gen. Jackson to be annoyed during the afternoon by shots from a piece of Federal artillery."

24. Talcott, *Lee's Strategy*, 20; Bigelow, *Chancellorsville*, 262; Fitzhugh Lee in Jones, ed., *Memorial Volume*, 315. Bigelow specifically suggests the influence of A. R. Wright's success on the railroad. In his report, Lee mentioned Wright's attack only in its place during the 1 May chronology (*Official Records*, pt. 1, p. 797).

25. James Power Smith, *Stonewall Jackson and Chancellorsville* (Richmond: R. E. Lee Camp #1, Confederate Veterans, 1904), 17; Douglas, *I Rode with Stonewall*, 220; Joseph Morrison to "My dear Sir," 29 October 1863, Charles William Dabney Papers, Southern Historical Collection. Morrison's account also declares that Lee preferred an attack in front, which he clearly did not; this error detracts from the aide's credibility.

26. Robert L. Dabney, *Life and Campaigns of Lieut.-Gen. Thomas J. Jackson* (New York: Blelock & Company, 1866), 672–75.

27. Long, *Memoirs*, 252–54; Jones, ed., *Memorial Volume*, 315; Walter H. Taylor, *Four Years with General Lee* (New York: D. Appleton and Company, 1878), 85. In a book three decades later, Taylor—perhaps in a fit of conciliatory zeal—wrote, "No one can say which of the two first suggested the movement," then intimated that it must have been Lee. Walter H. Taylor, *General Lee, His Campaigns in Virginia* (Norfolk, Va.: for sale by the Nusbaum Book and News Company [printed by Press of Braunworth & Company of Brooklyn, New York], 1906), 165.

28. *Official Records*, pt. 1, p. 798.

29. Lee to A. T. Bledsoe, 28 October 1867, in Long, *Memoirs*, 253–54; Lee to Mrs. T. J. Jackson, 25 January 1866, Roll 5, Jedediah Hotchkiss Papers, Library of Congress. Lee told Mary Anna Jackson in a passage typical of his conciliatory attitude that he wished Dabney had "treated certain points more mildly."

30. Talcott, *Lee's Strategy*, 4; Dodge, *Chancellorsville*, 63; John J. Garnett, "General Robert E. Lee," *Frank Leslie's Popular Monthly* 42 (July 1896), 10; Bigelow, *Chancellorsville*, 264.

31. Talcott, *Lee's Strategy*, 19; Smith, *Stonewall Jackson*, 18; Morrison letter, 29 October 1863 (for Hill's presence); Dodge, *Chancellorsville*, 62.

32. Talcott, *Lee's Strategy*, 7–8, 10, 12. The suggestion that Lee's query at this very late juncture, "What do you propose to do?," indicated deference to Jackson's wishes, founders on the rest of the stilted exchange. Lee hardly needed Jackson's help, for instance, in figuring out who would be left to him if all of Jackson's corps went on the mission.

33. Taylor, *General Lee*, 166; Alexander, *Fighting for the Confederacy*, 199; Alexander, *Military Memoirs*, 328–29; A. H. Nelson, *The Battles of Chancellorsville and Gettysburg* (Minneapolis: Alanson H. Nelson, 1899), 32.

34. Wilson, *Chancellorsville*, 32; Bates, *Chancellorsville*, 191; Dodge, *Chancellorsville*, 64. Dodge pointed out cogently in mitigating his criticism that "in case of failure, each wing had open ground and good roads for retreat, to form a junction towards Gordonsville."

35. Nelson, *Chancellorsville*, 32; Dodge, *Chancellorsville*, 63–64.

36. Bigelow, *Chancellorsville*, 374,

37. James Reid Cole, *Miscellany* (Dallas: Ewing B. Bedford Press, 1897), 217; Bigelow, *Chancellorsville*, 278; Justus Scheibert, *Seven Months in the Rebel States During the North American War, 1863* (Tuscaloosa, Ala.: Confederate Publishing Company, 1958), 75n.

38. *Official Records*, pt. 2, p. 765; Bigelow, *Chancellorsville*, 484.

39. Colonel Everard Meade Field (Twelfth Virginia) in George S. Bernard, comp., *War Talks of Confederate Veterans* (Petersburg, Va.: Fenn & Owen, 1892), 71–73; *Official Records*, pt. 2, p. 799.

40. R. E. Wilbourn to R. L. Dabney, 12 December 1863, Charles William Dabney Papers, Southern Historical Collection; Jedediah Hotchkiss, *Make Me a Map of the Valley: The Civil War Journal of Stonewall Jackson's Cartographer* (Dallas: Southern Methodist University Press, 1973), 138.

41. Wilbourn letter, 12 December 1863; Hotchkiss, *Make Me a Map*, 138–39; *Official Records*, pt. 2, p. 769.

42. Charles Marshall, *An Aide-de-Camp of Lee*, ed. Sir Frederick Maurice (Boston: Little, Brown, 1927), 172; Frank H. Foote, "Chancellorsville, Part Borne in That Struggle by Posey's Mississippi Brigade," *Philadelphia Weekly Times*, 8 August 1885.

43. Scheibert, *Seven Months*, 70, 75–76. The Prussian also described in his narrative some exciting episodes that occurred near Lee.

44. Bigelow, *Chancellorsville*, 375.

45. *Official Records*, pt. 1, p. 800; Alfred Lewis Scott memoir, 16, Virginia Historical Society, Richmond; McIntosh, *Chancellorsville*, 48; Taylor, *General Lee*, 177: Marshall, *Aide-de-Camp*, 172–73.

46. McIntosh, *Chancellorsville*, 49; Scheibert, *Seven Months*, 73; *Official Records*, pt. 1, p. 800–801. Lee's language in his report about hopes to renew the attack is: "Our preparations were just completed when further operations were arrested by intelligence received from Fredericksburg."

47. London *Times*, 16 June 1863; Alfred Lewis Scott memoir, 18, Virginia Historical Society; *Official Records*, pt. 2, pp. 769–70.

48. *Official Records*, pt. 1, p. 802; Hotchkiss and Allan, *Chancellorsville*, 91–92; Bigelow, *Chancellorsville*, 482.

49. *Official Records*, pt. 2, p. 770; Alexander, *Military Memoirs*, 356; Alexander, *Fighting for the Confederacy*, 213; McIntosh, *Chancellorsville*, 57.

50. *Official Records*, pt. 1, p. 802; Alexander, *Military Memoirs*, 357; R. W. York to G. W. Custis Lee, 28 November 1872, Private Collection of Vicki Heilig, Germantown, Maryland. York became major of his regiment two months after Chancellorsville.

51. Dodge, *Chancellorsville*, 208; *Official Records*, pt. 1, p. 802.

52. Alexander, *Military Memoirs*, 358.

53. McIntosh, *Chancellorsville*, 58; Alexander, *Fighting for the Confederacy*, 215; Bigelow, *Chancellorsville*, 482. A gauge of Alexander's relief is that, while he normally was not given to gushing in prose, he used seven exclamation points in this passage within less than four printed lines.

54. Everard H. Smith, ed., "The Civil War Diary of Peter W. Hairston," *North Carolina Historical Review* 67 (January 1990): 77. Porter Alexander (*Military Memoirs*, 360) argued fervently that J. E. B. Stuart should have been promoted to fill the vacancy.

55. Stephen M. Weld, *War Diary and Letters of Stephen Minot Weld* (Cambridge, Mass.: privately printed, 1911), 396.

56. Thomas J. Warren letter, 10 May 1863, Warren Papers, South Caroliniana Library, University of South Carolina, Columbia; *Official Records*, pt. 1, p. 805; Jubal A. Early to R. E. Lee, 20 November 1868, Box 25, undated folder, John W. Daniel Papers, University of Virginia.

57. Taylor, *Four Years*, 83; Taylor, *General Lee*, 173; Garnett, "Lee," 13; Hotchkiss and Allan, *Chancellorsville*, 114; McIntosh, *Chancellorsville*, 4.

58. Dodge, *Chancellorsville*, 123; Hamlin, *Chancellorsville*, ix; Bigelow, *Chancellorsville*, 488, 12.

59. Cecil Battine, *The Crisis of the Confederacy* (London: Longmans, Green, and Company, 1905), 95.

Lee in Pennsylvania

GENERAL JAMES LONGSTREET

It has been my purpose for some years to give to the public a detailed history of the campaign of Gettysburg from its inception to its disastrous close. The execution of this task has been delayed by reason of a press of personal business, and by reason of a genuine reluctance that I have felt against anything that might, even by implication, impugn the wisdom of my late comrades in arms. My sincere feeling upon this subject is best expressed in the following letter, which was written shortly after the battle of Gettysburg, when there was a sly undercurrent of misrepresentation of my course, and in response to an appeal from a respected relative, that I would make some reply to my accusers:

> CAMP, CULPEPPER COURT-HOUSE, July 24th, 1863.
>
> *My Dear Uncle:*—Your letters of the 13th and 14th were received on yesterday. As to our late battle I cannot say much. I have no right to say anything, in fact, but will venture a little for you, alone. If it goes to aunt and cousins it must be under promise that it will go no further. The battle was not made as I would have made it. My idea was to throw ourselves between the enemy and Washington, select a strong position, and force the enemy to attack us. So far as is given to man the ability to judge, we may say, with confidence, that we should have destroyed the Federal army, marched into Washington and dictated our terms, or, at least, held Washington, and marched over as much of Pennsylvania as we cared to, had we drawn the enemy into attack upon our carefully-chosen position in its rear. General Lee chose the plans adopted; and he is the person appointed to choose and to order. I consider it a part of my duty to express my views to the commanding general. If he approves and adopts them, it is well; if he does not, it is my duty to adopt his views, and to execute his orders as faithfully as if they were my own. I cannot help but think that great results would have been obtained had my views been thought better of; yet I am much inclined to accept the present condition as for the best. I hope and trust that it is so. Your programme would all be well

enough, had it been practicable, and was duly thought of, too. I fancy that no good ideas upon that campaign will be mentioned at any time, that did not receive their share of consideration by General Lee. The few things that he might have overlooked himself were, I believe, suggested by myself. As we failed, I must take my share of the responsibility. In fact, I would prefer that all the blame should rest upon me. As General Lee is our commander, he should have the support and influence we can give him. If the blame, if there is any, can be shifted from him to me, I shall help him and our cause by taking it. I desire, therefore, that all the responsibility that can be put upon me shall go there, and shall remain there. The truth will be known in time, and I leave that to show how much of the responsibility of Gettysburg rests on my shoulders.

Most affectionately yours,

J. LONGSTREET.

To A. B. LONGSTREET, LL.D., Columbus, Ga.

I sincerely regret that I cannot still rest upon that letter. But I have been so repeatedly and so rancorously assailed by those whose intimacy with the commanding general in that battle gave an apparent importance to their assaults, that I feel impelled by a sense of duty to give to the public a full and comprehensive narration of the campaign from its beginning to its end; especially when I reflect that the publication of the truth cannot now, as it might have done then, injure the cause for which we fought the battle. The request that I furnish this history to the WEEKLY TIMES comes opportunely, for the appeal just made through the press by a distinguished foreigner for all the information that will develop the causes of the failure of that campaign, has provoked anew its partisan and desultory discussion, and renders a plain and logical recital of the facts both timely and important.

After the defeat of Burnside at Fredericksburg, in December, it was believed that active operations were over for the winter, and I was sent with two divisions of my corps to the eastern shore of Virginia, where I could find food for my men during the winter, and send supplies to the Army of Northern Virginia. I spent several months in this department, keeping the enemy close within his fortifications, and foraging with little trouble and great success. On May 1st, I received orders to report to General Lee at Fredericksburg. General Hooker had begun to throw his army across the Rappahannock, and the active campaign was opening. I left Suffolk as soon as possible, and hurried my troops forward. Passing through Richmond, I called to pay my respects to Mr. Seddon, the Secretary of War. Mr. Seddon was, at the time of my visit, deeply considering the critical condition of Pemberton's army at Vicksburg, around which General Grant was then decisively drawing his lines. He informed me that he had in contemplation a plan for concentrating a succoring army at Jackson, Mississippi, under the command of General Johnston, with a view of driving Grant from before Vicksburg by a direct issue-at-arms. He suggested that possibly my corps might be needed to make the army strong enough to handle Grant, and asked me my views. I replied that there was a better plan, in my judgment, for relieving Vicksburg than by a direct assault upon Grant. I proposed that the army then concentrating at Jackson, Mississippi, be moved swiftly to Tullahoma, where General Bragg was then located with a fine army, confronting an army of about equal strength under General Rosecrans, and that at the same time the two divisions of my corps be hurried forward to the same point. The simultaneous arrival of these reinforcements would give us a grand army at Tullahoma. With this army General Johnston might speedily crush Rosecrans, and that he should then turn his force toward the north, and with his splendid army march through Tennessee and Kentucky, and threaten the invasion of Ohio. My idea was that, in the march through those States, the army would meet no organized obstruction; would be supplied with provisions and even reinforcements by those friendly to our cause, and would inevitably result in drawing Grant's army from Vicksburg to look after and protect his own territory. Mr. Seddon adhered to his original views; not so much, I think, from his great confidence in them, as from the difficulty of withdrawing the force suggested from General Lee's army. I was very thoroughly impressed with the practicability of the plan, however, and when I reached General Lee I laid it before him with the freedom justified by our close personal and official relations. The idea seemed to be a new one to him, but he was evidently seriously impressed with it. We discussed it over and over, and I discovered that his main objection to it was that it would, if adopted, force him to divide his army. He left no room to doubt, however, that he believed the idea of an offensive campaign was not only important, but necessary.

At length, while we were discussing the idea of a western forward movement, he asked me if I did not think an invasion of Maryland and Pennsylvania by his own army would accomplish the same result, and I replied that I did not see that it would, because this movement would be too hazardous, and the campaign in thoroughly Union States would require more time and greater preparation than one through Tennessee and Kentucky. I soon discovered that he had determined that he would make some forward movement, and I finally assented that the Pennsylvania campaign might be brought to a successful issue if he could make it offensive in strategy, but defensive in tactics. This point was urged with great persistency. I suggested that, after piercing Pennsylvania and menacing Washington, we should choose a strong position, and force the Federals to attack us, observing that the popular clamor throughout the North would speedily force the Federal general to attempt to drive us out. I recalled to him the battle of Fredericksburg as an instance of a defensive battle, when, with a few thousand men, we hurled the whole Federal army back, crippling and demoralizing it, with trifling loss to our own troops; and Chancellorsville as an instance of an offensive battle, where we dislodged the Federals, it is true, but at such a terrible sacrifice that half a dozen such victories would have ruined us. It will be remembered that Stonewall Jackson once said that "we sometimes fail to drive the enemy from a position. They always fail to drive us." I reminded him, too, of Napoleon's advice to Marmont, to whom he said, when putting him at the head of an invading army, "Select your ground, and make your enemy attack you." I recall these points, simply because I desire to have it distinctly understood that, while I first suggested to General Lee the idea of an offensive campaign, I was never persuaded to yield my argument against the Gettysburg campaign, except with the understanding that we were not to deliver an offensive battle, but to so maneuvre that the enemy should be forced to attack us—or, to repeat, that our campaign should be one of offensive strategy, but defensive tactics. Upon this understanding my assent was given, and General Lee, who had been kind enough to discuss the matter with me patiently, gave the order of march.

The movement was begun on the 3d of June. McLaws' Division of my corps moved out of Fredericksburg, for Culpepper Court House, followed by Ewell's Corps, on the 4th and 5th of June. Hood's Division and Stuart's cavalry moved at the same time. On the 8th, we found two full corps (for Pickett's Division had joined me then), and Stuart's cavalry, concentrated at Culpepper Court House. In the meantime a large force of the Federals, cavalry and infantry, had been thrown across the Rappahannock, and sent to attack General Stuart. They were encountered at Brandy Station, on the morning of the 9th, and repulsed. General Lee says of this engagement: "On the 9th, a large force of Federal cavalry, strongly supported by infantry, crossed the Rappahannock at Beverly's ford, and attacked General Stuart. A severe engagement ensued, continuing from early in the morning until late in the afternoon, when the enemy was forced to recross the river with heavy loss, leaving four hundred prisoners, three pieces of artillery, and several colors in our hands." The failure of General Lee to follow up his advantage by pouring the heavy force concentrated at Culpepper Court House upon this detachment of the Federals, confirmed my convictions that he had determined to make a defensive battle, and would not allow any casual advantage to precipitate a general engagement. If he had had any idea of abandoning the original plan of a tactical defensive, then, in my judgment, was the time to have done so. While at Culpepper, I sent a trusty scout (who had been sent to me by Secretary Seddon, while I was at Suffolk), with instructions to go into the Federal lines, discover his policy, and bring me all the information he could possibly pick up. When this scout asked me very significantly where he should report, I replied: "Find me, wherever I am, when you have the desired information." I did this because I feared to trust him with a knowledge of our future movements. I supplied him with all the gold he needed, and instructed him to spare neither pains nor money to obtain full and accurate information. The information gathered by this scout led to the most tremendous results, as will soon be seen.

General A. P. Hill, having left Fredericksburg as soon as the enemy had retired from his front, was sent to follow Ewell, who had marched up the Valley and cleared it of the Federals. My corps left Culpepper on the 15th, and with a view of covering the march of Hill and Ewell through the Valley, moved along the east side of the Blue Ridge, and occupied Snicker's and Ashby's gaps, and the line of the Blue Ridge. General Stuart was in my front and on my flank, reconnoitering the movements of the Federals. When it was found that Hooker did not intend to attack, I withdrew to the west side, and marched to the Potomac. As I was leaving the Blue Ridge, I instructed General Stuart to follow me, and to cross the Potomac at Shepherdstown, while I crossed at Williamsport, ten miles above. In reply to these instructions, General Stuart informed me that he had discretionary powers from General Lee; whereupon I withdrew. General Stuart held the gap for a while, and then hurried around beyond Hooker's army, and we saw nothing more of him until the evening of the 2d of July, when he came down from York and joined us, having made a complete circuit of the Federal army. The absence of Stuart's cavalry from the main body of the army, during the march, is claimed to have been a fatal error, as General Lee says: "No report had been received (on the 27th) that the enemy had crossed the Potomac, and the absence of the cavalry rendered it impossible to obtain accurate information." The army, therefore, moved forward, as a man might walk over strange ground with his eyes shut. General Lee says of his orders to Stuart: "General Stuart was left to guard the passes of the mountains and to observe the movements of the enemy, who he was instructed to harass and impede as much as possible, should he attempt to cross the Potomac. In that event, General Stuart was directed to move into Maryland, crossing the Potomac on the east or west of the Blue Ridge, as in his judgment should be best, and take position on the right of our column as it advanced."

My corps crossed the Potomac at Williamsport, and General A. P. Hill crossed at Shepherdstown. Our columns were joined together at Hagerstown, and we marched thence into Pennsylvania, reaching Chambersburg

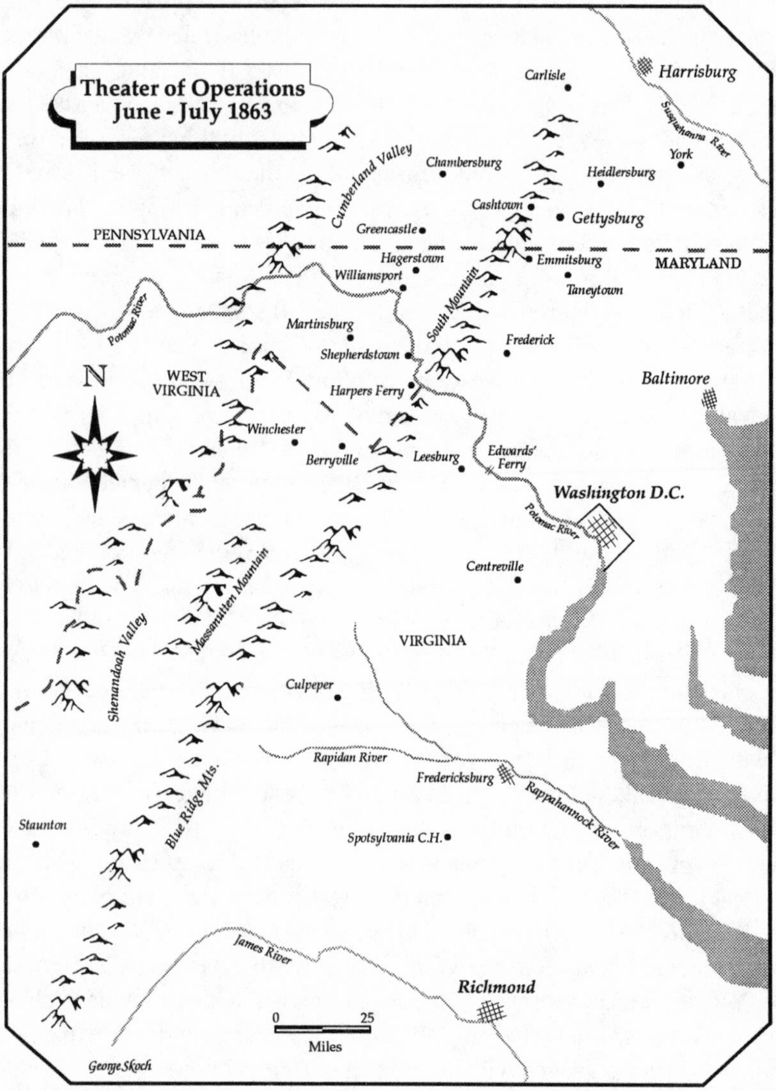

on the evening of the 27th. At this point, on the night of the 29th, information was received by which the whole plan of the campaign was changed. We had not heard from the enemy for several days, and General Lee was in doubt as to where he was; indeed, we did not know that he had yet left Virginia. At about ten o'clock that night, Colonel Sorrell, my chief-of-staff, was waked by an orderly, who reported that a suspicious person had just been arrested by the provost marshal. Upon investigation, Sorrell discovered that the suspicious person was the scout Harrison that I had sent out at Culpepper. He was dirt-stained, travel-worn, and very much broken down. After questioning him sufficiently to find that he brought very important information, Colonel Sorrell brought him to my headquarters and awoke me. He gave the information that the enemy had crossed the Potomac, marched northwest, and that the head of his column was at Frederick City, on our right. I felt that this information was exceedingly important, and might involve a change in the direction of our march. General Lee had already issued orders that we were to advance toward Harrisburg. I at once sent the scout to General Lee's headquarters, and followed him myself early in the morning. I found General Lee up, and asked him if the information brought by the scout might not involve a change of direction of the head of our column to the right. He immediately acquiesced in the suggestion, possibly saying that he had already given orders to that effect. The movement toward the enemy was begun at once. Hill marched toward Gettysburg, and my corps followed, with the exception of Pickett's Division, which was left at Chambersburg by General Lee's orders. Ewell was recalled from above—he having advanced as far as Carlisle. I was with General Lee most of that day (the 30th). At about noon, the road in front of my corps was blocked by Hill's Corps and Ewell's wagon train, which had cut into the road from above. The orders were to allow these trains to precede us, and that we should go into camp at Greenwood, about ten miles from Chambersburg. My infantry was forced to remain in Greenwood until late in the afternoon of the 1st; my artillery did not get the road until two o'clock on the morning of the 2d.

General Lee spent the night with us, establishing his headquarters, as he frequently did, a short distance from mine. General Lee says of the movements of this day: "Preparation had been made to advance upon Harrisburg; but, on the night of the 29th, information was received from a scout that the enemy had crossed the Potomac, was advancing northward, and that the head of his column had already reached South Mountain. As our communication with the Potomac were thus menaced, it was resolved to prevent its further progress in that direction by concentrating our army on the east side of the mountains." On the morning of the 1st, General Lee and myself left his headquarters together, and had ridden three or four miles, when we heard heavy firing along Hill's front. The firing became so heavy that General Lee left me and hurried forward to see what it meant. After attending to some details of my march, I followed. The firing proceeded from the engagement between our advance and Reynold's Corps, in which the Federals were repulsed. This rencontre was totally unexpected on both sides. As an evidence of the doubt in which General Lee was enveloped, and the anxiety that weighed him down during the afternoon, I quote from General R. H. Anderson the report of a conversation had with him during the engagement. General Anderson was resting with his division at Cashtown, awaiting orders. About ten o'clock in the morning he received a message notifying him that General Lee desired to see him. He found General Lee intently listening to the fire of the guns, and very much disturbed and depressed. At length he said, more to himself than to General Anderson: "I cannot think what has become of Stuart; I ought to have heard from him long before now. He may have met with disaster, but I hope not. In the absence of reports from him, I am in ignorance as to what we have in front of us here. It may be the whole Federal army, or it may be only a detachment. If it is the whole Federal force we must fight a battle here; if we do not gain a victory, those defiles and gorges through which we passed this morning will shelter us from disaster."

When I overtook General Lee, at five o'clock that afternoon, he said, to my surprise, that he thought of attacking General Meade upon the heights the next day. I suggested that this course seemed to be at variance with the plan of the campaign that had been agreed upon before leaving Fredericksburg. He said: "If the enemy is there to-morrow, we must attack him." I replied: "If he is there, it will be because he is anxious that we should attack him—a good reason, in my judgment, for not doing so." I urged that we should move around by our right to the left of Meade, and put our army between him and Washington, threatening his left and rear, and thus force him to attack us in such position as we might select. I said that it seemed to me that if, during our council at Fredericksburg, we had described the position in which we desired to get the two armies, we could not have expected to get the enemy in a better position for us than that he then occupied; that he was in strong position and would be awaiting us, which was evidence that he desired that we should attack him. I said, further, that his weak point seemed to be his left; hence, I though that we should move around to his left, that we might threaten it if we intended to maneuvre, or attack it if we determined upon a battle. I called his attention to the fact that the country was admirably adapted for a defensive battle, and that we should surely repulse Meade with crushing loss if we would take position so as to force him to attack us, and suggested that, even if we carried the heights in front of us, and drove Meade out, we should be so badly crippled that we could not reap the fruits of victory; and that the heights of Gettysburg were, in themselves, of no more importance to us than the ground we then occupied, and that the mere possession of the ground was not worth a hundred men to us. That Meade's army, not its position, was our objective. General Lee was impressed with the idea that, by attacking the Federals, he could whip them in detail. I reminded him that if the Federals were there in the morning, it would be proof that they had their forces well in hand, and that with Pickett in Chambersburg, and Stuart out of reach, we should be somewhat in detail. He, however, did not seem to abandon the idea of attack on the next day. He seemed under a subdued excitement, which occasionally took possession of him when "the hunt was up," and threatened his superb equipoise. The sharp battle fought by Hill and Ewell on that day had given him a taste of victory. Upon this point I quote General Fitzhugh Lee, who says, speaking of the attack on the 3d: "He told the father of the writer [his brother] that he was controlled too far by the great confidence he felt in the fighting qualities of his people, who begged simply to be 'turned loose,' and by the assurances of most of his higher officers." I left General Lee quite late on the night of the 1st. Speaking of the battle on the 2d, General Lee says, in his official report: "It had not been intended to fight a general battle at such a distance from our base, unless attacked by the enemy; but, finding ourselves unexpectedly confronted by the Federal army, it became a matter of difficulty to withdraw through the mountains with our large trains."

When I left General Lee on the night of the 1st, I believed that he had made up his mind to attack, but was confident that he had not yet determined as to when the attack should be made. The assertion first made by General Pendleton, and echoed by his confederates, that I was ordered to open the attack at sunrise, is totally false. Documentary testimony upon this point will be presented in the course of this article. Suffice it to say, at present, that General Lee never, in his life, gave me orders to open an attack at a specific hour. He was perfectly satisfied that, when I had my troops in position, and was ordered to attack, no time was ever lost. On the night of the 1st I left him without any orders at all. On the morning of the 2d, I went to General Lee's headquarters at daylight, and renewed my views against making an attack. He seemed resolved, however, and we discussed the probable results. We observed the position of the Federals, and got a general idea of the nature of the ground. About sunrise General Lee sent Colonel Venable, of his staff, to General Ewell's headquarters, ordering him to make a reconnoissance of the ground in his front, with a view of making the main attack on his left. A short time afterward he followed Colonel Venable in person. He returned at about nine o'clock, and informed me that it would not do to have Ewell open the attack. He, finally, determined that I should make the main attack on the extreme right. It was fully eleven o'clock when General Lee arrived at this conclusion and ordered the movement. In the meantime, by General Lee's authority, Law's Brigade, which had been put upon picket duty, was ordered to rejoin my command, and, upon my suggestion that it would be better to await its arrival, General Lee assented. We waited about forty minutes for these troops, and then moved forward. A delay of several hours occurred in the march of the troops. The cause of this delay was that we had been ordered by General Lee to proceed cautiously upon the forward movement, so as to avoid being seen by the enemy. General Lee ordered Colonel Johnston, of his engineer corps, to lead and conduct the head of the column. My troops, therefore, moved forward under guidance of a special officer of General Lee, and with instructions to follow his directions. I left General Lee only after the line had stretched out on the march, and rode along with Hood's Division, which was in the rear. The march was necessarily slow, the conductor frequently encountering points that exposed the troops to the view of the signal station on Round Top. At length the column halted. After waiting some time, supposing that it would soon move forward, I sent to the front to inquire the occasion of the delay. It was reported that the column was awaiting the movements of Colonel Johnston, who was trying to lead it by some route by which it could pursue its march without falling under view of the Federal signal station. Looking up toward Round Top I saw that the signal station was in full view, and, as we could plainly see this station, it was apparent that our heavy columns was seen from their position, and that further efforts to conceal ourselves would be a waste of time.

I became very impatient at this delay, and determined to take upon myself the responsibility of hurrying the troops forward. I did not order General McLaws forward, because, as the head of the column, he had direct orders from General Lee to follow the conduct of Colonel Johnston. Therefore, I sent orders to Hood, who was in the rear and not encumbered by these instructions, to push his division forward by the most direct route, so as to take position on my right. He did so, and thus broke up the delay. The troops were rapidly thrown into position, and preparations were made for the attack. It may be proper just here to consider the relative strength and position of the two armies. Our army was fifty-two thousand infantry; Meade's was ninety-five thousand. These are our highest figures, and the enemy's lowest. We had learned on the night of the 1st, from some prisoners captured near Seminary Ridge, that the First, Eleventh, and Third Corps had arrived by the Emmetsburg road, and had taken position on the heights in front of us, and that reinforcements had been seen coming by the Baltimore road, just after the fight of the 1st. From an intercepted dispatch, we learned that another corps was in camp, about four miles from the field. We had every reason, therefore, to believe that the Federals were prepared to renew the battle. Our army was stretched in an elliptical curve, reaching from the front of Round Top around Seminary Ridge, and enveloping Cemetery Heights on the left; thus covering a space of four or five miles. The enemy

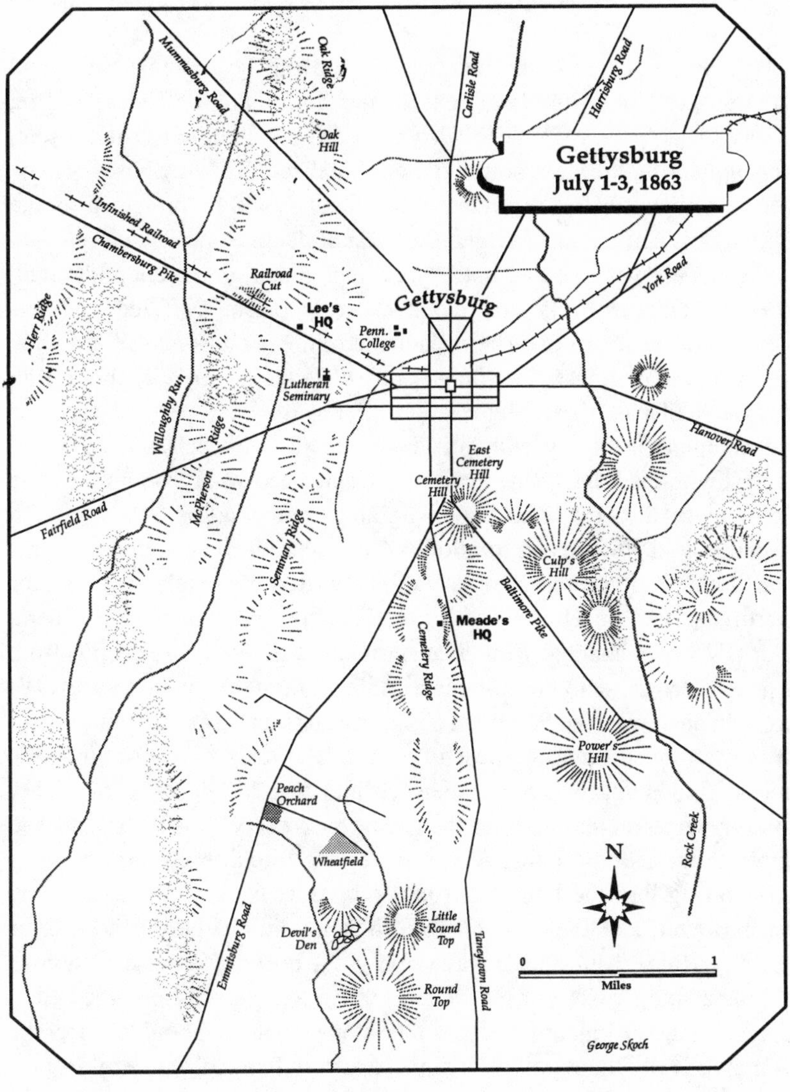

occupied the high ground in front of us, being massed within a curve of about two miles, nearly concentric with the curve described by our forces. His line was about one thousand four hundred yards from ours. Any one will see that the proposition for this inferior force to assault and drive out the masses of troops upon the heights, was a very problematical one. My orders from General Lee were "to envelop the enemy's left, and begin the attack there, following up, as near as possible, the direction of the Emmetsburg road."

My corps occupied our right, with Hood on the extreme right, and McLaws next. Hill's Corps was next to mine, in front of the Federal centre, and Ewell was on our extreme left. My corps, with Pickett's Division absent, numbered hardly thirteen thousand men. I realized that the fight was to be a fearful one; but being assured that my flank would be protected by the brigades of Wilcox, Perry, Wright, Posey, and Mahone, moving *en echelon,* and that Ewell was to co-operate by a direct attack on the enemy's right, and Hill to threaten his centre, and attack if opportunity offered, and thus prevent reinforcements from being launched either against myself or Ewell, it seemed possible that we might possibly dislodge the great army in front of us. At half-past three o'clock the order was given General Hood to advance upon the enemy, and, hurrying to the head of McLaws' Division, I moved with his line. Then was fairly commenced what I do not hesitate to pronounce the best three hours' fighting ever done by any troops on any battle-field. Directly in front of us, occupying the peach orchard, on a piece of elevated ground that General Lee desired me to take and hold for his artillery, was the Third Corps of the Federals, commanded by General Sickles. My men charged with great spirit and dislodged the Federals from the peach orchard with but little delay, though they fought stubbornly. We were then on the crest of Seminary Ridge. The artillery was brought forward and put into position at the peach orchard. The infantry swept down the slope and soon reached the marshy ground that lay between Seminary and Cemetery Ridges, fighting their way over every foot of ground and against overwhelming odds. At every step we found that reinforcements were pouring into the Federals from every side. Nothing could stop my men, however, and they commenced their heroic charge up the side of Cemetery Ridge. Our attack was to progress in the general direction of the Emmetsburg road, but the Federal troops, as they were forced from point to point, availing themselves of the stone fences and boulders near the mountain as rallying points, so annoyed our right flank that General Hood's Division was obliged to make a partial change of front so as to relieve itself of this galling flank fire. This drew General McLaws a little further to the right than General Lee had anticipated, so that the defensive advantages of the ground enabled the Federals to delay our purposes until they could occupy Little Round Top, which they just then discovered was the key to their position. The force thrown upon this point was so strong as to seize our right, as it were, in a vice.

Still the battle on our main line continued to progress. The situation was a critical one. My corps had been fighting over an hour, having encountered and driven back line after line of the enemy. In front of them was a high and rugged ridge, on its crest the bulk of the Army of the Potomac, numbering six to one, and securely resting behind strong positions. My brave fellows never hesitated, however. Their duty was in front of them and they met it. They charged up the hill in splendid style, sweeping everything before them, dislodging the enemy in the face of a withering fire. When they had fairly started up the second ridge, I discovered that they were suffering terribly from a fire that swept over their right and left flanks. I also found that my left flank was not protected by the brigades that were to move *en echelon* with it. McLaws' line was consequently spread out to the left to protect its flank, and Hood's line was extended to the right to protect its flank from the sweeping fire of the large bodies of troops that were posted on Round Top.[1] These two movements of extension so drew my forces out, that I found myself attacking Cemetery Hill with a single line of battle against no less than fifty thousand troops.

My two divisions at that time were cut down to eight or nine thousand men, four thousand having been killed or wounded. We felt at every step the heavy stroke of fresh troops—the sturdy regular blow that tells a soldier instantly that he has encountered reserves or reinforcements. We received no support at all, and there was no evidence of co-operation on any side. To urge my men forward under these circumstances would have been madness, and I withdrew them in good order to the peach orchard that we had taken from the Federals early in the afternoon. It may be mentioned here, as illustrative of the dauntless spirit of these men, that when General Humphreys (of Mississippi) was ordered to withdraw his troops from the charge, he thought there was some mistake, and retired to a captured battery, near the swale between the two ridges, where he halted, and when ordered to retire to the new line a second time, he did so under protest.[2] Our men had no thought of retreat. They broke every line they encountered. When the order to withdraw was given, a courier was sent to General Lee, informing him of the result of the day's work.

Before pursuing this narrative further, I shall say a word or two concerning this assault. I am satisfied that my force, numbering hardly thirteen thousand men, encountered during that three and a half hours of bloody work not less than sixty-five thousand of the Federals, and yet their charge was not checked nor their line broken until we ordered them to withdraw. Mr. Whitelaw Reid, writing a most excellent account of this charge to the Cincinnati *Gazette,* says: "It was believed, from the terrific attack, that the whole rebel army, Ewell's Corps included, was massed on our centre and left, and so a single brigade was left to hold the rifle-pits on the right, and the rest hurried across the little neck of land to strengthen our weakening lines." He describes, too, the haste with which corps after corps was hurried forward to the left to check the advance of my two-thirds of one corps. General Meade himself testifies (see his official report) that the Third, the Second, the Fifth, the Sixth, and the Eleventh Corps, all of the Twelfth, except one brigade, and part of the First Corps, engaged my handful of heroes during that glorious but disastrous afternoon. I found that night that four thousand five hundred and twenty-nine of my men, more than one-third of their total number, had been left on the field. History records no parallel to the fight made by these two divisions on the 2d of July at Gettysburg. I cannot refrain from inserting just here an account of the battle of the 2d, taken from a graphic account in the New York *World.* It will be seen that the correspondent treats the charge of my thirteen thousand men, as if it were the charge of the whole army. The account is as follows:

> He then began a heavy fire on Cemetery Hill. It must not be thought that this wrathful fire was unanswered. Our artillery began to play within a few moments, and hurled back defiance and like destruction upon the rebel lines. Until six o'clock the roar of cannon, the rush of missiles, and the bursting of bombs filled all the air. The clangor alone of this awful combat might well have confused and awed a less cool and watchful commander than General Meade. It did not confuse him. With the calculation of a tactician, and the eye of an experienced judge, he watched from his headquarters, on the hill, whatever movement under the murky cloud which enveloped the rebel lines might first disclose the intention which it was evident this artillery firing covered. About six o'clock P.M. silence, deep, awfully impressive, but momentary, was permitted, as if by magic, to dwell upon the field. Only the groans—unheard before—of the wounded and dying, only a murmur, a warning memory of the breeze through the foliage; only the low rattle of preparation of what was to come embroidered this blank stillness. Then, as the smoke beyond the village was lightly borne to the eastward, the woods on the left were seen filled with dark masses of infantry, three columns deep, who advanced at a quick step. Magnificent! Such a charge by such a force—full forty-five thousand men, under Hill and Longstreet—even though it threatened to pierce and annihilate the Third Corps, against which it was directed, drew forth cries of admiration from all who beheld it. General Sickles and his splendid command withstood the shock with a determination that checked but could not fully restrain it. Back, inch by inch, fighting, falling, dying, cheering, the men retired. The rebels came on more furiously, halting at intervals, pouring volleys that struck our troops down in scores. General Sickles, fighting desperately, was struck in the leg and fell. The Second Corps came to the aid of his decimated column. The battle then grew fearful. Standing firmly up against the storm, our troops, though still outnumbered,

> gave back shot for shot, volley for volley, almost death for death. Still the enemy was not restrained. Down he came upon our left with a momentum that nothing could check. The rifled guns that lay before our infantry on a knoll were in danger of capture. General Hancock was wounded in the thigh, General Gibbon in the shoulder. The Fifth Corps, as the First and Second wavered anew, went into the breach with such shouts and such volleys as made the rebel column tremble at last. Up from the valley behind, another battery came rolling to the heights, and flung its contents in an instant down in the midst of the enemy's ranks. Crash! crash! with discharges deafening, terrible, the musketry firing went on. The enemy, re-forming after each discharge with wondrous celerity and firmness, still pressed up the declivity. What hideous courage filled the minutes between the appearance of the Fifth Corps and the advance to the support of the rebel columns of still another column from the right, I cannot bear to tell. Men fell, as the leaves fall in autumn, before those horrible discharges. Faltering for an instant, the rebel columns seemed about to recede before the tempest. But their officers, who could be seen through the smoke of the conflict galloping, and swinging their swords along the lines, rallied them anew, and the next instant the whole line sprang forward, as if to break through our own by mere weight of numbers. A division from the Twelfth Corps, on the extreme right, reached the scene at this instant, and at the same time Sedgwick came up with the Sixth Corps, having finished a march of nearly thirty-six consecutive hours. To what rescue they came their officers saw and told them. Weary as they were, barefooted, hungry, fit to drop for slumber, as they were, the wish for victory was so blended with the thought of exhaustion that they cast themselves, in turn, *en masse* into line of battle, and went down on the enemy with death in their weapons and cheers on their lips. The rebel's camel's back was broken by this "feather." His line staggered, reeled, and drifted slowly back, while the shouts of our soldiers, lifted up amid the roar of musketry over the bodies of the dead and wounded, proclaimed the completeness of their victory.

It may be imagined that I was astonished at the fact, that we received no support after we had driven the Federals from the peach orchard and one thousand yards beyond. If General Ewell had engaged the army in his front at that time (say four o'clock) he would have prevented their massing their whole army in my front, and while he and I kept their two wings engaged, Hill would have found their centre weak, and should have threatened it while I broke through their left and dislodged them. Having failed to move at four o'clock, while the enemy was in his front, it was still more surprising that he did not advance at five o'clock with vigor and promptness, when the trenches in front of him were vacated, or rather held by one single brigade (as General Meade's testimony before the Committee on the Conduct of the War states). Had he taken these trenches and scattered the brigade that held them, he would have found himself in the Federals' flank and rear. His attack in the rear must have dislodged the Federals, as it would have been totally unexpected—it being believed that he was in front with me. Hill, charging upon the centre at the same time, would have increased their disorder and we should have won the field. But Ewell did not advance until I had withdrawn my troops, and the First Corps, after winning position after position, was forced to withdraw from the field with two corps of their comrades within sight and resting upon their arms. Ewell did not move until about dusk (according to his own report). He then occupied the trenches that the enemy had vacated (see General Meade's report). The real cause of Ewell's non-compliance with General Lee's orders was that he had broken his line of battle by sending two brigades off on some duty up the York road. General Early says that my failure to attack at sunrise was the cause of Ewell's line being broken at the time I did attack. This is not only absurd, but impossible. After sunrise that morning, Colonel Venable and General Lee were at Ewell's headquarters discussing the policy of opening the attack with Ewell's Corps. They left Ewell with this definite order: that he was to hold himself in readiness to support my attack when it was made. It is silly to say that he was ready at sunrise, when he was not ready at four o'clock when the attack was really made. His orders were to hold himself in readiness to co-operate with my attack when it was made. In breaking his line of battle he rendered himself unable to support me when he would have been potential. Touching the failure of the supporting brigades of Anderson's Division to cover McLaws' flank by *echelon* movements, as directed, there is little to be said. Those brigades acted gallantly, but went astray early in the fight. General Anderson, in his report, says: "A strong fire was poured upon our right flank, which had become detached from McLaws' left." General Lee, alluding to the action of these two brigades, says: "But having become separated from McLaws, Wilcox's and Wright's Brigades advanced with great gallantry, breaking successive lines of the enemy's infantry, and compelling him to abandon much of his artillery. Wilcox reached the foot and Wright gained the crest of the ridge itself, driving the enemy down the opposite side; but having become separated from McLaws, and gone beyond the other two brigades of the division they were to attack in front and on both flanks, and compelled to retire, being unable to bring off any of the captured artillery, McLaws' left also fell back, and it being now nearly dark, General Longstreet determined to await the arrival of Pickett." So much for the action of the first day.

I did not see General Lee that night. On the next morning he came to see me, and, fearing that he was still in his disposition to attack, I tried to anticipate him, by saying: "General, I have had my scouts out all night, and I find that you still have an excellent opportunity to move around to the right of Meade's army, and maneuvre him into attacking us." He replied, pointing with his fist at Cemetery Hill: "The enemy is there, and I am going to strike him." I felt then that it was my duty to express my convictions; I said: "General, I have been a soldier all my life. I have been with soldiers engaged in fights by couples, by squads, companies, regiments, divisions, and armies, and should know, as well as any one, what soldiers can do. It is my opinion that no fifteen thousand men ever arrayed for battle can take that position," pointing to Cemetery Hill. General Lee, in reply to this, ordered me to prepare Pickett's Division for the attack. I should not have been so urgent had I not foreseen the hopelessness of the proposed assault. I felt that I must say a word against the sacrifice of my men; and then I felt that my record was such that General Lee would or could not misconstrue my motives. I said no more, however, but turned away. The most of the morning was consumed in waiting for Pickett's men, and getting into position. The plan of assault was as follows: Our artillery was to be massed in a wood from which Pickett was to charge, and it was to pour a continuous fire upon the cemetery. Under cover of this fire, and supported by it, Pickett was to charge.

Our artillery was in charge of General E. P. Alexander, a brave and gifted officer. Colonel Walton was my chief of artillery; but Alexander, being at the head of the column, and being first in position, and being, beside, an officer of unusual promptness, sagacity, and intelligence, was given charge of the artillery. The arrangements were completed about one o'clock. General Alexander had arranged that a battery of seven eleven-pound howitzers, with fresh horses and full caissons, were to charge with Pickett, at the head of his line, but General Pendleton, from whom the guns had been borrowed, recalled them just before the charge was made, and thus deranged this wise plan. Never was I so depressed as upon that day. I felt that my men were to be sacrificed, and that I should have to order them to make a hopeless charge. I had instructed General Alexander, being unwilling to trust myself with the entire responsibility, to carefully observe the effect of the fire upon the enemy, and when it began to tell to notify Pickett to begin the assault. I was so much impressed with the hopelessness of the charge, that I wrote the following note to General Alexander: "If the artillery fire does not have the effect to drive off the enemy or greatly demoralize him, so as to make our efforts pretty certain, I would prefer that you should not advise General Pickett to make the charge. I shall rely a great deal on your judgment to determine the matter, and shall expect you to let Pickett know when the moment offers."

To my note the General replied as follows: "I will only be able to judge the effect of our fire upon the enemy by his return fire, for his infantry is but little exposed to view, and the smoke will obscure the whole field. If, as I infer from your note, there is an alternative to this attack, it should be carefully considered before opening our fire, for it will take all of the artillery ammunition we have left to test this one thoroughly; and, if the result is unfavorable, we will have none left for another effort; and, even if this is entirely successful, it can only be so at a very bloody cost." I still desired to save my men, and felt that if the artillery did not produce the desired effect, I would be justified in holding Pickett off. I wrote this note to Colonel Walton at exactly 1:30 P.M.: "Let the batteries open. Order great precision in firing. If the batteries at the peach orchard cannot be used against the point we intend attacking, let them open on the enemy at Rocky Hill." The cannonading which opened along both lines was grand. In a few moments a courier brought a note to General Pickett (who was standing near me) from Alexander, which, after reading, he handed to me. It was as follows: "If you are coming at all, you must come at once, or I cannot give you proper support; but the enemy's fire has not slackened at all; at least eighteen guns are still firing from the cemetery itself." After I had read the note, Pickett said to me: "General, shall I advance?" My feelings had so overcome me that I would not speak, for fear of betraying my want of confidence to him. I bowed affirmation, and turned to mount my horse. Pickett immediately said: "I shall lead my division forward, sir." I spurred my horse to the wood where Alexander was stationed with artillery. When I reached him, he told me of the disappearance of the seven guns which were to have led the charge with Pickett, and that his ammunition was so low that he could not properly support the charge. I at once ordered him to stop Pickett until the ammunition had been replenished. He informed me that he had no ammunition with which to replenish. I then saw that there was no help for it, and that Pickett must advance under his orders. He swept past our artillery in splendid style, and the men marched steadily and compactly down the slope. As they started up the ridge, over one hundred cannon from the breastworks of the Federals hurled a rain of canister, grape, and shell down upon them; still they pressed on until half way up the slope, when the crest of the hill was lit with a solid sheet of flame as the masses of infantry rose and fired. When the smoke cleared away, Pickett's Division was gone. Nearly two-thirds of his men lay dead on the field, and the survivors were sullenly retreating down the hill. Mortal man could not have stood that fire. In half an hour the contested field was cleared and the battle of Gettysburg was over.

When this charge had failed, I expected that, of course, the enemy would throw himself against our shattered ranks and try to crush us. I sent my staff officers to the rear to assist in rallying the troops, and hurried to our line of batteries, as the only support that I could give them, knowing that my presence would impress upon every one of them the necessity of holding the ground to the last extremity. I knew if the army was to be saved, those batteries must check the enemy. As I rode along the line of artillery, I observed my old friend Captain Miller, Washington Artillery, of Sharpsburg record, walking between his guns and smoking his pipe as quietly and contentedly as he could at his camp-fire. The enemy's skirmishers were then advancing and threatening assault. For unaccountable reasons, the enemy did not pursue his advantage. Our army was soon in compact shape, and its face turned once more toward Virginia. I may mention here that is has been absurdly said that General Lee ordered me to put Hood's and McLaws' Divisions in support of Pickett's assault. General Lee never ordered any such thing.[3] After our troops were all arranged for assault, General Lee rode with me twice over the lines to see that everything was arranged according to his wishes. He was told that we had been more particular in giving the orders than ever before; that the commanders had been sent for, and the point of attack had been carefully designated, and that the commanders had been directed to communicate to their subordinates, and through them to every soldier in the command, the work that was before them, so that they should nerve themselves for the attack, and fully understand it. After leaving me, he again rode over the field once, if not twice, so that there was really no room for misconstruction or misunderstanding of his wishes. He could not have thought of giving any such an order. Hood and McLaws were confronted by a largely superior force of the enemy on the right of Pickett's attack. To have moved them to Pickett's support, would have disengaged treble their number of Federals, who would have swooped down from their rocky fastnesses against the flank of our attacking column, and swept our army from the field. A reference to any of the maps of Gettysburg will show from the position of the troops that this would have been the inevitable result. General Lee and myself never had any deliberate conversation about Gettysburg. The subject was never broached by either of us to the other. On one occasion it came up casually, and he said to me (alluding to the charge of Pickett, on the 3d), "General, why didn't you stop all that thing that day?" I replied that I could not, under the circumstances, assume such a responsibility, as no discretion had been left me.

Before discussing the weak points of the campaign of Gettysburg, it is proper that I should say that I do so with the greatest affection for General Lee, and the greatest reverence for his memory. The relations existing between us were affectionate, confidential, and even tender, from first to last. There was never a harsh word between us. It is, then, with a reluctant spirit that I write a calm and critical review of the Gettysburg campaign, because that review will show that our commanding general was unfortunate at several points. There is no doubt that General Lee, during the crisis of that campaign, lost the matchless equipoise that usually characterized him, and that whatever mistakes were made were not so much matters of deliberate judgment as the impulses of a great mind disturbed by unparalleled conditions. General Lee was thrown from his balance (as is shown by the statement of General Fitzhugh Lee) by too great confidence in the prowess of his troops and (as is shown by General Anderson's statement) by the deplorable absence of General Stuart and the perplexity occasioned thereby. With this preface I proceed to say that the Gettysburg campaign was weak in these points—adhering, however, to my opinion that a combined movement against Rosecrans, in Tennessee, and a march toward Cincinnati would have given better results than could possibly have been secured by the invasion of Pennsylvania: First, the offensive strategical, but defensive tactical, plan of the campaign, as agreed upon, should never have been abandoned after we entered the enemy's country. Second, if there ever was a time when the abandonment of that plan could have promised decisive results, it was at Brandy Station, where, after Stuart had repulsed the force thrown across the river, we might have fallen on that force and crushed it, and then put ourselves in position, threatening the enemy's right and rear, which would have dislodged him from his position at Fredericksburg, and given us the opportunity for an effective blow. Third, General Stuart should not have been permitted to leave the general line of march, thus forcing us to march blindfolded into the enemy's country; to this may be attributed, in my opinion, the change of the policy of the campaign. Fourth, the success obtained by the accidental rencontre on the 1st, should have been vigorously prosecuted, and the enemy should have been given no time to fortify or concentrate. Fifth, on the night of the 1st, the army should have been carried around to Meade's right and rear, and posted between him and his capital, and we could have maneuvred him into an attack. Sixth, when the attack was made on the enemy's left, on the 2d, by my corps, Ewell should have been required to co-operate by a vigorous movement against his right, and Hill should have moved against his centre. Had this been done, his army would have been dislodged, beyond question. Seventh, on the morning of the 3d it was not yet too late to move to the right and maneuvre the Federals into attacking us. Eighth, Pickett's Division should not have been ordered to assault Cemetery Ridge on the 3d, as we had already tested the strength of the position sufficiently to admonish us that we could not dislodge him. While the co-operation of Generals Ewell and Hill, on the 2d, by vigorous assault at the moment my battle was in progress, would, in all probability, have dislodged the Federals from their position, it does not seem that such success would have yielded the fruits anticipated at the inception of the campaign. The battle, as it was fought, would, in any result, have so crippled us that the Federals would have been able to make good their retreat, and we should soon have been obliged to retire to Virginia with nothing but victory to cover our waning cause.

The morals of the victory might have dispirited the North, and aroused the South to new exertions, but it would have been nothing in the game being played by the two armies at Gettysburg. As to the abandonment of the tactical defensive policy that we had agreed upon, there can be no doubt that General Lee deeply deplored it as a mistake. His remark, made just after the battle, "It is all my fault," meant just what it said. It adds to the nobility and magnanimity of that remark, when we reflect that it was the utterance of a deep-felt truth, rather than a mere sentiment. In a letter written to me by General Lee, in January, 1864, he says: "Had I taken your advice at Gettysburg, instead of pursuing the course I did, how different all might have been." Captain T. J. Gorie, of Houston, Texas, a gentle man of high position and undoubted integrity, writes to me upon this same point as follows: "Another important circumstance which I distinctly remember was in the winter of 1864, when you sent me from East Tennessee to Orange Court-House with dispatches for General Lee. Upon my arrival there, General Lee asked me in his tent, where he was alone with two or three Northern papers on his table. He remarked that he had just been reading the Northern official report of the battle of Gettysburg; that he had become satisfied, from reading those reports that, if he had permitted you to carry out your plans on the third day, instead of making the attack on Cemetery Hill, we would have been successful." I cannot see, as has been claimed, why the absence of General Lee's cavalry should have justified his attack on the enemy. On the contrary, while they may have perplexed him, I hold that it was additional reason for his not hazarding an attack. At the time the attack was ordered, we were fearful that our cavalry had been destroyed. In case of a disaster, and a forced retreat, we should have had nothing to cover our retreat. When so much was at stake as at Gettysburg, the absence of the cavalry should have prevented the taking of any chances.

As to the failure of Stuart to move with the army to the west side of the Blue Ridge, I can only call attention to the fact that General Lee gave him discretionary orders. He doubtless did as he though best. Had no discretion been given him, he would have known and fallen into his natural position—my right flank. But authority thus given a subordinate general, implies an opinion on the part of the commander that something better than the drudgery of a march along our flank might be open to him, and one of General Stuart's activity and gallantry should not be expected to fail to seek it. As to Ewell's failure to prosecute the advantage won the 1st, there is little to be said, as the commanding general was on the field. I merely quote from his (General Ewell's) official report. He says: "The enemy had fallen back to a commanding position that was known to us as Cemetery Hill, south of Gettysburg, and quickly showed a formidable front there. On entering the town, I received a message from the commanding general to attack the hill, if I could do so to advantage. I could not bring artillery to bear on it; all the troops with me were jaded by twelve hours' marching and fighting, and I was notified that General Johnson was close to the town with his division, the only one of my corps that had not been engaged, Anderson's Division, of the Third Corps, having been halted to let them pass. Cemetery Hill was not assailable from the town, and I determined, with Johnson's Division, to take possession of a wooded hill to my left, on a line with and commanding Cemetery Hill. Before Johnson got up the Federals were reported moving to our left flank—our extreme left—and I could see what seemed to be his skirmishers in that direction. Before this report could be investigated by Lieutenant T. T. Turner, of my staff, and Lieutenant Robert Early, sent to investigate it, and Johnson placed in position, the night was far advanced." General Lee explains his failure to send positive orders to Ewell to follow up the flying enemy as follows: "The attack was not pressed that afternoon, the enemy's force being unknown, and it being considered advisable to await the arrival of the rest of our troops. Orders were sent back to hasten their march, and, in the meantime, every effort was made to ascertain the numbers and positions of the enemy, and find the most favorable point to attack."

Pursuit "pell-mell" is sometimes justified in a mere retreat. It is the accepted principle of action in a rout. General Early, in his report of this day's work, says "the enemy had been routed." He should, therefore, have been followed by everything that could have been thrown upon his heels, not so much to gain the heights, which were recognized as the rallying point, but to prevent his rallying at all in time to form lines for another battle. If the enemy had been routed, this could and should have been done. In the "Military Annals of Louisiana" (Napier Bartlett, Esq.), in the account of this rout, he says: "Hays had received orders, through Early, from General Ewell (though Lee's general instructions were subsequently the reverse) to halt at Gettysburg, and advance no further in case he should succeed in capturing that place. But Hays now saw that the enemy were coming around by what is known as the Baltimore road, and were making for the heights—the Cemetery Ridge. This ridge meant life or death, and for the possession of it the battles of the 2d and 3d were fought. * * * Owing to the long detour the enemy was compelled to make, it was obvious that he could not get his artillery in position on the heights for one or two hours.

The immediate occupation of the heights by the Confederates, who were in position to get them at the time referred to, was a matter of vital importance. Hays recognized it as such, and presently sent for Early. The latter thought as Hays, but declined to disobey orders. At the urgent request of General Hays, however, he sent for General Ewell. When the latter arrived, many precious moments had been lost. But the enemy, who did not see its value until the arrival of Hancock, had not yet appeared in force." General Hays told me, ten years after the battle, that he "could have seized the heights without the loss of ten men." Here we see General Early adhering to orders when his own conviction told him he should not do so, and refusing to allow General Hays to seize a point recognized by him as of vast importance, because of technical authority, at a moment when he admitted and knew that disregard of the order would only have made more secure the point at issue when the order was given.

Before closing this article, I desire to settle finally and fully one point, concerning which there has been much discussion, viz.: The alleged delay in the attack upon the 2d. I am moved to this task, not so much by an ambition to dissolve the cloud of personal misrepresentation that has settled about my head, as by a sense of duty which leads me to determine a point that will be of value to the historian. It was asserted by General Pendleton, with whom the carefulness of statement or deliberateness of judgment has never been a characteristic, but who has been distinguished for the unreliability of his memory, that General Lee ordered me to attack the enemy at sunrise on the 2d. General J. A. Early has, in positive terms, indorsed this charge, which I now proceed to disprove. I have said that I left General Lee late in the night of the 1st, and that he had not then determined when the attack should be made; that I went to his headquarters early the next morning, and was with him for some time; that he left me early after sunrise and went to Ewell's headquarters, with the express view of seeing whether or not the main attack should be made then, and that he returned about nine o'clock; and that after discussing the ground for some time, he determined that I should make the main attack, and at eleven o'clock gave me the order to prepare for it. I now present documents that sustain these assertions.

The first letter that I offer is from Colonel W. H. Taylor, of General Lee's staff. It is as follows:

NORFOLK, VA., April 28th, 1875.

Dear General—I have received your letter of the 20th instant. I have not read the article of which you speak, nor have I ever seen any copy of General Pendleton's address; indeed, I have read little or nothing of what has been written since the war. In the first place, because I could not spare the time, and in the second, of those of whose writings I have heard, I deem but very few entitled to any attention whatever. I can only say, that I never before heard of the "sunrise attack" you were to have made, as charged by General Pendleton. If such an order was given you I never knew of it, or it has strangely escaped my memory. I think it more than probable that if General Lee had had your troops available the evening previous to the day of which you speak, he would have ordered an early attack; but this does not touch the point at issue. I regard it as a great mistake on the part of those who, perhaps because of political differences, now undertake to criticise and attack your war record. Such conduct is most ungenerous, and I am sure meets the disapprobation of all good Confederates with whom I have had the pleasure of associating in the daily walks of life.

Yours, very respectfully,

W. H. TAYLOR.

TO GENERAL LONGSTREET.

The next letter is from Colonel Charles Marshall, of General Lee's staff, who has charge of all the papers left by General Lee. It is as follows:

BALTIMORE, MD., May 7th, 1875.

Dear General—Your letter of the 20th ultimo was received, and should have had an earlier reply, but for my engagements preventing me from looking at my papers to find what I could on the subject. I have no personal recollection of the order to which you refer. It certainly was not conveyed by me, nor is there anything in General Lee's official report to show the attack on the 2d was expected by him to begin earlier, except that he notices that there was not proper concert of action on that day. * * * *

Respectfully,

CHARLES MARSHALL.

TO GENERAL LONGSTREET, New Orleans.

Then a letter from General A. S. Long, who was General Lee's Military Secretary:

BIG ISLAND, BEDFORD, VA., May 31st, 1875.

Dear General—Your letter of the 20th ultimo, referring to an assertion of General Pendleton's, made in a lecture delivered several years ago, which was recently published in the *Southern Historical Society Magazine* substantially as follows: "That General Lee ordered General Longstreet to attack General Meade at sunrise on the morning of the 2d of July," has been received. I do not recollect of hearing of an order to attack at sunrise, or at any other designated hour, pending the operations at Gettysburg during the first three days of July, 1863. * * *

Yours, truly, A. S. LONG.

TO GENERAL LONGSTREET.

I add the letter of Colonel Venable, of General Lee's staff, which should of itself be conclusive. I merely premise it with the statement that it was fully nine o'clock before General Lee returned from his reconnoissance of Ewell's lines:

UNIVERSITY OF VIRGINIA, May 11th, 1875.

GERNERAL JAMES LONGSTREET:

Dear General—Your letter of the 25th ultimo, with regard to General Lee's battle order on the 1st and 2d of July at Gettysburg, was duly received. I did not know of any order for an attack on the enemy at sunrise on the 2d, nor can I believe any such order was issued by General Lee. About sunrise on the 2d of July I was sent by General Lee to General Ewell to ask him what he thought of the advantages of an attack on the enemy from his position. (Colonel Marshall had been sent with a similar order on the night of the 1st.) General Ewell made me ride with him from point to point of his lines, so as to see with him the exact position of things. Before he got through the examination of the enemy's position, General Lee came himself to General Ewell's lines. In sending the message to General Ewell, General Lee was explicit in saying that the question was whether he should move all the troops around on the right, and attack on that side. I do not think that the errand on which I was sent by the commanding general is consistent with the idea of an attack at sunrise by any portion of the army. Yours, very truly,

CHAS. S. VENABLE.

I add upon this point the letter of Dr. Cullen, Medical Director of the First Corps:

RICHMOND, VA., May 18th, 1875.

GENERAL JAMES LONGSTREET:

Dear General—Yours of the 16th ult. should have received my immediate attention, but before answering it, I was desirous of refreshing my memory of the scenes and incidents of the Gettysburg campaign by conversation with others who were with us, and who served in different corps of the command. It was an astounding announcement to the survivors of the First Army Corps that the disaster and failure at Gettysburg was alone and solely due to its commander, and that had he obeyed the orders of the commander-in-chief that Meade's army would have been beaten before its entire force had assembled, and its final discomfiture thereby made certain. It is a little strange that these charges were not made while General Lee was alive to substantiate or disprove them, and that seven years or more were permitted to pass by in silence regarding them. You are fortunate in being able to call upon the Adjutant General and the two confidential officers of General Lee's staff for their testimony in the case, and I do not think that you will have any reason to fear their evidence.

They knew every order that was issued for that battle, when and where attacks were to be made, who were slow in attacking, and who did not make attacks that were expected to be made. I hope, for the sake of history and for your brave military record, that a quietus will at once be put on this subject. I distinctly remember the appearance in our headquarter camp of the scout who brought from Frederick the first account that General Lee had of the definite whereabouts of the enemy; of the excitement at General Lee's headquarters among couriers, quartermasters, commissaries, etc., all betokening some early movement of the commands dependent upon the news brought by the scout. That afternoon General Lee was walking with some of us in the road in front of his headquarters, and said: "To-morrow, gentlemen, we will not move to Harrisburg as we expected, but will go over to Gettysburg and see what General Meade is after." Orders had then been issued to the corps to move at sunrise on the morning of the next day, and promptly at that time the corps was put on the road. The troops moved slowly a short distance, when they were stopped by Ewell's wagon trains and Johnson's Division turning into the road in front of them, making their way from some point north to Cashtown or Gettysburg. How many hours we were detained I am unable to say, but it must have been many, for I remember eating a lunch or dinner before moving again. Being anxious to see you I rode rapidly by the troops (who, as soon as they could get into the road, pushed hurriedly by us, also), and overtook you about dark at the hill this side of Gettysburg, about half a mile from the town. You had been at the front with General Lee, and were returning to your camp, a mile or two back. I spoke very exultingly of the victory we were thought to have obtained that day, but was surprised to find that you did not take the same cheerful view of it that I did; and presently you remarked, that it would have been better had we not fought than to have left undone what we did. You said that the enemy were left occupying a position that it wo .ld take the whole army to drive them from, and then at a great sacrifice. We soon reached the camp, three miles, perhaps, from Gettysburg, and found the column near by. Orders were issued to be ready to march at "daybreak," or some earlier hour, next morning. About three o'clock in the morning, while the stars were shining, you left your headquarters and rode to General Lee's, where I found you sitting with him *after sunrise* looking at the enemy on Cemetery Hill. I rode then into Gettysburg, and was gone some two hours, and when I returned found you still with General Lee. At two or three o'clock in the day I rode with you toward the right, when you were about to attack, and was with you in front of the peach orchard when Hood began to move toward Round Top. General Hood was soon wounded, and I removed him from the field to a house near by. * * * I am yours, very truly,

J. S. D. CULLEN.

I submit next an extract from the official report of General R. H. Anderson:

> Upon approaching Gettysburg, I was directed to occupy the position in line of battle which had first been vacated by Pender's Division, and to place one brigade and battery of artillery a mile or more on the right. Wilcox's Brigade and Captain Ross' battery, of Lane's battalion, were posted in the detached position, while the other brigades occupied the ground from which Pender's Division had first been moved. We continued in position until the morning of the 2d, when I received orders to take up a new line of battle, on the right of Pender's Division, about a mile and a half further forward. In taking the new position, the Tenth Alabama Regiment, Wilcox's Brigade, had a sharp skirmish with the body of the enemy who had occupied a wooded hill on the extreme right of my line. * * * Shortly after the line had been formed, I received notice that Lieutenant General Longstreet would occupy the ground on my right, and that his line would be in a direction nearly at right angles with mine, and that he would assault the extreme left of the enemy and drive him toward Gettysburg.

From a narrative of General McLaws, published in 1873, I copy the following:

> On the 30th of June, I had been directed to have my division in readiness to follow General Ewell's Corps. Marching toward Gettysburg, which it was intimated we would have passed by ten o'clock the next day (the 1st of July), my division was accordingly marched from its camp and lined along the road in the order of march by eight o'clock the 1st of July. When the troops of Ewell's Corps (it was Johnson's Division in charge of Ewell's wagon trains, which were coming from Carlisle by the road west of the mountains) had passed the head of my column, I asked General Longstreet's staff officer, Major Fairfax, if my division should follow. He went off to inquire, and returned with orders for me to wait until Ewell's wagon train had passed, which did not happen until after four o'clock P.M. The train was calculated to be fourteen miles long, when I took up the line of march and continued marching until I arrived within three miles of Gettysburg, where my command camped along a creek. This was far into the night. My division was leading Longstreet's Corps, and, of course, the other divisions came up later. I saw Hood's Division the next morning, and understood that Pickett had been detached to guard the rear. While on the march, about ten o'clock at night, I met General Longstreet and some of his staff coming from the direction of Gettysburg, and had a few moments conversation with him. He said nothing of having received an order to attack at daylight the next morning. Here, I will state, that until General Pendleton mentioned it about two years ago, when he was on a

lecturing tour, after the death of General Lee, I never heard it intimated even that any such order had ever been given.

I close the testimony on this point by an extract from a letter from General Hood. He writes:

> I arrived with my staff in front of the heights of Gettysburg shortly after daybreak, as I have already stated, on the morning of the 2d of July. My division soon commenced filing into an open field near me, when the troops were allowed to stack arms and rest until further orders. A short distance in advance of this point, and during the early part of the same morning, we were both engaged in company with Generals A. P. Hill and Lee in observing the position of the Federals. General Lee, with coat buttoned to the throat, sabre belt around his waist, and field-glasses pendant at his side, walked up and down in the shade of large trees near us, halting, now and then, to observe the enemy. He seemed full of hope, yet at times buried in deep thought. Colonel Freemantle, of England, was esconced in the forks of a tree not far off, with glasses in constant use, examining the lofty position of the Federal army. General Lee was seemingly anxious that you should attack that morning. He remarked to me: "The enemy is here, and if we do not whip him, he will whip us." You thought it better to await the arrival of Pickett's Division, at that time still in the rear, in order to make the attack, and you said to me, subsequently, while we were seated together near the trunk of a tree: "General Lee is a little nervous this morning. He wishes me to attack. I do not wish to do so without Pickett. I never like to go into a battle with one boot off."

Having thus disproved the assertions of Messrs. Pendleton and Early in regard to this rumored order for a sunrise attack, it appears that they are worthy of no further recognition; but it is difficult to pass beyond them without noting the manner in which, by their ignorance, they marred the plans of their chief on the field of battle. Mr. Pendleton robbed Pickett's Division of its most important adjunct, fresh field artillery, at the moment of its severest trial, and thus frustrated the wise and brilliant programme of assault planned by General Alexander, and without the knowledge of that officer. (See narrative of General Alexander in the *Southern Historical Monthly* for September, 1877.) General Early broke up General Lee's line of battle on the 2d of July by detaching part of his division on some uncalled-for service, in violation of General Lee's orders, and thus prevented the co-operative attack of Ewell, ordered by General Lee.

It is proper to discuss briefly, at this point, the movements of the third day. The charge of that day, as made by General Pickett, was emphatically a forlorn hope. The point designated by General Lee as the point of attack, seemed to be about one mile from where he and I stood when he gave his orders. I asked him if the distance that we had to overcome under a terrific fire was not more than a mile. He replied: "No, it is not more than fourteen hundred yards." So that our troops, when they arose above the crest, had to advance this distance under the fire of about half of the Federal army before they could fire a shot. Anything less than thirty thousand fresh veterans would have been vainly sacrificed in this attempt. The force given me for this work was Pickett's Division (or rather a part of it), about five thousand five hundred men, fresh and ready to undertake anything. My supporting force of probably eight thousand men, had bloody noses and bruised heads from the fight of the previous day, and were not in physical condition to undertake such desperate work. When fresh they were the equals of any troops on earth; but every soldier knows that there is a great difference between fresh soldiers and those who have just come out of a heavy battle. It has been charged that the delay of the attack on the 3d was the cause of the failure of Ewell to co-operate with Pickett's attack. Colonel Taylor says that Ewell was ordered to attack at the same time with me, mine being the main attack. He says: "General Longstreet's dispositions were not completed as soon as expected. * * * General Ewell, who had orders to co-operate with General Longstreet, and who was, of course, not aware of any impediment to the main attack, having reinforced General Johnson, during the night of the 2d, ordered him forward early the next morning. In obedience to these instructions, General Johnson became hotly engaged before General Ewell could be informed of the halt that had been called upon our right."

Let us look at the facts of this. Instead of "making this attack at daylight," General Ewell says: "Just before the time fixed for General Johnson's advance, the enemy attacked him to regain the works captured by Stuart the evening before." General Meade, in his official report, says: "On the morning of the 3d, General Geary, having returned during the night, attacked, at early dawn, the enemy, and succeeded in driving him back, and reoccupying his former position. A spirited contest was maintained along this portion of the line all the morning, and General Geary, reinforced by Wharton's Brigade, of the Sixth Corps, maintained his position, and inflicted very severe loss on the enemy." Now to return to my end of the line. At about sunrise General Lee came to me and informed me that General Pickett would soon report to me, and then ordered that his troops were to be used as a column of assault, designating the point of assault, and that portions of the Third Corps were to be used in support. About seven o'clock General Pickett rode forward and stated that his troops would soon be upon the field, and asked to be assigned his position. Colonel W. W. Wood, of Pickett's Division, in his account of the day, says: "If I remember correctly, Pickett's Division and the artillery were all in position by eleven A.M." Hence, we see that General Geary attacked General Ewell at least one hour before I had received my orders for the day; that at the very moment of my receiving these instructions General Ewell was engaged in a "spirited contest;" that this contest had continued several hours before General Pickett's troops came upon the field, and that the contest was virtually over before General Pickett and the artillery were prepared for the battle. When these arrangements were completed, and the batteries ordered to open, General Ewell had been driven from his position, and not a footstep was made from any other part of the army in my support. That there may have been confusion of orders on the field during the second and third days, I am not prepared to deny; but there was nothing of the kind about the headquarters of the First Corps.

I have not seen the criticism of the Comte de Paris upon the campaign, but I gather from quotations that he adduced as one of the objections to the invasion of Pennsylvania, that the Federals would do superior fighting upon their own soil. The Confederates, whom I have read after, deny that this is true. Although not technically correct, the Comte is right in the material point. The actual fighting on the field of Gettysburg, by the Army of the Potomac, was not marked by any unusual gallantry, but the positions that it occupied were held with much more than the usual tenacity of purpose.

There is little to say of the retreat of General Lee's army to the Potomac. When we reached South Mountain, on our retreat, we learned that the Federal cavalry was in strong force, threatening the destruction of our trains then collecting at Williamsport, and that it was also intercepting our trains on the road, and burning some of our wagons. Upon the receipt of this intelligence General Lee ordered me to march as rapidly as possible to the relief of our trains. By a forced march we succeeded in clearing the road, and reached Williamsport in time to save our supply trains. We then took position covering the crossing there and at Falling Water, a short distance below. As the other corps arrived they were assigned positions, and we went to work as rapidly as possible to strengthen our line with field works. On the 13th, General Lee informed me that the river had fallen sufficiently at Williamsport to allow us to ford, and that the bridge at Falling Water had been repaired, and that he would, that night, recross the river with his entire army. I suggested, as a matter of convenience, and to avoid confusion, that it might be better to pass the trains over that night, with everything not essential to battle, and let his troops remain in position until the night of the 14th; that, if the rest of his line was as strong as mine, we could easily repulse any attack that might be made, and thus recover some of the prestige lost by the discomfiture at Gettysburg. After we crossed the Potomac we soon found that the Federals were pushing along the west side of the Blue Ridge, with the purpose of cutting off our retreat to Richmond. General Lee again sent my corps forward to prevent this effort on the part of General Meade, and we succeeded in clearing the way and holding it open for the Third Corps, that followed us. General Ewell, however, was cut off, and was obliged to pass the mountains further south. The First Corps reached Culpepper Court-House on the 24th.

In the month of August, 1863, while lying along the Rapidan, I called General Lee's attention to the condition of our affairs in the West, and the progress that was being made by the army under General Rosecrans in cutting a new line through the State of Georgia, and suggesting that a successful march, such as he had started on, would again bisect the Southern country, and that when that was done the war would be virtually over. I suggested that he should adhere to his defensive tactics upon the Rapidan, and reinforce from his army the army lying in front of Rosecrans—so that it could crush that army, and then push on to the West. He seemed struck with these views, but was as much opposed to dividing his army as he was in the spring when I first suggested it. He went down to Richmond to arrange for another offensive campaign during the fall. While there several letters passed between us, only two of which I have preserved in connected form. The result of this correspondence was, however, that I was sent with two divisions—Hood's and McLaws'—to reinforce our army then in Georgia. The result of this movement was the defeat of Rosecrans, at Chickamauga, when the last hope of the Confederacy expired with the failure of our army to prosecute the advantage gained by this defeat. The letters are appended herewith:

(Confidential.) [*Copy.*]

RICHMOND, August 31st, 1863.

LIEUTENANT GENERAL J. LONGSTREET,
Headquarters Army of West Virginia:

General—I have wished for several days past to return to the army, but have been detained by the President. He will not listen to my proposition to leave tomorrow.

I hope you will use every exertion to prepare the army for offensive operations, and improve the condition of men and animals. I can see nothing better to be done than to endeavor to bring General Meade out and use our efforts to crush his army while in the present condition.

The Quartermaster's Department promise to send up three thousand bushels of corn per day, provided the cars can be unloaded and returned without delay. I hope you will be able to arrange it so that the cars will not be detained. With this supply of corn, if it can be maintained, the condition of our animals should improve.

Very respectfully and truly yours,

[Signed] R. E. LEE, General.

[*Copy.*]

HEADQUARTERS, September 2d, 1863.

General—Your letter of the 31st is received. I have expressed to Generals Ewell and Hill your wishes, and am doing all that can be done to be well prepared with my own command. Our greatest difficulty will be in preparing our animals.

I don't know that we can reasonably hope to accomplish much *here,* by offensive operations, unless we are strong enough to cross the Potomac. If we advance to meet the enemy on this side, he will, in all probability, go into one of his many fortified positions. These we cannot afford to attack.

I know but little of the condition of our affairs in the West, but am inclined to the opinion that our best opportunity for great results is in Tennessee. If we could hold the defensive here with two corps, and send the other to operate in Tennessee, with that army, I think that we could accomplish more than by an advance from here.

The enemy seems to have settled down upon the plan of holding certain points by fortifying and defending, while he concentrates upon others. It seems to me that this must succeed, unless we concentrate ourselves, and at the same time make occasional show of active operations at all points.

I know of no other means of acting upon that principle at present, except to depend upon our fortifications in Virginia, and concentrate with one corps of this army, and such as may be drawn from others, in Tennessee, and destroy Rosecrans' army.

I feel assured that this is practicable, and that greater advantages will be gained than by any operations from here.

I remain, general, very respectfully, your obedient servant,

[Signed] JAMES LONGSTREET, Lieut. General.

GENERAL R. E. LEE, Commanding, etc.

It will be noticed by those who have watched the desultory controversy maintained upon this subject, that after I had proved the fallacy of General Pendleton's and General Early's idea of a sunrise attack, they fall back upon the charge that I delayed bringing my troops into action, waiving all question of an order from General Lee. I have shown that I did not receive orders from General Lee to attack until about eleven o'clock on the 2d; that I immediately began my dispositions for attack; that I waited about forty minutes for Law's Brigade, by General Lee's assenting authority; that by especial orders from General Lee, my corps marched into position by a circuitous route, under the direction and conduct of Colonel Johnson, of his staff of engineers; that Colonel Johnson's orders were to keep the march of the troops concealed, and that I hurried Hood's Division forward in the face of those orders, throwing them into line by a direct march, and breaking up the delay occasioned by the orders of General Lee. I need only add that every movement or halt of the troops on that day was made in the immediate presence of General Lee, or in his sight—certainly within the reach of his easy and prompt correction. I quote, in this connection, the order that I issued to the heads of departments in my corps on the 1st. I present the order as issued to Colonel Walton, of the artillery, similar orders having been issued to the division commanders:

> [*Order.*]
>
> HEADQUARTERS FIRST ARMY CORPS,
> NEAR GETTYSBURG, July 18–5:30 P.M.
>
> *Colonel*—The commanding general desires you to come on to-night as fast as you can, without distressing your men or animals. Hill and Ewell have sharply engaged the enemy, and you will be needed for to-morrow's battle. Let us know where you will stop to-night. * * * Respectfully,
>
> G. M. SORRELL, A. A. General
>
> To COLONEL J. B. WALTON, Chief of Artillery.

I offer, also, a report made by General Hood touching this march. He says:

> While lying in camp near Chambersburg, information was received that Hill and Ewell were about to come into contact with the enemy near Gettysburg. My troops, together with McLaws' Division, were at once put in motion, upon the most direct road to that point, which we reached, after a hard march, at or before sunrise on July the 2d. So imperative had been our orders to hasten forward with all possible speed, that on the march my troops were allowed to halt and rest only about two hours during the night from the 1st to the 2d of July.

It appears to me that the gentlemen who made the above-mentioned charges against me have chosen the wrong point of attack. With their motives I have nothing to do; but I cannot help suggesting that if they had charged me with having precipitated the battle, instead of having delayed it, the records might have sustained them in that my attack was made about four hours before General Ewell's. I am reminded, in this connection, of what a Federal officer, who was engaged in that battle, said to me when we were talking over the battle, and the comments it had provoked. He said: "I cannot imagine how they can charge you with being late in your attack, as you were the only one that got in at all. I do not think their charge can be credited."

In conclusion, I may say that it is unfortunate that the discussion of all mooted points concerning the battle was not opened before the death of General Lee. A word or two from him would have settled all points at issue. As it is, I have written an impartial narrative of the facts as they are, with such comments as the nature of the case seemed to demand.

NOTES

1. The importance of Round Top, as a *point d' appui,* was not appreciated until after my attack. General Meade seems to have alluded to it as a point to be occupied, "if practicable," but in such slighting manner as to show that he did not deem it of great importance. So it was occupied by an inadequate force. As our battle progressed, pushing the Federals back from point to point, subordinate officers and soldiers, seeking shelter, as birds fly to cover in a tempest, found behind the large boulders of its rock-bound sides, not only protection but rallying points. These reinforcements to the troops already there, checked our advance on the right, and some superior officer, arriving just then, divined from effect the cause, and threw a force into Round Top that transformed it, as if by magic, into a Gibraltar.

2. The troops engaged with me in the fight of the 2d were mostly Georgians, as follows: The four Georgia brigades of Generals Benning, Anderson, Wofford, and Semmes, General Kershaw's South Carolina Brigade, General Law's Alabama Brigade, General Barksdale's (afterward General Humphrey's) Mississippi Brigade, and General Robertson's Texas Brigade.

3. Colonel Taylor says that General Lee, in his presence, gave me orders to put Hood's and McLaws' Divisions in this column of attack. This I deny, and do not suppose he will claim that any one else heard the order. If the reader will examine any of the maps of Gettysburg, he will see that the withdrawal of these two divisions from their line of battle would have left half of General Lee's line of battle open, and by the shortest route to his line of supplies and retreat. Fully one-half of his army would have been in the column of assault, and half of Meade's army would have been free to sally out on the flank of our column, and we should have been destroyed on that field of battle, beyond a doubt. Of course, if we assume that Meade would place his army in line of battle, and allow us to select our point of attack, we could have massed against it, and rushed through. But this assumption would be absurd. The only way for those divisions to have been moved, was to have attacked the heights in front. But this attack had been tried, and failed the day before. If Pickett had shown signs of getting a lodgment, I should, of course, have pushed the other divisions forward to support the attack. But I saw that he was going to pieces at once. When Colonel Freemantle (Her Majesty's service) approached me (see his account), and congratulated me on Pickett's apparent success, I told him that his line would break in a moment—that he was not strong enough to make a serious impression. My assertion was correct. To have rushed forward my two divisions, then carrying bloody noses from their terrible conflict the day before, would have been madness.

Reply to General Longstreet

JUBAL A. EARLY

[We had intended to have published in this No. of our Papers General Longstreet's letter to the Philadelphia *Times*. For while we are, of course, under no obligation to *copy what is published elsewhere,* we are desirous of getting at the whole truth, and wish to give every side a fair hearing. But the great length of General Longstreet's article compells us to postpone it for another issue. Meantime, General Longstreet's paper has been widely circulated, and it is due to fairness and a proper desire to aid the search for truth that we should give, as we do without note or comment of our own, the following rejoinder of General Early.]

After the foregoing review was in the hands of the printer, an article entitled "The campaign of Gettysburg," purporting to be by General James Longstreet, appeared in the Philadelphia *Weekly Times* of November the 3rd, which requires some notice at my hands. That article is not from General Longstreet's own pen, as is very apparent to those who are familiar with his style of writing, and of the fact I have the assurance from a quarter that leaves no doubt on the subject. The data and material for the article, however, were furnished by him and put in form by another. He is therefore responsible for its statements and utterances. The excuse for the appearance of the article is stated as follows:

After giving a letter, written on the 24th of July, 1863, to his uncle, he says:

> "I sincerely regret that I cannot still rest upon that letter. But I have been so repeatedly and so rancorously assailed by those whose intimacy with the Commanding General in that battle gives an apparent importance to their assaults, that I feel impelled by a sense of duty to give to the public a full and comprehensive narration of the campaign from its beginning to its end; especially when I reflect that the publication of the truth cannot now, as it might have done then, injure the cause for which we fought the battle."

The temper towards General Lee in which the article was written, or rather procured to be written, is shown by the following extract from an editorial notice of some additions to the article received after it was in print, contained in the same number of the *Times:*

The editor says:

> The letter from General Longstreet which accompanies these enclosures dwells particularly upon a point which he wishes to have his readers understand, as the justification of his present narrative. It is that while General Lee on the battle field assumed all the responsibility for the result, he afterwards published a report that differs from the report he made at the time while under that generous spirit. General Longstreet and other officers made their official reports upon the battle shortly after its occurrence, and while they were impressed with General Lee's noble assumption of all the blame; but General Lee having since written a detailed and somewhat critical account of the battle—and the account from which General Longstreet's critics get all their points against him—Longstreet feels himself justified in discussing the battle upon its merits. It is in recognition of his soldiery modesty that the substance of his letter is given here; the article is its own sufficient justification.

This is a direct imputation upon the motives that governed Gen. Lee in writing his detailed report, if it does not impeach his veracity, and place him among General Longstreet's assailants.

General Longstreet ranks me among the assailants whose attacks call for this vindication of himself and criticism of General Lee, and in that connection he says:

> It was asserted by General Pendleton, with whom the carefulness of statement or deliberateness of judgment has never been a characteristic, but who has been distinguished by the unreliability of his memory, that General Lee ordered me to attack the enemy at sunrise on the 2nd. General J. A. Early has, in positive terms, endorsed this charge, which I now proceed to disprove.

General Longstreet is exceedingly careless in his statements, as I have had occasion before to demonstrate, and, while to some it may be a matter of surprise when I assert that there is no foundation whatever for the statement that I endorsed either General Pendleton's or anybody else's assertion that the order was given by General Lee to General Longstreet to attack at sunrise on the morning of the 2d of July at Gettysburg, those familiar with the controversy that arose out of a bitter assault by General Longstreet on myself will not be at all astonished. In my official report, dated in the month of August, 1863, after giving an account of the operations of the 1st of July,

I say: "Having been informed that the greater portion of the rest of our army would move up during the night, and that the enemy's position would be attacked on the right and left flanks very early next morning, I gave orders to General Hays to move his brigade, under cover of the night, from the town into the field on the left of it, where it would not be exposed to the enemy's fire, and would be in position to advance on Cemetery Hill when a favorable opportunity should occur. This movement was made, and Hays formed his brigade on the right of Avery, and just behind the extension of the low ridge on which a portion of the town if located. The attack did not begin in the morning of next day, as was expected, and in the course of the morning I rode with Gen. Ewell to examine and select a position for artillery."

Here is a statement of a fact while its recollection was fresh in my memory, and it cannot surely be said that it was made for the purpose of attacking General Longstreet's war record "because of political differences," or from any other motive.

On the 19th of January, 1872, the anniversary of General Lee's birth, I delivered an address at Washington and Lee University, by invitation of the faculty, and in that address, after speaking of the fight on the 1st at Gettysburg, I said:

> General Lee had ordered the concentration of his army at Cashtown, and the battle on this day, brought on by the advance of the enemy's cavalry, was unexpected to him. When he ascertained the advantage that had been gained, he determined to press it as soon as the remainder of his army arrived. In a conference with General Ewell, General Rodes and myself, when he did reach us, after the enemy had been routed, he expressed his determination to assault the enemy's position at daylight on the next morning, and wished to know whether we could make the attack from our flank—the left—at the designated time. We informed him of the fact that the ground immediately in our front, leading to the enemy's position, furnished much greater obstacles to a successful assault than existed at any other point, and we concurred in suggesting to him that, as our corps (Ewell's) constituted the only troops then immediately confronting the enemy, he would manifestly concentrate and fortify against us during the night, as proved to be the case, according to subsequent information. He then determined to make the attack from our right on the enemy's left, and left us for the purpose of ordering up Longstreet's corps in time to begin the attack at dawn next morning. That corps was not in readiness to make the attack until 4 o'clock in the afternoon of the next day. By that time Meade's whole army had arrived on the field and taken its position. Had the attack been made at daylight, as contemplated, it must have resulted in a brilliant victory, as all of Meade's army had not then arrived, and a very

> small portion of it was in position. A considerable portion of his army did not get up until after sunrise, one corps not arriving until 2 o'clock in the afternoon; and a prompt advance to the attack must have resulted in his defeat in detail. The position which Longstreet attacked at four was not occupied by the enemy until late in the afternoon, and Round Top Hill, which commanded the enemy's position, could have been taken in the morning without a struggle. The attack was made by two divisions, and though the usual gallantry was displayed by the troops engaged in it, no material advantage was gained.

This constituted my sole criticism on Longstreet's operations on the 2nd day. In speaking of the assault on the 3rd day, I said:

> On the next day, when the assault was made by Pickett's division in such gallant style, there was again a miscarriage in not properly supporting it according to the plan and orders of the Commanding-General. You must recollect that a Commanding-General cannot do the actual marching and fighting of his army. These must, necessarily, be entrusted to his subordinates, and any hesitation, delay, or miscarriage in the execution of his orders, may defeat the best-devised schemes. Contending against such odds as we did, it was necessary, always, that there should be the utmost dispatch, energy, and undoubting confidence in carrying out the plans of the Commanding-General. A subordinate who undertakes to doubt the wisdom of his superior's plans, and enters upon their execution with reluctance and distrust, will not be likely to ensure success. It was General Jackson's unhesitating confidence and faith in the chances of success that caused it so often to perch on his banners, and made him such an invaluable executor of General Lee's plans. If Mr. Swinton has told the truth, in repeating in his book what is alleged to have been said to him by General Longstreet, there was at least one of General Lee's corps commanders at Gettysburg who did not enter upon the execution of his plans with that confidence and faith necessary to success, and hence, perhaps, it was not achieved.

The foregoing constituted all the criticisms I had made on Gen. Longstreet's operations at Gettysburg, or on any other theatre during the war, previous to the controversy before alluded to. The views in regard to the delay in the attack on the 2nd had been repeated more succinctly in notes to my own report, which was published in the September and October numbers of the *Southern Magazine* for the year 1872. No where do I assert that General Lee had ordered General Longstreet to make the attack at sunrise, or at any other specific time. I merely state that he had announced to Generals Ewell, Rodes and myself his purpose to attack at dawn on the morning of the 2nd, and that he had left us for the purpose of ordering up

Longstreet's troops to begin the attack at that time. I do not know what were the specific orders given to Longstreet, and in that respect I am as good a witness for him as either of those he has produced, who simply do not know what were the orders given, nor when they were given. These orders were manifestly given in person, and no living man can say precisely what they were, except General Longstreet, if he indeed recollects them.

I was prompted to make the remarks I did make in my address at the Washington and Lee University from the fact that I had read Mr. Swinton's "Campaigns of the Army of the Potomac," and discovered that his criticisms on General Lee's conduct of the battle of Gettysburg, which are amplified in those now made in General Longstreet's name with a great similarity of expression in several respects, was based on information given by the latter to Mr. Swinton after the war. I here give some extracts from Swinton's book:

On page 340 he says:

> Indeed, in entering on the campaign, General Lee expressly promised his corps commanders that he would not assume a tactical offensive, but force his antagonist to attack him. Having, however, gotten a taste of blood in the considerable success of the first day, the Confederate commander seems to have lost that equipoise in which his faculties commonly moved, and he determined to give battle.

There is a foot note to this statement as follows:

> This and subsequent revelations of the purposes and sentiments of Lee I derive from General Longstreet, who, in a full and free conversation with the writer after the close of the war, threw much light on the motives and conduct of Lee during this campaign.

On pages 340–1, he says:

> Longstreet, holding the right of the Confederate line, had one flank securely posted on the Emmetsburg road, so that he was really between the Army of the Potomac and Washington, and by marching towards Frederick could undoubtedly have manœuvered Meade out of the Gettysburg position. This operation Gen. Longstreet, who foreboded the worst from an attack on the army in position, and was anxious to hold General Lee to his promise, begged in vain to be allowed to execute.

To this there is a foot note as follows:

> The officer named is my authority for this statement.

On page 358 there is this foot note:

> The absence of Pickett's division on the day before made General Longstreet very loth to make the attack; but Lee, thinking the Union force

> was not all up, would not wait. Longstreet urged in reply that this advantage (or *supposed* advantage, for the Union force *was* all up) was countervailed by the fact that *he* was not all up either, but the Confederate commander was not minded to delay. My authority is again General Longstreet.

These uncontradicted statements by Swinton, the genuineness of which is now verified by similar statements under General Longstreet's direct authority, not only justified me in the remarks I made, but imperatively demanded a defence of General Lee against the severe criticisms based on them, in the address delivered on the occasion referred to, which necessarily involved a review of his military career. When General Longstreet had thus thrown down the gauntlet, he had no right to complain that a friend of General Lee took it up.

After he had begun to muddy the stream at as early a period as twenty days after the battle of Gettysburg, by his letter to his uncle, and when he resumed the work then begun immediately after the war by his communications to Mr. Swinton, his complaint now of being "rancorously assailed by those whose intimacy with the Commanding-General in that battle gives an apparent importance to their assaults," brings to mind very forcibly the fable of the wolf and the lamb.

In February, 1876, he made a bitter assault on myself, among others, in a long article published in a New Orleans paper, the gravimen of his complaint against me being the remarks about Gettysburg contained in my address which I have given.

I replied to him, and I think I demonstrated beyond all question that he was responsible for the loss of the battle of Gettysburg.

I did not in either of my articles in reply to him assert that an order was given him to attack at sunrise on the 2nd. As before stated, I do not know what orders were given him, nor when they were given. I only know the declared purpose of General Lee, and I cannot believe that he did not take every step necessary to carry that purpose into effect, as every consideration required the attack on the morning of the 2nd to be made at the very earliest hour practicable.

The testimony General Longstreet has adduced is very far from establishing the fact that General Lee did not direct the attack to be made by him at a much earlier hour than that at which it was made.

Before referring to that testimony, I desire to say that the statement contained in the article in the *Times,* that the information of the crossing of the Potomac by the Federal army was received from a scout on the night of the 29th of June is erroneous. Gen. Longstreet's own report, as well as General Lee's detailed one, show that the information was received on the night of the 28th. If it had not been received until the night of the 29th, it would have been impossible for the order to return to reach me at York by the way of Carlisle in time for me to begin my march back early enough on the 30th to reach Gettysburg in time for the fight on the 1st of July. The fact was that I received the order on the morning of the 29th at York, with the information that the enemy had crossed the Potomac and was moving north.

The statements of Colonel Taylor and Marshall, and of General Long, as given by General Longstreet, that they knew nothing of an order to attack at "sunrise," amount to nothing. They had no personal knowledge of the orders that were given, or of the time when they were given. That is all their testimony amounts to. But General Longstreet omits a very important and significant part of General Long's letter. That letter, a copy of which I have, goes on to say, immediately after the part given by General Longstreet:

> As my memory now serves me, it was General Lee's intention to attack the enemy on the second of July as early as practicable; and it is my impression that he issued orders to that effect. I inferred that such was the case from the instructions that Gen. Lee gave me on the evening of the first and very early on the morning of the second of July.

See also General Long's letter to me in the August number of the Southern Historical Society Papers.

The letter of Colonel Venable is as follows:

> UNIVERSITY OF VIRGINIA, *May* 11, 1875.
>
> *General* JAMES LONGSTREET:
>
> DEAR SIR: Your letter of the 25th ultimo, with regard to Gen. Lee's battle order on the 1st and 2nd of July at Gettysburg, was duly received. I did not know of any order for an attack on the enemy at sunrise on the 2nd, nor can I believe any such order was issued by General Lee. About sunrise on the 2nd of July I was sent by General Lee to General Ewell to ask him what he thought of the advantages of an attack on the enemy from his position. (Colonel Marshall had been sent with a similar order on the night of the 1st.) General Ewell made me ride with him from point to point of his lines, so as to see with him the exact position of things. Before he got through the examination of the enemy's position General Lee came himself to General Ewell's lines. In sending the message to General Ewell, General Lee was explicit in saying that the question was whether he should move all the troops around on the right and attack on that side. I do not think that the errand on which I was sent by the Commanding-General is consistent with the idea of an attack at sunrise by any portion of the army.
>
> Yours, very truly,
>
> CHAS. S. VENABLE.

Can Colonel Venable or any one else believe that General Lee had formed no definite opinion as to how he should attack the enemy until after his return at 9 A.M. on the 2nd from Ewell's line? That, in fact, he did not make up his mind how to begin the attack until 11 A.M., when General Longstreet says the peremptory order was given to him? If that was the case, then he exhibited a remarkable degree of indecision and vascillation, and the responsibility for the procrastination and delay that occurred must rest on him, and on him alone.

That Colonel Venable is sincere in his opinions I do not doubt, but I think his reasoning is illogical and his deductions erroneous.

That General Lee made up his mind promptly to attack the enemy in his position on the Gettysburg Heights, there can be no doubt.

General Longstreet says:

> When I overtook General Lee at 5 o'clock that afternoon, he said, to my surprise, that he thought of attacking General Meade upon the heights the next day. I suggested that this course seemed to be at variance with the plan of the campaign that had been agreed upon before leaving Fredericksburg. He said: If the enemy is there to-morrow we must attack him.

He then goes on to give a long list of the reasons he urged against the attack, and says of General Lee:

> He, however, did not seem to abandon the idea of attack on the next day. He seemed under a subdued excitement which occasionally took possession of him when "the hunt was up," and threatened his superb equipoise. The sharp battle fought by Hill and Ewell on that day had given him a taste of victory.

Is this Swinton, or Longstreet, or the writer for the *Times?*

It is very clear to my mind that when General Lee found Longstreet so averse to an attack, he rode over to see Ewell, and then ensued that conference of which I have given an account. I can now fully understand the import of his expressions in regard to Longstreet, and his anxiety for the attack to be made by Ewell's corps.

When he rode back from that conference he found Longstreet, for the latter says: "I left General Lee quite late on the night of the first." And he further says: "When I left General Lee on the night of the first, I believe that he had made up his mind to attack, but was confident that he had not yet determined as to when the attack should be made."

Now, General Lee had announced to Ewell, Rodes, and myself his purpose to attack at daylight or as soon thereafter as practicable, and asked whether we could not attack with our corps at that time. No man knew better than he the value of time, and the supreme necessity of attacking before Meade's whole army was up, and is it credible that in talking to Longstreet about the attack he did not once intimate that he desired to attack as early as practicable on the morning of the 2nd, before Meade's army should all be up? Swinton says: "The absence of Pickett's division on the day before made General Longstreet very loth to make the attack; but Lee thinking the Union force was not all up, would not wait." This information he says he got from Longstreet. Is it not very certain, then, that General Lee was determined to make the attack before Meade's army was all up, and discussed with Longstreet the necessity of making the attack before Meade had time to concentrate? Longstreet's continued reluctance to make the attack, manifested no doubt on General Lee's return from Ewell's line, must have caused the sending of Colonel Marshall to Ewell on the night of the first, after the conference I have spoken of.

Longstreet says:

> On the morning of the 2nd I went to General Lee's headquarters at daylight and renewed my views against making an attack. He seemed resolved, however, and we discussed the results.

General Lee had been firmly resolved for near twelve hours to attack the enemy, and to attack him before all of his troops had been concentrated, and is it to be credited for a moment that he had not then made up his mind when he should attack, nor where, nor how? Is it not palpable that, finding Longstreet so persistently averse to the attack, and so loth to take the steps necessary to begin it, he again sent Col. Venable to Ewell to see whether, after viewing the position by daylight, he could not make the attack from his flank. Let us see what General Hood says in his letter to Longstreet. He says:

> I arrived with my staff in front of the heights of Gettysburg shortly after daybreak, as I have already stated, on the morning of the 2d of July. My division soon commenced filing into an open field near me, where the troops were allowed to stack arms and rest until further orders. A short distance in advance of this point, and during the early part of that same morning, we were both engaged, in company with Generals Lee and A. P. Hill, in observing the position of the Federals. General Lee—with coat buttoned to the throat, sabre-hilt buckled around the waist, and field-glasses pending at his side—walked up and down in the shade of large trees near us, halting now and then to observe the enemy. He seemed full of hope, yet at times buried in deep thought.
>
> Colonel Freemantle, of England, was ensconced in the forks of a tree not far off, with glass in constant use, examining the lofty position of the Federal army.

> General Lee was seemingly anxious that you should attack that morning. He remarked to me: "The enemy is here, and if we don't whip him he will whip us." You thought it best to await the arrival of Pickett's division—at that time still in the rear—in order to make the attack; and you said to me subsequently, whilst we were seated together near the trunk of a tree: "The General is a little nervous this morning; he wishes me to attack; I do not wish to do so without Pickett. I never like to go into battle with one boot off."
>
> Thus passed the forenoon of that eventful day when in the afternoon, about 3 o'clock, it was decided to no longer await Pickett's division, but to proceed to our extreme right and attack up the Emmettsburg road.

Can there longer be any question that General Lee wanted Longstreet to begin the attack very early in the morning—as early as possible, and that the latter threw every obstacle in the way? Doubtless, after sending Colonel Venable to Ewell, General Lee's impatience at Longstreet's opposition to the attack and the delay in the movement of his troops caused him to ride over to Ewell's line to see for himself if it was not practicable to make the attack from that flank. Upon being satisfied that it could not be made to advantage there he rode back and gave the peremptory order—which, Longstreet says, was given at 11 A.M., though he did not begin the attack until about 4 P.M. If, as Colonel Venable supposes, General Lee had been undecided or vascillating as to how, when, and by whom the attack should be made, from 5 P.M. the day before until 11 A.M. of the 2d, when Longstreet acknowledges the receipt of the order, then Longstreet's opinion that "there is no doubt that General Lee during the crisis of that campaign lost the matchless equipoise that usually characterized him, and that whatever mistakes were made were not so much matters of deliberate judgment as the impulses of a great mind disturbed by unparalleled conditions"—that is, in plain English, that General Lee had lost his senses—has some foundation to rest on.

All who know General Lee's mode of giving directions to his subordinates, can well understand how he indicated his purposes and wishes, without resorting to a technical order, and doubtless he indicated to General Longstreet in that way his desire for him to make the attack, and make it at the earliest practicable moment, and did not resort to the peremptory order until the time indicated by General Longstreet. To rely on that is standing upon a mere technicality. But when the order was given at 11 A.M., as acknowledged, why was it that it required until 4 P.M. to begin? The pretense that he made the attack with great promptness, because he attacked before any one else on that day, is simply ridiculous. Every one else was waiting for him to begin, as the orders required them to do. General

Ewell, in his report, in speaking of a contemplated movement by Johnson on our extreme left, says:

> Day was now breaking, and it was too late for any change of plans. Meantime orders had come from the General Commanding for me to delay my attack *until I heard General Longstreet's guns open on the right.*

He is here speaking of the morning of the 2d; and would Col. Venable have us believe that General Lee had not then made up his mind that Longstreet should open the attack, or communicated his intention to the latter?

There is one thing very certain, and that is that either General Lee or General Longstreet was responsible for the remarkable delay that took place in making the attack. I choose to believe that it was not General Lee, for if any one knew the value of promptness and celerity in military movements he did. It is equally certain that the delay which occurred in making the attack lost us the victory.

It was very natural that Longstreet's corps should be selected to assume the initiative on the 2nd day at Gettysburg. Neither of his divisions had been at the recent battles at Chancellorsville and Fredericksburg, except McLaws', and that division, with the exception of Barksdale's brigade, had not been as heavily engaged there as the other troops. Ewell's corps had captured Winchester and cleared the valley on its advance into Pennsylvania, and two of its divisions, as well as two of Hill's, had been heavily engaged on the first.

Can it be that General Longstreet apprehended that if the advantage gained on the first day was promptly and vigorously prosecuted the chief glory of the battle would devolve on the two corps which had first encountered the enemy and brought him to bay, and hence desired to change the theatre of the battle that was inevitable?

A careful study of the testimony of Meade and his officers, contained in the 1st volume, 2nd series, of the Congressional Report on the Conduct of the War, will satisfy any one that the bulk of the Federal army that was up was massed on the right, confronting Ewell's corps, all the forenoon of the 2nd, and that the Round Tops, the key to the position on the enemy's left were unoccupied until Longstreet's movement began at 4 P.M. The distance which Longstreet's corps had to march from its camp of the night of the 30th, to reach the town of Gettysburg itself, could not have exceeded 15 miles, and it had the whole day of the 1st to make it, though it was somewhat delayed by Johnson's division of Ewell's corps, which got the road first, by moving more promptly it is presumed. The Fifth corps of Meade's army was 23 miles from Gettysburg at the close of the fight on the first day, and the Sixth corps was 36 miles away, yet the former reached the field on the morning of the 2nd, and the latter at 2 P.M.

To show that a great opportunity to inflict a crushing defeat on Meade's army was lost by the failure to make the attack in the morning, I here reproduce what I said on that point in the discussion with General Longstreet which has been mentioned, as follows:

> That General Lee was correct in selecting the enemy's left for his attack, there can be no question, for that was the weakest and most assailable part of the enemy's line. That the possession of Round Top by us would have rendered the position at Gettysburg untenable by the enemy, is proved by the testimony of Meade himself, contained in the same volume of Reports on the Conduct of the War from which I have already quoted, and to which I will refer hereafter by page alone, to prevent unnecessary repetition. On page 332, in describing the attack on Sickles, Meade says: "At the same time that they threw immense masses on Sickles' corps, a heavy column was thrown upon the Round Top Mountain, which was the key-point of my whole position. If they had succeeded in occupying that, it would have prevented me from holding any of the ground which I subsequently held to the last." That Sickles did not occupy the position assaulted by General Longstreet until late in the afternoon, is proved by the testimony of Hancock and others. On page 406, Hancock says: "Every thing remained quiet, except artillery firing and engagements with pickets on our front, until about four o'clock that afternoon, when General Sickles moved out to the front." After stating that he had made a reconnoissance to ascertain whether an attack could be made on our left, Warren on page 377, says: "Soon afterwards I rode out with General Meade to examine the left of our line, where Gen. Sickles was. His troops could hardly be said to be in position." On page 332, Meade says he arrived on the ground where Sickles was, "a few minutes before 4 o'clock in the afternoon." That Round Top was unoccupied until after Longstreet's attack began, is proved by the testimony of Warren, who says, on page 377: "I then went, by General Meade's direction, to what is called Bald Top, and from that point I could see the enemy's lines of battle. I sent word to General Meade that we would at once have to occupy that place very strongly. He sent as quickly as possible, a division of General Sykes' corps; but before they arrived the enemy's line of battle—I should think a mile and a half long—began to advance, and the battle became very heavy at once. The troops under General Sykes arrived barely in time to save Round Top Hill, and they had a very desperate fight to hold it." During all the forenoon the bulk of Meade's troops which had arrived were massed on the right (enemy's), as Meade contemplated an attack from that flank—Hancock's corps connected with Howard's, and Sickles was on the left of

Hancock, but he did not go into position until the afternoon. On page 405, Hancock says: "I was placed on the line connecting Cemetery Hill with Little Round Top Mountain, my line, however, not extending to Round Top, probably only about half way. General Sickles was directed to connect with my left and the Round Top Mountain, thus forming a continuous line from Cemetery Hill (which was held by Gen. Howard) to Round Top Mountain."

These arrangements were not made until the morning was considerably advanced.

On page 331, Meade after stating his purpose to make an attack from his right says:

"Major General Slocum, however, reported that the character of the ground in front was unfavorable to making an attack; and the Sixth corps having so long a distance to march, and leaving at nine o'clock at night, did not reach the scene until about two o'clock in the afternoon. Under these circumstances I abandoned my intention to make an attack from my right, and as soon as the Sixth corps arrived, I directed the Fifth corps, then in reserve on the right, to move over and be in reserve on the left."

It was a division of the Fifth corps (General Syke's) that rescued the Round Top from the grasp of our assaulting column. Does not this show how weak the left was in the morning, and how easy it would have then been for our troops on the right to have gotten possession of the key to the position? That General Lee's plans were thwarted by the delay on the right, can any man doubt? On the occasion of the dedication of the Cemetery for the Federal soldiers killed at Gettysburg, Edward Everett, in the presence of President Lincoln, some of his cabinet, many members of Congress and officers of the army, and an immense concourse of citizens, delivered an address, in which he thus graphically describes the effect of the delay that took place:

"And here I cannot but remark on the Providential inaction of the rebel army. Had the conflict been renewed by it at daylight on the 2nd of July, with the First and Eleventh corps exhausted by battle, the Third and Twelfth weary from their forced march, and the Second, Fifth, and Sixth not yet arrived, nothing but a miracle could have saved the army from a great disaster. Instead of this the day dawned, the sun rose, the cool hours of the morning passed, and a considerable part of the afternoon wore away without the slightest aggressive movement on the part of the enemy. Thus time was given for half of our forces to arrive and take their places in the lines, while the rest of the army enjoyed a much needed half-day's repose."

It is to be presumed that before preparing an address that was to assume a historical character, Mr. Everett had obtained accurate knowledge of all that transpired within the Federal lines from the most authentic sources, and doubtless he presents a true picture of the actual condition of things.

If General Lee was responsible for the delay the effects of which were so graphically described by Mr. Everett, if, in fact, his mind was undecided and vascillating as to when, where, and how he should begin, then his conduct on that occasion was at war with his whole character and history. Who can believe it? I repeat here a remark I have made on another occasion when vindicating General Lee against a charge of want of decision and boldness in action: "There is another reason, which to me is a most potent one; and that is because I know that the boldest man in his strategic movements and his tactics on the field of battle, in all the Army of Northern Virginia, Stonewall Jackson not excepted, was General Robert E. Lee." I cannot believe, therefore, that he omitted to do anything necessary to carry out his avowed purpose of attacking the enemy at a very early hour on the morning of the 2nd, which every consideration so imperatively demanded, except to supersede General Longstreet with another commander of the First corps; and then the question arises: Where could one of sufficient rank have been found?

General Longstreet, or his annalist, has copied from the "Military Annals of Louisiana," a book I never heard of before, an absurd story about General Hays' having sent for me at the close of the fight on the 1st and urged an immediate advance on the heights, in which it is said that, though I agreed with Hays, I refused to allow him to seize those heights, because orders had been received from General Lee through Ewell to advance no further than Gettysburg, if we succeeded in capturing that place. As I have shown in my "Review," I received no orders whatever on that day from either General Ewell or General Lee until after the whole fighting was over, except the simple order on the march to move towards Gettysburg, the previous orders being to concentrate at Cashtown. General Longstreet says, in this connection: "General Hays told me ten years after the battle that he 'could have seized the heights without the loss of ten men.' " How mistaken General Hays was in making such a remark will abundantly appear from the facts I have already given in my "Review," and the statement of Bates in regard to the precautions taken by Steinwehr, whose division, of 4,000 men, occupied the heights immediately confronting Hays, whose brigade was considerably less than 1,400 strong at the close of the fight.

General Longstreet further says, after giving his evidence to prove that no order was given for an attack at sunrise:

> Having thus disproved the assertions of Messrs. Pendleton and Early in regard to this rumored order for a surprise attack, it appears that they are worthy of no further recognition; but it is difficult to pass beyond without noting the manner in which, by their ignorance, they marred the plans of their chief on the field of battle.

After referring to the removal of some seven pieces of artillery from one part of the field to another, as the manner in which General Pendleton, by his "ignorance," "marred the plans" of General Lee, General Longstreet is made to say: "General Early broke up General Lee's line of battle on the 2d of July, by detaching part of his division on some uncalled-for service, in violation of General Lee's orders, and thus prevented the co-operative attack of Ewell ordered by General Lee."

This statement must have been compiled by Gen. Longstreet's annalist from the copy of his assault on me which was furnished, for General Longstreet himself would hardly have reiterated it after I had so effectually exploded it in our controversy. My official report, as well as the very full statement contained in my "Review," show that two of my brigades were placed, on the afternoon of the 1st, before General Lee came to our part of the line, on the York road, to guard against a flank movement apprehended in that direction. They never were in the line on the 2nd at all, but Gordon's brigade was sent for on the 2nd, Stuart's cavalry having arrived, and got back just as Hays' and Hoke's brigades were moving to the assault of Cemetery Hill. The repetition of this statement is simply ridiculous, and shows how hard General Longstreet and his apologists are pressed. General Longstreet has not disproved the assertion made by General Pendleton that an order was given for the attack at sunrise. That assertion made by General Pendleton, and not by myself, was contained in an address delivered by him one year after mine had been delivered. General Longstreet has merely shown that four of General Lee's staff officers knew of no such order, but neither did they know what order was given, nor when any order was given for the attack. He omits to give a very significant part of General Long's letter, which tends to show that some order must have been given for an attack early on the morning of the 2nd. The question, therefore, rests on an issue of veracity between General Longstreet and General Pendleton. The latter was General Lee's chief of artillery, who had very important duties to perform in regard to posting the artillery for the impending battle, and it was very natural that General Lee should communicate to him the time when the battle was to open, and what orders had been given in regard thereto. It was not necessary to communicate the same facts to the staff-officers, whose statements are given. General Pendleton professes to have obtained the information as to the order from General Lee himself, and I am disposed to side with him on the question of veracity, just as I am disposed to side with Colonel Taylor on the direct issue of veracity raised by General Longstreet with him in regard to the order for the use of Hood's and McLaws' divisions in the attack made on the 3d.

General Lee's statement of his orders in regard to this latter attack would imply that the orders originally given in regard to it were to make it with Longstreet's whole corps, and is therefore corroborative of Colonel Taylor's statement.

It is to be observed here that General Longstreet has heretofore denied the authenticity of General Lee's detailed report, first published in the *Historical Magazine,* New York, then in the *Southern Magazine,* Baltimore, and lastly among the Southern Historical Society Papers from another copy, which confirms the genuineness of the first. The article now given under the sanction of his name quotes partly from the preliminary report given in the Appendix to Bates' History of the Battle of Gettysburg and partly from the detailed report; but it appears that he thinks the latter was written in a different spirit from that in which the preliminary report was written, and being a "somewhat critical account of that battle," from it his "critics get all their points against him." In speaking of "Ewell's inaction," he says:

> Having failed to move at 4 o'clock, while the enemy was in his front, it was still more surprising that he did not advance at 5 o'clock with vigor and promptness, when the trenches in front of him were vacated, or rather held by one single brigade, as General Meade's testimony before the Committee on the Conduct of the War states.

By this statement General Longstreet or his vicarious cronicler has endeavored to show that while the fighting was progressing on the enemy's left, our right, Ewell's corps, was confronted by only one brigade. This attempt to pervert Meade's testimony shows how little credit any of the statements or arguments contained in the article are entitled to.

Here is what Meade says in his testimony, page 333:

> During these operations upon the left flank, a division and two brigades of the Twelfth corps, which held the right flank, were ordered over for the purpose reinforcing the left. Only one brigade, however, arrived in time to take any part in the action, the enemy having been repulsed before the rest of the force came up. The absence of this large proportion of the Twelfth corps caused my extreme right flank to be held by one single brigade of the Twelfth corps, commanded by General Greene. The enemy perceiving this, made a vigorous attack upon General Greene, but were held at bay by him for some time, until he was reinforced by portions of the First and Eleventh corps, which were adjacent to him, when he succeeded in repulsing them.

In his official report, Bates' Battle of Gettysburg, page 240, Meade says:

> An assault was, however, made about eight P.M. on the Eleventh corps, from the left of the town, which was repelled by the assistance

> of troops from the Second and First corps. During the heavy assault upon our extreme left, portions of the Twelfth corps were sent as reinforcements. During their absence the line on the extreme right was held by a very much reduced force. This was taken advantage of by the enemy, who, during the absence of Gracy's division of the Twelfth corps, advanced and occupied part of the line.[1]

It was then on the extreme right from which troops were taken, so as to leave only one brigade there. This was at Culp's Hill and on the right of it (the enemy's), where the sides of the hill were wooded and exceedingly rugged. This part of the line confronted Johnson's division, while Cemetery Hill itself was held by the First and Eleventh corps, which Butterfield shows in his testimony numbered more than 10,000 men on the 4th of July, after all the fighting on the 2nd and 3rd. In addition, the Second corps, Hancock's, was on the left of the Eleventh corps, connecting with it. That corps had three divisions, only one of which was sent to the enemy's left during Longstreet's attack. The attack mentioned by Meade as having been made on the Eleventh corps, when troops from the Second and First corps came to its assistance, was the attack made by my two brigades described in my "Review."

That attack began sooner than Meade states. It began about sunset (see Bates), and my brigades were compelled to retire probably about or a little after 8 P.M. It will be seen that there is a very gross perversion, in the article of Meade's testimony. Instead of there being only one brigade to hold the trenches in front of Ewell, there was a force fully equal to the entire strength of Ewell's corps at that time, with two divisions of Hancock's corps in easy supporting distance. This attempt of General Longstreet or his apologist to misrepresent the facts for the purpose of casting censure on General Ewell, is wholly unjustified by any criticisms of the latter on him, and demonstrates how utterly unreliable the whole article is for historical purposes.[2]

The statement by General Alexander, who was only a colonel of artillery at Gettysburg, that the responsibility of ordering Pickett when to begin the charge on the third day was devolved on him, with permission even to abstain from giving the order or "advise," as it is called, while General Longstreet himself shrank from the responsibility properly attached to him, has excited profound astonishment. That statement is now confirmed by Gen. Longstreet's own version of the matter, and it becomes abundantly apparent that the orders and plans of General Lee did not receive from him that hearty support which was absolutely necessary to success.

I desire to say in conclusion, that I do not wish to be understood as in any manner reflecting upon the conduct of that superb body of men who constituted the First corps of the Army of Northern Virginia. Their part on this occasion, so far as devolved on them, was performed in a manner becoming soldiers battling for the righteous cause in which they were enlisted.

I must add that I have never at any time entertained the feeling that would exalt the soldiers from one state at the expense of those from another. It was my fortune to command at some time or other during the war soldiers from every Confederate state, including Kentucky and Missouri, except the state of Texes, and I also commanded the Maryland troops. I could cite instances in which the troops who fought under me from each of those states, respectively, performed the most brilliant and daring feats. As the soldiers from North Carolina, especially, have taken exception to the remarks and statements of others, I will take occasion to say, that every infantry organization from that state belonging to the Army of Northern Virginia, prior to my departure from it on my Valley campaign, had at some time been under my command, and there was but a very brief interval when I did not have North Carolina soldiers under me. I can say in all sincerity, that there were no better troops from any state in all that grand army than the North Carolina soldiers, and of all that bright galaxy of heroes who yielded their lives for their country's cause while serving with that army, the names of Anderson, Branch, Pender, Daniel, Ramseur, and Gordon of the cavalry, will stand among the foremost.

There was enough glory won by the Army of Northern Virginia for each state to have its full share and be content with it, and there is no occasion to wrangle over the distribution of the honors.

J. A. Early.

NOTES

1. It will be seen by this statement of General Meade's, the witness adduced by General Longstreet to show that all the troops from Ewell's front except one brigade had been allowed, by "Ewell's inaction," to be thrown against him, that only one brigade from that point arrived in time to take part in the action on the enemy's left, Meade adding: "The enemy having been repulsed before the rest of the force came up."

2. The following is another instance of a perversion of the testimony by General Longstreet or his compiler. In referring to Colonel Taylor's account of the delay in the attack from our right on the 2d, the article proceeds:

> He (Colonel Taylor) says: "General Longstreet's dispositions were not completed as early as was expected; [it appears that he was delayed by apprehensions that his troops would be taken in reverse as they advanced]. General Ewell, who had orders to co-operate with General Longstreet, and

who was, of course, not aware of any impediment to the main attack, having reinforced General Johnson during the night of the 2d, ordered him forward early the next morning. In obedience to these instruction, General Johnson became hotly engaged before General Ewell could be informed of the halt that had been called on our right."

Let us look at the facts of this. Instead of "making this attack at daylight," General Ewell says: "Just before the time fixed for General Johnson's advance the enemy attacked him to regain the works captured by Stuart the evening before."

This is all that is given of Ewell's statement, and then follows an extract from Meade's testimony. The part of Colonel Taylor's statement, put in brackets above, was omitted in the article. Here is Ewell's whole statement as contained in his report:

> I was ordered to renew my attack at daylight Friday morning, and as Johnson's position was the only one affording hopes of doing this to advantage, he was reinforced by Smith's brigade of Early's division, and Daniel's and Rodes' (old) brigades of Rode's division.
>
> Half an hour after Johnson attacked (on Friday morning), and when too late to recall him, I received notice that General Longstreet would not attack until 10 o'clock; but, as it turned out, his attack was delayed till after 2 o'clock. Just before the time fixed for Johnson's advance the enemy attacked him to regain the works captured by Stuart the evening before. They were repulsed with very heavy loss, and he attacked in turn, pushing the enemy almost to the top of the mountain, when the precipitous nature of the hill and an abattis of logs and stones, with a very heavy work on the crest of the hill, stopped his further advance. In Johnson's attack the enemy abandoned a portion of their works in disorder, and as they ran across an open space to another work, were exposed to the fire of Daniel's brigade at sixty or seventy yards. Our men were at this time under no fire of consequence, their aim was accurate, and General Daniel thinks that he killed there, in half an hour, more than in all the rest of the fighting.
>
> Repeated reports from the cavalry on our left that the enemy was moving heavy columns of infantry to turn General Johnson's left, at last caused him, about 1 P.M., to evacuate the works already gained. These reports reached me, also, and I sent Captain Brown, of my staff, with a party of cavalry to the left, to investigate them, who found them to be without foundation; and General Johnson finally took up a position about three hundred yards in rear of the works he had abandoned, which he held under a sharp fire of artillery and exposed to the enemy's sharpshooters until dark.

Meade's testimony is not at all inconsistent with this statement of facts; but by wresting our short statement of Ewell's from the context and adding Meade's, the false impression is sought to be made that Johnson did not attack at all. General Longstreet complains of "Ewell's inaction" on the 2d. What must be thought of his inaction from daylight to 2 P.M. on the 3d?

Letter on Causes of Lee's Defeat at Gettysburg

EDWARD PORTER ALEXANDER

MONTGOMERY, ALA., *March 17th*, 1877.

Rev. J. WM. JONES, *Sec'y:*

DEAR SIR: I have your favor of the 27th ult., enclosing copy of letter from ———, giving an outline of his views of the campaign and battle of Gettysburg, and inviting my comments thereon. I take great pleasure in giving them in the same frank spirit in which they are asked, and asking no one to accept them to whom they do not commend themselves, and not pretending to know *every thing* about it.

My rank and position during that campaign was colonel of artillery, commanding a battalion of six batteries attached as reserve to Longstreet's corps; and on the field of Gettysburg I was placed by General Longstreet in command of all of his artillery on the field as chief of artillery for the action. As I had belonged to the United States Engineer Corps before the war, and as General Longstreet at that time had no engineer officers on his staff, I was frequently called on, also, during the campaign, as an engineer officer. I mention these facts only that you may form an idea of my personal opportunities of observation and information.

And now as to the questions of ——— in their order:

First. Was the invasion a mistake? The proof of the pudding is the eating, and that test has certainly condemned it. I must also say frankly that my recollection is, that while the whole army went across the Potomac in the highest spirits, they were due more to confidence in General Lee than to an entire accordance of all of the prominet officers in the wisdom of the invasion. I remember conversations on the matter while on the march with one of the most gallant major-generals of the army—General Hood—in which he suggested all of the very grave considerations against it which are so forcibly put by ———. General Longstreet has also stated to me since (although during the campaign I do not remember a word or sign from him indicating any doubt in its success) that he urged similar considerations, very earnestly, upon General Lee, when the campaign was being discussed, and was only persuaded out of them by the understanding that we were not to deliver an *offensive* battle, but to so manoeuvre that Meade would be forced to attack us. Remember, in this connection, one of Stonewall Jackson's last speeches: "Our men *sometimes* fail to drive the enemy out of their positions, but they *always* fail to drive us." Such a confidence on General Lee's part would probably not have been misplaced, for he carried the best and largest army into Pennsylvania that he ever had in hand. The morale and spirit of the men was simply superb, as shown by the fight they made and the orderly and successful retreat after the battle. General Lee, in his report, has given the reasons which led him to plan the invasion. Whether he then fully appreciated all of the objections to it which can now be pointed out I do not know, but, even if he did, I can imagine his confidence in defeating the enemy in a decisive battle, by *forcing them to attack us,* as so great, and as based on such reasonable grounds, as to fully justify the movement. For it must be remembered that there were great objections to be found to his standing still and allowing the enemy to take the initiative.

Second question. I fully agree as to the necessity to General Lee of defeating the Federal army, and *perhaps* that army would fight better on its own soil than in Virginia, and would, therefore, be easier to defeat in Virginia; but bear in mind that the *great* condition to *assure* its defeat was to force it to attack General Lee. Moreover, he did manoeuvre in Virginia inviting an attack, but in vain—at least he gave Hooker opportunities which were not availed of, and no disposition shown to act on them during the few days they remained open. It is also very certain that General Lee could never have established his army in Pennsylvania with his communications open so as to get supplies, even of ammunition; but yet I think he could easily have so manoeuvred as to force Meade to attack him. A position covering Fairfield would have given him the Valley to support himself on, and would have been so threatening to Washington, Baltimore, Philadelphia and Harrisburg that *public clamor would have forced Meade to try and dislodge him.* We had ammunition enough for one good fight, and in a victory would capture enough for the next. If Lee was to cross the Potomac at all, I don't think the crossing should necessarily have been dependent on a previous victory. A subsequent one would have answered all purposes, and in all human probabilities it was nearly as certain.

They could have been forced to attack us, and they never had driven us from a field since the war began. Excellent positions also were to be found everywhere in that section, which was a lime stone country, well cleared and abounding in long parallel ridges like the Seminary ridge or Cemetery ridge at Gettysburg. So much for the general plan of the campaign; and before proceeding to the next questions of ———, relating more to the incidents of the battle itself, it is in order to inquire why the original plan was changed and an offensive battle delivered. And, on this subject, I know little or nothing that is not contained in General Lee's report. My general recollection is that we considered the enemy very slow in moving upon us, and took our time every where to give him opportunities to attack, if he desired, and that the concentration which was ordered at Gettysburg was intended as an offer of battle to him. In making this concentration Hill's corps unexpectedly came in collision with Reynolds' corps, and the thing began. Reynolds' corps was not expected there, and our information of the enemy's movements was incomplete on account of the absence of all of the cavalry, or nearly all, with General Stuart, who, instead of being between us and the enemy, was on a raid around him. In this way the action began, and the first day's success stimulated the second day's effort. This effort should have been successful, and would have been, but for delays and faults of detail in its execution. These have been the subject of much crimination and recrimination among survivors as to the greater or less responsibility of them, but, to history, of course the general commanding is the responsible party. I will write frankly all that I know about them personally further on. It is sufficient to say here that, as I have already implied, the battle was lost by them, and, in fact, under the conditions existing when the actual conflict was joined, success was *almost impossible.*

Even after the second day's battle, in my humble judgment, it was possible to have withdrawn from the offensive and taken the defensive, and forced Meade to assault us, and to have given him a crushing defeat. I may be mistaken, and I do not by any means set up as a military critic in general, but, as we did offer battle on the 4th, and again for several days near Hagerstown, on the retreat (while waiting to construct a bridge over the Potomac), and as Meade did at last feel bound to attack us, but just a day too late to do it, I think a similar course might have been successfully pursued after the action of the second. Whether it was discussed I do not know, but I do know that Longstreet was very averse to the assault by Pickett's division on the third. He only expressed his opinion about it, so far as I know, after the division was launched, but the circumstances which I will detail presently led me to infer that he had discussed the matter fully with General Lee. And now I will give what details of the battle itself fell under my personal observation, which may assist in an understanding of the whole matter, and I will be very careful to give nothing unqualifiedly of which I am not personally certain.

My command, with the greater portion of Longstreet's corps, was in camp at Chambersburg from Saturday, June 27th, to Tuesday, June 30th, and on the latter date we moved in direction of Gettysburg, about 10 miles, and about 2 P.M. encamped at a small village called Greenwood. General Lee was in camp very near us during the same afternoon. On Wednesday, July 1st, we (the reserve artillery) remained in camp all day, and heard nothing of the battle which was begun at Gettysburg until about dark, when orders were received to march at 2 A.M. on the 2d for Gettysburg. Pickett's division of infantry had been left behind at Chambersburg, Hood's and McLaws' divisions had marched before us, and when we took the road at 2 A.M. (my batallion, 26 guns, and the Washington Artillery, 10 guns, I think, forming the artillery reserve,) we had a clear road and bright moonlight, and saw nothing of the infantry. About 8 or 9 A.M. we reached the vicinity of the field, and the guns were halted in a wood, and I reported in person to Generals Lee and Longstreet, who were together on a hill in rear of our lines. I was told that we were to attack the enemy's left flank, and was directed to take command of my own batallion—Cabell's batallion (with McLaws' division), 18 guns; Henry's batallion (with Hood's), 18 guns—leaving the Washington Artillery in reserve, and to reconnoitre the ground and co-operate with the infantry in the attack. I was especially cautioned in moving up the guns to avoid exposing them to the view of a signal station of the enemy's on Round Top mountain. I do not remember seeing or hearing any thing at this time of Longstreet's infantry, nor did I get the impression that General Lee thought there was any unnecessary delay going on. I had just arrived, and knew nothing of the situation, and my instructions were to reconnoitre the flank to be attacked, and choose my own positions and means of reaching them. This duty occupied me, according to the best of my recollection, one or two hours, when I rode back, and in person conducted my own batallion to the school-house on Willoughby run. At one point the direct road leading to this place came in sight of the enemy's signal station, but I turned out of the road before reaching the exposed part, and passing through some meadows a few hundred yards, regained the road without coming in sight. I then went about hunting up the other batallions which were attached to the infantry in order to give them all their positions for opening the attack. While thus engaged I came upon the head of an infantry column, which I think was Hood's division, standing halted in the road where it was in sight of Round Top. They had been instructed to avoid being seen, and finding that the road on which they had been sent came at this point in full view of the signal station, they had halted, in finding themselves already exposed, and sent back to General Lee or Longstreet for orders. For some reason, which I cannot now recall, they would not turn back and follow the tracks of my guns, and I remember a long and tiresome waiting; and at length there came an order to turn back and take another road around by "Black Horse Tavern," and I have never forgotten that name since. My general recollection is that nearly three hours were lost in that delay and countermarch, and that it was about 4 P.M. when Hood became engaged heavily on our extreme right flank, with Henry's batallion aiding him, while, with 18 guns of my own batallion and Cabell's 18, I attacked Hooker's corps at the Peach Orchard. McLaws' division was, during this, in the woods in our rear, our batteries firing from the edge next the Peach Orchard—my own probably 500 yards and Cabell's 700 yards distant. We were so engaged probably for an hour, when McLaws charged and carried the Peach Orchard, my batteries following him closely and going into action in and around the Orchard, and the firing was kept up thence till after dark.

Note—I have just found copy of a brief-dairy kept by Colonel G. Moxley Sorrel, Adjutant-General of Longstreet's corps, from which I copy the following entries, showing movements of the infantry divisions more accurately:

JUNE 30TH.—Moved (from Chambersburg) for Greenwood, where we camped at night, Pickett being left back at Chambersburg.

JULY 1ST.—Moved out from Greenwood on the Gettysburg road, passing through Cashtown and New Salem; arrive within two miles of Gettysburg; during the day A. P. Hill's corps is sharply engaged; also Ewell on the left. The enemy is driven steadily back, and the lines occupied by Rodes' division. McLaws, Hood, and the artillery are now moving up and Pickett is ordered from Chambersburg.

JULY 2D AND 3D.—See Battle Reports of General Longstreet.

JULY 4TH.—After the disasters of yesterday the morning opens very quietly, our troops occupying their original positions. There is not even the usual light skirmishing. Both armies appear thoroughly exhausted. Preparations are apparent for a backward movement by the right. The wagons are sent to Cashtown. The movement begins at dark, A. P. Hill leading and our corps following him in the order—1st. Reserve artillery; 2d. Pickett; 3d. McLaws; 4th. Hood. The troops move all night and the next day (5), when they camp in the afternoon near Monterey Springs. The retirement of our forces is not molested by the enemy. They evidently believed in building a golden bridge for a flying enemy.

Before daylight on the morning of the 3d I received orders to post the artillery for an assault upon the enemy's position, and later I learned that it was to be led by Pickett's division and directed on Cemetery Hill. Some of the batteries had gone back for ammunition and forage, but they were all brought up immediately, and by daylight all then on the field were posted.

Dearing's battalion (with Pickett's division) reported sometime during the morning. The enemy fired on our movements and positions occasionally, doing no great damage, and we scarcely returned a shot. The morning was consumed in waiting for Pickett's division, and possibly other movements of infantry. While forming for the attack, I borrowed from General Pendleton, General Lee's chief of artillery, seven 12 pounder howitzers, belonging to the Third corps, under Major Richardson, which I put in reserve in a selected spot, intending them to accompany Pickett's infantry in the charge to have the advantage of fresh horses and men and full chests of ammunition for the critical moment, in case the batteries engaged in the preliminary cannonade should be so cut up and exhausted as to be slow in getting up. About 11 A.M. the skirmishers in A. P. Hill's front got to fighting for a barn in between the lines, and the artillery on both sides gradually took part until the whole of Hill's artillery in position, which I think was 63 guns, were heavily engaged with about an equal number of the enemy's guns for over a half hour, but not one of the 75 guns which I then had in line was allowed to fire a shot, as we had at best but a short supply of ammunition for the work laid out. In this connection note that the number of rounds which is carried with each piece in its limber and caisson is, including canister, about 130 to 150—about enough for one hour and a half of rapid firing. I am *very sure* that our ordnance trains did not carry into Pennsylvania a reserve supply of more than 100 rounds per gun additional, and I don't believe they had over 60 rounds to a gun. I have never seen the figures, but I was myself chief of ordnance of the army from August, 1861, to November, 1862, and was very familiar with the extent and capacity of the ordnance trains. When nearer Richmond we seldom had a reserve of over 50 rounds per gun, the difficulty of transportation always limiting us to the utmost economy in its use, and in the trains devoted to its carriage. Gradually the cannonade just referred to died out as it began, and the field became nearly silent, but writers have frequently referred to "the cannonade preceding the assault" as having begun at 11 o'clock and lasted for some hours, being misled by this affair. About 12 M. General Longstreet told me that when Pickett was ready, he would himself give the signal for all our guns to open (which was to be two guns from the Washington Artillery, near the center of our line), and meanwhile he desired me to select a suitable position for observation, and to take with me one of General Pickett's staff, and exercise my judgment in selecting the moment for Pickett's advance to begin. Complying, I selected the advanced salient angle of the wood in which Pickett's line was now formed, just on the left flank of my line of 75 guns. While occupying this position and in conversation with General A. R. Wright, commanding a Georgia brigade in A. P. Hill's corps, who had come out there for an observation of the position, I received a note from

General Longstreet, which I copy from the original still in my possession, as follows:

HD. QRS., *July 3rd,* 1863.

COLONEL:

If the artillery fire does not have the effect to drive off the enemy or greatly demoralize him so as to make our efforts pretty certain, I would prefer that you should not advise General Pickett to make the charge. I shall rely a great deal on your good judgment to determine the matter, and shall expect you to let General Pickett know when the moment offers.

Respectfully,

J. LONGSTREET, *Lieut.-General.*

To Colonel E. P. ALEXANDER, *Artillery.*

This note at once suggested that there was some alternative to the attack, and placed me on the responsibility of deciding the question. I endeavored to avoid it by giving my views in a note, of which I kept no copy, but of which I have always retained a vivid recollection, having discussed its points with General A. R. Wright as I wrote it. It was expressed very nearly as follows:

GENERAL:

I will only be able to judge of the effect of our fire on the enemy by his return fire, for his infantry is but little exposed to view and the smoke will obscure the whole field. If, as I infer from your note, there is any alternative to this attack, it should be carefully considered before opening our fire, for it will take all the artillery ammunition we have left to test this one thoroughly, and, if the result is unfavorable, we will have none left for another effort. And even if this is entirely successful it can only be so at a very bloody cost.

Very respectfully, &c.,

E. P. ALEXANDER, *Colonel Artillery.*

To this note I soon received the following reply—the original still in my possession:

HD. QURS., *July 3rd,* 1863.

COLONEL:

The intention is to advance the infantry if the artillery has the desired effect of driving the enemy's off, or having other effect such as to warrant us in making the attack. When that moment arrives advise General P., and of course advance such artillery as you can use in aiding the attack.

Respectfully,

J. LONGSTREET, *Lieut.-General, Commanding.*

To Colonel ALEXANDER.

This letter again placed the responsibility upon me, and I felt it very deeply, for the day was rapidly advancing (it was about 12 M., or a little later), and whatever was to be done was to be done soon. Meanwhile I had been anxiously discussing the attack with General A. R. Wright, who said that the difficulty was not so much in *reaching* Cemetery Hill, or taking it—that his brigade had carried it the afternoon before—but that the trouble was to hold it, for the whole Federal army was massed in a sort of horse shoe shape and could rapidly reinforce the point to any extent, while our long, enveloping line could not give prompt enough support. This somewhat reassured me, as I had heard it said that morning that General Lee had ordered "every brigade in the army to charge Cemetery Hill," and it was at least certain that the question of supports had had his careful attention. Before answering, however, I rode back to converse with General Pickett, whose line was now formed or forming in the wood, and without telling him of the question I had to decide, I found out that he was entirely sanguine of success in the charge, and was only congratulating himself on the opportunity. I was convinced that to make any half-way effort would insure a failure of the campaign, and that if our artillery fire was once opened, after all the time consumed in preparation for the attack, the only hope of success was to follow it up promptly with one supreme effort, concentrating every energy we possessed into it, and my mind was fully made up that *if the artillery opened Pickett must charge.* After the second note from General Longstreet, therefore, and the interview with Pickett, I did not feel justified in making any delay, but to acquaint General Longstreet with my determination. I wrote him a note, which I think I quote verbatim, as follows: "General: When our artillery fire is doing its best I shall advise General Pickett to advance." It was my intention, as he had a long distance to traverse, that he should start not later than fifteen minutes after our fire opened. About this time, too, to be sure that Richardson with his seven 12-pounder howitzers should be promptly on hand, I sent for him to come up through the woods and be ready to move ahead of Pickett's division in the advance. To my great disappointment I learned just as we opened fire, and too late to replace him, that General Pendleton had sent four of his guns, without my knowledge, to some other part of the field, and the other three had also moved off and could not be found. Probably, however, the presence of guns in the head of this column would only have resulted in their loss, but it would have been a brilliant opportunity for them, and I always feel like apologizing for their absence.

It was 1 P.M. by my watch when the signal guns were fired, the field at that time being entirely silent, but for light picket firing between the lines, and as suddenly as an organ strikes up in a church, the grand roar followed from all the guns of both armies. The enemy's fire was heavy and secure, and their accounts represent ours as having been equally so, though our rifle guns were comparatively few and had only very defective ammunition. As an illustration, I remember that the casualties in my own battalion (26 guns) were about 147 men and 116 horses in the two days' actions, and about 80 per cent of the wounds were from artillery fire. General A. S. Webb, U. S. A., who commanded a brigade on Cemetery Hill, told me, after the war, that a Federal battery, coming into action on the Hill, lost from our artillery fire 27 out of 36 horses in about ten minutes. Average distances I should suppose were about 1,400 yards. We had some casualties from canister. I had fully intended giving Pickett the order to advance as soon as I saw that our guns had gotten their ranges, say, in ten or fifteen minutes, but the enemy's fire was so severe that when that time had elapsed I could not make up my mind to order the infantry out into a fire which I did not believe they could face, for so long a charge, in such a hot sun, tired as they already were by the march from Chambersburg. I accordingly waited in hopes that our fire would produce some visible effect, or something turn up to make the situation more hopeful; but fifteen minutes more passed without any change in the situation, the fire on neither side slackening for a moment. Even then I could not bring myself to give a peremptory order to Pickett to advance, but feeling that the critical moment would soon pass, I wrote him a note to this effect: "If you are coming at all you must come immediately or I cannot give you proper support; but the enemy's fire has not slackened materially, and at least 18 guns are still firing from the Cemetery itself."

This note (which, though given from memory, I can vouch for as very nearly verbatim) I sent off at 1:30 P.M., consulting my watch. I afterwards heard what followed its receipt from members of the staff of both Generals Pickett and Longstreet, as follows: Pickett on receiving it galloped over to General Longstreet, who was not far off, and showed it to General L. The latter read it and made no reply. (General Longstreet himself, speaking of it afterwards, said that he knew the charge had to be made, but could not bring himself to give the order.) General Pickett then said: "General, shall I advance?" Longstreet turned around in his saddle and would not answer. Pickett immediately saluted, and said, "I am, going to lead my division forward, sir," and galloped off to put it in motion; on which General L. left his staff and rode out alone to my position. Meanwhile, five minutes after I sent the above note to Pickett, the enemy's fire suddenly slackened materially, and the batteries in the Cemetery were limbered up and were withdrawn. As the enemy had such abundance of ammunition and so much better guns than ours that they were not compelled to reserve their artillery for critical moments (as we almost always had to do), I knew that they must have felt the punishment a good deal, and I was a good deal elated by the sight. But to make sure that it was a withdrawal for good, and not a mere change of position or relieving of the batteries by fresh ones, I waited for five minutes more, closely examining the ground with a large glass. At that time I sent my courier to Pickett with a note: "For God's sake come quick; the 18 guns are gone"; and, going to the nearest gun, I sent a lieutenant and a sergeant, one after the other, with other messages to same effect. A few minutes after this, Pickett still not appearing, General Longstreet rode up alone, having seen Pickett and left his staff as above. I showed him the situation, and said I only feared I could not give Pickett the help I wanted to, my ammunition being very low, and the seven guns under Richardson having been taken off. General Longstreet spoke up promptly: "Go and stop Pickett right where he is, and replenish your ammunition." I answered that the ordnance wagons had been nearly emptied, replacing expenditures of the day before, and that not over 20 rounds to the gun were left—too little to accomplish much—and that while this was being done the enemy would recover from the effect of the fire we were now giving him. His reply was: "I don't want to make this charge; I don't believe it can succeed. I would stop Pickett now, but that General Lee has ordered it and expects it," and other remarks, showing that he would have been easily induced, even then, to order Pickett to halt. It was just at this moment that Pickett's line appeared sweeping out of the wood, Garnett's brigade passing over us. I then left General Longstreet and rode a short distance with General Garnett, an old friend, who had been sick, but, buttoned up in an old blue overcoat, in spite of the heat of the day, was riding in front of his line. I then galloped along my line of guns, ordering those that had over 20 rounds left to limber up and follow Pickett, and those that had less to maintain their fire from where they were. I had advanced several batteries or parts of batteries in this way, when Pickett's division appeared on the slope of Cemetery Hill, and a considerable force of the enemy were thrown out, attacking his unprotected right flank. Meanwhile, too, several batteries which had been withdrawn were run out again and were firing on him very heavily. We opened on these troops and batteries with the best we had in the shop, and appeared to do them considerable damage, but meanwhile Pickett's division just seemed to melt away in the blue musketry smoke which now covered the hill. Nothing but stragglers came back. As soon as it was clear that Pickett was "gone up," I ceased firing, saving what little ammunition was left for fear of an advance by the enemy. About this time General Lee came up to our guns alone and remained there a half hour or more, speaking to Pickett's men as they came straggling back, and encouraging them to form again in the first cover they could find. While he was here Colonel Fremantle, of the Coldstream Guards, rode up, who afterwards wrote a very graphic account of the battle and of incidents occurring here, which was published in Blackwood's Magazine. A little before this, Heth's division, under Pettigrew, had been advanced also, but I cannot recall the moment or the place where I saw them, but only the impression on my mind, as the men passed us, that the charge must surely be some misapprehension of orders, as the circumstances at the moment made it utterly impossible that it could accomplish any thing, and I thought what a pity it was that so many of them were about being sacrificed in vain. It was intended, I believe, that Pettigrew should support Pickett's right flank, but the distance that had to be traversed in the charge got such and interval between the two that Pickett's force was spent and his division disintegrated before Pettigrew's got under close fire. I have always believed that the enemy here lost the greatest opportunity they ever had of routing General Lee's army by prompt offensive. They occupied a line shaped somewhat like a horse shoe. I suppose that the greatest diameter of the horse shoe was not more than one mile, and the ground within was entirely sheltered from our observation and fire, with communications by signals all over it, and they could concentrate their whole force at any point in a very short while and without our knowledge. Our line was an enveloping semi-circle, over four miles in development, and communication from flank to flank even by courier was difficult, the country being well cleared and exposed to the enemy's view and fire, the roads all running at right angles to our lines, and some of them at least broad turnpikes which the enemy's guns could rake for two miles. Is it necessary now to add any statement as to the superiority of the Federal force or the exhausted and shattered condition of the Confederates for a space of at least a mile in their very center, to show that a great opportunity was thrown away? I think that General Lee himself was quite apprehensive that the enemy would "ri poote," and that it was that apprehension which brought him alone out to my guns where he could observe all the indications.

Note.—In Fremantle's account he tells of General Lee's reproving an artillery officer for spurring his horse severely when it shied at the bursting of a shell. The officer was my ordnance officer and acting adjutant, Lieutenant F. M. Colston, now of Baltimore, and the shying was not at the bursting of a shell, but, just at that time there was a loud cheering in the enemy's line, a little on the right, and General Lee requested Colston to ride towards it and discover if it indicated an advance. Colston's horse cut up because it did not want to leave my horse, the two being together a great deal on the march and in the camp. General Lee then spoke to him, as Fremantle narrates; and the cheering turned out to be given to some general officer riding along the Federal line.

In the above narrative I have given all the light I can throw on the subjects of enquiry in the 4th and 5th questions of ———'s letter, the 1st and 2d having been previously discussed. The 3d question relates to the lack of co-ordination between the attacks of the 2d July; and a similar lack of co-ordination is equally patent in the attacks on the 3d. I attribute it partially to the fact that our staff organizations were never sufficiently extensive and perfect to enable the Commanding-General to be practically present every where and to thoroughly handle a large force on an extended field, but principally it was due to the exceedingly difficult shape in which our line was formed, the enemy occupying a center and we a semi-circumference, with poor and exposed communications along it. I believe it was simply *impossible* to have made different attacks from the flanks and center of the line we occupied and over the different distances which would have to be traversed and which should be so simultaneous that the *squeeze* would fall on the enemy at all points at the same time. And in this connection, I think that the very position which we took and every feature of the three days' conflict shows the absurdity of a story told by Swinton, who is generally very fair and above giving anecdotes suitable only for the marines. He says that some of our brigades were encouraged to the charge by being told that they were to meet only Pennsylvania militia, but on getting very near the enemy's line they "recognized the bronzed features of the veterans of the Army of the Potomac," (I quote from memory) and were at once panic-struck. Such stories are not only absurd, but, in a history, are in bad taste, having a tendency to provoke retorts. The above has been written in piece-meal in leisure moments during the past month, and with scarcely the opportunity to read it over, which must be my apology for its deficiencies; but as narrative of what fell under my personal knowledge, it may assist ——— in understanding some of the points of his enquiries, and is at your service for that or any other purpose.

Very respectfully, yours,

E. P. ALEXANDER.

Why Was Gettysburg Lost?

DOUGLAS SOUTHALL FREEMAN

Would Meade attack? Every man in the Army of Northern Virginia put that question to himself on the morning of the 4th of July, and no man knew the answer. If the Federals had the strength to take the initiative, they would find the Confederates frightfully extended, bleeding, and almost without ammunition. Should the Union commander for any reason withhold attack, another dawn would find Lee on his way back to Virginia, moving as fast as he could without endangering his wagon-train.

As the anxious hours passed without any sign of a Union offensive, the plans for the withdrawal took form. Instead of following the long route back to Chambersburg and thence to Hagerstown, the army was to go southwestward to Fairfield and westward to Greencastle. Stuart was to send a brigade or two of cavalry to hold the passes west of Cashtown on the Chambersburg pike, so that the Federal horse could not advance by that line and get ahead of the slower-moving Southern infantry before it reached the Potomac. The rest of the Confederate troopers were to use the Emmitsburg road and protect the rear and left flank of the army. The wounded were to leave as soon as practicable. Hill was to follow. Then Longstreet was to take up the march and was to guard the prisoners. Ewell would cover the rear. All the wagons not used in transporting the wounded were to form a single train, placed midway the column. To prevent all misunderstandings, Lee issued these orders explicitly and in writing.[1]

A hundred troublesome details absorbed the weary commander of the defeated army. In an effort to relieve himself of the burden of 4000 unwounded prisoners, he dispatched a flag of truce proposing an exchange, but Meade prudently declined.[2] Engineers were sent back to select a line in rear of Hagerstown, in case the enemy pursued vigorously;[3] the wounded were painfully assembled with great difficulty, and an artillery force was provided to supplement the escort, which consisted of Imboden's cavalry.[4] A brief report was prepared for the President.[5]

To add to the difficulties of the retreat, a torrential rain began to fall ominously about 1 P.M. and delayed the start of the ambulance train.[6] Final preparations had to be made in a blinding storm. When at last the wounded were on their way, in rough wagons that were as torturing as the rack,[7] fully 5000 sulkers and sick contrived to march with them. Lee could not readily prevent this, but he was most solicitous that no panic or sense of demoralization spread among the troops. When "Sandie" Pendleton brought the daily report of the Second Corps, he said to Lee encouragingly, "General, I hope the other two corps are in as good condition for work as ours is this morning." Lee was fond of "Sandie," but talk of this sort was apt to create dangerous impressions, so he looked steadily at young Pendleton and said coldly, "What reason have you, young man, to suppose they are not?"[8] To sustain the morale, he moved about as calmly as if the withdrawal of the army in the face of the foe were a simple summer's-day field manœuvre. He had little to say, but when he rode past the camps of the Texans and was welcomed with their loyal cheer, he was not too much absorbed in his own sombre thoughts to raise his hat in acknowledgment of their greeting.[9] In the afternoon, while the storm raged, Lee, without a tremor visible to any one, surveyed from one of the ridges the tragic scene of the defeat;[10] and when, in the evening, he stopped at Longstreet's bivouac on the roadside, his remark was the same as that with which he had met Pickett on the field after the fatal charge: "It's all my fault," he said, "I thought my men were invincible."[11] Longstreet had lost his sullenness in the face of the disaster to the army, and though he and Lee did not talk of the battle, Longstreet calmly voiced his sobered opinion to Colonel Fremantle. The assault had failed, he said, because it had not been made with a sufficient number of men. He made no reference then to the rejection of his plan of moving by the right in an effort to get between the enemy and Washington.[12]

The next day, July 5, was sixteen daylight hours of purgatory. The rain was falling as heavily as ever; the men were muddy, wet, and hungry.[13] So slowly did the other corps drag themselves along the blocked road that it was 2 A.M. before Ewell left the field of Gettysburg, and 4 P.M. by the time he reached Fairfield,[14] which was less than nine miles from his starting point. Even then, some of his wagons were lost.[15] Ewell was so outraged by this that he wished to turn back and get immediate revenge, but Lee refused to countenance such a foolish adventure. "No, no, General Ewell," he said, "we must let those people alone for the present—we will try them again some other time."[16] The rain continued during the night of July 5–6,[17] but as the leading corps was then through the mountains it was able to move, unabashed, at greater speed than it had ever made before in putting distance between itself and its old adversary. "Let him who will say it to the contrary," one Texas recruit confided in a letter to his wife, "we made Manassas time from Pennsylvania."[18]

At 5 o'clock on the afternoon of the 6th, Longstreet's corps, which was then the van, succeeded in reaching Hagerstown.[19] Lee rode with it and found to his vast relief that the ambulance train had arrived at Williamsport that day with the wounded. But the elements had again done battle against the South: the pontoon bridge below the town had been broken up by a raiding party, and the Potomac, swollen by the rains, was far past fording. The army, its wounded and its prisoners, were cut off from Virginia soil. More than that, a mixed force of Federal cavalry and artillery had appeared in the rear and had threatened the capture of the wagons and their pain-racked loads. The teamsters had been organized, however, to support Imboden, two regiments of infantry that had been returning from Winchester had been rushed up, and the attack had been held off until Stuart had arrived with his cavalry. The Federals had then been repulsed.[20] Despite this success, the situation was worse than serious. The raging river was so high that some days, perhaps a week, would pass before it was fordable. The country roundabout had already been foraged; few supplies could be collected. Meade, in Lee's opinion, was certainly pursuing in the hope of attacking before he crossed the Potomac. Any long delay would involve another battle in Maryland, and a disaster with the river at flood would mean annihilation.[21]

Lee's first thought was for his wounded. He gave orders that all the ferry-boats in the vicinity should be collected so that he might use them in transporting the sufferers to the south bank.[22] The wagons must wait until the river subsided or until the pontoon bridge could be reconstructed,[23] and if Meade attacked, the army must prepare to give battle once more to the Federals.[24] Fortunately, the engineers had found and had laid out an admirable defensive line. It extended from Downsville, which lies three miles south of Williamsport, northward in front of that town to the Conocoheague. Both flanks were well covered.[25]

The men in the ranks were not conscious of the danger they faced, or else they defied it. They were in sight of their own country once more and their morale seemed unimpaired, thin as were the ranks.[26] "We are all right at Hagerstown," one of Lee's staff officers wrote his sister reassuringly, "and we hope soon to get up another fight."[27] Another young soldier maintained, "The army is in fine spirits and confident of success when they again meet the enemy."[28] Lee himself reported the condition of the army good "and its confidence unimpaired."[29] The bands began to play again,[30] and the soldiers renewed their jests. Some of the men were not so mindful as Lee had commanded in respecting the property of the Maryland farmers, and had to be given stern orders not to forage or to steal horses.[31] Finding one battalion of artillery burning fence rails, Lee sent for the major and asked if a copy of General Orders No. 73 had reached him. The officer admitted that he had received those famous instructions against damaging the property of civilians. "Then, sir," said Lee, "you must not only have them published, but you must see that they are obeyed."[32]

In the press of duties in front of Williamsport, Lee found the loss and suffering of his men brought home to him. On June 26, his own son, Rooney Lee, wounded at Brandy Station, had been taken from his bed at "Hickory Hill," Hanover County, by a Federal raiding party, and had been carried to Fort Monroe, where he was held as a hostage for the good treatment of some Federal officers who had been threatened with death as a measure of retaliation. Lee's warmth of feeling for Rooney made the capture of his son a deep personal sorrow, and he hastened, busy as he was, to send comforting words to the soldier's young wife.[33]

Not for a moment, however, did Lee let his concern for Rooney or his uneasiness for his troops shake his equanimity. No trace of resentment was there in his dealings with the men who had failed him. He greeted Longstreet cordially as "my old war horse."[34] In fact, for months thereafter Lee showed more than usual warmth to Longstreet, as if to make it plain that he did not blame him and did not countenance any whispering against Longstreet that might cause dissension in the army.[35] When Captain Ross, the Austrian observer, came to call, Lee talked of Gettysburg as if all the fault had been his own. He told Ross that if he had been aware that Meade had been able to concentrate his whole army, he would not have attacked him, but that the success of the first day, the belief that Meade had only a part of his army on the field, and the enthusiasm of his own troops had led him to conclude that the possible results of a victory justified the risks. He added that his lack of accurate knowledge of the enemy's concentration was due to the absence of Stuart's cavalry.[36] In writing to the President, he was full of fight and urged once more that Beauregard's army be brought to the upper Rappahannock for a demonstration on Washington.[37] "I hope," he said, "Your Excellency will understand that I am not in the least discouraged, or that my faith in the protection of an all-wise Providence, or in the fortitude of this army, is at all shaken. But, though conscious that the enemy has been much shattered in the recent battle, I am aware that he can be easily reinforced, while no addition can be made to our numbers. The measure, therefore, that I have recommended is altogether one of a prudential nature."[38]

This was written on the 8th of July. The next night an officer who had escaped from the Federals at Gettysburg arrived with news that the enemy was marching on Hagerstown.[39] This confirmed Lee's belief that Meade intended to attack him north of the Potomac,[40] and he prepared accordingly.

His cavalry were thrown out as a wide screen and the infantry were moved into the lines prepared for them.[41] In person he supervised the posting of Longstreet's men; he issued a stirring appeal to the army to meet once more the onslaughts of the enemy.[42] He did not lose grip on himself, but to Colonel Alexander, who observed him on many fields, Lee never appeared as deeply anxious as on July 10.[43] The wounded and the prisoners were not yet across the river; supplies sufficed only from day to day because the flood waters made it impossible to operate some of the flour mills; forage was getting very scarce, and the horses were subsisting only on grass and standing grain.[44]

The Federals had been approaching cautiously,[45] but by the 12th they grew bolder[46] and appeared in considerable strength around Boonsboro and Sharpsburg.[47] Lee's mind wavered between hope and anxiety. "Had the river not unexpectedly risen," he wrote his wife, "all would have been well with us; but God, in His all-wise providence, ruled otherwise, and our communications have been interrupted and almost cut off. The waters have subsided to about four feet, and if they continue, by tomorrow, I hope, our communications will be open. I trust that a merciful God, our only hope and refuge, will not desert us in this hour of need, and will deliver us by His almighty hand, that the whole world may recognize His power and all hearts be lifted up in adoration and praise of His unbounded loving-kindness. We must, however, submit to His almighty will, whatever that may be."[48]

Lee's prayers seemed answered on the 13th. Jackson's handyman, the resourceful Major J. A. Harman, had torn down old warehouses and had constructed a number of crude boats that had been floated down to Falling Waters, where some of the original pontoons had been recovered.[49] With these a crossing had been laid—"a good bridge" in Lee's thankful eyes,[50] a "crazy affair" to the more critical Colonel Sorrel.[51] The river at Williamsport was still deep but fordable, at last, by infantry. Lee determined not to delay a day in reaching a wider field of manœuvre on the south shore of the forbidding Potomac. To expedite his movement he decided to use both the ford and the pontoons—Ewell to cross by the former route, and the trains and the rest of the army by the bridge.[52] Longstreet demurred at this withdrawal, because there was a chance of fighting a defensive battle on ground to his liking, but Lee overruled him and personally directed the preparations for the crossing.[53]

That afternoon, as if to defeat the whole difficult enterprise, rain began to descend heavily. By nightfall the river seemed to be pouring from the skies.[54] As Ewell's road to Williamsport was hard-surfaced, his progress was steady, but at the ford there was much confusion.[55] Nerves grew raw under the strain.[56] A new road had been cut to the bridge at Falling Waters and under the downpour this soon became so heavy that the wagons began to stall. Instead of the swift march for which Lee had hoped, there was a virtual blockade.[57] Hours passed while drenched and wretched thousands stood wearily waiting for the trains to move on. All night the laboring teams struggled through the mire, and soldiers strained at the hub-deep wheels. Lee sat on his horse at the north end of the brigade, encouraging the men until even his strong frame grew weary.[58] "The best standing points were ankle-deep in mud," Longstreet recorded, "and the roads half-way to the knee, puddling and getting worse. We could only keep three or four torches alight, and those were dimmed at times when heavy rains came."[59] Toward morning the report was that Ewell's column would soon be in Virginia; but at Falling Waters dawn found the rear of the wagon train still swaying uneasily on the pontoon bridge. Longstreet and Hill were yet to cross, with every prospect of being attacked while on the march. Leaving Longstreet to direct the movement on the north side of the river,[60] Lee went to the southern shore to expedite the clearing of the bridge, and there he waited while the survivors of Longstreet's corps tramped through the rain. It was the last time Lee ever passed over that stream as a soldier.

Finally the rear brigade of Longstreet's corps reached the bridge-head. Only Hill and the cavalry remained behind. Lee's anxiety was not wholly relieved, for, while he was grateful that so large a part of the army had escaped, he believed it certain that Meade would attack Hill. When Colonel Sorrel rode up and reported that Longstreet's last file had passed, Lee bade him return and urge the Third Corps to make the utmost haste and not to halt unless compelled to do so. Soon Sorrel came back and announced that the road was clear. Hill, he said, was only three-quarters of a mile from the bridge.

"What was his leading division?" Lee inquired.

"General Anderson, sir," Sorrel answered.

"I am sorry, Colonel; my friend Dick is quick enough pursuing, but in retreat I fear he will not be as sharp as I should like."

At that moment the echo of a heavy gun rolled up the river gorge. "There!" the General exclaimed. "I was expecting it—the beginning of the attack!"[61]

But instead of halting or stampeding at the sound, Hill's tired troops continued their steady tramp across the bridge. Ere long General Lee learned that only the rear division, Heth's, was in contact with the enemy, and that it was holding its own. At one time Heth dispatched an officer to request that Pender's division be sent back to reinforce him, but when ordered to continue his movement, he contrived to reach the river with no other loss than that of the stragglers and sick whom he had not been able to push on ahead of him.[62] "As the bulk of the rearguard of the army safely passed over the shaky bridge," one observer testified, "as it swayed to and fro, lashed by the current, [Lee] uttered a sigh of relief, and a great weight seemed taken from his shoulders. Seeing his fatigue and exhaustion, General Stuart gave him some coffee; he drank it with avidity, and declared, as he handed back the cup, that nothing had ever refreshed him so much."[63]

The final operation had been more harrowing, in the opinion of General Lane, than even the first stages of the retreat from Gettysburg.[64] Men had become so weary that they had fallen asleep in the rain and mud whenever the column had halted.[65] One South Carolina colonel who had been in all of Lee's campaigns, pronounced it the severest march his men had ever made.[66] Heth had required twelve torturing hours to cover seven miles.[67] But the retreat was over! The Potomac stood between the battered Army of Northern Virginia and the disappointed Federals. Many were the regrets that the Confederates had been "allowed to escape." Loud were the protests that Meade had not pushed his pursuit vigorously.[68]

As the army manifestly must have rest, Lee moved it on the 15th to the vicinity of Bunker Hill.[69] His expectation was to advance into Loudoun County, but the swollen Shenandoah prevented an early crossing.[70] Forced to remain temporarily where he was, Lee sent out men and horses, threshed wheat, carried it to the mills, ground it, and, with the beef captured in Pennsylvania, contrived to give a sufficient ration to the hungry army.[71] Thousands of the cavalrymen were dismounted because their horses had not been shod and had become lame. Robertson's brigade had been diminished, chiefly on this account, to a bare 300.[72] Lee collected horseshoes as rapidly as practicable, reduced transportation once more, procured corn for animals that had not tasted it since Gettysburg, and did what he could at so great a distance from Richmond to refit the troops.[73]

Before Lee could make more than a start in the never-ending work of reorganization, Meade crossed the Potomac east of the Blue Ridge and advanced his cavalry to the passes into Loudoun. Fearing that this might presage an attempt to keep him in the Valley while the enemy moved on Richmond, Lee promptly made counter-dispositions and placed Longstreet in Manassas and Chester Gaps before the enemy could take them.[74] With the waters lowered somewhat, a pontoon bridge was then thrown over the Shenandoah, Longstreet's remaining troops crossed, passed through Chester Gap, and reached Culpeper on July 24. Hill followed. Ewell, who was left in the Valley in the hope of picking off a force at Martinsburg, then moved to Madison Court-house, where he arrived on July 29. A force left at Manassas Gap had an affair with the enemy, but drew off with no great difficulty and rejoined the main army. The enemy shifted to Warrenton, and from that base on the night of July 31–August 1 sent a cavalry column and some infantry across the Rappahannock. The Confederate horse promptly opposed this advance; but as the Federal movement might be the initial step in a manœuvre to catch him between the Rappahannock and the Rapidan, or else to resume operations in front of Fredericksburg, Lee decided to transfer his whole army south of the Rapidan. This was accomplished by August 4, on which date the Gettysburg campaign may be said to have come to its conclusion, with the opposing troops holding almost the very ground whence Jackson had started the first stage of Lee's offensive a year previously.[75] The rapid changes of position during this last phase of the campaign were made with little loss and in good spirit. There was, however, the inevitable reaction that follows open campaigning, and among the North Carolina conscripts some desertions occurred.[76] To disappointed civilian eyes, the morale of the troops seemed lower than usual.[77] Even Major Walter Taylor, who was more familiar with the temper of the tired men, had already been compelled to admit that the army was better satisfied when on Southern soil.[78] By the second week in August, this reaction was past, and the spirits of officers and men were high again. "This is a grand old army!" Taylor wrote proudly, soon after Lee's headquarters had been established at Orange and the two armies had become inactive.[79] "No despondency here," he exclaimed, "though we hear of it in Richmond."[80]

Disappointment was, indeed, general at the capital, and there was much questioning throughout the South.[81] Lee refused to accept this as justified, and remarked that little value was to be attached to popular judgment of victories or of defeats. He told Major Seddon that after Fredericksburg and again after Chancellorsville, he had been greatly depressed because he could not follow up either success, but the country had been jubilant over the outcome of both battles.[82] "As far as I am concerned," he said of one series of hostile complaints, "the remarks fall harmless," but he felt that censure of the army did harm at home and abroad.[83] When General Pickett filed a report in which he complained of the lack of support given him in the charge, Lee returned the document. "You and your men have covered yourself with glory," he said, "but we have the enemy to fight and must carefully, at this critical moment, guard against dissensions which the reflections in your report would create. I will, therefore, suggest that you destroy both copy and original, substituting one confined to casualties merely. I hope all will yet be well."[84] In preparing his own report the following January, he struck from Major Marshall's draft all specific criticism.[85]

Despite Lee's example and influence, criticism of the Confederate operations at Gettysburg was not silenced in 1863 and has been expressed at intervals ever since. Where confined to the actual military details of the campaign, this criticism is easily analyzed, for no other American battle has been so fully studied, and concerning none is there more general agreement on the specific reasons for the failure of the losing army.

The invasion itself was, of course, a daring move, but, in the circumstances that Lee faced, politically and in a military sense, it probably was justified. The first mistake was in connection with Stuart's operations. To recapitulate this point, Lee intended to allow his cavalry commander latitude as to where he should enter Maryland. He is not to be blamed for giving Stuart discretion, nor is Stuart justly subject to censure for exercising it. But the *Beau Sabreur* of the South, by pushing on after he had encountered resistance east of the Bull Run Mountains, violated orders and deprived Lee of his services when most needed. He should have turned back then, as Lee had directed him to do should he find his advance hindered by the Federal columns. Stuart erred, likewise, in taking with him all the cavalry brigades that had been accustomed to doing the reconnaissance work of the Army of Northern Virginia. General Lee, for his part, was at fault in handling the cavalry left at his disposal. He overestimated the fighting value of Jenkin's and of Imboden's brigades, which had little previous experience except in raids, and he failed to keep in close touch with Robertson and Jones, who remained behind in Virginia.[86] Once in Pennsylvania, Lee's operations were handicapped not only because he lacked sufficient cavalry, but also because he did not have Stuart at hand. He had become dependent upon that officer for information of the enemy's position and plans and, in Stuart's absence, he had no satisfactory form of military intelligence. It is not enough to say with General Early, in exculpation of Stuart, that Lee found the enemy in spite of the absence of his cavalry.[87] Had "Jeb" Stuart been at hand, Lee would have had early information of the advance of the Federals and either would have outfooted them to Gettysburg or would have known enough about their great strength to refrain from attacking as he did. The injudicious employment of the Confederate horse during the Gettysburg campaign was responsible for most of the other mistakes on the Southern side and must always remain a warning of the danger of permitting the cavalry to lose contact with an army when the enemy's positions are unknown. In its consequences, the blunder was more serious than that which Hooker made at Chancellorsville in sending Stoneman on a raid when he should have had his mounted forces in front and on the flank of the XI Corps.[88]

The second reason for the Confederate defeat manifestly was the failure of Ewell to take Cemetery Hill when Lee suggested, after the Federal defeat on the afternoon of July 1, that he attack it. Had Ewell thrown Early forward, without waiting for Johnson, he probably could have taken the hill at any time prior to 4 P.M. or perhaps 4:30. Ewell hesitated because he was unfamiliar with Lee's methods and had been trained in a different school of command. Jackson, who had always directed Ewell's operations, had been uniformly explicit in his orders and had never allowed discretion unless compelled to do so; Lee always trusted the tactical judgment of his principal subordinates unless he had to be peremptory. Ewell, moreover, was of a temperament to take counsel, and was puzzled and embarrassed when told to capture Cemetery Hill "if practicable." Lee could not be expected to change his system for Ewell, nor could Ewell be expected to change his nature after only two months under Lee.

The third reason for defeat was the extent of the Confederate line and the resultant thinness. Lee's front on the second day, from Hood's right, opposite Round Top, to the left of Johnson, was slightly more than five miles in length. Communication between the flanks was slow and difficult. Co-ordination of attack was almost impossible with a limited staff.[89] Lee should have held to the decision reached late on the afternoon of the 1st and considered again on the morning of the 2d. He should have abandoned all attempts against the Culp's Hill position. By concentrating his attacks from Cemetery Hill to Round Top, he would have increased the offensive strength of his line by at least one-third. In doing this, he would not have subjected himself to a dangerous enfilade from Cemetery Hill, because he had sufficient artillery to put that hill under cross-fire from Seminary Ridge and from Gettysburg. Lee finally discarded the plan of shortening his line on the representation of Ewell that Johnson could take Culp's Hill—an instance where the advantage that would certainly have resulted from a concentrated attack was put aside for the uncertainty of a *coup* on the flank.

The fourth reason for the defeat was the state of mind of the responsible Confederate commanders. On July 2, Longstreet was disgruntled because Lee refused to take his advice for a tactical defensive. Determined, apparently, to force a situation in which his plan would have to be adopted in spite of Lee, he delayed the attack on the right until Cemetery Ridge was crowded with men, whereas if he had attacked early in the morning, as Lee intended, he probably could have stormed that position and assuredly could have taken Round Top. Longstreet's slow and stubborn mind rendered him incapable of the quick daring and loyal obedience that had characterized Jackson. Yet in the first battle after the death of "Stonewall" it seemed the course of wisdom to substitute the First for the Second Corps as the "column of attack" because its staff and line were accustomed to working together. Longstreet's innate lack of qualification for duty of this type had been confirmed by his period of detached duty. He was never the same man after he had deceived himself into thinking he was a great strategist.

It was Lee's misfortune at Gettysburg that he had to employ in offensive operations a man whose whole inclination was toward the defensive.

But this indictment of Longstreet does not relieve Lee of all blame for the failure on the second day at Gettysburg. His greatest weakness as a soldier was displayed along with Longstreet's, for when Longstreet sulked, Lee's temperament was such that he could not bring himself either to shake Longstreet out of his bad humor by a sharp order, or to take direction of the field when Longstreet delayed. No candid critic of the battle can follow the events of that fateful morning and not have a feeling that Lee virtually surrendered to Longstreet, who obeyed only when he could no longer find an excuse for delay. Lee's one positive order was that delivered about 11 o'clock for Longstreet to attack. Having done this much, Lee permitted Longstreet to waste the time until after 4 o'clock. It is scarcely too much to say that on July 2 the Army of Northern Virginia was without a commander.

The conclusion is inevitable, moreover, that Lee allowed operations to drift on the morning of the 2d, not only because he would not deal sternly with Longstreet but also because he placed such unquestioning reliance on his army that he believed the men in the ranks could redeem Longstreet's delay. If Longstreet was insubordinate, Lee was overconfident. This psychological factor of the overconfidence of the commanding general is almost of sufficient importance to be regarded as a separate reason for the Confederate defeat.[90]

The mind of Ewell was similarly at fault on July 2. Although he had then been given his direct orders by Lee in person, Ewell either did not comprehend the importance of the task assigned him or else he was unable to co-ordinate the attacks of his three divisions, two of which were under commanders almost as unfamiliar with their duties as he was. Ewell's attacks were those of Lee at Malvern Hill, or those of McClellan at Sharpsburg, isolated, disjointed, and ineffective. Had Early and Rodes engaged when Johnson made his assault, there is at least a probability that Early could have held Cemetery Hill. If he had done so, the evacuation of Cemetery Ridge would have been necessary that night, or else Pickett's charge could have been driven home with the help of a shattering Confederate fire from the captured eminence.

Fifth and most fundamental among the reasons for Lee's failure at Gettysburg was the general lack by the reorganized army of co-ordination in attack. Some of the instances of this on July 2 have already been given. To these may be added the failure of A. P. Hill's corps to support the advance of Wright and of Wilcox when the attack of the First Corps reached the front of the Third. General Wilcox maintained that Anderson's division was badly handled then and that the captured ground could have been retained if

Anderson had been on the alert.[91] Wilcox may have been in error concerning some of the details, but the impression left by the operations of Hill's corps is that they were not unified and directed to the all-important object of seizing and holding Cemetery Ridge. An even greater lack of co-ordination was apparent on the 3d. It was imperative on the last day of the battle that the three corps act together with absolute precision, for every one must have realized that another repulse would necessitate a retreat. Yet the reorganized army did not fight as a single machine. Longstreet could have had Pickett on the field at dawn and could have attacked when Ewell did; but he was still so intent on carrying his own point and moving by the right flank, that he devoted himself to that plan instead of hurrying Pickett into position. When Longstreet would not attack with his whole corps, Lee made the mistake of shifting his attack northward, and of delivering it with parts of two corps. Pickett and Pettigrew advanced together almost as well as if they had belonged to the same corps, but there was no co-ordination of their support. The men at the time—and critics since then—seem to have been so intent on watching the charge that they have forgotten the tragic fact that after the two assaulting divisions reached Cemetery Ridge they received no reinforcements. Probably it was the course of wisdom not to have rushed Anderson forward along with Pickett and Pettigrew, but there has never been any satisfactory explanation why Wilcox's advance was delayed or the whole of Anderson's division was not thrown in when it was apparent that Pickett and Pettigrew would reach the enemy's position. It was probably to this that Lee referred, on the night of July 3, in his conversation with General Imboden.[92] There were risks, of course, in hurling all the troops against Cemetery Ridge, and leaving none in reserve, but Lee had done the same thing at Gaines's Mill and at Second Manassas, and in both instances had driven the enemy from the field. Similarly, the advance of the left brigade of Pettigrew's division was ragged and uncertain from the moment it started, yet nothing was done by Hill or by Longstreet to strengthen that flank or to create a diversion. On the front of Ewell that day there was no co-ordination of his attack with Longstreet, or even co-ordination of his own divisions. Two of Ewell's divisions waited while Johnson wore himself out on Culp's Hill during the morning, and then, in the afternoon, those two in turn were repulsed. Ewell was ready to assault when the day was young, but Longstreet was not then willing. When Longstreet at last was forced into action, Ewell was half-crippled.

Lack of co-ordination was displayed in the artillery as well. So much has been written of the volume of the fire delivered against Cemetery Ridge that few students of the battle have stopped to count the batteries that were not utilized. Colonel Jennings C. Wise has computed that fifty-six of Lee's field-pieces were not employed at all on July 3, and that eighty of the eighty-four guns of the Second and Third Corps were "brought into action on a mathematically straight line, parallel to the position of the enemy and constantly increasing in range therefrom to the left or north."[93] Nearly the whole value of converging fire was neglected. Furthermore, the Confederates lost the greatest opportunity of the battle when they did not dispose their artillery to blast the Federals from Cemetery Hill. That eminence stands at the northwestern turn of the long Federal line, the "bend of the fish-hook," and is open to attack by artillery on an arc of more than 200 degrees from the northeast, the north, the northwest, and the west. A concentrated bombardment on the 2d would have driven the Federals from the hill and would have made its capture easy. Once in Confederate hands, it could have been a *point d'appui* for an attack on Cemetery Ridge. A short cannonade of Cemetery Hill on the 3d, more or less a chance affair, played havoc with the Federal batteries stationed there and indicated what might have happened under a heavier fire.[94] It is almost incredible that this opening was overlooked by the chief of artillery of the army or by the gunners of the Second and Third Corps. There are only two possible explanations. One is that General Pendleton devoted himself to reconnaissance, chiefly on the right, instead of studying the proper disposition of the guns. The other is that the lines of the two corps chanced to join in front of Cemetery Hill, so that liaison was poor. Neither Colonel Lindsay Walker of the Third nor Colonel John Thompson Brown of the Second seems to have realized to what extent the hill was exposed.

Southern critics of Gettysburg, admitting all these mistakes, have been wont to say that while each error was serious, the battle would not have been lost if any one of the blunders had been avoided. There is a probability at least as strong that few of the mistakes would have occurred if Jackson had not died and a reorganization of the army had not thereby been made necessary. Then it was that Lee was compelled to place two-thirds of the troops under corps commanders who had never directed that many men in battle; then it was that the sentimental demand of the South led him to put at the head of the reduced Second Corps the gallant Ewell who had never served directly under Lee and was unfamiliar with his discretionary methods; then it was that new division commanders were chosen; then it was that the staff, which was always too small, was divided among generals who were unacquainted with the staff personnel, with the troops, and even with the field officers; then it was that Longstreet, by the ill-chance of war, was cast for the rôle of the irreplaceable Jackson and became the appointed leader of the column of attack, the duty of all others for which he was least suited. Read in the light of the aftermath, the story of the reorganization of May, 1863, thus becomes one of the major tragedies of the Confederacy and explains why the death of Jackson was the turning-point in the history of the Army of Northern Virginia.

Such, in brief, were the principal Confederate mistakes at Gettysburg and some of the reasons for them as they appear to the student after seventy years.[95] How did those errors appear to Lee? What was his judgment of the battle and of the campaign? Said he: " . . . the loss of our gallant officers and men . . . causes me to weep tears of blood and to wish that I never could hear the sound of a gun again."[96] More than 23,000 Southerners had been killed, wounded, and captured by the enemy from the beginning of the campaign at Brandy Station to the return to the lines on the Rapidan (June 9–August 4).[97] Five guns had been lost, approximately fifty wagons and more than thirty flags.[98] Lee believed, however, that the enemy had paid a price in proportion,[99] and he was far from thinking that invasion had been fruitless. Much of what he hoped to achieve had been accomplished—the enemy had been driven from the Shenandoah Valley, the hostile forces on the coast of Virginia and the Carolinas had been reduced, the Federal plan of campaign for the summer had been broken up, and there was little prospect of a resumption of the offensive that year by the Union forces in Virginia.[100] He was no more prepared to admit a crushing defeat than Meade was to claim one,[101] and perhaps he shared the philosophical view later expressed by General Early that if the army had remained in Virginia it would have been forced to fight battles with losses as heavy as those of Gettysburg.[102] As criticism spread, Lee was quick to absolve his men of all responsibility for failure to attain the full objective. The army, he wrote Mrs. Lee on July 15, "has accomplished all that could be reasonably expected. It ought not to have been expected to perform impossibilities, or to have fulfilled the anticipations of the thoughtless and unreasonable."[103] In his preliminary report of July 31 he said: "The conduct of the troops was all that I could desire or expect, and they deserved success so far as it can be deserved by heroic valor and fortitude. More may have been required of them than they were able to perform, but my admiration of their noble qualities and confidence in their ability to cope successfully with the enemy has suffered no abatement from the issue of this protracted and sanguinary conflict."[104] He hoped that the final reports would "protect the reputation of every officer,"[105] and he was determined not to blame any of his subordinates. "I know," he said, "how prone we are to censure and how ready to blame others for the non-fulfilment of our expectations. This is unbecoming in a generous people, and I grieve to see its expression."[106] He felt that he had himself been at fault in expecting too much of the army. His confidence in it, he frankly confessed, had carried him too far[107]—an opinion that was shared by some of the men in the ranks.[108] Overlooking all the tactical errors and all the mistakes due to the state of mind of his subordinates, he went straight to the underlying cause of failure when he said it was due primarily to lack of co-ordination. On July 13, in a long letter to President Davis, he summed up his views:

> [The army] in my opinion achieved under the guidance of the Most High a general success, though it did not win a victory. I thought at the time that the latter was practicable. I still think if all things would have worked together it would have been accomplished. But with the knowledge I then had, and in the circumstances I was then placed, I do not know what better course I could have pursued. With my present knowledge, and could I have foreseen that the attack on the last day would have failed to drive the enemy from his position, I should certainly have tried some other course. What the ultimate result would have been is not so clear to me."[109]

After reflecting fully on the outcome in the comparative quiet of his camp at Orange Courthouse, he decided that he should ask to be relieved of the command of the army. In the course of a deliberately written letter to the President he said:

> The general remedy for the want of success in a military commander is his removal. This is natural, and, in many instances, proper. For, no matter what may be the ability of this officer, if he loses the confidence of his troops disaster must sooner or later ensue.
>
> I have been prompted by these reflections more than once since my return from Pennsylvania to propose to Your Excellency the propriety of selecting another commander for this army. I have seen and heard of expression of discontent in the public journals at the result of the expedition. I do not know how far this feeling extends in the army. My brother officers have been too kind to report it, and so far the troops have been too generous to exhibit it. It is fair, however, to suppose that it does exist, and success is so necessary to us that nothing should be risked to secure it. I therefore, in all sincerity, request Your Excellency to take measures to supply my place. I do this with the more earnestness because no one is more aware than myself of my inability for the duties of my position. I cannot even accomplish what I myself desire. How can I fulfill the expectations of others? In addition I sensibly feel the growing failure of my bodily strength. I have not yet recovered from the attack I experienced the past spring. I am becoming more and more incapable of exertion, and am thus prevented from making the personal examinations and giving the personal supervision to the operations in the field which I feel to be necessary. I am so dull in making use of the eyes of others I am frequently misled. Everything, therefore, points to the advantages to be

derived from a new commander, and I the more anxiously urge the matter upon Your Excellency from my belief that a younger and abler man than myself can readily be obtained. I know that he will have as gallant and brave an army as ever existed to second his efforts, and it would be the happiest day of my life to see at its head a worthy leader—one that would accomplish more than I could perform and all that I have wished. I hope Your Excellency will attribute my request to the true reason, the desire to serve my country, and to do all in my power to insure the success of her righteous cause.

I have no complaints to make of any one but myself. I have received nothing but kindness from those above me, and the most considerate attention from my comrades and companions in arms. To Your Excellency I am specially indebted for uniform kindness and consideration. You have done everything in your power to aid me in the work committed to my charge, without omitting anything to promote the general welfare. I pray that your efforts may at length be crowned with success, and that you may long live to enjoy the thanks of a grateful people.[110]

Lee said nothing to any one of this letter, though its language indicates that it was written with an eye to its possible publication in case the President saw fit to relieve him of command. There is not a hint in any other contemporary paper that he had asked to be relieved, though there had been a rumor, about ten days before, that he had resigned.[111]

He had not long to wait for the President's decision. In a reply to General Pemberton, who had sustained a far worse defeat, Mr. Davis had said on August 9, "My confidence in both [you and Lee] has not been diminished because 'letter writers' have not sent forth your praise on the wings of the press."[112] On August 12 or 13, Lee received from Mr. Davis a long answer in which the chief executive deplored the clamor of the times and then continued:

But suppose, my dear friend, that I were to admit, with all their implications, the points which you present, where am I to find that new commander who is to possess the greater ability which you believe to be required? I do not doubt the readiness with which you would give way to one who could accomplish all that you have wished, and you will do me the justice to believe that if Providence should kindly offer such a person for our use, I would not hesitate to avail of his services.

My sight is not sufficiently penetrating to discover such hidden merit, if it exists, and I have but used the language of sober earnestness when I have impressed upon you the propriety of avoiding all unnecessary exposure to danger, because I felt our country could not bear to lose you. To ask me to substitute you by some one in my judgment more fit to

> command, or who would possess more of the confidence of the army, or of the reflecting men of the country, is to demand an impossibility. . . ."[113]

That ended it! Lee had to go on. Perhaps it was fortunate for the South that his request to be relieved of command did not become known, for the mere suggestion of such a possibility might have created discontent akin to mutiny in the Army of Northern Virginia. There probably was no exaggeration in the statement of one veteran, years afterward, that "the army would have arisen in revolt if it had been called upon to give up General Lee."[114]

The discussion of Gettysburg, however, did not end with this private exchange of letters. It continued into the winter and to the close of General Lee's life. To Longstreet's credit be it said that he did not criticise his chief at the time or argue in public the alleged virtues of his plan of operations which he continued to believe superior to Lee's. In a letter to his uncle, three weeks after the battle, he expressed willingness to assume his share of the responsibility—all of it, in fact.[115] He claimed at a later date that Lee asked him after the campaign, "Why didn't you stop all that thing that day?"[116] Subsequently, also, he maintained that Lee told a staff officer of the First Corps in the winter of 1863–64 that if Longstreet had been permitted to carry out his plan, instead of making the attack on Cemetery Ridge, he would have been successful. In east Tennessee, again, Longstreet showed a friend a letter in which Lee was quoted as saying, "Oh, General, had I but followed your advice, instead of pursuing the course that I did, how different all would have been."[117] But in the face of charges that these statements were torn from their context, and in spite of a challenge to produce the originals, Longstreet remained silent.[118] Not until General Lee had been dead for years did General Longstreet make the remarkable assertion that he "would and could have saved every man lost at Gettysburg."[119] It was still later that Longstreet wrote that Lee was "excited and off his balance" at Gettysburg "and labored under that oppression until enough blood was shed to appease him."[120]

Since the publication of the official reports and of the narratives of the leading Confederate participants has shown the full measure of Longstreet's sulking, it has often been asked why Lee did not arrest him for insubordination or order him before a court-martial. The answer is quite simple: When Lee said, "It is all my fault," he meant exactly what he said. He undoubtedly considered himself to blame for the result. He was in command. If his orders were obeyed, the fault was with his plan; if his orders were not obeyed he was culpable for permitting them to be disregarded—so he must have reasoned. Even if this had not been his feeling he still would not have rid himself of Longstreet, for the simple reason that he had no one with whom to replace him. Grave as were Longstreet's faults, and costly as his peculiarities proved to be at Gettysburg, he was Lee's most experienced lieutenant and, after Jackson's death, the ablest, once he could be induced to go into action. Had he been removed, any successor then available would have disclosed other faults perhaps more serious. Lee displayed not the slightest difference in his manner toward Longstreet after the campaign: he was as friendly as ever and, as always,[121] determined to make the best of his subordinate's idiosyncrasies.

Lee made little comment on Gettysburg during the war. In talking with General Heth, who was one of the few generals in the army whom he called by his first name, Lee expressed conviction that the invasion of Pennsylvania was sound policy, and said that he would again enter that state if able to do so. He also remarked to Heth, when the *dicta* of the arm-chair strategists were under discussion, "After it is all over, as stupid a fellow as I am can see the mistakes that were made. I notice, however, that my mistakes are never told me until it is too late, and you, and all my officers, know that I am always ready and anxious to have their suggestions."[122]

When the war had ended, General Lee was still reticent in writing and speaking to strangers about Gettysburg or about any other of his battles, and never went further than to say to them that if the assault could have been co-ordinated success could have been attained.[123] In conversation with close friends, he would sometimes be more communicative. In April, 1868, he discussed with Colonel William Allan the invasion of Pennsylvania, explained in some detail his reasons for taking the offensive, and then, according to Allan's contemporaneous memorandum, went on:

> He [Lee] found himself engaged with the Federal Army . . . unexpectedly, and had to fight. This being decided on, victory would have been won if he could have gotten one decided simultaneous attack on the whole line. This he tried his utmost to effect for three days, and failed. Ewell he could not get to act with decision. Rodes, Early, Johnson, attacked, and were hurt in detail. Longstreet, Hill, etc., could not be gotten to act in concert. Thus the Federal troops were enabled to be opposed to each of our corps, or even divisions, in succession. As it was, however, he inflicted more damage than he received, and he broke up the Federal summer campaign.[124]

Discussing the battle with Governor John Lee Carroll of Maryland, Lee is quoted—though at second-hand—as saying that the battle would have been gained if General Longstreet had obeyed the orders given him, and had made the attack early instead of late. Lee was also credited with saying in the same conversation, "General Longstreet, when once in a fight, was a most brilliant soldier; but he was the hardest man to move I had in my army."[125]

The literal accuracy of various parts of these statements may be questioned, but it is certain that in the last years at Lexington, as Lee viewed the Gettysburg campaign in some perspective, he concluded that it was the absence of Jackson, not the presence of Ewell or of Longstreet, that made the Army of Northern Virginia a far less effective fighting machine at Gettysburg than at Chancellorsville. Not long before his death, in a long conversation with his cousin Cassius Lee of Alexandria, the General said that if Jackson had been at Gettysburg he would have held the heights that Ewell seized.[126] And one afternoon, when he was out riding with Professor White, he said quietly, "If I had had Stonewall Jackson with me, so far as man can see, I should have won the battle of Gettysburg." That statement must stand. The darkest scene in the great drama of Gettysburg was enacted at Chancellorsville when Jackson fell.[127]

NOTES

1. U.S. War Department, *The War of the Rebellion: A Compilation of the Official Records of the Union and Confederate Armies*, 127 vols., index, and atlas (Washington DC: GPO, 1880–1901), ser. 1, vol. 27, pt. 2, p. 311 [set hereafter cited as *Official Records;* all citations to series 1].

2. *Official Records*, vol. 27, pt. 1, p. 78; Jubal A. Early, *Lieutenant General Jubal Anderson Early, C. S. A.: Autobiographical Sketch and Narrative of the War Between the States* (Philadelphia: J. B. Lippincott Company, 1912), 276.

3. Clement A. Evans, ed., *Confederate Military History*, 12 vols. (Atlanta: Confederate Publishing Company, 1899), 3:420.

4. Robert Underwood Johnson and Clarence Clough Buel, eds., *Battles and Leaders of the Civil War*, 4 vols. (New York: 1887), 3:422 [set hereafter cited as *Battles and Leaders*].

5. *Official Records*, vol. 27, pt. 2, p. 298.

6. *Battles and Leaders*, 3:423; A. J. L. Fremantle, *Three Months in the Southern States: April–June, 1863* (New York: John Bradburn, 1864), 274; G. Moxley Sorrel, *Recollections of a Confederate Staff Officer* (New York and Washington: The Neale Publishing Company, 1905), 171; *Official Record*, vol. 27, pt. 2, pp. 966–67.

7. *Battles and Leaders*, 3:424.

8. *Official Records*, vol. 27, pt. 2, p. 1048; Susan P. Lee, *Memoirs of William Nelson Pendleton* (Philadelphia: J. B. Lippincott Company, 1893), 295.

9. J. M. Polk, *Memories of the Lost Cause* (Austin TX: n.p., 1905), 18.

10. Fremantle, *Three Months*, 254; FitzGerald Ross, *A Visit to the Cities and Camps of the Confederate States* (Edinburgh and London: W. Blackwood and Sons, 1865), 71.

11. William Miller Owen, *In Camp and Battle with the Washington Artillery of New Orleans* (Boston: Ticknor & Company, 1885), 256.

12. Fremantle, *Three Months*, 274.

13. Bartlett Yancey Malone, *The Diary of Bartlett Yancey Malone*, ed. William Whatley Pierson Jr. (Chapel Hill: North Carolina Historical Society, 1919), 38; William S. White, "A Diary of the War; or, What I Saw of It," in *Contributions to a History of the Richmond Howitzer Battalion* (Richmond: J. W. Randolph & English, 1883–86), 211–12.

14. *Official Records*, vol. 27, pt. 2, pp. 448, 471.

15. Fremantle, *Three Months*, 277.

16. William S. White, "A Diary of the War," 211–12.

17. Fremantle, *Three Months*, 280.

18. John C. West, *A Texan in Search of a Fight* (Waco TX: Press of J. S. Hill and Company, 1901), 96.

19. *Official Records*, vol. 27, pt. 2, p. 361.

20. *Official Records*, vol. 27, pt. 2, pp. 322, 107 ff.; John H. Worsham, *One of Jackson's Foot Cavalry* (New York: The Neale Publishing Company, 1912), 168; Armistead L. Long, untitled manuscript account of 1863 campaign [in possession of Long's heirs in Lynchburg, Virginia, at the time Freeman Published *R. E. Lee;* Freeman supplied no page for his citations to this source]. Long noted that "the teamsters of the train acted with great gallantry on this occasion. They were armed and acted as infantry."

21. *Official Records*, vol. 27, pt. 2, pp. 309, 322–23.

22. *Official Records*, vol. 27, pt. 2, p. 322; pt. 3, p. 983.

23. *Battles and Leaders*, 3:422.

24. *Official Records*, vol. 27, pt. 2, p. 300.

25. A. L. Long, 1863 campaign manuscript; George B. Davis, "From Gettysburg to Williamsport," in *Papers of the Military Historical Society of Massachusetts*, 14 vols. (Boston: published by the Society, 1895–1918), 3:461–62.

26. *Battles and Leaders*, 3:367 (quoting E. P. Alexander).

27. Walter H. Taylor to his sister, 7 July 1863. In the possession of W. H. Taylor III, Norfolk, Virginia, at the time Freeman wrote *R. E. Lee*, this and other Taylor letters have been published as Walter Taylor, *Lee's Adjutant: The Wartime Letters of Colonel Walter Herron Taylor, 1862–1865*, ed. R. Lockwood Tower (Columbia: University of South Carolina Press, 1995). Where possible, citations will be to the published letters. For the letter cited in this note, see Taylor, *Lee's Adjutant*, 59.

28. Randolph H. McKim, *A Soldier's Recollections* (New York: Longmans, Green, and Company, 1903), 181. Compare J. William Jones, *Life and Letters of Robert Edward Lee, Soldier and Man* (New York and Washington: The Neale Publishing Company, 1906), 253: "I never saw the soldiers of the Army of Northern Virginia more anxious to fight or more confident of victory than they were at Hagerstown."

29. *Official Records*, vol. 27, pt. 2, p. 299.

30. Walter Clark, ed., *Histories of the Several Regiments and Battalions from North Carolina in the Great War 1861–65*, 5 vols. (Raleigh: E. M. Uzzell, Printer and Binder, 1901), 2:399.

31. *Official Records*, vol. 27, pt. 3, pp. 982–83, 987.

32. J. William Jones and others, eds., *Southern Historical Society Papers*, 52 vols. (Richmond: published by the Society, 1876–1959), 37:142.

33. *Official Records*, vol. 27, pt. 2, pp. 796–97; Fremantle, *Three Months*, 287; [Judith McGuire], *Diary of a Southern Refugee* (New York: E. J. Hale and Son, 1867), 224; Robert E. Lee Jr., *Recollections and Letters of General Robert E. Lee* (New York: Doubleday, Page & Company, 1904), 98 ff.; personal account of the incident given the writer by Honorable Henry T. Wickham, then a boy at "Hickory Hill"; J. William Jones, *Personal Reminiscences, Anecdotes, and Letters of Gen. Robert E. Lee* (New York: D. Appleton and Company, 1874), 399; Jones, *Life and Letters of Lee*, 277–78. Fortunately, Rooney Lee stood the journey without relapse. By 2 Aug. 1863, Lee heard from a returning surgeon that his son was walking about on crutches. Later in the summer, a Federal general in Libby prison sought through Reverend T. V. Moore to arrange a special exchange between Rooney Lee and himself, but Lee opposed such special exchanges and wrote Mr. Moore that he could not seek for his son a favor that could not be asked for the humblest soldier in the army (Jones, *Personal Reminiscences of Lee*, 184).

34. *Battles and Leaders*, 3:428.

35. See Douglas Southall Freeman, *R. E. Lee: A Biography*, 4 vols. (New York: Charles Scribner's Sons, 1934–36), 3:168.

36. Ross, *Cities and Camps*, 80. It was at this time that Lee explained to Scheibert his theory of the high command and his belief that the commanding general should not attempt to direct the battle tactically. See Freeman, *Lee*, 2:347.

37. *Official Records*, vol. 27, pt. 2, p. 300. President Davis and Adjutant General Cooper had already vetoed this proposal, which Lee had advanced before he entered Pennsylvania (see Freeman, *Lee*, 3:47). Unknown to Lee, however, Mr. Davis's answer had been taken from the courier by Captain Ulrich Dahlgren and had been forwarded to General Meade. The assurance this letter gave him that he had nothing to fear in the way of an advance from Virginia on Washington is alleged to have been one of the reasons for Meade's decision to remain at Gettysburg and to receive Lee's final assault there (Edward Porter Alexander, *Military Memoirs of a Confederate* [New York: Charles Scribner's Sons, 1907], 367; *Southern Historical Society Papers*, 8:523; *Official Records*, vol. 27, pt. 1, p. 75 ff.).

38. *Official Records*, vol. 27, pt. 2, p. 300.

39. This officer was lieutenant Thomas L. Norwood of the Thirty-seventh North Carolina (*Official Records*, vol. 27, pt. 3, p. 991).

40. *Official Records*, vol. 27, pt. 2, p. 353.

41. *Official Records*, vol. 27, pt. 2, p. 300; pt. 3, pp. 994–95.

42. *Official Records*, vol. 27, pt. 2, p. 301.

43. Alexander, *Military Memoirs*, 439–40.

44. *Official Records*, vol. 27, pt. 2, pp. 300, 301, 327; James Longstreet, *From Manassas to Appomattox* (Philadelphia: J. B. Lippincott Company, 1896), 429.

45. Meade believed that Lee had taken up a succession of strong positions (Charles A. Page, *Letters of a War Correspondent* [Boston: L. C. Page and Company, 1898], 35).

46. Henry G. Pearson, *James S. Wadsworth of Geneseo* (New York: Charles Scribner's Sons, 1913), 231.

47. A. L. Long, 1863 campaign manuscript.

48. R. E. Lee Jr., *Recollections and Letters*, 101–2; compare *Official Records*, vol. 27, pt. 2, p. 301.

49. *Battles and Leaders*, 3:428.

50. *Official Records*, vol. 27, pt. 2, p. 323.

51. Sorrel, *Recollections*, 171.

52. *Official Records*, vol. 27, pt. 2, p. 323.

53. Longstreet, *Manassas to Appomattox*, 429; *Official Records*, vol. 27, pt. 3, p. 1001.

54. Alexander, *Military Memoirs*, 440; Malone, *Diary*, 38; William H. Stewart, *A Pair of Blankets* (New York: Broadway Publishing Company, 1911), 113.

55. Compare *Official Records*, vol. 27, pt. 2, pp. 448–49.

56. Major Venable was sent to the ford to report on conditions there. When he came back to headquarters he announced with disgust and in a loud voice that things were going badly at Williamsport. Lee rebuked him hotly for speaking of such an important matter in a tone that could be heard by every passing soldier. The General's manner was so severe that Venable went off in a huff. Busy as Lee was, he observed that he had offended his loyal subordinate, and when he went to his tent to drink a glass of buttermilk, he sent for Venable to join him. The major came but refused to be mollified by the General's oblations. At dawn the next day, when Lee's staff was with him on the south bank, Major Venable, still smarting under Lee's reprimand, lay down and went to sleep. Seeing him exposed to the storm, Lee took off his own poncho and quietly put it over the officer. Needless to say, when Venable awakened and found what Lee had done, he forgot his pique and set down the episode in the book of his remembrance as another example of the thoughtfulness of his chief (Armistead L. Long, *Memoirs of Robert E. Lee* [New York: J. M. Stoddart & Company, 1886], 301).

57. Longstreet, *Manassas to Appomattox*, 429.

58. John Esten Cooke, *A Life of Gen. Robert E. Lee* (New York: D. Appleton and Company, 1871), 333.

59. Longstreet, *Manassas to Appomattox*, 429.

60. Longstreet, *Manassas to Appomattox*, 429–30.

61. Sorrel, *Recollections*, 171–72.

62. The total number left on the Maryland shore was put at not more than 500, though General Kilpatrick, who commanded the Federal cavalry that attacked Heth, insisted he captured an entire brigade. Heth's heaviest loss was in the

person of General Pettigrew, who was mortally wounded in a brush with a small cavalry detachment that was allowed to approach the lines in the belief that it was Confederate (*Official Records*, vol. 27, pt. 2, pp. 303–4, 310, 323–34, 640 ff.; A. L. Long, 1863 campaign manuscript; R. E. Lee, *Lee's Dispatches: Unpublished Letters of General Robert E. Lee, C. S. A., to Jefferson Davis and the War Department of the Confederate States of America, 1862–65* [New York and London: G. P. Putnam's Sons, 1915], 105–6). Lee put a mild censure in his report on the withdrawal of Fitzhugh Lee's cavalry without notice to Heth, though, as usual, he did not name the responsible officer (*Official Records*, vol. 27, pt. 2, p. 323).

63. Cooke, *Life of Lee*, 333.

64. *Official Records*, vol. 27, pt. 2, p. 667.

65. *Official Records*, vol. 27, pt. 2, p. 667.

66. *Official Records*, vol. 27, pt. 2, p. 374. This was Colonel James D. Nance of the Third South Carolina.

67. *Official Records*, vol. 27, pt. 2, p. 640.

68. *Official Records*, vol. 27, pt. 1, pp. 92–94; George Gordon Meade, *The Life and Letters of George Gordon Meade*, 2 vols. (New York: Charles Scribner's Sons, 1913), 2:134; John Sedgwick, *Correspondence of John Sedgwick*, 2 vols. [New York]: Printed for C. and E. B. Stoeckel [by the De Vinne Press, 1902–3], 2: 132, Pearson, *James Wadsworth*, 235 ff.; Henry H. Humphreys, *Andrew Atkinson Humphreys: A Biography* (Philadelphia: The John C. Winston Company, 1924), 203–4.

69. *Official Records*, vol. 27, pt. 3, p. 1106.

70. *Official Records*, vol. 27, pt. 2, p. 324.

71. *Official Records*, vol. 27, pt. 3, p. 1049; Spencer Glasgow Welch, *A Confederate Surgeon's Letters to His Wife* (New York and Washington: The Neale Publishing Company, 1911), 60.

72. *Official Records*, vol. 27, pt. 3, p. 1106.

73. *Official Records*, vol. 27, pt. 2, pp. 302, 611, 653–54, 676; pt. 3, pp. 1011, 1015.

74. *Official Records*, vol. 27, pt. 2, p. 324; pt. 3, pp. 1020, 1024–5, 1026–27.

75. Lee's official reports of these movements will be found on *Official Records*, vol. 27, pt. 2, pp. 305, 310, 312, in *Official Records*, vol. 29, pt. 2, p. 624, and in Lee, *Lee's Dispatches*, 106–8. Longstreet's report is in *Official Records*, vol. 27, pt. 2, p. 362; Ewell's in *Official Records*, vol. 27, pt. 2, p. 449; Early's in *Official Records*, vol. 27, pt. 2, pp. 472–3; Hill's in *Official Records*, vol. 27, pt. 2, p. 609. For the correspondence see *Official Records*, vol. 27, pt. 3, pp. 1031, 1035, 1037, 1039, 1040, 1049, 1051, 1075. See also Early, *Autobiographical Sketch and Narrative*, 284 ff.; John B. Jones, *A Rebel War Clerk's Diary at the Confederate States Capital*, 2 vols. (Philadelphia: J. B. Lippincott & Company, 1866), 1:390, 2:6.

76. George W. Beale, *A Lieutenant of Cavalry in Lee's Army* (Boston: The Gorham Press, 1918), 120–21; *Official Records*, vol. 27, pt. 3, p. 1052; Jones *Rebel War Clerk*, 2:4. In *The American Issue*, Virginia Edition, 21 Feb. 1925, an amusing incident of the march to Culpeper was reported. One of Lee's veterans, on passing

his home, presented the whole family to the General. The soldier's mother, Mrs. Simms, produced a bottle of old blackberry wine and hospitably asked the General if he would refresh himself. Lee declined but suggested that his staff officers might be glad to taste her vintage. When Mrs. Simms offered it to them, they approved it so heartily that the rearmost had to content himself with wistfully smelling the bottle. The "cup that General Lee declined" has been preserved and was long in the possession of Reverend Doctor B. W. N. Simms, of Waxahatchie, Texas.

77. Thomas A. Ashby, *The Valley Campaigns* (New York: The Neale Publishing Company, 1914), 244–45.

78. Compare W. H. Taylor, 17 July 1863: "Our men, it must be confessed, are far better satisfied when operating on this side of the Potomac. . . . They are not accustomed to operating in a country where the people are inimical to them, and certainly every one of them is today worth twice as much as he was three days ago. I am persuaded that we cannot without heavy acquisitions to our strength invade successfully for any length of time" (Taylor, *Lee's Adjutant*, 61–62).

79. Lee was at Culpeper from 23 July to 4 Aug., on which day he moved to Orange Courthouse (compare *Official Records*, vol. 29, pt. 2, p. 624).

80. Walter H. Taylor, 8 Aug. 1863, in Taylor, *Lee's Adjutant*, 65–69.

81. Thomas C. De Leon, *Four Years in Rebel Capitals* (Mobile: The Gossip Printing Company, 1890), 257.

82. *Southern Historical Society Papers*, 4:153.

83. Lee to Davis, 31 July 1863, in Lee, *Lee's Dispatches*, 108–9.

84. *Official Records*, vol. 27, pt. 3, p. 1075. General Pickett either complied with this request or else gave strict instruction that the MS of his report should not be printed, for it has never appeared. When Arthur Crew Inman issued Pickett's war letters in 1928 under the title *Soldier of the South* (Boston and New York: Houghton Mifflin Company), he even omitted, at the instance of Mrs. Pickett, part of a letter of 4 July in which General Pickett expressed some of the criticisms he made in his report (Inman, *Soldier of the South*, 61–62 n.). It is plain that Pickett's complaint was that his attack was not properly supported by Pettigrew and by Trimble. Major Walter Taylor was of the same mind. In a letter of 17 July 1863 to his brother (Taylor, *Lee's Adjutant*, 60), he attributed Pickett's repulse to the strength of the Federal position—"a sort of Gibralter"—and to the action "of the division on his left," which, said Taylor, "failed to carry the works in its front and retired without any sufficient cause, thereby exposing Pickett's flanks."

85. Charles Marshall, *An Aide-de-Camp of Lee*, ed. Sir Frederick Maurice (Boston: Little, Brown, and Company, 1927), 181; Marshall quoted by McIntosh in *Southern Historical Society Papers*, 37:94–95. Compare Freeman, *Lee*, 3:233 and Appendix III.

86. It was not, apparently, until after the retreat from Gettysburg had begun that Lee had a just estimate of Imboden's troopers. He then told Stuart "they are unsteady, and, I fear, inefficient" (*Official Records*, vol. 27, pt. 3, p. 985).

87. Compare *Southern Historical Society Papers*, 4:269–70.

88. In 1896, General C. A. Battle, in a public address, asserted that Lee ordered

Stuart before a court of inquiry for his absence during the Gettysburg campaign, but this was not the case. The court convened to hear evidence regarding the loss of certain wagons in Fitz Lee's brigade (Taylor Papers in possession of W. H. Taylor III, Norfolk, Virginia, at the time Freeman wrote *R. E. Lee*).

89. Compare Alexander in *Southern Historical Society Papers*, 4:110.

90. See Freeman, *Lee*, 3:155.

91. See Freeman, *Lee*, 3: Appendix III—3.

92. See Freeman, *Lee*, 3:134.

93. Jennings C. Wise, *The Long Army of Lee*, 2 vols. (Lynchburg VA: J. P. Bell Company, 1915), 2:666–67.

94. Alexander, *Military Memoirs*, 417–18, 426–28.

95. The "Gettysburg controversy" of 1876–79 evoked much bitter but intelligent criticism of the campaign in *Southern Historical Society Papers* 4, 5, 6, and 7. The material there has never been invalidated. General Trimble supplied a good critique in *Southern Historical Society Papers*, 26:116–28, and McIntosh in *Southern Historical Society Papers*, 37:74–143. Cecil W. Battine, *The Crisis of the Confederacy: A History of Gettysburg and the Wilderness* (London and New York: Longmans, Green, and Company, 1905), is more tactical than strategical in his approach. Greely S. Curtis's "Gettysburg" in *Papers of the Military Historical Society of Massachusetts*, 3:356–65 and Thomas L. Livermore's "The Gettysburg Campaign" in *Papers of the Military Historical Society of Massachusetts*, 13:485–542, are authoritative. Alexander's account, *Military Memoirs*, 363 ff., is admirable in every way.

96. Jones, *Life and Letters of Lee*, 278; compare *Official Records*, vol. 27, pt. 2, p. 1049.

97. The loss in the infantry and artillery at Gettysburg was 20,486, including prisoners not listed by the Confederates but reported by the Federals. At Winchester, the casualties numbered 252; in the minor engagements, they were 316, and among the cavalry, 1817 (*Official Records*, vol. 27, pt. 2, pp. 337, 346, 712 ff.). Estimating the number captured at Falling Waters on 14 July at 500, the total is 23,371.

98. *Official Records*, vol. 27, pt. 1, p. 85; pt. 2, p. 354; *Official Records*, vol. 51, pt. 2, pp. 758–59.

99. He was correct in this. During the same period from 9 June to 4 Aug., the Federals had lost about 3500 killed, wounded, and captured at Winchester, 200 at Berryville and Martinsburg on the Confederate advance toward the Potomac, and 23,049 at Gettysburg. The casualties in the cavalry engagements raised the aggregate to 28,129 (*Official Records*, vol. 27, pt. 1, pp. 168ff; pt. 2, p. 442). Apparently no detailed Federal return was ever made of losses at Winchester,

100. *Official Records*, vol. 27, pt. 2, p. 302. Compare R. E. Lee Jr., *Recollections and Letters*, 108 (15 July 1863).

101. Compare Meade to his wife, 8 July 1863: "I never claimed a victory, though I stated that Lee was defeated in his efforts to destroy my army (Meade, *Life and Letters*, 2:133).

102. Early, *Autobiographical Sketch and Memoir*, 286.

103. R. E. Lee Jr., *Recollections and Letters*, 108.

104. *Official Records*, vol. 27, pt. 2, p. 309.

105. Lee to Davis, 31 July 1863, in Lee, *Lee's Dispatches*, 109.

106. Lee to Davis, 8 Aug. 1863, in *Official Records*, vol. 51, pt. 2, p. 752.

107. "I alone am to blame in perhaps expecting too much of its prowess and valour."—Lee to Davis, 31 July 1863 (Lee, *Lee's Dispatches*, 110). Compare Lee to Margaret Stuart, 26 July 1863: "The army did all it could. I fear I required of it impossibilities" (Jones, *Life and Letters of Lee*, 283). Compare also Longstreet, *Manassas to Appomattox*, 401, quoting General Lee, on the authority of Fitz Lee, as telling Captain Sidney Smith Lee that "he was controlled too far by the great confidence he felt in the fighting qualities of his people, and by assurances of most of his higher officers."

108. Compare West, *Texan in Search of a Fight*, 96: "I think General Lee never would have attacked the enemy in their position in the mountain side except for the splendid condition of his army, and his confidence in its ability to accomplish anything he chose to attempt." This was a contemporary letter.

109. Lee, *Lee's Dispatches*, 110.

110. *Official Records*, vol. 51, pt. 2, pp. 752–53.

111. Jones, *Rebel War Clerk*, 1:389.

112. John C. Pemberton manuscripts, kindly loaned the writer by John C. Pemberton of New York, through Mrs. H. Pemberton Rhudy of Philadelphia.

113. *Official Records*, vol. 29, pt. 2, p. 640.

114. C. Irvine Walker, *The Life of Lieutenant General Richard Heron Anderson* (Charleston SC: Art Publishing Company, 1917), 149–50.

115. James Longstreet to Doctor A. B. Longstreet, 24 July 1863, quoted in [A. K. McClure, ed.,] *The Annals of the War Written by Leading Participants North and South* (Philadelphia: The Times Publishing Company, 1879), 414–15.

116. *Philadelphia Times*, 27 July 1879, 8.

117. Longstreet, *Manassas to Appomattox*, 400.

118. *Southern Historical Society Papers*, 5:192, 279; Taylor Papers in the possession of W. H. Taylor III at the time Freeman wrote *R. E. Lee*. It is highly significant that in *Battles and Leaders*, 3:349, Longstreet himself gave a different version of what Lee was alleged to have said in this letter. He there quoted Lee as saying to him, "If only I had taken your counsel, even on the 3d, and had moved around the Federal left, how different all might have been."

119. *Battles and Leaders*, 3:349.

120. Longstreet, *Manassas to Appomattox*, 383–84.

121. Longstreet in *Washington Post*, 11 June 1893, 10.

122. *Southern Historical Society Papers*, 4:153, 159–60.

123. Lee to William M. McDonald, 15 April 1868: "As to the battle of Gettysburg, I must again refer you to my official accounts. Its loss was occasioned by a combination of circumstances. It was commenced in the absence of correct intelligence. It was continued in the effort to overcome the difficulties by which we were surrounded, and it would have been gained could one determined and

united blow have been delivered by our whole line. As it was, victory trembled in the balance for three days, and the battle resulted in the infliction of as great an amount of injury as was received and in frustrating the Federal campaign for the season" (Jones, *Personal Reminiscences of Lee*, 266–67). Compare also Lee to B. H. Wright, 18 Jan. 1869, printed in Jones, *Life and Letters of Lee*, 452–53, without the name of the addressee, which, however, appears in Lee's Lexington letterbook: "The failure of the Confederate army at Gettysburg was owing to a combination of circumstances, but for which success might have been reasonably expected."

124. Allan's memorandum in Marshall, *An Aide-de-Camp of Lee*, 250.

125. *Southern Historical Society Papers*, 5:193. The "governor" to whom this was reported to have been stated by General Lee is identified from a letter of General Fitz Lee's in the Taylor Papers (in possession of W. H. Taylor III at the time Freeman wrote *R. E. Lee*). Compare a somewhat similar comment by Lee on Longstreet's slowness quoted by Colonel McIntosh on the authority of Colonel Marshall in *Southern Historical Society Papers*, 37:106.

126. R. E. Lee Jr., *Recollections and Letters*, 415. The reference would seem to be to the attack of Early on the afternoon of 2 July, but it is possible that Lee was misunderstood and that he had in mind the opportunity of seizing Cemetery Hill that was lost on the afternoon of 1 July.

127. Henry M. Field, *Bright Skies and Dark Shadows* (New York: Charles Scribner's Sons, 1890), 303–4, quoting Professor White. This remark affords an excellent illustration of the manner in which Lee's undramatic observations were sometimes swollen into bombast. Lee's statement to White was simple and characteristically cautious in wording, but in *Southern Historical Society Papers*, 12:111–12, the language has been "dressed" to this: "If I had had Stonewall Jackson at Gettysburg, I should have won there a great victory, and if we had reaped the fruits within our reach, we should have established the independence of the Confederacy." The version given by Jones, *Personal Reminiscences of Lee*, 156, was almost rhetorical: "If I had had Stonewall Jackson at Gettysburg, we should have won a great victory. And I feel confident that complete success there would have resulted in the establishment of our independence."

R. E. Lee and *July 1 at Gettysburg*

ALAN T. NOLAN

Although President Jefferson Davis approved of the Army of Northern Virginia's moving into Maryland and Pennsylvania in 1863, the Gettysburg campaign was General Robert E. Lee's idea. In 1914, Douglas Southall Freeman wrote that Lee's "army . . . had been wrecked at Gettysburg."[1] This catastrophic consequence was the result of leadership failures on the part of the army commander. The first of these was strategic; the second involved a series of errors in the execution of the campaign.

In regard to strategy, it is apparent that the drama of Gettysburg and the celebrated controversies associated with the battle have obscured the primary question about the campaign: Should it have been undertaken; should Lee have been in Pennsylvania in 1863? When questioning Lee's campaigns and battles, one is frequently confronted with the assertion that he had no alternative. Accordingly, before addressing the question of the wisdom of Lee's raid into Pennsylvania, one must consider whether he had an alternative.

On the eve of the campaign, during the period following Chancellorsville, Lee's army remained near Fredericksburg on the Rappahannock facing Joseph Hooker's Army of the Potomac, located on the north side of that river. In this situation, Lee had at least three possible options: to attack Hooker across the river, which surely would have been problematical, to assume the defensive as he had at Fredericksburg in December 1862 and was to do again in 1864; or to undertake a raid into the North. The most likely of these choices was surely the middle course—to assume the defensive and force the Army of the Potomac to come after him. Lee apologists, committed to the "no alternative" thesis, would exorcise this option. The analysis of Colonel Charles Marshall, Lee's aid-de-camp and military secretary, is illustrative. In an effort to justify the campaign, Marshall carefully constructed the no alternative argument. He identified the same three choices for Lee set forth above. Rejecting the choice of Lee's attacking across the river, he eliminated the defensive option by the naked assertion that had Lee stood on the defensive south of the river he "was bound to assume . . . the enemy would abandon his effort to dislodge him from his position at Fredericksburg, and would move his army to Richmond by water." This, Marshall insisted, would have required Lee to retreat to defend Richmond. Based on this assumption, Marshall eliminated the defensive option and, as if by magic, concluded that there was no alternative to the Gettysburg raid. That the Federals would not have moved against Lee but would, instead, have proceeded directly to Richmond by water is simply Marshall's hypothesis. In fact, the evidence since the 1862 withdrawal from the Peninsula pointed to the North's commitment to the overland route.[2]

The Southern army's need for food is the premise of another no alternative justification for Lee's moving into Maryland and Pennsylvania. The South's supply problems were severe, as Robert K. Krick has graphically stated.[3] Collecting supplies and living off the Northern country was surely a motive for the campaign. But the Army of Northern Virginia was sustained in Virginia from July 1863 until April 1865, so it was not necessary to go North for food and forage. If supplying the army had really been the motive for the campaign, a raid by small, mobile forces rather than the entire army would have had considerably more promise and less risk.

Since there was an alternative, we may return to the primary question: Should Lee have undertaken the campaign at all? This question cannot be meaningfully considered in the abstract. It must be considered within the context of the larger question of the appropriate grand strategy of the war from the standpoint of the Confederacy. In this larger respect, the concern is not military strategy in the sense of a campaign or battle, that is, operational strategy. Rather, it is grand strategy, that is, to paraphrase Carl von Clausewitz, the art of employing military forces to attain the objects of war, to support the national policy of the government that raises the military forces. In evaluating a general's performance, the only significant inquiry is whether the general's actions related positively or negatively to the war objective and national policy of his government.

The statements of two Confederate leaders describe quite different theories of the South's grand strategy to win the war: E. Porter Alexander, chief of ordnance of the Army of Northern Virginia and later chief of artillery of Longstreet's First Corps, has described the South's appropriate grand strategy in this way:

> When the South entered upon war with a power so immensely her superior in men & money, & all the wealth of modern resources in machinery and transportation appliances by land & sea, she could entertain but one single hope of final success. That was, that the desperation of her resistance would finally exact from her adversary such a price in blood & treasure as to exhaust the enthusiasm of its population for the objects of the war. We could not hope to *conquer* her. Our one chance was to wear her out.[4]

This fairly describes a defensive grand stategy—to wear the North out instead of trying to defeat the North militarily.

The second view was Lee's. It may be found in two letters to President Davis. The first, written en route to Gettysburg, is dated June 25, 1863, at Williamsport, Maryland. Lee states: "It seems to me that we cannot afford to keep our troops awaiting possible movements of the enemy, but that our true policy is, as far as we can, so to employ our own forces as to give occupation to his at points of our selection." He further argues that "our concentration at any point compels that of the enemy." It is important that this letter was concerned with Confederate military forces on a wide range of fronts, including Virginia, North Carolina, and Kentucky. Since it contemplates drawing Federal armies to Confederate points of concentration to "give occupation" to the Federals, the letter is a prescription for military confrontation. It is therefore a statement of an offensive grand strategy, whether the confrontation at the "point of concentration" was to take the form of the tactical offensive or defensive on the part of the South. The second letter to Davis is dated July 6, 1864, shortly after the siege of Petersburg began. Lee wrote: "If we can defeat or drive the armies of the enemy from the field, we shall have peace. All our efforts and energies should be devoted to that object."[5]

This, then, was Lee's view of the way, as Clausewitz defined grand strategy, for the Confederacy "to attain the objects of [the] war." The South was to pursue the military defeat of the North. Lee's offensive grand strategic sense is reiterated again and again in his dispatches to Davis, the War department, and his fellow general officers. These dispatches, in the *Official Records* and *The Wartime Papers of R. E. Lee,* bristle with offensive rhetoric and planning: "striking a blow," "driving the enemy," "crushing the enemy."[6]

Any doubt that Lee was committed to the offensive as the South's appropriate grand strategy is presumably eliminated when one considers the most obvious source for identifying his grand strategic thinking, the campaigns and battles of the Army of Northern Virginia. Consistent with the grand strategy that he said he believed in and repeatedly planned and advocated, Lee from the beginning embraced the offensive. Appointed to command the Army of Northern Virginia on June 1, 1862, he turned at once to the offensive, beginning with major engagements on the Peninsula—Mechanicsville, Gaines's Mill, Frayser's Farm, and Malvern Hill. Following on the heels of the Seven Days, the Second Bull Run campaign was strategically offensive in an operational sense although, except for Longstreet's counterattack on August 30, it may be classified as defensive from a tactical standpoint. At Antietam Lee stood on the defensive, but the Maryland campaign was strategically offensive; his moving into Maryland assured a major battle in that state. At Chancellorsville, he chose not to retreat when confronted by the Federal pincer movement. Instead, he repeatedly attacked, and the Federals retreated back across the river.

The point is not that each of these campaigns and battles represented an error by Lee. Driving the Federals away from Richmond in 1862, for example, may have been required to maintain Southern morale and to avoid the practical consequences of losing the capital. The point is that the offensive pattern is plain. Lee believed that the South's grand strategic role was offensive.

Lee's grand strategy of the offensive, to defeat the North militarily as distinguished from prolonging the contest until the North gave it up, created a profound problem. It was not feasible and, indeed, was counterproductive to the Confederacy's "objects of war." Curiously, that Lee's attack grand strategy was misplaced is suggested by his own awareness of factors that argued against it. The primary reason the attack grand strategy was counterproductive was numbers, and Lee was sensitive to the South's manpower disadvantage and its implications. A letter of January 10, 1863, to Secretary of War James A. Seddon, between his victory at Fredericksburg and Ambrose E. Burnside's abortive Mud March, reflects this awareness. "I have the honor to represent to you the absolute necessity that exists . . . to increase our armies, if we desire to oppose effectual resistance to the vast numbers that the enemy is now precipitating upon us," Lee wrote. "The great increase of the enemy's forces will augment the disparity of numbers to such a degree that victory, if attained, can only be achieved by a terrible expenditure of the most precious blood of the country."[7]

Further recognition of the numbers problem appears in Lee's letter of June 10, 1863, to Davis, after Chancellorsville and at the outset of the Gettysburg campaign:

> While making the most we can of the means of resistance we possess . . . it is nevertheless the part of wisdom to carefully measure and husband our strength, and not to expect from it more than in the ordinary course of affairs it is capable of accomplishing. We should not therefore conceal from ourselves that our resources in men are constantly diminishing, and

> the disproportion in this respect between us and our enemies, if they continue united in their effort to subjugate us, is steadily augmenting. The decrease of the aggregate of this army as disclosed by the returns affords an illustration of this fact. Its effective strength varies from time to time, *but the falling off in its aggregate shows that its ranks are growing weaker and that its losses are not supplied by recruits.* (Emphasis added)[8]

The *Official Records* are full of Lee's analyses of his strength problems. These communications predict that unless his army was reinforced, "the consequences may be disastrous" and include such statements as "I cannot see how we are to escape the natural military consequences of the enemy's numerical superiority."[9]

Consciousness of his numerical disadvantage, of the ever-increasing Federal disproportion, did not mute Lee's commitment to the grand strategic offensive. Nor did that grand strategy permit his army to "husband our strength." During the Seven Days' battles on the Peninsula, George B. McClellan lost approximately 9,796 killed and wounded, 10.7 percent; Lee's casualties were 19,739 men, 20.7 percent of his army. Although Federal casualties in killed and wounded at Second Bull Run exceeded Lee's by approximately 1,000 men, the Army of Northern Virginia lost in excess of 9,000, almost 19 percent as compared to 13.3 percent for the Federals. In spite of McClellan's ineptitude, Lee lost almost 12,000 men, 22.6 percent, at Antietam, immediately following losses in excess of 1,800 at South Mountain on September 14. McClellan's Antietam casualties were 15.5 percent. At Chancellorsville, Lee lost almost 11,000 of 57,000 effectives, in excess of 18 percent, a much higher proportion than Joseph Hooker's 11.4 percent.[10]

These statistics show the serious attrition of Lee's limited numbers. In addition, Lee's losses were mostly irreplaceable, as he was aware. Finally, his losses also seriously affected his army's leadership. "The Confederates' ability to operate as they moved northward was affected by the loss of much mid-level command," Robert K. Krick has written. "The heart of the Confederate Army was starting to feel this difficulty for the first time just *before* Gettysburg. To the tremendous losses of the successful but costly campaign in the summer of 1862 . . . were added the victims of the dreadful bloodshed at Chancellorsville" (emphasis added).[11] Clearly, the Federals' increasingly disproportionate strength was the result of Northern reinforcements, but it was also exacerbated by Lee's heavy, disproportionate, and irreplaceable losses. Had Lee taken the defensive, the increasing Federal manpower advantage would have been slowed.

It is appropriate to contrast the alternative grand strategy of the defensive. In 1986, historians Richard E. Beringer, Herman Hattaway, Archer

Jones, and William N. Still, Jr., noted that "no Confederate army lost a major engagement because of the lack of arms, munitions, or other essential supplies." These authors then summarized the case as follows:

> By remarkable and effective efforts the agrarian South did exploit and create an industrial base that proved adequate, with the aid of imports, to maintain suitably equipped forces in the field. Since the Confederate armies suffered no crippling deficiencies in weapons or supply, their principal handicap would be their numerical inferiority. But to offset this lack, Confederates, fighting the first major war in which both sides armed themselves with rifles, had the advantage of a temporary but very significant surge in the power of the tactical defensive. In addition, the difficulties of supply in a very large and relatively thinly settled region proved a powerful aid to strengthening the strategic defensive. Other things being equal, if Confederate military leadership were competent and the Union did not display Napoleonic genius, the tactical and strategic power of the defense could offset northern numerical superiority and presumably give the Confederacy a measure of military victory adequate to maintain its independence.[12]

British observers sensed the feasibility of the grand strategy of the defensive as the war began. Harking back to their own experience in America, they did not see how the South could be conquered. The War of Independence analogy is not perfect, but it is illustrative. The military historian Colonel George A. Bruce has pointed out that George Washington "had a correct insight into the minds of his own people and that of the enemy, the strength of resolution of each to endure heavy burdens, looking forward with certainty to the time when the public sentiment of England, led by Chatham and Burke, would be ready to acknowledge the Colonies as an independent nation. With these views he carried on the war for seven years, all the way from Boston to Yorktown, on a generally defensive plan, the only one pointing to the final goal of independence."[13] The Americans, on the grand strategic defensive, lost many battles and retreated many times, but they kept forces in the field to avoid being ultimately defeated, and they won because the British decided that the struggle was either hopeless or too burdensome to pursue.

A Confederate defensive grand strategy would have been premised on E. Porter Alexander's conservative principle "to wear her [the North] out," to "exact . . . such a price in blood & treasure as to exhaust the enthusiasm of its population." To contribute to this wearing out, it was essential for Lee to maintain the viability of his army, to keep it in the field as a genuine force. That viability depended on his retaining sufficient relative strength for mobility and maneuver so as to avoid a siege and also to undertake timely and promising operationally strategic offensives and the tactical offensive. Lee could have accomplished these things had he pursued a defensive grand strategy. And despite Southern manpower disadvantages, this grand strategy was at the outset feasible because of the North's logistical task and the relative power that the rifled gun afforded the defense.

It is to be emphasized that the grand strategy of defense would not have required Southern armies always to be on the strategic operational or tactical defensive. As the British military historian Major General J. F. C. Fuller points out, "It is possible to develop an offensive tactics from a defensive strategy."[14] Thus, if Lee's grand strategic sense of the war had been defensive, he could nevertheless on appropriate occasions have pursued offensive campaigns and offensive tactics in the context of that defensive grand strategy. The Revolution again provides an illustration. Although pursuing a grand strategy of defense, the Americans were sometimes aggressive and offensive, for example, at Trenton, Saratoga, Yorktown.

The Federal manpower superiority would also have been less significant had Lee assumed the defensive in 1862–63, as evidenced by what happened in the overland campaign in 1864–65. Despite his prior losses and the great Northern numerical superiority, Lee's defense in 1864, again in Alexander's words, exacted "a price in blood" that significantly affected "the enthusiasm of [the North's] population" for continuing the war.[15] Indeed, Lee demonstrated in 1864 the feasibility of the grand strategy of the defense. Had he adopted the defensive earlier he would have had available a reasonable portion of the more than one hundred thousand officers and men that he lost in the offensives in 1862 and 1863, including Gettysburg. With these larger numbers he could have maintained mobility and avoided a siege.

It is in the context of grand strategy that one must view the primary issue regarding Gettysburg, that is, whether Lee should have been there at all. The Gettysburg campaign, Lee's most audacious act, is the apogee of his grand strategy of the offensive. The numerous reasons for the campaign offered by Lee and the commentators are well known: the necessity to upset Federal offensive plans, avoidance of a siege of the Richmond defenses, alleviation of supply problems in unforaged country, encouragement of the peace movement in the North, drawing the Federal army north of the Potomac in order to maneuver, even the relief of Vicksburg. Some or all of these reasons may have contributed to the decision, but fighting a battle was plainly inherent in the campaign because of the foreseeable Federal reaction and because of Lee's intent regarding a battle.

In his outline report dated July 31, 1863, Lee stated that "It had not been intended to fight a general battle at such a distance from our base, unless attacked by the enemy." The foreseeable Federal reaction to Lee's presence in loyal states suggests that the "unless attacked" provision was meaningless. As Hattaway and Jones point out: "Lee could have been under no illusion that he could bring off such a protracted campaign without a battle. . . . If he raided enemy territory, it would be politically if not strategically imperative for the Union army to take the offensive."[16] And on June 8, 1863, in a letter to Secretary of War Seddon, he spoke of the "difficulty & hazard in taking the aggressive with so large an army in its front, entrenched behind a river where it cannot be advantageously attacked" and of drawing the enemy out into "a position to be assailed." In the outline report, the same report in which he stated that "it had not been intended to fight a general battle at such a distance from our base," he wrote of his intent to "transfer the scene of hostilities north of the Potomac": "It was thought that the corresponding movements on the part of the enemy to which those contemplated by us would probably give rise, might offer a fair opportunity to *strike a blow* at the army then commanded by General Hooker, and that in any event that army would be compelled to leave Virginia" (emphasis added).[17]

The point is that the Gettysburg campaign involved substantial and unacceptable risks for Lee's army. His northern-most base in Virginia was to be Winchester, after it was taken by Richard S. Ewell. Winchester was ninety miles from Staunton, the available rail terminus. For this reason, and simply because of the distances involved, the extended lines of communication, and the necessity to recross the Potomac, these risks extended to the loss of the Army of Northern Virginia. In any event, assuming victory, the Gettysburg campaign was bound to result in heavy Confederate casualties, as Lee surely knew because of his losses in previous victories and at Antietam. Such foreseeable losses at Gettysburg were bound to limit his army's capacity to maneuver, to contribute to the risk that his army would be fixed, and to increase the risk of his being driven into siege in the Richmond defenses. Lee had repeatedly said that a siege would be fatal to his army.[18]

Colonel Charles Marshall, whose writings originated many of the still-current rationalizations of Lee's generalship, set forth what he called "Lee's Military Policy." Having identified the critical importance of the defense of Richmond, Marshall wrote that Lee sought "to employ the enemy at a distance and prevent his near approach to the city." The Maryland campaign and Gettysburg fit this purpose, according to Marshall. But having identified the Confederacy's inherent strength problem, Marshall states that Lee was "unwilling to incur the risks and losses of an aggressive war having for its object the destruction of the enemy." Indeed, wrote Marshall: "General Lee thought that to expose our armies to the sacrifices of great battles the object of which was only to disperse or destroy those of the enemy would soon bring the Confederacy to the verge of exhaustion. Even victory in such engagements might prove disastrous. The North could readily raise new armies, while the means of the South were so limited that a few bloody victories might leave it powerless to continue the struggle."[19]

These are fine words, a prescription for a defensive strategy, but surely they do not describe Lee's military policy. For an accurate description of Lee's leadership one may again consult Major General Fuller, who in 1929 characterized Lee's strategy: "He rushed forth to find a battlefield, to challenge a contest between himself and the North."[20] This is why Lee went north in 1863. It was a continuation of his offensive grand strategy, to "defeat or drive the armies of the enemy from the field." Win, lose, or draw, the Gettysburg campaign was a strategic mistake because of the inevitable casualties that the Army of Northern Virginia could not afford.

> In regard to defective execution, it is plain that if an army commander is to undertake a high-risk, strategically offensive maneuver, he had better do it with great care, especially if he is moving into enemy territory with extended lines of communication and endemic relative manpower problems. The fact is that Lee proceeded at Gettysburg without essential control of his army in three crucial respects—reconnaissance, the onset of the battle, and the renewal of the battle on the afternoon of July 1.

In his detailed report of January 1864, Lee made the following statements relating to the reconnaissance: "It was expected that as soon as the Federal Army should cross the Potomac, General Stuart would give notice of its movements, and nothing having been heard from him since our entrance into Maryland, it was inferred that the enemy had not yet left Virginia." This report also recounts Lee's learning from a scout on the night of June 28 that the Army of the Potomac had crossed the river and was approaching South Mountain. Colonel Marshall, who drafted the relevant orders as well as Lee's reports, also states that Lee "had not heard from him [Stuart] since the army left Virginia, and was confident from that fact, in view of the positive orders that Stuart had received, that General Hooker had not yet crossed the Potomac."[21] The facts challenge both the candor of Lee's report and the assumption that Stuart's silence meant that the Army of the Potomac was not following Lee.

In the first place, Lee should have assumed that the Federal army would place itself between him and Washington, by that time a well-developed pattern in the Virginia theater. In addition, dictating the movements of the Army of the Potomac was one of the premises of Lee's movement north. In his outline report of July 31, 1863, Lee stated as an objective of the campaign "the transfer of the scene of hostilities north of the Potomac." He intended, he wrote, that his movement north would provoke "corresponding movements on the part of the enemy . . . and that in any event that army would be compelled to leave Virginia." Lee reiterated the substance of these expectations in his detailed report of January 1864.[22] And as he proceeded, Lee knew considerably more than he admitted in his January 1864 report.

On June 18, Lee advised Davis that "the enemy has been thrown back from the line of the Rappahannock, and is concentrating, as far as I can learn, in the vicinity of Centreville. The last reports from scouts indicate that he is moving over toward the Upper Potomac." Centreville is about halfway to the Potomac from Fredericksburg. Thus Lee was aware that the Federals were on the move. On June 19, in another communication to Davis, Lee reported that "indications seem to be that his [the enemy's] main body is proceeding toward the Potomac, whether upon Harper's Ferry or to cross the river east of it, is not yet known." On the following day from Berryville, Virginia, having reported the location of the parts of his own army—Ewell was by this time across the river—Lee again reported what he knew of the Federals: "The movement of the main body . . . is still toward the Potomac, but its real destination is not yet discovered." Three days later, on June 23, another dispatch went to Davis: "Reports of movements of the enemy east of the Blue Ridge cause me to believe that he is preparing to cross the Potomac. A pontoon bridge is said to be laid at Edward's Ferry, and his army corps that he has advanced to Leesburg and the foot of the mountains, appear to be withdrawing." This letter also reported that Ewell was "in motion toward the Susquehanna" and that A. P. Hill's and James Longstreet's corps were nearing the Potomac.[23]

Two more dispatches bear on Lee's expectations. On June 22, in the first of his controversial dispatches to Stuart, he stated that "I fear he [the enemy] will steal a march on us, and get across the Potomac before we are aware." And on June 25, he advised Davis from opposite Williamsport, "I think I can throw General Hooker's Army across the Potomac."[24] From these statements it is apparent that Lee knew that his plan was working—the enemy was following him across the Potomac and out of Virginia. He would have the opportunity to "strike a blow."

On June 22 the much-debated issue of Stuart's orders arose. Lee's cavalry force included, in addition to horse artillery, six brigades under Stuart: Wade Hampton's, Beverly H. Robertson's, William E. "Grumble" Jones's, Fitzhugh Lee's, A. G. Jenkins's, and W. H. F. Lee's, the last-named temporarily commanded by Colonel John R. Chambliss, Jr. Jenkins moved with Ewell, screening the front of the advance, while Robertson and Jones were to guard the mountain passes behind the army. Hampton, Fitz Lee, and

Chambliss were to ride with Stuart. Also with the Army of Northern Virginia was Brigadier General John D. Imboden's command of four regiments.[25]

Setting aside postwar recollections of conversations and concentrating on the contemporaneous written word, Lee's June 22 communication to Stuart is the first relevant document. This letter, written at Berryville, begins with a direct inquiry regarding the enemy: "Do you know where he is and what he is doing?" The letter then identifies specific assignments for the cavalry brigades with Stuart: "If you find that he [the enemy] is moving northward, and that two brigades can guard the Blue Ridge and take care of your rear, you can move with the other three into Maryland, and take position on General Ewell's right, place yourself in communication with him, guard his flank, keep him informed of the enemy's movements, and collect all the supplies you can for the use of the army."[26]

Lee's June 22 letter to Stuart was sent to General Longstreet for forwarding to Stuart. Lee's letter to Longstreet that accompanied it is lost, but Longstreet's letter of transmittal to Stuart, dated 7:00 P.M. on June 22, refers to Lee's writing of Stuart's "passing by the rear of the enemy" and included advice from Longstreet: "If you can get through by that route, I think that you will be less likely to indicate what our plans are than if you should cross by passing to our rear."[27]

On the following day, June 23, another directive went from Lee to Stuart. Written at 5:00 P.M., it contained the following relevant provisions:

> If General Hooker's army remains inactive, you can leave two brigades to watch him, and withdraw with the three others, but should he not[28] appear to be moving northward I think you had better withdraw this side of the mountain tomorrow night, cross at Shepherdstown the next day, and move to Fredericktown.
>
> You will, however, be able to judge whether you can pass around their army without hindrance, doing them all the damage you can, and cross the river east of the mountains.
>
> In either case, after crossing the river, you must move on and feel the right of Ewell's troops, collecting information, provisions, etc.[29]

This order, like that of June 22, included the instruction to the cavalryman to feel Ewell's right and give Lee information. Since Lee knew his plan was working and the Federals were following him and were to cross the Potomac, information should have been his concern. In the circumstances, any commander in control of his army would have issued instructions to Stuart that were short, single-minded, and not discretionary. In the June 22 communication, Lee had asked a question regarding the enemy: "Do you know where he is and what he is doing?" He should have told Stuart that this question needed a prompt answer and that Stuart's one task was to keep him constantly informed of the enemy's movements. Lee did not do this, and taken together the orders contain the following problems:

1. No time sequences were specified; no deadlines were stated by which time Stuart was to perform his tasks or make reports.

2. Four missions for the brigades with Stuart were identified in the two orders—guarding Ewell's flank, keeping Ewell informed of the enemy's movements, collecting supplies for the army, and inflicting all possible damage on the Federals.

3. Stuart was to "judge whether you can pass around their army without hindrance." Even Colonel Marshall acknowledges that it was left to "Stuart to decide whether he can move around the Federal army."

4. The reference to Stuart's then "cross[ing] the river east of the mountains" is not specific as to location. Sir Frederick Maurice says that "Lee certainly meant that Stuart was to cross *immediately* east of the mountains, so as to be close to the right flank of the army," but that is not what the communication says.[30]

What fair and reasonable conclusions may be drawn in view of these problems with the orders? In the first place, the orders were ambiguous and uncertain with regard to such critical matters as the times and places of Stuart's movements. Second, contrary to the assertion of some writers, in riding around the Federal army Stuart was manifestly not acting on his own. That ride was expressly contemplated by Lee and was expressly left to Stuart's judgment. Third, regardless of other problems of interpretation, Stuart could not perform reconnaissance adequately with so many other tasks to perform. Two of these tasks indeed contradicted the reconnaissance function and minimized the likelihood of success in the performance of that function. Collecting provisions and doing damage to the enemy were sure to draw the cavalry away from the intelligence task and delay its progress, which they did. These collateral missions diminished the intelligence function and diluted the significance of that function. Their existence was bound to have contributed to Stuart's judgment that the ride around the Federals was a reasonable thing to do. Fourth, pushing east around the Union army was inconsistent with protecting the Confederate army's right. Stuart could not effectively protect Ewell's right and at the same time place eighty-five thousand Federals between himself and Ewell.

A fifth conclusion may be drawn regarding the orders to Stuart. Those orders are usually considered in the context of Lee's need for information concerning the movements of the Federal army. They are not analyzed in reference to the movements of the Confederate army after the orders were issued to Stuart. Such an analysis is appropriate.

Lee's entire army was on the move in June 1863. The army commander moves an army and knows where all of its parts are or are supposed to be. The individual parts do not necessarily know where the rest of the army is. A commander in control of his army may not rationally leave the movement of a detached unit up to that unit's commander, in this case Stuart, and then proceed to move the rest of the army and hope that the detached unit will be able to find its way to the moved or moving main body. The army commander is responsible for keeping the detached unit informed. Lee made no plan or timely effort to do this. In his June 22 communication to Stuart, Lee told the cavalry leader that the army's advance, Ewell's corps, was to move toward the Susquehanna River via Emmitsburg and Chambersburg. The June 23 order stated that "the movements of Ewell's corps are as stated in my former letter. Hill's first division will reach the Potomac to-day, and Longstreet will follow tomorrow."

These messages were the last Stuart received from Lee before the cavalry moved out on the night of June 24 to begin the fateful ride around the Federals. Thus there was justice to Stuart's complaint in his defensive official report that when he started east he understood that the rest of the army was moving toward the Susquehanna. Accordingly, he stated that when he swung north he moved toward York to rendezvous, only to discover that the Confederates had left that area. His sole source of information regarding the Confederate army's location was Northern newspapers. Finally, on the night of July 1, he received a dispatch from Lee telling him that the army was at Gettysburg.

There is a final conclusion that may be drawn regarding reconnaissance. Stuart had been given the discretion to "pass around their army," with no time or distance limitations. Having in mind that Lee knew the Federal army was following him, a reconnaissance contingency plan was surely in order. There was also justification for Stuart's statement in his report that if cavalry "in advance of the army the first day of Gettysburg" was wanted, "it must be remembered that the cavalry [Jenkins's brigade] specially selected for advance guard to the army by the commanding general on account of its geographical location at the time, was available for this purpose." Kenneth P. Williams's observation is fair: "There were still three cavalry brigades near at hand that he [Lee] could have called upon for mounted service: Imboden's operating toward the west, and those of B. H. Robertson and W. E. Jones guarding the passes below the Potomac that soon needed little or no guarding. There seems to be no excuse for Lee's finding himself at Chambersburg on the 28th without a single regiment of cavalry."[31]

This, then, was the Confederate reconnaissance failure as the armies moved toward July 1, 1863, and this failure was essentially Lee's.

The second leadership error in execution on July 1 concerns the onset of the battle. Coddington states that "to say that Stuart's late arrival was a major cause of Lee's defeat is a little too pat an answer to the question of why the Confederates lost the battle." There were other command failures. Colonel Marshall speaks of the Gettysburg campaign as involving the "risk [of] the battlefield which chance might bring us during a movement northward."[32] As it turned out, it was simply a chance battlefield.

In his July 31, 1863, outline report, part of which has been previously quoted, Lee states: "It had not been intended to fight a general battle at such a distance from our base, unless attacked by the enemy, but, finding ourselves unexpectedly confronted by the Federal Army, it became a matter of difficulty to withdraw through the mountains with our large trains. At the same time, the country was unfavorable for collecting supplies while in the presence of the enemy's main body. . . . A battle thus became in a measure unavoidable."[33]

In their essentials, these words bear little resemblance to what Lee in fact intended or what in fact occurred. In the same report, he stated that his movement was intended to require Hooker to move with him and that this "might offer a fair opportunity to strike a blow" at the Federals. With regard to the "unless attacked" condition of the report, Lee was not attacked. His forces initially attacked and were the aggressor for three days. As a result of the initial attack, a battle occurred on July 1, not by plan but by chance.

Had Lee seriously intended to avoid a chance battle, he could have so instructed his corps commanders. The *Official Records* contain no such circular. Lee's reports do not say that he had issued any such order. Nor do the reports of Hill, Ewell, or Longstreet. Even after he learned on the night of June 28 that the Army of the Potomac had, as he expected, crossed the river, there is no evidence of warning orders. No such orders were forthcoming before July 1, and the battle and the battlefield were left to chance until it was too late because he had not asserted control over his army. This was his second failure of control.

Lee provided a laconic account of the start of the battle in his official report dated July 31, 1863. "The leading division of Hill met the enemy in advance of Gettysburg on the morning of July 1," he wrote. "Driving back these troops to within a short distance of the town, he there encountered a larger force, with which two of his divisions became engaged. Ewell, coming up with two of his divisions by Heidlersburg road, joined in the engagement." The battle thus began without Lee's knowing the location of other elements of the Federal army and without the Confederate army's being closed up. On June 30 Henry Heth had sent James J. Pettigrew's brigade from Cashtown to Gettysburg and discovered the enemy, principally cavalry, there. Lee was at Chambersburg. Hill's November 1863 report states: "A courier was then dispatched with this information to the general commanding . . . ; also to General Ewell, informing him, and that I intended to advance the next morning and discover what was in my front." As Coddington notes, Hill's "announcement seemed not to have disturbed the commanding general."[34]

As that fateful July 1 began, conservative instincts came over Lee, and he briefly and belatedly asserted himself to control events. Thus Ewell's 1863 report of the campaign recites that at Heidlersburg on the night of June 30 he received Lee's order to proceed to Cashtown or Gettysburg "as circumstances might dictate," together with a note from Hill saying that he was at Cashtown. On July 1, Ewell reported that he started for Cashtown and Hunterstown. Receiving a note from Hill telling of his advance on Gettysburg, Ewell ordered Robert E. Rodes's and Jubal A. Early's divisions toward that place. Ewell notified Lee of these movements and was informed by Lee that, "in case we found the enemy's forces very large, he did not want a general engagement brought on till the rest of the army came up." Ewell's report continued: "By the time this message reached me, General A. P. Hill had already been warmly engaged with a large body of the enemy in his front, and Carter's artillery battalion, of Rodes' division, had opened with fine effect on the flank of the same body, which was rapidly preparing to attack me, while fresh masses were moving into position in my front. It was too late to avoid an engagement without abandoning the position already taken up, and I determined to push the attack vigorously."[35] In short, Lee's attempt at control came too late because of his failure to react to Hill's June 30 communication and because of the onrush of events.

Lee's renewal of the battle on July 1 constitutes the third error in execution. He apparently did make a second effort at control when he became aware of the fighting at Gettysburg. This awareness, Coddington states, occurred while Lee rode from Chambersburg to Cashtown, where he and his party heard the sound of cannon fire to the east. Walter H. Taylor adds that at Cashtown Lee received a communication from Hill and that he then sent instructions to Heth to avoid a general engagement but to ascertain the enemy's force and report immediately. A. L. Long confirms the Cashtown report from Hill but states that it was a request for reinforcements and that Lee rushed Richard H. Anderson's division forward. General W. N. Pendleton, who was with Lee, mentions the sound of cannon fire. He reports further that the command party hastened toward Gettysburg and that, "arriving near the crest of an eminence more than a mile west of the town . . . we took positions overlooking the field. It was, perhaps, 2 o'clock, and the battle was raging with considerable violence. . . . Observing the course of events, the commanding general suggested whether positions on the right could not be found to enfilade the valley between our position and the town and the enemy's batteries next the town."[36]

Pendleton's account suggests that if Lee, aware of Heth's morning attack, instructed Heth to avoid a general engagement, he abandoned this caution when he reached the field. And Coddington, relying on Heth's postwar account, confirms Lee's decision to commit the Confederates to the afternoon attack. Coddington tells of Heth's observation of Rodes's becoming engaged and states: "[Heth] took the trouble to find Lee and seek his permission to attack in coordination with Rodes. Lee refused the request on the grounds that Longstreet was not up. Returning to his division, Heth saw the enemy shifting his weight to meet Rodes's attack. He again sought Lee's consent to give assistance, and this time received it. These meetings of the two generals occurred before the grand assault all along the Union line."[37]

Thus did Lee permit the renewal of the battle in the afternoon of July 1 in spite of his lack of knowledge of the Federal army's whereabouts and the absence of his own First Corps, which meant that he did it without having reason to believe that he had sufficient manpower to deprive the Federals of the high ground south of the town. Laxness with respect to reconnaissance and his lack of control of Hill's movements had caused him to stumble into a battle. The renewal of the battle represents Lee's third failure with respect to the events of July 1. It committed him to a major confrontation on this particular ground. The need for food and forage did not require his renewal of the battle on July 1 any more than they did on the days following July 1. Porter Alexander, referring to July 2 and the retreat to the Potomac, notes that the Confederates foraged successfully for more than a week in a restricted area of Pennsylvania. He also states that it was feasible for the Confederates to have abandoned Seminary Ridge on the night of July 1 or on July 2: "The onus of attack was upon Meade. . . . We could even have fallen back to Cashtown & held the mountain passes . . . & popular sentiment would have forced Meade to take the aggressive."[38] This was even more true in the early afternoon of July 1, when Lee authorized the all-out Confederate attack on Seminary Ridge, without sufficient troops of his own on hand to keep going and without knowledge of the whereabouts of the rest of the Federal army.

At the close of the day, the net effect of his command failure was that Lee was on the battlefield and in the battle that chance had brought him. As a consequence, he was significantly disadvantaged: he confronted an enemy that occupied what Porter Alexander called a "really wonderful position," with interior lines; Lee's line was a long exterior line, a difficult one from which to organize a coordinated attack; and four of his divisions, as Lee reported, were "weakened and exhausted by a long and bloody struggle."[39]

Committed to the Lee tradition, a number of commentators in the *Southern Historical Society Papers* and elsewhere have attempted to rationalize his command failures in regard to July 1. As has been indicated, Stuart's absence is a major thrust of these efforts. Blaming Hill, in spite of Lee's knowledge on June 30 of Hill's planned movements on July 1, is another. Lee's advocates also attempt to moot the issue of his command failures by placing blame on Ewell. They argue that these failures would have been irrelevant if only Ewell had pushed on late on July 1 and seized Cemetery Hill or Culp's Hill. It is argued that this could have been readily accomplished. A number of Confederate officers said so—after the war and when the Lee tradition of invincibility was being formed.[40] A good lawyer may reasonably be skeptical of the *Southern Historical Society Papers* as evidence. Written after the facts during the creation of the Lost Cause tradition, their value as history is surely limited. Like the patriarchal stories of the Old Testament, such accounts have ideological rather than historical value. They nevertheless require a response.

An initial difficulty in regard to the controversy about Ewell's conduct concerns identification of the issue. The advocates on both sides insist on debating whether or not Ewell would have been successful. This is inevitably a hypothetical question and therefore inappropriate for historical inquiry. Properly framed, the issue historically can only be whether Ewell made a reasonable decision in the circumstances. There is a second problem. Those who criticize Ewell frequently resort to a contention that is also inappropriate: regardless of the facts, Ewell "should have tried." They forget that Ewell was not a Civil War student. He was a general officer responsible for the consequences of his acts and for the lives of his soldiers. Finally, the partisans frequently overlook the fact that there was more involved for the Confederates than simply getting on the heights. There was also the question of whether they would be able to stay if the Federals were to mount a prompt effort to drive them off.

With the foregoing considerations in mind, one may pursue the question of whether Ewell made a rational decision. This is a matter of the evidence with respect to four factors: the nature of the terrain, the Federal forces opposed, the manpower available to Ewell, and the orders given to Ewell by Lee.

The terrain confronting Ewell may be seen today looking up from the area of the Culp House and the low ground immediately to the west of that house. The heights are precipitous, irregular, and complex, marked by hollows and ravines. An attacking force would have been advancing uphill against defenders with ample places from which to effect an ambush.

In considering the Federal forces opposed—and the troops Ewell could have used—the identification of precise times of day is an impossible task. Any discussion of the issue is limited by inability to state exactly when either Federal or Confederate units were available. Nevertheless, Federals to oppose an attack were on the heights or very close by during the general time period in which Ewell was considering the question:

1. One brigade of Adolph von Steinwehr's division and Michael Wiedrich's battery had been on Cemetery Hill since the arrival of the Eleventh Corps.

2. The remnant of the Iron Brigade, approximately seven hundred men, had been sent from Cemetery to Culp's Hill and was entrenching there in a strong position.

3. The 7th Indiana of Lysander Cutler's brigade, five hundred rifles, which had not been engaged, had arrived and had been sent to Culp's Hill with the members of that brigade who had come through the day's fighting.

4. The remaining effectives from the First Corps and Eleventh Corps, "basically intact" according to Harry W. Pfanz, were present. There were skirmishers in the town at the base of Cemetery Hill.

5. The Federals had a total of forty guns and ample ammunition on the heights.

6. Henry W. Slocum's Twelfth Corps was close by, approximately one mile from the scene. John W. Geary's division was on the Federal left by approximately 5:00 P.M.; the first division was on the Federal right at about the same time.[41]

Confederate perceptions of this opposition are illuminating. In his 1863 report, Rodes stated that before "the completion of his defeat before the town, the enemy had begun to establish a line of battle on the heights back of the town, and by the time my line was in a condition to renew the attack, he displayed quite a formidable line of infantry and artillery immediately in my front, extending smartly to my right, and as far as I could see to my left, in front of Early." Ewell's 1863 report was similar: "The enemy had fallen back to a commanding position known as Cemetery Hill . . . and quickly showed a formidable front there. . . . I could not bring artillery to bear on it."[42] There were, in short, substantial forces opposed to Ewell, in infantry and artillery, placed on imposing terrain.

With regard to the manpower available for the attack, each of the Confederate corps on hand was missing a division. In the case of Ewell, Edward "Allegheny" Johnson's division was not present. It arrived at a late hour. From Hill's corps, Anderson's division did not come up until after the day closed. Lee's detailed report describes the four divisions that had participated in the July 1 fight as "already weakened and exhausted by a long and bloody struggle." Hill reported that his two divisions were "exhausted by some six hours hard fighting [and that] prudence led me to be content with what had been gained, and not push forward troops exhausted and necessarily disordered, probably to encounter fresh troops of the enemy." Ewell's report similarly noted that "all the troops with me were jaded by twelve hours' marching and fighting."[43] And the Confederate reports uniformly state that the Southern units had lost formation at the conclusion of the movement that drove the Federals from Seminary Ridge. Ewell's task was not simply to continue an organized assault that was ongoing. He would have been required to marshal forces and undertake a new movement against the heights.

Douglas Southall Freeman, Lee's great advocate, is always anxious to rationalize Lee's failures at the expense of his lieutenants. In *Lee's Lieutenants*, he criticizes Ewell for not mooting Confederate problems on the first day by taking the heights. He describes in detail Ewell's communications at this hour and his efforts to organize the forces with which to attack. Having recounted Lee's advising Ewell that none of Hill's troops were available on Ewell's right, Freeman states: "All of this meant that if Cemetery Hill was to be taken, Ewell must do it with his own men." Noting then that Early had detached two brigades under John B. Gordon to operate on Ewell's left, Freeman says: "Still again, the force with which Ewell could attack immediately was small. . . . Two Brigades of Early, then, and the tired survivors of Rodes's confused charges—these were all Ewell had for the attack till Johnson arrived. Nor would this force . . . have any support from the right."[44] Even Freeman concedes that Ewell did not have significant numbers for the attack.

Finally, what were Ewell's orders? Lee's detailed report identifies them and also their logic:

> It was ascertained . . . that the remainder of that army [the Federal army] . . . was approaching Gettysburg. Without information as to its proximity, the strong position which the enemy had assumed could not be attacked without danger of exposing the four divisions present, already weakened and exhausted by a long and bloody struggle, to an overwhelming number of fresh troops. General Ewell was, therefore, instructed to carry the hill occupied by the enemy, if he found it practicable, but to avoid a general engagement until the arrival of the other divisions of the army. . . . He decided to await Johnson's division, which . . . did not reach Gettysburg until a late hour.[45]

In *Lee's Lieutenants*, Freeman covers this issue in a chapter titled "Ewell Cannot Reach a Decision."[46] Surely this is nonsense. Pursuant to Lee's order, Ewell decided that it was not "practicable" to attack. Lee was on Seminary Ridge and available. The plain fact is that he did not issue a peremptory order to Ewell for the reasons he states in his report: the Federal army was approaching, but its proximity was unknown; the "strong position" of the enemy; the worn condition of the Confederate forces available; the risk of the presence of overwhelming and fresh Federal troops; and the desire to avoid a general engagement.

It is unhistoric to conclude that Ewell was necessarily wrong in his judgment. His decision was reasonable in the circumstances, and that responds to the only historically appropriate question concerning Ewell's conduct.

One can only conclude that Lee's movement across the Potomac was a grave strategic error. In addition, in reference to the first day of the battle, there were significant command failures on Lee's part that were destructive to the Confederate chances of victory at Gettysburg.

NOTES

1. Douglas Southall Freeman, ed., *Lee's Dispatches: Unpublished Letters of General Robert E. Lee, C. S. A., to Jefferson Davis and the War Department of the Confederate States of America, 1862–1865* (1915; rev. ed., Grady McWhiney, New York: G. P. Putnam's Sons, 1957), xxxvii.

2. Maj. Gen. Sir Frederick Maurice, ed., *An Aide-de-Camp of Lee, Being the Papers of Colonel Charles Marshall* (Boston: Little, Brown, 1927), 190. Although concerned with the overland campaign of 1864–65, Andrew A. Humphreys's discussion of the water route alternative illuminates the considerations affecting the choice of routes toward Richmond. See Humphreys, *The Virginia Campaign of '64 and '65: The Army of the Potomac and the Army of the James* (New York: Charles Scribner's Sons, 1883), 6–9.

3. Robert K. Krick, "Why Lee Went North," in Morningside Bookshop, *Catalogue Number Twenty-Four* (Dayton, Ohio, 1988), 10.

4. Edward Porter Alexander, *Fighting for the Confederacy: The Personal Recollections of General Edward Porter Alexander*, ed. Gary W. Gallagher (Chapel Hill: University of North Carolina Press, 1989), 415.

5. U. S. War Department, *The War of the Rebellion: A Compilation of the Official Records of the Union and Confederate Armies*, 127 vols., index, and atlas, (Washington DC: GPO, 1880–1901), ser. 1, vol. 27, pt. 3, p. 932 (hereafter cited as *Official Records*; all references are to volumes in series 1); Clifford Dowdey and Louis H. Manarin, eds., *The Wartime Papers of R. E. Lee* (Boston: Little, Brown, 1961), 816.

6. *Official Records*, vol. 29, pt. 1, p. 405; *Official Records*, vol. 51, pt. 2, p. 761; Dowdey and Manarin, eds., *Wartime Papers*, 675.

7. Dowdey and Manarin, eds., *Wartime Papers*, 388–89.

8. Dowdey and Manarin, eds., *Wartime Papers*, 508.

9. Dowdey and Manarin, eds., *Wartime Papers*, 843–44.

10. These data are taken from Thomas L. Livermore, *Numbers and Losses in the Civil War in America, 1861–65* (1901; reprint, Dayton, Ohio: Morningside House, 1986), 86, 88–89, 92, 98.

11. Krick, "Why Lee Went North," 11.

12. Richard E. Beringer, Herman Hattaway, Archer Jones, and William N. Still Jr., *Why the South Lost the Civil War* (Athens, Ga.: University of Georgia Press, 1986), 9, 16.

13. Lt. Col. George A. Bruce, "The Strategy of the Civil War," in *Papers of the Military Historical Society of Massachusetts*, 14 vols. and index (1895–1918; reprint, Wilmington, N.C.: Broadfoot Publishing Company, 1989–90), 13:469.

14. Maj. Gen. J. F. C. Fuller, *The Generalship of Ulysses S. Grant* (1929; reprint, Bloomington: Indiana University Press, 1958), 365.

15. On the question of Northern morale in the early summer of 1864, see Lt. Col. Alfred H. Burne, *Lee, Grant and Sherman* (New York: Charles Scribner's Sons, 1939), 65, and William H. Swinton, *Campaigns of the Army of the Potomac: A Critical History of Operations in Virginia, Maryland and Pennsylvania, from the Commencement to the Close of the War, 1861–1865* (New York: Charles Scribner's Sons, 1882), 494–95. Swinton's perceptive study argued that after Cold Harbor the outlook in the North was so gloomy "that there was at this time great danger of a collapse of the war. The history of this conflict truthfully written will show this."

16. *Official Records*, vol. 27, pt. 2, p. 308; Herman Hattaway and Archer Jones, *How the North Won: A Military History of the Civil War* (Urbana: University of Illinois Press, 1983), 398.

17. Dowdey and Manarin, eds. *Wartime Papers*, 505; *Official Records*, vol. 27, pt. 2:305.

18. *Official Records*, vol. 27, pt. 3, pp. 868–69; *Official Records*, vol. 40, pt. 2, p. 703.

19. Maurice, ed., *Aide-de-Camp of Lee*, 73, 68.

20. Fuller, *Generalship of Grant*, 377.

21. *Official Records*, vol. 27, pt. 2, p. 316; Maurice, ed., *Aide-de-Camp of Lee*, 217.

22. *Official Records*, vol. 27, pt. 2, p. 313.

23. *Official Records*, vol. 27, pt. 2, p. 970.

24. *Official Records*, vol. 27, pt. 3, pp. 913, 931.

25. Edwin B. Coddington, *The Gettysburg Campaign: A Study in Command* (New York: Charles Scribner's Sons, 1968), 594–95.

26. *Official Records*, vol. 27, pt. 3, p. 913. For Lee's order to Stuart and Longstreet's transmittal letter, see Gary W. Gallagher, ed., *The First Day at Gettysburg: Essays on Union and Confederate Leadership* (Kent, Ohio: Kent State University Press, 1992), 141–43.

27. *Official Records*, vol. 27, pt. 3, p. 915.

28. It is apparent that the word "not" was unintended. Read literally, the orders of June 23 set forth different movements for Stuart depending on the same facts: "if General Hooker's army remains inactive" and "should he [Hooker] not appear to be moving northward." This almost certainly represented a careless ambiguity, but it seems not to have been a critical one. In both of the orders printed in the *Official Records*, Stuart was to feel Ewell's right and give him information. Virtually all writers have ignored this seemingly misplaced "not" in Lee's instructions to Stuart. An exception is Coddington, who in *The Gettysburg Campaign*, 108, overlooks the possibility of a simple error and speculates that perhaps Lee "considered it possible that Hooker would move southward to threaten Richmond, in which case Stuart's occupation of Frederick, a town equidistant from Baltimore and Washington, would be an effective deterrent."

29. *Official Records*, vol. 27, pt. 3, p. 923.

30. Maurice, ed., *Aide-de-Camp of Lee*, 208 n.

31. *Official Records*, vol. 27, pt. 2, pp. 207–8; Kenneth P. Williams, *Lincoln Finds a General: A Military Study of the Civil War*, 5 vols. (New York: Macmillan, 1949–59), 2:666.

32. Coddington, *Gettysburg Campaign*, 207; Maurice, ed., *Aide-de-Camp of Lee*, 191.

33. *Official Records*, vol. 27, pt. 2, p. 308.

34. Ibid., 307, 607; Coddington, *Gettysburg Campaign*, 264.

35. *Official Records*, vol. 27, pt. 2, p. 444.

36. Coddington, *Gettysburg Campaign*, 280; Walter H. Taylor, *Four Years with General Lee* (1877; reprint, Bloomington: Indiana University Press, 1962), 280; A. L. Long *Memoirs of Robert E. Lee: His Military and Personal History* (New York: J. M. Stoddart, 1886), 275–76; *Official Records*, vol. 27, pt. 2, pp. 348–49.

37. Coddington, *Gettysburg Campaign*, 309.

38. Alexander, *Fighting for the Confederacy*, 233–34.

39. Alexander, *Fighting for the Confederacy*, 234; *Official Records*, vol. 27, pt. 2: 317.

40. These postwar recollections by John B. Gordon, Henry Kyd Douglas, James Power Smith, Isaac R. Trimble, Jubal A. Early, Walter H. Taylor, and others are cited in Douglas Southall Freeman, *Lee's Lieutenants: A Study in Command*, 3 vols. (New York: Charles Scribner's Sons, 1942–44), 3:92–102.

41. *Official Records*, vol. 27, pt. 1, pp. 721, 277, 283, 704, 758–59, 777, 825; Harry W. Pfanz, *Gettysburg—The Second Day* (Chapel Hill: University of North Carolina Press, 1987), 38–39.

42. *Official Records*, vol. 27, pt. 2, pp. 555, 445.

43. *Official Records*, vol. 27, pt. 2, pp. 470, 607, 445.

44. Freeman, *Lee's Lieutenants*, 3:97–98.

45. *Official Records*, vol. 27. pt. 2, pp. 317–18.

46. Freeman, *Lee's Lieutenants*, 3:90–105.

“If the Enemy Is There, We Must Attack Him”: R. E. Lee and the Second Day at Gettysburg

GARY W. GALLAGHER

No aspect of R. E. Lee’s military career has sparked more controversy than his decision to pursue the tactical offensive at Gettysburg. Lee’s contemporaries and subsequent writers produced a literature on the subject notable for its size and discordancy. Unwary students can fall victim to the hyperbole, dissembling, and self-interest characteristic of many accounts by participants. The massive printed legacy of the “Gettysburg Controversy,” with its blistering critiques of James Longstreet and “Old Pete’s” clumsy rejoinders, demands special care. Even many modern writers unfurl partisan banners when they approach the topic. Despite the size of the existing literature, Lee’s decision to resume offensive combat on July 2 remains a topic worthy of study. Before passing judgment on his actions, however, it is necessary to assess the merits of earlier works—an exercise that underscores the contradictory nature of the evidence and the lack of interpretive consensus among previous writers.

The Army of Northern Virginia went into Pennsylvania at its physical apogee, supremely confident that under Lee’s direction it could triumph on any battlefield. LeRoy Summerfield Edwards of the 12th Virginia Infantry struck a common note in a letter written near Shepherdstown on June 23: “[T]he health of the troops was never better and above all the *morale* of the army was never more favorable for offensive or defensive operations . . . victory will inevitably attend our arms in any collision with the enemy.” British observer A. J. L. Fremantle detected a similar outlook when he spoke to a pair of officers from Louisiana on that same day. Recuperating from wounds suffered in fighting at Winchester during the march northward, these men gave Fremantle "an animated account of the spirits and feeling of the army. At no period of the war, they say, have the men been so well equipped, so well clothed, so eager for a fight, or so confident of success. . . ."[1]

Two weeks and more than twenty-five thousand casualties later the picture had changed considerably. The soldiers still believed in Lee, but they had lost their almost mystical faith in certain victory. Randolph H. McKim, a young Marylander in Richard S. Ewell's Second Corps, betrayed such sentiment in his diary shortly after Gettysburg: "I went into the last battle feeling that victory *must* be ours—that such an army could not be foiled, and that God would certainly declare himself on our side. *Now* I feel that unless He sees fit to bless our arms, our valor will not avail." Stephen Dodson Ramseur, a brigadier in Robert E. Rodes's division, reacted similarly to the shock of Gettysburg. "Our great campaign," wrote Ramseur a month after the battle, "admirably planned & more admirably executed up to the fatal days at Gettysburg, has failed. Which I was not prepared to anticipate." Although insisting that Gettysburg did not spell the doom of the Confederacy, he believed it foreshadowed other crises the South must overcome to gain independence. Ramseur looked "the thing square in the face" and stood ready "to undergo dangers and hardships and trials to the end."[2]

Staggering losses and a shift in morale thus grew out of Lee's decision to press for a decisive result on the field at Gettysburg. Some Southerners immediately questioned his tactics. "Gettysburg has shaken my faith in Lee as a general," Robert Garlick Hill Kean of the War Department wrote in his diary on July 26, 1863. "To fight an enemy superior in numbers at such terrible disadvantage of position in the heart of his own territory, when the freedom of movement gave him the advantage of selecting his own time and place for accepting battle, seems to have been a great military blunder. . . . and the result was the worst disaster which has ever befallen our arms—." Brigadier General Wade Hampton used comparably strong language in a letter to Joseph E. Johnston less than a month after the battle. The Pennsylvania campaign was a "complete failure," stated Hampton, during which Lee resorted to unimaginative offensive tactics. "The position of the Yankees there was the strongest I ever saw & it was in vain to attack it." Hampton had expected the Confederates to "choose our own points at which to fight" during the expedition, but "we let Meade choose his position and then we attacked."[3]

More restrained in his disapproval was James Longstreet, who informed his uncle Augustus Baldwin Longstreet confidentially in late July 1863 that the "battle was not made as I would have made it. My idea was to throw ourselves between the enemy and Washington, select a strong position, and force the enemy to attack us." Through such a defensive stance, thought Longstreet, the Confederates might have "destroyed the Federal army, marched into Washington, and dictated our terms, or, at least, held Washington and marched over as much of Pennsylvania as we cared to, had we drawn the enemy into attack upon our carefully chosen position in his rear."[4]

The early postwar years witnessed a rapid escalation of the debate over Lee's generalship at Gettysburg. Longstreet served as a catalyst for an outpouring of writing, the opening salvo of which appeared the year after Appomattox in William Swinton's *Campaigns of the Army of Potomac*. A Northern journalist, Swinton interviewed Longstreet and drew heavily on his opinions to portray Lee's tactics at Gettysburg as misguided and contrary to a precampaign pledge to "his corps-commanders that *he would not assume a tactical offensive*, but force his antagonist to attack him." Lee's assaults on the second day were a "grave error" explained by overconfidence in the prowess of his soldiers, fear that withdrawal without battle would harm morale in the Army of Northern Virginia and among Southern civilians, and contempt for the Army of the Potomac. Having "gotten a taste of blood in the considerable success of the first day," suggested Swinton in language similar to that used elsewhere by Longstreet, "the Confederate commander seems to have lost that equipoise in which his faculties commonly moved, and he determined to give battle."[5]

Other early postwar accounts also highlighted questions about Lee's aggressive tactics. Edward A. Pollard, the staunchly pro-Southern editor of the *Richmond Examiner* during the war, alluded in 1866 to "a persistent popular opinion in the South that Gen. Lee, having failed to improve the advantage of the first day, did wrong thereafter to fight at Gettysburg." Granting the "extraordinary strength" of the Federal position, Pollard nonetheless asserted that the superlative morale of Lee's army might have justified the attempt to drive Meade's army from the field.[6] James D. McCabe, Jr.'s, generally appreciative *Life and Campaigns of General Robert E. Lee,* also published in 1866, argued that after July 1 the Confederate army "had before it the task of storming a rocky fortress stronger than that against which Burnside had dashed his army so madly at Fredericksburg, and every chance of success lay with the Federals." Citing Swinton's work as corroboration, McCabe endorsed Longstreet's proposal to shift around the Federal left and invite attack from a position between the Union army and Washington. "There are those who assert that General Lee himself was not free from the contempt entertained by his men for the army they had so frequently vanquished, and that he was influenced by it in his decision upon this occasion," added McCabe in reference to Lee's resumption of assaults on July 2. "This may or may not be true. It is certain that the decision was an error."[7]

The interpretive tide turned in Lee's favor shortly after the general's death. Led by Jubal A. Early, a number of former Confederates eventually mounted a concerted effort in the Southern Historical Society's *Papers* and elsewhere to discredit Longstreet (whose Republicanism made him an especially inviting target) and prove Lee innocent of all responsibility for the debacle at Gettysburg. Speaking at Washington and Lee University on the anniversary of Lee's birth in 1872, Early disputed the notion that the Confederates should have refrained from attacking after July 1. "Some have thought that General Lee did wrong in fighting at Gettysburg," remarked Early in obvious reference to Longstreet's views, "and it has been said that he ought to have moved around Meade's left, so as to get between him and Washington. . . . I then thought, and still think, that it was right to fight the battle of Gettysburg, and I am firmly convinced that if General Lee's plans had been carried out in the spirit in which they were conceived, a decisive victory would have been obtained, which perhaps would have secured our independence."

As the most prominent member of the Lost Cause school of interpretation, Early won a deserved reputation as Lee's most indefatigable defender and Longstreet's harshest critic. He blamed defeat on Longstreet's sulking sloth in mounting the assaults on July 2. Lee expected the attacks to begin at dawn, insisted Early (a charge Longstreet easily proved to be literally untrue—though Lee certainly wanted the attacks to commence as early as possible); Longstreet began the offensive about 4:00 P.M., by which time Meade's entire army was in place. "The position which Longstreet attacked at four, was not occupied by the enemy until late in the afternoon," concluded Early, "and Round Top Hill, which commanded the enemy's position, could have been taken in the morning without a struggle."[8]

Although few veterans of the Army of Northern Virginia spoke publicly against Lee during the postwar years, many did not share Early's views. Benjamin G. Humphreys, who commanded the 21st Mississippi Infantry in William Barksdale's brigade on the second day at Gettysburg, revealed sharp disagreement with the Lost Cause writers in comments he scribbled in the margins of his copy of Walter Taylor's *Four Years with General Lee.* Humphreys deplored the "necessity of hunting out for a 'scapegoat' " to guarantee that the " 'infallibility' of Lee must not be called into question." The commanding general "took upon himself all the blame for Gettysburg," observed Humphreys mockingly, "was that not an evidence of his infallibility?"[9]

Lee himself said little publicly beyond his official report. The fighting on July 1 had escalated from a meeting engagement to a bitter contest involving two corps on each side, during the course of which the serendipitous arrival of Ewell's leading divisions had compelled the Federals to withdraw through Gettysburg to high ground below the town. "It had not been intended to deliver a general battle so far from our base unless attacked," wrote Lee in apparent confirmation of Longstreet's assertion that he had envisioned acting on the tactical defensive in Pennsylvania, "but coming unexpectedly upon the whole Federal Army, to withdraw through the mountains with our extensive trains would have been difficult and dangerous." Nor could the Confederates wait for Meade to counterattack, "as the country was unfavorable for collecting supplies in the presence of the enemy, who could restrain our foraging parties by holding the mountain passes with local troops." "A battle had, therefore, become in a measure unavoidable," concluded Lee, "and the success already gained gave hope of a favorable issue."[10]

Lee offered the last hopeful statement despite a firm understanding of the terrain. "The enemy occupied a strong position," he conceded, "with his right upon two commanding elevations adjacent to each other, one southeast and the other, known as Cemetery Hill, immediately south of the town. . . . His line extended thence upon the high ground along the Emmitsburg Road, with a steep ridge in rear, which was also occupied. This ridge was difficult of ascent, particularly the two hills above mentioned as forming its northern extremity, and a third at the other end, on which the enemy's left rested." Stone and rail fences affording protection to defenders, together with generally open approaches three-quarters of a mile wide, complicated any plan of assault. Yet offensive thoughts dominated Lee's thinking. When Ewell declined to strike at Cemetery Hill late on the afternoon of July 1, the commanding general opted to await the arrival of Longstreet's two leading divisions: "It was determined to make the principal attack upon the enemy's left. . . . Longstreet was directed to place the divisions of McLaws and Hood on the right of Hill, partially enveloping the enemy's left, which he was to drive in." A. P. Hill would engage the Union center with a demonstration, while Ewell's troops would do the same on the enemy's right with an eye toward exploiting any opening.[11]

Almost matter-of-fact in its explication of the reasons for resuming attacks on July 2, Lee's report contains no hint that he considered the decision a bad one. Five years after the battle, he responded to a query about Gettysburg in a similar vein: "I must again refer you to the official accounts. Its loss was occasioned by a combination of circumstances. It was commenced in the absence of correct intelligence. It was continued in the effort to overcome the difficulties by which we were surrounded, and it would have been gained could one determined and united blow have been delivered by our whole line."[12]

Several secondhand accounts also suggest that Lee never deviated from the tenor of his report. Colonel William Allan, former chief of ordnance in the Second Corps, made notes of a conversation with Lee on April 15, 1868, wherein Lee talked passionately about Gettysburg. Lee had hoped to avoid a general battle in Pennsylvania, recorded Allan, but "Jeb" Stuart's absence caused the opposing forces to stumble into one another on July 1. The commanding general "found himself engaged with the Federal army therefore, unexpectedly, and had to fight. This being determined on, victory w[oul]d have been won if he could have gotten one decided simultaneous attack on the whole line." Lee also observed that his critics "talked much of that they knew little about" and, in a likely reference to William Swinton's book, stated that he doubted Longstreet ever said Lee "was under a promise to the Leut. Generals not to fight a general battle in Pa. . . . He never made any such promise, and he never thought of doing any such thing."[13]

Nearly two years later, Lee again "spoke feelingly" about Gettysburg with Allan. "Much was said about risky movements," noted Allan. Lee believed that "everything was risky in our war. He knew oftentimes that he was playing a very bold game, but it was the only *possible* one." This justification of risk, though not specifically tied to any phase of the campaign, certainly could apply to Lee's pursuing assaults after the first day. As in his earlier pronouncements on the subject, Lee seemed content with his principal decisions. He still maintained that Stuart's failure had precipitated the fighting, and the fact that he "never c[oul]d get a simultaneous attack on the enemy's position" sealed the result.[14]

Accounts by Brigadier General John D. Imboden and Major John Seddon further buttress an image of Lee as comfortable with his tactical conduct at Gettysburg. Early on the morning of July 4, wrote Imboden in the 1880s, he met with Lee at army headquarters outside Gettysburg. The conversation turned to the failed assaults on July 3: "I never saw troops behave more magnificently than Pickett's division of Virginians did to-day in that grand charge upon the enemy," averred Lee. "And if they had been supported as they were to have been . . . we would have held the position and the day would have been ours." It is reasonable to infer from this passage that Lee also viewed the resumption of the offensive on July 2 as correct. Major Seddon, a brother of the Confederate secretary of war, met with Lee shortly after Gettysburg and subsequently related his conversation to Major General Henry Heth. Heth quoted Seddon as stating that Lee acknowledged a heavy loss at Gettysburg but pronounced it "no greater than it would have been from the series of battles I would have been compelled to fight had

I remained in Virginia." After making this observation, Lee rose from his seat and with an "emphatic gesture said, 'and sir, we did whip them at Gettysburg, and it will be seen for the next six months that *that army* will be as quiet as a sucking dove.' "[15]

A smaller body of evidence portrays Lee as subject to doubts about his tactical moves at Gettysburg. Perhaps best known is Fremantle's description of Lee's response to Brigadier General Cadmus M. Wilcox as the latter brought his brigade out of the fight on July 3: "Never mind, General, *all this has been MY fault*—it is *I* that have lost this fight, and you must help me out of it in the best way you can."[16] Whether or not Lee meant the entire battle when he spoke of "this fight," his comment can be extended to the decision to keep attacking after July 1. In early August 1863, Lee informed President Davis that he was aware of public criticisms of his generalship at Gettysburg. "I do not know how far this feeling extends in the army," wrote Lee. "My brother officers have been too kind to report it, and so far the troops have been too generous to exhibit it. It is fair, however, to suppose that it does exist, and success is so necessary to us that nothing should be risked to secure it." Offering to step down as commander of the army, Lee implicitly recognized that he had erred in Pennsylvania: "I cannot even accomplish what I myself desire. How can I fulfill the expectations of others?"[17]

Two additional vignettes, though both hearsay, merit mention. Henry Heth remembered after the war that he and Lee discussed Gettysburg at Orange Court House during the winter of 1863–64. "After it is all over, as stupid a fellow as I am can see the mistakes that were made," said the commanding general somewhat defensively. "I notice, however, my mistakes are never told me until it is too late, and you, and all my officers, know that I am always ready and anxious to have their suggestions." Captain Thomas J. Goree of Longstreet's staff recalled in an 1875 letter to his old chief a similar episode at Orange Court House in the winter of 1864. Summoned to Lee's tent, Goree found that the general had been looking through Northern newspapers. Lee "remarked that he had just been reading the Northern official reports of the Battle of Gettysburg, that he had become satisfied from reading those reports that if he had permitted you to carry out your plans on the 3d day, instead of making the attack on Cemetery Hill, we would have been successful."[18] Because Longstreet first argued for a movement around the Federal flank on July 2, it is possible that in retrospect Lee also considered the assaults of the second day to have been unwise.

Many later writings about Gettysburg by Confederate participants followed furrows first plowed by Jubal Early and his cohorts in their savaging of James Longstreet. They insisted that Longstreet disobeyed Lee's orders to attack early on July 2, dragged his feet throughout that crucial day, and was slow again on July 3. Had "Old Pete" moved with dispatch, the Confederates would have won the battle and perhaps the war. No questioning of Lee's commitment to bloody offensive action after July 1 clouded the simplistic reasoning of these authors, typical of whom was former Second Corps staff officer James Power Smith. In a paper read before the Military History Society of Massachusetts in 1905, Smith recounted the conference among Lee and his Second Corps subordinates on the evening of July 1. Events of that day dictated further attacks, stated Smith. "There was no retreat without an engagement," he affirmed. "Instead of the defensive, as he had planned, General Lee was compelled to take the offensive, and himself endeavor to force the enemy away. It was not by the choice of Lee nor by the foresight of Meade that the Federal army found itself placed on lines of magnificent defence." Persuaded that Ewell's corps lacked the power to capture high ground on the Union right, Lee concluded that Longstreet would spearhead an effort against the enemy's left on July 2. "Then with bowed head he added, 'Longstreet is a very good fighter when he gets in position, but he is *so slow*.'" This last comment, a staple of the Lost Cause canon with no direct supporting evidence from Lee's own hand, anticipated the further argument that Lee's sound planning ran aground on the rock of Longstreet's lethargic movements.[19]

Longstreet defended himself against his tormentors ineptly, launching indiscreet counterattacks that often strayed widely from the truth and provoked further onslaughts against his character and military ability. One notorious example of his poor judgment will suffice: "That [Lee] was excited and off his balance was evident on the afternoon of the 1st," claimed Longstreet in his memoirs, "and he labored under that oppression until enough blood was shed to appease him." Such statements provoked a massive response from Longstreet's critics, creating a body of evidence that would damn him in the eyes of many subsequent historians.[20]

The writings of Brigadier General Edward Porter Alexander stood in notable contrast to the emotional approach of many former Confederates. Easily the most astute military analyst among Lee's lieutenants, he sometimes is perceived as an apologist for Longstreet because he served for much of the war as chief of artillery in the First Corps. In fact, Alexander probed in brilliantly dispassionate fashion Lee's generalship at Gettysburg. He thought a casual reading of Lee's report "suggests that the aggressive on [the] second day seemed forced upon him, yet the statement is very much qualified by the expression 'in a measure,' & also by the reference to the hopes inspired by our partial success." Alexander bluntly declared that "no real difficulty" prevented Lee's shifting to the defensive on July 2 and maneuvering in such a manner as to force Meade to attack. Lee's reference to his trains failed to impress Alexander, who as the army's former chief of ordnance possessed an excellent grasp of the difficulties of moving large numbers of wagons.

With an engineer's love of precision, Alexander reckoned "it a reasonable estimate to say that 60 per cent of our chances for a great victory were lost by our continuing the aggressive. And we may easily imagine the boon it was to Gen. Meade . . . to be relieved from the burden of making any difficult decision, such as what he would have had to do if Lee had been satisfied with his victory of the first day; & then taken a strong position and stood on the defensive." Expressing astonishment that "the strength of the enemy's position seems to have cut no figure in the consideration [of] the question of the aggressive," Alexander labeled Meade's good fortune "more than impudence itself could have dared to pray for—a position unique among all the battlefields of the war, certainly adding fifty per cent to his already superior force, and an adversary stimulated by success to an utter disregard of all physical disadvantages. . . ."

These opinions aside, Alexander believed that victory eluded the Confederates on July 2 only because Longstreet's assaults began so late. Professing no doubt that the offensive could have started sooner, he expressed equal certainty that "Gen. Lee much desired it to be made very much earlier." Longstreet's preference to await the arrival of Evander M. Law's brigade, to which Lee acceded, and the delay occasioned by Southern infantry near Black Horse Tavern coming into view of Federal signalmen on Little Round Top slowed the flanking march. Present on the field the entire time and "apparently consenting to the situation from hour by hour," Lee bore a major portion of responsibility for the late opening of the attacks by Alexander's reading of the evidence.[21]

Modern writers have continued to explore Lee's choice to resume offensive operations on July 2. Easily the most influential of Lee's biographers is Douglas Southall Freeman. After discussing Lee's conferences with Ewell and Longstreet on the evening of July 1, Freeman asked, "But was it wise to attack at all? What alternatives were there?" Freeman listed four available courses of action: Lee could take up a defensive position on the field and invite attack from Meade; he could retreat to the western side of South Mountain; he could move around the Union left as Longstreet urged, placing the army between the Federals and Washington; or he could mount another series of attacks in the hope of achieving a complete victory. The first two alternatives Freeman dismissed quickly with a paraphrase of Lee's official report. The third he termed impractical, citing the opinions of "nearly all military critics"—the roster of whom include Jubal Early, William Allan,

Armistead L. Long, and other stalwart members of the Lost Cause school of interpretation. With unintended irony, Freeman admitted in a footnote that George G. Meade " was the only critic who agreed with Longstreet. He said that Longstreet's proposal was . . . the step he feared Lee would take. . . ."[22]

Freeman thus brought himself to the fourth option. Once again paraphrasing Lee, he concluded: "Strategically, then, Lee saw no alternative to attacking the enemy before Meade concentrated, much as he disliked to force a general engagement so early in the campaign and at such a distance from Virginia." Tactically, Freeman approved of Lee's plan to use the divisions of McLaws and Hood to deliver the heaviest blow on the Union left, with Ewell's corps doing what it could against the enemy's far right. Little did Lee know, contended Freeman, that as he anticipated another day's combat his plans already were being undone. In a statement worthy of Jubal Early, Lee's great biographer closed his chapter on July 1: "The battle was being decided at that very hour in the mind of Longstreet, who at his camp, a few miles away, was eating his heart away in sullen resentment that Lee had rejected his long-cherished plan of a strategic offensive and a tactical defensive." That sullenness manifested itself in a performance on July 2 so sluggish "it has often been asked why Lee did not arrest him for insubordination or order him before a court-martial." Freeman answered that an absence of qualified officers forced Lee to make do with Longstreet, warts and all, even as he lamented the absence of "Stonewall" Jackson.[23]

Other historians offer a mixture of praise and censure for Lee's decision to attack on July 2. Clifford Dowdey, whom one reviewer aptly called "the last *Confederate* historian," endorsed Lee's offensive inclination, observing that Lee apparently never thought of shifting to the defensive. Dowdey emphasized the need for a quick Confederate triumph: "[Lee's] thinking was shaped by the background of the South's waning strength, by the present illustration of the attrition in high command, and by the need for a decisive victory away from home. . . . His men were driving the enemy, and, though Ewell had kept them from clinching the victory today, Lee thought only of how to complete it the next day." Poor execution robbed the army of success on July 2, but the decision to seek that success had been correct.[24] Frank E. Vandiver echoed Dowdey, with the twist that a spell of ill health in Pennsylvania rendered Lee edgy and more inclined to seek a quick resolution. His physical ailments and Longstreet's stubbornness left Lee "generally irritated and he's determined that he is going to attack." "He has every reason for wanting to do that," judged Vandiver, "he has his army in Pennsylvania, it's at its finest strength and gear and this is the time to cast the die. Across the field is a Union general, George G. Meade, who has been in command of the Army of the Potomac only two weeks [*sic*], doesn't know much about his army and might be unready to fight a major engagement."[25]

Even the British historian J. F. C. Fuller, widely known as a severe critic of Lee, essentially accepted the rationale in the general's official report of the campaign. The "defective supply arrangements and the absence of his cavalry (to disengage himself) compelled him to fight," wrote Fuller, "and to fight an offensive action in place of a defensive one; for, as he had to live on the country, it was impossible for him to stand still for any length of time." Fuller believed that an inability to move and forage simultaneously ruled out Longstreet's option. This approval of the decision to attack on July 2 contrasted sharply with Fuller's estimate of Lee's tactical blueprint, which he considered "a thoroughly bad plan" with little prospect of success.[26]

H. J. Eckenrode and Bryan Conrad generally treated Lee favorably in their harsh biography of Longstreet (their real hero was Stonewall Jackson), but at Gettysburg these authors deviated from their usual pattern. They found that the commanding general "blundered into battle" and once committed "showed no genius in the manner in which he conducted it, making no feints and relying on frontal attacks on a formidable position."[27]

Few historians probed the questions of Gettysburg more judiciously than Edwin B. Coddington, Harry W. Pfanz, and Alan T. Nolan—yet their careful examinations produced differing conclusions. Coddington weighed Lee's options for July 2, took into account the explanations in his official report, and resolved that although Lee's expressed concern about his trains and living off the countryside had some validity, the general perhaps overstated the dangers of withdrawal. The key to Lee's action was psychological—he and his army would not retreat unless pushed. "They had just achieved a smashing success against a part of the Union army," wrote Coddington, "and now was the time for them to finish the job. The stakes were high, and they might never again have as good an opportunity." Coddington viewed the decision as perfectly in keeping with the pattern of offensive combat forged by Lee and his army in previous campaigns.[28]

Pfanz agreed that Lee's decision to keep attacking was reasonable. Longstreet's proposed flanking movement posed logistical problems, Stuart was unavailable to screen the march, and the whereabouts of much of the Union army remained unknown; moreover, a "shift to the left and away from the valley that sheltered the Confederate line of communications was virtually out of the question." A defensive stand would transfer the initiative to Meade, who might circumscribe Southern foraging while calling up Union reinforcements, and thus "did not seem a practical course of action."

"In General Lee's words," Pfanz stated in summary, "a battle had, therefore, become in a measure unavoidable." Nolan disagreed strongly, attributing rationales for Lee's aggressive behavior after July 1 to an unpersuasive school of apologists for the Southern chief. "When all is said and done, the commentators' rationalizations of Lee's most daring offensive thrusts seem contrived," insisted Nolan. "Although these commentators are aware that Lee's efforts were unsuccessful, costly, and destructive to the South's chances of victory in the war, they are committed to the Lee tradition and seem to strain to absolve him."[29]

Lee's decision to pursue the offensive on July 2 manifestly has produced such cacophonous opinions as to confuse the most earnest student. But despite the contradictory shadow cast by this imposing mass of material—and accepting the fact that definitive answers are impossible at a distance of more than a century and a quarter—it remains worthwhile to train a close lens on the crucial questions: Was it reasonable for Lee to renew assaults on July 2? On the basis of his knowledge at the time, did aggressive tactics offer the best chance for the type of sweeping success on Northern soil that might propel the Confederacy toward independence?

The situation at the end of the first day of fighting is well known. Lee had arrived on the field early in the afternoon and, in the words of Walter H. Taylor of his staff, "ascertained that the enemy's infantry and artillery were present in considerable force. Heth's division was already hotly engaged, and it was soon evident that a serious engagement could not be avoided."[30] Only two of Heth's brigades actually had experienced serious fighting at that point, however, and Lee found himself witness to a meeting engagement rather than a general battle. It soon became apparent that the positioning of units from Richard S. Ewell's Second Corps, which were arriving on the northern end of the field, afforded the Confederates a tactical edge that Lee promptly exploited to good advantage. By 4:30 P.M., Southern attackers had driven the Federals to defensive lines along the high ground south of Gettysburg. Lee watched the action from atop Seminary Ridge, sensed the makings of a striking victory, and shortly after 5:00 P.M. instructed Ewell to seize the heights below town if practicable. For a variety of reasons, Ewell decided not to do so. Why Lee refused to commit some of A. P. Hill's troops—especially the fresh division of Richard H. Anderson—to a final joint assault with Ewell's brigades remains a mystery; the upshot was that daylight expired with Union troops firmly entrenched on Cemetery Hill.[31]

About 5:00 P.M., James Longstreet found Lee on Seminary Ridge. Dismounting and taking out his field glasses, Longstreet scanned the high ground that eventually would constitute the famous Union fish hook. Impressed by the strength of the enemy's position, Longstreet soon engaged

Lee in an increasingly tense conversation. The only eyewitness testimony about this exchange comes from Longstreet, who left three versions that agree in substance but differ in detail. Longstreet suggested to Lee that the Confederates move around the Federal left and take up a defensive position between the Army of the Potomac and Washington; once situated, they could force Meade to attack them and then seek an opening for a counterstroke. This proposed movement, claimed Longstreet in all of his later writings, conformed to an agreement between himself and Lee to pursue a strategic offensive but remain on the tactical defensive in Pennsylvania. He therefore was surprised at Lee's response: "If the enemy is there to-morrow, we must attack him." Loath to embrace aggressive tactics, Longstreet persisted in his arguments. But Lee did not "seem to abandon the idea of attack on the next day. He seemed under a subdued excitement, which occasionally took possession of him when 'the hunt was up'. . . . The sharp battle fought by Hill and Ewell on that day had given him a taste of victory."[32]

James Power Smith of Ewell's staff presently joined Lee and Longstreet with news that Jubal Early and Robert Rodes believed they could take the high ground south of Gettysburg if supported on their right. Thinking Hill's troops too exhausted for such duty, Lee asked Longstreet if the leading elements of the First Corps were near enough to assist. According to Smith, Longstreet "replied that his front division, McLaws, was about six miles away, and then was indefinite and noncommital."[33] Disappointed with Longstreet's response, Lee instructed Smith to tell Ewell "he regretted that his people were not up to support him on the right, but he wished him to take the Cemetery Hill if it were possible; and that he would ride over and see him very soon."[34]

Lest Smith's reading be deemed suspect because of his well-known antipathy toward "Old Pete," it is important to note that a trio of witnesses friendly to Longstreet also sketched a man deeply upset about the prospect of attacking on July 2. G. Moxley Sorrel of Longstreet's staff remembered that the lieutenant general "did not want to fight on the ground or on the plan adopted by the General-in-Chief. As Longstreet was not to be made willing and Lee refused to change or could not change, the former failed to conceal some anger." Raphael J. Moses, commissary officer of the First Corps, wrote in his unpublished autobiography that later in the evening Longstreet expounded at length to Fremantle about the enemy's position, insisting that "the Union army would have greater advantages at Gettysburg than we had at Fredericksburg." Fremantle himself noted that over supper on July 1, "General Longstreet spoke of the enemy's position as being, 'very formidable.' He also said that they would doubtless intrench themselves strongly during the night."[35] Of Longstreet's deep misgivings there can be no doubt; nor is it likely that his words and gestures failed to convey his feelings to Lee.

Sometime after 5:30 P.M., Longstreet departed and Lee rode toward Ewell's end of the line. Lee must have worried about the attitude of his senior lieutenant, whose friendship he valued and upon whom he had relied heavily since calling him "the staff of my right hand" in the wake of the Seven Days.[36] Although he knew from a reconnaissance by Armistead L. Long of his staff that Federals held Cemetery Hill in strength, Lee also wondered why firing had slackened along the Second Corps front. He had instructed Ewell to take that high ground if possible, and his postwar conversations with William Allan clearly indicated deep dissatisfaction at Ewell's failure to press his assaults. Walter Taylor's memoirs confirm that Lee was unhappy: "The prevailing idea with General Lee was, to press forward without delay; to follow up promptly and vigorously the advantage already gained. Having failed to reap the full fruit of the victory before night, his mind was evidently occupied with the idea of renewing the assaults upon the enemy's right with the dawn of day on the second."[37]

Lee thus reached Second Corps headquarters north of Gettysburg in a testy mood. He and the principal commanders of Stonewall Jackson's old corps gathered after dusk in the arbor of a small house near the Carlisle road. The ensuing conversation deepened Lee's frustration with his lieutenants. "It was evident from the first," recalled Jubal Early in the fullest eyewitness account of the meeting, "that it was his purpose to attack the enemy as early as possible the next day." Early maintained that "there was not the slightest . . . difference of opinion" about Lee's idea of continuing the offensive; however, all three Second Corps leaders argued against their troops spearheading the assaults. They had been impressed with the strength of Cemetery Hill, which Ewell's official report characterized as "a commanding position." Early took the lead in pointing to the Union left as the most vulnerable target.[38] Because Lee believed two of A. P. Hill's divisions had been fought out on July 1, the response of Ewell and his subordinates meant that the First Corps, headed by a suddenly peevish Longstreet, would perform the hardest work the following day.

Early averred in a controversial part of his account that Lee exhibited distress at the thought of relying on Longstreet: "When General Lee had heard our views . . . he said, in these very words, which are indelibly impressed on my memory: 'Well, if I attack from my right, Longstreet will have to make the attack;' and after a moment's pause, during which he held his head down in deep thought, he raised it and added: 'Longstreet is a very good fighter when he gets in position and gets everything ready, but he is *so slow*.' " This assertion, with its claim of precise accuracy nearly fifteen years after the alleged quotation was uttered, reeks of Lost Cause special pleading and lacks support from evidence closer to the event.[39] It is quite simply beyond belief that Lee would criticize his senior lieutenant in front of junior officers. Still, it is reasonable to assume that Lee did not relish the prospect of entrusting his assaults on July 2 to a man obviously opposed to resuming the offensive—and his facial expression may well have indicated as much to Early and the others.

Lee spent a long night working out details for the next day's fighting. Lack of enthusiasm among his subordinates for continuing the tactical offensive must have grated on him. The Army of Northern Virginia had built its formidable reputation on a series of impressive victories that with few exceptions included a large aggressive component. Had not the odds at the Seven Days or Second Manassas been less favorable for Southern success? And what of Chancellorsville? On all of those fields the army's offensive spirit had made the difference. Now Lee faced the prospect of planning a battle with substantive doubts regarding key Confederate commanders.

Although he strongly favored retaining the initiative, those doubts kept other options open. Longstreet's desire to flank the Federals remained on his mind. George Campbell Brown of Ewell's staff recalled in 1870 that Lee instructed him on the night of July 1 to tell Ewell "not to become so much involved as to be unable readily to extricate his troops." "I have not decided to fight here," stated Lee, " and may probably draw off by my right flank. . . . so as to get between the enemy & Washington & Baltimore, & force them to attack us in position."[40] During his meeting with the officers of the Second Corps, Lee had proposed moving their troops to the right but dropped the idea when Early argued, among other things, that it would hurt morale to give up ground won through hard combat. Lee returned to this idea later, however, sending Ewell orders "to draw [his] corps to the right." A second conference with Ewell, during which the corps chief expressed a willingness to attack Culp's Hill, persuaded Lee to leave the Second Corps in position on the left.[41] As stated before, the commanding general's final plan for July 2 called for Longstreet to make the principal attack against the Union left while Hill and Ewell supported him with secondary assaults against the enemy's center and right. Lee admonished Ewell to exploit any opportunity to convert his offensive into a full-blown attack.[42]

Few episodes in Lee's career reveal more starkly his natural aggressiveness. He had examined closely the imposing Federal position later described so graphically in his official report. Even the most optimistic scenario would project heavy casualties in an attempt to seize that ground. Jedediah Hotchkiss's journal records that on the morning of July 2, Lee discussed the upcoming assault at Second Corps headquarters and was not "very sanguine of its success. He feared . . . a great sacrifice of life." Lee knew from prisoners that two Union corps had been defeated on July 1, but he lacked information about the location of the bulk of the enemy's forces. In the absence of sound intelligence from his cavalry, he surmised only that the balance of Meade's army "was approaching Gettysburg."[43] His senior subordinate had disagreed sharply with the suggestion that offensive operations be resumed on July 2. Officers in the Second Corps were willing enough for Longstreet's soldiers to mount assaults but preferred a supporting role for their own men. In sum, powerful arguments could be raised against continuing the offensive.

Why did Lee choose to overlook all of them? His own explanations are unconvincing. Raphael Moses mentioned that Lee objected to Longstreet's flanking maneuver "on account of our long wagon and artillery trains"; as noted above, Lee also asserted in his official report that "to withdraw through the mountains with our extensive trains would have been difficult and dangerous." Lee further postulated a logistical crisis should he take a defensive position and await Meade's attack—his men had stripped the immediate region clean of supplies, and the enemy might use local troops to frustrate Southern efforts to forage on a large scale.[44]

Porter Alexander countered both of these points in one telling passage. "Now when it is remembered that we stayed for three days longer on that very ground, two of them days of desperate battle, ending in the discouragement of a bloody repulse," wrote the artillerist in the 1890s, "& then successfully withdrew all our trains and most of the wounded through the mountains; and finding the Potomac too high to ford, protected them all & foraged successfully for over a week in a very restricted territory along the river . . . it does not seem improbable that we could have faced Meade safely on the 2nd at Gettysburg without assaulting him in his wonderfully strong position." David Gregg McIntosh, like Alexander an artillerist who held Lee in the highest esteem, similarly dismissed the obstacles to Lee's pulling back on July 2: "The fact that he was able to do so after the battle, justifies the belief that Longstreet was right in his opinion that an attack in front was not advisable, and that General Lee committed an error in determining upon that course."[45]

Lee's notion that local units posed a serious threat to his army strains credulity. Jubal Early's memoirs captured the attitude of Confederates in the Army of Northern Virginia toward such troops. Describing a clash with soldiers of the 26th Pennsylvania Militia several days before the battle of Gettysburg, "Old Jube" identified them as "part of Governor Curtin's contingent for the defence of the State, . . . [who] seemed to belong to that class of men who regard 'discretion as the better part of valor.' "

It was a good thing the regiment fled quickly, added Early sarcastically, "or some of its members might have been hurt, and all would have been captured." Those who did fall into Southern hands received paroles the next day and were "sent about their business, rejoicing at this termination of their campaign." George Templeton Strong of the United States Sanitary Commission took an equally derisive view of the Pennsylvania militia. On learning that they were mustering in strength, Strong wrote an acidic entry in his diary on June 30: "Much good they would do, to be sure, in combat with Lee's desperadoes, cunning sharp-shooters, and stark, hard-riding moss troopers."[46] Furthermore, correspondence on July 2–3 among Secretary of War Stanton and various Union commanders involved with local troops leaves no doubt about the ineffectiveness of the latter.[47] Had Lee decided to forage on either side of the South Mountain range, it is almost certain that his soldiers could have handled local Federal troops with impunity.

Even offensive moves by a combination of local forces and units from the Army of the Potomac—a remote possibility due to problems of transportation and morale among the former—should not have given Lee undue pause. His decision to attack on July 2 betrayed confidence that his soldiers could take a strong position from the enemy. It makes no sense to assert that those men would fail to hold a position against attacks from the same foe. Porter Alexander turned to a quotation from Stonewall Jackson in emphasizing this point: "We did sometimes fail to drive them out of position, but they *always* failed to drive us."[48]

What of Lee's dismissal of Longstreet's proposed flanking movement? Possible weaknesses in the plan must be given consideration (though Lee did not mention any in his report). If Longstreet envisioned a strategic rather than a tactical shift around Meade's left, the Army of Northern Virginia might have opened its own left flank to the Federals. Moreover, lines of supply and communication west of South Mountain might have been somewhat vulnerable.

But no such dangers would have obtained had Lee remained on the victorious field of July 1. As Porter Alexander put it, "We had a fine defensive position on Seminary Ridge ready at our hand to occupy. It was not such a really *wonderful* position as the enemy happened to fall into, but it was no bad one, & it could never have been successfully assaulted." To the west lay even stronger ground in the passes of South Mountain. A fragment of Lee's army had been driven from such gaps on September 14, 1862; however, the Army of Northern Virginia in July 1863 possessed the numbers and morale to hold the eastern face of the mountain indefinitely, all the while foraging in the lush Cumberland Valley. Had Lee fallen back to South Mountain "with all the prestige of victory," thought Alexander, "popular sentiment would have forced Meade to take the aggressive."[49] The likely result of Northern assaults would have been a bloody repulse followed by some type of Confederate counterattack. Readily at hand was the example of Second Manassas, where Jackson had fixed the Federals with assaults on August 28, 1862, gone on the defensive the next day, and set the stage for Longstreet's smashing counterattack on the thirtieth.

The difficulty of Meade's situation after July 1 should be kept always in mind. Abraham Lincoln and the Republicans could not tolerate for long the presence of the most famous Rebel army on Northern soil. As early as June 14, a day before the first elements of the Army of Northern Virginia crossed the Potomac at Williamsport, Secretary of the Navy Gideon Welles sketched a very uneasy Union leadership. Noting "scary rumors abroad of army operations and a threatened movement of Lee upon Pennsylvania," Welles described Secretary of War Edwin M. Stanton as "uneasy" and Lincoln as fearful that thousands of Federal troops in the Shenandoah Valley would be lost—"Harper's Ferry over again." The next day Welles mentioned a "panic telegraph" from Pennsylvania's governor, Andrew G. Curtin, and rumors of Rebels in Chambersburg, Pennsylvania: "I can get nothing satisfactory from the War Department. . . . There is trouble, confusion, uncertainty, where there should be calm intelligence."[50]

The onus was on the Federals to force Lee away from Pennsylvania. Meade's initial orders underscored his responsibility as head of "the covering army of Washington as well as the army of operation against the invading forces of the rebels." Should Lee menace either Washington or Baltimore, stated General in Chief Henry W. Halleck in a telegram to Meade on June 28, "it is expected that you will either anticipate him or arrive with him so as to give him battle."[51] The crucial part of this order is that Meade was *to give* battle rather than simply await the enemy's moves. Lee's comment that a battle had become "in a measure unavoidable" after July 1 applied far more realistically to Meade than to himself.

Clearly a number of factors militated against Lee's attacking on July 2. Just as clearly, a defensive posture might have opened the way for a decisive counterattack. The prudent decision would have been to shift to the defensive following the tactical victory on July 1. From such a posture, Lee would retain great freedom of action following a likely Union attempt to defeat the Army of Northern Virginia through offensive tactics. The Confederates could have stayed north of the Potomac for a protracted period of time, thus adding logistical and political accomplishment to any military success. Finally, had Lee opted for the tactical defensive after the first day's battle, thousands of men shot down in assaults on July 2–3 would have been in the ranks for further service.

But acceptance of these statements does not prove that Lee made a foolish decision. A victory on Northern soil might aggravate internal dissension in the North and thus weaken Union resolve. Within the context of dwindling Confederate manpower (a state of affairs Lee's aggressive generalship had helped to produce), there was reason to believe the Army of Northern Virginia would never again face the Army of the Potomac on such relatively equal terms. Lee had seen his men perform prodigious feats on a number of battlefields—most recently against intimidating odds at Chancellorsville. The overriding influence in his choosing to resume the offensive on July 2 might have been a belief that the splendid Southern infantry could overcome the recalcitrance of his lieutenants, the difficulties of terrain, and everything else to achieve great results. Lee's subsequent comments that failures of coordination brought defeat suggest that he never doubted his soldiers might have won the fight. Fourteen years after the campaign, Henry Heth said simply, "The fact is, General Lee believed the Army of Northern Virginia, as it then existed, could accomplish anything."[52]

Ample testimony about soaring confidence in the Army of Northern Virginia lends credence to Lee's opinion, none more dramatically than Fremantle's description of morale on the night of July 1. Over supper that evening, recorded Fremantle, Longstreet discussed the reasons attacks might fail; however, in the ranks "the universal feeling in the army was one of profound contempt for an enemy whom they have beaten so constantly, and under so many disadvantages." Lee's great faith in his own men implied a degree of scorn for the Federals, an attitude noted by Fremantle's fellow foreign observer, Captain Justus Scheibert of the Prussian army: "Excessive disdain for the enemy . . . caused the simplest plan of a direct attack upon the position at Gettysburg to prevail and deprived the army of victory."[53]

If Lee did experience any regret about his decision to remain on the offensive after the first day's victory, perhaps it stemmed from a sense that he had asked the men to do so much despite obvious signs of trouble among his top lieutenants. Two of Lee's statements at the time illustrate this point. He wrote Mrs. Lee on July 26, 1863, that the army had "accomplished all that could reasonably be expected." "It ought not to have been expected to perform impossibilities, or to have fulfilled the anticipations of the thoughtless and unreasonable," admitted the general in a sentence that could well be taken as self-criticism. Five days later Lee wrote a preliminary report for Adjutant General Samuel Cooper in which he praised the "heroic valor and fortitude" of his troops. "More may have been required of them than they were able to perform," he acknowledged, "but my admiration of their noble qualities and confidence in their ability . . . has suffered no abatement. . . ."[54]

R. E. Lee confronted a crucial choice on the evening on July 1, 1863. His selection of the tactical offensive for July 2 reflected his predilection for aggressive action. Porter Alexander thought even Napoleon failed to surpass "some of the deeds of audacity to which Gen. Lee committed himself" and saw Gettysburg as an example of Lee's unnecessarily taking "the most desperate chances & the bloodiest road."[55] Without question Lee *did* gamble a very great deal on the throw of his offensive dice after July 1. He ruled out defensive maneuvers that might have opened breathtaking possibilities, and in the process he bled the future offensive edge from his magnificent army. It is not unfair to state from the safe confines of historical perspective that Lee erred in his decision. Many of his own contemporaries realized as much at the time. But it *is* unfair to look at the grisly result and argue that his actions were entirely unreasonable. Momentum and morale count heavily in warfare, and it was probably those two factors that motivated Lee to a significant degree. Had Southern infantry solidified the first day's victory through successful assaults on July 2, as they almost did, many of Lee's critics would have been silenced.

NOTES

1. Joan K. Walton and Terry A. Walton, eds., *Letters of LeRoy S. Edwards Written During the War Between the States* (N.p., [1985]), [57]; Arthur James Lyon Fremantle, *Three Months in the Southern States: April–June, 1863* (1863; reprint, Lincoln: University of Nebraska Press, 1991), 231–32.

2. Randolph H. McKim, *A Soldier's Recollections: Leaves from the Diary of a Young Confederate* (1910; reprint; Washington, DC: Zenger Publishing, 1983), 182; Stephen Dodson Ramseur to Ellen Richmond, Aug. 3, 1863, folder 7, Stephen Dodson Ramseur Papers, Southern Historical Collection, Wilson Library, University of North Carolina, Chapel Hill.

3. Robert Garlick Hill Kean, *Inside the Confederate Government: The Diary of Robert Garlick Hill Kean*, ed. Edward Younger (New York: Oxford University Press, 1957), 84; Wade Hampton to Joseph E. Johnston, July 30, 1863, quoted in Herman Hattaway and Archer Jones, *How the North Won: A Military History of the Civil War* (Urbana: University of Illinois Press, 1983), 414.

4. James Longstreet to Augustus Baldwin Longstreet, July 24, 1863, reproduced in part in J. William Jones et al., eds., *Southern Historical Society Papers*, 52 vols. and 3-vol. index (1876–1959; reprint, Wilmington, NC: Broadfoot Publishing, 1990–92), 5:54–55. This letter also appeared in the *New Orleans Republican* on Jan. 25, 1876, in the *New York Times* four days later, and in Longstreet's article "The Campaign of Gettysburg" in the *Philadelphia Weekly Times*, Nov. 3, 1877 (the *Weekly Times* article also appeared under the title "Lee in Pennsylvania" in Editors of the *Philadelphia Weekly Times, The Annals of the War Written by Leading*

Participants North and South [Philadelphia, 1879], 414–46 [the last work cited hereafter as *Annals of the War*]).

5. William Swinton, *Campaigns of the Army of the Potomac: A Critical History of Operations in Virginia, Maryland and Pennsylvania, from the Commencement to the Close of the War, 1861–1865* (1866; rev. ed., New York: Charles Scribner's Sons, 1882), 340–41. Swinton credited "a full and free conversation" with Longstreet as his source for "revelations of the purposes and sentiments of Lee." In Editors of the *Philadelphia Weekly Times*, "Lee in Pennsylvania," 433, Longstreet used almost precisely the same language as Swinton when he observed: "There is no doubt that General Lee, during the crisis of that campaign, lost the matchless equipose that usually characterized him, and that whatever mistakes were made were not so much matters of deliberate judgment as the impulses of a great mind disturbed by unparalleled conditions."

6. Edward A. Pollard, *The Lost Cause: A New Southern History of the War of the Confederates* (New York: E. B. Treat and Company, 1866), 406–7. Pollard's assessment of Lee is a bit harsher in his *Lee and His Lieutenants, Comprising the Early Life, Public Services, and Campaigns of General Robert E. Lee and His Companions in Arms, with a Record of Their Campaigns and Heroic Deeds* (New York: E. B. Treat and Company, 1867).

7. James D. McCabe Jr., *Life and Campaigns of General Robert E. Lee* (St. Louis: National Publishing, 1866), 393–95.

8. Jubal A. Early, *The Campaigns of Gen. Robert E. Lee. An Address by Lieut. General Jubal A. Early, before Washington and Lee University, January 19th, 1872* (Baltimore: John Murphy and Company, 1872), 30–32. Fitzhugh Lee, J. William Jones, and William Nelson Pendleton were among Longstreet's chief critics. For the early arguments in the Gettysburg controversy, see vols. 4–6 of the *Southern Historical Society Papers.* Useful modern treatments include Thomas L. Connelly, *The Marble Man: Robert E. Lee and His Image in American Society* (New York: Alfred A. Knopf, 1977); William Garrett Piston, *Lee's Tarnished Lieutenant: James Longstreet and His Place in Southern History* (Athens: University of Georgia Press, 1987); and Glenn Tucker, *Lee and Longstreet at Gettysburg* (Indianapolis: Bobbs-Merrill, 1968).

9. Frank E. Everett Jr., "Delayed Report of an Important Eyewitness to Gettysburg—Benjamin G. Humphreys," *The Journal of Mississippi History* 46 (Nov. 1984): 318.

10. U.S. War Department, *The War of the Rebellion: A Compilation of the Official Records of the Union and Confederate Armies*, 127 vols., index, and atlas (Washington, DC: GPO, 1880–1901), ser. 1, vol. 27, pt. 2:318 (hereafter cited as *Official Records*; all references are to volumes in series 1).

11. *Official Records*, vol. 27, pt. 2, pp. 318–19.

12. Robert E. Lee Jr., *Recollections and Letters of General Robert E. Lee* (1904; reprint, Wilmington, NC: Broadfoot Publishing, 1988), 102. Lee wrote to Major William M. McDonald of Berryville, Virginia.

13. Transcript of conversation between R. E. Lee and William Allan, Apr.

15, 1868, pp. 13–15, William Allan Papers, Southern Historical Collection. Lee apparently misconstrued Longstreet's comment about an agreement not to fight an offensive battle, interpreting it as a claim that Lee had agreed to fight no battle at all.

14. Transcript of conversation between R. E. Lee and William Allan, Feb. 18, 1870, pp. 20–21, William Allan Papers, Southern Historical Collection.

15. John D. Imboden, "The Confederate Retreat from Gettysburg," in *Battles and Leaders of the Civil War*, ed. Robert Underwood Johnson and Clarence Clough Buel, 4 vols. (New York: Century, 1887), 3:421 (this set hereafter cited as *Battles and Leaders*), Henry Heth, "Letter from Major-General Henry Heth of A. P. Hill's Corps, A.N.V.," in *Southern Historical Society Papers* 4:154–55.

16. Fremantle, *Three Months*, 269. For other eyewitness versions of Lee's accepting full responsibility for the defeat while greeting survivors of the Pickett-Pettigrew assault, see Charles T. Loehr, *War History of the Old First Virginia Infantry Regiment, Army of Northern Virginia* (1884; reprint, Dayton, Ohio: Press of Morningside Bookshop, 1978), 38 (Loehr recalls Lee saying to Pickett, "General, your men have done all that men could do, the fault is entirely my own."), and Robert A. Bright, "Pickett's Charge. The Story of It as Told by a Member of His Staff," in *Southern Historical Society Papers* 31:234 (Bright has Lee say, "Come, General Pickett, this has been my fight and upon my shoulders rests the blame.").

17. R. E. Lee to Jefferson Davis, Aug. 8, 1863, in *Official Records*, vol. 51, pt. 2, p. 752. Lee also alluded to public disapproval in his talk with John Seddon: "Major Seddon, from what you have observed, are the people as much depressed at the battle of Gettysburg as the newspapers appear to indicate?" Seddon answered in the affirmative, whereupon Lee stated forcefully that popular sentiment misconstrued events on the battlefield—Fredicksburg and Chancellorsville were hollow victories yet lifted morale, whereas Gettysburg accomplished more militarily but lowered morale. Heth, "Letter from Major-General Henry Heth," 153–54.

18. Heth, "Letter from Major-General Henry Heth," 159–60; Thomas Jewett Goree to James Longstreet, May 17, 1875, in Thomas Jewett Goree, *The Thomas Jewett Goree Letters*, vol. 1, *The Civil War Correspondence*, ed. Langston James Goree V (Bryan, Texas: Family History Foundation, 1981), 285–86. Longstreet asked Goree for his recollections of Gettysburg in a letter of May 12, 1875. A portion of Goree's reply of May 17 (with several errors of transcription) appears on p. 400 of Longstreet's *From Manassas to Appomattox: A Memoir of the Civil War in America* (Philadelphia: J. B. Lippincott, 1896).

19. James Power Smith, "General Lee at Gettysburg," in *Papers of the Military Historical Society of Massachusetts*, 14 vols. and index (1895–1918; reprint, Wilmington, N.C.: Broadfoot Publishing, 1989–90), 5:393. The charge that Lee considered Longstreet slow was common in Lost Cause literature. For example, Fitzhugh Lee's "A Review of the First Two Days' Operations at Gettysburg and a Reply to General Longstreet by Fitzhugh Lee," in *Southern Historical Society Papers* 5:193, quotes an unnamed officer who stated that Lee called Longstreet, "the hardest man to move I had in my army," and Douglas Southall Freeman, *R. E.*

Lee: A Biography, 4 vols. (New York: Charles Scribner's Sons, 1934–36), 3:80, cites W. Gordon McCabe, who in old age remarked to Freeman that Lee had told his son Custis that Longstreet was slow. No direct evidence from Lee's hand supports this contention; however, William Preston Johnston made a memorandum of a conversation with Lee on May 7, 1868, in which he claimed that Lee, in the context of a discussion of the second day of the Battle of the Wilderness, observed that "Longstreet was often slow." William G. Bean, ed., "Memoranda of Conversations Between General Robert E. Lee and William Preston Johnston, May 7, 1868, and March 18, 1870," *Virginia Magazine of History and Biography* 73 (Oct. 1965): 478. Because it is impossible to confirm when Johnston reconstructed his conversations with Lee, his undated memorandum should be used with care.

20. Longstreet, *From Manassas to Appomattox*, 384. The best analysis of Longstreet's part in the Gettysburg controversy is Piston, *Lee's Tarnished Lieutenant*, esp. chaps. 7–9. Piston concludes (p. 150) that "Longstreet's efforts to defend his military reputation had been futile."

21. Edward Porter Alexander, *Fighting for the Confederacy: The Personal Recollections of General Edward Porter Alexander*, ed. Gary W. Gallagher (Chapel Hill: University of North Carolina Press, 1989), 277–78. See Also Edward Porter Alexander, *Military Memoirs of a Confederate: A Critical Narrative* (New York: Charles Scribner's Sons, 1907), 387–89.

22. Freeman, *R. E. Lee*, 3:81–82.

23. Freeman, *R. E. Lee*, 82–84, 159–60. Freeman offered a significantly different analysis in *Lee's Lieutenants: A Study in Command*, 3 vols. (New York: Charles Scribner's Sons, 1942–44), 3:173–74, finding that Longstreet's "attitude was wrong but his instinct was correct. He should have obeyed orders, but the orders should not have been given."

24. Clifford Dowdey, *Death of a Nation: The Story of Lee and His Men at Gettysburg* (New York: Alfred A. Knopf, 1958), 155, 239–40. The reviewer was Richard B. Harwell, whose blurb appears on the dustjacket of Dowdey's *Lee* (Boston: Little, Brown, 1965).

25. Frank E. Vandiver, "Lee During the War," in *1984 Confederate History Symposium*, ed. D. B. Patterson (Hillsboro, Tex.: Hill Junior College, 1984), 17. Vandiver listed a series of physical factors: "Lee at Gettysburg was infirm, had been thrown from his horse a couple of weeks before and had sprained his hands; he may have been suffering from infectious myocarditis, did have diarrhea and stayed mainly in his tent." There is slim evidence to support such a catalog of ailments.

26. J. F. C. Fuller, *Grant and Lee: A Study of Personality and Generalship* (1933; reprint, Bloomington: Indiana University Press), 197. Fuller disliked Lee's tactical plan because it "depended on the earliest possible attack and the most careful timing to effect co-operation; further, *Lee's* troops were by no means concentrated, and to make things worse he issued no written orders."

27. H. J. Eckenrode and Bryan Conrad, *James Longstreet: Lee's War Horse* (1936; reprint, Chapel Hill: University of North Carolina Press, 1986), 213.

28. Edwin B. Coddington, *The Gettysburg Campaign: A Study in Command* (New York: Charles Scribner's Sons, 1968), 362.

29. Harry W. Pfanz, *Gettysburg: The Second Day* (Chapel Hill: University of North Carolina Press, 1987), 26–27; Alan T. Nolan, *Lee Considered: General Robert E. Lee and Civil War History* (Chapel Hill: University of North Carolina Press, 1991), 98.

30. Walter H. Taylor, *Four Years with General Lee* (1877; reprint, Bloomington: Indiana University Press, 1962), 93.

31. For discussions of Lee on the first day at Gettysburg, see Alan T. Nolan, "R. E. Lee and July 1 at Gettysburg," and Gary W. Gallagher, "Confederate Corps Leadership on the First Day at Gettysburg: A. P. Hill and Richard S. Ewell in a Difficult Debut," in *The First Day at Gettysburg: Essays on Confederate and Union Leadership*, ed. Gary W. Gallagher (Kent, Ohio: Kent State University Press, 1992).

32. The quotations are from the first of Longstreet's three accounts in Editors of the *Philadelphia Weekly Times*, "Lee in Pennsylvania," 421. See also James Longstreet, "Lee's Right Wing at Gettysburg," in *Battles and Leaders*, 3:339–40, and Longstreet, *Manassas to Appomattox*, 358–59. Douglas Southall Freeman, among others who sought to discredit Longstreet, made much of the fact that each of the three narratives employed somewhat different language in recounting this episode. Freeman, *R. E. Lee*, 3:74–75. The most important point, however, is that all three versions concur in juxtaposing Longstreet's defensive and Lee's offensive inclinations.

33. Smith, "General Lee at Gettysburg," 391. This account was reprinted under the same title in *Southern Historical Society Papers*, 33:135–60.

34. James Power Smith, "With Stonewall Jackson in the Army of Northern Virginia," in *Southern Historical Society Papers*, 43:57–58. Smith presented a slightly different version of the discussion between Lee and Longstreet here, adding: "I was the only other person present at this interview between Lee and Longstreet on the afternoon of the first day of the Battle of Gettysburg." The version cited in the preceding note does not mention Lee's disappointment at Longstreet's reply.

35. G. Moxley Sorrel, *Recollections of a Confederate Staff Officer* (1905; reprint, Wilmington, NC: Broadfoot Publishing, 1987), 157; Raphael J. Moses, "Autobiography," pp. 60–61, no. 529, Southern Historical Collection; Fremantle, *Three Months*, 256.

36. The quotation is from Thomas J. Goree to My Dear Mother, July 12, 1862, in Goree, *Goree Letters*, 164. In *Lee and His Lieutenants*, 420, Edward A. Pollard described the relationship between Lee and Longstreet as "not only pleasant and cordial, but affectionate to an almost brotherly degree; an example of beautiful friendship in the war that was frequently remarked by the public."

37. Armistead L. Long to Jubal A. Early, Apr. 5, 1876, reproduced in "Causes of the Defeat of Gen. Lee's Army at the Battle of Gettysburg—Opinions of Leading Confederate Soldiers," in *Southern Historical Society Papers*, 4:66; transcript of conversation between R. E. Lee and William Allan, Apr. 15, 1868, pp. 13–14,

William Allan Papers, Southern Historical Collection; Taylor, *Four Years with General Lee*, 96.

38. Jubal A. Early, "Leading Confederates on the Battle of Gettysburg. A Review by General Early," in *Southern Historical Society Papers*, 4:271–75. For descriptions of the ground in the official reports of Second Corps officers, see *Official Records*, vol. 27, pt. 2, pp. 445 (Ewell), 469–70 (Early), and 555 (Rodes).

39. Early, "A Review by General Early," 273–74.

40. George Campbell Brown Memoir, pp. 70–71, Brown-Ewell Papers, Tennessee State Library and Archives, Nashville, Tennessee. Brown admitted that he could not fix precisely the time of his meeting with Lee, suggesting that it might even have taken place on the night of July 2. His "strong impression" was that it was on the night of the first, however, and it seems far more likely that Lee was considering a flanking movement then—with Longstreet's arguments fresh in his mind—rather than after the second day's fighting.

41. Early, "A Review by General Early," 272–73; *Official Records*, vol. 27, pt. 2, p. 446.

42. *Official Records*, vol. 27, pt. 2, pp. 318–19.

43. Jedediah Hotchkiss, *Make Me a Map of the Valley: The Civil Way Journal of Stonewall Jackson's Topographer*, ed. Archie P. McDonald (Dallas, TX: Southern Methodist University Press, 1973), 157; *Official Records*, vol. 27, pt. 2:317.

44. Moses, "Autobiography," 61; *Official Records*, vol. 27, pt. 2, p. 318.

45. Alexander, *Fighting for the Confederacy*, 233; David Gregg McIntosh, "Review of the Gettysburg Campaign, By One Who Participated Therein," in *Southern Historical Society Papers*, 37:140.

46. Jubal A. Early, *Lieutenant General Jubal Anderson Early, C.S.A.: Autobiographical Sketch and Narrative of the War Between the States* (1912; reprint, Wilmington, NC: Broadfoot Publishing, 1989), 257–58; George Templeton Strong, *Diary of the Civil War, 1860–1865*, ed. Allan Nevins (New York: Macmillan, 1962), 327.

47. For a sampling of this correspondence, see *Official Records*, vol. 27, pt. 3:494–508.

48. Alexander, *Fighting for the Confederacy*, 234.

49. Alexander, *Fighting for the Confederacy*, 234.

50. Gideon Welles, *Diary of Gideon Welles, Secretary of the Navy Under Lincoln and Johnson*, ed. Howard K. Beale, 3 vols. (New York: W. W. Norton, 1960), 1:328, 330.

51. *Official Records*, vol. 27, pt. 1, p. 61.

52. Heth, "Letter from Major-General Henry Heth," 160.

53. Fremantle, *Three Months*, 256; Justus Scheibert, *Seven Months in the Rebel States During the North American War, 1863*, ed. William Stanley Hoole (Tuscaloosa, AL: Confederate Publishing, 1958), 118.

54. Lee, *Recollections and Letters*, 109; *Official Records*, vol. 27, pt. 2, p. 309.

55. Alexander, *Fighting for the Confederacy*, 91–92.

"A Mere Question of Time": Robert E. Lee from the Wilderness to Appomattox Court House

NOAH ANDRE TRUDEAU

In April 1864, as Lt. Gen. Ulysses S. Grant set in motion his coordinated strategy for defeating the Confederacy, Gen. Robert E. Lee considered his military options in northern Virginia. Characteristically, his impulse was aggressive. "If Richmond could be held secure against the attack from the east," he told Jefferson Davis on 15 April, "I would propose . . . to . . . move right against the enemy on the Rappahannock." This was, Lee believed, the only action that could upset the designs of the enemy. "Should God give us a crowning victory there," he continued, "all their plans would be dissipated."[1]

It had been a winter of frustration for the fifty-seven-year-old commander of the Confederacy's finest fighting army. He scarcely had weathered the political fallout from his Gettysburg defeat when called upon to detach nearly a third of his army for service in a distant theater of the war. In early September 1863, the veteran infantry of Lt. Gen. James Longstreet's First Corps, along with its nearly indispensable commander, filed onto trains that would carry them west and into battle.

Mere weeks after Gettysburg, the soldiers left behind were again in the field, taking part in a series of expeditions against their old foe, the Army of the Potomac. The operations in Culpeper, Fauquier, and Prince William counties in October and November led to no decisive engagement. There were small but fierce clashes at Bristoe Station and Rappahannock Station, but the net result of a fall season of hard marching and countermarching was to leave the two armies pretty much as they had been.[2]

Lee fell seriously ill in this period with heart and rheumatic problems, a situation aggravated by his almost constant sparring with Richmond for more troops and supplies. He had sent Longstreet to Braxton Bragg with the understanding that the troops would be returned speedily once the crisis had passed. "I want you badly and you cannot get back too soon," Lee told Longstreet just five days after the men of the First Corps had helped bring victory at Chickamauga. Yet it would not be until early April 1864 that Longstreet's soldiers finally were released, and late into the month before the Confederacy's strained transportation system could return them to northern Virginia.[3]

Also at this time Lee was having to handle the matter of serious desertions from the ranks of his army, and he had to fend off a half-hearted attempt by President Jefferson Davis to reassign him as replacement for Braxton Bragg in the West, a post that eventually went to Joseph E. Johnston.[4]

Throughout all this, as he watched the hostile camps grow across the Rapidan River, Lee constantly tried to peer into the mind of his opponent. "Their plans are not sufficiently developed to discover them," he wrote Jefferson Davis on 30 March, "but I think we can assume that if Genl Grant is to direct operations on this frontier he will concentrate a large force on one or more lines, & prudence dictates that we should make such preparations as are in our power." Lee had few additional details by 5 April, but was sufficiently alarmed by the continuing buildup that he warned Davis the signs tended "to show that the great effort of the enemy in this campaign will be made in Virginia."[5]

Lee sketched his strategy in a 3 February message to Davis. He at once discounted the possibility of making any serious move into the North. "We are not in a condition, & never have been, in my opinion, to invade the enemy's country with a prospect of permanent benefit," he said. Nor did he believe that a decisive field victory was likely. "But we can alarm & embarrass him to some extent," continued Lee, "& thus prevent his undertaking anything of magnitude against us." Bedeviled by a lack of supplies and the poor condition of his cavalry, Lee continued to wait and watch until, in the early hours of 4 May 1864, word came from his signal station on Clark's Mountain that the great Union army was moving.[6]

Two of Lee's three infantry corps were spread along the Rapidan—Richard S. Ewell's Second Corps farthest east, posted to cover Somerville Ford (a dozen or so miles from Germanna Ford, where the right column of the two-column Federal advance would cross), and A. P. Hill's Third Corps farther west with headquarters at Orange. About ten miles south of Hill were Longstreet's men, camped around Gordonsville. By mid-morning, 4 May, Lee knew enough about the enemy's line of march to begin to move his infantry eastward—Ewell following the Orange Turnpike, Hill the Orange Plank Road, and Longstreet angling to come into line on Hill's right.

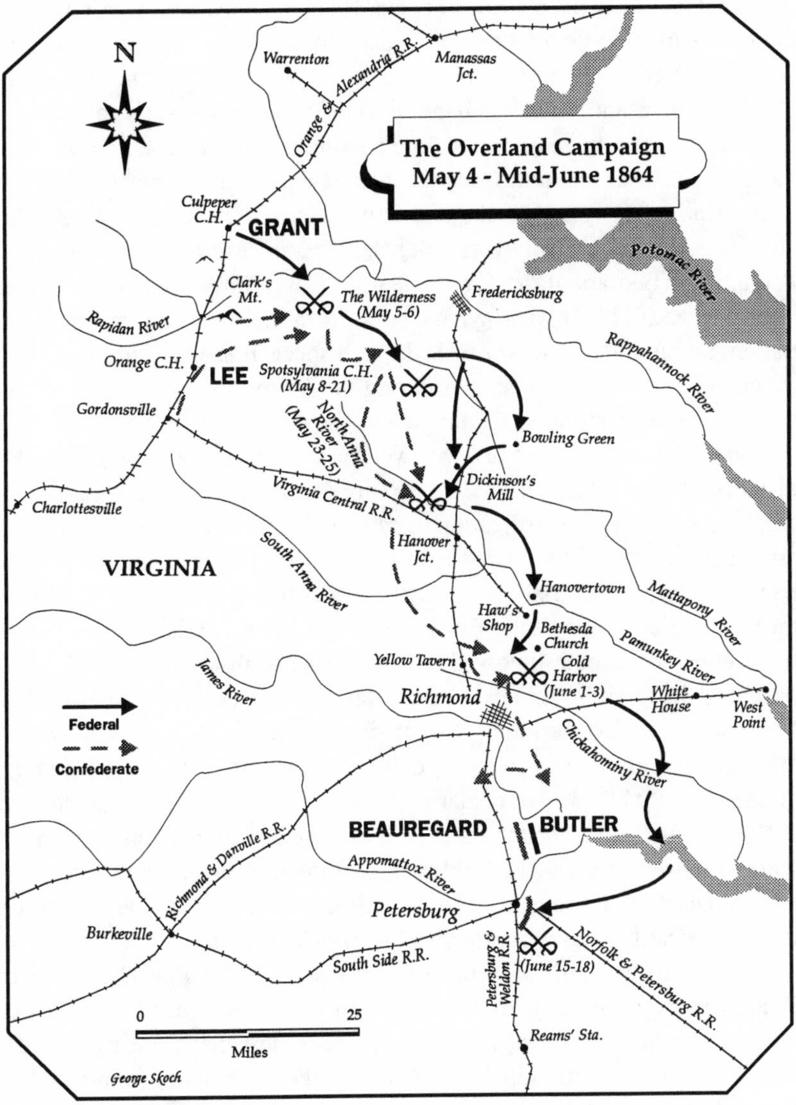

Lee anticipated the Federals would either turn toward him to fight or away from him to seize Fredericksburg, but he was not expecting to hear that the Union columns were instead pushing south, thus presenting their flank. He spoke on the evening of 4 May to Ewell's artillery chief, A. L. Long, who later recalled that Lee "expressed himself surprised that his new adversary had placed himself in the same predicament as 'Fighting Joe'

[Hooker] had done the previous Spring. He hoped the result would be even more disastrous to Grant than that which Hooker had experienced."[7]

It was Lee's intention to bring Grant to battle, but not before all the Confederate infantry were on hand. With Longstreet at least a day's march away, Lee had to move his units close enough to be able to strike on 6 May, but not so close as to ignite a general engagement before Longstreet arrived. Complicating matters, Ewell's and Hill's corps were moving on parallel courses with several miles of often tangled underbrush between them. Perhaps worried about the fragile health of his Third Corps commander, Lee rode with Hill on 4 May, and tried, in a message sent at 8:00 P.M., to convey his intentions to Ewell. In retrospect, it seems that his closing statement expressing his desire to bring the enemy to battle "as soon now as possible," communicated an urgency to Ewell that he did not intend.[8]

On the morning of 5 May, as Ewell pushed his corps to within picket distance of the Federal Fifth Corps camped around Wilderness Tavern, he received a disturbing clarification from Lee via Maj. Campbell Brown. The army commander did not want Ewell "to get his troops entangled so as to be unable to disengage them, in case the enemy were in force." A follow-up message confirmed this. Ewell instructed his brigadiers "not to allow themselves to become involved, but to fall back slowly if pressed." This produced in Ewell's officers a near-fatal lack of resolution to hold their line, and when that portion of it south of the Orange Turnpike was heavily attacked around 1:00 P.M., it nearly collapsed. Writing of this series of events after the war, Maj. Brown declared, "I don't believe brigades would have been so easily broken had it not been for the general understanding that we were to retire . . . if attacked in force." It took a brilliant counterattack by John B. Gordon's brigade, coupled with the leveling effect of the Wilderness itself, to permit Ewell to reestablish his lines by 3:00 P.M.[9]

Although physically present with Hill's column along the Orange Plank Road, Lee exercised little direct control on 5 May. Between three and four o'clock he sent a suggestion to Maj. Gen. Henry Heth that he push forward to where the east-west-running Plank Road met the north-south-running Brock Road. Heth should do so only if he could avoid a general engagement. Heth demurred without firm orders, which Lee declined to provide. The issue became moot at 4:00 P.M. when Heth was suddenly attacked by Union troops pressing west along the Plank Road. The savage fighting ceased after nightfall, and only darkness prevented a substantial Northern victory.[10]

Lee's activities on this critical night were curious to say the least. Despite knowing the Third Corps had been roughly handled in the day's fighting, and in the face of several requests from A. P. Hill to allow him to regroup his scattered command, Lee insisted that the men be left undisturbed, despite

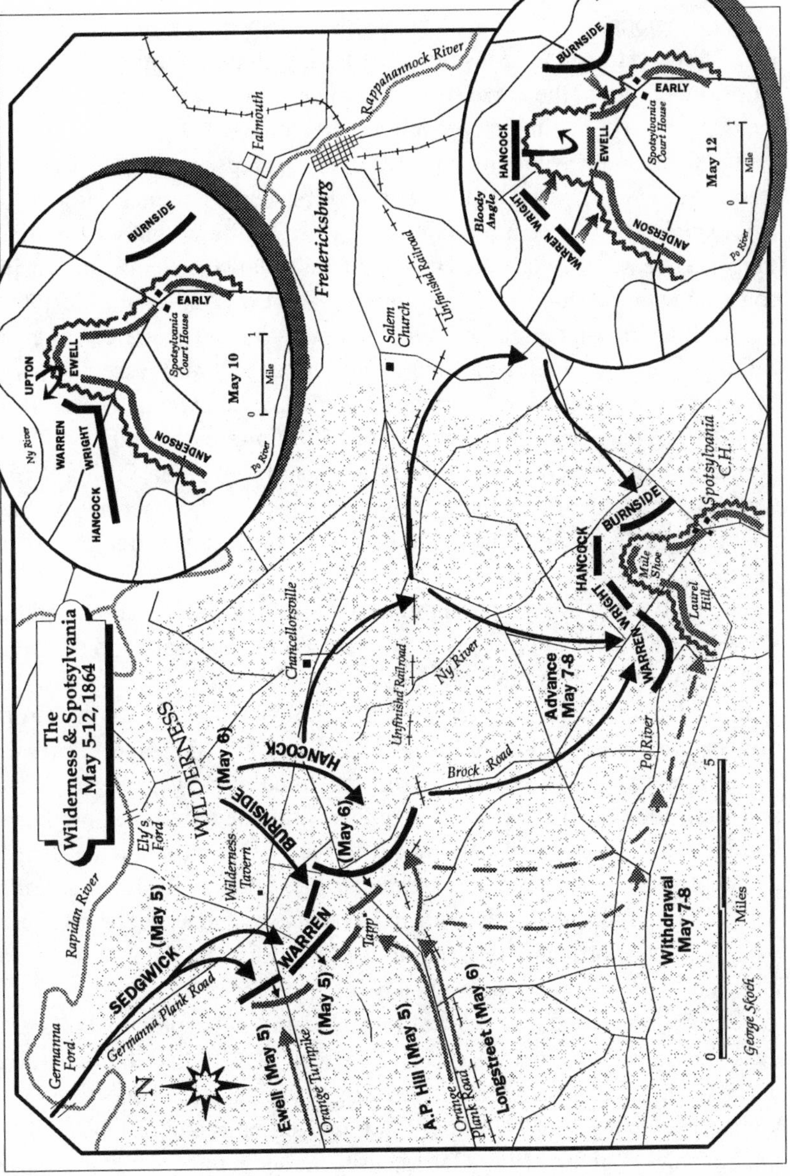
The Wilderness & Spotsylvania
May 5-12, 1864
Germanna Ford
Germanna Plank Road
Rapidan River
Ely's Ford
WILDERNESS
Wilderness Tavern
Chancellorsville
Orange Turnpike
Orange Plank Road
SEDGWICK
(May 5)
WARREN
(May 5)
Ewell (May 5)
A.P. Hill (May 5)
Longstreet (May 6)
BURNSIDE
(May 6)
HANCOCK
(May 6)
Tapp
Brock Road
Unfinished Railroad
Ny River
Po River
Advance
May 7-8
Withdrawal
May 7-8
Salem Church
Fredericksburg
Falmouth
Rappahannock River
HANCOCK
WRIGHT
WARREN
BURNSIDE
Mule Shoe
Laurel Hill
Spotsylvania C.H.
0
5
Miles
George Skoch
May 10
UPTON
EWELL
WARREN
WRIGHT
HANCOCK
BURNSIDE
EARLY
ANDERSON
Spotsylvania Court House
Ny River
Po River
May 12
HANCOCK
EWELL
WRIGHT
WARREN
BURNSIDE
EARLY
ANDERSON
Bloody Angle
Spotsylvania Court House
0
1
Mile

Lee's learning from a staff officer sent to contact Longstreet that the First Corps had halted at dusk and would not resume its march until 1:00 A.M. The lone mounted officer had taken more than ninety minutes to reach Longstreet, yet Lee based his plans for 6 May on the assumption that a full corps, marching in the dark over unfamiliar roads, would be able to cover the distance in something approaching three hours.[11]

Douglas Southall Freeman passes over this lapse with almost no comment, suggesting Lee's intention that the First Corps entrench a line behind Hill explains his inaction the night of 5 May. While virtually no evidence suggests Lee was incapacitated this night, his failure to exercise any positive command control in a clearly perilous situation was indeed curious.[12]

U. S. Grant, on the other hand, meant to strike a blow. Before retiring for the night he ordered an all-out assault for 4:30 A.M. Pressed by Meade for a ninety-minute delay, Grant agreed to allow an extra half-hour. It was near 5:00 A.M. when attacks went forward along both roadways. In the northern sector, where Ewell faced portions of the Union Fifth and Sixth Corps and had dug in, the Federals were repulsed without serious problem. Along Hill's disordered, unstrengthened line, the results were dramatically different.[13]

By 6:30 A.M., Hill's men, fighting with stubborn desperation, had been shoved back to the twelve guns of William T. Poague's battalion of artillery that Lee had ordered established in a last stand position at the Widow Tapp farm. It was here that Lee berated Samuel McGowan's South Carolina brigade for running "like a flock of geese." Only the timely arrival of Longstreet's corps as a compact striking force made it possible to blunt and then stop the Union tide. During this action occurred the now famous incident as Lee appeared determined to lead Longstreet's Texas Brigade personally in a sacrificial counterattack. Lee knew well the value of his personal presence on a battlefield, and like any shrewd leader he recognized when a little theatricality was required. His gesture did the job; the Texans attacked with great fury, taking heavy losses in the process.[14]

Lee doubtless had instilled an offensive spirit in his principal officers—even the sometimes quarrelsome Longstreet. Hardly had the Federal advance been stopped when he was dividing his force to send one portion of it around the enemy's left flank via an unfinished railroad bed located by the army's chief engineer, Maj. Gen. Martin Luther Smith. While this assault was being staged, Lee visited Ewell and urged him to press matters on his front, something the one-legged general was reluctant to do. By the time Lee returned to the Orange Plank Road, Longstreet's attack was underway.[15]

In a striking parallel to Chancellorsville, Longstreet's force hit the Union flank and began to press it toward the center. Unlike at Chancellorsville, no wildfire of panic spread through the Federal ranks; instead, a sulky retreat carried the Federals back to the Brock Road, where a line of half-finished breastworks provided the nucleus for Northern officers to rally their regiments.

Even as his flanking force was fighting in the woods, Longstreet advanced his main line. When the two came together confusion and a dangerous loss of the assault's momentum resulted. Accompanied by his staff and several key officers, Longstreet rode forward to straighten things out and reinvigorate the attack. In another parallel to Chancellorsville, his mounted party was mistaken for enemy cavalry and fired upon. Longstreet fell, seriously wounded, and some with him were killed. When word of this reached Lee, the Confederate commander was strangely uninformed about affairs in the southern sector. According to Lt. Col. Moxley Sorrel of Longstreet's staff, Lee "was not in sufficient touch with the actual position of the troops to proceed with it as [Longstreet] . . . would have been able to do."[16]

Lee now believed a single strong blow at the weakened Federal line would give him the "crowning victory" needed to restore stalemate along the Rapidan. It took several hours to organize thirteen brigades into a striking force and send them against the enemy along the Brock Road. The Union troops (most from Maj. Gen. Winfield Scott Hancock's Second Corps) had used the lull to refill empty ammunition pouches and improve the breastworks, so that when the Rebel attack came it was beaten back, though not without difficulty in places. The significance of Lee's failure here should not be underestimated. As historian Edward Steere observed, "The last great charge that Lee was ever to launch with an expectation of destroying the Army of the Potomac had recoiled in defeat." On the Confederate left, a flanking attack devised by John B. Gordon began too late in the day and with too little force to do more than sweep up a few hundred prisoners and start rumors of a disaster, which were decisively quashed at Grant's and Meade's headquarters.[17]

With the exception of reconnaissance probes, both sides rested during the daylight hours of 7 May, though the quiet was deceptive. On the Union side, Grant issued orders early in the day for the army to change position after dark for a march toward a new destination: Spotsylvania Court House. Throughout the day Lee received fragmentary reports of Federal activity that supported several conflicting interpretations. The Union army might be retreating toward Fredericksburg, or moving on to Spotsylvania. Because Federal engineers had removed the pontoon bridges across the Rapidan, Lee knew Grant's men would not retrace their steps. Although Douglas Southall Freeman contends that Lee correctly read Grant's mind by ordering his First Corps, now under Maj. Gen. Richard H. Anderson, to Spotsylvania, the evidence indicates that he miscalculated Grant's resolve to fight it out on this line.

Lee's orders sending Anderson south suggested no urgency and left discretion as to starting time, allowing until 3:00 A.M., 8 May, to get underway. It was Anderson's own choice (likely motivated by his desire to make a good showing in his first outing as a corps commander) to leave at 10:00 P.M., 7 May, and the chance circumstance that his line of march passed through still-burning woods, thus precluding any rest stops, accounts for his timely arrival at Spotsylvania to turn back the Federal advance. As late as the morning of 8 May, Lee was advising Richmond that the "enemy had abandoned his position and is moving toward Fredericksburg."[18]

Once Lee recognized the true direction of the blue columns, he sent orders to the other units still in the Wilderness to hurry to Anderson's aid and then rode south, arriving at Spotsylvania in the early afternoon. By this time, Anderson's infantry and cavalry under Maj. Gen. Fitzhugh Lee had stopped the most significant Federal thrusts. The commanding general did witness the final Union attacks of the day across the face of Laurel Hill, a poorly coordinated attempt by portions of the enemy Fifth and Sixth Corps countered by the timely arrival of the lead elements of Ewell's corps.

Although the Federal move to Spotsylvania was serious, Lee faced an even greater challenge this day—the near collapse of his core command structure. Longstreet was badly wounded and out of action for the rest of the summer; Ewell, already showing the strain of the campaign, was barely holding up; then word arrived that A. P. Hill was too ill to lead his corps. Jubal Early replaced Hill in temporary command, but Lee had to make plans, knowing that two-thirds of his starting corps commanders were out of action.[19]

The next few days at Spotsylvania saw Lee react to a series of attacks that came boiling out of the blue behemoth curled up on either side of the Brock Road. On the night of 9 May, the Federal Second Corps attempted to swing around his left flank. Slow to cross the Po River, these Federals were already falling back the next day when a Confederate counterattack struck them, taking two of Hancock's cannon in the process. A series of frontal assaults came on 10 May against Lee's entrenched lines, which stretched east from the Brock Road, jogged out into the famous "Mule Shoe" salient, then twisted back to shield the court house village. Lee's soldiers repulsed attacks undertaken by the Union Fifth and Second Corps, but a storming party of hand-picked men from the Sixth Corps led by Col. Emory Upton punched through the western face of the salient and failed only for want of support.[20]

The relative ease with which Lee's men stopped these heavy assaults attested to their fighting ability, the multiplying effect good entrenchments bestowed upon defenders, and Lee's superb eye for defensible terrain. Yet the Confederate commander took no action when presented with a potentially dangerous salient within his defensive scheme. The position, occupied during the evening and night of 8–9 May by Edward Johnson's division of Ewell's corps, jutted out a good mile from the tight curve of the rest of the line. Lee's chief engineer, M. L. Smith, decided it could be held only if strongly bolstered with artillery. Lee agreed, but at least one of the artillerists sent into the position declared that it was "a wretchedly defective line."[21]

During the cold and rainy night of 11 May, Lee learned that a large body of men was moving behind the enemy's lines. Scouts reported some activity on the Confederate left and even more on the right. To Henry Heth, Lee said, "My opinion is the enemy are preparing to retreat tonight to Fredericksburg. I wish you to have everything in readiness to pull out at a moment's notice, but do not disturb your artillery, until you commence moving. We must attack these people if they retreat."

A very short time afterward, following a meeting with General Ewell and his staff, Lee reversed himself and, according to Maj. Campbell Brown, "directed General Ewell to withdraw from the trenches and General Long to do the same with the artillery." Only after Ewell suggested that his men would be better off this night in the relative comfort of their trench bunkers than out in the open, did Lee agree to delay implementing the first half of his order.[22]

The guns departed, and when the drizzly dawn of 12 May arrived and nearly twenty thousand Union soldiers from Hancock's corps poured out of the mist in a great assault against the salient, almost no Southern cannon opposed them. Apprised of the attack, Lee realized he had terribly misjudged the enemy's intentions and turned at once to personal leadership. First with John B. Gordon's men, and then with Nathaniel Harris's Mississippians, Lee appeared at the head of columns advancing into the maelstrom in the salient. In very few engagements preceding those in the spring of 1864 did Lee feel the need to expose himself so recklessly. Whether in private punishment for his mistakes or as a gesture calculated to inspire troops facing suicidal assignments, Lee threw himself forward.[23]

Had the attacks planned by Grant against the Confederate flanks been driven home with half the determination shown by Hancock, Lee would have faced utter disaster. But Burnside's inept handling of his assignment to press from the east and Warren's refusal to add to the body count on Laurel Hill allowed Lee to rush reinforcements into the salient. These fierce counterattacks, an almost complete breakdown of Union tactical control of the assault force, and the fact that trench systems favor defenders allowed Lee's fighters to stall, then reverse the Federal advance.

To Lee's credit, by midday he recognized the futility of further counterattacks and rushed to complete a shorter line of works dug across the neck of the salient, into which he moved his troops early on the morning of 13 May. Though Grant's Federals had virtually wiped out one division, they had not broken through Confederate lines.[24]

More bad news awaited Lee. Most of his cavalry and its incomparable chief, Maj. Gen. "Jeb" Stuart, had left him two days earlier to pursue a large Union raiding force under Philip H. Sheridan that was moving against Richmond. Stuart turned Sheridan away from the capital in a free-flowing melee near Yellow Tavern, but at the cost of his own life. "He never brought me a piece of false information," was Lee's response when first informed of the loss, later adding, "I can scarcely think of him without weeping."[25]

Lee spent the next few days reorganizing his battered command structure and responding to Federal attempts to gain little points of advantage with quick, strong counterstrokes. His calls to Richmond for reinforcements elicited excuses from Jefferson Davis. A subsidiary component of Grant's grand design had Maj. Gen. Benjamin Butler's Army of the James threaten the Confederate capital from the south via a peninsula between the James and Appomattox Rivers known as Bermuda Hundred. Rebel defenders rallied under the overall command of Gen. P. G. T. Beauregard, who refused to release any of his units to Lee. Only when the Army of the Potomac drew closer to Richmond did Davis see any merit to Lee's requests.[26]

Starting late in the evening of 20 May, the Army of the Potomac began to slide away from Spotsylvania, a process that took nearly twenty-four hours to complete. In the evening of the twenty-first, assured that the Federals had committed themselves, Lee put his own forces on roads leading toward Richmond. His destination was the south bank of the North Anna River. To lure Lee away from his entrenchments into a stand-up fight, Grant had risked Hancock's Second Corps by sending it a day's march ahead of the rest of the army, but Lee ignored the bait.[27]

The ride to the North Anna exhausted Lee, who managed only a few hours of sleep each night. Early on the morning of 22 May, he paused near Dickinson's Mill on the Telegraph Road to send an explanation to Jefferson Davis about the need to concede the territory between Spotsylvania and the North Anna to the Federals without a challenge. He cited the difficult terrain ("a wooded country . . . where nothing is known beyond what can be ascertained by feeling") and his worry that Sheridan's cavalry might yet imperil the Confederate capital. In a letter written the next day to his wife, Lee set down some additional reasons: "We have the advantage of being nearer our supplies & less liable to have our communication . . . cut by his cavalry & he is getting farther from his base."[28]

Despite the record of his recent encounters with Grant's style of generalship, Lee reached the North Anna convinced he had won some breathing space. His orders to corps commanders stressed the need to rest their men and did not mention the possibility of taking up a defensive position along the river. So it must have been with a mixture of surprise, resignation, and fatalism that he watched from the porch of the Ellington House as the first lines of Yankee skirmishers came down the Telegraph Road toward the river early on 23 May.[29]

Any prospect of holding the river line disappeared by nightfall when Lee learned that Federals had crossed upstream near Jericho Mill. Misled by poor intelligence that grossly underestimated the enemy's numbers, A. P. Hill (again commanding the Third Corps) sent a division to engage what turned out to be a full corps. His men failed to prevent a Union lodgment that effectively flanked any line Lee hoped to hold along the river bank. Something of his frustration over this turn of affairs can be gleaned from his angry debriefing of A. P. Hill regarding this engagement: "Why did you not do as [Stonewall] Jackson would have done—thrown your whole force upon these people and driven them back?"[30]

That night, even as Lee's health began to fail, he met with his general officers and engineers to examine the changed tactical situation. He repositioned his army and set it to digging a fresh line of earthworks, which resembled an inverted V with its point pinned to high ground along the river's south bank at a place known as Ox Ford. The two wings of the V ran southward to natural anchors, creating something of a vacuum both east and west of the position, into which Lee expected the Federals to march. Once the enemy wings crossed the river they would be separated from each other, with Lee's compact force between. Using the defensive advantage of entrenchments, Lee planned to leave a skeleton force to man one face of the V, while the rest of his army attacked the Federals opposite the other. Grant obligingly let his troops rush into the Confederate snare.[31]

North Anna should have been the tactical victory Lee had sought in the Wilderness and Spotsylvania, an opportunity to "fall upon them unexpectedly [and] . . . derange their plans." But the decisive attack never happened. According to Col. Charles Venable of Lee's staff, "In the midst of these operations on the North Anna, General Lee was taken sick and confined to his tent. As he lay prostrated by his sickness, he would often repeat: 'We must strike them a blow—We must never let them pass us again.' "[32]

Once Grant recognized the danger he halted the advance, allowing Union soldiers time to dig entrenchments that in a short time were strong enough to extract a heavy price from any Confederate attackers. It is significant that Lee apparently believed he could trust none of his corps commanders—

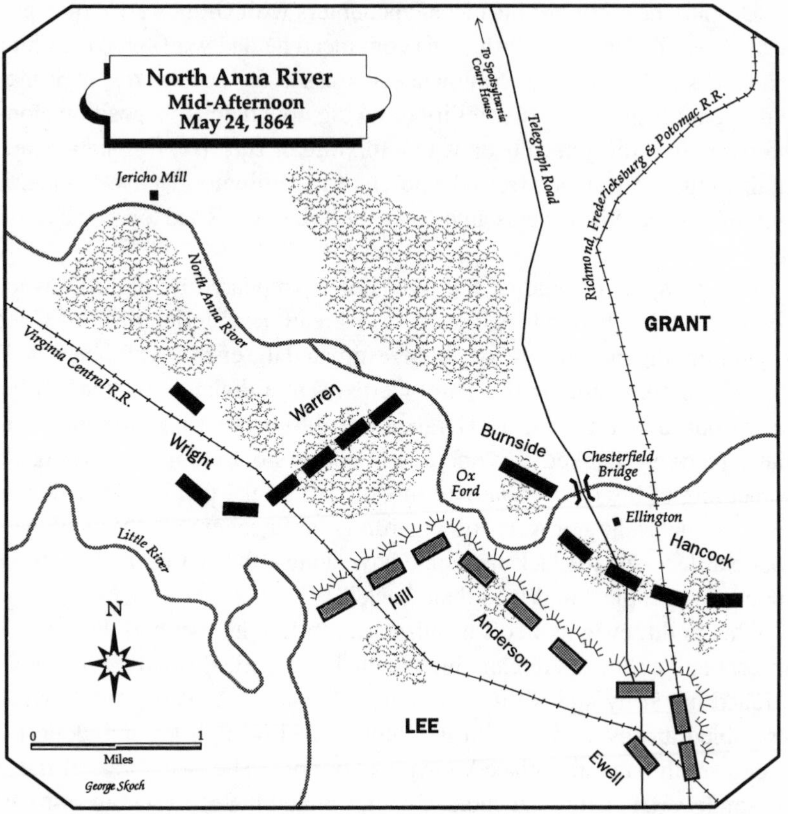

Anderson, Ewell, and Hill—to manage this operation. How else can one explain the fact that the moment he took to his cot the plan died stillborn?

As the Union force pulled back across the North Anna, then continued its sidle around Lee's right flank by pushing along the far bank of the Pamunkey River, the Confederate chief (now traveling in a carriage) dropped his army back toward Richmond to a position near Atlee's Station. There he waited to see where Grant intended to turn against the capital. The crisis in his command flared again when Richard Ewell reported himself too ill to continue. Lee assigned Jubal Early to Ewell's place, making the appointment official on 29 May.[33] Thus far in this seemingly endless campaign, Lee had seen personnel changes at the top of two corps, three divisions, and fourteen brigades. And he had yet to settle on a replacement for the fallen Stuart. In a letter to his wife written on 29 May, Lee expressed the wish that "God will give me strength for all He wishes me to do."[34]

On 28 May, major units of the Union and Confederate cavalries clashed near Haw's Shop, east of Richmond, signaling the Army of the Potomac's intention to cross the Pamunkey River near Hanovertown. Upon receipt of this intelligence, Lee posted two corps across the enemy's direct route in a north-south line behind the protective marshes of Totopotomoy Creek.

Now secure in his post as commander of the Second Corps, Jubal Early wasted little time demonstrating his own fondness for the offensive. On 30 May, he led his command around the left flank of the Union line and struck it near Bethesda Church. A combination of faulty coordination with other Southern units, poor tactical field management on Early's part, and the opposition of Federal general Gouverneur K. Warren, who excelled on the defensive, resulted in nearly 1,200 Confederate casualties for no commensurate gain in position or intelligence. At about the same time Early's troops were engaged, Lee learned that a contingent of enemy infantry brought up from Butler's army on Bermuda Hundred had landed at White House, fifteen miles below Hanovertown. Roads led west from that point like a dagger slipping in under his right flank. A rapid march by these Union troops would threaten his rear and possibly even cut him off from Richmond.[35]

Events of the next four days, 31 May–3 June, showed only too clearly that the offensive power of the Army of Northern Virginia had been ground away during the Overland Campaign, while at the same time its defensive abilities remained undiminished. On 1 June, Lee effected a junction between Anderson's corps of his army and Robert F. Hoke's division, recently pried away from Beauregard, to secure the strategically important crossroads near Cold Harbor. Through a Federal mix-up, the troops landed at White House had marched in the wrong direction, leaving only lightly armed cavalrymen under Phil Sheridan at Cold Harbor. Once more, inept coordination among the different Confederate forces, and a tactical error by Anderson in allowing a large untested South Carolina regiment to spearhead his attack, let Sheridan's fast-firing troopers shatter the leading wave and hold their position long enough for infantry reinforcements from Grant's Totopotomoy line to join them. Unable to dislodge this Federal incursion, the Confederates began to dig a defensive line, sections of which near Cold Harbor fell later in the day to a heavy enemy assault.[36]

The Yankee attack expected for 2 June did not materialize, though not for want of effort. Grant had ordered assaults and selected his favorite shock force—Hancock's corps—to lead. That meant a long night march for Hancock's men, not enough of whom arrived in time on 2 June to mount the offensive. Grant rescheduled the attack for 3 June, and Lee's men used the unexpected respite to deadly advantage, laying out a defensive position that created a nearly perfect killing ground in their front.[37]

The Confederate victory that followed on 3 June at Cold Harbor owed more to the almost innate ability of the Southern soldiers to dig and defend than to any alignment or positioning Lee had determined. Indeed, reading his brief report of the action, sent to Richmond that evening, one is tempted to conclude that Lee was as surprised as his men at their "easy" win. "Our loss today has been small, and our success, under the blessing of God, all that we could expect," noted Lee.[38]

As this front settled into a spiteful stalemate, Lee turned his attention to the Shenandoah Valley, where a Confederate advantage won at the battle of New Market on 15 May was threatened seriously by the sudden appearance of 20,000 Federals under Maj. Gen. David Hunter. Writing on 6 June to Jefferson Davis, Lee urged that "some good officer should be sent into the Valley at once to take command there and collect all the forces, . . . & endeavor to drive the enemy out." He reluctantly offered to return the 2,100 men he had "borrowed" from that theater, but pointedly did not mention the possibility of contributing any more. Three days later Lee confirmed reports that a "large force of cavalry" under Sheridan had left Grant's army on 7 June and was likely engaged in a cooperative operation with Hunter's Valley army. He also indicated that he had sent off two of his own cavalry divisions—Wade Hampton's and Fitzhugh Lee's—to intercept Sheridan.[39]

By 11 June, Lee was receiving heavy pressure from Richmond to do more to regain the advantage in the Shenandoah Valley. A message sent that day revealed his dilemma. Replying to a suggestion from Braxton Bragg, now Davis's military adviser, Lee reckoned it would take a full corps to redress the balance, knowing only too well from where that corps must come. While it was not in his nature to diametrically oppose the will of his superiors, Lee pointed out the great risks that would accompany the detachment of many men. As he put it, "If it is deemed prudent to hazard the defense of Richmond, the interests involved by thus diminishing the force here, I will do so. I think this is what the enemy would desire." Lee bowed to the inevitable and, on the morning of 13 June, sent a slimmed-down version of his Second Corps under Jubal Early off to the Valley.[40]

While Lee held out no hope of going over to the offensive at Cold Harbor ("To attack him here I must assault a very strong line of entrenchments and run great risk to the safety of the army," he reported), he did desire to catch the enemy off balance when Grant tried to shift his massive army. Lee cautioned Richard Anderson on 4 June that should the enemy begin such a movement, the thing to do would be "to move down and attack him with our whole force." To this end Lee urged Anderson to maintain a special vigilance over the enemy positions to provide a timely warning of such an occurrence. A circular from Anderson's headquarters two days later underscored Lee's anxieties in this regard by stating it was "probable that the enemy is engaged in a movement from our front which we must follow with the utmost promptitude." A directive issued the next day stressed that "General Lee is exceedingly anxious to be advised of any movement the enemy may undertake." "We must destroy this army of Grant's before he gets to the James River," he had confided to Jubal Early. "If he gets there, it will become a siege, and then it will be a mere question of time."[41]

While Lee pressed his subordinates to keep a close watch on the enemy and waged a losing battle with Richmond over reinforcing the Shenandoah Valley, a stream of messages passed from Beauregard to the capital requesting the return of troops he had "loaned" the Army of Northern Virginia to meet the crisis at Cold Harbor. In one communication sent to Richmond at 9:30 A.M. on 9 June from his headquarters north of Petersburg, Beauregard reported an attack on the Cockade City. "The return soon as practicable of my troops sent to General Lee is again urged on War Department," Beauregard wrote. Later that day, after weak enemy assaults had been turned back, his anxiety, if anything, had increased. "Necessity for troops here still urgent," he insisted. While Lee received no copies of these messages, it seems highly unlikely that he remained unaware of the appeals. Although Beauregard's partisans later accused Lee of negligence in not responding more quickly to the threats against Petersburg, Douglas Southall Freeman's analysis of the communications between Beauregard and Richmond and Beauregard and Lee supports his thesis that Lee "gave Beauregard in every instance the help that general asked for defense."[42]

Amidst all of this Lee still found the time on 12 June to undertake the personally painful task of keeping Richard Ewell from returning to command the Second Corps, soon to head into the Shenandoah Valley. Skeptical of Ewell's stamina to undertake a vigorous campaign, Lee tactfully recommended his assignment to command Richmond's defenses, a recommendation that was followed.[43]

On the morning of 13 June, Lee awoke to learn that Grant's army had slipped away during the night. According to Eppa Hunton, one of George E. Pickett's brigadiers, "It was said that General Lee was in a furious passion— one of the few times during the war. When he did get mad he was mad all over."[44]

Two years earlier, faced with a different opponent and less numerical disparity, but in much the same tactical situation, Lee had directed an aggressive pursuit of the enemy then en route to the James River. This time, however, Lee held back, allowing only the most tenuous contact between the two forces. Why was he suddenly so reluctant to strike with everything he had? On a strategic level the answer lies with a transformation of Lee's goals and objectives. In early May, when a tactical victory along the Rapidan River line offered the only chance to disrupt seriously the enemy's strategic planning, Lee was prepared to risk all. But after Cold Harbor, when such a victory no longer could alter the strategic situation, Lee looked instead to the fall elections in the North and the prospect that the Lincoln administration would lose. He had made this point in a letter to his wife a year earlier, predicting that there "will be a great change in public opinion at the North. The Republicans will be destroyed & I think the friends of peace will become so strong as that the next administration will go on that basis. We have only therefore to resist manfully."[45]

In order for the Confederacy to bargain effectively with the new Union government, it needed viable armies in the field; consequently, Lee's impulse after Cold Harbor was to preserve his force. He turned to a defensive-offensive mode, that is, to defend against any enemy action that threatened his position and to be ready to undertake a limited offensive should an opportunity arise. The prospect of an unlimited offensive was no longer to be considered. As one student of his campaign recently concluded, "Lee probably calculated that even if he attacked and was successful initially the casualties inflicted on his army when Grant counterattacked would be self-defeating."[46]

In reviewing Lee's command decisions during the course of the Overland Campaign, it is hard not to conclude that the terrible stresses of the period seriously undermined both his self-confidence and his military judgment. His miscalculations on the night of 7 May in the Wilderness and on 11 May at Spotsylvania might have been fatal had not chance and circumstances dictated otherwise. The erosion in his command structure, the crushing administrative burdens he carried with little staff support, and his own poor health all contributed to this diminished performance. He remained throughout an inspirational figure to his men, and at several critical junctures the sheer power of his presence tipped the balance toward the Confederates. Yet there must have been times when only Lee's deep religious faith kept him going. For all the human flaws he revealed during this campaign, he also demonstrated the qualities of stern duty and self-sacrifice that would make his character so appealing to succeeding generations.

Lee's unwillingness to press Grant's army as it marched to the James allowed his opponent to send a striking force from Butler's and Meade's armies against Petersburg with the confident expectation that the vital railroad hub would drop into his hands. It did not. Inept Union tactical leadership, a brilliant defense by Beauregard, and the cumulative effect of the terrible losses suffered during the preceding five weeks by the Army of the Potomac allowed Petersburg's hard-pressed defenders to hold until the Army of Northern Virginia arrived. By the time Lee showed up in person on 18 June, the Federal high tide had passed. When an ebullient Beauregard pressed Lee with plans for a counterstroke, the Confederate chieftain rejected them. According to Beauregard's staff officer Alfred Roman, "General Lee refused his assent, on the ground that his troops needed rest, and that the defensive having been thus far so advantageous to him against Grant's offensive . . . at Petersburg, he preferred continuing the same mode of warfare."[47]

The operations that followed at Petersburg, from mid-June 1864 to early April 1865, are too extensive to be treated here in any detail. Yet one chronological division does suggest itself, namely, before and after the Northern elections of 1864. Between 19 June and 4 November the Union forces confronting Petersburg mounted four major operations south of the Appomattox and four north of the James against Richmond. In the same period, Lee organized five counterstrokes designed to frustrate these operations, only one of which was successful. While the larger Union actions generally receive the lion's share of attention, it would be appropriate here to examine each of Lee's efforts to understand better his performance in this period.

The four significant Union operations against Petersburg were Burnside's assault of 30 July (popularly known as "The Crater"), Warren's expedition of 18–21 August against the Weldon Railroad, Meade's flanking action of 29 September–2 October (variously known as the battle of Peeble's Farm or Poplar Spring Church), and Hancock's movement of 27 October to cut the South Side Railroad. Lee played only an indirect role at the Crater because it lay within Beauregard's jurisdiction; took an even less active part for the same reason in the Weldon Railroad combat; and contributed virtually nothing to countering either Meade's operation in September or Hancock's in October. In every case the Union offensives found Lee elsewhere, usually handling the military situation north of the James.

On two occasions, however, Lee did organize a limited offensive strike south of the Appomattox. The first took place on 24 June. It followed hard on the heels of a disastrous Union attempt to disrupt the Weldon Railroad by swinging the Second Corps westward to the rail line that stretched south from the city. It took only three brigades under Brig. Gen. William Mahone, attacking the left flank of the Second Corps on 22 June, to rout all three of its divisions, taking sixteen hundred prisoners, four cannon, and eight stands of colors. Immediately after that engagement, Lee met with the chief of artillery for the First Corps, E. P. Alexander, to see if something could be done to break the Union grip on the Cockade City. The two examined the Union right flank, which rested on the south bank of the Appomattox River

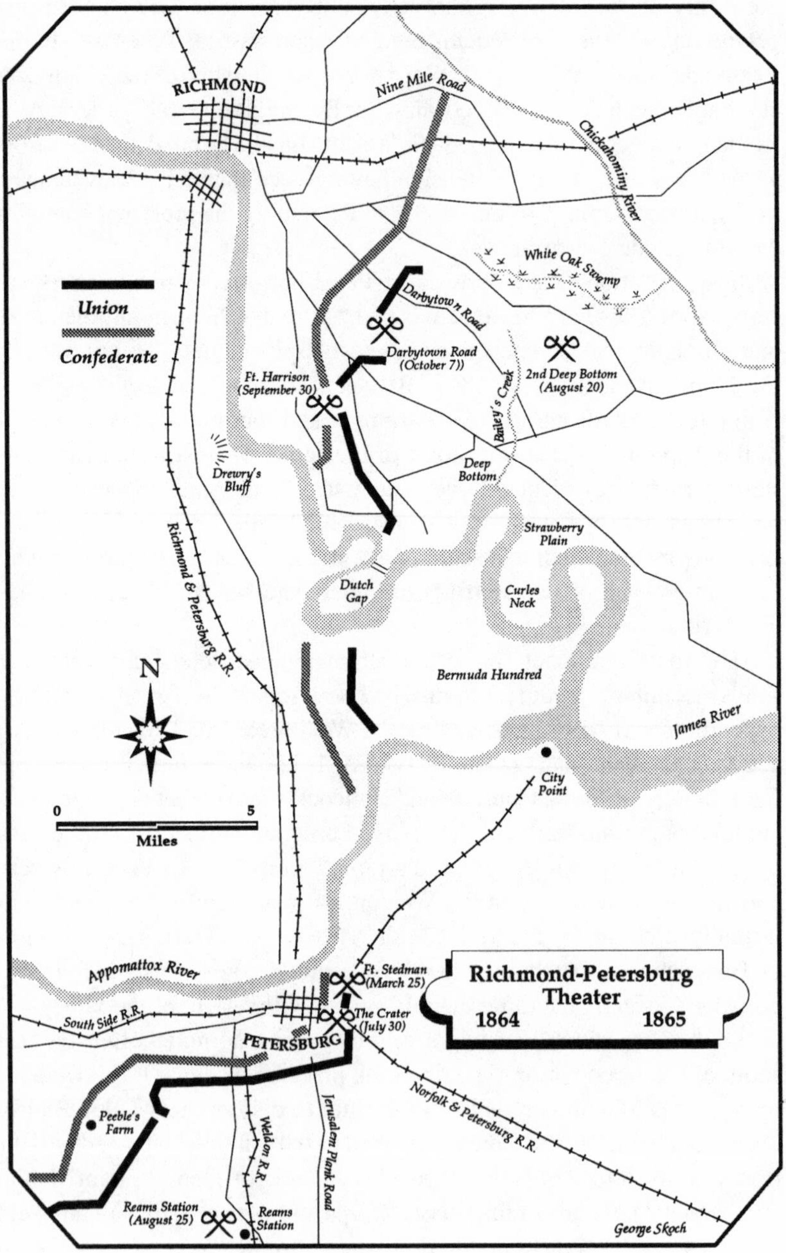
RICHMOND
Nine Mile Road
Chickahominy River
White Oak Swamp
Darbytown Road
Union
Confederate
Darbytown Road
(October 7))
Ft. Harrison
(September 30)
2nd Deep Bottom
(August 20)
Bailey's Creek
Deep
Bottom
Drewry's
Bluff
Richmond & Petersburg R.R.
Strawberry
Plain
Dutch
Gap
Curles
Neck
Bermuda Hundred
N
James River
City
Point
0
5
Miles
Appomattox River
Ft. Stedman
(March 25)
Richmond-Petersburg
Theater
1864
1865
South Side R.R.
The Crater
(July 30)
PETERSBURG
Norfolk & Petersburg R.R.
Peeble's
Farm
Weldon R.R.
Jerusalem Plank Road
Reams Station
(August 25)
Reams
Station
George Skoch

and was dominated by Confederate positions on the opposite side. Lee and Alexander devised a plan to smother that flank with artillery fire, attack head-on with infantry, turn it, and roll it up as far south as they could go.[48]

Because Beauregard exercised operational control over that area, Lee had to sell the idea to the Creole officer and then let him execute it. The plan required Charles W. Field's division from Lee's command to coordinate in the assault with Robert F. Hoke's division under Beauregard, an integration of forces no more successful than that attempted on 1 June at Cold Harbor. Alexander did pull off his part by providing a punishing artillery barrage. According to a Northern reporter present, with the "exception of Gettysburg, the war has not afforded another instance of so many guns concentrated upon one point and firing so rapidly for such a length of time." But Field and Hoke failed to mesh, and the leading units in the attack were trapped between the lines without support and lost many men captured. In his review of the action, Lee commented that there "seems to have been some misunderstanding as to the part each division was expected to have performed." Charles Venable of Lee's staff later reflected, "And thus the whole plan, so well conceived and so successful in its beginning, was given up to the sorrow of the commanding general."[49]

Lee's only other offensive action at Petersburg in the preelection period took place after Beauregard's failure to erase a Union lodgment on the Weldon Railroad achieved on 18 August and maintained in the face of fierce Confederate counterattacks on that and the next two days. U. S. Grant provided Lee with an opening when he immediately sought to capitalize on his newly won advantage by sending portions of Hancock's corps south along the rail line to wreck it. Unlike the previous days, when Confederate scouts consistently underestimated the size of the Union force, Southern patrols under the able leadership of Wade Hampton supplied Lee with accurate intelligence regarding the size and disposition of the Federals.

Hampton suggested the Yankees had isolated themselves and were vulnerable to a combined cavalry-infantry strike. At first Lee believed it too risky to send such a force so far outside his own entrenched lines, but after reflection he decided it a gamble worth taking. Left unchallenged, the Union troops could cut his remaining road and rail supply links, effectively starving the defenders out of Petersburg and Richmond. Even then Lee was cautious, initially assigning only one infantry division to accompany Hampton. Once he pushed his chips onto the table, Lee proved willing to raise the stakes rather than leave the game. He eventually added portions of two other divisions to the force and placed A. P. Hill in overall command.[50]

When their scouts apprised them of the impending danger, Hancock's Federals hastily took up a poorly sited defensive position near Reams

Station. Hill attacked them there on the afternoon of 25 August. The first assaults were thrown back, but a panic in one of Hancock's regiments allowed the attackers to penetrate the perimeter and slowly collapse the position. A substantial Confederate victory resulted in Federal losses of more than 2,600 (most of them prisoners) compared to 720 for Hill, halted Northern plans to further disrupt Petersburg's supply lines, boosted Confederate morale, and bought Lee another month.[51]

It was north of the James where Lee concentrated his planning and energies. As historian Richard J. Sommers observed, "Rightly or wrongly, numerous legitimate military, political, economic, and psychological considerations compelled Lee to defend the city." Even though the great preponderance of Union men and material threatened Petersburg, it was east of Richmond where Lee mapped out three offensives ambitiously designed to clear the enemy from that side of the river. Grant's siege positions at Petersburg gave him the advantage of interior lines stretching up from the city, across the neck of Bermuda Hundred, and through to an area on the north side known as Deep Bottom. This advantage made it possible for him to shift great numbers of men rapidly from one flank to the other. To counter these moves, Lee's soldiers had to cover a greater distance using a far weaker transportation web. A Federal presence at Deep Bottom also made it difficult, if not impossible, for Lee to send raiding parties down along the river to interdict the steady stream of transports hauling supplies to Grant at City Point.[52]

Lee revealed acute sensitivity to his Richmond flank on 26 July when Grant staged an expedition made up of Hancock's Second Corps and two divisions of Sheridan's cavalry. Shackled by Hancock's lackluster leadership and Sheridan's near indifference to his assignment, the operation accomplished little before withdrawing on 29 July. But Lee had reacted. At the time Grant's movement began, Confederate defenses north of the James consisted of elements of Kershaw's division of R. H. Anderson's First Corps and a portion of Cadmus M. Wilcox's division from A. P. Hill's command. In response to the Federal move, Lee summoned from the Petersburg lines all of Henry Heth's division and two of his cavalry divisions, leaving behind just three divisions to face three corps. That the Federals were unable to capitalize on this disparity at the battle of the Crater is a story best told elsewhere.[53]

Meanwhile, Lee's investment of men in the Shenandoah Valley initially paid dividends, thanks to Jubal Early's aggressive campaign. It took four days for Early's veterans to march and ride as far as Lynchburg, where they promptly scattered the Union force under David Hunter that had so frightened Richmond. By mid-July, Early had raided into Maryland, and on 11 July his men stood outside Washington after rolling over a smaller force under Maj. Gen. Lew Wallace that had tried to stop them two days before near Frederick. Early found Washington's defenses too tough to crack, so he fell back into the Valley where a part of his force defeated 9,500 Federals in the battle of Second Kernstown on 24 July.[54]

Early was accomplishing all that Lee had hoped, diverting attention from the Petersburg front, protecting the granaries of the Shenandoah farmlands, and forcing Grant to dispatch or divert troops from the James River theater toward the Valley. The balance began to shift on 1 August when Grant appointed Philip Sheridan to command all Federal troops opposed to Early. Along with Sheridan, Grant sent two divisions of cavalry from the Army of the Potomac at Petersburg, units which began their movement north via steamers on 4 August. Confederate scouts spotted the flotilla of forty-six transports and reported their movement to Lee.[55]

Suddenly, Lee's bet had been called and raised, and he now had to see it or fold. "I fear that this force is intended to operate against General Early," Lee informed Jefferson Davis on 4 August, "and when added to that already opposed to him, may be more than he can manage." Lee rode into Richmond two days later to confer with Davis and Richard H. Anderson. The decision was made to detach from Lee's command Joseph B. Kershaw's infantry division, Wilfred E. Cutshaw's artillery battalion, and Fitzhugh Lee's cavalry division to reinforce Early. On 11 August, Lee increased the pot again by ordering Wade Hampton to take another cavalry division to Anderson.[56]

According to Fitzhugh Lee, the commanding general's purpose in doing this was "to induce Grant to send troops to Sheridan equivalent to [a] . . . whole corps. In that case Lee would again re-enforce Early and transfer the principal scene of hostilities to the Potomac." Once again, however, Lee seriously misread his opponent. Grant responded not with more men for Sheridan but another expedition up from Petersburg to the Deep Bottom area.[57]

Grant's second Deep Bottom expedition was, like the first, entrusted to Hancock—who this time had infantry units from the Tenth Corps to augment the forces he had used in July. The operation got underway on 13 August. Similar to the earlier effort, Hancock's plan called for a turning movement by the troops coming off the river near Deep Bottom, pushing along the east bank of Bailey's Creek, and swinging in toward Richmond along either the Darbytown or Charles City Roads. In an eerie echo of previous events, Union command leadership was ambiguous in its goals, conservative in its execution, and equally unsuccessful in its efforts.[58]

An incident involving Lee during this little-known operation throws some light on his state of mind. According to a Georgia soldier named John C. Reed, Lee was positioned in the rear of the battle lines when a short-lived Federal breakthrough caused some Confederate units to break and run. Reed recalled how Lee rode among the stragglers and skulkers and spoke to each one, "harshly demanding that he show his wound." When a tall soldier with his hat pulled down over his eyes refused to halt at Lee's command, the general "showed great anger and hemmed the man by wheeling his horse across him." Lee again insisted that the soldier show blood. This time the man raised his hat to reveal an ugly wound. Reed remembered that Lee "did not apologize for his injurious words, but he told him where he could find some water near, and bade him go there forthwith and bathe his forehead well."[59]

This time Lee was determined to punish the Federals for threatening Richmond. Working with a hastily recalled Wade Hampton, he drew up what one historian of the campaign has called "an ambitious plan to drive Hancock's force back to the river." Hampton's riders were to flank the Federal position and then, supported by infantry, roll up the line. Nothing went as planned. Through a combination of miscues and miscommunications, the cavalry's attack did not get under way until nearly six hours after the scheduled start. The synchronized infantry assault waited until it was too dark to be effective. Fighting ceased at dusk, ending another of Lee's offensive designs. By dawn, 21 August, most of the Federal force had been withdrawn.[60]

At almost the same time, Lee's gamble in sending Anderson to support Early failed because Sheridan and Grant recognized its purpose. Sheridan bided his time, patiently sitting on the defensive, knowing that sooner or later Lee would recall Anderson. On 15 September, Anderson received orders to send his infantry and artillery on roads leading south. Four days later Sheridan and Early met in battle outside Winchester, beginning a series of engagements that would mark the finish of Lee's Valley strategy. By the end of the month he would have to send Kershaw's men back north, not to insure a victory but to stave off impending defeat.[61]

Lee's crystal ball had failed him badly in the Shenandoah Valley. Despite Early's protests that "the enemy's force is very much larger than mine," Lee persistently believed the actual disparity was slight. He guessed that Sheridan fielded around twelve thousand men at a time when the actual count was nearly double that. Nevertheless, prodded by Lee, Early took all the reinforcements sent to him and in mid-October risked a decisive battle at Cedar Creek. The result was ruin for the Southern cause. In the end, it was Lee's fatal half-measures and indecision during the latter phase of the Valley campaign that led to defeat and caused historian Richard J. Sommers to brand it "one of the worst miscalculations he ever made." By mid-November, Lee gave up on the Valley, ordering the return to

Petersburg of what remained of Kershaw's division and the Second Corps, now commanded by John B. Gordon.[62]

Grant proved more adept at playing the Valley game. Following receipt of news of Sheridan's victory over Early at Fisher's Hill on 22–23 September, Grant moved up by one week an offensive planned to prevent Lee's sending any more troops into the Valley. The resulting operation, while marginally successful outside Petersburg, broke the pattern of Union failure north of the James when, on 29 September, troops from Butler's Army of the James stormed and captured Fort Harrison, one of the major bastions in Richmond's outer ring of fortifications.[63]

The breadth of front Lee had to cover with a limited number of troops virtually guaranteed that any serious move against his lines would provoke a crisis requiring an all-out effort at restoration. In a 2 September letter to Jefferson Davis, Lee explained, "As matters now stand we have no troops disposable to meet movements of the enemy or strike when opportunity presents, without taking them from the trenches and exposing some important point." Both Lee and Grant knew the two-edged value of entrenchments. While the earthen mounds made it possible for relatively small numbers of men to defend a position against a frontal assault, they also allowed an offensive-minded general to mass his troops into mobile columns behind sheltering works from which they then were free to operate against the enemy's weak points. Although the Union operation at Petersburg is often referred to as a siege, there was never a complete encirclement of that last citadel, so Lee always had to worry about two widely separated flanks—one below Petersburg, the other near Richmond. As Sommers concluded, "Counterpunching, striking back, looking—hoping—for an opening and all the while trying to fend off the Northerners' blows: To such measures was Lee now reduced."[64]

According to Lee's nephew-biographer Fitzhugh, "General Lee was very sensitive about his lines being broken." Lee planned and launched two limited offensives to regain what he had lost on 29 September. Interestingly, both sought to integrate an Army of Northern Virginia unit with one not of his command (Field's and Hoke's divisions respectively), both were essentially converging assaults, and both failed. The first, on 30 September, was designed to recapture Fort Harrison. Of this attempt, an officer on Lee's staff later wrote, "Our effort to retake [Fort Harrison] was not an energetic nor systematic one. We could & should have retaken it, but matters were not executed as well as they were planned." Lee's second, and indeed last, offensive north of the James, was aimed at the flank of the defensive line established by Butler after his victory at Fort Harrison. It took place a week after the first offensive but would have occurred sooner had Lee not been diverted by events at Petersburg. The staff assessment of the 30 September failure can serve as well as an epitaph for the fighting on 7 October along the Darbytown and New Market Roads that cost Lee one of his most promising officers, John Gregg of the Texas Brigade.[65]

Whatever hope Lee harbored of preserving the status quo until the Northern elections of 1864 evaporated in the wake of Union victories at Mobile Bay in August and at Atlanta in early September. Lincoln's reelection presented Lee with perhaps the most difficult dilemma a military man must face—knowledge that the only possible resolution to the conflict no longer lay on the battlefield but rather in the political sphere. Realizing he could not deliver further victories to the Confederate cause, was it Lee's duty to pressure the politicians to seek a negotiated settlement, or should he narrowly define his responsibilities to simple military functions? Clifford Dowdey, one of Lee's modern biographers, phrased it this way: "Lee was being forced into a dilemma as to the nature of his duty—to the constituted authority who legally represented the falling country or to the men who looked to him for leadership."[66]

Perhaps the most significant effort that brought the war to the peace table in this post-election period occurred on 3 February 1865, at the so-called Hampton Roads Conference. The initiative for the talks had come from Francis P. Blair Sr., Andrew Jackson's old adviser and long a power in the Democratic Party, who advocated a hair-brained scheme to unite the warring factions in a common expedition against Mexico. Abraham Lincoln and Jefferson Davis used Blair's mission for their own political ends. Lincoln's aim appears to have been a serious effort to present the leaders of the Confederacy with advantageous economic terms to end their secession, while Davis's effort was a more cynical manipulation of the process aimed at reinvigorating the Southern will to fight by forcing the North into a policy of unconditional surrender. Davis guaranteed that the talks would fail by refusing to allow his three commissioners even to discuss the possibility of rejoining the Union, a point that Lincoln had said from the beginning was a *sine qua non.* Lee played no role in the talks, while it was through a personal intervention by U. S. Grant that a pre-conference impasse was broken and both sides brought to the table. As a part of his larger campaign to build consensus, Davis also acceded to pressure from his Congress and appointed Lee commander in chief of all Confederate armies. It was a hollow, self-serving gesture. Said a Texas soldier of the appointment: "Now it was too late; the Confederacy was gasping for breath, its armies were scattered, disorganized, and, practically, commanderless, and there was not time to gather together and weld the fragments into fighting machines." A staff officer added that Lee's promotion was a "mockery of rank no longer of any value."[67]

Lee did play a part in an attempt by some military men on both sides to restart the peace process. This time the initiative came from the Federal general E. O. C. Ord, successor to Benjamin Butler in command of the Army of the James, who on 21 February met between the lines with his prewar friend James Longstreet. Ord proposed a military convention, a cease-fire to allow the politicians time to negotiate. Longstreet passed Ord's proposal up the chain of command to Richmond, where, on 22 February, Lee was authorized to write Grant to suggest a meeting to discuss such a convention. Lee was enough of a political realist to know that without flexibility on the Southern side there would be no discussions. "My belief is that [Grant] . . . will consent to no terms, unless coupled with the condition of our return to the Union," he told Davis on 2 March. Lee was not far wrong. Grant also had passed Ord's proposal on to his superiors and was promptly instructed to have "no conference with General Lee, unless it be for . . . some minor and purely military matter."[68]

It was about this time that Lee met with the president pro tem of the Confederate Congress, Robert M. T. Hunter. According to Hunter, Lee indicated: "[I]f I thought there was a chance for any peace which would secure better terms than were likely to be given after a surrender at discretion, he thought it my duty to make the effort." Lee rejected any suggestion that he openly support such an initiative because "it would be almost equivalent to surrender." Hunter pressed Lee at least to make a personal appeal directly to Jefferson Davis. Said Hunter, "To this he made no reply. In the whole of this conversation he never said to me he thought the chances were over; but the tone and tenor of his remarks made that impression on my mind."[69]

Lee's official dispatches in the early months of 1865 provide some insights into his outlook and the nature of the problems he faced. On 27 January, he felt compelled to call to the attention of Secretary of War James Seddon, "the alarming frequency of desertions from the army." A follow-up message on 8 February catalogued the deplorable conditions of food and clothing supply in the Army of Northern Virginia. "If some change is not made and the Commissary Department reorganized, I apprehend dire results," he declared. Eleven days later, after pondering the seemingly inexorable progress made by Sherman in his march to the sea and the threat he now posed to North and South Carolina, Lee concluded, "I fear it may be necessary to abandon all our cities, & preparation should be made for this contingency." Then, on 9 March, in an assessment of the overall situation to John C. Breckinridge, newly appointed secretary of war, Lee concluded that "the legitimate military consequences of [the enemy's numerical and material] . . . superiority have been postponed longer than we had reason to anticipate."[70]

This clear-headed view contrasts sharply with Lee's decision to undertake an all-out offensive at Petersburg. Planned at Lee's request by John B. Gordon, the attack on the enemy entrenchments near Union Fort Stedman was tactically brilliant, but strategically flawed. According to his only report of this action, Lee was "induced to assume the offensive from the belief that the point assailed could be carried without much loss, and the hope that . . . I could . . . cause . . . Gen. Grant . . . so to curtail his lines, that upon the approach of Genl Sherman, I might be able to hold our position with a portion of the troops, and with a select body unite with Genl Johnston and give him battle." The assumptions made here are baffling, especially as Lee's own experiences in the field against Grant would have validated none of them. Sherman was 150 miles to the south and not moving (and would not move until 10 April); and Grant, now heavily reinforced by the troops he had recalled from the Valley, could be counted upon to be anything but passive. There is something irrational about this whole enterprise that smacks of desperation and delusion—two qualities not usually associated with Lee's generalship. Even biographer Dowdey, one of Lee's most eloquent defenders, could only describe his avid support of Gordon's plan as "cloudy-minded."[71]

Gordon's failed assault on Fort Stedman cost Lee between twenty-five hundred and four thousand casualties, and in its aftermath the Federals achieved small but significant gains of position along other portions of the Petersburg siege lines. One of those became the jumping off point for the wedge assault made on 2 April by the Union Sixth Corps, which broke Lee's line west of Petersburg and resulted in the death of A. P. Hill. The loss of these lines, compounded by Sheridan's defeat of George E. Pickett at Five Forks on 1 April, made Lee's position untenable. With less than twenty-four hours's notice to the Davis government, Lee ordered all troops assigned to defend Richmond and Petersburg to begin a prearranged withdrawal, which got underway late on 2 April. It was during the preparations for this movement that Lee received a note from Jefferson Davis asking for more time. Lee's uncharacteristic response was to tear the letter into pieces with the comment, "I am sure I gave him sufficient notice."[72]

The Confederate retreat to Appomattox Court House has acquired the aspects of legend. The image persists of a small, ragged band of stalwart fighters valiantly fending off the Yankee hordes until they were at last cornered near the small Virginia county seat whose name has become synonymous with the end of the Civil War. Yet a thorough modern study by Christopher M. Calkins suggests that many of these assumptions simply do not stand up.

While this is not the place to examine in detail the facts assembled for the series of appendices Calkins prepared for his book *The Final Bivouac,* it would be a fair summary to say that ample supplies of clothing and subsistence were generally on hand in the spring of 1865. What was lacking, Calkins contends, was an effective method of distributing them. Some of the blame here must lie with Lee, who, despite his oft-quoted protests to Richmond on the subject of supply, took no effective steps to improve distribution within the Army of Northern Virginia. As Calkins says, "It appears that the condition of the men in Lee's army varied from command to command during the siege. This could be attributed to the state from which they hailed, their position along the defense line, and their own leadership."[73]

It should be noted too that even though Lee had several times warned Richmond of the imminence of his withdrawal from Petersburg, and of the fact that he had prepared and distributed in advance a plan of retreat for all units under his command, he made no effective attempt to provide rations for his troops in anticipation of this move. Lest the argument be advanced that there were no rations to pass out, Confederate sources quoted by Calkins indicate that on the night of 2 April there were 300,000 in Richmond, 80,000 at Farmville, and 180,000 at Lynchburg.[74]

The size of the force that Lee led from Petersburg and Richmond also has generated much speculation. Southern accounts, prone to exaggerate the disparity in numbers, place the total between 25,000 and 35,000 men. Factoring backward from the number known to have surrendered at Appomattox, adding those captured during the campaign accounted for by Federal prisoner-of-war rolls, noting those killed or wounded, and adding a modest figure of 100 desertions per day of the retreat, Calkins arrives at a total of approximately 58,000. So it was not an insubstantial force that left the Richmond-Petersburg trenches on 2 April, and for the most part units marched according to a plan laid down several weeks earlier. What failed was the structure of command within this mass of men. While some units preserved discipline and morale, many others trudged along more by instinct than conviction. The heart of the Confederate cause had stopped beating long before its military and political leaders acknowledged the fact.[75]

Lee's basic retreat strategy—to steal a day's march on the enemy so he could turn south through Burkeville for an eventual link-up with Joseph E. Johnston's army—was the only one with even a remote chance of success. Yet Lee himself doomed this plan when, on 4 April, he decided to halt at Amelia Court House to reprovision his army. The stop accomplished none of Lee's intended objectives. He was unable to draw enough provender from the region to supply his army, and the one-day head start he lost was turned

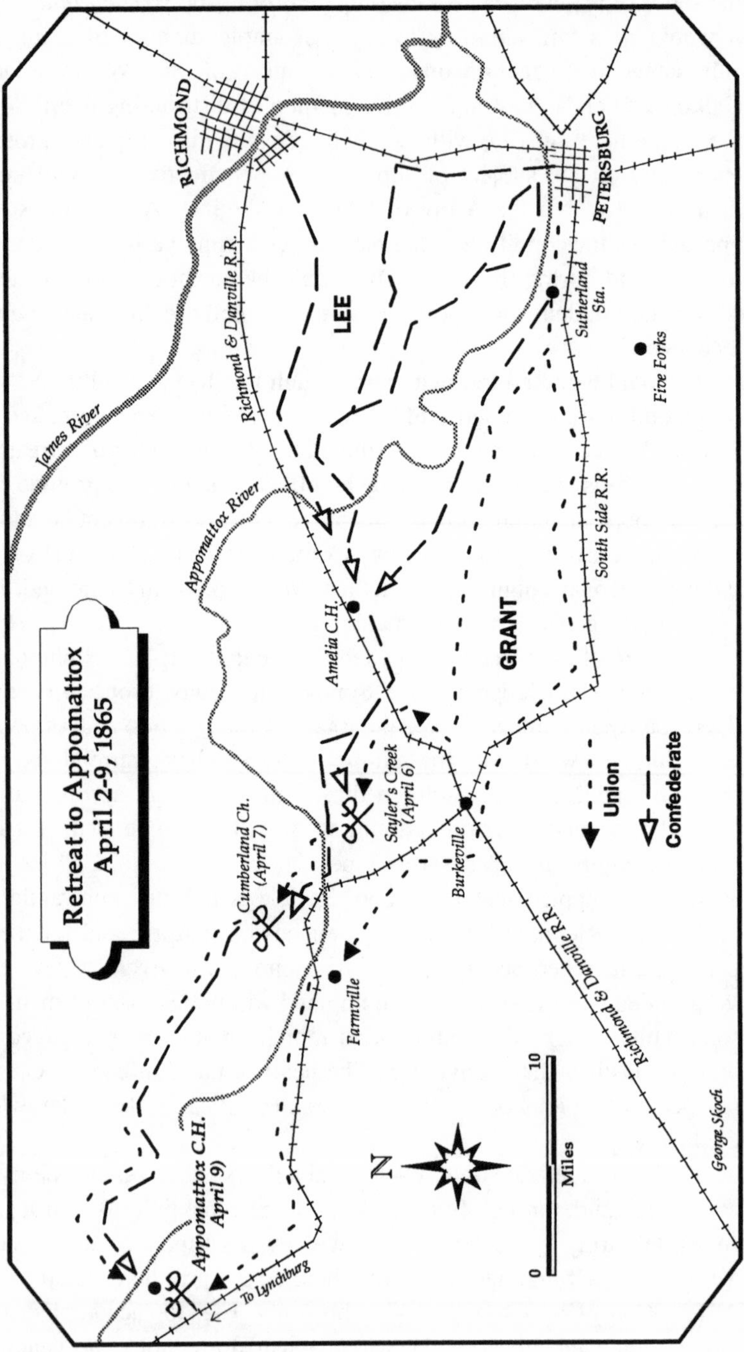

Retreat to Appomattox
April 2-9, 1865
RICHMOND
PETERSBURG
James River
Appomattox River
Richmond & Danville R.R.
LEE
GRANT
Sutherland Sta.
Five Forks
South Side R.R.
Amelia C.H.
Sayler's Creek (April 6)
Cumberland Ch. (April 7)
Burkeville
Farmville
Appomattox C.H. (April 9)
To Lynchburg
Union
Confederate
N
Miles
0
10
George Skoch

to advantage by closely pursuing Federals who blocked his best route south and forced him off to the west, farther and farther away from joining hands with Johnston.

The decision that made surrender inevitable took place on 7 April, when Lee opted to move through Farmville to the north side of the Appomattox River. As part of his instructions about the rear guard to artillerist E. P. Alexander, Lee showed him a map of the region. Alexander later wrote of this moment:

> The most direct & shortest road to Lynchburg from Farmville did not cross the river as we had done, but kept up the south side near the railroad. The road we were on bent up & then back, & was evidently longer, finally recrossing the head waters of the river & rejoining the straighter road at Appomattox Court House. I pointed to that place, & said it looked as if there we might have [the] most trouble. . . . The gen. said, "Well there is time enough to think about that. Go now & attend to these matters here."[76]

Clearly the end was near. On the day after he had been forced to divert to the west, and in the wake of a disastrous fight by his rear guard along Sailor's Creek that cost him 7,700 men, Lee told an emissary from Jefferson Davis, "A few more Sailor's Creeks and it will be over—ended—just as I have expected it would end from the first."[77]

Much of the combat of this last campaign was more reactive than planned. Lee exercised no direct control over the larger actions fought during the retreat—either at Sailor's Creek on 6 April or at Cumberland Church on the seventh. The only battle he did command to be fought, apart from that outside Appomattox Court House on the morning of 9 April, he seems to have recognized as futile even as he ordered it. On the night of 8 April, Lee met with corps commanders Longstreet and Gordon, along with cavalry chief Fitzhugh Lee, to plan the next day's effort. To have any chance of moving south, the army would have to follow the roads stretching in that direction from Appomattox Court House. A Federal force of unknown size and composition stood in the way. If the enemy was merely a cavalry advance, the Confederate army should be able to bull its way through, though it would have to abandon its supply train. If, however, sizable Union infantry units lay ahead, the prospects for a breakout were slim. It was a contentious meeting, and Gordon was certain that infantry blocked his front, while Lee insisted it did not. Lee overrode any objections and ordered the morning attack to proceed.[78]

The chronology of events on the morning of 9 April is revealing. Gordon's attack got underway at around 5:00 A.M. with a series of skirmishing probes that lasted for about two hours. The general advance began about

7:00 A.M., and by 9:00 A.M. had cleared the escape road for the rest of the army to follow. The fighting up to this point had been against Yankee cavalry and horse artillery; infantry units from the Twenty-fourth, Twenty-fifth, and Fifth Corps were closing but would not come into contact with Gordon's men until nearly 9:30 A.M. While all this unfolded, Robert E. Lee, at about 8:30 A.M., rode out through the lines of Longstreet's corps (which constituted his rear guard) in the hope of meeting with U. S. Grant to discuss "the restoration of peace," as he had proposed in a message sent to the Northern general-in-chief on 8 April. Lee met a Federal courier bearing a note written by Grant earlier that morning which rejected the proposed agenda because, as Grant explained, "I have no authority to treat on the subject of peace." Lee had tried, in his letter, to shift the subject from the surrender of the Army of Northern Virginia to a wide-ranging discussion aimed at a broad peace settlement. Why he chose this tack, after predicting its failure during the Longstreet-Ord discussions in February, was never explained.[79]

Upon receipt of Grant's note rejecting any "peace" talks, Lee at once accepted the inevitable. Turning to his staff officer, Charles Marshall, Lee said, "Well, write a letter to General Grant and ask him to meet me to deal with the question of the surrender of my army." It was about this time that Gordon's men made contact with the approaching Federal infantry, effectively ending the attempt to break out.[80]

The moving events that ensued at the McLean House are too well known to be recounted here. Much has been said about Lee's humanity in refusing even to consider ordering his army to scatter and continue the conflict in a guerrillalike fashion. In so acting, Lee responded no differently than any of his peers when presented with similar options. To the Confederate officer class, the prospect of social disorder was far more terrifying than the shame of surrender. Joseph E. Johnston actually defied an order from Jefferson Davis to scatter his army and instead surrendered it for that very reason. Also rejecting the guerrilla option were Richard Taylor and Edmund Kirby Smith. Lee's action was quite in line with this way of thinking.[81]

Throughout his active service in the Confederate military, Lee had drawn a rather firm line between his military duties and any larger responsibilities. On the day after he signed the official surrender of his army, Lee met with Grant at Grant's request. The substance of the meeting is best described by Grant himself:

> Lee said to me that the South was a big country and that we might have to march over it three or four times before the war entirely ended, but that we would now be able to do it as they could no longer resist us.

> He expressed it as his earnest hope, however, that we would not be called upon to cause more loss and sacrifice of life; but he could not foretell the result. I then suggested to General Lee that there was not a man in the Confederacy whose influence with the soldiery and the whole people was as great as his, and that if he would now advise the surrender of all the armies I had no doubt his advice would be followed with alacrity. But Lee said that he could not do that without consulting the President first. I knew there was no use to urge him to do anything against his idea of what was right.[82]

Eleven days after he had surrendered to Grant at Appomattox, and five days after returning to a now-occupied Richmond, Lee wrote Jefferson Davis a letter. After reviewing the sorry condition of his army at the start of that last retreat, and reflecting on the profound war-weariness that permeated the Confederacy, Lee ended with words he could never bring himself to say to Davis in person: "To save useless effusion of blood, I would recommend measures be taken for suspension of hostilities and the restoration of peace."[83]

In his book *Lee Considered,* Alan T. Nolan wondered why Lee did not do more to end the war once he realized it could not be won. Nolan pointed to Lee's refined sense of military duty, quoting Clifford Dowdey regarding his "sense of . . . pride of a professional in his craft, [that] caused him to practice meticulously the techniques of command long after any military purpose could be achieved." Nolan's arguments found an eerie pre-echo in the angry words of veteran *New York Times* reporter E. A. Paul, who, in June 1865, wrote that the "world . . . will . . . hold [Lee] . . . to account for the blood spilled since last Winter, when he testified before a committee of the rebel Senate that the cause for which he was the military head was a failure. For every drop of blood shed since that time Robert E. Lee should be held answerable."[84]

Lee never answered to Federal authorities. After the surrender, with his sense of duty satisfied and his military obligations discharged, Lee adapted to the changed circumstances more quickly than many of his brother officers. An exchange of letters between Lee and the Rev. William H. Platt of Petersburg, written in May 1865, is revealing, both for its intimation of the Lee legend and doctrine of the Lost Cause soon to emerge, and Lee's own attitude toward the future.

In his letter, Platt wrote:

> The grateful hearts of millions will ever bless you for struggling so long and so nobly for their right of self government. You, no more than Napoleon and other great commanders, could do impossibilities. The enemy exceeded us vastly in numbers and other resources of war and

exhaustion was inevitable. The Powers of the world, misunderstanding us, coldly left us to expire. Our Confederate nationality is gone, but not the glory of its brief existence and history. Whatever we have lost, our honor is safe.

Lee replied:

God has thought it fit to afflict us most deeply and his chastening hand is not yet stayed. How great must be our Sins and how unrelenting our obduracy. We have only to submit to His gracious will and pray for His healing mercy. Heaven's power could not long have withstood the overwhelming force opposed to us. . . . It is however useless to look back now that the South is willing to have peace. I hope it may be accorded on a permanent basis; that the affections and interests of the Country may be united and not a forced & hollow truce formed to be broken at the first convenient opportunity. To this end all good men should labor.[85]

NOTES

1. Robert E. Lee, *The Wartime Papers of R. E. Lee*, ed. Clifford Dowdey and Louis H. Manarin (Boston: Little, Brown, 1961), 666, 700.

2. For more detailed studies of these engagements, see William D. Henderson, *The Road to Bristoe Station* (Lynchburg VA: H. E. Howard, 1987), and Martin F. Graham and George F. Skoch, *Mine Run: A Campaign of Lost Opportunities* (Lynchburg VA: H. E. Howard, 1987).

3. Lee, *Wartime Papers*, 605; James Longstreet, *From Manassas to Appomattox: A Memoir of the Civil War in America* (Philadelphia: J. B. Lippincott, 1896), 547–48.

4. Lee, *Wartime Papers*, 592, 642.

5. Lee, *Wartime Papers*, 666, 675, 688, 690.

6. Lee, *Wartime Papers*, 667; B. L. Wynn, "Lee Watched Grant at Locust Grove," *Confederate Veteran* 21 (February 1913): 68; Jedediah Hotchkiss, *Virginia, Confederate Military History*, ed. Clement A. Evans, 12 vols. (Atlanta: Confederate Publishing Company, 1899), 3:433.

7. Edward Steere, *The Wilderness Campaign* (Harrisburg PA.: Stackpole, 1960), 73–87; Armistead Lindsay Long, *Memoirs of Robert E. Lee* (New York and Philadelphia: J. M. Stoddart & Company, 1886), 327.

8. U.S. War Department, *The War of the Rebellion: A Compilation of the Official Records of the Union and Confederate Armies*, 127 vols., index, and atlas (Washington DC: GPO, 1880–1901), ser. 1, vol. 36, pt. 2, p. 948 [hereafter cited as *Official Records*, all references are to series 1 unless otherwise indicated].

9. Percy G. Hamlin, *"Old Bald Head" (General R. S. Ewell): The Portrait of a Soldier* (Strasburg VA: Shenandoah Publishing House, 1940), 170; Samuel J. Martin, *The Road to Glory: Confederate General Richard S. Ewell* (Indianapolis: Guild Press of Indiana, 1991), 281; *Official Records*, vol. 36, pt. 1, p. 1070; Campbell

Brown, "Memoranda—Campaign of 1864," undated manuscript, Tennessee State Library, Nashville.

10. Henry Heth, *The Memoirs of Henry Heth*, ed. James L. Morrison (Westport CN: Greenwood Press, 1974), 182–83.

11. Heth, *Memoirs*, 183–84; Steere, *Wilderness Campaign*, 309–31.

12. Douglas Southall Freeman, *R. E. Lee: A Biography*, 4 vols. (New York: Charles Scribner's Sons, 1934–35), 3:285.

13. Ulysses S. Grant, *Personal Memoirs of U.S. Grant*, 2 vols. (New York: C. L. Webster & Company, 1886), 2:195.

14. Steere, *Wilderness Campaign*, 335–45.

15. Steere, *Wilderness Campaign*, 388; Robert E. Lee to John B. Gordon, 22 February 1868, Special Collections, University of Georgia, Athens.

16. G. Moxley Sorrel, *Memoirs of a Confederate Staff Officer* (New York and Washington: Neale Publishing Company, 1905), 244–45.

17. Steere, *Wilderness Campaign*, 427.

18. Freeman, *Lee*, 3:304; Lee, *Wartime Papers*, 724; *Official Records*, vol. 36, pt. 1:1041.

19. Freeman, *Lee*, 3:304.

20. William D. Matter, *If It Takes All Summer: The Battle of Spotsylvania* (Chapel Hill: University of North Carolina Press, 1988), 124–67.

21. *Official Records*, vol. 36, pt. 1, p. 1071; Charles S. Venable, "The Campaign from the Wilderness to Petersburg," in *Southern Historical Society Papers*, 52 vols. and 3-vol. index, ed. J. William Jones et al. (1876–1959; reprint, Wilmington NC: Broadfoot Publishing Company, 1990–92), 14:527; James A. Walker, "The Bloody Angle," in *Southern Historical Society Papers*, 21:233; Thomas H. Carter, "Colonel Thomas H. Carter's Letter," in *Southern Historical Society Papers*, 21:239; W. W. Old, "Trees Whittled Down at Horseshoe," in *Southern Historical Society Papers*, 23:21; Edward Porter Alexander, *Military Memoirs of a Confederate: A Critical Narrative* (1907; reprint, Bloomington: Indiana University Press, 1962), 516.

22. Douglas Southall Freeman, *Lee's Lieutenants: A Study in Command*, 3 vols. (New York: Charles Scribner's Sons, 1942–44), 3:397–98; Heth, *Memoirs*, 186–87; Brown, "Memoranda."

23. Matter, *If It Takes All Summer*, 189–202; Robert W. Hunter, "Major-General Johnson at Spotsylvania," in *Southern Historical Society Papers*, 33:339; John Esten Cooke, *A Life of General Robert E. Lee* (New York: D. Appleton and Company, 1871), 397.

24. Matter, *If It Takes All Summer*, 202–68.

25. Freeman, *Lee*, 3:326–27.

26. Matter, *If It Takes All Summer*, 271–305; Lee, *Wartime Papers*, 737–44.

27. Michael J. Miller, *Even to Hell Itself: The North Anna Campaign, May 21–26, 1864* (Lynchburg VA: H. E. Howard, 1989), 1–22.

28. Lee, *Wartime Papers*, 745–46, 748.

29. Miller, *Even to Hell Itself*, 23–60.

30. Miller, *Even to Hell Itself*, 61–68; Hotchkiss, *Virginia*, 460.

31. Miller, *Even to Hell Itself*, 88–98.

32. Venable, "Wilderness to Petersburg," 535.

33. Freeman, *Lee's Lieutenants*, 3:498–99.

34. Lee, *Wartime Papers*, 756.

35. Freeman, *Lee's Lieutenants*, 3:502–3.

36. Freeman, *Lee's Lieutenants*, 505–7; Andrew A. Humphreys, *The Virginia Campaign of '64 and '65: The Army of the Potomac and the Army of the James* (New York: Charles Scribner's Sons, 1883), 173–77.

37. Humphreys, *Virginia Campaign*, 178–79.

38. Lee, *Wartime Papers*, 764.

39. Jeffry D. Wert, *From Winchester to Cedar Creek: The Shenandoah Campaign of 1864* (Carlisle PA: South Mountain Press, 1987), 7; Lee, *Wartime Papers*, 767, 771.

40. Lee, *Wartime Papers*, 775.

41. Lee, *Wartime Papers*, 765, 775; *Official Records*, vol. 36, pt. 3, pp. 877–78; J. William Jones, *Life and Letters of Robert Edward Lee, Soldier and Man* (New York and Washington: Neale Publishing Company, 1906), 40.

42. *Official Records*, vol. 36, pt. 3, pp. 878–79, 884–85; Freeman, *Lee*, 3:445–46.

43. Lee, *Wartime Papers*, 776.

44. Eppa Hunton, *Autobiography of Eppa Hunton* (Richmond VA: William Byrd Press, 1933), 113.

45. Lee, *Wartime Papers*, 437–38.

46. Brian H. Reid, "Another Look at Grant's Crossing of the James, 1864," *Civil War History* 39 (December 1993): 315.

47. Alfred Roman, *Military Operations of General Beauregard in the War Between the States, 1861 to 1865; Including a Brief Personal Sketch and Narrative of His Services in the War with Mexico, 1846–8*, 2 vols. (New York: Harper & Brothers, 1884), 2:247.

48. *Official Records*, vol. 40, pt. 3, p. 678; Humphreys, *Virginia Campaign*, 227–29; Freeman, *Lee*, 3:454; *Official Records*, vol. 40, pt. 1, p. 805.

49. *New York Tribune*, 28 June 1864; *Official Records*, vol. 40, pt. 1, p. 799; Venable, "Wilderness to Petersburg," 540.

50. Freeman, *Lee's Lieutenants*, 3:589; John Horn, *The Destruction of the Weldon Railroad: Deep Bottom, Globe Tavern, and Reams Station, August 14–25, 1864* (Lynchburg VA: H. E. Howard, 1991), 119–20.

51. Humphreys, *Virginia Campaign*, 279–83.

52. Richard J. Sommers, *Richmond Redeemed: The Siege at Petersburg* (Garden City NY: Doubleday, 1981), 2, 210.

53. Humphreys, *Virginia Campaign*, 247–50; Michael A. Cavanaugh and William Marvel, *The Battle of the Crater: "The Horrid Pit" June 25–August 6, 1864* (Lynchburg VA: H. E. Howard, 1989), 28–36.

54. Wert, *Winchester to Cedar Creek*, 7–8.

55. *Official Records*, vol. 42, pt. 2, pp. 38–39, 1161.

56. *Official Records*, vol. 42, pt. 2, p. 1161; Wert, *Winchester to Cedar Creek*, 33.

57. Fitzhugh Lee, *General Lee* (New York: Appleton and Company, 1894), 337.

58. Humphreys, *Virginia Campaign*, 268–72; Horn, *Destruction of the Weldon Railroad*, 9–53.

59. John C. Reed, "Journal," undated manuscript, Alabama Department of Archives and History, Montgomery.

60. Horn, *Destruction of the Weldon Railroad*, 49–51.

61. Wert, *Winchester to Cedar Creek*, 41.

62. Wert, *Winchester to Cedar Creek*, 139, 174; Sommers, *Richmond Redeemed*, 422.

63. Sommers, *Richmond Redeemed*, 5.

64. Sommers, *Richmond Redeemed*, 207.

65. Lee, *General Lee*, 321–22; Sommers, *Richmond Redeemed*, 137, 148; Noah A. Trudeau, "Darbytown Road Debacle," *America's Civil War* (May 1992): 30–36.

66. Clifford Dowdey, *Lee* (Boston: Little, Brown, 1965), 532.

67. Julian S. Carr, *The Hampton Roads Conference* (Durham NC: n.p., 1917), 3–36; J. B. Polley, *Hood's Texas Brigade: Its Marches, Its Battles, Its Achievements* (New York and Washington: Neale Publishing Company, 1910), 272; Cooke, *Life of Lee*, 436.

68. Freeman, *Lee's Lieutenants*, 3:643; Lee, *Wartime Papers*, 911; *Official Records*, vol. 42, pt. 2, p. 802.

69. Robert M. T. Hunter, "The Peace Commission—Mr. Hunter's Reply," in *Southern Historical Society Papers*, 4:308–9.

70. Lee, *Wartime Papers*, 886, 890, 904–5, 913.

71. Lee, *Wartime Papers*, 916–17; Dowdey, *Lee*, 532.

72. Dowdey, *Lee*, 544.

73. Christopher M. Calkins, *The Final Bivouac: The Surrender Parade at Appomattox and the Disbanding of the Armies, April 10–May 20, 1865* (Lynchburg VA: H. E. Howard, 1988), 193.

74. Calkins, *Final Bivouac*, 196.

75. Calkins, *Final Bivouac*, 201, 208.

76. Edward Porter Alexander, *Fighting for the Confederacy: The Personal Recollections of General Edward Porter Alexander*, ed. Gary W. Gallagher (Chapel Hill: University of North Carolina Press, 1989), 525.

77. John S. Wise, *The End of an Era* (Boston: Houghton Mifflin, 1899), 429.

78. Frank P. Cauble, *The Surrender Proceedings: Appomattox Court House, April 9, 1865* (Lynchburg VA: H. E. Howard, 1987), 14.

79. Christopher M. Calkins, *The Battles of Appomattox Station and Appomattox Court House, April 8–9, 1865* (Lynchburg VA: H. E. Howard, 1987), 211; Cauble, *Surrender Proceedings*, 12, 16, 23.

80. Charles Marshall, *An Aide-De-Camp of Lee, Being the Papers of Colonel Charles Marshall, Sometime Aide-De-Camp, Military Secretary, and Assistant Adjutant General on the Staff of Robert E. Lee, 1862–1865*, ed. Major General Sir Frederick Maurice (Boston: Little, Brown, 1927), 254.

81. Dowdey, *Lee*, 573; *Official Records*, vol. 47, pt. 3, p. 836; pt. 3, p. 1275; Robert L. Kerby, *Kirby Smith's Confederacy: The Trans-Mississippi South, 1861–1865* (New York: Columbia University Press, 1972), 50.

82. Grant, *Memoirs*, 2:497.

83. Lee, *Wartime Papers*, 939.

84. Alan T. Nolan, *Lee Considered: General Robert E. Lee and Civil War History* (Chapel Hill: University of North Carolina Press, 1991), 118–33; *New York Times*, 4 June 1865.

85. William H. Platt to Robert E. Lee, 5 May 1865, Lee Headquarters Papers, Virginia Historical Society, Richmond; Robert E. Lee to William H. Platt, 16 May 1865, Civil War Times Collection, United States Military History Institute, Carlisle, Pennsylvania.

★ IV ★

THE WRITTEN RECORD

The R. E. Lee *200*: An Annotated Bibliography of Essential Books on Lee's Military Career

T. MICHAEL PARRISH

Compiled with advice from Gary W. Gallagher and Robert K. Krick, this list offers a general guide to the broad range of primary and secondary books concerning R. E. Lee's actions and reputation as a soldier.

1.
Adams, Charles Francis. *Lee at Appomattox, and Other Papers.* Boston, 1902. Reprint (revised), Boston, 1903. Reprint, Irvine CA, 1989.
Includes a description of Lee's decision to surrender his army rather than resort to guerrilla warfare; based on eyewitness testimony.

2.
———. *Lee's Centennial: An Address Delivered at Lexington, Virginia.* Boston, 1907. Reprint, with introduction by Douglas Southall Freeman, Chicago, 1948.
A climactic speech in the consecration of Lee's heroic image, ironically fashioned by a prominent New Englander who admired Lee as a shining example of the selfless leadership desperately needed in the twentieth century.

3.
Adams, Michael C. C. *Our Masters the Rebels: A Speculation on Union Military Failure in the East, 1861–1865.* Cambridge MA, 1978. Reprint, titled *Fighting for Defeat: Union Military Failure in the East, 1861–1865.* Lincoln NE, 1992.

A study of the intimidating effect Lee and his lieutenants enjoyed upon a succession of habitually cautious and often bewildered Federal adversaries.

4.
Alexander, Bevin. *Lost Victories: The Military Genius of Stonewall Jackson.* New York, 1992.
A study notable for its daring argument that Jackson's victories went wasted at least four times because of Lee's refusal to consider Jackson's larger strategic vision for making rapid strikes against the North.

5.
Alexander, Edward Porter. *Fighting for the Confederacy: The Personal Recollections of General Edward Porter Alexander.* Ed. Gary W. Gallagher. Chapel Hill NC, 1989.
By far the best testimony by a member of the Army of Northern Virginia's high command, combining personal and professional insights sometimes critical of Lee, thus proving the author's rare genius and utter integrity.

6.
———. *Military Memoirs of a Confederate: A Critical Narrative.* New York, 1907. Reprint, with introduction by T. Harry Williams, Bloomington IN, 1962. Reprint, with introduction by Maury Klein, Dayton OH, 1990. Reprint, with introduction by Gary W. Gallagher, New York, 1993.
A thoughtful analysis of Lee's campaigns, by his brilliant chief of artillery.

7.
Allan, William. *The Army of Northern Virginia in 1862.* Boston, 1892. Reprint, with introduction by Robert K. Krick, Dayton OH, 1984.
The first comprehensive scholarly study of Lee's army, written with surprising objectivity by one of Stonewall Jackson's former officers.

8.
Anderson, Nancy S., and Dwight Anderson. *The Generals.* New York, 1988 and 1989.
An interesting attempt at a dual biography of Lee and Grant, gradually intertwining their lives and their climactic confrontation in Virginia.

9.
Beringer, Richard E., Herman Hattaway, Archer Jones, and William N. Still Jr., *Why the South Lost the Civil War.* Athens GA, 1986. Abridged edition, titled *The Elements of Confederate Defeat*, Athens GA, 1988.

A controversial book whose quartet of eminent scholars asserts that the Confederacy failed militarily because its people lacked the collective will to win at any cost.

10.

Bigelow, John, Jr. *The Campaign of Chancellorsville: A Strategic and Tactical Study.* New Haven CT, 1910. Reprint, Dayton OH, 1983 and 1991.
Still by far the best purely military account of Lee's masterpiece, enhanced by a stunning array of beautiful maps.

11.

Blackford, Susan L., comp. *Memoirs of Life In and Out of the Army in Virginia During the War Between the States.* 2 vols. Lynchburg VA, 1894–96. Reprint, titled *Letter's from Lee's Army*, edited and abridged by Charles M. Blackford III, with notes by Charles M. Blackford, New York, 1947.
An outstanding collection of personal recollections and supporting materials, including correspondence between an officer in the Second Virginia Cavalry and his wife.

12.

Blackford, William Willis. *War Years with Jeb Stuart, by Lieut. Colonel W. W. Blackford, C.S.A.* New York, 1945. Reprint, Baton Rouge LA, 1993.
An exciting memoir by a well-bred Virginia cavalry officer who served on Stuart's staff.

13.

Boritt, Gabor S., ed. *Why the Confederacy Lost.* New York, 1992.
A superb collection of essays by leading scholars who probe all the major themes of the Confederate struggle, with Lee placed squarely at the storm center.

14.

Bradford, Gamaliel. *Confederate Portraits.* Boston, 1917. Reprint, Boston, 1942.
A path-breaking series of biographical sketches, including one on Longstreet, another on Stuart, and a final chapter on the Battle of Gettysburg.

15.

———. *Lee the American.* Boston, 1912. Reprint (revised), Boston, 1927.
A sympathetic and insightful study of Lee's character and psychology as a selfless soldier worthy of wide admiration.

16.
Bridges, Leonard Hal. *Lee's Maverick General: Daniel Harvey Hill.* New York, 1961. Reprint, with introduction by Gary W. Gallagher, Lincoln NE, 1991.
An accurate portrait of one of Lee's most troublesome division commanders.

17.
Brock, Robert A., ed. *Gen. Robert Edward Lee: Soldier, Citizen, and Christian Patriot.* Richmond, 1897.
A voluminous collection of woefully neglected essays covering Lee's entire life, several of which are written by officers who served under Lee during the war.

18.
Burne, Alfred H. *Lee, Grant and Sherman, The Last Phase: A Study in Leadership in the '64–65 Campaign.* Aldershot, England, 1938. Reprint, New York, 1939.
An overlooked, although somewhat unorthodox, study of the Civil War's greatest commanders, graced with an introduction by Douglas Southall Freeman.

19.
[Caffey, Thomas E.] *Battle-fields of the South, from Bull Run to Fredericksburg; with Sketches of Confederate Commanders, and Gossip of the Camps. By an English Combatant.* 2 vols. London, 1863. Reprint, New York, 1864. Reprint, Alexandria VA, 1984.
One of the most quotable accounts by a foreigner who observed Lee and his officers personally.

20.
Calkins, Christopher M. *The Battles of Appomattox Station and Appomattox Court House, April 8–9, 1865.* Lynchburg VA, 1987.
A straightforward scholarly account of Lee's final campaign.

21.
———. *The Final Bivouac: The Surrender Parade at Appomattox and the Disbanding of the Armies, April 10–May 20, 1865.* Lynchburg VA, 1988.
A detailed description of the collapse and surrender of Lee's once magnificent army.

22.
Casdorph, Paul D. *Lee and Jackson: Confederate Chieftains.* New York, 1992.

An attempt to explain the unlikely chemistry that bonded two proud men possessing apparently differing personalities.

23.
Chambers, Lenoir. *Stonewall Jackson.* 2 vols. New York, 1959. Reprint, Wilmington NC, 1988.
The fullest, most scholarly biography to date of Lee's uniquely eccentric, utterly matchless corps commander.

24.
Clark, Walter, ed. *Histories of the Several Regiments and Battalions from North Carolina, in the Great War of 1861–'65.* 5 vols. Raleigh, 1901. Reprint, Wendell NC, 1982. Reprint, Wilmington NC, 1991.
A treasure trove of information on the North Carolinians in Lee's army, arguably his most important source of manpower, with much oblique commentary on Lee's generalship.

25.
Coddington, Edwin B. *The Gettysburg Campaign: A Study in Command.* New York, 1968. Reprint, with introduction by Jacob E. Cooke, Dayton OH, 1979.
A massive, erudite, thoroughly enjoyable narrative of Lee's pivotal campaign; still the best single work on the subject.

26.
Connelly, Thomas L. *The Marble Man: Robert E. Lee and His Image in American Society.* New York, 1977. Reprint, Baton Rouge, 1978.
A sometimes outrageous but often original and persuasive critical study, more useful for its modernistic attack on the Lee mystique than for its fadish attempt to psychoanalyze the man.

27.
Connelly, Thomas L., and Archer Jones. *The Politics of Command: Factions and Ideas in Confederate Strategy.* Baton Rouge, 1973. Reprint, Baton Rouge, 1982.
An innovative and intently argued scholarly analysis of the entire sweep of Confederate military policy, including much on Lee's ideas and actions.

28.
Connelly, Thomas L., and Barbara Bellows. *God and General Longstreet: The Lost Cause and the Southern Mind.* Baton Rouge, 1982.
A strong indictment of former Confederates—especially Virginians who served with Lee—blaming them for constructing the mythic Lost Cause for their own selfish purposes.

29.
Cooke, John Esten. *A Life of Gen. Robert E. Lee.* New York, 1871. Reprint, New York, 1887. Reprint titled *Robert E. Lee*, New York, 1899.
A loosely woven biography whose potency springs from many incidents recounted from personal knowledge of Lee and his officers.

30.
———. *Wearing of the Gray: Being Personal Portraits, Scenes and Adventures of the War.* New York, 1867. Reprint, with introduction by Philip Van Doren Stern, Bloomington IN, 1959. Reprint, New York, 1968. Reprint, Gaithersburg MD, 1988.
A potpourri of stories and vignettes told with literary flourish by one of Jeb Stuart's staff officers; its best portions describe Stuart, Wade Hampton, Stonewall Jackson, John S. Mosby, Turner Ashby, P. G. T. Beauregard, Jubal A. Early, and other colorful personalities, as well as Lee himself. Cooke's wartime letters, titled *Outlines from the Outpost*, edited by Richard B. Harwell, Chicago, 1961, compliment this volume.

31.
Current, William N., ed. *Encyclopedia of the Confederacy.* 4 vols. New York, 1993.
A gigantic scholarly effort presenting a wide range of articles by leading authorities on all major campaigns and battles; contains much basic information on Lee, his generals, and his army, plus bibliographies of the best books and articles on each subject.

32.
Dabney, Robert L. *Life and Campaigns of Lieut.-Gen. Thomas J. Jackson.* 2 vols. London, 1864–66. Reprint, New York, 1866. Reprint, Harrisonburg VA, 1976 and 1988.
The first full biography of Lee's indispensable corps commander, authored by a devout clergyman and staff officer who probably knew and understood Jackson better than any other man.

33.
Davis, Burke. *Gray Fox: Robert E. Lee and the Civil War.* New York, 1956. Reprint, New York, 1981. Reprint, New York, 1993.
One of the most flattering evaluations of Lee the commander; a good book for young readers.

34.
———. *To Appomattox: Nine April Days, 1865.* New York, 1959.
A popular account of the Appomattox campaign.

35.
Davis, Jefferson. *The Papers of Jefferson Davis.* Ed. Lynda L. Crist and Mary S. Dix. Vol. 7: 1861 [and] vol. 8: 1862. Baton Rouge, 1992 [and] 1994.
The latest volumes in an ongoing series that has achieved status as one of the most impressive scholarly editions of collected letters and documents on any Civil War figure. Jefferson Davis, *Jefferson Davis Constitutionalist: His Letters, Papers, and Speeches*, ed. Dunbar Rowland, 10 vols. (Jackson: Mississippi Department of Archives and History, 1923) includes letters relating to Lee's Confederate service that are not printed in full in *The Papers of Jefferson Davis.*

36.
———. *The Rise and Fall of the Confederate Government.* 2 vols. New York, 1881. Reprint, Richmond, 1938. Reprint, New York, 1988. Reprint, with foreword by James M. McPherson, New York, 1990.
President Davis's legalistic defence of the Confederacy's claims to nationhood and his own part in its political and military struggle, with some important allusions to his particularly successful reliance on Lee's genius.

37.
Davis, Jefferson, and Alexander H. Stephens. *Robert E. Lee.* Ed. Harold B. Simpson. Hillsboro TX, 1966 and 1983.
Brief anecdotal estimations of Lee's strength of character and martial acumen as only Davis and Stephens could have known them.

38.
Davis, Varina Howell. *Jefferson Davis, Ex-President of the Confederate States of America: A Memoir by His Wife.* 2 vols. New York, 1890. Reprint, with introduction by Craig L. Symonds, Baltimore, 1990.
A characteristically opinionated account from the unique perspective of the first lady of the Confederacy, with some revealing commentary on Lee's dealing with President Davis.

39.
Davis, William C. *Breckinridge: Stateman, Soldier, Symbol.* Baton Rouge, 1974. Reprint, Baton Rouge, 1992.
A superb biography of a soldier-statesman who served admirably in the Army of Tennessee before going east to fight in Virginia; in early 1865 he became secretary of war, dealing closely with Lee during the Confederacy's final chaotic months.

40.
———. *Jefferson Davis: The Man and His Hour.* New York, 1991.
A splendid biography filled with insight into Lee's unique ability to work well with the otherwise testy Confederate chief executive.

41.
Davis, William C., ed. *The Confederate General.* 6 vols. Harrisburg PA, 1991.
The best collection of scholarly biographical sketches and photographs of the entire roster of Confederate general officers.

42.
———. *The Image of War: 1861–1865.* 6 vols. New York, 1981–1984.
The greatest photographic history of the Civil War; an exquisite presentation of more than four thousand images, most of them previously unpublished, with essays by leading authorities; includes many excellent photographs of Lee, the Army of Northern Virginia's officers and men, and their fields of operations.

43.
de Butts, Mary Custis Lee, ed. *Growing Up in the 1850s: The Journal of Agnes Lee.* Chapel Hill NC, 1984.
A remarkable compilation and editing of the personal journal of one of Lee's daughters, with some of Lee's antebellum letters included as well.

44.
Douglas, Henry Kyd. *I Rode with Stonewall.* Chapel Hill NC, 1940. Reprinted numerous times by the publisher.
The single most quotable source on Jackson, the result of youthful impressions forever captured in the author's mind (although sometimes with minor inaccuracies), and vividly conveyed.

45.
Dowdey, Clifford. *Death of a Nation: The Story of Lee and His Men at Gettysburg.* New York, 1958. Reprint, Baltimore, 1988 and 1992. Reprint, Lincoln NE, 1993.
Although probably the weakest of Dowdey's several books, it contains a useful annotated bibliography.

46.
———. *Lee.* Boston, 1965. Reprint, Gettysburg, 1991.
A compelling, laudatory one-volume biography too often caught in the shadow of Douglas Southall Freeman's *R. E. Lee.*

47.
———. *Lee's Last Campaign: The Story of Lee and his Men against Grant, 1864.* Boston, 1960. Reprint, Wilmington NC, 1988. Reprint, with introduction by Robert K. Krick, Lincoln NE, 1993.
A solid account of the horrific campaign that began with the Wilderness and resulted in the siege of Petersburg.

48.
———. *The Seven Days: The Emergence of Lee.* Boston, 1964. Reprint, New York, 1978. Reprint, Wilmington NC, 1988. Reprint, with introduction by Robert K. Krick, Lincoln NE, 1993.
Although dated in some respects, a superbly crafted narrative of the entire campaign, placing Lee in the forefront where he belongs.

49.
Early, Jubal A. *The Campaigns of Gen. Robert E. Lee. An Address by Lieut. General Jubal A. Early, before Washington and Lee University, January 19th, 1872.* Baltimore, 1872.
The takeoff point for Lee's status as a Lost Cause demigod, delivered by the utterly irascible, always calculating, largely effective officer Lee enjoyed calling affectionately "my bad old man."

50.
———. *Lieutenant General Jubal Anderson Early: Autobiographical Sketches and Narrative of the War Between the States.* Philadelphia, 1912. Reprint, titled *War Memoirs*, with introduction by Frank E. Vandiver, Bloomington IN, 1960. Reprint, with original title, with introduction by Gary W. Gallagher, Wilmington NC, 1989, and New York, 1991. Reprint, with introduction by Craig M. Symonds, Baltimore, 1989.
The slightly slanted but extremely detailed and forceful memoirs of the gifted, stubborn, outspoken Early.

51.
Eckenrode, H. J., and Bryan Conrad. *James Longstreet: Lee's War Horse.* Chapel Hill NC, 1936. Reprint, with introduction by Gary W. Gallagher, Chapel Hill, 1986.
A highly critical portrait of the headstrong Longstreet, centering on his warm but strained relationship with Lee.

52.
Eckert, Ralph L. *John Brown Gordon: Soldier, Southerner, American.* Baton Rouge, 1989.

A fine scholarly biography of one of Lee's best officers, a Georgian who rose to corps command despite his lack of West Point training.

53.
Elliott, Joseph C. *Lieutenant General Richard Heron Anderson: Lee's Noble Soldier.* Dayton OH, 1985.
The best biography of Anderson, perhaps Lee's most underrated corps commander.

54.
Evans, Clement A., ed. *Confederate Military History.* 13 vols. Atlanta, 1899. Reprint of "extended edition," 17 vols. and 2-vol. index, Wilmington NC, 1987–89.
Especially valuable for Jedediah Hotchkiss's 692-page volume on Virginia, as well as for the excellent biographical sketches of officers of nearly all grades in the volumes of the "extended edition."

55.
Ewell, Richard Stoddert. *The Making of a Soldier: Letters of General R. S. Ewell.* Ed. Percy G. Hamlin. Richmond, 1935. For reprint, see item 82 below.
Includes some of Ewell's private wartime letters.

56.
Farwell, Byron. *Stonewall: A Biography of General Thomas J. Jackson.* New York, 1992.
A well-written, full-length biography, yet limited by its exclusive reliance on published sources.

57.
Foote, Shelby. *The Civil War: A Narrative.* 3 vols. New York, 1958–74. Reprinted numerous times by the publisher.
An American epic of vast popularity, sensitively crafted from a Southern slant; several of its most memorable passages focus on Lee and his army.

58.
Foster, Gaines M. *Ghosts of the Confederacy: Defeat, the Lost Cause, and the Emergence of the New South.* New York, 1987.
A fine scholarly study, placing the Lost Cause in its rich, uniquely Southern social and political setting.

59.
Frassanito, William A. *Antietam: The Photographic Legacy of America's Bloodiest Day.* New York, 1978.

A remarkable comparison of wartime and modern photographic images of the bloody battlefield in Maryland.

60.
———. *Gettysburg: A Journey in Time.* New York, 1975.
A landmark in Civil War historical studies; the first example of Frassanito's technique of haunting juxtaposition between original and modern battlefield photographs.

61.
———. *Grant and Lee: The Virginia Campaigns, 1864–1865.* New York, 1986.
The most extensive of the author's studies of the photographic legacy of the greatest battles fought by the Army of Northern Virginia.

62.
Freeman, Douglas Southall. *Lee's Lieutenants: A Study in Command.* 3 vols. New York, 1942–44. Reprinted numerous times by the publisher.
The perfect complement to Freeman's monumental biography, as valuable for its penetrating character studies of Lee's officers as for its analysis of his varyingly successful relationships with them.

63.
———. *R. E. Lee: A Biography.* 4 vols. New York, 1934–35. Reprinted numerous times by the publisher.
One of the greatest of all American biographies—the vital starting point for any reader—limited not so much by Freeman's generous admiration as by his determination to confine Lee to a "fog of battle" that presents little context for involving the thoughts and actions of his enemies.

64.
Fremantle, Sir Arthur James Lyon. *Three Months in the Southern States: April–June, 1863.* Edinburgh and London, 1863. Reprint, New York, 1864. Reprint titled *The Fremantle Diary*, edited by Walter Lord, Boston, 1954. Reprint, Alexandria VA, 1984. Reprint, with introduction by Gary W. Gallagher, Lincoln NE, 1991.
The best memoir by a foreigner in the Confederacy, including a thrilling account of Gettysburg, with some truly memorable personal encounters with Lee and his generals.

65.
Fuller, J. F. C. *Grant and Lee: A Study in Personality and Generalship.* London, 1933. Reprint, Bloomington IN, 1957. Reprint, Bloomington, 1982.

A classic comparison that rates Grant the superior commander for his expansive realization of the political dimension inherently necessary in military strategy in order for a democratic society to wage a long and costly war; foreshadows modern critics who fault Lee's strategic vision.

66.
Furgurson, Ernest B. *Chancellorsville, 1863: The Souls of the Brave.* New York, 1992.
A popular, highly readable account of the battle in which Lee solidified his reputation for tactical brilliance.

67.
Gallagher, Gary W. *Stephen Dodson Ramseur: Lee's Gallant General.* Chapel Hill NC, 1985.
An excellent full biography—based on a substantial body of private letters—of Lee's splendid young division commander who died at Cedar Creek in 1864.

68.
Gallagher, Gary W. ed., *Antietam: Essays on the 1862 Maryland Campaign.* Kent OH, 1989.
Includes introductory and concluding essays by Gallagher, and an essay by Robert K. Krick criticizing Lee's decision to strike northward into Maryland.

69.
———. *The First Day at Gettysburg: Essays on Confederate and Union Leadership.* Kent OH, 1992.
Includes an essay by Alan T. Nolan on Lee, another by Gallagher on A. P. Hill and Richard Ewell, and a concluding essay by Robert K. Krick on the "failures" of Lee's brigade commanders.

70.
———. *The Fredericksburg Campaign: Decision on the Rappahannock.* Chapel Hill NC, 1995.
A fine group of scholarly essays on the conduct and consequences of the battle that saw Lee make excellent use of defensive superiority.

71.
———. *The Second Day at Gettysburg: Essays on Confederate and Union Leadership.* Kent OH, 1993.
Highlighted by Gallagher's essay on Lee and Krick's essay on Longstreet.

72.
———. *The Third Day at Gettysburg and Beyond.* Chapel Hill NC, 1994.
The concluding volume in the outstanding series on Gettysburg; includes William Garrett Piston's analysis of the Lee-Longstreet debate over Confederate tactics on 3 July, 1863.

73.
Georg, Kathleen R., and John W. Busey. *Nothing But Glory: Pickett's Division at Gettysburg.* Hightstown NJ, 1987. Reprint (revised), Gettysburg, 1993.
A kaleidoscopic account based on exhaustive research of primary sources.

74.
Glatthaar, Joseph T. *Partners in Command: The Relationships between Leaders in the Civil War.* New York, 1993.
Includes a pungent chapter titled "Lee, Jackson, and Confederate Success in the East."

75.
Gordon, John B. *Reminiscences of the Civil War.* New York, 1903. Reprint, Alexandria VA, 1981. Reprint, with introduction by Ralph L. Eckert, Baton Rouge, 1993.
Self-serving and superficial in many respects, yet permanently valuable for Gordon's telling of his rise to stature as one of Lee's best field commanders.

76.
Goree, Thomas Jewett. *The Thomas Jewett Goree Letters. Vol. I: The Civil War Correspondence.* Ed. Langston J. Goree. Bryan TX, 1981. Reprint titled *Longstreet's Aide: The Civil War Letters of Major Thomas J. Goree*, edited by Thomas W. Cutrer, Charlottesville VA, 1995.
The extremely rich correspondence of one of Longstreet's key staff officers; a gold mine of inside information on Lee and his officers.

77.
Gorgas, Josiah. *The Civil War Diary of Josiah Gorgas.* Ed. Frank E. Vandiver. University AL, 1947.
A jewel of a primary source, providing the personal observations and actions of the Confederacy's chief of ordnance, a wizard of resourcefulness who kept Lee's army supplied with a continual stream of munitions.

78.

Grant, Ulysses S. *Personal Memoirs of U. S. Grant.* 2 vols. New York, 1885–86. Reprint, edited by E. B. Long, 2 vols. in 1, New York, 1952. Reprint, with introduction by William S. McFeely, 2 vols. in 1, New York, 1982.

A straightforward and honest account by Lee's most challenging adversary.

79.

Griffith, Paddy. *Battle Tactics of the Civil War.* New Haven, 1989.

A scholarly work, crucial to an understanding of the difficult military context in which Lee operated, which argues that Civil War commanders were the last to rely on a Napoleonic-style of armed conflict.

80.

Grimes, Bryan. *Extracts of Letters of Major-Gen'l Bryan Grimes to His Wife, Written While in Active Service in the Army of Northern Virginia. Together with Some Personal Recollections of the War, Written by Him after Its Close, etc.* Comp. Pulaski Cowper. Raleigh, 1883. Reprint, Raleigh, 1884. Reprint, with introduction by Gary G. Gallagher, Wilmington NC, 1986.

A brief but sensitive source on one of Lee's best generals; descriptive of the Appomattox campaign.

81.

Hagerman, Edward. *The American Civil War and the Origins of Modern Warfare: Ideas, Organization, and Field Command.* Bloomington IN, 1988.

A sophisticated counterbalance to Paddy Griffith, *Battle Tactics of the Civil War*, asserting that Lee and other successful commanders fought an essentially modern mode of warfare by relying increasingly on more firepower, trench fortifications, and strategic maneuvering on a grand scale.

82.

Hamlin, Percy G. *"Old Bald Head" (General R. S. Ewell): The Portrait of a Soldier.* Strasburg VA, 1940. Reprint, combined with Ewell's *The Making of a Soldier*, with introduction by Gary W. Gallagher, Gaithersburg MD, 1988.

An accurate biography of the unlucky, indecisive, and often unwell officer who replaced Stonewall Jackson as commander of Lee's Second Corps.

83.
Hartwig, D. Scott. *The Battle of Antietam and the Maryland Campaign of 1862: A Bibliography.* Westport CT, 1990.
A useful list of primary and secondary publications, although not as comprehensive as Richard Sauers's work on Gettysburg.

84.
Hassler, Warren W., Jr. *Crisis at the Crossroads: The First Day at Gettysburg.* University AL, 1970. Reprint, Gaithersburg MD, 1986.
A good scholarly summary of Gettysburg's strangely fateful first day.

85.
Hassler, William W. *A. P. Hill: Lee's Forgotten General.* Richmond, 1957. Reprint (revised), Richmond, 1962. Reprint, Chapel Hill NC, 1984.
A creditable, well-written portrait of Hill, a relatively neglected figure in Lee's orbit of high-ranking officers up until the time this book was first published.

86.
Hattaway, Herman, and Archer Jones. *How the North Won: A Military History of the Civil War.* Urbana IL, 1983.
A sweeping analysis of the strategy and tactics employed by the Union and Confederacy alike, detailed in its arguments and judicious in its conclusions, but critical of Lee as an overall strategist when compared to Grant.

87.
Henderson, G. F. R. *The Civil War, A Soldier's View: A Collection of Civil War Writings.* Ed. Jay Luvaas. Chicago, 1958. Reprint, Chicago, 1968.
A series of collected works, including a complete reprint of the author's *The Campaign of Fredericksburg* (London, 1886), plus shorter pieces on Gettysburg and the Wilderness.

88.
———. *Stonewall Jackson and the American Civil War.* 2 vols. London, 1898. Reprint, 2 vols. in 1, New York, 1949. Reprint, with introduction by Thomas L. Connelly, New York, 1988.
After nearly a century, a truly classic military study that provides the clearest analysis of Jackson's command decisions and actions, despite the author's intense admiration for his subject.

89.
Hennessy, John J. *Return to Bull Run: The Campaign and Battle of Second Manassas.* New York, 1993.

The definitive account of the battle that many consider Lee's most brilliant victory; based on research into every conceivable source.

90.
Heth, Henry. *The Memoirs of Henry Heth.* Ed. James L. Morrison Jr. Westport CT, 1974.
The extensive recollections of one of Lee's most underrated subordinates—a talented, often rash division commander who gravitated to the thick of the fighting throughout the war.

91.
Hood, John Bell. *Advance and Retreat: Personal Experiences in the United States and Confederate States Armies.* New Orleans, 1880. Reprint, edited by Richard N. Current, Bloomington IN 1959. Reprint, with introduction by Richard M. McMurry, New York, 1993.
Apologetic but revealing for its arguments by the meteoric young officer whose misdirected imitation of Lee's audacity ended in disaster; especially good on the first two years of the war.

92.
Horn, Stanley F., ed. *The Robert E. Lee Reader.* New York, 1949.
A Lee omnibus comprising extracts from letters and other firsthand sources, most of them previously published.

93.
Hotchkiss, Jedediah. *Make Me a Map of the Valley: The Civil War Journal of Stonewall Jackson's Topographer.* Ed. Archie P. McDonald. Dallas, 1973. Reprint, Fort Worth, 1988.
The wartime journal of Jedediah Hotchkiss; a primary source whose odd title almost belies its excellence.

94.
Hotchkiss, Jedediah, and William Allan. *The Battle-fields of Virginia: Chancellorsville, Embracing the Operations of the Army of Northern Virginia.* New York, 1867. Reprint, Baltimore, 1985.
A brief study, important because the authors had been on the scene as participants, more so because of Hotchkiss's peerless talent as Jackson's cartographer.

95.
Howard, McHenry. *Recollections of a Maryland Confederate Soldier and Staff Officer under Johnston and Lee.* Baltimore, 1914. Reprint, with introduction by James I. Robertson Jr., Dayton OH, 1975.
A vital source on Jackson's corps, the author having served on the staffs of Charles S. Winder, Isaac R. Trimble, and George H. Steuart.

96.
Hubbell, John T., ed. *Battles Lost and Won: Essays from Civil War History.* Westport CT, 1975.
Contains Thomas L. Connelly's essay, "Robert E. Lee and the Western Confederacy: A Criticism of Lee's Strategic Ability"; and Albert Castel's retort, "The Historian and the General: Thomas L. Connelly vs. Robert E. Lee.'

97.
Jackson, Mary Anna. *Life and Letters of General Thomas J. Jackson (Stonewall Jackson).* New York, 1892. Reprint (revised), titled *Memoirs of Stonewall Jackson*, Louisville KY 1895. Reprint, with introduction by Lowell Reidenbaugh, Dayton OH, 1976.
Notable for its intimate letters and revealing commentary by Jackson's wife.

98.
Johnson, Robert Underwood, and Clarence Clough Buel, eds. *Battles and Leaders of the Civil War.* 4 vols. New York, 1884–88. Reprinted numerous times by various publishers.
An unsurpassed, often magical assemblage of largely evenhanded articles by former Confederate and Union officers as well as some common soldiers, studded throughout with the finest Civil War combat illustrations ever published; with heavy coverage of Lee and his campaigns.

99.
Johnston, Angus James, II. *Virginia Railroads in the Civil War.* Chapel Hill NC, 1961.
Crucial for an understanding of communications, supply, and transportation in the strategic context of the entire Eastern Theater of operations.

100.
Johnston, Joseph E. *Narrative of Military Operations, Directed, during the Late War Between the States, by Joseph E. Johnston, General, C.S.A.* New York, 1874. Reprint, with introduction by Frank E. Vandiver, Bloomington IN, 1959. Reprint, New York, 1990.
The personal memoirs of one of Lee's peers in the Confederate army's early high command, a sometime rival who soon proved as despicable to Jefferson Davis as Lee proved indispensable.

101.
Jones, Archer. *Civil War Command and Strategy: The Process of Victory and Defeat.* New York, 1991.
The culmination of decades of research, thinking, and writing about Civil War strategy and tactics, by one of the few scholars capable of taking a tempered critical look at Lee the commander.

102.
Jones, J. William. *Christ in the Camp; Or Religion in Lee's Army.* Richmond, 1887. Reprint, Harrisonburg VA, 1986.
Still the most compelling factual account, despite its potent evangelical flavor, with frequent commentary on the centrality of Lee's spiritual convictions.

103.
———. *Life and Letters of Robert Edward Lee, Soldier and Man.* New York, 1906. Reprint, Harrisonburg VA, 1986.
A haphazard compilation of many of Lee's letters as well as stories about Lee, by a clergyman whose personal devotion and friendship to the general enhances its value.

104.
———. *Personal Reminiscences, Anecdotes, and Letters of Gen. Robert E. Lee.* New York, 1874. Reprint, New York, 1875 and 1876. Reprint, Baton Rouge, 1990.
Useful for its many letters and conversational encounters between Lee and his comrades, but only if consulted carefully.

105.
Jones, J. William, ed. *Army of Northern Virginia Memorial Volume.* Richmond, 1880. Reprint, with introduction by James I. Robertson Jr., Dayton OH, 1976.
A compilation of stirring speeches by some of Lee's best officers, including Jubal A. Early, John W. Daniel, Fitzhugh Lee, Henry A. Wise, and John B. Gordon, with many interesting details of their roles in the army's campaigns.

106.
Jones, J. William, et al., eds. *Southern Historical Society Papers.* 52 vols. and index. Richmond, 1876–1959. Reprinted several times by various publishers.
Along with the *Official Records*, the most important source of primary material on the Army of Northern Virginia; filled with superb postwar reminiscences and letters by former Confederates.

107.
Jones, John B. *A Rebel War Clerk's Diary at the Confederate States Capital.* 2 vols. Philadelphia, 1866. Reprint, edited by Howard Swiggett, 2 vols., New York, 1935. Reprint (condensed), ed. Earl Schenck Miers, 2 vols. in 1, New York, 1958. Reprint, 2 vols., Alexandria VA, 1982. Reprint (Miers's edition), Baton Rouge, 1991.
An immensely important firsthand account of Jefferson Davis's actions as Confederate commander-in-chief and Lee's ultimate effectiveness militarily and politically.

108.
Kean, Robert Garlick Hill. *Inside the Confederate Government: The Diary of Robert Garlick Kean, Head of the Bureau of War.* Ed. Edward Younger. New York, 1957. Reprint, Baton Rouge, 1993.
A good complement to John B. Jones's firsthand account; this book chronicles the turmoil in the Confederate government and high command.

109.
Klein, Maury N. *Edward Porter Alexander.* Athens GA, 1971.
A good biography that does justice to Lee's heady young artillery commander.

110.
Krick, Robert K. *Lee's Colonels: A Biographical Register of the Field Officers of the Army of Northern Virginia.* Dayton OH, 1979. 4th edition (revised), Dayton OH, 1992.
An astonishing compilation of biographical and military information on the middle echelon of Lee's remarkable officer corps, the result of relentless research by the leading expert on all components of the Army of Northern Virginia and its operations.

111.
Lee, Fitzhugh. *General Lee.* New York, 1894. Reprint, New York, 1904. Reprint, with introduction by Gary W. Gallagher, Wilmington NC, 1989, and New York, 1994.
A biography valuable mainly for the many extracts from Lee's private letters but also something of a capstone to the anti-Longstreet argument, written by the talented cavalry commander who also happened to be General Lee's nephew.

112.
Lee, Robert Edward. *Lee's Dispatches: Unpublished Letters of General Robert E. Lee, C.S.A. to Jefferson Davis and the War Department . . .*

1862–1865. Ed. Douglas Southall Freeman. New York, 1915. Reprint, with additional dispatches included and foreword by Grady McWhiney, New York, 1957.
A crucial edition of primary sources necessary for an appreciation of Lee's military decision making and his influence on President Davis.

113.
———. *The Wartime Papers of R. E. Lee.* Ed. Clifford Dowdey and Louis H. Manarin. Boston, 1961. Reprint, New York, 1987.
An enviable compilation of Lee's letters and telegrams, free of too many editorial notes, thus allowing the documents to speak for themselves.

114.
Lee, Robert Edward [Jr.]. *Recollections and Letters of General Robert E. Lee, by His Son.* New York, 1904. Reprint (revised), with introduction by Gamaliel Bradford, New York, 1924. Reprint titled *My Father, General Lee,* with introduction by Philip Van Doren Stern, Garden City NY, 1960. Reprint, with introduction by Gary W. Gallagher, Wilmington NC, 1988.
The best compilation of Lee's family letters and most personal reflections, especially during the war and afterward, edited and commented upon by his son.

115.
Lee, Susan P. *Memoirs of William Nelson Pendleton, D.D. . . . Chief of Artillery, Army of Northern Virginia.* Philadelphia, 1893. Reprint, Harrisonburg VA, 1991.
The detailed, although rather dry, reminiscences of an aging officer who by all accounts was a far better clergyman than he was a military man.

116.
Long, Armistead L., and Marcus J. Wright, eds. *Memoirs of Robert E. Lee: His Military and Personal History.* Philadelphia, 1886. Reprint, New York, 1887. Reprint, Secaucus NJ, 1983 and 1992.
Somewhat disjointed, often shallow and incorrect in its facts, but still filled with telling stories of Lee in camp and battle; Long was one of Lee's closest staff officers.

117.
Longstreet, Helen D. *Lee and Longstreet at High Tide: Gettysburg in the Light of the Official Records.* Gainesville GA, 1904. Reprint, Wilmington NC, 1989.

A self-conscious apology for husband James Longstreet against his army of postwar detractors.

118.

Longstreet, James. *From Manassas to Appomattox: Memoirs of the Civil War in America.* Philadelphia, 1896. Reprint, edited by James I. Robertson Jr., Bloomington IN, 1960. Reprint, with introduction by Jeffry D. Wert, New York, 1992.

The important personal account by Lee's argumentative corps commander, especially vital to an understanding of his fiery resentment toward his many postwar critics.

119.

Luvaas, Jay, and Harold W. Nelson, eds. *The U.S. Army War College Guide to the Battle of Antietam: The Maryland Campaign of 1862.* Carlisle PA, 1987.

A handy reference, valuable for its numerous maps and succinct commentary.

120.

———. *The U.S. Army War College Guide to the Battle of Gettysburg.* Carlisle PA, 1986. Reprint titled *The Gettysburg Guide,* New York, 1987.

A useful summary narrative and guide to detailed maps.

121.

———. *The U.S. Army War College Guide to the Battles of Chancellorsville and Fredericksburg.* Carlisle PA, 1988. Reprint, New York, 1989.

A basic battlefield guide together with fairly good maps, covering two of Lee's greatest victories.

122.

McCabe, James D., Jr. *Life and Campaigns of General Robert E. Lee.* New York, 1867.

An early study valuable mainly for quotations from contemporary news accounts and statements by officers close to Lee.

123.

McClellan, Henry B. *The Life and Campaigns of Maj. General J. E. B. Stuart.* New York, 1885. Reprint titled *I Rode with Jeb Stuart*, with introduction by Burke Davis, Bloomington IN, 1958. Reprint, New York, 1969. Reprint, Dayton OH, 1987.

The best work by an officer who served with Stuart.

124.
[McClure, Alexander K., ed.] *The Annals of the War, Written by Leading Participants North and South.* Philadelphia, 1879. Reprint, Dayton OH, 1988. Reprint, with introduction by Gary W. Gallagher, New York, 1994.
An outstanding collection of essays by Confederate and Union officers, several of whom served with or fought against Lee.

125.
McKim, Randolph Harrison. *The Soul of Lee, by One of His Soldiers.* New York, 1918.
Written by a talented staff officer and chaplain who enjoyed the opportunity to observe Lee fairly often during the war.

126.
McKinney, Tim. *Robert E. Lee at Sewell Mountain: The West Virginia Campaign.* Charleston WV, 1990.
A thorough description of Lee's early failure culminating at Cheat Mountain in September 1861.

127.
McMurry, Richard M. *John Bell Hood and the War for Southern Independence.* Lexington KY, 1982. Reprint, Lincoln NE, 1991.
An outstanding critical biography of the young officer who sought most brazenly to duplicate Lee's charismatic audacity.

128.
———. *Two Great Rebel Armies: An Essay in Confederate Military History.* Chapel Hill NC, 1989.
A creative argument for the Army of Northern Virginia's superiority in leadership and fighting ability as compared to the Army of Tennessee.

129.
McWhiney, Grady, ed. *Grant, Lee, Lincoln and the Radicals: Essays on Civil War Leadership.* Evanston IL, 1964. Reprint, New York, 1966.
Contains Charles P. Roland's seminal essay, "The Generalship of Robert E. Lee."

130.
McWhiney, Grady, and Perry D. Jamieson. *Attack and Die: Civil War Military Tactics and the Southern Heritage.* University AL, 1982.
One of the most controversial yet scholarly books on the military side of the Civil War, concentrating on the frequent use of costly frontal assaults by Southern commanders.

131.
Mapp, Alf J., Jr. *Frock Coats and Epaulets.* New York, 1963.
Includes a well-written ninety-page essay titled "Robert E. Lee: Man of Disciplined Fire."

132.
Marshall, Charles. *An Aide-de-Camp of Lee: Being the Papers of Colonel Charles Marshall . . . on the Staff of Robert E. Lee, 1861–1865.* Ed. Sir Frederick Maurice. Boston, 1927.
An essential primary source on Lee in his role as any army organizer, although vague in some details.

133.
Matter, William D. *If It Takes All Summer: The Battle of Spotsylvania.* Chapel Hill NC, 1988.
An exhaustive description of the desperately bloody fighting between Lee's and Grant's veteran armies.

134.
Maurice, Sir Frederick. *Robert E. Lee, the Soldier.* Boston, 1925. Reprint, New York, ca. 1976.
A competent study of Lee's abilities as a commander, interestingly juxtaposed to the awful combat of the First World War, from the viewpoint of an eminent British military expert.

135.
Meredith, Roy. *The Face of Robert E. Lee in Life and in Legend.* New York, 1947. Reprint, New York, 1981.
Still the prime reference on Lee in portraiture and photographs, begging to be revised and greatly expanded.

136.
Military Historical Society of Massachusetts. *Papers of the Military Historical Society of Massachusetts.* 14 vols. Boston, 1895–1918. Reprint, with index volume, Wilmington NC, 1989–90.
A magnificent collection of essays on various campaigns and battles, especially concerning the Eastern Theater, by scholars and former soldiers, including several who served under Lee, such as William Allan, McHenry Howard, and James Power Smith.

137.
Miller, Francis T., ed. *The Photographic History of the Civil War.* 10 vols. New York, 1911–12. Reprint, 10 vols. in 5, New York, 1957.

A classic, multivolume photographic history of the war, emphasizing the fighting in the East, supported by scores of essays too often neglected, many by former Confederate and Union participants.

138.
Miller, William J. *Mapping for Stonewall: The Civil War Service of Jed Hotchkiss.* Washington DC, 1993.
A fine biographical treatment of Jackson's most vital staff officer, based on a large body of excellent Hotchkiss manuscripts.

139.
Miller, William J., ed. *The Peninsula Campaign of 1862: Yorktown to the Seven Days.* Campbell CA, 1993.
A volume of scholarly essays, notable for Steven W. Woodworth's analysis of Lee and Davis during the Seven Days, and Edwin C. Bearss's account of Stuart's famous "ride around McClellan."

140.
Mosby, John S. *The Memoirs of Colonel John S. Mosby.* Ed. Charles Wells Russell. Boston, 1917. Reprint, with preface by Virgil Carrington Jones, Bloomington IN, 1959. Reprint, New York, 1968. Reprint, Gaithersburg MD, 1992. Reprint, New York, 1992.
Important primarily because many of Mosby's personal wartime letters appear verbatim, yet otherwise less exciting than the earlier book by the dashing partisan cavalry commander.

141.
———. *Mosby's War Reminiscences, and Stuart's Cavalry Campaigns.* New York, 1887. Reprint, Boston, 1887. Reprint, New York, 1958. Reprint, New York, 1987. Reprint, Rupert ID, 1992.
Based on a series of entertaining lectures by Mosby, whom Lee mentioned in his wartime reports and correspondence more than any other Confederate officer.

142.
———. *Stuart's Cavalry in the Gettysburg Campaign.* New York, 1908. Reprint, Gaithersburg MD, 1987.
The case for Stuart, beginning with the fight at Brandy Station and concluding with the cavalry commander's subsequent conduct—which disappointed Lee so deeply—during the Gettysburg campaign.

143.
Murfin, James V. *The Gleam of Bayonets: The Battle of Antietam and the Maryland Campaign.* New York, 1965. Reprint, Baton Rouge, 1982.

A good rendition of the subject, full of deprecation for McClellan and perhaps too generous toward Lee.

144.
Nagel, Paul C. *The Lees of Virginia: Seven Generations of an American Family.* New York, 1990.
The best modern study of the Lee family, with a heavy emphasis on Lee's personal life as it suffered and endured the hardships of war.

145.
Neely, Mark E., Jr., Harold Holzer, and Gabor S. Borritt. *The Confederate Image: Prints of the Lost Cause.* Chapel Hill NC, 1987.
Enlightening for its interesting explanations of Lee's powerful reputation in the popular art of the South during the war and long afterward.

146.
Nolan, Alan T. *Lee Considered: General Robert E. Lee and Civil War History.* Chapel Hill NC, 1991.
A superb legal brief, one-dimensional and frequently repetitive in its presentation of evidence, making it unquestionably one of the most hard-hitting and provocative works of its kind; a revisionist indictment of Lee's character as well as his generalship.

147.
Osborne, Charles C. *Jubal: The Life and Times of General Jubal A. Early, CSA, Defender of the Lost Cause.* Chapel Hill NC, 1992.
A book whose energy matches its subject, although hardly a full picture of Early's "life and times."

148.
Paret, Peter, ed. *Makers of Modern Strategy from Machiavelli to the Nuclear Age.* Princeton NJ, 1986.
Contains Russell F. Weigley's essay "American Strategy from Its Beginnings to the First World War," a brief summary that includes some cogent conclusions about Lee as a military strategist.

149.
Pfanz, Harry W. *Gettysburg: Culp's Hill and Cemetery Hill.* Chapel Hill NC, 1994.
A thoroughly researched and detailed account of the three days of fighting along the northern end of Lee's bloodiest battlefield.

150.
———. *Gettysburg: The Second Day.* Chapel Hill NC, 1987.

A definitive scholarly study of the action on the Confederate right that lasted most of the second day at Gettysburg, representing Lee's best tactical efforts to win the battle.

151.
Piston, William Garrett. *Lee's Tarnished Lieutenant: James Longstreet and His Place in Southern History.* Athens GA, 1987.
A successful rehabilitation of Longstreet's reputation, painting him as a victim of the Lost Cause's effusive admiration of Lee.

152.
Pollard, Edward A. *Lee and His Lieutenants; Comprising the Early Life, Public Service, and Campaigns of General Robert E. Lee and His Companions in Arms.* New York, 1867. Reprint titled *The Early Life, Campaigns, and Public Services of Robert E. Lee*, New York, 1870 and 1871.
Important for its immediacy in describing how Lee was viewed by his contemporaries.

153.
Rhea, Gordon C. *The Battle of the Wilderness, May 5–6, 1864.* Baton Rouge, 1994.
The most exhaustive account of the bloody collision between Lee and Grant, critical of both commanders for their operational decisions.

154.
Rhodes, Charles D. *Robert E. Lee, West Pointer.* Richmond, 1932.
Useful as a description of Lee as a cadet and later as superintendent.

155.
Rister, Carl C. *Robert E. Lee in Texas.* Norman OK, 1946.
A fine scholarly account, now much in need of a modern overhaul, describing Lee's fitful antebellum career on the Texas frontier where he resisted Indian incursions in West Texas and grappled with Mexican bandidos along the lower Rio Grande.

156.
Robertson, James I., Jr. *General A. P. Hill: The Story of a Confederate Warrior.* New York, 1987.
One of the half-dozen truly outstanding modern biographies of a Confederate officer, rich in scholarly analysis and just as deftly composed.

157.
———. *Stonewall Jackson: A Biography.* New York, 1996.
A full study by a major historian of the Confederacy and of Lee and his army.

158.
Roland, Charles P. *Reflections on Lee: A Historian's Assessment.* Harrisburg PA, 1995.
A perceptive study by a consummate historian of the South and the Civil War.

159.
Ross, Fitzgerald. *A Visit to the Cities and Camps of the Confederate States.* Edinburgh and London, 1865. Reprint, edited by Richard B. Harwell, Urbana IL, 1958.
An English officer's detailed record of travels during 1863 and 1864, particularly revealing for his close contact with Lee and his subordinates during and after the Gettysburg campaign; filled with trenchant critical observations.

160.
Sanborn, Margaret. *Robert E. Lee: A Portrait, 1807–1861* [and] *Robert E. Lee: The Complete Man, 1861–1870.* 2 vols. Philadelphia, 1966–67.
The result of a somewhat worshipful attitude toward Lee, yet with many telling anecdotes of his personal habits and beliefs.

161.
Sanger, Donald B., and Thomas R. Hay. *James Longstreet: I. Soldier, II. Politician, Officeholder, and Writer.* Baton Rouge, 1952. Reprint, Gloucester MA, 1968.
A sympathetic portrait of the controversial general in whom Lee entrusted great authority.

162.
Sauers, Richard A. *The Gettysburg Campaign, June 3–August 1, 1863: A Comprehensive, Selectively Annotated Bibliography.* Westport CT, 1982.
One of the most nearly definitive bibliographies ever produced on any aspect of American military history, the author having spent years tracking down nearly three thousand books, pamphlets, and magazine and newspaper articles.

163.
Scheibert, Justus. *Sieben Monate in den Rebellen-Staaten, wahrend des Nordamerikanischen Krieges, 1863.* Stettin [Germany], 1868. Reprint in English titled *Seven Months in the Rebel States during the North American War, 1863*, trans. Joseph C. Hayes and ed. William Stanley Hoole, Tuscaloosa AL, 1958.

A perceptive account by a Prussian officer; includes excellent material on Lee during the Gettysburg campaign.

164.
Scott, Winfield. *Memoirs: Written by Himself.* 2 vols. New York, 1867.
Includes a brief but invaluable estimation of Lee's talents as displayed during the Mexican War and subsequent service to the United States Army.

165.
Sears, Stephen W. *Landscape Turned Red: The Battle of Antietam.* New York, 1983.
A masterful use of a wide range of sources, especially common soldiers' writings, on Lee's controversial push across the Potomac and the great slaughter that resulted.

166.
———. *To the Gates of Richmond: The Peninsula Campaign.* New York, 1992.
An extremely full and detailed rendition of the series of battles that first gave Lee status as the Confederacy's greatest general.

167.
Simpson, Harold B. *Cry Comanche: The 2nd U.S. Cavalry in Texas, 1855–1860.* Hillsboro TX, 1979.
The only complete study of the frontier military unit in which Lee served dutifully with several other future Confederate generals, including Albert Sidney Johnston, John Bell Hood, and Edmund Kirby Smith.

168.
Smith, Gene. *Lee and Grant: A Dual Biography.* New York, 1984.
A popular account comparing and contrasting the Civil War's two peerless field commanders.

169.
Snow, William P. *Southern Generals, Who They Are, and What They Have Done.* New York, 1865. Reprint titled *Lee and His Generals,* New York, 1867. Reprint, New York, 1982.
Includes a critical chapter on Lee analyzing his martial abilities from a contemporary standpoint.

170.
Sommers, Richard J. *Richmond Redeemed: The Siege at Petersburg.* Garden City NY, 1981.

A mind-boggling presentation with a superior reputation as an exercise in exacting military detail, although describing only a part of a single movement by Grant's army against the Virginia stronghold Lee held for many months.

171.
Sorrell, G. Moxley. *Recollections of a Confederate Staff Officer.* New York and Washington, 1905. Reprint, ed. Bell I. Wiley, Jackson TN, 1958. Reprint, with introduction by Edwin C. Bearss, Dayton OH, 1978. Reprint, Wilmington NC, 1991. Reprint, with introduction by Neil C. Mangum, New York, 1992.
A pleasant memoir by Longstreet's chief of staff, replete with stories of Lee and his methods of command.

172.
Steere, Edward. *The Wilderness Campaign.* Harrisburg PA, 1960. Reprint, with introduction by John Miller Jr., Gaithersburg MD, 1987. Reprint, with introduction by Robert K. Krick, Mechanicsburg PA, 1994.
A competent modern scholarly work, heavy on intricate tactical details.

173.
Stephens, Robert G., Jr., ed. *Intrepid Warrior: Clement Anselm Evans, Confederate General from Georgia. Life, Letters, and Diaries of the War Years.* Dayton OH, 1992.
A useful biography of a capable brigadier who took over command of John B. Gordon's division; most valuable for the numerous letters printed in full throughout.

174.
Stern, Philip Van Doren. *Robert E. Lee, the Man and the Soldier: A Pictorial Biography.* New York, 1963.
A book devoted to reproducing scores of photographs and contemporary illustrations documenting Lee's entire life.

175.
Stewart, George R. *Pickett's Charge: A Microhistory of the Final Attack at Gettysburg, July 3, 1863.* Boston, 1959. Reprint, Dayton OH, 1980 and 1983.
A gripping account describing the superabundant bravery of the men who responded to Lee's most lamentable tactical decision.

176.
Stiles, Robert. *Four Years under Marse Robert.* New York, 1903. Reprint, with introduction by Robert K. Krick, Dayton OH, 1977 and 1988.

A first-rate artillery officer's account of service in the Army of Northern Virginia, personal in its details and insightful in its descriptions of Lee's actions.

177.
Stuart, James Ewell Brown. *The Letters of Major General James E. B. Stuart.* Comp. Adele H. Mitchell. Carlisle PA, 1990.
A surprisingly good collection of Stuart's private and official letters, although unevenly edited.

178.
Taylor, Walter H. *Four Years with General Lee.* New York, 1877. Reprint with introduction, notes, and index by James I. Robertson Jr., Bloomington IN, 1962.
An argumentative apology for the Army of Northern Virginia's numerical weakness against increasingly heavy odds, yet chocked full of Taylor's letters, stories, and evaluations of Lee's generalship and dauntless character.

179.
———. *General Lee: His Campaigns in Virginia, 1861–1865, with Personal Reminiscences.* Norfolk VA, 1906. Reprint, Dayton OH, 1975. Reprint, with introduction by Gary W. Gallagher, Lincoln NE, 1994.
An expansive complement to Taylor's earlier book, made more valuable by its graphic recollections and mature judgments.

180.
———. *Lee's Adjutant: The Wartime Letters of Colonel Walter Heron Taylor, 1862–1865.* Edited by R. Lockwood Tower. Columbia SC, 1995.
A superb collection of letters filled with insights about Lee and his army, written from the vantage point of a young officer who served at Lee's headquarters throughout the war.

181.
Thomas, Emory M. *Bold Dragoon: The Life of J. E. B. Stuart.* New York, 1986.
One of the best modern biographies of any of Lee's subordinates, exploring fully and accurately Stuart's personal relationship with his commander.

182.
———. *Robert E. Lee: A Biography.* New York, 1995.
A perceptive biography that achieves excellent balance between Lee's personal and professional lives.

183.
Thomason, John W., Jr. *Jeb Stuart.* New York, 1930. Reprint, New York, 1958. Reprint, New York, 1992. Reprint, with introduction by Gary W. Gallagher, Lincoln NE, 1994.
A classic biography full of literary verve and splashed with the characteristic illustrations that have made the author as famed for his artistry as for his writing.

184.
Trudeau, Noah Andre. *Bloody Roads South: The Wilderness to Cold Harbor.* Boston, 1989.
A successful narrative history based on research in a wide range of sources.

185.
———. *The Last Citadel: Petersburg, Virginia, June 1864–April 1865.* New York, 1991. Reprint, Baton Rouge, 1993.
An admirably researched and energetic account of the agonizing siege that enabled Lee to prolong the war nearly a year longer than he might otherwise have done.

186.
Tucker, Glenn. *High Tide at Gettysburg: The Campaign in Pennsylvania.* Indianapolis, 1958. Reprint (revised), Dayton OH, 1973 and 1988.
The most readable account of Lee's dramatic plunge northward and the epic struggle at Gettysburg.

187.
Tucker, Glenn. *Lee and Longstreet at Gettysburg.* Indianapolis, 1968. Reprint, Dayton OH, 1986 and 1989.
A vigorous attempt to exonerate Longstreet for his alleged refusal to attack at dawn on the second day of battle, blaming several of Lee's other subordinates for incompetence and exposing their subsequent efforts to frame Longstreet.

188.
U. S. War Department. *The War of the Rebellion: A Compilation of the Official Records of the Union and Confederate Armies.* 127 vols., index, and atlas. Washington DC, 1880–1901. Reprinted several times by various publishers.
A storehouse of military reports, correspondence, battlefield orders, and official documents comprising the most important basic primary sources available for both the Union and Confederate army operations.

A new series of volumes, titled *Supplement to the Official Records of the Union and Confederate Armies* (Wilmington NC, 1994–), promises to enhance the greatness of the original collection by providing thousands of items overlooked by or unknown to the original compilers.

189.

Vandiver, Frank E. *Mighty Stonewall.* New York, 1957. Reprint, College Station TX, 1988.

A lively yet thoroughly scholarly portrait of the strange, inscrutable genius, Jackson; a most enjoyable biography.

190.

———. *Rebel Brass: The Confederate Command System.* Baton Rouge, 1956. Reprint, New York 1969 and 1977. Reprint, Baton Rouge, 1993.

A path-breaking, evaluation of the interaction of politics and military decision making by Davis, Lee, and other Southern leaders.

191.

Weigley, Russell F. *The American Way of War: A History of United States Military Strategy and Policy.* New York, 1973.

A solid survey of American military history, including an outstanding chapter titled "Napoleonic Strategy: R. E. Lee and the Confederacy" and another titled "A Strategy of Annihilation: U. S. Grant and the Union."

192.

Wellman, Manly Wade. *Giant in Gray: A Biography of Wade Hampton of South Carolina.* New York, 1949. Reprint, Dayton OH, 1980.

A laudatory but generally accurate portrait of Lee's genteel cavalry commander, one of the few non–West Pointers who achieved greatness in the Confederate army.

193.

Wert, Jeffry D. *General James Longstreet, The Confederacy's Most Controversial Soldier: A Biography.* New York, 1993.

An ardent defense of Longstreet's character and military capacity, both during and after the war.

194.

Whan, Vorin, E., Jr. *Fiasco at Fredericksburg.* State College PA, 1961. Reprint, Gaithersburg MD, 1986.

Although relatively brief, still the only monograph on this easy defensive victory for Lee.

195.
White, Henry Alexander. *Robert E. Lee and the Southern Confederacy, 1807–1870.* New York, 1897. Reprint, New York, 1969. Reprint, St. Clair Shores MI, 1971. Reprint, Irvine CA, 1992.
The first truly scholarly biography of Lee, written by a professor at Washington and Lee University who knew Lee after the war and benefitted from the use of information provided by Lee's family, friends, and former officers.

196.
Wilson, Charles Reagan. *Baptized in Blood: The Religion of the Lost Cause, 1865–1920.* Athens GA, 1980.
An admirable scholarly explanation of the fervent course of postwar Southern patriotism that helped create legions of Lee devotees.

197.
Winston, Robert W. *Robert E. Lee: A Biography.* New York, 1934.
A creditable, fairly scholarly biography; the author delved into primary sources and spoke to "old soldiers" who knew Lee.

198.
Wise, Jennings C. *The Long Arm of Lee: The History of the Artillery of the Army of Northern Virginia, with a Brief Account of the Confederate Bureau of Ordnance.* 2 vols. Lynchburg VA, 1915. Reprint, with foreword by L. Van Loan Naisawald, 2 vols. in 1, New York, 1959. Reprint, with introduction by Gary W. Gallagher, Richmond, 1988.
A massive study of perhaps the most underrated aspect of Lee's powerful army.

199.
Wolseley, Garnet Joseph. *The American Civil War: An English View.* Ed. James A. Rawley. Charlottesville VA, 1964.
A collection of essays by Britain's leading military expert during the Victorian era; including a memorable account of his visit with General Lee during the fall of 1864. Supplemented and reinforced by Wolseley's seldom-cited *General Lee* (Rochester NY, 1906).

200.
Zinn, Jack. *Lee's Cheat Mountain Campaign.* Parsons WV, 1974.
The first serious study of Lee's ill-fated command early in the war.

Contributors

The introduction contains information about the nineteenth-century authors in this collection, including Edward Porter Alexander, George A. Bruce, Jubal A. Early, Francis Lawley, James Longstreet, and Viscount Wolseley.

Albert Castel, a Civil War historian living and writing in Hillsdale, Michigan, has published numerous articles and several books, including *General Sterling Price and the Civil War in the West, A Frontier State at War: Kansas, 1861–1865, The Presidency of Andrew Johnson, William Clarke Quantrill: His Life and Times*, and *Decision in the West: The Atlanta Campaign of 1864* (co-winner of the Lincoln Prize).

Thomas L. Connelly, a native of Nashville, Tennessee, who became a leading interpreter of the military history of the Confederacy, spent most of his teaching career at the University of South Carolina and wrote a number of books, among them *Army of the Heartland: The Army of Tennessee, 1861–1862, Autumn of Glory: The Army of Tennessee, 1862–1865, The Marble Man: Robert E. Lee and His Image in American Society*, and (with Archer Jones) *The Politics of Command: Factions and Ideas in Confederate Strategy.*

William C. Davis is the author or editor of more than twenty-five books on the Civil War, including *Jefferson Davis, The Man and His Hour, The Image of War: 1861–1865, Breckinridge: Statesman, Soldier, Symbol*, and *A Government of Our Own: The Making of the Confederacy.*

Douglas Southall Freeman, a native Virginian who edited the *Richmond News Leader* for more than three decades (1915–1949), published, among other titles, *R. E. Lee: A Biography* and *Lee's Lieutenants: A Study in Command*, 4- and 3-volume works, respectively, that made him the most influential historian of the Confederate military effort.

GARY W. GALLAGHER is a member of the Department of History at Pennsylvania State University. He has published widely on the Civil War, including *Stephen Dodson Ramseur: Lee's Gallant General*, *Fighting for the Confederacy: The Personal Recollections of General Edward Porter Alexander*, *The Third Day at Gettysburg and Beyond*, and *The Fredericksburg Campaign: Decision on the Rappahannock.*

D. SCOTT HARTWIG, who studied under E. B. Long at the University of Wyoming, has published several articles on the Battle of Gettysburg as well as *The Battle of Antietam and the Maryland Campaign of 1862: A Bibliography.*

ROBERT K. KRICK grew up in California but has lived and worked on the Virginia battlefields for more than twenty years. He has written dozens of articles and ten books, the most recent being *Stonewall Jackson at Cedar Mountain* and *Conquering the Valley: Stonewall Jackson at Port Republic.*

ALAN T. NOLAN, an Indianapolis lawyer, is a graduate of Indiana University and the Harvard Law School. He is a Fellow of the Company of Military Historians, a Trustee of the Indiana Historical Society, and a member of the Indianapolis Civil War Round Table. His publications include *The Iron Brigade* and *Lee Considered: General Robert E. Lee and Civil War History.*

T. MICHAEL PARRISH, an archivist at the Lyndon Baines Johnson Library, received his doctorate from the University of Texas at Austin. He is author of *Richard Taylor: Soldier Prince of Dixie* and coauthor of *Confederate Imprints: A Bibliography.*

CAROL REARDON is the military historian at Pennsylvania State University and author of numerous articles and essays as well as *Soldiers & Scholars: The U.S. Army and the Uses of Military History, 1865–1920.*

CHARLES P. ROLAND, a Tennessean and specialist in Southern, Civil War, and military history, taught at Louisiana State University, Tulane University, and the University of Kentucky, and held the presidency of the Southern Historical Association. His many publications include *Albert Sidney Johnston: Soldier of Three Republics*, *The Confederacy*, *An American Illiad: The Story of the Civil War*, and *Reflections on Lee: A Historian's Assessment.*

NOAH ANDRE TRUDEAU, a historian, is the director for cultural programs at National Public Radio in Washington DC. His published work includes a trilogy on the Civil War: *Bloody Roads South: The Wilderness to Cold Harbor, May–June 1864, The Last Citadel: Petersburg, Virginia, June 1864–April 1865*, and *Out of the Storm: The End of the Civil War, April–June 1865*.

★ ★ ★

Index